MW00529393

Judgment Day Must Wait

Jehovah's Witnesses— A Sect Between Idealism and Deceit

Poul Bregninge

YBK Publishers
New York

ISBN: 978-1-936411-23-8

First English proofreading: J. Turner Stilson
Proofreading, selected chapters: Brian Kutscher, Jerry Leslie, James Parkinson and Jim Whitney
Editing for US publication: Dawn M. Johnson, Word Edge (http://www.word-edge.com)
Cover illustration by Jørgen Bregninge describes a new catastrophic year with great potential for renewed activity about to emerge from the apocalyptic idea's inexhaustible store: the year, 2034.

YBK Publishers, Inc.
39 Crosby Street
New York, NY 10013
www.ybkpublishers.com

Bregninge, Poul.
  Judgment day must wait : Jehovah's Witnesses : a sect between idealism and deceit / Poul Bregninge.
    pages cm
  Includes bibliographical references and index.
  ISBN 978-1-936411-23-8 (pbk. : alk. paper)
  1. Jehovah's Witnesses--Controversial literature. I. Title.
  BX8526.5.B74 2013
  289.9'2--dc23
                          2013020961

Manufactured in the United States of America for distribution in North and South America
or in the United Kingdom or Australia when distributed elsewhere.

For more information, visit
www.ybkpublishers.com

In memory of my parents

Gerda Marie Bregninge née Bilde
who, in 1953–1954, refused to receive a blood transfusion
for a life-saving operation. She died in February 1954,
scarcely forty years old.

Hans Eigil Bregninge showed me the road to freedom
by his example. He died in 1995
at eighty-nine years of age.

I noticed (and how many times!) that anything
that was unusual, fantastic, often obviously clumsily
concocted, pleased the people much more than
serious stories about the real truth. But when
I told Khokhol about this he grinned and said:
'But that will pass, the main thing is for people to learn how
to think for themselves—then they might get near the truth.

—Maxim Gorky, *My Universities*,[1] 1923

The Story of the Jehovah's Witnesses is to be seen and understood
in light of the Adventist churches' development in the United States
in the mid and latter half of the 1800s.

Contents

Preface

Religion is a profoundly fascinating phenomenon that can bring out both the best and the worst in people. On the one hand religion represents faith, hope and love, generosity, unselfishness and many other such noble qualities. On the other hand, tyrannical behavior, suppression, brainwashing and superstition often follow and sometimes lead. All human phenomena can be studied under the magnifying glass of religion, and perhaps even more so in this area than in others.

In 1966, Poul Bregninge wrote the book *Jehovas Vidner under anklage* (Jehovah's Witnesses on Trial) in his native Danish. He has followed up this book with a retrospective glance at the beginnings of this movement, as well as a thorough update on how "Jehovah's organization" has evolved since the publishing of his first book. The origins of this movement are clarified as we are taken back to the middle of the 19th century and the life and teachings of C. T. Russell, a man who was deeply indebted to the Adventists, but who, on the other hand, was very critical towards all other church societies.

Despite its less-than charitable treatment of the adherents, with brainwashing tactics, heresy hunting and a theocratic dictatorship in which everything is run by the headquarters in Brooklyn, Jehovah's organization has still managed to grow in size; it now numbers more than seven million baptized members. And this in spite of the fact that many have either left or been expelled. Both variants are often tragic for the unfortunate individual, as relationships are often subjected to such strains that families and marriages are ruined, and informing on loved ones is not an uncommon feature to Jehovah's Witness life.

Along the way, this sect has had many problems, partly because they, for some reason, constantly rely on calculations. These calculations have been concerned with both the exact number of saved ("anointed"), as well as the precise date for the end of the world, in which the Witnesses will rejoice in the misfortune of the rest of us, as we lay dying, gutted and skinned, while beasts and birds eat our flesh. One of these precise dates was the year 1914, a year the Witnesses arrived at via complex calculations based on Biblical prophecies. This assertion of the Witnesses has not yet been officially disclaimed, but they seem to be getting there. Later, the great battle of Armageddon, which marks the end of the world as we know it, was calculated to happen in 1975. Unfortunately, as seen from the Witnesses' point of view, this year turned out to be a very peaceful year.

Why then, this fascination with calculations? One of the reasons might be that in the years preceding this glorious, violent event, the number of adherents has (*every* time) grown rapidly, as they get to join in this self-righteous fascination of being "latter-day holy ones." But of course, they too are eventually let down, as nothing ever happens, and like many Witnesses over the years, they too have had to face their very personal Armageddon, realizing they wouldn't have had to abandon having children or getting an education, after all. In addition to this, Society leadership even seems to have doubted their own predictions, as they have always made secret plans for damage control and excuses in the aftermath of their Armageddon-fiascos.

In many ways, reading the material Poul Bregninge here presents is like gazing into a dreadful abyss. But still, it is imperative that these kinds of books are written, as this harmful sect is still enlisting new members. This is why the book has devoted the last chapter on how to argue with the Jehovah's Witnesses, so that the reader can learn how to beat them at their own game. The chapter offers the most absurd reading, with arguments and counterarguments that no sane person could ever take seriously. Yet, considering the fact that some are still allowing themselves to be led into this darkness, it might be a good idea to know how to fight back. The way the Jehovah's Witnesses approach the Bible is—as is the case with all fundamentalists—selective and self-centered. Everything is interpreted according to their own already established motives, ideas and desires and with disregard for the resulting absurdities. But this is exactly why it might be beneficial to play along and pretend to take them seriously.

Poul Bregninge has written a necessary book.

Jan Lindhardt[2]

Acknowledgements

My appreciation and gratitude to the following:

Jan Lindhardt, the author and former Bishop at Roskilde Cathedral, Denmark, who wrote the Foreword.

Mogens Müller, professor at the University of Copenhagen, who has advised me about church history issues and assisted me with recommendations, encouragements, etc., for which I owe him great thanks.

Carl Olof Jonsson, Swedish author, whose story I tell in Chapter 28. He contributed with important details and a very rare pamphlet.

Barbara Anderson, former employee at the Watchtower Headquarters in New York, who contributed with her remarkable experiences and sensational report.

David Mace assisted me from 2008 to 2012 with vital quotations from the original English Watchtower publications.

Øyvind Midteng of Norway, who is a school teacher, translated the Preface, the Introduction and around six of the subsequent chapters, which have since undergone some changes.

Roberto di Stefano of Geneva, Switzerland, contributed with his European angle of Jehovah's Witnesses (Chapter 33).

Jan Turner Stilson, a historian, author and archivist at the Church of God General Conference, McDonough, Georgia. In 2010–2012 Jan performed the first proofreading of the entire English manuscript. She also provided vital information about the Age-to-Come movement.

Jim Whitney, a former Witness familiar with Jehovah's Witnesses' history, rhetoric and terminology, proofread the first 200 pages of the manuscript. Jim contributed with criticism and several notes.

Brian Kutscher, James Parkinson and *Jerry Leslie*, who I came in contact with in 2011, are all connected with a contemporary Bible Student association in the US that emerged from C. T. Russell's original association. They helped me with a critical review of chapters 11 through 17. Brian read the proofs of chapters 22 and 23 and he also contributed high quality images. This does not necessarily imply that these men endorse my views and conclusions—rather the contrary.

Also special thanks to *Dawn Johnson*, and her business Word Edge in Stillman Valley, Illinois, for a brilliant Americanization of the entire manuscript.

In no particular order thanks to the following:

Jette Svane who shared her very personal story (Chapter 29), helped with graphs, calculations and other important contributions.

"Eve" contributed with her very private story (Chapter 31).

"Ruth" told of her feelings and conflicts in relation to her parents who were still in the "Truth" (Summary).

"Beroea," a Jehovah's Witness elder, updated me on the *present* status of the Jehovah's Witnesses worldwide (Chapter 38).

John Roller, former Resource Center Coordinator at the Advent Christian General Conference of America provided insight into new and important information about C. T. Russell; *Mark M. Mattison* contributed with important documentation about Russell's contact with Adventists early in his career.

From *David Krogh*, registrar at Atlanta Bible College, McDonough, Georgia, I received with gratitude a copy of W. H. Wilson's, *Cunningly Devised Fables of Russellism* (Chapter 4).

Dr. Keld M. Homburg, director of the Transfusion Center at Storstrømmen Hospital, Denmark, advised me about blood transfusion.

Also thanks to *Leif Wæber* who helped me with calculations and statistics.

Appreciation also goes to the photographer, *Poul Dal*, who told his story and assisted with research (Chapter 30).

Joergen Larsen, former director of Jehovah's Witnesses in Denmark, now deceased, allowed me to meet him on "neutral grounds" (a restaurant); *Thorben Thöger Andersen*, elder of a congregation in Copenhagen, Denmark, supplied me with *invaluable* documentation and material in English, which have been crucial for this book.

Thanks also go to *John Pedersen* and *Sven Hagen Jensen* at the Seventh Day Adventist Church in Denmark, who gave me free access to the church's library and helped with information.

Also thanks to the psychoanalyst *Jean-Christian Delay* with whom I discussed various psychological aspects; *Gitte Jakobsen*, consultant for SISO[3]—Knowledge Centre for Social Efforts concerning Sexual Abuse of Children.

Professor P. G. Lindhardt recommended publication of my first book in 1966, which at the time was very important for me. It was of course the reason why I asked his son, *Jan Lindhardt*, to write the preface to *Judgment Day Must Wait*.

Last but not least, thanks to my wife, *Birgit*, for her proofreading and constructive criticism, as well as patience and encouragement, while I again was writing about the Jehovah's Witnesses.

It took *too much* time.

Introduction

Between Idealism and Deceit

Originally, this book was intended to be an updated version of my previous book, *Jehovah's Witnesses On Trial*,[4] which was released in Copenhagen forty-six years ago—six years after my wife and I had left the movement, the Jehovah's Witnesses. However, after having worked on this new Danish-English project since the summer of 2003, it soon became clear to me the task was much greater than I originally had imagined, and soon a completely new book was taking form. That the book got a brand new title is due to the fact that its general theme circulates around Judgment Day's *conspicuous absence*.

Even though the book's ostensible subject is the Jehovah's Witnesses movement, its range of concern is really a much more comprehensive consideration of church history. The topic concerns more than some idealistic and overwrought Christians in late-19th-century America who believed that Christ had (invisibly) returned to earth. In reality, the movement had simply recycled the motives and arguments that originally constituted the central revelations of the first Christians, namely the message that the world was very near its end: Mankind, first-century Jews *and* Gentiles, could be saved through conversion to Christianity, by means of which they would ascend to heavenly life on Judgment Day. History repeated itself in countless variations, and 2,000 years later it came, in the Jehovah's Witnesses' view, to mean that *millions of now-living people would never die*. It was an alluring message at a time when one of the most terrible wars the world had ever seen, indeed the first war ever to be called a World War, was raging.

At its basic level, this book deals with fundamentalism, which in our own time is ravaging the world like a plague. This fundamentalism erects concrete walls around its adherents by maintaining outdated perceptions and radical ideas which catastrophically affect current and future generations.

To provide a striking example of such fundamentalism was the task I under-took in 2003—a hopeless project on a hopeless case, as I, against all odds, tried to instill a new kind of hope.

Critical but Fair

From the start, this book was not intended as a scholarly treatise, and for this reason I, as far as possible, sought to avoid footnotes and foreign words. How-ever, the revised version, including this English one, has many more footnotes that have been converted to endnotes at the back of the book. They contain only supplementary and more detailed information; their primary goal is to support the main text. By presenting the subject in this way, I hope the book can and will be read by as many as possible. It is a compromise between the personally experienced and the clinical unreadable. Yet despite my personal engagement, I have tried for a fair but critical treatment of the subject. Or at least that is what I hoped to achieve.

Work on the manuscript resulted not only in a re-acquaintance with the reli-gious community of my childhood, but also in *yet another confrontation* with that community. Unlike the first time I wrote about this subject, in this instance I have included the stories of a number of other Witnesses who broke with the movement in the 1990s and still experience confrontational situations, giving them the opportunity to express the details of their journeys. Still, it is not the confrontation with the Witnesses alone which is interesting, but rather the rev-elation that a relatively tiny American religious movement, through the reuse of the early Christian Church's apocalypticism, has been able to invoke the whole world's attention in the 19th, 20th and 21st centuries.

As I encountered these elements of my past again, I noted with astonishment and gratitude that, while I had left the fundamentalist beliefs of this movement light years before, the Witnesses steadfastly moved in the same old grind I had experienced more than fifty years earlier. Ravages of time, however, left traces in the movement's history and doctrines, which I will try to show.

Now, I thank my God and Creator for the fact that I had the strength to break free from this mental prison. So who then do I consider my creator, in addition to my parents and thousands of generations backwards in time? I don't know. But this is a lesser problem, as long as one can deal with one's own existence and live life to its fullest extent. Even though I make my own reflections con-cerning the origin and function of religion, reflections in which I still have not committed to dismissing the religious experience completely, religion is not a cause of private concern for me anymore.

Still, the origins of the idea of God are not the subject of this book, even though human beings' abuse of them stands in the center.

Background and Motives

My basic motivations for writing this book are many and complex, but the primary reasons rest in my own past, a past which, after the religious constraints of my childhood, quickly came full circle around how I could free myself from the Jehovah's Witnesses. The book is written on this background of personal experiences. Breaking free was of vital necessity, a life-struggle that came to shape the rest of my life. I confronted the movement's "black tide of mud of occultism,"[5] Biblical fundamentalism and pseudoscientific thoughts, and quickly found an acceptable explanation for my presence on this planet, a natural and scientific one, which soon took the form of a kind of "revelation" for me. It was a long and tough process toward freedom, which I finally conquered for my little family and me.

When I published my first book on the Witnesses in 1966, we were able to put the past behind us. Not until 2003, thirty-seven years later, did I decide to write a new book on my old topic. Not because I wasn't done with the topic, but because I wanted to penetrate deeper into the substance. The topic simply fascinated me. How did it all start and how has the movement progressed since we left?

Although the present investigation is motivated at a personal level and, therefore some could perceive as a personal vendetta, this is not the intention. Still, I recognize, of course, that my exposition is *engaged* and often *critical*; this has been impossible to avoid. Maybe I come closest to my motives when I write that my investigation has been motivated from a heartfelt surprise over what human beings, in spite of any reason, can be brought to believe in and fight for—even martyrdom!

As a phenomenon, the Jehovah's Witnesses are hugely well known—far beyond what the movement's size warrants. Their history is at the same time extremely interesting, fascinating and frightening. Psychologically speaking, however, the movement's own self-understanding is enormously exaggerated. From a world perspective it is largely inconsequential, and therefore, its importance must be acknowledged for its value to the individuals who—to have order and meaning in their lives—engage themselves in its community and activities.

A Sect Characterized by Delusions

When I think of the hundreds of thousands of well-meaning people who have played supporting roles in this bizarre "divine comedy" of the Jehovah's Witnesses, which the leaders of the movement in the course of time have directed and performed, I realize the history of the Witnesses is no less than a tragedy to all the people who have allowed themselves to be persuaded. Their lives are an urgent example of the costs that personal surrender to a religious organization may entail. The costs, as far as victims are concerned, are difficult to imagine. Hundreds of thousands have vainly spent all their time on the ideas of the movement. They have let themselves be swept away by belief in eternal life in a utopia-like new world where only the chosen ones, the ones that eventually crawl out from the smoldering ruins of Armageddon's devastating chaos, come to live.

The members find themselves in a conceptual world which is characterized by delusions, and after all these years, it has become impossible for them to grasp their own situation, both intellectually and psychologically. The systematic subversive and detrimental influence, to which they are constantly exposed, causes their real "I" to be overlaid with a weight of organizational material, absurd doctrines, unreasonable obligations, rules and prohibitions, all of which are done to keep them detached from everything considered normal and indispensable by the rest of society. Worst of all: Independent thinking is systematically treated with hatred.

And so, the story of Jehovah's Witnesses, who have been seized and restrained by a utopian idealism that developed into a worldwide movement, is a report of mankind's folly, and its only real goal now seems to be growing to an *even bigger* movement.

The discrepancies between the reliability of what the leaders prophesied and what they demanded of the membership have been too grave. But the leaders always start afresh, when the memory of their last fiasco has finally been suppressed and the calculations and *the* date again changed, arguing that the "light is getting brighter" and that Jehovah only gradually "reveals his truths."

Most surprising is that the members, without question, have accepted these never-ending revisions of the doctrines from the early days of the movement. The only possible explanation for this must be that, in spite of the deception, they simply *needed* to believe in the unbelievable—this illusion of the impossible—which could camouflage lives that to some extent lacked meaning and content. They became unconscious consumers of exhortations and absurd prohibitions on all human normality. They created and accepted a "surrogate reality" because there is something about this life they do not dare to face—as the female psychiatrist (Madeleine Stowe) said to the main character (Bruce Willis) in the apocalyptic science fiction movie, *Twelve Monkeys.*

The condition of vulnerability came from deep roots. After the Middle Ages and the collective loss of faith in the centuries that followed—a consequence of the Age of Enlightenment, criticisms of religion, and Darwin's theory of evolution—people were like castaways, floundering in a spiritual sea of sorts, scouting for means of rescue. Because of this newfound freedom to believe in everything between heaven and earth, a freedom that left them in a state of profound hopelessness, many people—who previously felt comfortable with religious authority—became easy victims for the many travelling salesmen of religion. In this state, they were ready and willing to accept almost anything, as long as it could provide them with a borrowed identity to help free them from all true moral responsibilities through submission to an authoritarian organization with all its strange teachings. They never truly understood this organization, but still willingly accepted it as the one indisputable truth. (Ref. Erich Fromm's *Escape from Freedom*)

Thus, with this study, I hope to provide a significant contribution to the reader's understanding that there is absolutely no reason to believe God has scheduled a worldwide destruction that will kill billions and is purported to take place within a relatively few years.

It is true the destruction of our world is being scheduled, but the scheduling isn't happening in heaven. Rather, it's happening at the East River's large berths in Brooklyn, New York, where Jehovah's Witnesses' executives continually develop and fine-tune this perverted idea. My ambition is that with this book I have provided a "key" so my reader—if the need should be present—may free himself from these coarse, ludicrous and bizarre fabrications, and perhaps become deprogrammed and return to the real "old" world, which is the *only one* that is realistic.

Poul Bregninge,
July 2013

Editor's Comment

As I Americanized Poul's self-translated manuscript I was reintroduced to a religion that I—like most Americans—often find at my front door and hastily dismiss. Poul's treatment of sect history, members' experiences and disquieting statistics was, without doubt, enlightening; it also braced my long-held suspicions about Christian denominations' use and misuse of biblical text for their own ends. *JDMW* is a sometimes-academic, often-documentary and endlessly human examination of a wholly manmade theocracy and its apocalyptic crimes of ideological and religious folly. Reading this book will make you wiser.

Dawn M. Johnson
Stillman Valley, Illinois

Practical Remarks

A list of source material can be found in the back of the book. This list also includes biographical notes on persons and topics that have had significance for the author's work. The full titles of the cited sources and the years of English publication can be found there, plus in some cases, print runs. The sources follow through the book in abbreviated form in parenthesis immediately after quoted matter. The publishing years of English editions are also cited after the abbreviated book titles. For example: (Life Everlasting 1966, p. 31–35). The full title of the source is then: *Life Everlasting—in Freedom of the Sons of God*, WTS, 1966 (please note that it is either Watchtower Bible and Tract Society of New York, Inc., or Watch Tower Bible & Tract Society of Pennsylvania that is the publisher; Watch Tower Bible & Tract Society of Pennsylvania holds all copyrights).

Especially with books by C. T. Russell in some cases two publication years are listed, as in this example: (*Studies* 2, 1917 (1889), p. 241, 242). The year in parenthesis is the source of citation, and the year in the extra parenthesis is the year of the original publication.

In the List of Publications, an overview of books and brochures published by the Watchtower Bible and Tract Society (WTS) can be found, as well as a list of other applied books, mainly theological.

In the author's text, the name Jehovah's Witnesses is written with initial capitals.

Punctuation and Formatting

As the situation often arises in the publications of the Jehovah's Witnesses, citations are quoted *within* citations; these citations within the citations are marked by 'singular' quotation marks. And when citations within citations in which yet *another* citation appears, for example a Biblical citation, these are marked with the standard quotation marks. Thus the format is one of alternating mark styles as each citation is embedded within another. The author's subjective comments are either marked by quotation marks or written in *italics*. All quotations from the Watchtower literature are cited with the punctuation used in the original publications.

Where [square brackets] occur within a citation, they signify that the content has been added by the author for reader clarification of the quoted material, but these brackets also appear in quotations from Jehovah's Witnesses' books and magazines and other instances where parenthetical elements are contained within parenthetical elements, etc.

A slash in the middle of a quote / indicates the author has annulled a line break in the quotation, so the quote appears coherent within the rest of the text.

The use of ellipsis points means a section of a citation has been omitted to save space only when the material is unrelated or redundant to the context of the discussion.

The titles of books, booklets and magazines are consequently shown in *italics*. If the name of a magazine is not shown in *italics*, the name has another meaning. For example, *The Watchtower*, which is the most commonly known publication of the Jehovah's Witnesses, is also used as a name/title (in abbreviated form) for the Watchtower Bible and Tract Society, which is the formal title of the book publishing company and top leadership of the worldwide organization of the Jehovah's Witnesses, for the time being still located in Brooklyn, New York. Due to the Society's location in Brooklyn, for simplicity, the Watch Tower Society is simply referred to as "Brooklyn" at various times throughout the book

Reprints

Quotations followed by a reference structured as follows (Reprints 3411), lower or higher, originate from seven volumes of reprints of *Zion's Watch Tower* and *The Watchtower* (new name in 1909). After the death of Charles Taze Russell, these reprints were produced by the Watch Tower Society. The last page of this collection is 6622. On each page found in the reprints are two page numbers. On the top of the page is the number from the original magazine; at the bottom is the page number of the reprint volume. Today these volumes can be found at various locations on the internet.

Bible Translations Used

Unless otherwise noted in connection with Bible quotations, the following are used: *Authorized* or *King James Version* (KJ) and the *Revised Standard Version* (RSV), 1971—the last, specifically in connection with chapter 39 of this book. If a quote comes from the Jehovah's Witnesses' own Bible translation, *New World Translation of the Holy Scriptures* (NWT 1984), it will be apparent in the context of the quote. If other translations are used, they are indicated.

Concerning Danish Scholarly Works not Available in English

In this book's text, particularly in chapters 2 and 39, the author refers to books written by Danish scholars, which English/American readers may not have a chance to read or verify. Therefore, on advice from Professor Mogens Müller, University of Copenhagen, the author has listed a number of articles from *The Anchor Bible Dictionary* that either deal with the issues addressed in the Danish historical and theological works or are supplemental to them. Moreover, in the bibliography other English works are listed which the author has read or used as reference works. This includes, for example, the following: Donald Guthrie: *New Testament Introduction*, 1981; D. A. Carson, Douglas J. Moo, and Leon Morris: *An Introduction to the New Testament*, 1994; *A Theology of the New Testament* by George Eldon Ladd, 1974 (reprinted in 1991); and Bart D. Ehrman's: *Jesus–apocalyptic prophet of the new millennium*, 1999. The last mentioned work is recommended as an introduction to the New Testament's eschatology dealing with the subject in a straightforward manner.

Internet Sources

Because the approach to information regarding specific topics is facilitated considerably through internet sources and research, the author has located and referenced such sources that have proven to be reliable. But one must naturally take the information from the internet with a pinch of salt, which is why the author also, where possible, has listed printed sources. Thus, all information has been cross-checked with multiple sources.

Using *Wikipedia*

From the author's location in Denmark it was difficult to locate a wealth of scholarly studies in English. But since the author considers *Wikipedia* (exposed for certain criticisms) as the general reader's friend, he has quoted from and referred to the treatment of various topics, especially when he found the illuminated issues relevant and informative.

Possible Criticism of this Book

With a view to a revised new edition of this book, I urge my readers to send comments that can deepen one or more points, which is assumed will increase the book's content and quality. Use the following email addresses:

bregningebook@gmail.com or pbpostkasse@mail.dk

Abbreviations

ACA: Advent Christian Association from 1860 to 1864. The name was later changed to Advent Christian Church or ACC.

ACC: Advent Christian Church from 1864 onward. Previously Advent Christian Association or ACA.

AD: *Anno Domini* (Latin), in the year of our Lord. Denotes years after Christ's birth in year 1.

BC: Before Christ. Denotes years before Christ's birth in year 1.

BCE: Before the Common Era. A more secular term to denote the years before Christ's birth.

CE: Common Era or Christian Era. A more secular term to denote the years after Christ's birth.

DK: The Kingdom of Denmark.

IBSA: The International Bible Students Association.

JW: Jehovah's Witnesses; known as Bible Students before 1931.

KJ: *King James Version.*

NT: New Testament.

NWT: *New World Translation*; began to appear from 1950.

RSV: Revised Standard Version of the whole Bible.

SDA: Seventh-day Adventists.

Studies: *Studies in the Scriptures*, C. T. Russell's book series consisting of six volumes.

WT: The magazine *The Watchtower.*

WTS: Watch Tower Bible & Tract Society of Pennsylvania.

ZWT: C. T. Russell's magazine, *Zion's Watch Tower*; started in 1879.

X-JW or Ex-JW: Former JW active in campaigns against Jehovah's Witnesses.

PART ONE

At the End of the World

"Everyone who has predicted the end of their world has intuited one aspect of Jesus' teaching that appears to be historically accurate— the more popular strands of Christianity and the outspoken protests of numerous theologians notwithstanding. For those anticipating the imminent end of their own world have been able to base their expectations on the words of the historical Jesus, a first-century apocalyptic prophet who expected the imminent end of his."

Bart D. Ehrman: *Jesus—Apocalyptic Prophet of the New Millennium,* Oxford University Press, 2001, p. 245

Chapter 1

Charles Taze Russell

—Prophet of the Millennial Reign

Our story begins in the 1870s in Pittsburgh, Pennsylvania, where the Monongahela and Allegheny rivers meet the Ohio River. Pittsburgh's geographical location proved to be significant to its growth in the late 19th century. Before the Europeans arrived, two Native American tribes lived there, Shawnee and Delaware.

Around the 1750s the British and the French considered the area strategically important for control of the Ohio River. In the 1740s, British settlers established commercial trading posts with the region's Indian tribes, and around the 1750s the French began building forts from Lake Erie to the Allegheny River. When the British began to establish themselves in French territory, today the Pittsburgh area, they not only had to struggle against the French, but also against their allies, the Indians.

In 1754 the British began to build a fort on the site, and that same year the French captured it and subsequently named it Fort Duquesne. When a British regiment of 150 men under the leadership of a 21-year-old Major George Washington came across a French contingent near the fort on a rainy night in late May 1754, the French commander Joseph Coulon de Jumonville was killed in the skirmish. This initiated the nine-year French and Indian War between French and British troops (1754–1763).

The wars in North America between the colonial powers France and England were part of the *Seven Years' War*, which actually involved all the European countries and eventually culminated in the American Revolutionary War (1775–1783); this war was later called the "first World War." Between 900,000 and 1,400,000 died during the Seven Years' War.

The British regained control of Fort Duquesne in 1758, but the French burned it down before surrendering. It was rebuilt under the name of Fort Pitt after English Prime Minister William Pitt, the elder. A town grew up around the fort, and by the end of the 18th century, the area had developed into a hotspot for trade and industry. Glass was in production from 1797 and iron from 1806.

Around 1800, Pittsburgh, as the town around Fort Pitt had been named, had 1,500 residents; by 1860, it had grown to more than 50,000.

From around 1870 until 1914, this area was one of the world's busiest, richest and most productive mining districts. Coal was transported down the river on an armada of barges. In addition to coal, iron and petroleum were produced, and natural gas piped up from underground fueled industrial ovens and furnaces. Pittsburgh became a capital for industrial magnates in the 1870s, and with the need for labor, the town grew rapidly.

Near Pittsburgh lay the neighboring city Allegheny, today also called Old Allegheny, which was incorporated into Pittsburgh in 1907. Old Allegheny is the urban and geographical center for the beginnings of this story.

If we were living in the late 19th century in Pittsburgh and Allegheny, we would see a completely modern society which offered promise of great change in the immediate future.

As a result of the area's vast natural resources, Pittsburgh soon came to be a center of political contrasts in America. I am mentioning this very deliberately, because the people of that time couldn't realize all these signs of an arising new era, a *new dawn*, that hung as smoke and noise in the air, and whose consequences would lead to new social conflicts. But they were aware of the tremendous progress in all areas that occurred everywhere in the flourishing "new world"—not least of which was in the area of technical developments.

Our main character at the start of this narrative, Charles Taze Russell, was a complicated personality. On the one hand, he was progressive and optimistic. On the other, he had a religious calling, based on the ancient religious texts of the Bible, with its Old and New Testament, both of which he reinterpreted in the most speculative of ways. Still, his works must, in my opinion, be viewed as nothing less than impressive, although his ideas were responsible for creating one of the most controversial religious movements of our time, and despite the fact that he stole and copied many of his ideas from his contemporaries. He founded the only religious movement ever to stem from Pittsburgh.

Despite my attempts to look favorably upon our protagonist's project, I cannot explain away that he was basically a rather verbose person, one who immoderately rose over everything and everybody, without possessing the required academic skills as ballast for his highly publicized messages. However, to characterize him as a *charlatan* would demand that the same, demeaning characterizations could be applied to many of his contemporaries, who, in the same manner as him, appealed more to *emotions* than *reason*. However, those who allowed themselves to be "captivated" by his preaching had mainly themselves to blame for being led astray—for they really were *led astray*.

For more than thirty-five years Charles Russell wrote about the millennial "dawn" based on his and others' complex calculations, which he also thought could be documented using the background of the contemporary social and geopolitical upheavals of the world, starting with the French Revolution of 1789–1799.

The many new inventions of his time, particularly those of industry, were considered miraculous signs of the gradual establishing of the Millennium, which, beginning with the year 1874 and within a 40-year long period of "harvesting," would make its presence increasingly noticeable. Then in 1914, it would all end with the full and final establishment of God's Kingdom— as Christians had asked of God for nearly 2,000 years—both in heaven and on earth. However, Russell and his followers represented just one of several smaller religious groups in the 19th century who were convinced Christ's second coming was imminent and that his return would usher the establishment of the Millennium.[6]

Russell's chronological system was extremely complex and the logic not always easy to comprehend. Although establishment of the Millennium apparently was to *begin* in 1874, this same period was also called the "Day of the Lord"[7] and the "time of trouble" and would be characterized by increasing political and social unrest, government crises, revolutions and wars, all culminating with the great battle of Armageddon in 1914. Both these periods would last forty years and end in 1914.

In 1889 Russell wrote that *the battle of the great day of God Almighty* had "already commenced" in 1878,[8] and this citation supports the assumption that it most likely was Russell's original viewpoint that the *battle* actually was a *period*, which would gradually worsen from 1874 onwards to its awful climax, the battle of Armageddon, slated to erupt in 1914. During this 40-year period many weapons would be manufactured, and the armies, which would battle in the final showdown, would be mobilized. Russell's apocalyptic timetable, based on earlier calculations of the Adventists, was not firmly fixed from the beginning and underwent many changes. In Russell's timetable, the so-called "time of the end" began as early as 1799, the final years of the French Revolution, and this period would also end in 1914. (*Studies* 2, 1917 (1889), p. 101)

When I write that the "harvest period" would last until 1914, I must also add that Russell originally—in his mission work from 1876 to 1878—learned that the harvest time was merely a shorter three-and-a-half-year period, beginning in 1874 and terminating in 1878, and then when nothing of what he had predicted happened, it was extended to 1881. He then increased the harvest time to last right up until 1914.

The *cornerstone* in Russell's "divine plan" was the so called "Gentile Times"— a period of 2,520 years beginning in 606 BC[9]—and would likewise end in October 1914, therefore, all Russell's timelines pointed toward 1914 as the year everything would be turned upside down in our world. In fact, 1914 was crucial for his future. He stood and fell with it. (*Studies* 2, 1917 (1889), p. 79)

Russell, of anyone, became *the* prophet and proselytizer of the Millennium when it came to the prophecy itself, but it was so-so with the fulfillments.

His supporters, who were unable to see through the speculative content of his teachings and who believed he had been chosen by God to assume a very special role as the Lord's "faithful and wise servant" caretaker of the elects' *spiritual food in due season*, loved him dearly and relied on him to the end.

In fact, Russell repeated, on a modern scale, what many others proclaimed throughout Christian church history: that humanity was living in its last days—also the fundamental tenet of the early Christian church but which the church has since largely neutralized and insulated in the creeds.

Throughout the centuries, various groups within the church and its periphery had time and again actualized the old dream of the return of Jesus Christ and Judgment Day, and Russell was merely one example of a modern offshoot with this particular infatuation or dream, and sides had to be chosen before it was too late. At first, however, there was plenty of time, because the so-called "harvesting period" would not end until October 1914.

But in that month, that year, it would surely all come to an end.

Did Russell Predict World War One?

In the course of writing this book, as my research reached the year 1916 and the demise of our main character, I was initially astonished at the claim presented by Russell's followers, who posthumously published the "Seventh Volume" of his life's work *Studies in the Scriptures* in 1917, that their leader had predicted the outbreak of the First World War.

My surprise was the result of reading the preface to the Seventh Volume of this work, where the authors quoted one of Russell's previous articles from his magazine *Zion's Watch Tower* of July 1, 1898, in which the term "world war," as it literally can be read in the Danish translation of the preface (in Danish *en Verdenskrig*), allegedly had been used. However, I found the claim suspect and approached one of my contacts, author Carl Olof Jonsson of Sweden, who was kind enough to provide me with copies of the above mentioned *Zion's Watch Tower*, in which the term "world war" was nowhere to be found. Instead, the original text of 1898 is "an era of general warfare," a term that certainly correlates much better with what Russell originally thought.

As I went deeper into this issue, I realized that even in this, an area which I had been willing to yield Russell *a bit of credit* (!), it turned out he most certainly had *not* prophesied a world war starting in late 1914. But bereaved Danish followers had of course—in light of the world events at that time—optimistically thought that they could give Russell's words a slant towards events as they unfolded after the start of the First World War. Of course, this is all too understandable in light of what *didn't* happen that year. (*Studies* 7, 1917; *ZWT*, 1898, column 207–298)

But before we continue, let's take a closer look at this strange story's earliest origin.

Russell's Beginnings

Charles Taze Russell was born in 1852 in Old Allegheny, a suburb of Pittsburgh at that time. He was the second son of Joseph L. and Eliza Birney Russell, both of Scottish-Irish descent. Charles' mother died when he was nine. He attended public school and was subsequently taught by private tutors, yet he never received any kind of formal, higher education. Still, he studied much more on his own, and his self-education became the basis for his unconventional studies of the Bible, and eventually, his attempts to find "Biblical truths," which the major Christian churches, in his view, had corrupted.

His parents raised him in the teachings of the Presbyterian Church, but at age fifteen, Charles left this church in favor of the Congregational Church, and later, the Young Men's Christian Association (YMCA). He was unable to find what he sought in any of these places (*Studies* 7, 1917, chapter 3; *WT*, 1916, p.170, 171).

The young Charles Russell was a searching soul and like so many others at the time, found himself in a religious crisis. He asked himself, under the influence of the deism and rationalism of his time, many reasonable questions, concerning, for example, that he could not reconcile the doctrine of pre-determination and an eternally burning hell with God's infinite love. Similarly, he could not reconcile the contradictory teachings of the various churches, and subsequently he developed doubts as to whether these teachings were compatible with Bible texts at all. Already at age seventeen, he supposedly stated that:

"A God that would use his power to create human beings whom he foreknew and predestinated should be eternally tormented, could be neither wise, just nor loving; his standard would be lower than that of many men" (*WT*, Dec. 1, 1916; *Proclaimers,* 1993, p. 43; original source missing in the *Proclaimers*).

This apparently reasonable view sounded appealing to a number of searching individuals, many of whom did not feel at home in the various church communities of the United States. This view, of course, rested on the underlying assumption that one could earnestly imagine a God subjected to the logic of human reason.

Russell's Protestant Heritage

The Presbyterian Church, in which Russell spent his childhood years, was one of the great free churches of America. The church originated in Scotland and came to America with the immigrants in the 1640s, establishing a strong presence particularly in Maryland, Virginia, Delaware, New York, New Jersey and Pennsylvania.[10] The teachings of this church were based on pious ideals, rationalism, order, and a clearly defined authoritarian structure. It based this structure on the principles of the charter of the Reformed Church, with the four offices of the New Testament: priest, teacher, deacon and elders. Today this church is found particularly in Switzerland, Holland, England and the United States.

The Presbyterian Church was founded by reformer John Calvin. Calvin was, in terms of personality, the incarnation of pure, genuine fanaticism. As a result of the Reformation initiated by Martin Luther, Calvin established a church regime in Geneva, Switzerland, which truly surpassed what other churches have achieved in terms of coercion and terror. Going to church became mandatory for all, and all entertainments were condemned. He would tolerate no opposition, and any who got in his way were swiftly dealt with and executed. In 1545, within the course of just three months, thirty-four death sentences were carried out. The process against Michael Servetus (Miguel Serveto Conesa), a mathematical genius who had raised objections against the trinity doctrine, resulted in the most severe punishment, as Servetus was literally tortured to death, an event which was applauded by a number of Protestants at the time.

Calvin had introduced *theocracy*, or God-rule, in Geneva, a despotic church regime based on a fundamentalist belief in the Bible as the supreme authority, not only for the church, but for the state as a whole. Exploring God's omnipotence and motives was inexcusable, for which reason the faithful were unable to contribute to their souls' salvation. Everything had been determined beforehand; everyone was predestined for either salvation or damnation, which was a concern for Catholicism with all its gifts of grace. For man, it was now all a matter of getting confirmation of being part of the elect, recognizable by certain marks in one's own life: strong faith, pious living and the will to eradicate those who are impure and sinful. Personal success in business was also a plus. Calvin restored the strictness of the Old Testament, resulting in intolerance against dissenters.

It is tempting here to also mention events in Salem, Massachusetts, in the late 1600s, where a veritable religious mass hysteria erupted. The Puritans favored the doctrine of predestination and believed God had predetermined who would be saved and who would burn eternally in Hell. It was deadly dangerous to preach a different doctrine in town. A critic of the church, Philip Ratcliffe, was beaten, had his ears cut off and run out of town. In 1692 the outrageous events culminated. A young girl, Betty, daughter of newly elected pastor Samuel Parris became ill, exhibiting "fits"—convulsions, contortions and outbursts of unintelligible speech. Other girls soon manifested the same symptoms, and the doctors could only find one reason: witchcraft. Nineteen "witches" were hanged on Gallows Hill. One defendant, Giles Cory, was tortured to death. Five others, including an infant, died in prison. From 1693 to 1706 Salem's residents came slowly to their senses. In 1697 a reconciliation day was held, "a day of atonement." In 1957 the state of Massachusetts apologized, and in 1992 they erected a memorial to the victims of witch hunting.[11]

These atrocities occurred 160 years before Russell was born.

According to Russell himself, his own critical attitude to Christian churches' development and decay eventually led him into a deist-rationalistic pattern of thought, characterized by a vigorous antipathy towards all religion. This was not uncommon in this era, and around 1868–1869, he supposedly openly declared himself a skeptic, in opposition to both the Bible and church creeds.

Deism involved the belief in a God who, although he might have created the world eons ago, had no involvement in his creation any longer and never intervened in the course of human affairs. Deism eventually led to the rationalism of the 17th century, strongly influencing the philosophical and religious ideas of the era. Rationalism finally nominated *reason* to be the decisive factor in all matters of dogma, God, miracles and so forth.

While the young Russell seemed undecided, exploring the religious arena as he did, he had far more success in the commercial field. Apparently, he was a born businessman, for already at age fifteen, he became a partner in his father's shop, J. L. Russell & Son, Gents' Furnishing Goods. Later, Charles Russell expanded his father's business, opening a whole chain of stores. Russell's skills as a businessman and organizer would eventually be invested in the religious movement and activity that was to become his life's work—The International Bible Students Association (IBSA). When Russell later retired from business life, he had made more than a quarter of a million dollars, a significant sum at the time. (*Gentile,* 2004, p. 47; *Divine Purpose,* 1959, p. 17)

That is, at least, the official version, but information suggests Russell continued with his "secular" investments and businesses up to around 1912–1913, three years before his death. We will encounter more on this topic later.

Russell Discovers the Adventists

Still searching for "the truth," *around* 1869[12] Russell first came in contact with one of the four or five Adventist Churches active at that time, the Advent Christian Church. This group had broken away from the original Adventist movement, which more or less collapsed after the Great Disappointment of October 1844. A renowned Adventist preacher, Jonas Wendell of Edenboro, Pennsylvania, who was associated with the above-mentioned church (previously a co-editor of an Adventist magazine, *The Watchman,* that preached the return of Christ in 1850), had come to Allegheny to speak at a meeting. Once more Wendell warned his listeners of the imminent coming of Christ in 1873. Russell listened with growing interest and later wrote about Wendell in retrospect:

"Seemingly by accident, one evening I dropped into a dusty, dingy hall in Allegheny, Pa., where I had heard that religious services were held, to see if the handful who met there had anything more sensible to offer than the creeds of the great churches. There, for the first time, I heard something of the views of Second Adventism, by Jonas Wendell, long since deceased" (*Studies* 7, 1917, p. 53; *Divine Purpose,* 1959, p.14; *Proclaimers,* 1993, p. 43, 44).

Whether Wendell (who died in 1873) really held a fiery judgment-day sermon on the theme of the approaching second coming of Christ on that evening in 1869,[13] or if he simply presented one of the intricate calculations the Adventists were still known for at this time, is difficult to say. In a reference to this first meeting with Wendell, Russell later wrote in the first volume of his magazine, *Zion's Watch Tower*, published from July 1879, that Wendell was "then preaching the burning of the world as being due in 1873."[14]

But, no matter the subject which Wendell was addressing, the message Wendell presented to his audience that evening certainly changed the course of young Russell's life. From that time on, Russell became what we could now label a *late* Second Adventist.[15] Just as William Miller, the founder of the Second Adventist movement, Russell had been "changed." He discarded his former deism and skepticism, and became absorbed by the subjects the Adventists had focused on for decades.

Ten years later, around 1879, Russell stated he had not been too enthusiastic about the "primitive" teachings of the Adventists, but this was probably a maneuver to distance himself from the Adventist movement, which at that time did not have high status in American society. However, the motivation behind Russell and his followers would soon be the same as that of many Adventists: A categorical belief in the doctrine that they were living in the "last days," the end of the "evangelical age," that the return of Jesus Christ was still on the program (even if it had already taken place—*invisibly* from 1874) and that the "chosen few" would be found through "harvesting work." The latter was a large-scale propaganda campaign of published writings, lectures and the organization of interested people to meet the objective that as many as possible be reached with the apocalyptically oriented message before it was too late—a clear copy of the Adventist beliefs and practices.

About 1884 Russell attributed that Adventists played a certain, if admittedly less prominent, role in God's plans:

"Odium attaches to the study of prophetic time by reason of past misapplications of it by 'Second Adventists' and others, and the consequent failures to realize the events expected to occur at stated times. We see, however, that even this has been a part of God's plan to obscure the subject to all but the class for whom it was intended, by permitting contempt and ridicule to attach to it, thus hindering the worldly wise and prudent from apprehending it.... Our Adventist friends have failed to recognize both the manner and the object of the Lord's return..." (*Studies* 2, 1916 (1889), p. 30).

In other words, God had "obscured" these matters for the Adventists because the Biblical truths they had been so near to "grasp" had obviously been reserved for Russell and his small selected group of followers in Allegheny (additional discussion of this later). In this way, the Adventist-friends performed a *preparatory work* that lasted more than thirty years and was a part of God's schedule. (*Studies* 2, 1917 (1889), p. 241, 242)

In reality, Russell was much more of an Adventist than he would have cared to admit at that time. The next chapter outlines the history of Adventism to elucidate the significance of Russell's encounter with Jonas Wendell and its important impact on the development of Russell's project. The reader may choose to bypass the chapter and come back to it later. Adventism's history is, however, in many ways a prerequisite for understanding the formation and development of *Russellism*.

Chapter 2

The Adventists Before and After 1844

The entire American immigrant culture's foundation rests on Puritan immigrants—out of England and Holland in the early 17th century (1600–1640)—who came to the New World with their anti-Catholic, anti-Protestant and anticlerical attitudes.[16] They wished to build a utopian society in the new world, so they could practice their religious perceptions in peace and without interference from larger churches. Their aim was nothing less than unlimited religious freedom—a product of European Enlightenment. In England, for example, they had been persecuted by the Church of England, Presbyterians and others. The Puritans looked to the New World and possible colonies where they could settle. With a story similar to the Puritans, the Anabaptists, who had been exposed to cruel persecutions in Switzerland around 1527, settled in Rhode Island. Thus, the colonies were typically characterized by specific religious denominations: Catholics, Protestants, Puritans, Quakers, Anabaptists, Baptists, Jews and others.

Most famous of these New World settlers are the *Pilgrim Fathers*, a group of Puritan separatists, who immigrated to Holland in 1609, but as a result of dissatisfaction with the more free conditions of that country, chose to depart Holland and come to the young Virginia colony. Off course following a rough Atlantic crossing further complicated by illness, they arrived in Cape Cod Bay in 1620. They founded the Plymouth Colony in 1621.

In 1607 an expedition led by John Smith and sent by The Virginia Company of London, a trading company, founded the first colony in America, Jamestown. The expedition's main purpose for coming to the new continent was to locate gold. King James the First of England sanctioned this expedition that ended in a human tragedy. The majority of its members died. They failed to locate precious minerals, yet they did discover another form of "gold" in the lucrative production of tobacco. The place they went ashore, Chesapeake Bay, lay on the coast of what later became Virginia.

In the course of time many new fundamentalist churches arose everywhere, especially emanating from the Baptist groups that also, because of persecution in Europe, had come to America in the first half of the 17th century. The Bible was their principal book and their daily pivot. It was ever-relevant and contained the truth about past, present and future. They were *Biblicists*[17] and interpreted the Bible literally. Many of these immigrant groups threw themselves into primitive ponderings that, for example, in the late 18th century were strongly inspired by the world political events of Napoleon's time. Many of these people began to scout for "the signs" mentioned in the "small apocalypses" of the Gospels—Matthew 24, Mark 13 and Luke 21—which should augur Christ's return and the end of the world. The Book of Daniel from the Old Testament and Revelation from the New Testament were and are central to these speculations, which particularly came to dominate the Adventist's Biblical interpretation in the 19th century—and later the Bible Students during the latter part of the century. (*Holmquist,* 1927, p. 97, *DK*; *The Last Trump*, p. 19-26)

The Millerites

Adventist supporters in America were initially known as "Millerites," a name derived from its founder William Miller, a Baptist. They came from many established churches in North America, but since there was talk about a widespread revival, it was not necessary to form a new religious community: This was just before Judgment Day's arrival! Therefore, Miller and his followers remained members in their respective churches until they were either thrown out or left of their own will. Although Adventism became widespread up through 1840–1844, it had many more opponents than supporters.[18] Opponents were especially found among university-trained theologians, but also among some of the leading preachers of the day, such as Moses Stuart, Charles G. Finney and Horace Bushnell. (Lindén, 1971, p. 49–52)

Researchers, who by virtue of their training knew the above mentioned signs for Christ's return, first and foremost, needed to be understood in the context of the time when they were written, had to distance themselves from the doomsday hysteria of the Millerites. Otis A. Skinner, pastor of the Fifth Universalist Society in Boston, refuted the Adventist teachings in his book *The Theory of William Miller,* 1840 (originally five discourses), which was based on the so-called "Preterist" view—*roughly* an early version of *the historical-critical method*.[19] Skinner basically argued that the "apocalyptic signs" in question exclusively revolved around events connected with the siege and destruction of Jerusalem in AD 70 and that predictions of Christ's return were concurrent with this destruction ("Christ came at the destruction of Jerusalem," p. 23); thus the Adventists' apocalyptic expectations were completely pointless.

The various texts of the New Testament are mainly comprised of letters from individuals to Christian congregations within the Roman Empire of that time, and a letter will always reflect the ideas and conceptions of its originating period in a number of primary and secondary areas, just as a letter from a Millerite, arguing for Christ's second coming in 1843–1844, would reflect the contemporary conceptions of that era. To summarize: The Christians of the first century believed, in essence, that apocalyptic events belonged to the very near future. A long-term future perspective did not exist in that century, but became topical later, as the reappearance failed to transpire.

Moses Stuart (1780–1852) was a professor, preacher and debater; he spent much of his time refuting the interpretation methods of Miller. This is particularly seen in Stuart's work *Hints on the Interpretation of Prophecy*, 1842, where Stuart noted the potential damage inflicted by non-educated people as they erroneously believed they could interpret extremely difficult Bible texts. In a revised edition of *Hints* from 1851, Stuart clashed with Adventist writer Rev. George Duffield of Detroit, author of the book *Millennium* or *Second Coming of Christ*, which supported Millerite doctrines.[20] (Lindén, 1971, p. 49, 50)

Swedish Seventh-day Adventist Ingemar Lindén emphasized that leading intellectuals of the time engaged in the debate, which reveals that the revival movement Miller set in motion must have been of *significant* proportion, at least significant enough to spark concerns among the general public. This may be difficult to imagine today, in our global, diverse world, but one must not forget that American society in the 1830s was still "virgin land," and the common religious conscience had not been stabilized and consolidated. At that time, the United States' population was only a fraction of what it is today. Chicago, which sprang up around Fort Dearborn, had a mere one hundred residents in 1820. It grew rapidly in the following decades, reaching 30,000 in 1850. In the 1840s, the overall population of the United States was seventeen million. Railroads had not yet been built on a large scale, which is why most traveled either on horseback or by carriage. (Gordon 1990, p. 54; Lindén 1971, p. 51)[21]

William Miller: Setting North America on Fire

The originator of Adventism, William Miller, was born in 1782 in Pittsfield, Massachusetts, and was raised in Low Hampton, New York. He was the eldest of sixteen children, and his father was unable to provide the schooling he himself had once dreamed of. At the time, there were only around twenty colleges in the United States, and private tutoring was usually reserved for the wealthy.

In 1803, at age twenty-one, William married and the couple moved to Poultrey, Vermont, where he became acquainted with certain prominent members of society. In 1809, Miller became constable, and later sheriff and justice of the peace; he was eventually appointed to the rank of lieutenant in the Vermont State Militia. Young William embraced the fashionable philosophy of deism, became a Freemason and also joined a literary society.

In 1812, England and the United States went to war. Miller received his rank of lieutenant and was promoted to captain in 1814. After the war, at age thirty-one, he left the army and returned to Low Hampton, New York, with his family to take possession of his late father's farm. The farm Miller inherited made him a man of means. He returned to the sermons of the Baptist Church, and from time to time he even took care of the reading, recitation and preaching. After a very emotional spiritual awakening, his religious engagement took on a more drastic shape. It was as if he had been transformed, changed; as if the inner dwellings of his soul had been restructured. He quickly replaced his former deistic conceptions with something that looked more like a Jesus-obsession. (Bliss, reprint 1988 (1853), p. 26; 67)

Miller now devoted all his time to Bible studies and religious topics from Genesis to Revelation, and around 1818, he concluded the second coming of Christ would occur in 1843. Miller investigated these matters more thoroughly from 1818–1823, and became convinced that the Bible was a "system of re-vealed truths." The return of Jesus Christ on clouds from heaven would occur *literally*,[22] followed by a cleansing of the earth or a weeding out of all evil, so that our planet, at the end of the millennial reign, would again become the home of the righteous. At the Second Coming, Jesus would raise the righteous dead from their graves, and they would join the presently living righteous ones, to live for all eternity—respectively, in heaven and after the thousand years on earth. The wicked, on the other hand, would die, only to be resurrected a thousand years later to receive their final judgment, along with Satan and his demons. (Gordon, 1990, p. 29-31; Lindén, 1971, p. 34-36)

Miller arrived at the date of Christ's second coming via an amateurish in-terpretation of the Book of Daniel 8:14: "Unto two thousand and three hundred days; then shall the sanctuary be cleansed." By juxtaposing the 2,300 days with the seventy weeks spoken of in Daniel 9 (the commandment of the resto-ration of Jerusalem in Daniel 9:24-27), he concluded that both the "days" and "weeks" had their starting point in the year 457 BC. In Deuteronomy 14:34 and Ezekiel 4:5-6, he discovered another *previously used* calculation formula: One prophetic "day" equaled one year. So, by starting at 457 BC and counting 2,300 years, Miller arrived at 1843. Therefore, in 1843, the world would be cleansed. (Knight, 1992, p.16, 17)

Starting in 1831, Miller spoke widely about his ideas. Although he was ner-vous about public appearances, he held as many as 800 lectures from 1834 to 1839 and managed to speak publicly despite his hesitation. As a modern Adventist historian puts it, "putting a whole country on fire" (Knight, 1995; Danish edition, p. 14).

Increasing the Preaching Work's Efficiency

In 1839, as Miller traveled the country giving lectures, he met a young, bold preacher from Boston, Joshua Vaughan Himes (1805-1895), who adhered to the Christian Connexion church (not to be confused with the modern Christian

Connexion founded by Dr. John Scott in the US in the last decade of the 20th century). Himes told Miller that if he wanted to spread his message more efficiently, he should focus on the larger cities in the US, and he offered Miller his assistance.

According to George R. Knight, a modern Seventh-day Adventist historian,[23] Himes was not only an advocate of educational reforms, but also a prominent pastor, and was at the time, it is said, a recognized leader in the interchurch movement to facilitate the earthly millennium through broad-based personal and social reform and progress. (Knight, 1992, p. 10-12)

Himes quickly rose to be one of the prominent leaders of the new movement, and quickly began publishing and editing the first Adventist magazine, *The Signs of the Times*, in March 1840. Soon, many other Adventist magazines[24] were being published; there was pressure in those years to spread the word because in their view the whole world had to have the last, final message. A comprehensive missionary work was initiated, and grand plans were made to prepare to spread Miller's sensational message. Grand campaigns were organized in Boston, Philadelphia, Portland (Maine), New York City, and further inland in Rochester and Buffalo, Detroit and Cleveland. In 1833, Miller had eight people aiding his efforts, but by 1844 the number had increased to 200 preachers and 500 public speakers. The crowds at the conventions were of considerable magnitude, as they often varied between 1,000 and 10,000. (Knight, 1992, p.10-12; Lindén, 1971, p. 38-39; Gordon, 1990, p. 55-56)

The movement aroused worldwide interest. In England, Edward Irving (1792–1834), a Presbyterian minister, started focusing his sermons on "the last days," and in 1832 he established a free church in London where he preached that the second coming of Christ was imminent. The Adventists were in contact with Irving for a while, but diverging opinions ended their collaboration.

The message of the Second Coming—or advent, hence the name of the movement the Second Adventists—resulted in extensive reactions around the world that are hard to imagine today. In 1844, over five million magazines and newspapers were reportedly shipped around the world by distributing material to ships' crews. The followers of the movement came from various Protestant Churches of North America, and at a large conference in Boston in 1840, approximately 200 clergymen from the various churches and denominations came together to discuss these matters. During 1844, another fifteen conferences were held.

Other methods were also implemented. Camp meetings were introduced in 1842, in Quebec, Canada, and in East Kingston, New Hampshire. The sum of $1,000 was collected to buy a new, large tent, fifty-five feet high, and 120 feet in diameter, one of the largest tents of its time. "The Great Tent" held from 3,000 to 6,000 people, and was put to use regularly up until 1844. From 1843 to 1844, 124 tent meetings were held with crowd sizes ranging from 2,000 to 15,000. It is estimated that as many as 500,000 people attended these tent meetings during this two-year period. (Lindén, 1971, p.40; Gordon, 1990, p. 70-73; Knight, 1992, p. 22; Bliss, reprint 1988 (1853), p. 180-181; Dean, 2004)

"Come out of Babylon"

Early in the 1840s, the Millerites had still not left their various churches. However, a growing, widespread critical attitude toward the Millerites is evident through Methodist clergyman Levi Stockman at a Methodist conference in Maine in 1843. Stockman was encouraged to abandon his Miller-inspired message, but he refused. Shortly before Stockman's death he was threatened with expulsion from the church, and his wife and children would lose his pension. Stockman was accused of heresy and ostracized. Events like these compounded the Millerites' ever-increasing desire to leave the larger church communities in favor of establishing one of their own, and it didn't take long before they were encouraged to leave "Babylon," a term that had thus far been reserved for the Catholic Church. But as of that time, the Protestants were also viewed as part of this great enemy of "true Christians."

"Babylon the great is fallen, is fallen.… Come out of her, my people, that ye be not partakers of her sins, and that ye receive not of her plaques." So goes the text of The Revelation of John 18:2-4.

That the churches were Babylon was obviously pure fantasy. The Revelation of John refers to the city of Rome at the end of the first century AD, in which the emperor Domitian instigated a brutal campaign of persecution and atrocities against the Christians. It was in this context that the Book of Revelation was written.[25]

In the summer of 1843 Charles Fitch, one of the so-called "Four Great" within the movement, established as fact—in his opinion—that Babylon was the Antichrist, and that anyone who refused to recognize Christ's imminent return was also Antichrist.

The message was not to be misunderstood and served to emphasize that the clergymen and ordinary churchgoers, who were opponents of the Adventists, also belonged to Babylon. If anyone would be assured of salvation before Christ's return, they had to leave their respective churches and join the Adventists. Fitch wrote this strong appeal:

"To come out of Babylon is to be converted to the true scriptural doctrine of the personal coming and kingdom of Christ.… If you are a Christian, come out of Babylon! If you intend to be found a Christian when Christ appears, come out of Babylon, and come out Now! … Come out of Babylon or perish." In other words; if one wished to stay alive and be saved, one had to become an Adventist. (Gordon, 1990, p. 86; Knight, 1992, p. 13)

The Millerites challenged all Christian denominations of North America in the same manner as Russell would some forty years later. And all the preachers of the various denominations, preachers who had at one time opened their doors for the Adventists and their message, now changed their attitude regarding the enlisting machinery of the Adventists. Miller wrote about this development, which he rejected: "From that time, the churches, as might have been expected, were closed against us" (Gordon, 1990, p. 86).

In January 1844, Miller was excluded from the Baptist Church. He had finally reached his point of no return. The lack of moderation within the movement became increasingly obvious, as outside criticism increased.

"The Great Disappointment"

Miller preached from the beginning that the second coming of Christ would occur "around 1843," in other words, the prediction was not a precise one. His followers wanted a more specific date, and eventually, in January 1843, Miller informed his followers that he, after a thorough examination of the prophecies of the Book of Daniel (8:14), had decided that Jesus Christ would return to earth sometime between March 21, 1843, and March 21, 1844, to "bring all his saints with him; and that then he will reward every man as his works shall be" (Bliss, reprint 1988 (1853), p. 172).

On March 9, 1844, the headlines of the Adventist paper *Western Midnight Cry*, read: "Prepare to meet your Maker." On March 25, 1844, Miller was devastated and remorseful. As one might have expected, absolutely nothing had happened.

The entire movement found itself in a state of emergency, but at this time, it did not dissolve. The Adventists awaited developments, but they did not know what to do or believe. Confusion reigned everywhere within the movement. (Lindén, 1971, p. 45)

Miller's colleague, Joshua V. Himes, refused to give up hope, although he acknowledged that they had been mistaken on the matter of the exact date. He tried to gain time by referring to the prophet Habakkuk, a so-called *late-Jewish* scripture from the Old Testament; the words are crucial to this type of doomsday cult:

"And the LORD answered me, and said, Write the vision, and make *it* plain upon tables, that he may run that readeth it" (Hab. 2:2-3; Knight, 1992, p. 15).

People in Miller's group made a desperate attempt to correct the date for the second coming of Christ, resetting it to April 18 or 19, 1844. There were still no signs of the movement's collapse. Everyone held their breath in eager expectation.

The so-called "Seventh-month movement" was therefore now formed, based on new, intricate calculations by leaders S. S. Snow and *George Storrs* (note the name). According to these new interpretations of the scriptures, the cleansing of the world by fire would not occur in the spring of 1844, but in the *fall*, to be precise, in *October*—a month that would become a mandatory ingredient in Charles Russell's time schedule and later in the Jehovah's Witnesses' permanent schedule fixture before 1975. (Lindén, 1971, p. 56)

The new date was presented at an energetic camp meeting in Exeter, New Hampshire, in August 1844.

S. S. Snow entered the meeting place on horseback, and a woman introduced him to the audience with the following words: "The Lord has servants here who have *meat in due season for his household*. Let them speak, and let the people hear them" (Gordon, 1990, p. 91; italics are mine).

Snow then presented the audience with a new date. The 2,300 "days" would expire on October 22, that year, which corresponded with the tenth day of the seventh month of the Jewish calendar. Miller had been correct about the date of March 21, but as it had been predicted in the parable of the ten virgins (Matthew 25:1-13), the Second Coming would not occur without a certain waiting period. The rescue attempt was a success, and the majority now accepted this new date. The disappointment over the previous date, March 21, seemed to have already been forgotten. The new slogan read: "Behold, the Bridegroom cometh! Christ is coming on the tenth day of the seventh month! Time is short, get ready! get ready!!" (Knight, 1992, p. 16; Lindén, 1971, p. 56; Gordon, 1990, p. 76-78)

The arch-Adventist George Storrs, who would later become a significant character in the development of Charles Russell's theories, wrote in the Adventist magazine *The Midnight Cry* with great eagerness concerning this new date:

"Beyond a doubt, in my mind, the tenth day of the seventh month, will witness the revelation of our Lord Jesus Christ in the clouds of heaven. We are then within a few days of that event. Awful moment to those who are unprepared—but glorious to those who are ready. I feel that I am making the last appeal that I shall ever make through the press" (Knight, 1992, p. 16).

Another fanatical leader, C. R. Gorgas of Philadelphia, must have had an intense desire to surpass the others in this immense folly, claiming to have experienced a vision in which he received information about the exact time of the Lord's return: Jesus would appear at three o'clock in the morning, October 22. Gorgas must have encouraged all the residents of Philadelphia to leave town, just as Lot had left Sodom before its destruction. (Gordon, 1990, p. 78)

After the disappointments of the spring of 1844, the Millerites now had a "new understanding" of the parable in Matthew 25:1-13, the parable of the five foolish brides and the five wise. The foolish brides had remembered to bring their lamps, but had forgotten the oil, whereas the wise ones had remembered both. As the bridegroom was late (March 21, 1844), they all became drowsy and fell asleep. When midnight came, someone cried out: "Behold, the bridegroom cometh; go ye out to meet him." They all woke up and prepared their lamps, but the foolish had no oil, and asked the wise if they could borrow some, but the wise had nothing to spare, and referred them to the merchant. While the foolish brides were gone, the wise went into the wedding hall and "the door was shut." When the foolish ones returned, they were rejected at the door: "Verily I say unto you, I know you not. Watch therefore, for ye know neither the day nor the hour wherein the Son of man cometh" (Matthew 10–13; KJ).

Appropriate words of warning, which Christian church leaders of the first century, especially after AD 70, may have used for maintaining discipline in the congregations.

In 1982 Ingemar Lindén, one of the best experts on the Seventh-day Adventists in the 20th century, wrote about the impact on the fans:

"The movement was saved, at least for a time, and the wheels began once more to gather speed. Millerism was headed against its dramatic climax: Christ would come at last on October 22. The hard-core Millerites invested their whole existence on that calculation. Many sold or gave away their property or money in full accord with their religious convictions" (Lindén: *Shut Door*, 1982, p. 14).[26]

On October 6, 1844, Miller and Himes, although somewhat reluctantly, decided to confirm the new date, only sixteen days prior to October 22. This may have been the result of certain political adaptation to the last vigorous effort of their followers. Again, Miller was overwhelmed with optimism and great expectations, as he in a letter to Himes exaltedly proclaimed: "I see that the time is correct.... My soul is so full I cannot write.... My doubts, and fearness, are all gone. I see that we are yet right. God's word is true; and my soul is full of joy" (Knight, 1992, p. 16; Gordon, 1990, p. 89-101).

Joshua Himes announced on October 16 that the offices of the magazine *The Advent Herald* would be closed because of what would come to pass one week later. The contemporary press wrote, in the aftermath of these events, that fanatical Adventists had dressed up in their white linen robes—ascension robes—tailor suited for this glorious event, in which they would ascend up into the heavens. If this story, one that would later make headlines around the world, was nothing more than journalistic exaggeration or if it was true is hard to say. But on Miller's property there most certainly is a large rock from which one can get a good view of the sky on cloudless nights. To this day, this rock bears the rather telling name: Ascension Rock. (Knight, 1992, p. 17; Gordon, 1990, p. 96)

During the last week before the second coming, many Millerites abandoned their daily work. The exact number of adherents who actually expected Christ's Second Coming on that day in October is uncertain, but scholars and researchers have estimated the number to be more than one million. (Lindén, 1971, p. 58; Dean, 2004)

The day passed and night came without incident. They waited all the way to midnight before going home, crestfallen and depressed.

In the Adventist journal *The Advent Review* dated August 1850, a mile-long article by Miller appears; it had been previously published in his magazine, *The Advent Herald*, on November 13, 1844. This article is important because it indicates a "new understanding" of the *nature* of Christ's Second Coming, which would become crucial for the Seventh-day Adventists (and later Russell)—something the editors, Himes, Bliss and Hale, also note in a footnote with the reprinted article. Namely, toward the end of the article Miller wrote under the heading "OUR POSITION":

"We cheerfully admit that we have been mistaken in the *nature* of the event we expected would occur on the tenth day of the seventh month; but we cannot yet admit that our Great High Priest did not on that very day, ACCOMPLISH ALL THAT THE TYPE WOULD JUSTIFY US TO EXPECT. WE NOW BELIEVE HE DID" (with capital letters exactly as it appeared in the journal).[27]

What Miller had in mind here is not entirely clear but it may have been the hint of a solution-model, whose fulcrum was the *manner* of Christ's return. This manner would soon materialize as the rescuing device they could cling to in the future.

However, the great inrush the movement had experienced halted after October 22. From all directions, laughter and ridicule descended upon the Millerites, and the movement disbanded. The followers either returned to their previous churches, to be reintegrated into normal, ordinary society, or they steamed on in new groups. Some refused to quit. Some still awaited a "new understanding."

By November 1844, Joshua Himes had taken the position, as Miller had already done—which since the second century AD has been relevant for all apocalyptic Christian believers—that although "we are near the end … we have no knowledge of a fixed date or definite time, but do most fully believe that we should watch and wait for the coming of Christ, as an event that may take place at any hour" (Knight, 1992, p. 20).

Miller resigned and constantly found exculpatory explanations that would mitigate criticism. Still, his excuses were merely a penitent reflection of his better days.

In *The Advent Herald* of December 11, 1844, Miller writes in a letter to editor Joshua Himes, organizational leader of the crumbling movement: "Dear Bro. Himes:—Be *patient*, establish your heart, for the coming of the Lord draweth nigh. For you have need of *patience*, that ye have done the will of God, ye might receive the promise. For yet a little while and He that shall come will come, and will not tarry. This is the time for *patience*, it is the last trial the dear Second Advent brethren are to experience…"

Also in the letter quoted above, Miller assured his friend that "[We] have done our work in warning sinners, and in trying to awake a formal church. God, in his providence has shut the door; we can only stir one another up to be patient…" Miller and his followers now resorted to claiming that on October 22, 1844, God had "shut the door" (as in the parable with the ten brides), and that no more could be saved. (Matthew 25:10; Knight, 1992, p. 18; 37; *Advent Herald*, p. 8, Dec. 11, 1844)

After the Great Disappointment, Joshua Himes tried to reorganize the disappointed Adventists at a conference held in Albany, New York, in April 1845. When this failed, he became leader of the Evangelical Adventists and their American Millennial Association (1858), which was in opposition to the Adventists who, among others, fought to reintroduce the Sabbath (the future Seventh-day Adventists). In 1863 Himes joined the Advent Christian Association, as this group called themselves prior to 1864, and accepted the specific beliefs of this group. Then he moved his family west to Buchanan, Michigan, where he became a leader among the Advent Christians and started a newspaper, *The Voice of the West* (later *Advent Christian Times*). In 1865 he became chairman of the newly formed American Advent Mission Society and further planned to start a school in Illinois. (Internet sources for Joshua V. Himes include guam. net, "Church History 16: William Miller 2"; and *Wikipedia*.)

But, for now, this story must return to those very dramatic days in 1844–1845.

Although most decided against setting new dates, some of the more prominent preachers did just that—among others, Joseph Bates and James White (later Seventh-day Adventists). The latter wrote in *The Day-Star*, September 1845, that all "will receive a certainty that before the tenth day of the seventh month 1845, our King will come." This date-fixation continued with new dates, almost every year, until 1875. (Lindén, 1971, p. 75; *Gentile* 2004, p. 42, 43)

The original Miller movement, whose supporters before the collapse numbered somewhere between 150,000 and one million, was reduced to about 50,000 core supporters, who did not return to their original churches. Eventually, they divided into some twenty-five independent Adventist churches, of which the most important were:

1. Evangelical Adventists (Miller and Himes)
This group was originally organized in 1858 under the name American Evangelical Advent Conference. One of their most important doctrines was in conformity with the major Protestant denominations—namely that the dead remained conscious and the wicked would be tormented for all eternity. They opposed Storrs so-called "conditionalism" or "conditional immortality" (more detail on this in the next chapter). They practically gave up on the second coming, but remained steadfast in the belief that, in principle, it was near. The group dissolved sometime around 1880.

2. Advent Christian Church (1860 to 1864: The Advent Christian Association)
This group, which had broken away from Miller and Himes' original movement around 1845, reorganized in 1860 after yet another Second-Coming fiasco in 1854. They advocated for Storrs *conditional immortality*, and were unwilling to abandon the belief in Christ's imminent return, as they were still occupied with it. They did not keep the Sabbath on Saturdays, as the Seventh-

day Adventists, but kept Sunday as a day of rest, like most other Christian denominations. This group is now the second-largest Adventist Church in the world, in 2009 numbering some 88,000 members in thirty-eight countries. Of this, 25,617 members are in the United States (compared with 28,300 in 1925), which actually means that in the US the church is in decline compared to, for example, the Seventh-day Adventists. Members of the Advent Christian Church today acknowledge that their church community probably is a *godfather* to the Jehovah's Witnesses. (John Roller, ACC; *Wikipedia* 2009)

3. Seventh-day Adventists (SDA)

From 1845, with the introduction of the Sabbath on Saturdays and acceptance of the "visions" of "prophetess" Ellen G. White, the SDA church established itself as an independent continuation of original Millerism, definitively organized between 1860 and 1863. Much like Miller and Himes, they ceased setting final dates for the second coming of Christ. This group remains the world's largest Adventist community, today numbering more than 16 million baptized members. Counting the large number of sympathizers, the SDAs number some 25 million adherents, with—reportedly—a yearly growth of one million adults baptized. (Source: SDA, Denmark)[28]

4. Life and Advent Union

In 1863, George Storrs and others broke away from the Advent Christian Association to form this group. One of their fundamental doctrines was that those who were not saved would never be resurrected; they also believed that the millennium reign (the thousand-year reign) *had passed*. Storrs became president, but left the small church community in 1871. Life and Advent Union reunited with the Advent Christian Church in 1964 (see #2 above).

5. Church of God

Also known as the Age-to-Come people, they were characterized by the belief that the return of Christ would occur at the "end of the evangelical age," and that His return would mark the beginning of an era of "reconstruction" (age of "restitution," in other words, the millennial reign), and that the government of Christ, with Jesus on the "throne of David" and the Jews in a leading role, would govern all the nations of the earth from Jerusalem. It is this thousand-year reign, and the coming millennium under the rule of Christ—the age-to-come—that gave this branch of the Adventist movement its name. The ideas of the Age-to-Come people were accepted by a number of Adventists in all the various churches. Under the name Churches of God in Jesus Christ according to the 1888 by-laws, they made attempts at uniting as an organization in 1869, 1870, 1888, 1889 and 1910. In 1921, this fellowship re-emerged under the name Church of God General Conference, also known as the Church of God of the Abrahamic Faith, despite great internal resistance against a formal, unified organization. (Arthur, 1970, p. 352-370; Hewitt, 1983, p. 274; and also in-depth information from C.O. Jonsson and J. Turner Stilson)

It was members of the Advent Christian Church or breakaways from the age-to-come movement, that Russell encountered in the years 1869–1879. Even though he personally never mentions the Age-to-Come people, so far I remember, it is my opinion that they, at least indirectly, must have put their characteristic brand on him. I have come to this conclusion based on the fact that many of Russell's ideas and those of one other excommunicated preacher from the Advent Christians (J. H. Paton) share some striking similarities with the doctrines of the Age-to-Come people (more on this in the following chapter). Before I explore this connection, a more thorough look at The Seventh-day Adventists, who partly developed ideas that more or less were shared by the other Adventist groups is needed. Some of their ideas may also indicate that Russell encountered this Adventist group around 1877 and some years thereafter.

The "Invisible" Return

The so-called "left wing" of the Adventist movement had resorted to putting faith in the "spiritual messages" and "visions" of their charismatic leaders, including the later-prominent Seventh-day Adventist, Ellen G. White, among others.

Ellen G. White and her husband James held the opinion that no ungodly person had any chance of being saved after October 22, 1844. The door to salvation had been closed or shut, and the majority of mankind had been left outside in the cold. This was less unfortunate when the program was changed to the so-called "open door," which was also communicated in visions supposedly sent from God. Today, Ellen White's role in all of this is a matter of increasing criticism, both inside and outside the Seventh-day Adventist movement. [29] (Lindén, 1971, p. 73-84; Lindén, 1983, p. 35; see also: Lindén: *Shut Door*, 1982, p. 13-32)

One of the groups, which is of particular interest and must be seen in direct relation to the teachings of Charles Russell, The Spiritualizers, claimed that October 22, 1844, had been the correct date and that Jesus *had* indeed returned to earth—but it had happened beyond the reach of the human eye, in other words, *invisibly*. Here we have the fundamental model for the basic, primary doctrines of both Charles Taze Russell and eventually, the Jehovah's Witnesses.

A similar view concerning the *invisibility of Christ* was presented by a member of Himes and Miller's group. Hiram Edson, previously a respected Methodist, received a vision in which he saw that Christ, "our High Priest," instead of leaving his heavenly temple to return to earth on October 22, 1844, went into the inner sanctum of the temple to complete an important task before he returned to earth. This was the key!

Edson's views were accepted and later became important to the Seventh-day Adventists' theology, as it explained why something other than the expected had happened at the "right" time. The October 1844 date had been correct all along, as leader Ellen G. White, who was still receiving "spiritual messages," confirmed.

Joseph Bates now became the spokesman for another strange view, namely that, before Jesus would judge the living and dead at his Second Coming, an "investigative judgment" would occur. (Knight, 1992, p. 22-39) This theory was also later incorporated into the doctrines of the Seventh-day Adventists.

These very specific doctrines, whose real task was to explain away the failure to return in 1844, are today under sharp criticism by Dr. Desmond Ford of Australia, a former Seventh-day Adventist leader there and in the United States.[30] (Lindén, 1983, p. 109; 125)

In 1980, Dr. Ford was stripped of his "ministerial credentials" and is no longer a member of the church. In the late 1990s, he applied for membership at a congregation in Australia but was rejected. He now leads the break-away group, Good News Unlimited.

Clarifications and Compromises

George Storrs, the Methodist preacher who joined the Millerites in 1842, contributed his ideas concerning the conditional immortality of the soul early in the history of the movement, and Storrs ideas on this issue became more or less established truths within the entire movement. In 1848, the White group—which evolved into the Seventh-day Adventists—arrived at a certain "political" clarification about what to believe and think. That same year, five basic doctrines were established (originators are noted in parenthesis):

1. The visible and personal second coming before the establishing of the millennial reign. (William Miller)
2. Jesus began his cleansing of the heavenly sanctuary on October 22, 1844, and this cleansing would culminate in the final confrontation with evil. (Hiram Edson)
3. The gift of prophecy was not limited to "Biblical times" only, but remained part of the present time. (This aspect must be viewed in relation to the prophet, Ellen G. White.)
4. The Sabbath was still to be kept. (Bates and James White, Ellen's spouse)
5. Immortality was not a birth-gift, but could only be received by accepting Jesus Christ as one's Savior. (George Storrs)

These dogmas corresponded to the various special perceptions of the factions, so it was presumably not for the sake of the original or "pure" Christian teachings that they adopted all these strange articles of faith, but rather for the sake of everything that might attract the members from outside groups and create harmony within the Seventh-day Adventists.

At that time, the Adventist's fundamental belief was that the warning should only sound until the Second Coming. But as of 1844, that event had been pushed into the future, because they had gotten the *new understanding* that Jesus as investigator had been performing an inspection since October 1844, called the Investigative Judgment, in the innermost sanctum of the heavenly temple. After the tenets had been accepted, the closed door, which for a while had stopped all extrovert activities of the Seventh-day Adventists, was again opened, and in addition they *organized*, which meant—as shown through Storrs' words, well-known in these circles—they immediately became "*Babylon!*"

This children's disease was apparently now overcome.[31]

In 1861, the American Civil War broke out, an event that Ellen G. White had *supposedly* foreseen in one of her visions. In 1862, the US government wanted to introduce mandatory military service for all young men, but the Adventists were allowed to refuse on the grounds of their religious conscience. The issue of conscientious objection is later found in both the Bible Students movement and the Jehovah's Witnesses.

Ellen G. White is believed to have used her visions to manage the movement in the direction she thought was the most pragmatic. In 1863 she again had a vision, whereby the Seventh-day Adventists became aware of their health in relation to the establishment of the Millennium. It was therefore decided that all members of the movement had to live a healthy life and abstain from pork and *blood* until Jesus returned. The surgeon John Harvey Kellogg established the Battle Creek Sanatorium; his brother Will K. Kellogg founded the Battle Creek Toasted Cornflake Company, later known as Kellogg's, which still produces and sells its famous cornflakes—a very tasty product. (Lindén 1971, p. 142; 312; see also Ingemar Lindén: *The Last Trump, p. 309-361, generally on Adventism, SDA and the Health Reform*)

J. H. Kellogg and Ellen G. White made the health issue, a popular cause at the time, their drawing card. Besides eating meat, the consumption of alcohol, tea, coffee and chocolate, as well as smoking tobacco, almost automatically resulted in *eternal damnation,* and thus all these things should not be done by the faithful; on the other hand, J. H. Kellogg praised the use of bran after every meal. Following a power struggle between Ellen G. White and one other prominent leader, A. G. Daniels, Kellogg was expelled from the organization in 1907. (Lindén, 1971, p. 309-334)

As early as the 1850s, Ellen G. White decided that they might very well be forced to wait for a while in the matter of the second coming of Christ. It appears the Seventh-day Adventists already, at an early stage in the history of their organization, had accepted the possibility that they too would be earthbound *for some time.* After the consolidation of their movement and organization in 1864, and after the restart of their missionary work, it could be argued that the "advent" was becoming a *formal* ingredient in the doctrines of the new church—exactly the same way as it happened for the Christian Church in the early centuries.

The fact that various Adventist churches as a whole are still dynamic more than 160 years after 1844 testifies to the incredible longevity of the apocalyptic idea and the apocalyptic movement's ability to spin a new yarn on earlier mistakes. And not without precedent, they now live in the realm of excitement the always theoretically close Judgment Day creates, but at the same time, the hour of truth is postponed indefinitely to reassure the congregation members, whose energy can now manifest itself within the framework of the growing organization.

So let us now return to this story's main course to see what Russell's circa-1869 encounter with independent Adventist preacher Jonas Wendell entailed—an encounter that fundamentally changed C. T. Russell's life.

Chapter 3

The Adventistic Connection[32]

In the early 1870s, Charles Taze Russell and his small group of likeminded followers initiated the movement today known as the Jehovah's Witnesses. The name Jehovah's Witnesses, however, was not used until 1931. Originally the group referred to themselves as Bible Students and later as International Bible Students.[33] Their common cause was a shared interest in the second coming of Christ and the world's forthcoming end. Young and energetic, C. T. Russell was a central figure in this small group or *class*, initially numbering approximately ten members: Charles Russell; his father and sister, Joseph Russell and Margaret Russell; William I. Mann; and William H. Conley and his wife Sarah Conley (nee Shaffer), as well as a few others. In fact, a source states that around 1870 Russell was not just a member but already led this small group—although it seems unlikely a young man could play such a crucial role at age eighteen, or at most twenty. (*Divine Purpose*, 1959, p. 14, 15)

The group, which was formed for Bible study only, discussed various doctrinal issues between 1870 and 1875, and supposedly, one of the most controversial doctrines of the Bible Students originated in the early days of this group: They discovered the second coming of Christ would occur *invisibly*. (*Proclaimers*, 1993, p. 43-49)

At least, this is how the Jehovah's Witnesses describe the early beginnings of the movement in the 1870s. But, in the shade of this official version of the events, some secrets lay hidden, secrets that hitherto have not been widely known. In fact, Russell forgot many details about the aforementioned "discovery," which was partly retrospective (written later) and partly not his own but due to his many Adventist connections. (Jonsson in *Quest*, 1988, nr. 1, p. 47-58)[34]

Years later, Russell had this to say about his encounter with the Adventists:

"We felt greatly grieved at the error of Second Adventists, who were *expecting Christ in the flesh* and were teaching that the world and all in it except Second Adventists would be burned up in 1873 or 1874, and whose time settings and disappointments and crude ideas generally of the object and manner of our Lord's coming more or less reproach on us and upon all who longed for and proclaimed His coming Kingdom" (*WT*, 1916, p. 170, 171; *Divine Purpose*, 1959, p. 15; italics are mine).

It is appropriate here to underscore that in his later writings Russell did not distinguish between the various Adventist groups of his time, even though he knew perfectly well there were different churches—for example the Seventh-day Adventists. Still, the "errors" he referred to were particularly common among the Adventists he knew, all of them being either members or expelled members of The Advent Christian Church.

A leading member of this, as of today, second-largest Adventist Church in the world, Dr. John Roller (at that time, Resource Center Coordinator inside ACC), informed me by email (May 2005) that it was common knowledge within his church that Russell, early in his career—probably sometime between 1872 and 1875—had applied for ministerial credentials at this church, only to be rejected. This information corresponds well with the young Russell's possible pattern of development. When he could not be appointed as a preacher of this church, he devoted his efforts to starting a new movement, consisting of, among others, members of the Advent Christians who were attracted to Russell's eschatological preaching. This may explain Russell's subsequent rejection of the Adventists—or "the Second Adventists" as he calls them.

In the following years (1875–1879), the Advent Christians, who around 1870 were the original Millerites' immediate heirs, were the subject of Russell's attempt to achieve a prominent position within small Adventist churches, and many members from the movement later went over to Russell. More on this as we proceed, but first, let's meet the person who made such a great impression on the seventeen-year-old Russell that he, shortly afterwards, converted to Adventism.

Jonas Wendell's Influence

According to Russell's own retrospective account, Jonas Wendell was the first Adventist he met:

"I have been a Bible student since I first had my attention called to the second coming of our Lord, by Jonas Wendell, a Second Advent Preacher, *about 1869*, who was then preaching *the burning of the world* as being due in 1873. But though he first awakened my interest on the subject, I was not a convert, either to the *time* he suggested nor to the events he predicted.... Thus growing in grace and knowledge for seven years, the year 1876 found us. Up to this time we persistently ignored *time*, and looked with pity upon Mr. Thurman's and Mr. Wendell's ideas (The latter was preaching the same time as Bro. Barbour; viz., The burning of the world in 1873.) We regarded those ideas as unworthy of consideration..." (*Supplement to Zion's Watch Tower*, July 1, 1879; italics about 1869 are mine).

I think Russell's meeting with Wendell was of greater importance for Russell than it was for Wendell, because this Adventist preacher became very important to Russell's development. It is true that Russell later mentioned Wendell as his "friend," but there is very little known about their real relationship. However, Russell's meeting with Wendell had a decisive influence on the rest of his life.

Did Russell later tell those Adventists, who flocked about him in 1879, that this important man, Jonas Wendell—who was well known as an independent preacher and generally accepted by the Advent Christians and with whom he was in some way associated—had been one of Russell's friends because he wanted to give an impression of his own importance? I don't know. It's only a guess. It would be both human and understandable. Still, perhaps Wendell and Russell had met a few times after the evening sermon in Allegheny in 1869.[35]

Jonas Wendell of Edenboro, Pennsylvania, was born in 1815 and died August 14, 1873. He was a zealous preacher, following in the footsteps of William Miller. Around 1843 he received "remission of sins" in Syracuse, New York, and afterwards united with the Methodist Episcopal Church. After the Millerites' Great Disappointment in 1844 he experienced periods of personal crisis, like many Adventists.

As noted earlier, Wendell was co-editor of an Adventist magazine, *The Watchman*, which was published just once in 1850 promoting Jesus Christ's return in the same year (they only produced one issue). Wendell had contacts with Adventists and similar groups everywhere. For example, in 1853 he participated in a conference in Rochester, New York, where John Thomas, leader of the Christadelphians and publisher of the magazine *Herald of the Kingdom and Age-to-Come*, was the featured speaker. Thomas was not a declared Adventist, but his views were close to both the Adventists and the Age-to-Come people, two groups which later very much inspired Russell. Thomas affected Russell both directly and indirectly, something I will try to show later.

Wendell was also engaged in the so-called "1854 movement," which taught the imminent coming of Christ in 1854; after this expectation had also failed, Wendell's "faith failed him," and he turned aside from "the Word" for several years.[36] Around 1865, Wendell's faith recovered by help of Adventist friend C. B. Turner, and Wendell now proclaimed 1868 as the time Christ would come again, *again*. When this also failed, Wendell published a little booklet of sixteen pages, *Present Truth, or, Meat in Due Season*, in 1870; his new prediction fixed the return to happen in 1873. This booklet contains all the usual calculation material typical for the Second Adventists: The "1,335 days" from the book of Daniel would not end in 1843 as Miller had predicted, but in 1873. Naturally it was pure fabrication, and the seventeen- or eighteen-year-old Russell was, according to his own account, very critical of Wendell's newest predictions.

Yet his interest on the subject was awakened.

Wendell was a true "end-timer," always occupied with speculations of the next year for Christ's return. This was obviously his way of making life more dramatic, more exciting. For him all the years—1843, 1844, 1850, 1854, 1866-1868, and at last 1873—were connected first with hope and fervent expectations, and then with despair and depression. This pattern was apparently typical for this Second-Adventist preacher, and I assume, many of his contemporary fellow believers, as well. (Pastor-Russell.com, July 30, 2008)

It is likely Wendell also contributed ideas to Russell's new movement as Russell read the booklet *Present Truth, or, Meat in Due Season*. The similarities are striking.[37]

Jonas Wendell was not the only Adventist who affected Russell, and Russell freely admitted this later on.[38] Of course, there's no shame in letting oneself be influenced by peers and contemporaries, whether the issue was religion or anything else, still in Russell's case, it appears that the issues extended beyond mere influence.

With his small group, Russell more or less constructed a new religious community by copying the contemporary Adventists, who were ever his main source of inspiration. It would later be revealed that Russell's primary method lay in adapting ideas and thoughts "borrowed" from others, whereby he became a kind of *eclectic*.[39] The end result was a *conglomerate* of Adventist ideas (and ideas of related groups like Age-to-Come and Christadelphians), interpretations and doctrines, all revolving around belief in the second coming of Christ, the dawn of the Millennium and the approaching end of the world. He never openly admitted it, but I assume that he, in this way, sought to recruit Adventists from different groups, and in particular the Advent Christians, to his own new association, which was founded on his new magazine, *Zion's Watch Tower*, first published in 1879.

It is likely the young Charles Russell, sometime after he attended Wendell's evening sermon in 1869,[40] had been trained in Adventist thoughts and doctrines by George W. Stetson who, according to *Proclaimer's*, was "an earnest student of the Bible and pastor of the Advent Christian Church in Edinboro, Pennsylvania" (*Proclaimers*, 1993, p. 45).

Like Russell, Stetson was Wendell's friend; it was Stetson who also wrote Jonas Wendell's obituary for *The World's Crisis* on September 10, 1873. Before Stetson died in 1879, it was his request that Charles Russell, his earlier bible student and now friend, would deliver the funeral speech. So, the 27-year-old Russell belonged, I assume, to this group of friends or colleagues. But whether Russell was at some time a real member of the Advent Christian Church remains unknown. Neither Wendell nor Russell can be found in the files of earlier members of this church. (John Roller, Aug. 2008; *Proclaimers*, 1993, p. 45)

Therefore, it is not easy to prove Russell's association with the Advent Christians. The ties between the Second Adventists were very loose at this time, although, as stated earlier, they were divided into many small churches, groups or sects. They were united across sectarian lines, and they had friendly social relations. So he could have been a member, or he had been accepted into the circle of Advent Christians in Allegheny. The latter is far more likely. I think this period was important for the education of the young, idealistic and very ambitious Charles Russell. With Wendell as a model, probably from 1869–1871 to about 1876–1877, Russell evolved as an *independent* Adventist, but in the last-mentioned two years he began working with a small, newly formed Adventist group that had broken away from the Advent Christian Church. And, as previously noted, in 1879 Russell started his own magazine; in this situation, it became important for him to demonstrate distance from the Adventists, while at the same time trying to attract them.

However, it is rather certain that a number of known Advent Christian members, who would later join Russell's group, had a decisive influence upon the course of his life. Other well-known Adventists from various groups would also have direct or indirect impact on the religious development of Charles Taze Russell and his doctrines. (*Proclaimers,* 1993, p. 45)[41]

George Storrs

Around 1872–1874, Russell most likely had very close ties to renowned Adventist George Storrs (1796-1879). Storrs published the *Bible Examiner* (1843–1863; re-published from 1871 to 1879), a magazine which Russell contributed to from 1876 to 1879.[42] Although Storrs was an old Second Adventist adventurer, he is spoken of kindly by today's Jehovah's Witnesses, most likely because of the sympathy Russell held for him. Storrs presumably became a father figure to the young Charles Russell.

Supposedly, Charles Russell and his father and sister were even re-baptized by Storrs sometime before or around 1874, which, if this is the case, must have been a private endeavor, as Storrs was an *independent* Adventist at that time. And, as is the case with Storrs, Russell too embraced an antipathy toward the concept of "organized religion" (John Roller), which was one of Storrs' hobbyhorses. In any case, it seems Storrs was a decisive factor in Russell's maturing process. That Storrs played a role in Russell's life can be seen in *Proclaimers*, published in 1993. Storrs is mentioned as an "associate of Russell," although I personally have doubts on whether their collaboration really was that extensive. (*Proclaimers,* 1993; see: Storrs, George, in Index, p. 745)

From Storrs, the young Russell learned much of what would eventually become, and remain, fixed inventory in the Jehovah's Witnesses' theology. Many beliefs and practices of the Witnesses, both past and present, were borrowed directly from Storrs: the yearly "memorial" celebrated at Easter, the doctrine of the restoration of an earthly paradise, and the teaching of conditional immortality. This latter doctrine involves the belief that man is not born with an immortal soul, but rather acquires this immortality by surrendering himself to God through Jesus Christ and in return receives eternal life as a gift from God. Those who reject this gift, the wicked, will eventually be destroyed in the "second death," the *lake of fire* (The Revelation of John 20:14). Storrs became the most prominent defender of "conditionalism," as well as the teaching that death is merely a sleep-like state of unconsciousness until the resurrection.

In 1842, Storrs worked as a travelling preacher for the Adventists. One other Adventist leader, Charles Fitch, accepted Storrs' new doctrines in January 1844, and others followed. Still, regarding these issues, Storrs faced strong opposition from William Miller. Storrs had been active among the Adventists who had revised Miller's original calculations after the disappointment of April 1844 and decided the second coming of Christ would not occur until October 1844. When this date also failed, Storrs was quick to abandon William Miller, as did a number of others. In return, Miller discarded Storrs' doctrine of conditional immortality.

Around 1853, Storrs flirted with the Age-to-Come Adventists, but then joined the Advent Christian Association, formed in 1860. In 1863, he left even this Adventist church to finally form his own, and that same year, the Life and Advent Union was established.

Storrs was a genuine idealist, a restless soul and quite a troublemaker, not easy to please. In 1871, he broke away from his own Life and Advent Union to resume publishing his old magazine from 1843, the *Bible Examiner*, to which Russell later contributed articles (Russell was thus, in a way, Storrs' employee, rather than vice versa). Storrs abandoned his previous article of faith—millions of people who had died without ever hearing the gospel of Christ would be eternally damned (so-called annihilationism). Rather, he concluded they too would be resurrected and granted life in an earthly paradise with the chance of acquiring immortality, *eternal life on paradise earth*, which is almost exactly what the Jehovah's Witnesses of today believe. Due to his many doctrinal revisions, among other things, Storrs lost a great deal of his authority.

Russell's critical attitude toward other churches and Christian organizations was partially a result of his collaboration with Storrs, and partially because it was typical for Adventists, as is also the case with the Jehovah's Witnesses today, to view all other major denominations as part of "Babylon the great." Storrs was known for statements such as "no church can be organized by man's invention but that it becomes Babylon *the moment it is organized*"—an opinion which, among other things, must be considered in light of the Adventists' difficulties with established churches in the US after the 1844 failure. Despite their differences of opinion, Russell still respected this aging preacher and businessman, fifty-six years his senior, a man who, in terms of Adventist adventures, was both a veteran and a pioneer. (Penton, 1986, p. 15-17; Steinhaug, 1993, 1.1; *ENCY.*, 1966. p. 1263; *Proclaimers,* 1993, p. 42-47; Knight, 1992, p. 63)

George Storrs died on December 28, 1879, at age eighty-three. Russell, twenty-seven at the time, wrote this eulogy:

"The Lord gave us many helps in the study of His word, among whom stood prominently, our dearly beloved and aged brother, George Storrs, who, both by word and pen gave us much assistance; but we ever sought *not to be followers of men*, however good and wise, but 'Followers of God, as dear children.' Thus growing in grace and knowledge for seven years, the year 1876 found us..."

It seems clear that Russell, in view of his close ties and friendship with Storrs, viewed the Adventists as *less-mature brothers* who still had reason to hope for salvation. Some other Second Adventists (Advent Christians) apparently, after Russell began to publish *Zion's Watch Tower*, served as advisers to him, including George Stetson, who also died in 1879 at age sixty-four.

Clearly, by 1879, Russell must have achieved considerable status among the Adventists.

Henry Grew

Beginning in 1807, Henry Grew served as a minister in the Baptist Church of Hartford, Connecticut, but because of his critical views, he left the Baptists in 1811 to devote his time to studying the Bible independently.

Henry Grew marked himself in a number of notable areas with future connections to Russell and Jehovah's Witnesses. Russell held an antitrinitarianism view partly gained from leading Advent Christians, and partly from Grew, who wrote against the doctrine of the Trinity in 1824. Also, leading Seventh-day Adventists Joseph Bates and James S. White, among others, were originally antitrinitarians (as Jehovah's Witnesses are today). In 1828 Grew also began struggling against Christians' participation in war, a position which Russell also later adopted.

Around 1835, Grew published a tract in which he criticized the teachings of immortality of the soul and the doctrine of eternal hellfire—a tract Storrs later stumbled across on a train journey. Grew concluded that, because the wicked do not possess immortality, they could not possibly be subjected to eternal torment in Hell. Only the just, those who have surrendered themselves to God through the Lord Jesus Christ, will receive immortality as a gift from God.[43]

The sequence of events is an almost chaotic puzzle, where pure coincidences united ideas that eventually ended with Russell, who thus became an "anti-heller."

From Grew, Charles Russell probably also inherited his antipathy towards the Freemasons, Odd Fellows and similar secret societies, although critics of our day argue that Russell himself, in a transition period, was a Freemason. Still, Russell could presumably not have been a member of a lodge, because in later years he encouraged his followers "to have nothing whatever to do with any of these semi-religious societies, clubs, orders, churches," as he considered all to be "parts of Babylon" (*Studies* 6, 1904, p. 580-581).

Nevertheless, I have some doubt, since American author Maurice Barnett, in a book available on the internet (viewed June 5, 2010), notes that much about

Russell indicates a connection with Masonic societies, as follows: "Russell, and other Witnesses, were influenced by more than the superstition of pyramidology and numerology. Masonic influence was evident in several ways, right up to the time of Russell's death and beyond. We will not go in to all the evidence but it is clear that Russell was a member of the York Rite Knights Templar. Early terms, such as 'Golden Age' and several symbols were taken from that background" (internet Archive: *Jehovah's Witnesses* by Maurice Barnett).

Seen with contemporary eyes, the elements adorning the Bible Students' magazine, books and buildings—such as the cross-and-crown symbol and the winged sun disc—in the late 1800s may be Masonic in origin. However, they might also have been an expression of speculation in occult symbols; this was in vogue in the 19th century, and their use might have been designed to attract new supporters. (See Barnett, among others.)

Maurice Barnett also notes that when one stands beside Russell's gravestone and looks toward the mini-pyramid at his burial site (built 1921), directly in the line of site is a large Masonic Temple. "What a coincidence," Barnett notes. But this Masonic Temple was, according to the secretary of Lodge 45, Pittsburgh, Pennsylvania, not built until 1987,[44] thus the so-called coincidence fades into history's misty veil. As a result, crucial evidence of Russell's connection with Freemasonry seems, unfortunately, to not yet have emerged. Perhaps one could find revealing archives on the case of the Brooklyn Watchtower buildings' concrete basements, but accessing them is ostensibly a bit of a problem.

Through Grew and others, Russell was presumably also inspired by Age-to-Come Adventists. Grew was in contact with their leader, Joseph Marsh, sometime around 1850; Marsh promoted the idea that the Jews would take a leading role in the future scenario of Christ's second coming. In time, this would be incorporated into Russell's *late*-Adventism. Around 1846, Marsh lingered with the shut-door concept for some time. (Arthur, 1970, p. 226-227; Lindén: *Shut Door* 1982, p. 22)

That the Jehovah's Witnesses of today still feel doctrinal kinship with Storrs and Grew is evident when reading their main publication, *The Watchtower Announcing Jehovah's Kingdom*,[45] in which the careers and temptations of these two individuals are portrayed in kind terms. It is clear, according to *The Watchtower*, that these two gentlemen were "working in the 'field' in preparation for the harvest," before the missionary work of the Bible Students commenced around 1879. (*WT*, Oct. 15, 2000, p. 25-30)

Chapter 4

Crucial Meeting
with Barbour

The Adventist who would influence Russell more than any other was Nelson H. Barbour, an independent Adventist from Rochester, New York. He was previously a prominent member of the Advent Christian Church. Sometime around 1874, Barbour was expelled from the church with another member, J. H. Paton; a few years later, Paton became one of Russell's closest associates—Paton also wrote the first *real* book for the new movement.[46]

While on a journey to Philadelphia in 1876,[47] Russell, as he describes it, *accidentally* stumbled across a magazine titled *Herald of the Morning*—published by none other than Nelson Barbour. Of this event, Russell later wrote:

"When I opened it I at once identified it with Adventism from the picture on its cover, and examined it with some curiosity to see what time they would next set for the burning of the world. But judge my surprise and gratification, when I learned from its contents that the Editor was beginning to get his eyes open on the subjects that for some years had so greatly rejoiced our hearts here in Allegheny—that the object of our Lord's return is not to destroy, but to bless all the families of the earth, and that *his coming would be thieflike, and not in flesh, but as a spirit-being, invisible to men...*" (*Conscience*, 1983, p. 143-144; *WT*, July 15, 1906; italics are mine).

Russell examined the magazine "with some curiosity," but I think evidence indicates he already knew of Barbour, as he did Jonas Wendell, who he met in 1869, and who also predicted Christ's second coming in 1873, which appears in his booklet, *Present Truth, or, Meat in Due Season*, published in 1873.[48] Also, Wendell seems, in some way, to have been one of Barbour's proselytes, but he was spared the new-return failure of 1873, as he died the same year. Working from the assumption that Barbour and Wendell knew *of* each other before Wendell's booklet was published, it seems likely that Russell was also acquainted with Barbour's existence and views *prior to* 1876—the year he allegedly first heard of him. Yet, Russell was keen to be perceived—by his adherents—to be at least Barbour's *equal*, his peer. I therefore think that Russell later deliberately understated Barbour's importance to him.[49]

Russell was *friends* with Wendell, who was *friends* with Stetson, who was *friends* with Russell. So, although the question could be perceived as controversial, it nevertheless appears inconceivable that he didn't know Barbour before he met him early in 1876. At least, he must in some way or another have heard of him, I think.

As early as 1867, Barbour argued for the 1873 date, and since Barbour's ideas were widely discussed and widespread among the Adventists, particularly within the Advent Christians, it again makes it unlikely that Russell first heard about Barbour in 1876. I think that Wendell, at an early stage, must have told his young friend about the controversial Barbour—whose ideas were debated eagerly among the Advent Christians.

But *if* Russell had heard about Barbour, he could not claim later that his little group—independently—had made the same discovery about the *invisible* return of Christ, as Barbour announced around 1875–1876. Therefore, it is my opinion—although I can't prove it—that Russell intentionally downplayed the significance of Barbour's influence on his own doctrinal developments.

Nonetheless, Russell immediately wrote to Barbour and declared his support. (*Gentile*, 2004, p. 42–59; *Conscience*, 1983, p. 145; *Radical Reformation*, p. 54–57, Spring 2008[50])

At the time Russell retrospectively wrote about his unexpected discovery, he had been a fully engaged member of Barbour's movement for four years, but by 1879 Russell needed to distance himself from Barbour and the other Second Adventists.

Nelson Horatio (probably not Homer) Barbour was born in 1823. From 1839 to 1843 he studied to be a physician at Temple Hill Academy in Geneseo, New York. He gave up his medical ambition and began studying for the Methodist Episcopal ministry under a man noted only as "Elder Ferris" but Barbour abandoned that too. Then Barbour joined Millerism and served as a preacher. After the Great Disappointment of 1844 he resumed his education and became a specialist in nerve disorders. Since he'd abandoned any further hopes of an imminent Second Coming, he travelled to Australia to dig for gold. In 1859 he returned to the United States via London. During his journey at sea, he and the ship's minister supposedly performed a systematic study of the prophecies of the Bible, after which Barbour concluded that Miller had simply made a calculation error.[51]

At the British Museum in London, he studied the *Horae Apocalypticae*, first published in 1844 (fifth edition, 1862)[52] by Edward Bishop Elliott, a minister at St. Mark's Church in Brighton; Elliott had predicted the Lord's return in 1866 and proposed, as others would too, *1914* as a possible year for this glorious event. In the same extensive work (2,611 pages), Elliott presented a chart, "World Chronology of the Bible," developed by Christopher Bowen, a minister who suggested that the year 1851 was 5,979 years after the creation of Adam (which *reportedly* occurred around the year 4129 BC, a year Russell would later adopt into his own calculations). Since that time, the Watchtower Society accepted 4026 BCE as the year of Adam's creation. This was used to support the Society's theory that Armageddon would occur by late 1975.

A Literal Creation, 6,000 Years before 1873

In the 18th century, Adventists held the notion that God created the world in six literal days, and at that time, almost 6,000 years prior, Adam had been created. Barbour added the missing years, twenty-one to be exact, to the 5,979 years, and consequently, 6,000 years after Adam's creation calculated to sometime around 1873.

Russell later developed his theories concerning the length of each creation day, calculating that each "day" must have been 7,000 years long. The seventh and last day of creation (and God's day of rest), which must have started around the time of Adam and Eve's creation, would in this way be the entire 7,000 years long when the thousand year reign (the millennial reign) had been added. (See: *What Pastor Russell Said*, approx. 1919, p. 758[53]) Combined, the seven days of creation (the day of rest included) would equal a full 49,000 years, an idea Russell had most likely inherited from William I. Mann, one of ten members in Russell's original Allegheny group. Russell combined this idea with a rather bizarre theory, promoted by one of the scientists at the time. (Jonsson, 2004; *ZWT*, Dec.1881, p.1–2)[54]

The scientist was professor Isaac Newton Vail. In Vail's 1874 pamphlet *Above the Firmament*, he promoted the bizarre theory that the earth had once been surrounded by a system of "rings"—rings that had eventually come crashing down in intervals. The last of these rings—or belts—was supposedly comprised of enormous amounts of water that had, as it crashed into the earth, caused the worldwide flood spoken of in Genesis (Vail further developed his ideas in *The Earth's Annular System*, 1902). Russell's successor, J. F. Rutherford, later presented and explained Vail's theory in his book *Creation*, in which Rutherford also combined this theory of the "annular system" with Russell's ideas concerning the combined length of the creation days, set to last a full 49,000 years (of which the last thousand years, the Millennium, began in 1874 as Russell had proposed). The fact that Vail's idea had been presented in *1874*, would later be *emphasized*, and was to be viewed as an especially significant event by Rutherford, since the "invisible return" of Christ had occurred in the same year. (*Creation*, 1927, p. 29; 49-50)[55] Today there is increasing interest in Vail's Water Vapor Canopy theory among Creationists in the United States.[56]

For now, back to Barbour:

By use of supplementary and highly speculative calculations, based on Daniel 12:11, 12 (1,290 and 1,335 days), as well as The Revelation of John 11:3 (1,260 days; the "days" reinterpreted to mean *years*), Barbour likewise arrived at 1873 for the second coming of Jesus Christ. (*Gentile*, 2004, p. 42-59)

After his return to the United States in 1859, Barbour promoted his discoveries from around 1867 onwards; in 1870 he published a small pamphlet, *Evidence for the Coming of the Lord in 1873*. He also published a number of articles in the Advent Christian magazine *World's Crisis*, which had ties to the semi-organized Advent Christians.

In December 1873 Barbour began publishing his own monthly magazine, *The Midnight Cry,* later *Midnight Cry and Herald of the Morning* (supposedly named after William Miller's publication from the 1840s), which particularly appealed to the Advent Christians. Many members of this group had again become preoccupied with calculating the exact date for the coming of Christ, inspired by Nelson Barbour, and over the course of a few years, Barbour's publication increased its monthly circulation from approximately 15,000 to 20,000 copies.

The "end-timers" were thriving again, and the level of expectation rose, just as in the good old days of William Miller. The Judgment Day scenario worked like a magnet, attracting the naive, gullible dreamers who had not abandoned hope of seeing the Lord in their lifetime. Many associated themselves with the Barbourite movement, which gained significant numbers. Some members of the group, it is said, met at Terry's Island through the fall of 1873 to await the return, but when the year passed without incident, Barbour moved the date forward to 1874 to avoid a total collapse of the little movement. (Schulz and Rachael De Vienne, 2008)

Again, in 1874, nothing happened, and following this new fiasco, which caused a significant defection from the movement, the circulation numbers of the *Midnight Cry* dropped to about 2,000 monthly copies (other sources say 200; *Gentile,* 2004, p. 46), and as neither Barbour nor his readers dared yet another date fiasco, the effort was made to find an acceptable explanation.

It was then, almost by chance, a solution to this "problem" was developed:

Barbour received a letter from one of his readers, B. W. Keith, in which Keith wrote about a new and relatively unknown translation of the New Testament, *The Empathic Diaglott*, by Benjamin Wilson, published in 1864. In this translation, the Greek word *parousia* in the Gospel of Matthew 24:3, 27, 37 and 39 had been rendered "presence" instead of "coming." Consequently, as of 1874, Jesus Christ was "invisibly present"—as opposed to "coming" in the flesh. (*Gentile,* 2004, p. 45; *Divine Purpose,* 1959, p. 18)

B. W. Keith, as previously noted, would later become one of Russell's co-workers as did many other Adventists.

Benjamin Wilson

Benjamin Wilson too was tied to the Adventist movement. Still, there is nothing to indicate that Wilson himself ever considered the translation of the noun in question, *parousia*, to be of particular significance, as Keith, Barbour and later Russell, all felt it implied—although Wilson unwittingly delivered the very *cornerstone* of Russell's *late*-Adventism (Adventism *after* 1870) development. That Wilson himself never considered this invisibility theory had any significance is further emphasized by Wilson's clearly favoring the idea that Jesus, upon his Second Coming, would govern the world from literal, earthly Jerusalem. In other words, he would, as a visible manifestation, be active in the *physical* world.

Benjamin Wilson was born in England in 1817 and died in the United States in 1900. While living in Halifax in northeastern England, he came—via his family, who had originally been Baptists—under the influence of Alexander Campbell's Restoration Movement. Wilson later joined Campbell's organization, the Disciples of Christ. In 1844, the Wilson family migrated to Geneva, Illinois, and established a local group of Campbell's organization. As Benjamin Wilson was a printer by trade, he began a printing business in Geneva, and published a local newspaper, *The Western Mercury*. In the years 1853 to 1865, he published an Age-to-Come, Adventist magazine, *The Gospel Banner and Millennial Advocate*, which reportedly was highly respected within Adventist communities.

Benjamin Wilson's father had held a department chair in Greek at Oxford, and it was largely due to him that Benjamin had been trained in New Testament Greek. It was on this background, without a proper university education, that Benjamin translated the New Testament, word for word, a so-called "interlinear" translation. His motives were to recreate the basic, simple Christian faith: "One Faith."

Wilson's translation was modeled on the German Dr. J. J. Griesbach's[57] translation of 1775–1777, and under each Greek line followed the English, word for word. In a narrow column on the right, Wilson placed his own modern English translation, with explanatory notes at the bottom of the page. Wilson's rendering of the Gospel of John 1:1 may shed light on the tendentious character of his work because he was an opponent to the Trinity doctrine.

The doctrine of trinitarianism is central in major Christian churches: The Father, the Son and the Holy Ghost represent both a unity and a trinity, which together constitutes God. They are three manifestations of the same God. Everyone is equally divine, omnipresent, omnipotent, infinitely wise, infinitely holy, infinitely loving and omniscient. The doctrine was, after great struggle, established as the basic tenet for the Church in the 4th century at the Council of Nicaea, and was incorporated in the article of faith for all Christians. The Trinity, however, was well established in the church's teachings long before the Council of Nicaea in AD 325.[58] About AD 180, Clement of Alexandria, head of the prime Christian university at the time, provided a clear definition of the Trinity which was well accepted throughout the majority of Christendom.

The word-for-word translation in Wilson's *Emphatic Diaglott*, reads: "In the beginning was the Word, and the Word was with the God, and *a god* was the

Word" (italics are mine). In the column on the right, however, he rendered it in accordance with the more conservative translations: "...and the Logos was God." The *King James Version* had: "...and the Word was God" (the Greek *Logos* means "Word" and is usually translated this way).

Wilson's antitrinitarianism is also evident in the Jehovah's Witnesses' Bible translation, the *New World Translation of the Holy Scriptures*, first published in 1950: "...and the Word was *a god*" (italics are mine; *The Kingdom Interlinear Translation of the Scriptures*, Watchtower Society, 1985, p. 401).

As a member of the Disciples of Christ, Benjamin Wilson was greatly influenced by Dr. John Thomas (1804–1871), who shared Wilson's antitrinitarian views, and even *assisted* him in the work on the *Emphatic Diaglott*, for which he received praise in Thomas's magazine, *The Herald of the Future Age*, in September 1855.

John Thomas founded the group known as the Christadelphians (the name means *Brothers in Christ*), whose doctrines and highly speculative last-days interpretations of the Book of Daniel and Revelation make them more than a little similar to the Jehovah's Witnesses of our time:

There is only one god; Jesus is his son, and the Holy Spirit is God's active force. In other words: Antitrinitarianism. Man does not exist after death in *any* form. Once Jesus returns, he will awaken the dead, *sleeping* successors (disciples, etc.), who will then help him govern, and bring justice and peace to the whole world. There is no such thing as an immortal soul, and there is no hell.

The prophecies of John Thomas can be studied in his 1849 book *Elpis Israel* (Israel's Hope), wherein he presented evidence (based on highly arbitrary interpretations of Daniel 11) for a coming war of conquest by the Russian Czar against Constantinople. Thomas prophesied this would lead to the Ottoman Empire's collapse in 1850; the scenario went unfulfilled as expected. Like the Age-to-Come-people, Thomas taught that Jesus, upon his arrival, would govern the world from literal Jerusalem.

I mention John Thomas and the Christadelphians because Russell read and published articles by Thomas. It is therefore plausible that Russell was also influenced by the views of this Adventist—or antitrinitarian—leader, just as he was by so many others. (More on this topic appears in an endnote associated with the last part of this chapter.) In fact: Many Age-to-Come people later went over to Russell, and his books witness to the influence from this movement. It was probably no coincidence that Russell's first book in his *Millennial Dawn* series was titled *The Plan of the Ages*. Russell also delivered four lectures at the 1895 Age-to-Come Conference in Iowa, where he received a small fee; this indicates he had friendly connections with this church.[59]

The events concerning the Watch Tower's acquisition of *The Emphatic Diaglott* around 1901 are somewhat unclear, but copyrights and printing blocks of the *Diaglott* were clearly, as part of some "arrangement" with the family of the late Benjamin Wilson, transferred from the publishing firm S. R. & Wells

Company (later, Fowler & Wells), New York, which for some years had printed *Diaglott* from the original printing plates, in the form of a gift to the Watch Tower Bible and Tract Society—also resulting in great frustration to Wilson's former fellow adherents of the Church of God. (Stilson; *WT*, Nov. 15, 1969)

The printing plates of the *Diaglott* were a prized "relic" for the Watch Tower Society, and it was the movement's main Bible translation for its first seventy years. It was not reprinted before 1927, but from that year and forward to 1993, 427,924 copies were produced. (Stilson; *WT*, Nov. 15, 1969; *Proclaimers*, 1993, p. 606-607)

Still, although the publishing rights to the *Diaglott* were sold to the Watchtower, Wilson never supported Russell, which is revealed by the following:

A number of Adventists were attracted to Russell's movement and doctrines. To confront this attraction or "drawing," Benjamin Wilson's nephew, W. H. Wilson—who had worked closely with Benjamin for several years—published a small, 30-page pamphlet in 1890, *Cunningly Devised Fables of Russellism*, all of which revolved around two central articles of faith: The resurrection of Christ *in the flesh* and the *visible* second coming of Christ. The pamphlet clearly demonstrates that the Wilson family considered Russell to be nothing less than a false prophet, particularly on the issue of the "invisible return" ("secret coming"; p. 23–27). Clearly, there is nothing to indicate that Benjamin Wilson held any sympathy for Russell and his "cunning" ideas. (Stilson)

On the other hand, for Barbour—and later, Russell—Wilson's translation of *parousia* became a decisive factor in their future religious development. And as Barbour and his followers *already* believed the calculations leading them to 1873–1874 in the first place were valid, they easily *read more into* Wilson's translation than Wilson had *ever* intended.

Consequently, it was the idea that Jesus would come again *visibly* that was wrong. Instead, from 1874 he was invisibly present—a "discovery" which, of course, was not particularly new; the Adventists had in a way used the same trick when nothing happened in October 1844. Jesus *had* come that year, but he had merely "moved from one heavenly apartment to another" (Stilson in: "An Overview… 1832–1871;" *ZWT*, Oct.–Nov. 1881, p. 3; *Gentile,* 2004, p. 47-50).[60]

"Time of the Gentiles"

Barbour had previously presented his so-called "time prophecies" and calculations as those before him had done. As early as 1823, in his book *Even Tide* John Aquila Brown[61] presented the length of the so-called "seven times" spoken of in Daniel 4; in Brown's opinion it would last a full 2,520 years. Supposedly, the period began in 604 BC and would end in 1917. Brown juxtaposed this calculation with the "time of the gentiles" found in Luke 21:24. The truth is these two Biblical expressions, "seven times" and "time of the gentiles," have absolutely nothing to do with each other, yet in a few years they would play *the decisive* role in the doctrinal development of the Bible Students, and eventually, the Jehovah's Witnesses.

Barbour decided Brown had been on the right track, but his calculations had been a few years off. Instead of 1917, Barbour arrived at 1914. As early as 1844, two other British pastors, Bowen and Elliott, noted that the seven times would end in 1914. Others, such as Robert Seeley in London (1849) and Dr. Joseph A. Seiss in the United States (1870), had also pointed to 1914. (Penton, 1986; *Proclaimers,* 1993, p. 46; 124)

Around 1872, Nelson Barbour participated in a conference in Worcester, Massachusetts, arranged by the Advent Christian Church. At this conference, the date for the second coming of Christ was discussed, and one year stood out from the others: *1873.* All the participants were in agreement concerning this particular year. In March 1872, the *Advent Christian Times* wrote: "The point on which there seemed to be any general unanimity was the ending of the thirteen hundred and thirty five years in 1873" (the 1,335 days in question are derived from Daniel 12, and have been abused by the Adventists as well as the Jehovah's Witnesses; footnote, *Gentile,* 2004, p. 45). In light of all this, it is highly probable that Russell knew of Barbour long before 1876, as Barbour's theories had been printed in a number of Adventist magazines. Russell most likely swore to *selective memory* when he later suggested that he had "stumbled across" Barbour's magazine and name in 1876.

To complete this picture, it should be added that Age-to-Come leader Joseph Marsh, with whom Wilson had both met and worked alongside in 1856, also speculated in terms of calculations and dates. He believed that the "time of the end" would amount to a period of seventy-five years, ending in 1873. Thus, this date was highlighted in a number of calculations by the Adventist communities. (footnote, *Gentile,* 2004, p. 45)

Also, it becomes increasingly clear, that Russell—as he acknowledged in the eulogy he wrote for Storrs—was a person who *followed men,* for he had been fully dependent on the calculations and theories of his predecessors, whom he had unscrupulously plagiarized.

Everything was now okay. The situation had been turned from failure to brilliant success, and this success was to be proclaimed far and wide. The fact that this "new" explanation to Christ's conspicuous absence could (and should) be characterized as merely a way of explaining *away* the lack of any visible second coming, was quickly brushed aside. Barbour coordinated the many calculations and presented them in his magazine, *Midnight Cry and Herald of the Morning,* in September 1875. The magazine proclaimed the glorious news that Jesus actually *had* come in 1874—not in the flesh, which is what Barbour and some of his fellow Advent Christians had expected—but in the spirit, or "secretly," as the Advent Christians sarcastically said!

At this point Russell is made aware of Barbour's views and Benjamin Wilson's translation of *parousia.* After this discovery, Russell is all enthusiasm, filled with confidence and joy. After all, this is what he and his small group of Bible Students in Allegheny *already* had pondered upon.

Yes, the young Russell was definitely among equals!

Meeting with Seiss

Joseph Augustus Seiss (1823–1904), a Lutheran theologian from Philadelphia, published the magazine *Prophetic Times* (1863–81), a distinguished "millennial journal" in the United States at the time, in which it was argued, contrary to the fundamental tenets of all the major denominations, that the resurrection of Christ had been in the spirit not in the flesh. Since 1856, Seiss described Jesus' second coming as an event that would occur in two distinct phases: One invisible *parusi* (coming), followed by a later visible manifestation.

One of Joseph Seiss' friends had—according to a later account by one of Russell's closest associates, Paul S. L. Johnson—asked the 54-year-old Seiss to invite the young Russell to hear his presentation and argument of Christ's "presence" since 1874, because Russell simply was *the* man that could help Seiss with a "better understanding on these matters" (*The Parousia Messenger*, 1938, p. 525). Actually, the situation was quite the opposite. As early as 1865, Seiss wrote an article for the *Prophetic Times* titled "The Manner of Christ's Coming." Russell's visit occurred early in 1877 and was most likely an attempt to obtain information, as well as strengthen his position among leading Adventists and his own small group of followers.

Russell brought his newly published book, *The Object and Manner of Our Lord's Return*, (printed in 50,000 copies and published by Barbour in 1877) to the meeting. The book bore a certain resemblance, both in title and content, to Seiss' article published in 1865. Here it should be noted that in 1875 Seiss' *Prophetic Times* was changed to *The Prophetic Times and Watch Tower*. Russell simply couldn't resist putting the name on his upcoming magazine to closely associate it with his competitors, and the intention seemed obvious: It was all about attaining authority from a prominent individual who had *already* achieved a position of significant status within the broad Adventist movement, even though he was an accepted Lutheran. Therefore, Seiss also appears to be one of the main suppliers of what would eventually become Russell's dogmas and basic tenets. (Jonsson in *Quest*, 2:1, 1989, p. 47-53; *Proclaimers*, 1993, p. 47)

So, now some evidence is seen that much of the contemporary Adventists' mindset contributed to Russell's "discovery" that when Jesus returned, it would be as an invisible spirit-creature. Russell's discovery was therefore the rediscovery of an already quite widespread Adventist idea. (Penton, 1986, p. 17-18; *Proclaimers*, 1993, p. 46; *Quest*, 1:2, 1989, p. 47-58)

Also Russell's ideas concerning the so-called "secret rapture,"[62] the transformation of the living saints who would ascend to heaven as spirit creatures in connection with the return of Christ, one invisible return and one more manifest (at Armageddon), was primarily borrowed from Joseph Seiss. This *two-stage* return of Christ was completely unknown to first-century Christians, but originated with evangelical Christians in the early 19th century.

From 1826–1830, Henry Drummond, owner of Albury Park in Surrey south of London, and other well-known millenarian scholars, among them Edward Irving founder of the "Catholic Apostolic Church" (a Free Church established in 1835[63]), developed the *secret rapture idea,* presumably based on a book, *The Coming of Messiah*, published in 1827. The book was authored by Spanish Jesuit priest Manuel Lacunza, who under the pseudonym of Rabbi Ben Ezra wrote about the *two-stage* coming of Christ in 1791. Edward Irving, Drummond's friend, translated the book. It was probably on this foundation of original *Jesuit thinking*[64] that Drummond and Irving, and later Seiss, Barbour and Russell, developed their speculative ideas around the secret rapture. Also others contributed early (in the 1830s) to the circulation of the idea, among them J. N. Darby,[65] who together with Irving, of many, is seen as the originator of the idea.

The idea of the saint's transformation at Christ's return must be studied in relation to Apostle Paul's first letter to the Thessalonians (4:15-17), but it is impossible to insert a meaning into the text, which at the same time is about a *two-stage* return of Christ, involving an *invisible* presence. Two thousand years ago, Paul wrote in plain, figurative language, referring to a current and hysterical expectation of Christ's imminent return among the members of the congregation in Thessalonica. Paul tried to reassure the Thessalonians that the "dead in Christ" and the yet-living saint's, virtually at the same moment, would be saved in good order "to meet the Lord in the air."

Based on Barbour's original timetable and doctrines,[66] Russell and Barbour initially agreed "the time of harvest," which would last from October 1874 to the spring of 1878, would end with "the transference"[67] (or the *rapture*) of the living saints. In the spring of 1878, when the rapture failed, Russell in his first article in *Herald of the Morning*, July 1878, advocated the idea that the saints (instead) would arise as spirit creatures immediately upon death, and that the harvest would last another 3-1/2 years, from spring of 1878 to autumn of 1881, at which time the transference (endnote ibid.) would take place. And after these two 3-1/2-year periods (1874 to 1881) which would total "seven years of *favor* to the church," the saints (supposedly including Russell, his wife Maria and his adherents) would ascend to heaven. This was at least, I think, what Russell's supporters thought, but I am not sure that deep down Russell himself believed in all this. Even in this matter, I suppose he was realistic enough to realize that Barbour's 1878 doctrine on the rapture was a blind trail, which in the future could spoil all Russell's efforts to create a new and efficient organization. (*ZWT*, May 1881; *Herald...*, July 1878)

If Barbour's apocalyptic thinking is placed into a timetable, it will presumably look like this: Barbour saw the entire period from 1874 to 1914 as "the time of trouble" (Daniel 12:1; Matthew 24:21). The invisible coming of Christ took place in October 1874, and the resurrection of the sleeping saints began in the spring of 1875. In the spring of 1878, when the harvest time (the 3-1/2 years) was to end, the yet living saints would be changed and led to the sky. From 1874 until 1914 (the time of trouble), the world would be increasingly afflicted by disease, earthquakes, wars, famine, etc. A worldwide "reign of terror" would assume power and terrorize the world until 1914 when violent events would culminate with God's war, the battle of Armageddon. After this, Christ would finally assume power and establish his kingdom.[68]

Barbour, who reportedly could be both a lion and a lamb, could not accept Russell's re-interpretation and came up with other ideas and new "light," and after a short but acrimonious disagreement—which must have taken place early in 1879 (just before Russell started on his own)—the two men went their separate ways. After this breach, Russell continued to advocate the rapture would come in the autumn of 1881, but the whole idea was, as one could expect, cancelled *just before* the unbelievable event.[69] The transformation, or *secret rapture*, doctrine is still—in different versions—an important part of the theology and history of the Jehovah's Witnesses.

The idea of a "secret rapture" in a modern variant is found in the bestselling series of novels written by Tim LaHaye and Jerry B. Jenkins, titled *Left Behind*. In the series, the saints are suddenly torn away regardless of whether they were located in an airplane or a submarine.

The Bible's Stone Witness in Egypt

Dr. Seiss' influence on Charles Russell did not end with the above doctrines. Years later, Russell published a series of books titled *The Millennial Dawn*—later *Studies in the Scriptures*—in which one of Dr. Seiss' other ideas came to play a prominent role.

In chapter ten of the third volume of *The Millennial Dawn*, originally published in 1891, Russell presented some very speculative and eccentric ideas concerning the Great Pyramid of Giza in Egypt. Again, in this case, Russell was probably strongly influenced by Seiss, who had previously published a book under the title, *The Great Pyramid, a Miracle in Stone* (1877).

To my astonishment, as I began scratching the surface of this subject, I discovered Dr. Seiss was merely one of Russell's many acquaintances doing research on the Great Pyramid. It appears Seiss was influenced by two other pyramid researchers, among them John Taylor, an English publisher; in 1859, Taylor published *The Great Pyramid: Why Was It Built? And Who Built It?*

Nevertheless one of the most important characters regarding research on the Great Pyramid seems to have been Charles Piazzi Smyth, royal-appointed astronomer in Edinburgh, Scotland. During journeys to Egypt, Smyth took exact measurements both inside and outside the Cheops pyramid. Russell must have become acquainted with Smyth during his collaboration with George Storrs, as Smyth wrote articles about the Great Pyramid in Storrs' magazine, *Bible Examiner*, as well as the magazine *Herald of Life and the Coming Kingdom*, published by the rather small Adventist Life and Advent Union church, which had been established by Storrs and others. It is highly probable that it was via Storrs, Smyth, Seiss, Taylor, Barbour and others, all seemingly with a weak spot for Adventism and other fantastic ideas, that Russell became involved in the theories concerning the Great Pyramid as "God's stone witness." Russell's involvement with this subject resulted in an attempt to surpass them all. As early as September 1883, in his new magazine, *Zion's Watch Tower*, Russell claimed God had placed the Great Pyramid as a *sign* in Egypt, but it was not until 1891 in the third volume of his book series *Millennial Dawn*, that Russell finally bit off more than he could chew. On page 314 in this volume, he writes:

"Viewed from whatever standpoint we please, the Great Pyramid is certainly the most remarkable building in the world; but in the light of an investigation which has been in progress for the past thirty-two years, it acquires new interest to every Christian advanced in study of God's Word; for it seems in a remarkable manner to reach, in harmony with all the prophets, an outline of the plan of God, past, present and future" (*Studies* 3, 1919 (1891), p. 314).

Based on the inner measurements of the halls and tombs of the pyramid, Russell arrived at the years 1874, 1881, 1910 and 1914. As a consequence, he expected increased troubles for his Bible Student movement in the year 1910 ["...but a trouble chiefly upon the Church may be expected about 1910 AD" (*Studies* 3, 1919 (1889), p. 363-364)].

Of course, none of these things happened in 1910.

Probably the original and more important inspiration for Russell was Barbour's magazine, *The Midnight Cry and the Herald of the Morning* (March 1874), in which editorial staff member John H. Paton wrote about Smyth's book, *Our Inheritance in the Great Pyramid*,[70] published in 1874. Paton, later a staff member at Russell's magazine, wrote in his review that Smyth's pyramid measurements, as seen through Paton's eyes, could be interpreted as prophecies about such years as 1875, 1881 and 1914. In this article is found perhaps the real basis or model for Russell's later pyramid speculations which, among other things, is reflected in the third volume of his book series. So, nearly the whole terminology Russell used in connection with this particular subject appears to have been inspired by or plagiarized from Barbour's magazine.

As previously mentioned, Charles Piazzi Smyth, well known and highly respected in his time, held the position of royal astronomer at the observatory in Edinburgh, Scotland, from 1846–1888, just as he also held a chair at the university in the same town. However, concerning the exploration of the Cheops pyramid as "God's messenger in stone," and the assumption that one could make predictions regarding the future based on the inner measurements of this pyramid, Smyth clearly compromised his scholarly integrity. Due to his more eccentric interests, Smyth was made a laughing stock in the academic community. This did not discourage Russell; Smyth's authority could still be used in promoting his own ideas. And of course, Russell himself traveled to Egypt to inspect the Great Pyramid. That was what all important men did at the time.

Russell's chapter on the Cheops pyramid numbered sixty-five pages, and in his attempt at providing some scholarly basis for his pyramid speculations, he had—before the publication—made his co-worker W. M. Wright approach the renowned astronomer to hear his opinion on Russell's theories (1889–90). Smyth was more than accommodating towards Russell, as he felt there was something new and positive in Russell's thoughts—thoughts Smyth might come to use in his own books, but perhaps that was only polite rhetoric.

As I used the internet to research Charles P. Smyth, to my surprise I discovered where the Watchtower Society, a few years after Russell's death in 1916, may have gotten the idea to erect a memorial at Russell's grave designed as a Cheops pyramid *en miniature*.[71] A similar stone is found on Smyth's grave at St. John's Church Yard, Sharow, Scotland.

Sometime after 1916, chapter ten in *Millennial Dawn*'s third volume was removed by the publishers, although in the foreword from 1916 Russell stated "the light of Truth is shining so clearly and the Divine Plan is so manifest that scarcely a word of the Volume would need to be changed if it were written to-day—twenty-six years later"[72] (Foreword, *Studies 3*, 1919 (1891)).

J. F. Rutherford, Russell's successor as President of the Watchtower Society (a.k.a. Bible Students), later discarded Russell's 35-year-old theory concerning the Cheops pyramid as the "Bible's stone witness," because the Bible Students now believed the Egyptian pyramids had been raised by demon worshippers as a "manifestation of Devil religion…" (*WT*, May 15, 1956; *Proclaimers,* 1993, p. 201).

Russell Adopts Barbour's Ideas

Let us finally return to the year 1876, the year Russell got so involved in Barbour's calculations and theories that he simply decided to adopt the whole thing—lock, stock and barrel, as the saying goes:

"Could it be that the time prophecies which I had so long despised, because of their misuse by Adventists, were really meant to indicate when the Lord would be invisibly present to set up his Kingdom?" (*Proclaimers*, 1993, p. 46)

Russell made arrangements to meet with Barbour in Philadelphia to evaluate the evidence for the second coming (presence) of Christ since 1874 and that the "harvest"—the gathering of the elect—would last until 1914. Barbour's co-editor, J. H. Paton, was also present at the meeting. At this time, Russell was twenty-three, Barbour approximately fifty-two. Barbour managed to convince Russell that Jesus Christ had been "invisibly present" since 1874, the resurrection of the "sleeping" saints had begun in the same year, the "harvest"—and the gathering of *new* saints—began in 1874 and would end in 1878, and the yet-living saints would be *transformed* (see endnote 68) to heaven to meet Jesus Christ in the spring of that year. From this point onwards, their respective groups united.

At this time Russell also wrote an article for the *Bible Examiner*, Storrs re-published magazine. In the article, Russell stated the "time of the gentiles" would expire in 1914, exactly the same year Barbour had noted

I do not think Russell could evaluate all the speculative doctrines that Barbour had developed over the years and which had been presented during their meeting. Therefore, Russell accepted the whole package, perhaps also because he had so little to offer himself; although after that time Russell most likely tried to convince his followers that he—in terms of Jesus' invisible coming—had drawn the same conclusion *before* Barbour. This was probably not entirely in accordance with actual events, but has since been indirectly suggested by the Watch Tower Society.

In 1877, Russell and Barbour co-authored a book titled *Three Worlds, and the Harvest of This World*. In it they explained and justified their mutual faith that: A. the second coming of Christ took place in 1874, and would be followed by a 3-1/2-year harvesting period, in the course of which the "elect" would be gathered, and late in the spring of 1878 *transferred* to heaven; and B. the "time of trouble," which commenced in 1874, concurrently with the "gentile times" (the period of 2,520 years) would end in 1914. And this: "...forty years upon which we have now [1877] entered is to be such 'a time of trouble as never was since there was a nation.' And during this forty years, the kingdom of God is to be set up (but not in the flesh, 'the natural first and afterwards the spiritual'), the Jews are to be restored [about 1881], the Gentile kingdoms broken in pieces 'like a potter's vessel,' and the kingdoms of this world become the kingdoms of our Lord and his Christ, and the judgment age introduced" (*Three Worlds*, 1877, p. 18; 83; 108; 124).[73]

Barbour authored this book. Russell covered the expenses, and on the front cover Barbour's name was in *bolder letters* than Russell's, which indicates that Russell's participation was subordinate to Barbour's. In fact their agreement stated Russell was in charge of the finances and Barbour wrote the book. Still, this joint effort of Russell and Barbour is significant, as the book contains a great many of the ideas Russell and his followers would preach and spread throughout the world for the following thirty-nine years (1877–1916). Even today, many of the ideas and linguistic terms used in *Three Worlds* are part of Jehovah's Witnesses' theology. (Penton, 1986, p. 22)

Barbour, Russell and others also attended an Advent Christian conference in 1877, the Alton Bay Conference, though their presence was less than welcoming (Schulz and Vienne, 2008). Also in 1877 the editor of the *Advent Christian Times*, who was also a spokesman for the Advent Christians, warned his subscribers against Barbour, Russell and Paton, who had particularly aimed their agitation toward this Adventist community in an attempt to cause division:

"One N. H. Barbour, called Dr. Barbour, with his confreres, J. H. Paton and C. T. Russell, is travelling around the country, going everywhere that they can find Adventists, and preaching that Jesus has come *secretly*, and will soon be revealed and mingling in their lectures a lot of 'Age-to-come' trash, all to subvert their hearers. They are not endorsed by Adventists, 'Age-to-come' folks, or anybody else, yet having some money and a few sympathizers they will probably run awhile. They have been to Ohio and Indiana and are working westward. We are credibly informed that one of them boasted in Union Mills, Ind., a few days since, that they would break up every Advent church in the land. We guess not. Their whole work is proselytizing. The Lord never sent them on their mission. Give them no place, and go not near them or countenance them" (*Advent Christian Times*, July 18, 1877; italics are mine; quotation provided by Carl Olof Jonsson in 2005).

Not only is this revealing when it comes to who Barbour, Paton and Russell considered their primary target group, it also shows, in an indirect manner, that the Advent Christians had been (or would potentially be) attracted to Barbour and Russell's claims concerning the "invisible presence" of Christ from 1874. Coming developments would show that the fear displayed by Russell's competitors in the "soul-saving business" was not the least unfounded.[74]

The following year, after they had finished *Three Worlds*, Russell and Barbour re-invigorated *The Herald of the Morning*, which had temporarily ceased publishing due to economic problems. Russell provided the necessary funds and became co-editor (assistant editor) and co-owner, while Barbour attended to content, printing and distribution.

The collaboration with Barbour lasted just two years. From the beginning they were an odd couple—both ambitious and eager to take the lead in their combined effort—the young, enterprising businessman Charles Russell, in his mid-twenties, and the more experienced Nelson Barbour, who had been part of all the previous second-coming fiascos.

All available information indicates that *beneath* their mutual undertaking was an almost constant power struggle. The main reason for the two men's cooperation problems prior to the breach can be attributed to the fact that the saint's *transference* to heaven in 1878 was not forthcoming. Another controversy heated their relationship: According to *Proclaimers* (p. 48) and other sources, Barbour denied the *ransom doctrine*—the substitutionary value of Christ's blood and death—in an article in *Herald of the Morning*, August 1878. In a subsequent article, titled "The Atonement," Russell defended the conservative view of the subject. This disagreement finally led to Russell's decision to break with Barbour. After a short power struggle, in which Paton supported Russell, Russell withdrew from the editorial office, and terminated his financial support of the magazine. Russell wrote:

"Now I leave the 'Herald' with you. I withdraw entirely from it, asking nothing from you.... Please announce in next No. of the 'Herald' the dissolution and withdraw my name" (*Proclaimers*, 1993, p. 48).

Barbour suggested that Russell and his supporters were the foolish virgins of Jesus' parable, and eventually abandoned *invisible presence* and returned to more standard Adventist positions. (*Studies* 7, 1917, p. 54; Schulz and Vienne, 2008)

Thus the two partners became enemies moving in different directions, a situation the young Russell found untenable, as he determined to gain a more important role than Barbour and Seiss in proclaiming the "good news" of Christ's *invisible* or "secret" *presence*.

To insure the attention would be directed exclusively towards him, Russell had to seek a new angle. The solution lay in establishing a new publication and a new association where he could be the sole sovereign—after adapting nearly all his competitors' ideas, of course.

As methods are concerned, the young Charles Russell seems to have been quite ruthless. But as they say, in war, love and politics, not to mention *religion*, all is fair, and as he had long since proven himself a prominent businessman from a young age, he knew all he needed to know about running any kind of operation.

Following his break with Barbour, Russell distanced himself from the Adventists, although he had plagiarized them on almost *every* doctrine. And in this willingness to adapt lay his strength, and also his weakness—as well as his inevitable downfall, remorselessly rising on the horizon.

Barbour, then a printer by trade, published his magazine until 1903 and continued to advocate for Age-to-Come views and further predictions for the return of Christ in 1881, 1886, 1905 and 1907. He died in 1905, at age eighty-three, and did not experience the last date-setting failure in 1907. (Schulz and Vienne, 2008)

Incredibly, after Russell's death in 1916, his heirs rushed, with arbitrary ease, to label Barbour as the "evil servant" mentioned in Matthew 24, because "Pastor Russell took the place of Mr. Barbour who became unfaithful and upon whom was fulfilled the prophecies of Matt. 24:48-51 and Zech. 11:15-17" (*Studies* 7, 1917, p. 54).

Chapter 5

Russell's
Earthly Organization
Takes Form

Russell must have understood nearly from the beginning that his relationship with Barbour was destined to fail, because just one month after Russell left the *Herald*, he published the first issue of his new magazine, *Zion's Watch Tower and Herald of Christ's Presence* in July 1879, even incorporating the word "Herald" in the new publication. The *Tower* symbolism, both in the name and on the front cover, was designed to alert the reader to the magazine's purpose and its editor and to show that the people responsible for the magazine's publication were *on guard*, constantly looking for the signs of Christ's "invisible presence."

While the Adventist magazines experienced hard times,—*The Advent Christian Times* published its last issue in 1878, and others were having difficulties too—Russell's magazine held its ground, and presumably is one of the world's most published religious magazines today (under the name *The Watchtower*), with vast circulation numbers.[75] Russell's Adventist endeavors thereby achieved success to a degree his competitors hardly could have imagined.

The title of the magazine was, I suppose, in part a plagiarism. George Storrs, Russell's previous mentor, published a book in the 1850s titled *The Watch Tower*, plus a subtitle.[76] And British clergyman E. B. Elliott, who mentioned the years 1866 and 1914 as possible years for Christ's second coming, might have also published a magazine under *The Watch Tower* title sometime around 1856. Even the title of Joseph Seiss' magazine, *Prophetic Times*, had had *Watch Tower* added to it in 1875. The term "Herald," known from Miller's *Advent Herald* and Barbour's magazine, also had a certain appeal. Thus we see how Russell combined established publication names to generate appeal among the always date-hungry Adventists (*Divine Purpose,* 1959, p. 296; *Proclaimers*, 1993, p. 48; *Gentile*, 2004, p. 60-61).

In 2008, when I first viewed a copy of the *Christian Times*, the Advent Christians' magazine, I was a little shocked to see the special crown-and-cross logo on the front of this magazine. It seemed that, in 1892, Russell had borrowed the symbol for the front page of his own journal. But I also learned the cross-and-crown image was commonly used by many denominations prior to and during the 19th century. So it is possible Russell simply used the logo as something familiar to many Adventist and nominal Christians (*Divine Purpose*, 1959, p. 296; see also Barbara Anderson's home page: www.watchtowerdocuments.com).

Russell was now sole editor of his own publication, and five other men— among them one named Keith, who had worked for Barbour and who had discovered Benjamin Wilson's *different* translation of the Greek *parousia*—wrote for the magazine on a regular basis. The entire stock of the first issue—6,000 copies—was shipped to Barbour's subscribers, free of charge. Russell had brought their addresses with him when he parted with Barbour. In addition to that mailing list, he had that of another Adventist magazine, *The Last Trump*. This subscriber list was given to Russell by the publication's editor, E. B. Rice.[77] Most likely Rice was affiliated with the Church of God Abrahamic Faith—or Age-to-Come people—as the name Rice is a common family name within this Adventist church. (Jonsson; Stilson)

From 1879 to 1890, *Zion's Watch Tower* subscribers began forming congregations, with members mainly recruited from the Advent Christian Church and the Age-to-Come Adventists. These congregations, referred to by Russell as *ecclesia* (Greek: church; congregation) or "classes," were all autonomous in congregational matters, and loosely organized; nevertheless, they accepted Russell's leadership. Each congregation elected its own leaders or administrators, a panel of seven so-called "elders."

From here forward events unfolded rapidly. Eventually, the subscribers to *Zion's Watch Tower* were encouraged to get organized: "Our readers," the announcement explained, "are much scattered, some places 2 and 3, and on up to 50. Many places they are totally unacquainted with each other.… The proposed meetings we would hope, might conduce to personal acquaintance…" (*Proclaimers*, 1993, p. 50).

Russell personally travelled from congregation to congregation. In 1881, he requested congregations report their locations so he could help the subscribers communicate with each other. In spite of this, at this time it was not Russell's *declared* intent to establish a "church" with a predominant priesthood and imposed articles of faith, something he made clear in an article in the *Zion's Watch Tower* of October–November 1881. He stressed that the Bible Students did not intend to form an "earthly organization," as they all, subscribers and publishers, were part of a heavenly organization: "We adhere only to the heavenly organization—'whose names are written in heaven' " (*Proclaimers*, 1993, p. 204-205).

The entire *concept* of "organization" was looked on with contempt in the circles where Russell recruited his followers; for instance, George Storrs had strong opposition to organized Christianity. According to Storrs, joining or creating an organization would immediately result in becoming part of Babylon. Therefore, the concept of organization was a sore issue among Russell's idealistic adherents, as many had the Adventist microbe in their blood. Eventually though, they would develop their organization to such a degree that Storrs would have turned over in his grave. Storrs, it seems, clearly saw where establishment of a formal organization could lead. Still, for Russell, establishing an organization was inevitable. It is simply a normal, social result of how humans cooperate, compete and evolve. That Russell had already concerned himself with the issue shows, although indirectly, that *this* was the area where the coming struggles would occur.

It was exactly what happened during the Seventh-day Adventists' formation in the early 1860s where the founders met opposition to a proper organization. The resistance was undoubtedly inspired by both George Storrs' warnings and the basic idealism connecting such organization with Babylon, the major Christian churches, which the Adventists had abandoned.

Russell's main publication, *Zion's Watch Tower*, was now the movement's focal point, but the tradition of tracts, leaflets and books published in parallel gradually came to dominate the movement's activities. The Bible Students released *Bible Students' Tracts*, and were faced with the dilemma of how to distribute these new publications.

"Are you preaching?" the subscribers were asked in 1881, whereby the magazine's publisher was indicating a *reward* was associated with this activity: "We believe that none of the little flock will be saved *except preachers...*" (*Proclaimers*, 1993, p. 51; italics are mine).

Before I move on, let's consider that quote for a moment.

It bears the strong implication that if one wanted to go to heaven (when the time came), there were certain requirements involved: One *had* to be active in the distribution of the literature of this newly founded organization. Evidence indicates that some were unhappy about these new conditions, but as the process shook out, the introduction of the preaching work contributed to separating "the tares" from "the wheat."

Russell needed "a thousand preachers," both men and women, who were not burdened by family responsibilities. As travelling booksellers or "colporteur evangelists," each would become a kind of *elite preacher*. By the year 1885, some 300 travelling colporteurs were active. These special preachers, the forerunners to the "full-time pioneers" or "publishers"[78] of our time, had increased to more than 47,000 pioneer-publishers (full-time preachers) by 1965, and by 2011 they numbered 895,844 (in 2004: 858,461). The Peak of Publishers in Kingdom Service occurred in 2011, according to the 2012 Yearbook, with 7,659,019 (*YB*, 2012). However, since the 1960s there has been a significant decrease in the number of hours a pioneer must spend in service. Around 1960, the requirement was 110 hours (Denmark: 100) per month, and in 2006 it was

50 hours. Jim Whitney, a former member who joined the Jehovah's Witnesses in the US in the late 1960s, shared this with me via email:

"When I first became a Jehovah's Witness in the late 1960s, a regular pioneer was required to put in 110 hours of field service. Sometime in the early 1970s it was lowered to 100 hours; subsequently to 90 hours; then 70 hours, and eventually, in 2006, the requirement was reduced to 50 hours for regular pioneers and 35 hours for 'Auxiliary Pioneers.' Also, in the late 1960s, the hourly requirement to remain an active and regular 'publisher' was 10 hours per month. Sometime in the early 1970s this requirement was dropped to no particular amount—except one must get at least one hour each month to be considered 'regular' and at least some time reported in any given six-month period to be considered 'active.' However, as of 2006 only fifteen minutes per month is needed to be treated as a 'regular publisher.' I left the Jehovah's Witnesses in 1993, and so I never was able to personally witness the results of this last hourly change."

Jim Whitney's information was new to me and the situation in no way resembled the time when I was a member—and pioneer. But it appears to support the fact that members wilt at the idea of preaching in their residential areas. It's actually nothing new. In *The Watch Tower* of October 1911, O. L. Sullivan wrote:

"Another important matter which appears to deserve notice is that in some places the brethren appear not to appreciate the privilege of service—in 'volunteering' in the distribution of the papers—not half as they should. Sometimes they hire boys to do it for them. The thought is that it would never do for them to risk their respectability by appearing on the street thus. It would endanger their popularity and thus injure their practice or trade, etc. It is, of course, all right to hand out medicine or goods to the public, 'but not the *truth,*' for the world approves the one and frowns upon the other. The boy may burn up the papers, and no one attend the meeting, and the Lord's cause languish and die, but what matters that so long as they retain their popularity and practice!"

Even the Lord's elect are only human.

Russell's Companies

In 1881, Russell formed a new company the Zion's Watch Tower Tract Society, to attend to the publishing activities of the newly formed organization. This company—or "the Society," as it is called by both members and leaders, and how I will refer to it (with a capital S) going forward—was legally registered in 1884, according to the laws of the Commonwealth of Pennsylvania. The Society is now named: Watch Tower Bible and Tract Society of Pennsylvania.

In 1884 the board consisted of seven members, among them were C. T. Russell (president), William I. Mann (vice president), and Russell's wife, Maria Frances Russell (secretary and cashier). To be nominated for a seat in the administration, one had to contribute a minimum of ten dollars. The contributor would gain one vote for every ten dollars contributed. When Russell died, he held 25,000 "votes," since some years prior (possibly 1898 or in 1911) he contributed $250,000 to the Society. (*WT*, April 15, 1955, p. 121; *Divine Purpose*, 1959, p. 27; 64)

Society vice president William I. Mann was, as stated earlier, part of the original Allegheny group and regularly wrote articles for *Zion's Watch Tower* between 1879 and 1888. It was Mann who developed the idea of the length of the Creation days (7,000 years for each), but after 1888, it appears Mann made no further contributions and he is no longer mentioned.[79]

First President of the Society

A prominent member of the organization in 1881, William Henry Conley (1840–1897), became the first president of the Society; he held the position until 1884. Joseph Russell, Charles' father, was the vice president of the new Society, while Charles was secretary and cashier. This arrangement was unknown to the Jehovah's Witnesses until 1993 when the Watch Tower Society published their history in the book *Jehovah's Witnesses—Proclaimers of God's Kingdom* (p. 576). This peculiar piece of information was made public almost by coincidence.[80]

William H. Conley was a bookkeeper for James M. Riter, owner of a Pittsburgh metal fabrication company. When Riter died in 1873, his brother formed a partnership with Conley, and the company's name changed to Riter & Conley Company. It became a highly respected supplier to the drilling, mining, manufacturing and marine industries. Conley was also a stockholder in and a director of the Third National Bank of Allegheny. He married Sarah Shaffer (1841–1908) who, like Conley, had been a member of Russell's initial group circa 1870–1874. Both were active in several Pittsburgh charities. (William H. Conley; sources on the internet: *Russell Not First President of Watchtower*, Freeminds; *facts about William Henry Conley*, True Knowledge, 2011; *Wikipedia*, 2009)

Barbara Anderson, a former employee working at the Watchtower's headquarters in Brooklyn, and now a leading active Ex-Jehovah's Witness, chanced upon this information while researching for the *Proclaimers* history book. She found the original constitution documents from 1881 signed by Russell's wife, Maria. This find became quite sensational when it was first revealed at Watchtower headquarters in 1990. (Read Barbara Anderson's full story in Chapter 32.)

Whether Conley contributed financially to the new association during the 1880–1881 period, or even if he held more stocks than Russell, is uncertain due to lack of sufficient documentation. Still, considering Russell indirectly encouraged his subscribers to contribute financially, one can certainly conclude that financial contributions were an important part of the Bible Student's activities in these early days of the Society just as they are today:

"We never solicit donations. Those who possess this world's goods and are wholly consecrated need only to know how they can use it. Donations to this fund should be specified" (*Divine Purpose*, 1959, p. 27).

By *legally registering* the Zion's Watch Tower Tract Society *in 1884*, when the breach with Conley had probably already occurred, Russell assumed the Society's presidency—presumably because of his substantial share of stocks at that time. However, there is insufficient evidence to determine if that was the case.

Conley had previously been an Advent Christian, a friend of Paton, and formerly George Stetson's friend—Stetson introduced Russell to the Conleys, but sometime around 1883–1884, Conley withdrew from the Society entirely due to doctrinal objections. George Peters, a Lutheran pastor, published his book *Theocratic Kingdom* in 1884. According to a note in the book, the author thanks Conley for financial help for the release. Subsequently, Conley and his wife are said to have joined the Presbyterian Church. Around 1884, Conley disappears from the records, only to reappear in 1894 in the *Zion's Watch Tower* (Russell's magazine), arguing that Russell was promoting "false teachings." In the magazine, Russell speaks of Conley as a member of his original Allegheny group, but does not disclose Conley's previous position as president of the Society. (*ZWT*, June 15, 1894) Conley died in 1897, but his demise was never mentioned in *Zion's Watch Tower*. (Maurice Barnett: *Jehovah's Witnesses;* available on the internet)

New Address and Name Change

Though the Pennsylvania company still formally functioned as the "mother-organization," the Society relocated its headquarters from Allegheny, near Pittsburgh, to Brooklyn, New York, in 1908. Allegheny was practically unknown, as Russell wrote in *Zion's Watch Tower*, and Pittsburgh was better known for smoke, dirt, steel and iron than for science, literature and religion. Chicago and St. Louis were central locations, but not appropriate from a religious view. And Boston, although "cultured and scientific," according to Russell had "a reputation for unorthodox fads regarding religious lines." Therefore, Russell concluded, "after seeking divine guidance," that Brooklyn, with its large middle-class population and numerous churches, was preferable. And it was probably a good choice, since the rapidly growing metropolis was regarded as the "most suitable center for the harvest work during the few remaining years" (*ZWT*, Dec. 15, 1908, p. 373; *Proclaimers*, 1993, p. 59).

Simultaneously, the magazine's name was changed from *Zion's Watch Tower* to *The Watch Tower*. The main reason for this seems to have been that subscribers and buyers might have perceived "Zion" in the title as "objectionable" and mistaken it for another New York periodical, *Zion City*, a publication by a Mr. Dowie and his followers. Russell's journal was often confused with this magazine and cast aside by readers supposing it was produced under Dowie's auspices, and in some manner affiliated with *Zion City*: "It appears, further, that African churches and papers use the word *Zion* extensively, which has led to the inquiry whether or not our Journal is published and generally read by *colored people*" (*ZWT*, Dec. 15, 1908; italics are mine).

In 1909, the daughter company People's Pulpit Association was founded to safeguard Russell's interests in New York. In 1939, its name was changed to Watchtower Bible and Tract Society of New York, Inc. In 1914, another daughter company was founded in England under the name "International Bible Students Association." All these companies were judicially subordinate to the Pennsylvania company, and received financial support from it. (*Divine Purpose*, 1959, p. 49)

New York is one of the world's finest seaport towns, open for Atlantic trade, with goods shipped up the Hudson River and on to the Great Lakes. If one consults an encyclopedia published circa 1916, one finds a metropolis whose skyline, with some imagination, resembles today's New York. The Watchtower Society could not have found a more suitable center for their headquarters in the *few remaining years*—or for the *following 100 years*[81]—even though land prices gradually grew sky high!

As I applied the finishing touches to my English manuscript, I learned via internet research that parts of the Watchtower headquarters' large and intricate building complex in Brooklyn was up for sale (see endnote 81), perhaps due to the global financial crisis. Actually, property sales have been ongoing since 2004 when the printing and shipping department was moved to Walkill, New York, because of profound reorganization of literature production. Several of the Watchtower's Brooklyn properties have already been sold or been placed on the market.

For now, let us return to events of the early 1880s.

Tower Publishing Company

The activity of the movement was associated with a huge spread of printed material—as was also the case with the Adventists—clearly showing the movement's Adventist heritage. In 1881, subscribers were asked to distribute free copies (more than one million) of the brochure *Food for Thinking Christians*, a special edition of the *Zion's Watch Tower* 162 pages long, a project in which Russell must have invested a substantial sum indeed.

Russell was an indefatigable writer. C. S. Braden, an American professor of religious studies, wrote in his book *These Also Believe,* published in 1960: "No other group has used so extensively, or perhaps so successfully, the printed page as means of propaganda. It was reported at the time of his death that more than 13,000,000 copies of his books had been distributed. One of them, *The Divine Plan of the Ages*, reached almost 5,000,000 circulation and *What the Scriptures Say about Hell*, 3,000,000" (Braden, 1960, p. 360).

In 1887, to reduce production costs as much as possible, Russell formed the Tower Publishing Company, which was transferred to the Russell-owned Watchtower Bible and Tract Society in 1898. According to information retrieved from the Bible Students, among its other publications, this company produced and distributed, Russell's book series *Millennial Dawn* (later: *Studies in the Scriptures*), published in six volumes with 9,384,000 copies printed between 1886 and 1916, the period when the company clearly became a publishing giant.

The International Bible Students subsequently produced and distributed religious materials—magazines, brochures, tracts and books—in huge editions. This circumstance indicates how the movement's publishing activities constitute an essential precondition of its economy and propaganda. And, apart from initial funding with Russell's own resources and secondly by donors' monetary gifts, sales of the Society's books and magazines by the virtually free-working preachers and colporteurs have acted as the movement's economic foundation. This might explain the vast literary production of the movement. As time passed, the Society gradually acquired all press tasks, built its own printing facilities and organized distribution. All in all a tremendous undertaking that required provisioning of large financial resources.

In a way, Russell founded a somewhat unconventional business. Viewing him as a business owner, he gave his "company" an ingenious design. While he enjoyed an employer's benefits, his employees or "preachers" practically volunteered for him, and if they didn't like the employment, they could just quit or be fired! In another section of this book, as I explore Russell's ownership of the movement's various companies, I will show how this characteristic of the publishing business was not entirely unusual.

The Jehovah's Witnesses are incredibly proud of their movement's strong growth since the beginning of the 1870s. But really, I think one could have expected a somewhat larger increase, especially when one considers that the end of the world should have come at least three times within the 20th century, and particularly when one notes the enormous number of hours the members have spent on propaganda and preaching work, for example 1,707,094,710 hours in 2011. (*YB*, 2012, pp. 40-51)

Yes: One billion, 707 million, 94 thousand and 710 *unpaid* working hours!

Coupled with this incredible human investment is the fact that *The Watchtower* magazine is published in more languages than Hans Christian Andersen's fairytales.

Confrontation with the Churches

An important part of Russell's approach to the dissemination of his message was confrontation with the clergy from churches in Pittsburgh and its environs, confrontations that eventually became a regular element of the movement's attempts to show itself to the world. Eventually, this strategy resulted in an intense clash with the "harlot church," an attack launched in one of the first issues of the *Zion's Watch Tower* as early as November 1879. As had his Adventist forerunners, Russell identified churches, and the Catholic Church in particular (although the Protestants weren't any better), as being "Babylon the Great," spoken of in Revelation 17:5.

Russell and his followers now favored provoking Babylon, because they wanted a showdown with the dogmas of the harlot church. Russell considered the doctrines of the immortal soul, eternal hellfire, the trinity and a number of others fundamental to the church had been adopted from pagan religion. These heathen ideas had been incorporated into the Christian church in the first centuries of its existence (which, as far as I know from my church history, sounds reasonable). According to Russell, the time had come to *cleanse* and *restore* "true" Christianity. Russell and his newly formed association expected great results from this offensive, which, truth be told, was nothing more than another enlistment campaign, further compounded because these activities often took place outside the church proper on Sundays after the sermons. Of course, the clergy from various churches weren't enthusiastic about this provocative soul fishing.

Russell believed these churches had been on the wrong track for centuries, and he assumed the duty of escorting them back into the Truth, naturally under his authoritative guidance as "Pastor" Charles Taze Russell.

As early as 1877, he invited the ministers of his native Allegheny and neighboring Pittsburgh to engage in public debate; according to Jehovah's Witnesses' own historical account, a number of clergymen accepted the challenge, however, all the ministers present refused to accept Russell's exhibited proofs for Christ's second coming in the form of a "present" *invisible* spirit.

Russell then encouraged the members of the area churches to break with their respective organizations, which formed the modern Babylon, as true Christians should. The practice and course of events were very Adventistic. But the request to break with established churches predated the Adventists. Martin Luther and other Protestants had more or less used the Babylon label, which at the time seemed a valid appellation for the Catholic Church. Still, according to Russell, the Protestant churches were not much better. In the November issue of *Zion's Watch Tower* of 1879, he wrote:

"[We] must go further and implicate, (not the individual members, but the church systems) other churches united to the Empires of earth. Every church claiming to be a chaste virgin espoused to Christ, but in reality united to and supported by the world (beast) we must condemn as being in scripture language a *harlot church*" (*ZWT*, Nov. 1879; Reprint 45; *Proclaimers*, 1993, p. 52).

Therefore, *Watch Tower* subscribers were encouraged to leave their respective churches: "If the church with which you are connected, lives in adulterous union with the world, you must, if you would keep your garments white, leave her" (*Proclaimers*, p. 52).

Russell had, for the most part, adopted the Adventist interpretation of Revelation as a text wherein our present day is described and predicted in great detail; therefore, the words spoken by the angel in Revelation 18:4 referred to the apostate churches of the 19th century: "Come out of her, my people, that ye be not partakers of her sins, and that ye receive not of her plagues" (KJ).

It's no wonder the local ministers took notice of this ambitious and pushy young man, so eager to fight. The scenario resembled a clash between generations. Russell wanted to "re-establish" fundamental Biblical "truths"—which was also quite typical of other contemporary Adventist-influenced groups—and he had nothing but contempt for the "higher Biblical criticism" predominant in the theological institutions of his time.

According to this "higher criticism," The Revelation of John is estimated to have been written circa AD 95, and since the symbolism of the Revelation text is very difficult to understand, yet possible to partially decipher, it leads to the question: What might such an obscure and symbolic text fit better than the city of Rome, the very capital of the "beast" (the Emperor), and the center of the persecution?

So Babylon in its original context was, beyond any doubt, the Emperor's Rome and *not* the Catholic Church, as subsequent apocalyptic preachers have proclaimed. That the Apocalypse of John had been in any way directed at the meager beginnings of the Catholic Church, which first (barely) emerged around AD 100–110, is illogical, as John then would have been referring to the young church in Rome which he probably knew or may have been affiliated with.

Of course, the name Babylon was not to be taken literally, but in the apocalyptic writing was used as a *cover name* for Rome, capital of the Roman Empire where so many Christians had died by order of ruthless emperors.

Also Grew and Storrs' ideas about so-called "conditional immortality" were now evident in Russell's campaign as he became the ideas' most effective advocate. In particular, belief in a fiery hell, where the wicked were tormented forever, became the subject of Russell's flaming campaigns. Since, as Russell believed, humans did not have mortal souls, they could not be tortured after their death. For this reason, Russell confronted the doctrine of Hell in a tract from 1889, *The Old Theology* (*Bible Students' Tracts*):

"The eternal torment theory had a heathen origin.... It remained for the great apostasy to tack to heathen philosophy the horrid details now so generally believed, to paint them upon the church walls, as was done in Europe, to write them in their creeds and hymns, and to so pervert the Word of God as to give a seeming divine support to the God-dishonoring blasphemy. The credulity of the present day, therefore, receives it as a legacy, not from the Lord, or the apostles, or the prophets, but from the compromising spirit which sacrificed truth and reason, and shamefully perverted the doctrines of Christianity, in an unholy ambition and strife for power and wealth and numbers. Eternal torment as the penalty for sin was unknown to the patriarchs of past ages; it was unknown to the prophets of the Jewish age; and it was unknown to the Lord and the apostles; but it has been the chief doctrine of Nominal Christianity since the great apostasy—the scourge wherewith the credulous, ignorant and superstitious of the world have been lashed into servile obedience to tyranny" (*Proclaimers,* 1993, p. 126-129).

These views—boldly expressed by a self-taught young man—made some impression, and they seem to have come from a fiery spirit determined to weed out everything he believed was foreign and not part of *original* Christianity and since the days of primitive Christendom was incorporated into the Catholic church, which more or less consciously occurred as part of the church's take-over strategy.

Russell seems to have hit on a general trend of the time, and the issues of hell, immortality of the soul and eternal torment were relatively easy game. Russell was totally uncompromising and argued straightforwardly:

"If the Bible does teach that eternal torture is the fate of all except the saints, it should be preached—yea, thundered from the housetops weekly, daily, hourly; if it does not so teach, the fact should be made known, and the foul stain dishonoring God's holy name removed" (*Proclaimers*, 1993, p. 126-127).

In 1903, it appears leading pastors and ministers met to discuss what measures could be taken about Russell's message. As early as 1846, a Protestant association, the Evangelical Alliance, was formed with the purpose of protecting the student candidates of theological institutions. Russell had no formal theological training and was not an ordained minister, although he referred to himself as "pastor"; the Evangelical Alliance probably decided, sometime around 1903, to counter Russell's many campaigns, particularly his unorthodox religious teachings. According to the Jehovah's Witnesses' presentation of their history, Dr. E. L. Eaton of the Methodist Episcopalian Church of Pittsburgh and L. S. White of the Disciples of Christ challenged Russell to a series of public debates in Allegheny's Carnegie Hall. Eaton wrote to Russell:

"I have thought that a public debate of some of those questions about which you and I differ, and which we both believe to be vital to the Christian system, would be of immense interest to the public..." [82]

And in contemporary, polite style, Russell's forthcoming reply: "I assure you that your courteous expressions and Christian sentiments are fully reciprocated by me. I agree with you that such a public discussion as you suggest—of our divergent views on the teachings of the Bible—ought to be profitable, stimulating to Bible study on our part as well as on the part of all Bible students hereabouts. I therefore accept your proposition…" (Read the continuation in the accompanying endnote).[83]

During the debates, Eaton must have defended the doctrine that the wicked are punished with eternal torment and sufferings, while Russell vigorously opposed the doctrine of Hell. He emphasized that the dead in their graves had no consciousness, but millions would be re-awakened during the coming resurrection. Russell stuck to his mantra that "death is death," and that "our dear ones, when they pass from us, are really dead, that they are neither alive with the angels nor with demons in a place of despair."

In Russell's view, it was unacceptable that a just, wise and loving god could ever condemn man to eternal punishment: "What is declared of our heavenly Father? That he is just, that he is wise, that he is loving, that he is powerful. All Christian people will acknowledge these attributes of the divine character. If this is so, can we find any sense of the word in which we could conceive of God as just and yet punishing a creature of His own hand to all eternity, no matter what the sin was? I am not an apologist for sin; I do not live in sin myself, and I never preach sin…. But I tell you that all these people around here that our brother [Dr. Eaton] says are making the air blue with their blasphemies of God and the holy name of Jesus Christ are all people who have been taught this doctrine of eternal torment. And all the murderers, thieves and evil doers in the penitentiaries, were all taught this doctrine…. These are bad doctrines; they have been injuring the world this long time; they are not a part of the Lord's teaching at all, and our dear brother has not gotten the smoke of the dark ages rubbed out of his eyes yet" (*Divine Purpose*, 1959, p. 37; *Proclaimers,* 1993, p. 128-131).

Russell must have appeared to be the winner after six debates, which one can well understand, and according to the Watchtower Society's account, members of Eaton's congregation later left in favor of Russell. That Russell's anti-hell campaign was a success on some level is shown by later references to the Bible Students as the "no-hellers." The pastors of different denominations despised Russell of a true heart, for he attacked not just one of the church's strongest means of discipline, but questioned the church's entire teachings and theological interpretation methods established through the centuries. On this issue, Russell may be viewed as progressive, but this endeavor was probably also responsible for adding to his opponent's motives for some of the exhausting lawsuits waged against him in the next few years. In 1911, E. L. Eaton published a 153-page book, *The Millennial Dawn Heresy: An Examination,* wherein Eaton casts another light on the debates in Pittsburgh, and the results differ from Russell's description in *Zion's Watch Tower* in 1903. In the book's foreword, Eaton writes retrospectively:

"Believing his whole system erroneous, and that it ought to be exposed, especially for those to whom it most strongly appealed—persons the least able to discover its errors—I proposed to him that we publicly debate those views which he was putting forth in opposition to the current theological opinions. Six debates were accordingly arranged, and these took place in Carnegie Music Hall, Allegheny City, in autumn of 1903. / These debates were printed in the city papers, the Pittsburgh *Gazette* containing the fullest reports of them. At the close these were gathered into one number of that paper of which a very large edition was printed and extensively circulated. I felt from the beginning that these reports—taken at the time by Mr. Russell's stenographer, I having no chance to edit my part of the debate—did not fairly represent my side of the issue. Since that time a large number of communications have reached me from different parts of the world, asking for literature upon the Millennial Dawn heresies; it is therefore a pleasure that I am permitted … to give to the public an ungarbled account of my reply to the false doctrines and extravagant inventions published by the 'Watch Tower Bible and Tract Society,' somewhat more vaguely known as 'Millennial Dawn'" (Eaton's Foreword to *The Millennial Dawn Heresy*, Evanston, Ill., April 1911; reprinted 1912, 1913 and 1916; *Divine Purpose*, 1959, p. 41-44).

Eaton, a conservative theologian building on his higher education, knew what he was talking about, and he obviously disagreed with Russell in almost all doctrine-related areas, which his book from 1911 also clearly shows.

Still, the Eaton-Russell debates, seen from Russell's point of view, had been a success, as evidenced in the report published in special editions of *The Pittsburgh Gazette* in 1904 and 1905 and offered for sale in *Zion's Watch Tower*. The issue from January 15, 1904, states:

"We have still special issue of the *Gazette* containing reports of the entire six debates. These can be supplied at 2¢. each, postpaid, or 50 or more at 1¢. each by express prepaid."

It is not difficult to understand that Charles Russell felt he fought for a manifest cause. A pastor present at one of the Eaton-Russell debates must, according to *Proclaimers*, afterwards have remarked to Russell: "I am glad to see you turn the hose on hell and put out the fire" (*Proclaimers*, 1993, p. 128-131).

Thus Russell achieved great success in his campaigns against the doctrine of Hell, which was a teaching in retreat at that time. Between 1905 and 1907 he toured the United States and Canada to lecture and repeatedly spoke about "to hell and back." He must have spoken to full houses everywhere, and when he treated the subject from a humorous angle, he also won a number of new supporters. (*Divine Purpose*, 1959, p. 43)

The extent of Russell's preaching was reflected in the newspaper media, which became increasingly important to helping him broadcast the message about the world's impending end and reach as many people as possible. At the time, a magazine called *The Continent* wrote that Russell's weekly newspaper article had a greater "circulation every week than those of any other living man; a greater, doubtless, than the combined circulation of the writings of all the priests and preachers in North America" (*Proclaimers*, 1993, p. 55-59).

Russell worked relentlessly and was quick to realize that the willingness of the newspapers to provide column space for him facilitated spreading his message to millions of readers. In 1904, an article titled "Newspaper Gospeling," published in his own magazine, stated his sermons were now printed in three newspapers: "Millions of sermons have thus been scattered far and near; and some at least have done good. If the Lord wills we shall be glad to see this 'door' keep open, or even open still wider."

In 1903, the breadth of Russell's newspaper gospeling, via some 200 newspapers, reached approximately fifteen million readers, and there is no reason to doubt the source material for these statistics. Through the following years Russell wrote articles bearing headlines such as: "Denying the Son of God," "The Time is at Hand—The New Day Dawns," "When Peace on Earth?," "Clergy Ordination Proved Fraudulent—No Divine Authority for It"—headlines as provocative as his other endeavors. (*Proclaimers*, 1993, p. 55-59)

The latter article, which I unfortunately could not access during my research because it can only be seen as a very small reproduction in *Proclaimers*, has this subheading: "Christian People Humbugged—Dignified False Pretense Christ's Kingdom Thereby Injured—Shackles of Ignorance and Superstition Forged—The Start of the Error—Its Motive—Its Bad Effects—The Proper Remedy" (1914). Interesting topics, particularly in view of Russell's libel suit against Rev. Ross in 1912 and 1913. Baptist Rev. J. J. Ross published a pamphlet in 1912 wherein he and others accused that Russell had never been appointed as "pastor" of an ecclesiastical authority. This subject receives more thorough treatment in Chapter 8.

In 1908, Russell wrote about "Evangelizing through newspapers" in *Zion's Watch Tower*:

"The newspaper has become the great factor in the daily life of the civilized world. The Lord seemed to point us to this way also of forwarding the interests of the Truth, and opened a wide door for us in connection with the publication of the debates. We have sought wisdom and grace to use this opportunity to the Lord's praise and to the finding of his people, and their liberation from the chains of error. The Lord has greatly blessed the effort so that at the present time the editor's weekly sermons are published in eleven newspapers regularly, representing a combined circulation of 402,000. This is equivalent to a circulation of 400,000 tracts per week, or 21,000,000 per year, with the advantage that it reaches people in a manner which some prefer; for quite a good many dislike to be seen receiving or reading a tract. Surely this is an excellent field, well worthy of cultivation as one of the best means of reaching the reading public" (*ZWT*, Dec. 15, 1908, p. 372, 373).

In 1908, Russell debated with other church leaders: An "elder" A. A. Bunner and "elder" L. S. White, who had debated Russell in Pittsburgh with Eaton. Russell also arranged to debate Rev. Dr. W. Dillon. Dillon sent his apologies; he was unable to debate due to another meeting he had forgotten. "Or possibly its importance seemed greater later on, as he thought of the questions for debate," Russell notes a little bit sarcastically in *Zion's Watch Tower*. Russell immediately telegraphed Pastor Dillon because it was too late to cancel the meeting, but "we received no reply from the reverend gentleman" (*ZWT*, Feb. 1908; reprint 4136).

There is no doubt that Russell and the Bible Student's very primitive, aggressive and church-hostile propaganda garnered Russell many friends and enemies. This confrontational strategy seems to have remained in use quite deliberately to our own time, since the movement's enemy images still—apart from the devil—are the Christian churches. This aspect of the movement's propaganda would rise to even higher levels under the leadership of Russell's successor, J. F. Rutherford, as the priesthood, politicians and capitalists—at the time often portrayed as a kind of *unholy trinity*—were systematically condemned in a jargon fitting the ideological exaggerations of the 20th century.

I suppose, however, that the church of today is not so important an opponent as Jehovah's Witnesses presume. Rather, the leaders of the churches no longer take the Jehovah's Witnesses seriously. Still, this opponent legend is part of the Witnesses' self-understanding, since the churches are seen as Satan's instrument of their persecution in the last days. And if no one seeks to persecute the Witnesses, then the Witnesses will deliver opportunity for it. After all, it's one of the "signs" from Matthew 24, and they must prove that we are living in the end time of this wicked old world.

In other words, persecutions from the 1870s and forward were *favored the end-time's signs* and the absence of them is, and was, a *bad sign*.

Chapter 6

Increasing Opposition

Although Russell, despite his declared intentions, was now in the process of forming a real organization, which was only democratically organized on the surface, it became gradually clear that he—when it came to the crunch—was not really a democratic-minded individual. This was because both his society and the movement, which were gradually linked together, had a basic commercial structure, with Russell as *principal* and *owner*.

Russell tenaciously defended his ownership of the Watch Tower Bible and Tract Society and, therefore, he was untouchable by anyone dissatisfied with his leadership. No doubt he acted wisely if, as we presuppose, his society and its subsidiaries, legally speaking, were a kind of economic activity. His company, the "Society," was shielded against "hostile takeover," because after 1884 and Conley's introductory presidential period, Russell held the majority of the shares. If hostile forces sought to wrest the Society from him, they had to first acquire the majority, unlikely with Russell controlling the largest portion. Any attempt to alter this fact would inevitably fail. Thus, when some of the senior managers tried to dismiss him in the early 1890s, the coup failed, and the rebels had to withdraw. They had not really grasped how firmly Russell sat in the saddle.

Over the years, and especially during litigations around 1913, when Russell faced his critics, among them the well-known New York tabloid *Brooklyn Daily Eagle* and Canadian Baptist pastor J. J. Ross, it was revealed that not only did Russell have full ownership of the Watch Tower Bible and Tract Society but also other companies with which he did business. He had—according to Ross—business interests in lead, asphalt and petroleum, among others. In the divorce proceedings between Russell and his wife, which started in 1896–1897 and resurfaced in 1906, Russell claimed to be without funds to pay his estranged wife alimony. This proved to be disastrous to him and the proceedings revealed that he was not at all without assets, as he asserted.

Siftings

Throughout the group's evolution, individuals or groups questioned Russell's leadership. When someone subsequently broke with him, it was called "siftings."

As early as 1880–1881, two co-editors broke with Russell. John H. Paton, author of the hardcover book *The Day Dawn*,[84] which was released by A. D. Jones of Pittsburgh in 1880, left Russell in 1881.[85] The Watch Tower Society was first founded in 1881. After John Paton broke with Russell, A. D. Jones tried to publish a new magazine, *Zion's Day Star,* with Russell in 1881. "Yet within one year it had gone boldly into infidelity," Russell wrote gloatingly. He considered these problems as demonstrations of a sifting, through which the *pure* and "unselfish" were selected. The opponents had "only served to test the quality and the strength of integrity of the channel God is using," the Watchtower Society notes today. These various attempts to overthrow the Pastor led to a gradual narrowing of the movement, which had only about 4,000 members circa 1891. (*Proclaimers*, 1993, p. 620-621; *Divine Purpose*, 1959, p. 44-45)

To retain the congregations formed via the *Watch Tower* subscribers, a new kind of missionary went out from the Society's headquarters; they were known as "pilgrims." They acted as traveling overseers and visited congregations to link the supporters closer together. The Pilgrims had no *real* salary, but the Society helped them with expenses: "They were simply provided with food and lodging by the local brothers, and to the extent necessary, the Society helped them with travel expenses" (*Proclaimers*, 1993, p. 222).

Russell's usual method was persuasion rather than coercion. Still, in 1905 he introduced Berean Studies, established training programs and associated methodological issues and answers through which he sought to gain greater control over the members. He warned, however, against "parrot-like" manners, but invited the congregations to free discussion to review the responses: "The questions should be discussed *freely by all* first, and then before proceeding to the next question the DAWN answer should be considered and discussed and understood. Never forget that the Bible is our Standard..." (*Divine Purpose*, 1959, p. 46; Penton, 1986, p. 32).

But this was untrue. Only Russell's interpretation of the Bible was the *real* "standard." If the supporters read only the Bible they would miss "the truths" Russell delivered through his magazines, brochures and books. (*ZWT*, Sept. 15, 1910, p. 298; *Facts and More Facts,* 1913, p. 41, 42)

That Russell, in his own opinion, played a very important role is illustrated when he refers to himself as "God's mouthpiece" in *Zion's Watch Tower* of July 15, 1906. (*Proclaimers*, 1993, p. 143)[86]

The Faithful and Wise Servant

The adherent's relationship with their elected "pastor" eventually led to a glorification of Russell, which was in contrast to Barbour's "evil servant" role. Therefore, we see an internal logic as some of Russell's most-ardent supporters, at an early stage, began to consider him *the* "faithful and wise servant" mentioned in the parable of the Gospel of Matthew 24:45 (KJ): "Who then is a faithful and wise servant, whom his lord hath made ruler over his household, to give them meat in due season?"[87]

Since the appearance of the first issue of *Zion's Watch Tower* in 1879, the magazine's purpose was associated with the role of this "servant," specifically to provide "spiritual food" for the elect. Russell himself argued in 1881, however true to say, that the "servant" was *all* the selected Christians: "We believe that every member of this body of Christ is engaged in the blessed work, either directly or indirectly, of giving meat in due season to the household of faith" (*Proclaimers*, 1993, p. 142,143).

The whole matter seems somewhat muddy, because there can be no doubt that Russell's supporters saw him personally to be *that* servant. The latest historical account from the Society meekly notes this view came to be "generally held by the Bible Students for some thirty years. Brother Russell did not reject their view, but he personally avoided making such an application of the text..." (*Proclaimers*, 1993, p. 143).

Maria Russell, who was a schoolteacher before marrying Charles, expressed that since "servant" is singular, while "household" and "fellow servants" are plural, the parable of Jesus must refer to her husband. Thus it is suggested that Russell may have come to indirectly accept the idea of his status. In *Zion's Watch Tower*, December 1895, Maria writes to George Woolsey, a Bible Student in New York:

"Now, if the Lord wished to indicate a chief servant of the truth, and fellow servants assisting in serving the meat in due season to the household of faith, he could not have chosen more precise language to convey such a thought. And, on the contrary, to ignore such an order and reasonableness in the account, to my mind throws the entire narrative into confusion, making the 'servants' (plural) and 'that servant' interchangeable terms" (Penton 1986, p. 33; and footnote 97, p. 315; *ZWT*, Dec. 1895; *ZWT*, July 1, 1906).

Note here that Russell—editorially—could have stopped Mrs. Russell's point of view from appearing in *Zion's Watch Tower* because it advocated a *new position* that was not consistent with his previous position. *But he did not.*

Note also that Russell discussed the question of who the servant was in the fourth volume of the *Millennial Dawn* series, published in 1897, and could have amended Maria's 1895 statements; he clearly could have written that this servant was *still* a collective group, as he wrote in 1881, yet he does not. Rather, he expressed himself in such an ambiguous way that the reader can add the missing words, for "our Lord, the great Servant of his people, will make choice of *one channel* for dispensing the meat in due season, though other channels or 'fellow-servants' will be used in bringing the food to the 'household.' But the servant is merely a steward, *and liable to be removed at any moment, should he fail...*" (*Studies* 4, 1915 (1897), p. 613, 614; italics are mine; Penton, 1986, p. 33 and notes p. 315).

And here, we are led to ask: Did Russell really write this?

Did Maria Russell Co-author Russell's Books?

Until 1893, Maria Russell played an active role as Russell's closest associate, and held what was nearly the second highest position in the Watch Tower Society, serving as treasurer and secretary. As Charles Russell's closest secretary, who assisted him with writing articles and answering readers' questions, she also acted as associate editor of *Zion's Watch Tower*. Beyond that it seems she also, to some not-fully elucidated extent, co-authored the first four volumes of the *Millennial Dawn* series, published from 1886 to 1897.

During the couple's divorce proceedings, which resumed during 1906–1907, Maria Russell revealed the extent of her commitment and involvement in her husband's editorial work, as the pair, *plus a few others*, were largely responsible for the *Zion's Watch Tower* content. According to B. W. Schulz, publisher of the internet-based *Watch Tower History*, this is incorrect because a brief glance at *Zion's Watch Tower* volumes through 1897 shows many others contributed articles to the magazine. Schulz writes: "Even a glancing acquaintance with the early issues of *The Watch Tower* shows this [that only few contributors wrote for the magazine] to be false."

After reading Schulz's objections in 2009, and the accusation that Maria Russell's testimony was *untrue*, I reviewed the entire 1894 volume of *Zion's Watch Tower (ZWT)*, and it appeared then that approximately twenty-seven people *outside* the magazine's editorial group, specifically the Russells, contributed various short articles or letters to the editors; among them was W. H. Conley, the first president of the Watch Tower Society, expressing himself for the first and last time in Russell's magazine following his resignation in 1884. Still, compared to the amount of text in *ZWT*, these contributions were *negligible*. Thus, we can conclude the editors (Charles and Maria) wrote the *vast majority* of the articles, which were often unmanageably voluminous.[88]

According to the court record from the divorce, Maria also testified she had "laid the plans for each of these volumes" and written "at least one-half the work," which perhaps was about half of the first three volumes and virtually the whole of the fourth, where Charles, according to Maria's testimony, subsequently made changes. This may be attributed in part to the conflict between the spouses, which began around the time the fourth volume was completed. I think Charles Russell most likely left the *servant reference* virtually as written in the fourth volume, presumably by Maria Russell, because it expressed the *grandiose role* of the "servant," something he was *unable to resist*, even though his wife had written it.

It is difficult to draw any final conclusion about all claims of authorship 100 years after the events. Yet, perhaps I can lift the veil on the incidents and proceedings, and then my reader may judge. Together with the general image I

Maria Frances Russell and Charles Taze Russell, circa 1894, photographed a few years before they separated (retouched photo courtesy of Brian Kutscher).

have gradually formed of Charles Taze Russell—most recently from the 1907 court record—a somewhat clearer picture of our protagonist has slowly come into focus, and it corresponds very well to the conclusions Maria Russell finally reached (see endnote).[89]

Maria Frances Ackley

Charles Russell met Maria Frances Ackley, a school teacher and active member in the local branch of the Methodist Episcopal Church, around the turn of the year 1878–1879. Maria Frances was born in 1850, making her two years older than Charles Russell. She graduated from high school, continued her education at the Pittsburgh Curry Normal School, and because of this "higher" education seemed a perfect partner for Russell (at least, if we think solely in terms of company operations). Apparently she had recently shown interest in Barbour's message and probably joined his movement before Russell broke with Barbour in 1879. Maria and Charles crossed paths at a meeting in Allegheny, where Russell had been speaking. Their infatuation seems to have been intense, perhaps even love at first glance, and before three months had elapsed they wed on March 13, 1879. John Paton performed the ceremony. (Penton, 1986, p. 35, 36; B. W. Schulz, *Watch Tower History*, April 22, 2008)

Mr. and Mrs. Russell's extensive activities in the organization were only sustained because the couple agreed to a celibate marriage from the start, without sexual consummation, and thus, without children. One might wonder at the couple's agreement to forego genuine married life, but when they committed to each other in 1879, they believed and their supporters believed that *very soon*—at the latest in 1881—they would be raptured into heaven (changed or transformed into heavenly life).

Therefore time, also at *that* time, was very short!

The *real* reason was presumably that Russell himself, as a starting point, had a principle view on the matter—perhaps also a decreased sexual energy (*libido*)[90]—which, because of his immense intellectual activity, may also be associated with repressed sexual needs that were sublimated into an endless chain of words (see also Penton, 1986, p. 35).

It is well-enough known among writers, artists, politicians, elite athletes and others that a huge commitment for a cause can steal energy from the sexual drive. And the era in which the Russells lived was also characterized by a lack of broad-mindedness in relation to sexual life, so there may have been many factors which influenced their relationship.

It seems reasonable, at this point, to note that the Russells appear to have adopted an orphan, Rose J. Ball, around 1884; she would later play a fateful role in the Russells' marriage. This girl, approximately twenty in 1893 and thus a young woman, worked as Russell's private secretary at his headquarters in Allegheny, where she was the only female staff member.

Maria Russell was apparently a remarkable woman, as one could not avoid noticing. Canadian Baptist pastor J. J. Ross, who saw Mrs. Russell in 1913 during a lawsuit brought against him by Charles Russell, seems to have been impressed by her. Perhaps he wanted to see her as a contrast to Russell, who Ross openly despised. Ross wrote:

"Mrs. Russell is a modest, intelligent, charming devoted Christian woman. One can see at a glance that she possesses a vastly superior intellect and personality to that of Mr. Russell." Naturally a rather subjective description, which I believe served his own purpose; as a Baptist pastor, he was *totally against* Russell (*Facts and More Facts*, 1913, p. 15).

The Russells' early relationship and the building of the organization occurred during the Victorian age, one characterized by a parochial and Puritan lifestyle, which (not surprisingly) corresponds to the appearance of today's Jehovah's Witnesses—the final product of Russell's activities. The whole Victorian behavior complex gave rise to strong double standards that marked social, economic and religious life, and especially, sexual life. Therefore, emancipated women were generally not very popular at this time.

Maria Russell's extensive involvement in the movement's many activities clearly generated a need for recognition from her husband, who apparently did not sufficiently grant her this honor. Much also suggests that Mrs. Russell increasingly disagreed with her husband about their celibate marriage, but beyond these very personal matters, economic motives and subsequent controversy regarding the Society's management also contributed to the disintegration of their relationship. Further, she was apparently viewed with some sympathy by leading members of the movement who believed Russell treated her with condescension. That the critics' sympathy influenced Maria Russell can hardly be denied, and it is very understandable in light of the marital difficulties she eventually experienced. However, Maria was so far loyal, even when the rebellion erupted in early 1894. (Penton, p. 35-37)

According to the Watchtower's own representation, there was a run-up to this early 1890s rebellion against Russell, and it manifested itself during the movement's annual meeting in Chicago, Illinois: "Some of the prominent workers set themselves in opposition to Pastor Russell in an attempt to seize control of the Society for themselves. Soon after the convention in Chicago, Illinois, in 1893, these conspirators planned to explode what they thought would be a bombshell that would end Russell's popularity and finish him as president of the Society" (*Divine Purpose*, 1959, p. 44-45).

The editors of *Proclaimers* wrote in 1993 that "individuals in responsible positions" had begun to consider themselves "as the channel of spiritual light." Others simply "gave in to the desire to exercise greater personal influence."

According to *Proclaimers*, the rebels called a meeting for April 5, 1894; it would not be held on association property, but somewhere else entirely. Mr. and Mrs. Russell were not invited, and only forty people attended the meeting. The written invitation was signed by Elmer Bryan, S. D. Rogers (later ostracized by the other three critics), J. B. Adamson and Otto von Zech, all trusted colporteurs in Russell's international association. *Proclaimers* states that the meeting proved to be "a malicious effort on the part of these conspirators to poison the minds of others by divulging what they surmised to be evil in Brother Russell's business affairs..." (p. 627). The rebels also claimed "Russell had too much authority (which they wanted for themselves)," and complained that he favored the printed material and "Bible-class meetings" over delivering discourses wherein "they might more readily expound personal views." The accusations appear to have been based on petty, insular matters, and for that reason "the bomb" apparently was a dud—Russell prevailed, of course. Still this would eventually prove to be a Pyrrhic victory. Although he subsequently stood with palms of victory, the events were—as seen through modern eyes—part of a series of forthcoming defeats, due solely to Russell's great self-importance. He wanted to maintain power over his and Maria's company at all costs. (*Divine*

Purpose, 1959, p. 44-45; *Proclaimers*, 1993, p. 624, 627; *The Bible Student Movement in the Days of C.T. Russell*, third edition, 1999, located on the internet, March 2011)

After a trip to New York City in 1894, the always outwardly loyal Maria Russell wrote a long article for the *Tower* in which she defended "the church" in Allegheny against the critics. Her well-formulated exaggerations leave no doubt about the critics' unholy alliances. They are characterized as "false brothers" performing "Satan's work"—these "brothers" had issued a critical circular, with copies distributed as far away as London. She also noted one of the rebels, Mr. Rogers, had introduced Mr. Barbour, "an old enemy of the cross of Christ and of Brother Russell," to the congregation in Rochester, New York, and thus tried to bring the adherents in Rochester "under the Influence of a bold and relentless enemy and his blasphemous teaching." In this, Maria's words became a tribute to her husband, whom she apparently still wanted to impress. (That Charles Russell responded with increasing suspicion is shown by subsequent events as featured in the next chapter.)

In a strange way Maria's article reflects the love-hate relationship with her husband, a relationship that was developing into a profound and jealous war between the spouses—one with potentially disastrous consequences for the movement's future under Russell's leadership.

Members of the Allegheny "church" had probably witnessed Charles' humiliation of Maria. Nevertheless, in the article she maintains her loyalty. She writes, among other things, that "Mr. Rogers falsely represented Mr. Russell as a liar, and his wife and all his household—the office helpers—as *compelled* by him, by force of circumstances, which he very specially and falsely particularized, to lie for him. He stated that he had seen Sister Russell weep bitter tears over Brother Russell's sins, though he never saw me in tears in his life; and for ten days previous to this despicable business he had been a witness of the peace and tranquility of our home, the hospitality of which he has so grossly abused" (*ZWT*, 1894, p. 167-169; reprints 1661).

In April 1894 she writes in a letter to the editor of *Zion's Watch Tower*:

"I take this opportunity to speak in defense of my husband against the bold attack of our enemies in maligning his character and misrepresenting our domestic relations. Our household is composed only of ourselves and our esteemed and beloved helpers in the WATCH TOWER Office, all of whom gladly bear witness to the tranquility and happiness of our home, save as intrusions of false brethren and busybodies occasionally disturb it. / Our home, so far from being a discordant one, is the reverse,—most happy" (*A Conspiracy Exposed*, April 25, 1894; reprints 3810).

Everything still seemed perfect on the surface.

Some of the dissenters who revolted against Russell's leadership before and after the 1893 meeting in Chicago did so because they perceived him as a "pope," and it appears they tried to get Maria Russell on their side afterward.

Sometime after the aforementioned incidents, Maria went on a lecture tour—including Chicago—to defend her husband against accusations of immoral behavior (or a "sort of misconduct," as the *Proclaimers* says), leveled by a former employee. Following this trip in 1895 she openly suggested that her husband was "the faithful and wise servant." So, in public she defended Russell and was loyal to him, but in private they continued to struggle intensely, especially in regard to her associate-editor role at the *Tower*, where issues and tensions with Charles gradually increased (*A Conspiracy Exposed*, April 25, 1894; reprints 3810; *Proclaimers*, 1993, p. 646; Penton, 1986, p. 35-40).

Yet, the conflicts seemed to remain private, as they did not surface in Maria's letters to Charles. In *Zion's Watch Tower*, she writes, caringly (circa August 15, 1895):

"My dear husband;—I arrived a few hours ago from Troy, on the 1:12 train and am safely and pleasantly sheltered with Sister Clark ... I have not had a chance to write you since I left New York, my stay in each place being so short that what little time I had with the friends was wholly occupied; and it has been midnight and after, almost every night before we retired.... It was a great pleasure to receive your letter on my arrival here, and to know that you are so thoughtful of me and that I have your prayers constantly.... I am trying to fulfill my mission as thoroughly as possible, but I must leave particulars until I return. I expect to hear from you next at Boston.... Your loving wife, MARIA F. RUSSELL" (Springfield, Massachusetts, July 25, '95; reprints 1850).

Her tone makes it difficult to envision that the Russells would soon enter into a conflict so fierce its results would have implications in the 21st century. One must conclude that everything was not as perfect and happy as it appears in Maria's letters. There was obviously something unsaid, kept hidden beneath surface tranquility—something in their "home" was certainly not as "happy" as they made it seem. In a short time this would become clear to members within the movement—and the bemused public.

Possibly, the supposedly belligerent Mr. Rogers had observed something during his visit. What this gentleman may have seen and heard was a hint of all that occurs in marriage that no one wants trumpeted to the winds. Still, the desire for power, in teams large or small, often overrides all humane consideration. The four rebels disappeared from view, but Maria Russell forged on.

Chapter 7

Maria Russell's *Uprising*

Up until this time (1894 to 1897), Maria Russell held a prominent position in the movement, and the following statement, found in an *Extra Edition of Zion's Watch Tower* from April 1894—and taken out of context (see endnote)—was probably published to calm her and any potential supporters:

"The affairs of the Society are so arranged that its entire control rests in the care of Brother and Sister Russell as long as they shall live" and further "that the management of the Tract Society would probably rest entirely in the hands of myself and Sister Russell so long as we live, as provided by the regulations of the Charter…" (*Extra Edition ZWT*, April 25, 1894, p. 57-59;[91] *Introduction to M.R.-Writings*, 2008).

Maria Russell had many important functions in the movement at this time, and because of her skills and education, she wrote many editorials for *Zion's Watch Tower*, in agreement with Russell's editorial and doctrinal principles. However, in the midst of the marital crisis (around 1896–1897), Charles Russell recast some of the articles she wrote in her capacity as associate editor. Maria insisted that he should reject the articles instead of rewriting them. He refused and accused her of supporting women's emancipation. She subsequently abandoned her associate editor's title.

These problems led to a committee of elders convening in the Bible Student's congregation in Allegheny; the committee held that neither she nor anyone else "had a right to interfere with Bro. Russell's Management of the Watch Tower: that it was his stewardship only, and that he alone was accountable for its management" (Penton, 1986, p. 35-38; *WT*, 1906; reprint 3812).

Unbearable for Maria Russell

In this gathering of conservative believers, consisting primarily of unlettered men, the women's rights movement was, at its least, unpopular, especially when a prominent "sister" was engaged in this liberation. An echo of this macho-chauvinist attitude from the 1890s is clearly sensed between the lines of a footnote in the Witnesses' history book from 1993:

"The Bible Students did not clearly understand at that time what the Witnesses now know from the Bible regarding men as teachers in the congregation. (1 Cor. 14:33, 34; 1 Tim. 2:11, 12) As a result, Maria Russell had been associate editor of the *Watch Tower* and a regular contributor to its columns" (*Proclaimers*, 1993, footnote, page 645).

Russell offers unnecessary details about events in his account in *Zion's Watch Tower* of June 1906. This presumably was the cause of Maria Russell's final separation from him; and his intention was, as far as I can judge, to exhibit and ridicule his wife:

"[The committee] suggested that they considered Mrs. Russell had the grandest of all opportunities in the world as my associate and co-laborer in the harvest work; they told her that personally they could think of no higher honor, and advised her to take this same view, that evidently was at one time her own view of the situation..." (*ZWT*, July 15, 1906). Her annoyance of the committee's reprimand of her is comprehensible, when you read more of Russell's humiliating report:

"Mrs. Russell was chagrined, broke down and wept, and left the room."

And he continued:

"She returned to the study [where the committee stayed] and there stated herself in substance that she could not agree with their decision, that she still had her own views, but that in deference to their advice she would endeavor to look at matters from their standpoint..."

The end of the story becomes clear as one reads further in Russell's unbalanced and very subjective report:

"I then asked her in their presence if she would shake hands. She hesitated, but finally gave me her hand. I then said, 'Now, will you kiss me, dear, as a token of the degree of change of mind which you have indicated?' Again she hesitated, but finally did kiss me and otherwise manifested a renewal of affection in the presence of this Committee..." (*ZWT*, July 15, 1906; reprint 3812, 3813).

The situation was unbearable for Maria, who may have felt she'd reached her breaking point. It is clear to us as readers how, in 1906 when Russell wrote this article, he obviously did not comprehend how greatly he compromised himself with this public display of Maria's humiliation. It is depressing reading. I certainly do not believe that a woman like Maria, who fought for women's rights, was proud and independent and opposed this committee—whose members probably exclusively consisted of gullible, pious men Russell had in his hollow hand—would adapt and subordinate herself in the long term.

And she did not.

For a short time, the Russells seemed to function in agreement, but it appears to have been a game of words only, completely without substance. Behind their differences were much deeper conflicts. Maybe they were in fact "incompatible," as Russell told her in 1895—after which he, it is said, offered her their common house, which she refused and, in the end, she got nothing at all. Although there is no evidence to suggest that he *truly intended* to leave the house to her.

Accusations of Envy and Vain Glory

Prior to the final separation, the couple corresponded privately during the summer of 1896. To her husband's great regret, Maria published these letters under the title of *Readers Attention* around 1903. This thirteen-page leaflet shows very clearly why the marriage hung by such a thin thread.

On July 8, 1896, Russell wrote the following to Maria; at the time, they still lived under the same roof:

"I decline a discussion.... I am convinced that our difficulty is a growing one generally—that it is a great mistake for strong-minded men and woman to marry such as are not too intellectual and high-spirited; for there never can, in the nature of things, be peace under present time conditions where the two are on an equality" (*Readers Attention,* 1903, p. 4; in the following, I refer again to this publication by only its page-numbers).

On July 9, Maria Russell wrote:

"I received your letter of Monday evening, and what a revelation it is of your real cause of your opposition to me–that it is envy, jealousy.... Is it possible that you are so full of envy and vain-glory, so desirous of out-rivaling everyone else, so full of that spirit of 'which shall be greatest?' which the Lord reproved in his early disciples, that you cannot brook being among your peers? Is it indeed possible that 'the nature of things' in your heart forbids your living at peace with one on an 'equality' with you, even though, as you confess, you never met as near your ideal? ... O my husband, beware of this spirit of pride, of strife and vain glory. I beg of you to fight against it or it will ruin you..." (p. 4-6).

On July 13, Charles replied:

"I must wait for some evidence of a true repentance in a full and hearty recantation, or else I must hold you at a distance and doubt your object and meaning and look for some solution of the meaning and object of your attack as I would with any other attacker and traducer" (p. 8).

Maria Commences the Battle

Under the heading, "None Support," the authors of the *Readers Attention* tract (perhaps four of Maria's friends, who witness the authenticity of the correspondence with their respective signatures and seals) wrote:

"These letters were followed by withdrawal of support, except upon humiliating conditions to which he knew his wife would never descend, and when he refused her even her clothing, claiming that it belonged to him, and she took the wife's privilege of supplying herself from the stores at his expense, he published the following notice in the Pittsburgh daily papers: / 'Notice.—The public is hereby cautioned to give credit to no one in my name except upon my specific written order, as I will not be responsible for such debts nor pay them.'"

(See full text of this tract in Appendix.)

Maria left Charles in November 1897:

"When Mrs. Russell left the house in the fall of 1897 to seek legal counsel of her brother [who practiced as a lawyer in Chicago] it was with full intent to return in a few days. And this was a very necessary prudential measure in view of a report he was causing to be circulated to the effect that she was of unsound mind, and of measures that were manifestly being taken to deal with her on this pretext. / To this danger she felt she was exposed unprotected. This measure, which she wisely took for self-protection, has resulted, unwittingly on her part, in permanent separation, with little hope, as the reader may judge, of any peaceable settlement" (p. 10, 11).

In April 1899, one and a half years later, she moved into a tenement house in Allegheny where her sister Emma lived. At the time, the Russells held joint ownership of the property. Mrs. Russell decided to stand on her legal rights. In the following note, she shortly informs her husband about her step: "Husband:—Acting on legal advice from one of the most eminent Pittsburgh attorneys I have taken up my abode at No. 79 [now No. 1004] Cedar Ave. Some furniture has been provided me and I am keeping house here by myself with occasional company of Mabel. I have no fears as I have good neighbors on both sides" (p. 12).

Mrs. Russell also informed him of her intent to let rooms in the house:

"I have taken down the 'To let' notice and purpose by renting the rooms to secure a little income, aside from which, as you know, I have none. If you take this matter kindly and feel like co-operating in it I feel sure it will be for your good no less than mine" (p. 12).

Charles Russell was furious:

"Dear Mrs. Russell:—Your note of the first inst., informing me that you had burglarized house No. 79 Cedar Ave. and had taken possession of the same, and intend to hold possession of it, and impliedly requesting that I give my assent, came duly...." Continuing, he wrote: "I regret that you have taken this step, and I now give you formal and legal notice to immediately remove from the said premises any of your belongings, for I can neither rent you the property nor permit you to occupy it..." (p. 12).

Proclaimers states, however, that Russell "provided her with a place to live and means of maintenance," which does not quite seem to match completely with Maria Russell's presentation of the case. However, the account in the Witnesses' history book from 1959 sounds a bit more true—note use of the verb "forced":

"When Mrs. Russell realized that no article of hers would be acceptable for publication unless it was consistent with the Scriptural views expressed in the *Watch Tower*, she became greatly disturbed and her growing resentment led her eventually to sever her relationship with the Society and also with her husband. This *forced* Russell to provide a separate home for her, which he did, providing financially for her support" (*Proclaimers*, 1993, p. 645; italics are mine; *Divine Purpose*, 1959, p. 45).

According to one of my sources, Russell and staff members from the Bible House in Allegheny responded by repossessing the tenement house where Maria Russell and several other women lived, and arbitrarily removed all the women's personal belongings. Russell soon was in court again, accused of violence and unwarranted action for having thrown the women out of their residence. He lost the case, apart from the charges of violence. (Penton 1986, p. 39; *Divine Purpose*, 1959, p. 45; *Proclaimers*, 1993, p. 645)

According to the *Readers Attention* tract, Mrs. Russell still lived in this house in 1903, four years after the above-mentioned events, "not receiving a dollar from her husband, *nor from the literary work so largely hers*" (p. 13, italics are mine). That the Society today claims this tract contains "gross misrepresentations" is really incomprehensible, because it contains only private letters written between the spouses in the summer of 1896. Apart from Maria's leaflet representing only a selection of the letters exchanged, the Society's documentation seems one-sided and incomplete. The humiliating incidents, in particular, which led to her fleeing to Chicago where she sought legal assistance from her brother, led to her final break with Russell.

That Maria Russell was very angry, yes, perhaps even *vindictive*, after these dramatic events in her life, is evidenced partly and reportedly by an attempt to arrogate the second-largest congregation of Bible Students in Chicago—partly through publication of *Readers Attention*—seems to be quite understandable (*Proclaimers*, 1993, p. 645: Penton, 1986, p. 39).

Charles Russell was undoubtedly furious. However, he allowed Maria to remain in her new home because he was increasingly concerned about his reputation in Allegheny and Pittsburgh. Furthermore, the house Maria now inhabited was, by definition, also *her* property.

They were not yet divorced.

"The Servant" Once More

At this point, it will be advantageous to return to the issue of "the servant," exploring details of the authorship of the "fourth volume," and the hints about the servant's identity. Some later time after the work's writing, Russell came to reveal *indirectly*, and perhaps unconsciously, he did not write this whole volume, and that Maria, to some extent, *probably* was co-author.

At the divorce proceedings in 1906, Charles Russell protested violently against his wife's testimony (regarding the authorship) and claimed among other things that he had not imagined "Mrs. Russell would be able to write the three volumes, or the fourth volume, or any of the volumes. If she has that ability I have never found out…" (*The Divorce Appeal*, p. 214; *Introduction to M.R.-Writings*, 2008).

The following may offer further enlightenment of this matter:

In 1909, Russell answered a question from a reader about who the servant really was, and the answer from him was as follows—and it is quite interesting: "As far as I know nearly *all the talk about 'that servant' has been by my enemies.* I have nothing to say about the subject. What I would say would not change matters anyway. You have your right to your opinion and they have their right to theirs. In the fourth chapter of the sixth volume of 'Millennial Dawn,' this Scripture is brought to your attention. *That is all that I have ever written on the subject.*" (The topic, "servant," is treated under "Servant—Who That Servant?" in *What Pastor Russell Said*, p. 644, first published in 1916-1917. The version I am quoting was probably released after 1916. There is no reference in the book about the quote's origin—except that it is from 1909. In the preface of *What Pastor Russell Said*, however, we find the book was printed near the time of Russell's death in 1916. Therefore, I must conclude the quote was originally taken from a *Souvenir Convention Report* from 1909. See endnote[92]; see also *Studies* 6, the sixth chapter, p. 274; italics are mine).

It sounds as if, prior to the sixth volume, Charles Russell had never written or suggested that he filled the role of the servant, which infers he *did not write the words about the servant in the fourth volume.* But he knew very well this topic had a *prominent place* in the fourth volume, a fact he seems to have disregarded.

Therefore, we may consider that if Maria Russell authored the fourth volume, or parts thereof, which this quote and other quotations seem to indicate, then the scenario makes more sense. She likely wrote the section about the "servant" in the fourth volume at the same time she proposed Russell in the role in *Zion's Watch Tower.* As she fled from Russell in 1897, taking refuge with her brother in Chicago and to enlist his aid against her husband, she was almost finished writing the fourth volume. It's reasonable to consider that she may have simply stopped at pages 613 and 614, where the identity of the servant indirectly is suggested, because she left Russell.

Note that the text in the fourth volume emphasizes that the servant may be "removed at any moment," if he is not a "humble and unassuming" servant and does not "think of claiming authorship or ownership of the truth." It resembles an idea: "authorship." Perhaps I am reading too much into the statement, yet if I focus only on the words, to me it seems they are *shaped* by Maria Russell, and in an enigmatic, subtle way, she may be initiating her campaign against Charles Russell: "Any other spirit and course would surely work a *change of steward.*" And then, referring to the text (maybe *her* text), and the words of the "evil servant" in Matthew 24:48-51 (*Studies* 4, 1915 (1897), p. 613, 614; *Studies* 4 and Russell's other books found on *Strictly Genteel* on the internet; italics are mine).

It is striking, isn't it? And more so when one considers she later appointed Russell the role of the "evil servant."[93] Therefore, we might even presume she was *ready in the wings*, if anyone should need her. She almost handed the arguments to the opposition on a silver platter—the opposition who, as noted earlier, didn't see "the Pastor" as *that* servant, but rather as a "pope."

The timing is too striking a coincidence to be ignored, and on that background Maria Russell's assertion that she wrote much of the first three volumes, and nearly the entire fourth, is weighty, indeed. This heavily supports her as a credible court witness during the 1906 divorce trial, which today strengthens the quality of her testimonies.

Moreover, Maria Russell was a capable writer and author who most likely could have written the fourth volume. The *Writings by Maria Russell*, published digitally in 2008 by Barbara Anderson, a considerable work of over 1,100 pages, included a larger, never-published, handwritten manuscript from 1906, *The Eternal Purpose*; it demonstrates clearly that Maria Russell was a *capable writer* who was by no means any less talented than Russell (which he suggested at one point in the trial). The same impression comes from reading *The Twain One*, published in 1906 (100 pages). Maria Frances Russell was a strong and articulate woman who, apart from antiquity's opinion about women, advocated for women's traditional rights from an ancient Christian perspective. (*The Twain One*, 1906, p. 77–82)

The variety of her writing substantiates that she had a broad range and was able to write about anything besides just doctrines and end-time dates. She was also something of a poet,[94] an engaged woman filled with emotions and religious feelings, which shines through in her work. She was an inspiring counterpart to Russell, and it seems, that was the very thing he refused to embrace.

I think it may be safe to conclude that Maria Russell, by all appearances, was a highly intelligent, idealistic and ambitious woman who unfortunately turned out to be her husband's *worst competitor*. When she couldn't get his recognition and love, she sought more influence over their shared company—at that time as much *her* lifeblood as it was his. She would show him and the Bible Students that she was truly capable.[95]

More Strife

Even as the trouble between the spouses fermented, another controversy emerged. In the showdown with Barbour around 1877–78, Russell had developed the "new covenant" dogma. Russell believed that the "church" could not be considered part of the new covenant, since all church members had to first be "raptured" into heaven, something Russell expected to happen in 1914 (previously 1881). Russell had, however, quickly abandoned his new thesis and returned to the traditional Christian view that the church was under the new covenant.

Russell's closest advisor at that time was Paul S. L. Johnson, a highly educated, 1895 graduate of Capital University in Columbus, Ohio. Shortly after graduation, Johnson attended Lutheran seminary—after converting from Judaism to Christianity—and became pastor at a Lutheran church. Johnson researched Russell's discarded viewpoint and encouraged Russell to reinstate the new-covenant dogma, which happened in January 1907. Many of his associates tried to get him to abandon the matter, but in vain.

Yet another contentious issue arose when Russell took an oath (the issue of the Vow); the controversy surrounded the issue of *proper relationship* between the sexes within the Bible Students and attracted much attention. Early in 1908, Russell swore by the Lord that he would "avoid being in a room with any female alone, unless the door of the room stand wide open—wife, children, mother and sisters excepted" (Penton, 1986, p. 41).

When he tried to sell this oath commitment to the employees in March 1908, it all went wrong. Each had to submit a letter confirming they had followed the request. Most did as Russell required, but some were resentful that Russell intended to publish the names of those who would not take the oath—something he subsequently promised not to do. Although he still insisted they kindly inform him of taking the oath, he offered this alternative to publishing names: "We will preserve an alphabetical list which may be of use some time" (Penton, 1986, p. 41).

The new covenant and the loyalty-list situation combined became a stumbling block for many of Russell's closest associates and they left the organization. This happened in 1909 with former head cashier E. C. Henninges,[96] who by that time was the movement's branch manager in Melbourne, Australia. Henninges wrote an open protest letter to Russell, urging him to abandon the new doctrine and investigate its legitimacy. When Russell refused, Henninges and most of the Melbourne congregation left the movement to form the New Covenant Fellowship. In the US out of approximately 10,000 Bible Students, hundreds also left the movement on this occasion and formed the New Covenant Believers. This group is known today as the Berean Bible Students Church and has less than 200 members (The New Covenant Believers, Bible Student Movement, *Wikipedia*, 2011).

Some of Russell's followers must have realized that if there was not a formalized opposition within the movement, it would end up in pure Babel. Still, such a challenge seemed unthinkable because it would reduce the divine authority of the faithful and wise servant (Russell). Member democracy within the Bible Students implied a contradiction, because such a course might lead the members through an election that could put into question "God's leadership" by Russell and—not unimportant—his ownership of *Zion's Watch Tower* and the Society.

Brick by immoveable brick the foundations for the dictatorship and the regimentation were laid.

Chapter 8

Relocation and New Problems

Mr. and Mrs. Russell were physically separated in 1897. In 1903 Maria Russell sought legal separation, and when the case went to trial in 1906 and again in 1908, the separation was legalized and the court ruled that Mrs. Russell would receive spousal support in the amount of $100 per month. While the Russells were separated at this point, they never divorced, yet in practice it was a divorce, if only from "bed and board." In this way she received alimony. Charles Russell was ordered to pay his estranged wife a compensation of several thousand dollars, but apparently refused to pay alimony because he, as he claimed, had "no money" and thus was unable to provide financial maintenance for her. J. F. Rutherford wrote about this situation in his little, 64-page book, *A Great Battle in the Ecclesiastical Heavens*, New York City, 1915:

"The property was his and he had the right to do with it as he pleased. That after their separation, acting in good faith and in harmony with their said agreement, he had transferred his property to said Society, and that he had not the means with which to pay the amount of alimony allowed by the Court."

However, Russell's reasoning was not accepted by the court since it established that he owned several hundred thousand shares in the Watch Tower Bible and Tract Society (Efraim Briem mentions a value of $317,000). Still, the disbursement was unnecessarily delayed for several years.

According to Rutherford, in 1908 Mrs. Russell tried to cancel transfer of the matrimonial common property to the Watchtower Society. Rutherford, however, indicates in his 1915 book that Charles Russell, during the divorce negotiations, testified that before the couple's marital problems began, they had consecrated everything they owned for the religious work of the Lord before the Watchtower Society organization, and they had agreed that all their property "should be turned over to" the Watch Tower Bible and Tract Society. As far as I can see, this agreement may have been concluded—provided the information is accurate—just before or immediately after 1894. (*Ecclesiastical Heavens*, 1915, p. 34; p. 16)

For five years Russell resisted his wife's demands for separation and alimony. In 1909 she appealed for an increase of her maintenance, at the very time when

Russell was about to move from Pittsburgh and the jurisdiction there. Possibly around this same time, he transferred all his assets to the Watchtower Society. According to his critics, the transfer was made to avoid paying maintenance to Maria. Finally, an appeals court ruled, reportedly with barely disguised anger, in favor of Mrs. Russell in 1911. The verdict, among other things, substantiated Charles Russell's allegedly arrogant and domineering behavior towards her, a behavior that, in the longer term, would have made life unbearable for her if she had remained in the marriage.

I cannot disprove the claims Rutherford makes in his book, and therefore, I cannot offer plausible argument that Russell transmitted his wealth to the Watchtower Society earlier than 1908 (but not before about 1893 and latest around 1909), before or shortly after Russell and his staff moved to New York.

So claim is against claim in this late-Victorian confrontation, one eagerly reported in the contemporary scandal press. This reveals a headstrong man who with beak and claws, denials and inaccurate information, and extreme stubbornness, stuck to his claim. At the same time, it leaves the impression of a woman who fought for her economic interests that, among other concerns, should be viewed against the background she to some extent helped draw as co-author of Russell's first four books, and those of her own also published by their joint company.

After the long and exhausting process of divorce was over, Russell and his staff moved to the new headquarters in Brooklyn, New York, in 1908. Russell had acquired property, rebuilt it and named it The Brooklyn Tabernacle. Russell's advisers had told him New York would be far superior to Pittsburgh when it came to establishing stronger contact with newspaper editors, an important part of Russell's extroverted activities. Therefore, New York with its large population was seen as the "most suitable center for the harvest work during the *few remaining years*" left before eruption of the apocalyptic war or perhaps for the *many years*, which would elapse *after* 1914, against the expectations of the majority of adherents in 1908. However, this was yet to be revealed. (*Proclaimers*, 1993, p. 59; *WT*, December 15, 1908; italics in quoted material are my emphasis)

Russell and his followers had much work to do if they were to reach the entire world's population and inform them all governments worldwide faced immediate downfall at the approaching Armageddon battle. In a few years 1914–1915 would arrive; there was little time to bring more people into the organization before the worldwide mission work was completed.

Russell may have "fled" Pittsburgh in favor of New York to escape the unsuitable limelight cast by his divorce, but in a few years it would be crystal clear that things weren't much better in New York. He got the coveted press attention, but in an entirely different manner than he had wanted or expected. In New York he soon became the central figure in a series of revealing articles and new lawsuits where everyone but Charles Russell was victorious.

A False Prophet

Also Dr. E. L. Eaton, pastor of the Methodist Episcopal Church in Pittsburgh who debated Russell publicly six times in 1903—a debate series which Russell and his followers believed they won—published a new book in 1911, *The Millennial Dawn Heresy: An Examination*, which was aimed squarely at Russell's "heretical" views.

Based on his interpretation of the Christian gospel, Eaton wrote indignantly:

"By reversing the divine law of interpretation, Millennial Dawn [synonymous with Russell's book series] has managed to build up a most false, extravagant, and fantastic system of doctrines, and is industriously trying to foist them upon the world as a substitute for the well-nigh universally accepted truth of Christianity. Putting one man's opinion over against millions of scholarly and godly men, and then founding that opinion upon a false and crude principle of interpretation—such is the propaganda that is now undertaken to enlighten the world under the name of Millennial Dawn!... We have noticed the tendency of all Millennialists to plunder the Bible, and especially the prophecies of the spread and triumph of the gospel, and the reign of the Messiah.... A noted Millennialist of New York [Russell] claims all the glowing descriptions of Messiah's kingdom and reign as having reference only to the Millennium.... This institution has taken practically the entire Bible as having written only for its pet hobby..." (*Millennial Dawn Heresy*, p. 10, 11 and 19; see also the section, "Confrontation with the Churches" in Chapter 5 of this book).

It is obvious that Russell seemed as a "thorn in the side" of contemporary theologians, who rightly regarded Russell as a *false prophet*, and this is why he had to be fought with all means. (And perhaps these theologians also used Russell to grab some of the limelight for themselves.) It's also obvious Russell had greater influence as a religious leader during his lifetime, than we can even imagine today. The six debates between Russell and Eaton alone demonstrate the point. Also, the Pittsburgh *Gazette's* debate reprints are pertinent. Apart from the Christian fundamentalists, hardly anyone today would agree with Eaton's views on the soul's immortality, Hell and other cardinal doctrinal points. But in 1911, Eaton's views were more commonly accepted. As seen in this context, Russell's campaigns against Hell represented a progress that ordinary people were tempted to engage in, without being aware that Russell's other "truths" and fantasies about future glories of the Millennium were pure speculations. So because of the growing opposition from the clerical side, the years 1911–1913 were preparatory years before Russell's final-battle years and retreat, 1914–1916. And although he loved the fight, it probably made short work of him in the end. (*Proclaimers*, 1993, p. 59)

The Case of "Miracle Wheat"

On January 1, 1913, *The Brooklyn Daily Eagle* began an attack on "Pastor" Russell, starting with the gradually well-known miracle-wheat case. By all accounts, the attack was inspired by Eaton's 1911 book, as well as the attack begun by Baptist pastor J. J. Ross in 1912, when he released a very controversial pamphlet, in which, among other things, the above mentioned miracle-wheat case was detailed.

In 1904, K. B. Stoner, a farmer who knew nothing of Russell, stated he had discovered a new, more-productive wheat variety, which he christened "miracle wheat." Experts speculate the new variety may have been a mutation. In 1907, an agricultural expert filed a report in praise of Stoner's wheat with the US Department of Agriculture. The case was reported in the press. Russell, who saw the new wheat as a "sign" of the millennial dawn, something he believed began to emerge in 1874 and would culminate in all its brilliance around and after October 1914, involved himself in the matter and wrote under the title "Miracle Wheat" in *Zion's Watch Tower* on the March 15, 1908:

"The public press is telling of the origin of 'Miracle Wheat' in answer to prayer. The description has the earmarks of truth to it, in that it gives the address of the man whose prayers are said to have been answered—'K. B. Stoner, a farmer of Fincastle, Botetourt county, Virginia.' It would appear from the account that the original stalk of wheat appeared in the midst of a crop of the ordinary kind, but with '142 heads of grain.' / We quote:—Mr. Stoner was amazed. It seemed incredible" (*ZWT*, March 15, 1908).

In 1911 two of Russell's Bible Students donated approximately ten hectoliters of wheat to the Watchtower Society to promote the Society's work, and on a proposal from the givers, the wheat was advertised for sale for one dollar per pound in *The Watch Tower*[97] of August 1, 1911:

"The notice in THE WATCH TOWER of June 15 that Brother Bohnet has 'miracle wheat' in abundance now, and that he will sell it at $1 per pound and donate the entire proceeds to our Tract Fund, has brought in many orders. These will be filled between August 15 and September 1. No limit as to supply has been noted. Sent by Express, prepaid, the price will be twenty-two pounds for $20; fifty-five pounds for $50; larger quantities at the latter rate. The merits of this wheat over the common variety have been mentioned in previous issues of THE WATCH TOWER."

Due to this case, the tabloid newspaper *The Brooklyn Daily Eagle* attacked Russell in a series of articles[98] in January 1913, even featuring a cartoon of Russell and calling him a "cheater." *The Eagle* was quite harsh with Russell, and he could only judge the attack from the viewpoint of his own grandiose self-image that tolerated neither a newspaper caricature of the kind the paper published, nor the harsh article also published on that occasion. Russell immediately sued the magazine, demanding $100,000 in damages—a terrifying amount at that time. Government experts examined the wheat, but found nothing remarkable about it. On January 29, 1913, *The Eagle* won the lawsuit. Russell was not present when the court handed down the verdict. *The Eagle's* many critical articles were annotated by Russell in *The Watch Tower* of February 15, 1913, the introductory lines of which read (see also: *1975 Yearbook of Jehovah's Witnesses*, p. 70):

"My suit against *The Eagle* for slanderous defamation of reputation has been decided in its favor. A Jury of twelve men have [*sic*] decided that *The Eagle* was justified in making its vicious onslaughts upon me, notwithstanding the Judge's Charge that, according to the law, the cartoon, at least, was a slanderous, vicious libel in fact. I am urged by my attorneys and petitioned by friends to take the case to the Court of Appeals…" (full article found in endnote, where it is revealed seven Catholics on the jury were blamed for the unfortunate outcome of Russell's legal action against *The Eagle*).[99]

Prior to the court battle, the magazine wrote that the trial would "show that 'Pastor' Russell's religious cult is nothing more than a money making scheme." In the end the case revealed him to the public as someone they shouldn't take seriously anymore (Martin and Klann, p. 14; this book is rather one-sided, no doubt affecting the objectivity of its data and representation).

Also, because of Russell's religious and legal dominance of his Society and the movement, he was basically considered guilty of the whole mess. Had he been a top executive of a multinational company (as he in a way was), everything would have been more understandable; but he was, in reality, supreme leader of a religious organization, which complicated matters because he *legally* was its owner. The press was critical and drilled relentlessly into Russell's methods.

Still, I cannot dismiss my opinion that there is some truth in Rutherford's assumption (from his 1915 pamphlet) that a unified front of "leading clergymen, representing numerous church denominations," and "certain Catholic bishops, priests and prelates" (Rutherford called them "allied *forces*") in some way united against Russell; of course—as Rutherford fails to address—this unified attack was caused by Russell's provocation of these other churches and leaders. In his 1915 pamphlet, Rutherford seems to base his argument and analysis on this starting point. (Rutherford's foreword, *Ecclesiastical Heavens*, p. 4 and 7, 1915)

Although Russell apparently did not personally profit from sale of the miracle wheat, it was still Russell who, formally speaking, collected profits totaling $1,800; this is provided he was the legal owner of the Watch Tower and Bible and Tract Society. Following criticism in the press, Russell offered, via his paper, to refund the buyers' money. However, none approached Russell or the Society to obtain refunds. In a later trial, addressed below, Russell conceded that there was a "particle of truth, just one grain of truth," in the criticism about the miracle wheat. (Penton, 1986, p. 43; *YB*, 1975, p. 71, *JVCD*, 2001)

Ross Accuses Russell

During the Russells' separation process from 1903–1911, it became clear C. T. Russell legally controlled and had power over the Watchtower Society, including full possession of the Society's resources. The assets in several of the subordinate companies, which Russell also owned, were controlled by a holding company where Russell held 990 shares out of 1,000. Two of his associates, J. A. Bohnet and E. C. Henninges, held the remaining ten shares—each valued at five dollars. (*Facts and More Facts*, 1913, p. 31–37)

In early 2009, I read Canadian Baptist minister J. J. Ross' pamphlet, *Some Facts and More Facts about the Self-Styled "Pastor" Charles T. Russell*, released in 1913 (subsequent page references are to this pamphlet).[100] I read the pamphlet eagerly, but soon remembered Ross' almost *uncompromisingly critical*, yes, even *hateful*, attitude towards Russell. Still, Ross succeeded with almost all his accusations against his opponent, "the cunning Brooklyn Pastor," which he called his hate object number one (p. 13).

Ross' pamphlet is a major source of information about the Hamilton case, which lasted from December 1912 to March 1913, and for that reason I decided to use it as the basis for my review of the case but only as a reference framework to summarize the main points, documented with quotations from the pamphlet. In fact, Ross published the pamphlet twice, the first in 1912, and then an updated 1913-version (as referenced here) released after Ross triumphed in the Hamilton court case.

The accusations in Ross' pamphlet led me to conclude they were the cause for Russell, on advice from legal advisor J. F. Rutherford, bringing libel proceedings against Ross in 1912. I know that Ross' second pamphlet against C. T. Russell is much discredited among today's Jehovah's Witnesses; this was also why I read Ross' pamphlet with a little more interest. Ross did not hold back. He hammered his points home, and in the end, was quite unchristian toward the "cunning pastor" from Brooklyn:

"In this leaflet I am to tell you something about the so-called 'Pastor' C. T. Russell, the founder and chief executive of 'Millennial Dawnism.' … He never attended the higher schools of learning, knows comparatively nothing of philosophy, systematic or historical theology, and is totally ignorant of the dead languages, and yet he is successful in making his disciples believe that the most difficult passages in the Old Testament and the book of Revelation are as simple as a sunbeam to him. 'Pastor' Russell was never ordained and has no church affiliation…. By thousands he is believed to be a religious fakir [*sic*][101] of the worst type, who goes about like the Magus of Samaria enriching himself at the expense of the ignorant. Years ago he gave himself the title of 'Pastor' and from this many have inferred that he was a properly approved minister of the gospel. In 1879, he married Miss Marie F. Ackley, who divorced him a few years ago on the ground of cruelty and of having wrong relations with other women. In court, she proved improprieties between her husband and one Rose Ball. Mrs. Russell is now living at Avalon, Pa." (p. 3, 4)

Ross continues:

"Wishing to frustrate the verdict of the court in giving his wife alimony, he [Russell] changed the names of his publications to 'Studies in the Scriptures,' [previously *Millennial Dawn*] and transferred the head office to Brooklyn, N. Y., where it is at the present time.... By the name 'International Bible Students Association,' the public is deceived into thinking that the institution is international in extent, that the governments of the world are behind it, and that it is made up of accredited representatives of all the denominations and theological colleges, when in fact the name stands only for the followers of one man, and not a scholar at that. That appellation is, therefore, a misnomer.... At the present time, the 'Brooklyn Eagle' has its talons in Russell, and shows him to be a most undesirable citizen" (p. 5).

Ross further states:

"By 'The Brooklyn Eagle,' he [Russell] stands charged with defrauding his wife of her dower interest, with having his name sensationally connected with those of other women, with giving himself out as an interdenominationalist, when, in fact, he is connected with none, but opposed to all, with publishing himself as giving addresses to great crowds in important places, where he has not spoken a word at all, with seeking to dupe certain ministers into supporting daring transactions, with being connected with lead, asphalt and turpentine companies, with selling or causing to be sold 'Miracle Wheat,' at $60 a bushel, with influencing the sick and dying to make their wills in his favor, with engineering the sale of a property worth $35,000 for $50 for the purpose of defrauding another.... Judging from his advertisements of himself, many do not think him normal, and so are persuaded that he is self-deceived" (p. 6).

And, finally:

"The teaching of these books subverts the faith of Christians of all evangelical denominations and substitutes for the truth as it is in Christ the destructive doctrines of one man, who is neither a scholar nor a theologian. The whole system of Russellism is anti-rational, anti-scientific, anti-Biblical, anti-Christian and a deplorable perversion of the Gospel of God's dear Son" (p. 7).

And thus, Ross makes his case in his pamphlet, and I am with him—up to a point.

Preliminary Hearing in Hamilton, Ontario, December 1912

First let me state that whatever appears to have happened around Russell, the divorce proceedings, the miracle-wheat proceedings and *The Brooklyn Daily Eagle's* and Ross' accusations against Russell, it is impossible to objectively determine anything about the cases or exactly why they happened. The parties naturally had their own subjective perceptions of what happened at the time, and now, 100 years later, we have only those records and perceptions to consult, since all the players are long deceased. Therefore, everything must be observed with restraint and balance. Still, the circumstantial evidence points in one direction where the truth must exist and enable us to draw our own conclusions.

One may ask why I have chosen to examine the case of *Russell v. Ross* so closely. The answer is a simple one: The case is essential to the Bible Students' history, and because it is still largely reflected on and debated in the media— and especially on the internet with international participation. The first event surrounding Russell's legal action was a preliminary hearing on December 9, 1912, in Hamilton, Ontario, where Russell was summoned to appear to make declaration that Ross' accusations, as found in his pamphlet, were untrue. "Under oath," as Ross writes, "he [Russell] positively and most emphatically denied every charge made against him" (p. 17).

The entirety of Ross' pamphlet was read aloud at the hearing, page by page, and Russell was repeatedly asked by the Crown Attorney: "Is this true," and his responses according to Ross' account, were in the negative throughout: "no, no, no," "wrong," "pronounced untrue," "it is not true," etc. And so it went until the miracle-wheat incident, to which Russell replied: "The item about the miracle wheat might be said to have a particle of truth...."

Here Ross writes (p. 17, 18) that the miracle-wheat incident was Russell's only concession to the accusations against him. In this, we see legal rationale and logic applied to its fullest as Ross notes: "By denying these charges, he [Russell] claimed for himself a high scholastic standing, having a knowledge of the dead languages, having taken a course in theology, systematic and historical theology, ordination, church affiliation and so on" (p. 18).

As to the question of whether Russell committed adultery, the grand jury noted on the warrant: "No Bill!"—Nothing to come after.[102] When Maria was asked whether she thought her husband had committed adultery, she said no. So, on this accusation at least, Ross' attack of Russell was on shaky ground.

It was a very subtle trial, whose purpose, in my view, was to skewer Russell because of his somewhat unconventional and anti-ecclesiastical preaching.

Russell had not received a higher education, a legacy that still characterizes the movement as it maintains anti-scholastic and antiquated attitudes. Russell was, in principle, unschooled, plain and straight forward, and his responses to the judge's rulings were not *sophisticated*—as they should have been if J. F. Rutherford had provided sufficient legal guidance. Or Rutherford's advice may have been ignored because Russell probably felt superior to his lawyer and the logic of the courtroom.

In this, Russell miscalculated completely.

The case moved forward rapidly, but there was, as far as I can deduce, some messiness after the preliminary hearing on December 9 when Russell had to declare his *complete disagreement* with Ross' allegations, before the court could really get started. What follows is my attempt to summarize events:

The first hearing occurred on December 2, 1912, and Russell filed summons for defamation of character (criminal, defamatory libel, p. 9) against Ross. Because of procedural errors in Hamilton (p. 9), and because of Russell's absence from various court hearings, the crucial cross-examination was postponed. On December 9, the initial interrogations took place, and Russell was forced to post a $500 cash security deposit so the information could be verified, and he was ordered to appear at a subsequent hearing in the High Court of Ontario, Canada, where the case would be completed. Due to procedural errors, the case would need to begin again. This is why Russell returned to Hamilton to submit a summons, after which he immediately left the city. The case resumed on February 7, 1913, but Russell failed to appear (p. 9): "We were informed that Mr. Russell was not in Canada that he could not be forced into the country, that for an unknown period he would be out of the United States and that the case could go on without his presence" (p. 9). Ross had somehow uncovered that Russell was on tour.

Determined to bring Russell in for the crucial cross-examination, Ross encouraged his attorney G. L. Staunton to extend the case, after which Russell was recalled for a new hearing. Russell, however, tried to avoid this proceeding, too. Mr. S. F. Washington, legal counsel for the prosecution in Hamilton, forwarded Ross an offer from Russell that if he (Ross) would give Russell a "mild" excuse, Russell would immediately drop all libel charges (p. 11). The determined Ross refused the request and replied that knowing all he did about Russell and his teachings, a heavy fine or term in jail would be preferable (p. 11).

In his reply to Russell, Ross expressed his sincere hope that Russell would implement the libel case; Ross even offered to pay for Russell's trip to Hamilton and the return to Brooklyn. According to Ross, the problem was that Russell ignored Ross' and the Hamilton court's summons to appear on February 28, 1913, and give testimony under oath, where he would also be subjected to cross-examination. At the time, Russell was still travelling outside the United States; but when he returned to New York, he immediately agreed to appear in the Hamilton court.

In his pamphlet, Ross writes about this correspondence:

"This letter was ignored by him until he was compelled later to notice it. This made it necessary to take an additional step in which an order was granted in the County Court for the appointment of a commission to go across the border to Brooklyn, N.Y., and to compel Mr. Russell to undergo cross-examination there. As soon as he was advised of this—*thinking doubtless* that it would be to his advantage and presuming that the Hamilton people did not know as much about him, his teachings and methods as the Brooklyn people did, he wrote the Crown Attorney that he would come to Hamilton and submit to cross-examination" (p. 13; italics are mine).

Ross continues his less-than-objective report:

"He came. He was put into the witness box by the defense. He was in the stand for nearly five hours, and at the conclusion of the examination, there being no other course the Magistrate again ordered a committal for trial. The cunning 'Brooklyn Pastor' seems not to have enjoyed this experience in a Canadian Court and his cross-examination by a Hamilton lawyer, and he seems also to have resolved that this experience should not be repeated. At all events, when he found himself safely back in Brooklyn and had a little time to recover himself, he wrote me a lengthy letter urging me to apologize and he would drop legal proceedings at once. His exact words are 'If you will apologize the error of your course, assuring me that you regret it and that you will do what you can to correct the misimpressions thus put forth, I will accept the apology and discontinue legal action against you forthwith" (p. 14).

An important hearing held on March 1, 1913, might have ended the whole affair, and perhaps would have settled it, if Ross had been satisfied that there was no cause for further proceedings. At that hearing, the court and the jury found "absolutely no ground for libel and handed down the verdict 'no bill' " (p. 15).[103] With Russell's libel case dismissed, Ross won the first round, but the defense was extremely upset by this development, since Ross and Staunton wanted the facts of their case published. They had gathered a great deal of material, intending to completely expose the "Pastor" by cross-examination. Maria Russell and other key witnesses were present at the March 1 hearing, but to Ross' annoyance there was no need for further proceedings.

(Speaking of excuses, from the available source material it was difficult to assess whether Russell's offer to Ross was made one or two times. But I run the risk and comfort myself with the truth that, at least in this case, I brought forth the important details in context and showed how Russell offered Ross an amicable solution.)

When I began to investigate the relationship between Ross and Russell, I gradually concluded that Ross' conscience was not *entirely* clear in these matters. Rather he, in my assessment, distorted the situation of Russell's response to the Hamilton court summons, and the controversy over Russell's mastery of New Testament Greek.

In the transcript of the cross-examination on March 17, 1913, which Ross cited in his pamphlet, he apparently altered one of Staunton's questions to Russell: "Do you know the Greek?" In reality, the question was, according to the official court transcript, "Do you know the Greek alphabet?"[104]

What Ross would gain by omitting the word "alphabet," I don't comprehend; maybe he left out the word on purpose, or perhaps he believed during his passionate writings that he, for the sake of clarity, could allow himself to omit the word. However, in retrospect, it seems petty.

Still, whether Greek or Greek alphabet, Russell quickly replied: "Oh, yes" (p. 18).

As a matter of fact, Russell worked with New Testament Greek words and their definitions in his books, something I have also done without being a specialist in dead languages (for example, *parousia*, which he, in his grandiose self-understanding completely misinterpreted). Presumably, Russell thought he could say "oh, yes" in this context. At this point, Russell must have begun to understand the situation in the courtroom, where the defense (Ross' lawyer, Staunton), much like *The Eagle,* wanted to put their claws in him, and that it would not do to give a smart reply (one he may not even have intended), but had to express himself seriously and accurately. In other words, he had to step off his pedestal and tell the truth, nothing but the truth.

Pressing on, Staunton rephrased his question in kinder terms: "Can you tell me the correct letters if you see them?"

Ross writes:

"Here he [Russell] was handed a copy of the New Testament in Greek, by Westcott & Hort, and asked to read the letters of the alphabet as they appear on the top of page 447. He did not know the alphabet. 'Now,' asked Mr. Staunton, 'Are you familiar with the Greek language?' 'No,' said Mr. Russell, without a blush. When he saw that he was caught, then he admitted that he knew nothing about Latin, and Hebrew and neither had he ever taken a course in Philosophy, Systematic Theology and neither had he ever attended any of the higher schools of learning. A trap had been set for him at every one of these points, and having been caught in the first, *he thought* it best for him to 'own up before he was shown up...' " (p. 18, 19; italics are mine).

Ross' hostility toward Russell is unmistakable.

In 1953, Baptist ministers Walter R. Martin and Norman H. Klann published a rather critical book on Jehovah's Witnesses: *Jehovah of the Watchtower.* Their representation of the testimony seems more objective; they included a transcript of the "Greek" issue:

Attorney Staunton: "Do you know the Greek alphabet?"

Charles Russell: "Oh yes."

Staunton: "Can you tell me the correct letters if you see them?"

Russell: "Some of them, I might make a mistake on some of them."

Staunton: "Would you tell me the names of those on top of the page, page 447, I have got here?"

Russell: "Well, I don't know that I would be able to."

Staunton: "You can't tell what those letters are, look at them and see if you know?"

Russell: "My way—" [he was interrupted at this point and not allowed to explain].

Staunton: "Are you familiar with the Greek language?"

Russell: "No."

(Martin and Klann, 1953, p. 20)

James Penton was quite critical of the proceedings in his book about Jehovah's Witnesses, *Apocalypse Delayed*; Penton believes it was Ross who "testi-fied falsely," and he stresses that "Ross misquoted his lawyer as asking Russell if he 'knew the Greek.' " Penton continues: "Actually what the lawyer, George Lynch-Staunton, asked was: 'Do you know the Greek alphabet?' Russell sim-ply answered, 'Oh, yes.' He made no claim whatsoever about knowing any-thing more of Greek or any other second language than that. Ross therefore distorted the truth" (Penton, 1986, p. 43).

On a website friendly to Jehovah's Witnesses, I found the following quote which addressed the issue of whether Russell perjured himself regarding his knowledge of New Testament Greek. In fairness, I have to bring it into this context:

"[There] was no question about matters. C. T. Russell had not committed perjury as Ross falsely charged after the trial. The case itself later went before a grand jury, which declined to return a bill of indictment. So, the case never went on for trial before the Supreme Court of Ontario. Under legal practice in Ontario, only the crown attorney is allowed to speak before the grand jury. We do not know how the case was presented to it or what caused that body to reject it. No decision ever was rendered on the merits of the case. In his subsequent writings, Ross treated this inconclusive result as though he had won a great vic-tory. He and others apparently chose to forget that Russell was not the man on trial" (*JW Apologetics Encyclopedia*; *Charges Against Charles Taze Russell*, Feb. 27, 2010).

Petroleum Company and Other Businesses

At the cross-examination on March 17, 1913, Attorney Staunton also addressed whether Russell still owned the Watchtower Society and, at least partly, other companies under his management from his headquarters in New York, includ-ing real estate. This particularly interested Ross because he wanted to prove that Russell by no means was without "money," as he claimed during the di-vorce process.

Under the sub-heading, "RUSSELL AND HIS BUSINESS CORPORA-TIONS" Ross' wrote in his 1913 pamphlet:

"Under his [Russell's] direct-examination by his attorneys, he was asked, 'Now if these charges did appear in the *Brooklyn Eagle*, are any one of them true?' 'They are not true,' was his most emphatic answer. 'Not true?' 'Not true.' But when he was forced into the witness box by the defense and learned that *we had the facts about these Companies on hand, and the charters of them in our possession*, he made a clean breast of the whole thing. He confessed being a stockholder in the Pittsburgh Asphaltum Co., which afterwards became the California Asphaltum Co., the organizer of the Selic Brick Co., which he 'en-tirely' managed from the Bible House on Arch Street, Pittsburg, the Brazilian Turpentine Co., in which he had a controlling interest, a Cemetery Company, located in Pittsburg, and the United States Coal and Coke Co., with capital stock of $100,000. It should have been most humiliating to swear to one thing and then, when facing the facts, again under oath to be compelled to confess to the very opposite. What do you call this?..." (p. 31, 32, emphasis mine).

"Is it strange," Ross notes later in his pamphlet, "that the jury brought down the verdict 'No bill?' "

In fact, that meant the jury did not find the information about Russell's various companies relevant or incriminating; Ross greatly disagreed with this. Russell's "interests" in the Watchtower Society and its subsidiaries were a central issue for Ross, and it appeared that Russell was not without money, as he had claimed in the divorce proceedings.

Russell did not comment in *The Watch Tower* on the question of the "secular" companies linked to The Watch Tower Society as far as I have been able to tell.

Was Russell Ordained?

After the questions about Russell's Greek proficiencies, Staunton addressed the issue of Russell's ordination: "Is it true that you were never ordained?"

Russell replied: "It is not true."

The court instructed Russell to provide a clear yes or no answer.

Staunton repeated the question: "Now, you never were ordained by a bishop, clergyman, presbytery, council, or any body of men living?"

Russell said, after a pause: "I never was."

In fact Russell had no reason to hesitate about this issue, for he did not believe in an episcopal "succession." The church was the modern Babylon, and represented the apostasy of the true, original Christianity. Russell was, as he himself expressed, elected pastor by his congregations, which strictly speaking would be acceptable—if one didn't know that he actually was the *absolute* owner of his pastorate, his Society and his movement. Anyone who questioned his powerful position soon learned Russell was clearly in charge. Or as Ross said: "He is always elected to the Presidency of this 'Religious' Society without opposition, in fact, he is always elected unanimously.... Russell financially and in every other way dominates that society and clearly *he is* that society..." (p. 33; italics are mine).

In fact, since Russell held the majority of voting shares, he could always choose himself. It was for this reason the opposition within had no chance of success up to that time—and would never get it as long as Russell alone held control.

Clearly, Ross and Staunton laid traps for Russell, and he managed to fall into almost all of them. In a large audience of ordinary listeners and supporters, he could say what he wished, but in the court he had to behave quite differently toward the issues raised. In the end, Russell lost the trial and Ross was upheld on all counts. (Martin and Klann, 1959, p. 18-22; Penton, 1986, p. 43)

Ross' verdict over Russell was hard and merciless, but understandable from Ross' assumptions as pastor in Hamilton, as well as those of colleagues in his and other church communities, on whose behalf he might have acted. For him, Russell was a completely irresponsible upstart who created a religious establishment built on an amateurish interpretation of the Bible and its original language. Ross had probably studied enough New Testament Greek to have the tools to expose the layman Charles Taze Russell's methods. It is not surprising that, for quite a long time, no articles or reports on the matter appeared in *The Watch Tower*. Had Russell won a clear victory over Ross, there would have been no end to the gloating and reports in *The Watch Tower*.

That Ross' criticism did make an impression on Russell is demonstrated in a smaller note in *The Watchtower* in 1914 where Russell writes about the "theological" level among the employees in the organization's headquarters, Bethel:

"We realize that here at Bethel, we have by far the strongest Theological School, with daily studies and recitations, in the whole world. I read only today in the *Christian Herald,* a challenging query as to how many of us were regularly ordained, where we got our education, how many of us had any understanding of Greek or Latin, etc. Now, all of us understand Greek better than most orthodox (?) ministers; and we could have some formal recognition of our ordination, perhaps referring it to the date of our individual consecration, believe it would serve to stop the mouths of many, and would give the truth much impetus in the public opinion, which would well serve the purpose in gathering the Lord's wheat" (*WT,* April 15, 1914; parenthetical question mark is part of the quote).

Russell's lawyer, J. F. Rutherford, tried to address both *The Eagle's* and Ross' claims in his 1915 book, *A Great Battle in the Ecclesiastical Heavens,* but it was a summarily parenthetical and propagandistic contribution to these events. However, it offers several additional details not to be found elsewhere. Today, the defense Rutherford offers is only interesting as a historical document of those years in the movement. At the time, it probably served to both prevent further member departures in the critical years just after 1914, and to counter the charges brought against Russell by J. J. Ross and *The Eagle*. Still, the release of Rutherford's book shows that in 1915 he and Russell considered both parties' allegations very serious. And they were![105]

As far as I know, Ross' arguments and claims have never been effectively refuted by the Watch Tower Society—apart from Rutherford's book and various mentions in the Jehovah's Witnesses' literature. As a result, Ross' pamphlet, which may seem an unfair and coarse (or even ill-mannered) criticism of Russell, is a noteworthy contribution to the collection of reproachful literature written by Russell's contemporaries. That Ross' pamphlet is discussed and quoted 100 years after publication is no small achievement for the writer.

According to Ross, Russell finally ceased defending himself, and in an internal circular letter of May 16, 1913, addressed to *The Watch Tower*'s readers, Russell apologized and explained again, according to *Facts and More Facts*, why he did not intervene against Ross in the Hamilton case (if Ross' account can be labeled accurate): "I did not think it worth while to sue Rev. Ross for money damages when he had no money" (p. 44).

For the Bible Students, the first official mention of Ross' campaign against Russell appeared in *The Watch Tower* on September 15, 1914, more than a year after the legal proceedings ended. In a long editorial letter, Russell replied to a letter from Mr. E. J. Coward.[106] Russell's reply may illuminate some of his motives for abandoning the case against Ross. In this answer, Russell takes up an argument similar to the one Ross used in his pamphlet, specifically, because Ross didn't own any property it was useless to sue and he couldn't be frightened into relenting. Quoting from Russell's letter to E. J. Coward (see above endnote reference with Russell's letter to Coward): "[H]e has no property, a suit for damages would not intimidate him nor stop him." Russell also found pursuing the case would be too expensive. He apparently realized he could not frighten Ross the way he had hushed other critical voices, including the *Washington Post* and *The Brooklyn Daily Eagle*, by demanding large damages. At the same time he overlooked the opportunity to not only seek financial settlement, but restoration of reputation. In the dispute between Russell and the *Washington Post*, the court sentenced the newspaper to pay Russell one dollar in damages—as settlements go, a humiliation for sure. On the other hand, if Russell had initiated a comprehensive defense against Ross' allegations, it could have backfired at the time he was focused on producing "The Photo Drama of Creation," a large-scale slideshow he labored over for years, and his other domestic campaigns. Continuing a trial, where he already knew the majority was against him, might expose too much dirt. (See also: *Ecclesiastical Heavens*, 1915, p. 35.)

When I first read Ross' pamphlet from 1913, I was impressed by his arguments, but when I looked deeper into the material, I could see why Ross is regarded with suspicion by the Watchtower Society and even by Ex-Witnesses— a suspicion I shared, even after so many years away from the movement. I needed to wade deep in the sediments of brainwashing, and view what Ross wrote about Russell without the old prejudices. Ross was a tough critic, and his merciless attack on Russell's self-understanding was sometimes unfair and unpleasant.

I eventually had to view Ross as a less-than-prime witness in connection with Russell, even though his two pamphlets contain important details needing to be studied and considered—by Russell's modern-day heirs as much as anyone. It is of further interest to note that, apparently, with the matter ended, Ross does not feel compelled to mention that a grand jury refused to re-hear the case, and it was subsequently not addressed in the Ontario Supreme Court.

When first published, Ross' pamphlets drew attention to Russell, and no doubt his advisers told him to let the matter die and be forgotten. Still, accounts of the trial appeared in *The Daily Eagle*, and despite a small print run of 25,000 copies, as J. F. Rutherford notes ironically in his 1915 book, the small tabloid newspaper is still frequently cited, 100 years later, as one finds through a simple internet search. Small editions or not, *The Eagle* had put its claws in a real "juicy booty!" (*Ecclesiastical Heavens*, 1915, p. 11)

Presumably, it was not only the history of Rose Ball, which follows, that got Russell to abandon the case against Ross, but that all the other accusations in Ross' pamphlet, if commonly known, could cause a catastrophic decrease in the number of Russell's supporters frighteningly close to the apocalyptic year 1914, which waited just beyond the horizon.

Quite a lot was at stake for Russell.

Rose J. Ball

Rose Ball, who Mr. and Mrs. Russell took in as their adopted daughter, seems to have been an intimate aspect of Maria Russell's separation from Charles because she was angry, dismayed and perhaps almost morbidly jealous of Russell's relationship with the young woman. Ross also brought public attention to this case in his 1913 pamphlet.

For a time, Rose worked as Russell's private secretary in the Bible House in Pittsburgh; this situation and the other factors Maria Russell presented under oath were apparently crucial to her separation from Charles. There were only rumors back then, and a certain feeling that Russell *clearly could have had reason* to feel offended regarding his honor regardless of whether Maria Russell spoke the truth. The mere fact that these rumors were presented during the divorce trial was enough to cast a shadow, and I don't think Reverend Ross, the collected clergy or the press wished "the cunning Brooklyn Pastor" (as Ross called him) any good will.

Beyond the reliability of Mrs. Russell's testimony in 1906, the story of Rose Ball was extremely bad publicity for Russell. If this story were taken from a novel, it might have value as commentary on complex human behavior, but history reflects only half the story in the expression of Maria Russell's views that can only be considered subjective. Nothing could be proven and Charles Russell simply denied everything. So then, had Mrs. Russell expressed the truth, or had her *vindictive imagination* run off with her, as it was later claimed?

Ross used Mrs. Russell's testimony regarding Rose Ball as evidence of Russell's dubious character, but Maria's testimony was rejected by the court at the separation hearing in 1906. The evidence was simply lacking, and the judge sentenced accordingly: "No Bill!"[107] The jury was to disregard this area of testimony, rescuing Russell from the burden of the accusation. During the trial

Mrs. Russell's attorney asked whether she believed Charles was guilty of adultery, she responded: "No!"

Paradoxically, this statement reinforces her overall credibility. Possibly she revealed knowledge of Charles Russell's behavior, on the basis that she *may have* known more but could not say so publicly. According to the court transcript, Rose Ball allegedly told Maria *her* version of events, and as a serious Christian woman, Maria could not possibly lie.[108] Or could she?

Viewed objectively, Ross' arguments are quite in-depth and particular; they present surprising details, yet are selective and abrasive, making them most useful as background material. Therefore, if I lose myself in *Russell v. Ross*, I fall short of my larger goal for this book.

In 1945, Brooklyn College professor H. H. Stroup concluded: "In reviewing the case today, an observer may perceive that the evidence of the prosecution was not as conclusive as the jury considered it to be" (Stroup, 1945, p. 9).

I believe Stroup was right in his observation, yet it's difficult to reach a definitive conclusion. Any investigation into the substance of the Russells' conjugal conflict encounters the wall of distortion and denial still surrounding Maria Russell with the researcher feeling "infected" as a consequence.

Thousands filled Pittsburgh's Carnegie Hall for Charles Taze Russell's funeral in 1916. A veiled Maria Russell walked up the aisle and placed a lilies-of-the-valley bouquet by the coffin. On the bouquet was written: "To My Beloved Husband." This very private expression of Maria's extremely mixed feelings came before the public's gaze, but it concerned only her. It should have been respected with compassion. Unfortunately, in the Society's view it became "Maria Russell's own belated acknowledgment [of Russell]…" (larger quote from *Proclaimers*, 1993, p. 646, can be found in the endnote).[109]

There is no doubt that Maria Russell remained emotionally attached to her husband, and presumably, in her own complicated way, both hated and loved him. But Maria's last words to her husband, as displayed on her funeral bouquet, stand as a sign that the truth *can*, and perhaps *must*, lie between her words and between the disparate positions of hatred and love.

Maria Frances Russell died in 1938 at age eighty-seven. There were few mourners at her coffin. She was interred at Royal Palm Cemetery where her sister Emma and husband Joseph Russell (Charles Russell's father) were buried.

Russell's Journeys

During *Russell v. Ross*, Ross suspected Russell's apparent reluctance to appear in court at Hamilton was a tactical choice. I will not deny that Russell may have been conflicted about appearing, but more likely it was his great travel activity, both domestic and international, that kept him away. However, for Ross, who wanted Russell exhibited and disclosed in a public courtroom, the matter was clear: Russell tried to avoid the consequences of his legal action against Ross, but as Ross opined, Russell realized a trial conducted in a small Canadian town was preferable to one in New York—so Russell appeared in court. In fact, evidence for such a conclusion is insufficient, indicating the idea is Ross' subjective interpretation and demonization of Russell's motives. Ross did not know Russell's motives at all; the circumstances of Russell's extensive travel activity seem to substantiate this.

Russell began traveling as early as 1876–1877 while a member of the Barbourites, Nelson Barbour's small movement.[110]

From about 1891 to 1914, Russell and his companions embarked on at least twelve world tours, visiting Canada, Ireland, Scotland, England, Russia and the Middle East, among others. In Russia, Italy, Turkey, Austria and Germany, Russell saw no fertile ground for the "truth," but he was more optimistic about Norway, Sweden, Denmark and Switzerland, and "especially England, Ireland and Scotland [were] fields ready and waiting to be harvested. These fields seem to be crying out, Come over and help us! [*sic*] and we know of no more hopeful parts in which to thrust in the sickle and reap," he concluded. (*YB*, 1993, p. 69-147)

In 1911–1912 Russell traveled to the Far East for four months escorted by a committee of seven men. Their official purpose was "to examine firsthand the conditions there." The committee was comprised of Russell's doctor, three retired dignitaries, a general, a professor and a judge, all very respectable and prestigious personalities; Russell must have felt that he was among equals.

Honolulu, Hawaii, was the group's first stop, but here, something was amiss. In February 1912, *The Brooklyn Daily Eagle* ran a story about "Pastor" Russell's "imaginary sermons" in Honolulu (among other places) that apparently never occurred.

The paper made a sensational story out of it:

The *Daily Eagle* telegraphed the *Hawaiian Star* newspaper in Hawaii, and the editor replied that Russell and his entourage were on the island "a few hours with a Bible Students' committee of foreign mission investigation, but did not make a public address as was anticipated" (Martin and Klann, 1959, p. 17).

Officially, the journey was part of Russell's attempt to spread his message all over the world—before the imminent battle of Armageddon; unofficially, it's been suggested that it was arranged to remove him from the negative press coverage in New York. Today the Jehovah's Witnesses explain *plausibly*—or at least it *sounds* convincing—that the Bible Students didn't expect to convert the entire world during this foreign evangelizing, but wanted to "give a witness and that this would serve toward the gathering of 'an elect few from *all* nations, peoples, kindreds and tongues for membership in [Christ's] Bride class...' " (*Proclaimers*, 1993, p. 420; see also *WT*, April 15, 1912).[111]

After Hawaii the group continued to Japan, China, the Philippines and India. In Tokyo, the *Japan Weekly Chronicle* viewed the visit as a "huge advertising scheme." *The Eagle* quoted the *Chronicle*, as follows: "These gentlemen arrived in Japan on Saturday the 30th December. On the following day 'Pastor' Russell delivered a sermon in Tokyo titled 'Where are the dead?' which, though the title is a little ambiguous, does not seem to have any special connection with the mission work. On Monday it assumed that the mission work in Japan was begun and finished, for the next day seems to have been devoted to travelling, and on Wednesday 'Pastor' Russell and his co-adjutors [assistants] left Kobe for China in the same vessel in which they arrived in Yokohama..." (Martin and Klann, 1959, p. 17).[112]

The committee, with Russell in the lead, proceeded into China and India, adding 4,000 miles to the already-lengthy tour. According to Penton—and a comment by Mrs. Russell[113]—Russell must have spared no comfort on his tours. However, considering his ownership role, he only used his personal fortune on these trips, which—if viewed objectively—may be justified by his desire to enlarge his internationally expanding religious activities. (*Proclaimers*, 1993, p. 419)

Nevertheless, the Far East tour seems somewhat extravagant today, as if it served every purpose other than "evangelizing" in foreign lands.

Worldwide, the Bible Students had high and ever-increasing expectations for what would follow when the "Gentile Times" ended. Undoubtedly they were also very tense, preoccupied by unanswerable questions: Would Armageddon follow immediately after October 1914—or 1915—and would the chosen few be raised to heavenly life, before it was too late?

At this time, however, Russell formulated new plans for the Bible Student's *long-term survival and future expansion*—plans he had so far kept to himself.

Chapter 9

Growing Concerns about 1914

In his 1889 book *The Time is at Hand*, the second volume of the *Millennial Dawn* series, Russell wrote about the date for the end of the world:

"In the preceding chapter we presented evidence showing that the 'Times of the Gentiles,' or their lease of dominion, will run fully out with the year AD 1914, and that by that time they will all be overturned and Christ's Kingdom fully established. That the Lord must be present, and set up his Kingdom, and exercise his great power so as to dash the nations to pieces as a potter's vessel, *before* AD 1914, is then clearly fixed..." (*Millennial Dawn* 2, 1907 (1889), p. 170).[114]

Russell left no doubt: *The governments of the world would all be overthrown in 1914.*

Manipulation

The above quotation remains in the republished and revised edition of Russell's massive work, continuously published under the title *Studies in the Scriptures* (the name of the series after 1904). But in the edition published after Russell's death in 1916 the above passage is manipulated so it better correlates with world events after the start of the First World War in August 1914. Below are the equivalent passages from the *corrected* version of 1917:

"In the preceding chapter we presented evidence showing that the 'Times of the Gentiles,' or their lease of dominion, will run fully out with the year AD 1914, and that at that time they will all be overturned* and Christ's Kingdom fully established. That the Lord must be present, and set up his Kingdom, and exercise his great power so as to dash the nations to pieces as a potter's vessel, is then clearly fixed..." The words, "*before* AD 1914," had been removed! (*Studies* 2, 1917 (1889), p. 170-171)

The correction is quite telling. The asterisk (*) in the middle of the passage refers to a footnote on the same page in the edited version; the publisher states:

"How long it will require to accomplish this overturning we are not informed, but have reason to believe the period will be short" (*Studies* 2, footnote, p. 170).

In the 1880s, with plenty of time until the anticipated date, Russell was confident in his calculations: 1914 would be the "farthest limit for the rule of imperfect man" (*Millennial Dawn* 2, 1889, p. 77).[115] The same sentence has been decisively rephrased in the revised English edition produced *after* 1916 (in the Danish version it was completely removed). In other words, the original language and intended meaning were adjusted so, at least for a short time, Russell remained in a better light. (*Millennial Dawn 2*, 1887/1894, p. 76, 77; *Studies* 2, 1916, p. 77)

However, in the years prior to 1904, Russell was apparently unshaken because of all that he expected to occur *before* 1914, as seen in his 1890 declaration in *Zion's Watch Tower*: "…that the Millennium of peace and blessing would be introduced by forty years of trouble, beginning slightly in 1874 and increasing until social chaos should prevail in 1914" (*ZWT*, October 1890; see also *ZWT*, Feb. 1890[116]).

In 1894 Russell wrote:

"We see no reason for changing the figure—nor could we change them if we would. They are, we believe, God's dates, not ours. But bear in mind that the end of 1914 is not the date for the *beginning*, but for the *end* of the time of trouble" (*ZWT*, July 15, 1894, p. 226; *Gentile*, 2004, p. 51).

Furthermore, he had promised his followers, the Saints, that "some time before the end of the overthrow the last member of the divinely recognized Church of Christ, the 'royal priesthood,' 'the body of Christ,' will be glorified with the Head; because every member is to reign with Christ, being a joint-heir with him of the Kingdom, and it cannot be fully 'set up' without every Member." The surrounding text on the page (81) leaves no doubt that the point of intersection and the time when the secular governments were to be overthrown is 1914. (*Millennial Dawn 2*, 1887/1894, p. 76, 77)

Without doubt, and well before 1914, Russell taught that the forty years of "harvesting" and the "great tribulation" period would culminate and end in 1914, and Christ's universal kingship would be established on earth immediately upon the expiry of this period. The above-cited lines, from Russell's hand, however, may indirectly indicate that both he and others questioned the reliability of his calculations. Still, he stubbornly stuck to his dates: They were not his, but God's!

Russell Begins to Climb Down

Around July 1904, a change in tone becomes evident, as in Russell's article "Universal anarchy—just before or after October 1914 AD," more than implies that the climax of the "great tribulation" could no longer be expected precisely in October 1914:

"We now expect that the anarchistic culmination of the great time of trouble which will precede the Millennial blessings will be *after* October, 1914 AD— very speedily thereafter, in our opinion—'in one hour,' 'suddenly,' because 'our forty years' harvest, ending October, 1914 AD, should not be expected to include the awful period of anarchy which the Scriptures point out to be the fate of Christendom" (*ZWT*, 1904, p. 197, 198; *Gentile*, 2004, p. 51; italics are mine).

There is little doubt how much importance the word "after" gained among Russell's followers, because the view revealed completely new interpretations and possibilities. He would neither disappoint the adherents nor diminish his standing. By using "after" he created uncertainty around the time of the "trans-formation" of the member-crowd to heavenly life, which, until the *Watch Tower* article of 1904, should have happened immediately after October 1914. Deep down in his soul he knew, however, that the time after 1914 would be *his* only real "Judgment Day."

In that same article, he wrote:

"Looking back to the prophetic testimony respecting the Times of the Gen-tiles, we perceive that our Lord's words, 'Jerusalem shall be trodden down of the Gentiles until the *Times of the Gentiles* be filled full,' give the Intimation that the determined *times*, or years, in which the empire of earth would be in the hands of Gentile governments was a fixed one from the Divine standpoint. And if, as we believe the Scriptures to teach, Gentile domination was provided for up to October, 1914, it would seem but a reasonable interpretation that Di-vine power would not be exercised to their dethronement until *after* the time allotted for their reign had ended—October, 1914" (*ZWT*, July 1, 1904, p. 198; see the preface to *Studies* 7, p. 5; the word "after" in the passage is accentuated in the original text, and therefore, in italics here).

The readers noticed it, and they understood that the "servant" had opened the door for a certain flexibility in the schedule; at this early stage in the prepa-rations for the coming Day of Judgment, Russell already attempted to ensure his growing undertaking and movement could continue beyond 1914, even if the earthly governments had not been overthrown and replaced by God's king-dom. We now know that he later suggested a delay of many years; the new predictions really were "elastic."

Placing the anticipated anarchistic culmination of the great tribulation *after* 1914, i.e., *after* the definite closure of the time of the gentiles, was something new. Up to this point, Russell—strongly inspired by his previous mentor and partner, Barbour—believed the period of 1874–1914 would be signified by increasing unrest and troubles, a great tribulation, culminating in worldwide anarchy and chaos. (*Three Worlds*, 1877, under the headline: "Bible Chronology")

It appears here, ten years before the deadline, that Russell acquired scruples and obviously wanted to protect himself. How long did he think the period of anarchy would last? That there was a change in the way he expressed himself is evident, and his readers quickly *reacted* to this change, of course.

Some people suggested, possibly out of sheer enthusiasm, that perhaps the chronology's foundation should be re-evaluated and that, instead of 607 BC, the time of the gentiles might have begun twenty years later, in 587 BC. After all, this was the scholarly accepted year for the first destruction of Jerusalem. With this adjustment, the time of the gentiles wouldn't expire until 1933, adding a cushion of numerous years before something happened—something which would provide some respite from the tribulation. By then, Russell would be an old man of eighty-one.

Russell remained steadfast on the expiration date of the time of the gentiles: "We know of no reason for changing a figure; to do so would spoil the harmonies and parallels so conspicuous between the Jewish and Gospel ages." Russell, however, had planted doubt; he and the Bible Students could call upon it if circumstances required—a trick, which eventually became a tiresome habit within the movement. Although Russell maintained the year 1914 was the end of the time of the gentiles—which he could completely and freely afford if the great tribulation time would be extended beyond that date—it's likely he was already mentally prepared that this extension could be explained by the classical argument of the *longsuffering* of God spoken of in 2 Peter 3:9, in the New Testament. (*Gentile*, 2004, p. 52; *ZWT*, Oct. 1, 1904)

On the other hand, today we can only speculate what was in Russell's mind at that time, but he had obligated himself to the view that the time of trouble would expire no later than October 1914, an absolute deadline which would be the "farthest limit for the rule of imperfect man." Russell thought the Millennium began around 1874, but before peace could come to earth, the world would have to experience the great tribulation. Extending the tribulation period beyond 1914 would disturb his alleged harmonious chronology, a chronology that would, consequently, collapse. In *Studies in the Scriptures*, Third Volume, Russell writes:

"Thus all the rays of prophecy converge upon this 'Time of the End,' the focal point of which is the 'Harvest'—the time of our Lord's presence and the establishment of his long promised Kingdom" (*Studies* 3, 1917 (1891), p. 130).

Approaching War

The anticipation of a future Great War on the European continent was common in the years 1870–1914. *The War* was reportedly the day's topic of conversations in the east and west for many years, and Russell kept well abreast of developments. He indulged himself in further guesswork and also commented on the possibility of a major war starting in Europe. Thus, in the *Zion's Watch Tower* of February 1885, he stated:

"Storm clouds are gathering thick over the old world. It looks as though a great European war is one of the possibilities of the near future" (Jonsson: *Guds tider och stunder,* 1985, p. 9; *ZWT,* Feb. 1885, p. 1).

In1887, he wrote:

"This all looks as though *next Summar* [sic] *would see a war on foot* which might engage every nation of Europe..." However, in the same article, he maintains 1914 as the deadline: "But let no one imagine that such a war will bring final results. It will be but one act in the drama—one skirmish in the 'Battle of the great day of God Almighty,' which covers the coming twenty-seven years" (*ZWT,* Feb. 1887, p. 2).

In 1892, Russell seems to have adopted a more cautious attitude, but he still believed that the greatly anticipated catastrophe could occur in 1905:

"[The] daily papers and the weeklies and monthlies, religious and secular, are continually discussing the prospects of war in Europe. They note the grievances and ambitions of the various nations and predict that war is inevitable at no distant day.... Even should a war or revolution break out in Europe sooner than 1905, we could not consider it any portion of the severe trouble predicted ... the ever-darkening war cloud will burst in all its destructive fury. *This culmination we do not expect, however, before about 1905, as the events predicted will require about that time, notwithstanding the rapid progress in these directions now possible*" (Jonsson: *Guds tider och stunder,* 1985, p. 9; *ZWT,* Jan. 15, 1892, p. 19-25; italics are mine).

Russell seems more cautious, yet open to the possibility of a rapid deterioration of the world situation. He was skilled in the art of double-talk, covering all exits and potential developments.

In the 1892 article, Russell also stated that, according to Scriptures, October 1914 would mark the end of the great battle: "The date of the close of that 'battle' is definitely marked in Scripture as October, 1914. It is already in progress, its beginning dating from October, 1874" (*Conscience,* 1983, p. 159).

As the years passed, Russell focused more and more on 1914—the *farthest limit* of the existence of the Gentile kingdoms. However, if all would be as Russell predicted, his time was short. The "great tribulation" and the "battle" were already underway in 1892, so there were only approximately twenty-two years to the climax.

In 1893, he wrote:

"A great storm is near at hand. Though one may not know exactly when it will break forth, it seems reasonable to suppose that it cannot be more than twelve or fourteen years yet future." This would take them to 1905–1907 and would be perfectly fine, since it was merely a guesstimate! (*ZWT,* 1893, p. 194; *Divine Purpose,* 1959, p. 52)

Russell did stick to October 1914, which gave him a little more time to prepare for the inevitable failure, as he undoubtedly increasingly feared.

During the great tribulation climax in 1914, all institutions would be subject to destruction, developed in the form of a worldwide revolution, since the "retribution" would come through the masses who, under revolutionary conditions, would overthrow all the secret societies: Freemasons, Odd Fellows, trade unions, guilds, trusts, "all societies secular and ecclesiastical," the unions and leagues, and stop the financial institutions and "the idolatry of money." He states emphatically: "The retribution, as we have seen, will come from the *Lord, through the uprising of the masses of the people*" (*Millennial Dawn* 2, 1889; quoted from *Studies* 2, 1917 (1889), pp. 139, 140; italics are mine).

Apparently, the masses would become God's tool during this great rebellion, but the overthrowing of all the governments, authorities, institutions and churches is not all that bad, since the majority of mankind seems to survive. And I must conclude, it is these "masses of the people" who apparently enjoy the benefits of the millennial blessings; this is because Russell had not yet developed any doctrine regarding the identity of the "great crowd" or the "great multitude," spoken of in Revelation (7:9). Russell's successor, J. F. Rutherford, would resolve and clarify this in his doctrine updates—more on this to come.

Russell wrote:

"But not until the great day of trouble is about closing—not until the Gentile kingdoms are ground to powder and utterly removed, no place being found for them (AD 1914, as shown in the preceding chapter)—not until great Babylon is utterly overthrown and her influence over the world broken—will the great mass of mankind come to realize the true state of the case. Then they will see that the great trouble *through which they will have passed* was that symbolically termed 'the battle of that great day of God Almighty' (Rev. 16:14)…" (*Millennial Dawn* 2, 1889; this exact passage also occurs in *Studies* 2, 1917, p. 140, 141; italics are mine).

Also Babylon—Catholic and Protestant churches—would be destroyed in October 1914. In the third book of Russell's series *Thy Kingdom Come*, first published in 1891, he wrote: "And, with the end of AD 1914, what God calls Babylon, and what men call Christendom, will have passed away, as already shown from prophecy" (*Conscience*, 1983, p. 158).

Altogether improbable expectations, except maybe those regarding 1905 when the first Russian Revolution began, but Russell undoubtedly felt something large was in store and the world stage could be witnessing a spectacle of unprecedented dimensions; and in a way, he was close to the truth when one considers the First World War initiated the terrible Bolshevik Revolution and the fall of the orthodox church in Russia. Did he have a sixth sense, or had he just kept abreast of news filled with rumors of war? Either way, the armies were thus aligned for the big blow.

Chapter 10

Moment of Truth

Russell's followers were now fully focused on the fateful year 1914—the year when the so-called *gentile times* would expire.

It was the moment of truth.

The tensions were extraordinary—despite Russell's last-minute vacillation—now that the "transformation" of the holy ones, the *remnant* of the 144,000 (those that were still alive) approached its final act.

The concept of the "remnant of the 144,000" may sound somewhat complex, but it isn't really when one looks at the details. The 144,000 were, according to the Bible Students, the few Christians "selected" during all the centuries from Jesus lifetime through our time with hopes of getting into heaven where they would reign with Christ for a thousand years. This select group is also referred to as "the little flock," or "the anointed." Around 1914, only the *remainder of the 144,000* was considered to still be on earth, and this remnant was, of course, Russell and his group of door-to-door preachers, the International Bible Students. Many of them expected—just as the Adventists had done before them—to literally ascend into heaven some day *after* October of 1914.[117]

Russell's successor, the "Judge" J. F. Rutherford, would later identify yet another group of people who would not ascend to heaven for Christ's kingship, but instead would be allowed to live eternally on earth after Armageddon: the so-called "great flock of other sheep" or the "great multitude," whose numbers would greatly surpass that of the "little flock." However, as late as 1927, members still believed those in the great multitude also had to go to heaven: "All the facts and the scriptures bearing upon the matter under consideration show that those who form the great multitude constitute a spirit class." They would, however, as "bridesmaids," occupy a lower position than the members of the 144,000; a change, one must say, that developed over time. (*WT*, January 15, 1927, p.19-20).[118]

But let us return to *the moment of truth*. In 1907 Russell wrote in *Zion's Watch Tower*:

"But let us suppose a case far from our expectations: suppose that AD 1915 should pass with the world's affairs all serene and with evidence that the 'very elect' had not all been 'changed' and without the restoration of natural Israel to favor under the New Covenant. (Rom. 11:12, 15) What then? Would not that prove chronology wrong? Yes, surely! And would not that prove a keen disappointment? Indeed it would! … What a blow that would be! One of the strings of our 'harp' would be quite broken! However, dear friends, our harp would still have all the other strings in tune and that is what no other aggregation of God's people on earth could boast" (*Gentile*, 2004, p. 52; *ZWT*, Oct. 1907, p. 294, 295).

But shortly before 1914, Russell desperately tried to fortify the safety valves again. In the October 1913 issue of *The Watch Tower* he wrote very cautiously:

"We are waiting for the time to come when the government of the world will be turned over to Messiah. We cannot say that it may not be either October, 1914, or October, 1915. It is possible that we might be out of the correct reckoning on the subject a number of years. We cannot say with certainty. We do not know. It is a matter of faith, and not of knowledge. 'We walk by faith, not by sight.'" (p. 308; reprint 5328)

Later in the same issue, he writes:

"So when October, 1914, comes or October, 1915, or some other date (the Lord knoweth) and the Gentile Times terminate, it does not follow that there will be an outburst that will revolutionize the world, all in a day. But we believe that it will do so not very long thereafter" (*WT*, Oct. 1913, p. 309; reprint 5329).

Concerning the church's ascent to heaven, he writes:

"As we understand this matter, the Church will be glorified before that time. When the lease expires, it would seem that the new tenants will be ready to take possession. And we cannot see how the new tenants could be ready to take possession unless they were glorified beforehand [dead!]. If they were still in the flesh, they would not be ready to take possession. So if the Church is here in 1915, we shall think that we have made some mistake. We do not understand how they will all die between now and the close of 1914—how so many people, all over the world—people of one mind—will all pass beyond the veil in so short a time. But we can see how the Lord might purposely leave us in a measure of ignorance in this matter. We do not know positively that the month of October, 1914, will see the Church all glorified, and the time of trouble ushered in. We merely say, Here are the *evidences*. Here are the proofs. Look at them for yourself and see what you then think. It is for each to accept or reject the facts" (*WT*, Oct. 1913, p. 308, 309; reprint 5329; consult this book's list of publications or view endnote).[119]

In October 1913, as Russell notes, the world's governments had little time left:

"The Federation may continue to prosper for a year yet, and accomplish everything that they are to accomplish before October, 1914; and the fall of Babylon will follow shortly after that date. That is one of the things due to come to pass at that time" (*WT*, Oct. 1913, p. 308; reprint 5329).

What his followers felt, one can only guess, and although free speech to some degree was actually allowed in the congregations of the Bible Students, probably very few dared speak their minds on this issue. As one, they identified themselves with and shared Russell's speculative ideas—until the creeping doubts came.

In January 1914, Russell reflected on his situation, and then suddenly allowed for the greatest margin of error conceivable, which may be said to represent something of a leap in time:

"If 1915 should go by without the passage of the church, without the time of trouble, etc., it would seem to some to be a great calamity. It would not be so with ourself [*sic*]. We shall be as glad as any one if we shall all experience our change from earthly to spirit conditions before 1915, and this is our expectation; but if this should not be the Lord's will, then it would not be our will. If in the Lord's providence the time should come *twenty-five years later*, then that would be our will" (italics are mine).

A little further along in the article Russell writes, however: "Have we been expecting the wrong thing at the right time? The Lord's will might permit this" (*WT*, January 1, 1914, p. 5; reprints 5275).

Of course, Russell could not know that twenty-five years later World War II would begin. At this point, his followers, still brimming with expectations for 1914, were prepared for the worst. Anything could happen.

A *Watch Tower* reader went even further, although perhaps the remarks should be viewed with the writer's fidelity in mind:

"Our dear brother and pastor ... We got the thought from reading the Nov. 15th WATCH TOWER, the article on 'What Course Should We Take?' that you had almost decided that the things we have been expecting in 1914 would not come to pass on time—since you said it is possible, but not probable. Now, dear Brother, if these things do not come to pass until 2014, instead of 1914, our faith in you will be as great as it ever has been.... May the dear Lord's richest blessings be upon you. In behalf of the Class, your brother in the Lord. N.B. Rankin:—Okla" (*WT*, January 1914, p. 31; reprints 5391).

It is quite clear that the nearer Russell came to the "deadline," the more intense the heat beneath his feet, and in some obscure corner of his soul, he seems to realize the consequences for his Society and the other enterprises—yes, his very existence—when his prophecies turned out to be nothing more than the hot-headed fantasies of a charlatan, and that beneath these fantasies lay even more complex motives.

Actually, I find it hard to imagine that at this time Russell still believed in his cause deep down; I believe he was realistic and found reason for serious concern. From his early days as an ambitious young man, a Titan, willing to storm the gates of heaven, he had grown into a much more cautious and thoughtful person. He was likely burdened by increasing doubts, and one can only blame him for not being forthright with his subscribers and supporters. From this point of view, he certainly deserves to be labeled a *charlatan*.

It's sensible to conclude that the members may have suffered their own growing doubts about the issue and that this reflected the "Pastor's" fickleness, as it now indirectly crept into his magazine. But of course, no one could be absolutely sure until 1914–1915 had passed. Not even Russell, who appeared to have a "relapse" at the outbreak of the First World War. Could he have gotten it right after all? Still, how he could have a relapse of this sort at this time, if his doubts had been sincere, is hard to grasp. Maybe it was about playing for the audience, and his being trapped in the spotlight. He still enjoyed the adherent's admiration, and they eventually placed him so high on the pedestal he could hardly descend. Thus, his followers were his reflection, the image and defense for his self-confidence. If they stumbled, he stumbled, and vice-versa. He so identified with his followers, they were—psychologically speaking—an extension of him, of his "self." It was on this connection his mental balance probably depended.

No matter what, he continued the game to its inexorable conclusion.

Long Term Investment

Evidence of Russell's wavering belief in his own calculations and predictions is amply exhibited by the eleventh-hour retractions in his publications, which even less-naive Bible Students could see right through if they desired to look. Furthermore, in 1912 Russell and his nearest co-workers set in motion a vast lantern-slide project, clearly not only intended for use *before* 1914 but also for the years *after*. The show was completed in 1914, and in just one year, eight million people in the US, Canada, United Kingdom and continental Europe viewed the presentation. Australia and New Zealand reported full houses (*Proclaimers*, p. 561, 562). The project was expensive, requiring vast financial investments and organizational efforts, supporting the idea that Russell and the other top figures of the Society had foreseen the need for a long-term survival strategy and fixed their gaze far beyond the "prophetic year" 1914. The statement (from *The Watch Tower* of January 1914) that if it was in the "Lord's providence the time should come *twenty-five years later*, then that would be our will," can be seen as nothing less than an indication of Russell's long-term plans for the movement—plans that can only be called bad faith, and were known only to Russell's closest associates.

Paradoxically, in 1959 leaders of the Watch Tower Society of New York wrote in defense of Russell's long term plans:

"To demonstrate that the witnesses did not believe the prophetic year of 1914 would end all their operations with respect to this earth, from 1912 to the beginning of 1914 the Watch Tower Society spent over $300,000 in preparing 'The Photo-Drama of Creation' to spread Bible knowledge to the masses of people from 1914 on" (*Qualified*, 1955, p. 310; italics are mine; excerpts of "The Photo-Drama of Creation" can be found on the internet).

Not even Russell would have had the audacity to make such a claim in public, but judging by the 1959 arguments, today's leaders of the Society may hold information and documents (if they can find them) proving that the movement's founder and president indeed had long-term plans for the future. On the other hand, the Society's statement may be nothing more than a *post-rationalization*, yet without further information, we must take them at their word! Nonetheless, in the end these long-term plans were an expression of incredible cynicism, for what do they say about Russell's concern for the faithful and dear supporters who anticipated important and decisive events around October 1914—or 1915?

If Russell truly believed 1914 was the final deadline, why didn't he invest *more* than $300,000? Particularly considering the terrible events he expected to unfold at the end of the forty years of great tribulation and the subsequent consequences for the world's population. According to J. J. Ross' allegations, Russell had even more money he could have used to spread his last-minute message. And if Christ came, what need did Russell have for money?

But perhaps I am a bit unfair here.

The sum of $300,000 was considerable at that time, yet this sizeable investment supports the assumption that Russell harbored great expansion plans for the years to come. Plus, *"The Photo-Drama of Creation"* was *not the last* investment for the future,[120] and yet the ordinary believers probably knew nothing about this, and so continued to preach the world's imminent end.

The quotation from 1955's *Qualified to Be Ministers*, as cited above, may make this situation more understandable: *"all their operations with respect to this earth"* is a somewhat cryptic way of convoluting the fact that the majority of the "Russellites" expected to be taken up to heaven sometime around October 1, 1914. Russell had promised *in writing* that the last "member" of Christ's Kingdom would be glorified around the end of 1914, and that the Kingdom could not possibly be made a reality "without every member" (*Studies* 2, 1917 (1889), p. 77). Such imprecise language shows Russell's careful hedging in all areas.

Also in the quote from 1955 one finds *"...the witnesses did not believe the prophetic year of 1914 would end all their operations..."* which appears to say that around 1914 the movement's members in no way expected their world would end in October 1914. But, if this truly is the case, why did A. H. Macmillan, Russell's close friend and co-worker, expect the end of the world during that first week of October 1914? In his biography, *Faith on the March*, Macmillan writes:

"That was a highly interesting time because a few of us seriously thought we were going to heaven during the first week of that October. At the Saratoga Springs convention quite a number were in attendance. Wednesday (September 30) I was invited to talk on the subject, 'The End of All Things Is at Hand; Therefore Let Us Be Sober, Watchful and Pray.' Well, as one would say, that was down my road. I believed it myself sincerely—that the church was 'going home' in October. During that discourse I made this unfortunate remark: 'This is probably the last public address I shall ever deliver because we shall be going home soon'" (Macmillan, 1957, p. 47).[121]

From this, it is evident Macmillan knew nothing of the plans to extend activities beyond 1914. On page forty-four of his biography, we find:

"C. T. Russell had no idea of building a strongly knit organization. At that time we saw no need for it. We expected 1914 would mark the end of this system of things on earth."

So, this raises the question: Why did the leaders of 1959 claim the investment in "The Photo-Drama of Creation" proved the members of the organization in 1914 *didn't* expect the world to end that year?

In the 1955 quote, Watch Tower Society leaders appear to admit the true intent of their *long-term strategy*, as it seems they intended, although this admission may be a sort of parapraxis. However, it seems evident that the Society's leadership of 1914 had either led or been involved in the plans for new initiatives and consolidation of efforts to ensure international growth in the years ahead while they waited to take the helm after Russell's demise. Still, it's nearly inconceivable that Russell wasn't aware of such plans, or that he hadn't approved them. Producing "The Photodrama of Creation" indicates just the opposite, as it was a grand-scale project, requiring vast finances—finances which Russell undoubtedly controlled.

The last passage from 1955 quoted above is revealing in other respects: The Watch Tower leadership was, of course, aware of the conflict between the official view that the "remaining" time was short (before Armageddon) and the long-term initiative to reach as many people as possible with their "gospel" to ensure organizational growth.

I believe that the closest we will ever get to the truth in these matters comes from the fact that the majority of Russell's followers, Macmillan among them, never understood the range of their leader's plans or the extent of pre-established excuses. For years they accepted Russell's cocksure claims and alleged unerring judgment, and identified themselves with his motives and beliefs to such a degree it became impossible for them to accept anything other than the *preferred* explanation, which always happened to be the very explanation they were eventually given. The tension increased throughout these years, reaching its climax in October 1914, but no matter how things had been twisted, rearranged or distorted, all remained convinced: *Something* had to happen.

It may also be true that many members sung the song of the movement but deep inside remained skeptical—we see the same in many religions today. In later chapters I will discuss this in more depth as I try to unravel the tangled threads woven by J. F. Rutherford's aggressive takeover of the Bible Students.

"We are now in a testing season..."

Of course, the Society had to make the most of the situation, and in its usual dramatic style, the near future was now proclaimed to be a "testing period." In *The Watch Tower* of November 1914, Russell writes:

"Let us remember that we are in a testing season.... If there is any reason that would lead any to let go of the Lord and His Truth and to cease sacrificing for the Lord's Cause, then it is not merely the love of God in the heart which has prompted interest in the Lord, but something else; probably a hoping that the time was short; the consecration was only for a certain time. *If so, now is a good time to let go*" (*Proclaimers*, 1993, p. 61; italics are mine).

It is quite telling how easily and arbitrarily the argument was inverted—and aimed directly at the followers. From this point onwards, faith in what was supposed to occur in 1914 no longer counted, rather the contrary, the belief that it would probably "still take a few years" became the focus. And if members were unwilling to be flexible about this, they could just get out. The majority probably went along with the new direction, giving it little thought, but for the really serious Russellites, those who viewed Charles Russell as the "faithful and wise servant" spoken of in Matthew 24, it must have been a bitter pill to swallow. Could it be that he had all the while been a *false* prophet?

Macmillan, who seemingly had blind faith in Russell, and who, in the course of his long life, willingly adapted to all the changes within the movement, was tasked with addressing the residents at Bethel in New York, a mere two days after delivering the speech he believed would be his last. His remarks on the matter:

"I found Psalm 74:9, 'We see not our signs: there is no more any prophet: neither is there among us any that knoweth how long.' Now that was different. In that talk I tried to show the friends that perhaps some of us had been a bit too hasty in thinking that we were going to heaven right away, and the thing for us to do would be to keep busy in the Lord's service until he determined when any of his approved servants would be taken home to heaven" (*Proclaimers*, 1993, p. 62).

Macmillan was of the "right brand," and he obediently adapted to the new course, even eighteen months after those October days of 1914, when Russell wrote in *The Watch Tower*:

"But, Brother Russell [it's Russell writing here], what is your thought as to the time of our change? Were you not disappointed that it did not come when we hoped that it would?' you will ask. No, we reply, we were not disappointed.... Brethren, those of us who are in the right attitude toward God are not disappointed at any of His arrangements. We did not wish our own will to be done; so when we found out that we were expecting the wrong thing in October, 1914, then we were glad that the Lord did not change His Plan to suit us" (*Proclaimers*, 1993, p. 62).

This line of arguing not only reflects that the "brothers," like Macmillan, had expected the "transformation" from flesh and blood to angelic spirit-creatures around October 1, 1914, but also that they were prepared to accept an adjustment of the timetable. Macmillan was fully aware of the new situation, and therefore concluded later: "Sometimes our expectations were for a specific date greater than the Bible provided a legal basis for" (*Proclaimers*, 1993, p. 637).

However, one day in the fall of 1916, Russell invited Macmillan to his office at Bethel (Brooklyn) to share some exciting new developments: "The work is increasing rapidly, and it will continue to increase, for there is a world-wide work to be done in preaching the 'gospel of the kingdom' in all the world." In less than four hours Russell informed Macmillan on what he saw to be the great work yet in front of them. (*Proclaimers*, 1993, p. 63)

The Photodrama of Creation, supposedly quite an accomplishment at the time, also served to distract Macmillan during these years, and it certainly helped him occupy the time he had left: "We were not particularly disturbed that not everything took place as we had expected, because we were so busy with the Photo-Drama work and with the problems created by the war" (Ibid., p. 63).

At this time, Russell supposedly knew that a continuance of the work was the *only* solution to this crisis, a crisis that certainly threatened to divide and dissolve the entire movement.

Around 1914, there were some 20,000 followers and 1200 congregations.

In 1915, attendance figures for the yearly Memorial, which is the only holiday the Witnesses celebrate, had slipped to 15,000, indicating a significant drop. Some 4,000–5,000 members appear to have left the movement between October 1914 and Easter 1915, despite Russell being in the midst of the events, attempting to calm the situation.

One can only say October 1914 was really a sharp corner for the movement.

In 1955, the Watchtower Society described the situation as follows:

"Individually, however, some who had shared in giving that warning were disappointed in that they incorrectly thought of themselves as due to go to heaven in 1914 to become part of the invisible Kingdom organization, little realizing that it was not until 1918 that it would become possible for any of the dead Kingdom heirs to be joined with Jehovah's enthroned Christ in heaven, at which latter time the 'first resurrection' was due to begin. Many also inaccurately thought that the world war which began in 1914 would merge into the 'battle of the great day of God Almighty,' Armageddon, and thus cleanse the earth of all opposition to righteousness. However, Jehovah's leading indicated that there was yet much work to be done by the anointed Christians on the earth" (*WT*, March 15, 1955).

Watch Tower politics is not for the faint of heart. If this statement reflects the general attitude of the leaders toward their frustrated followers at the time, I certainly don't blame those followers for packing their bags and jumping ship. It was a good time to let go.

Stagnation

Increasing opposition—both internally and externally—now resulted in a reduction of activities. In 1914, the preaching work culminated in record sales, just as expected, but from 1915–1917, the movement stagnated and even declined. (*Divine Purpose*, 1959, p. 58)

While 1914 saw 71,385,037 brochures and 992,845 books sold, the correlating numbers for 1916 were a mere 30,547,172 brochures and 452,713 books—less than half for each.

Around October 1, 1916, in the preface to the second volume of *Studies in the Scriptures*, Russell's primary work—previously titled *Millennial Dawn*—he tried to calm the Bible Students. Using the outbreak of the First World War as an excuse, Russell emphasized the difficulty of making predictions about the future.

"Promptly in August," he wrote, in the passage cited below, even though no one had previously heard or read about August being a noteworthy month—but what was a couple of months, give or take:

"We could not, of course, know in 1889, whether the date 1914, so clearly marked in the Bible as the end of the Gentile lease of power or permission to rule the world, would mean that they would be fully out of power at that time, or whether, their lease expiring, their eviction would begin. The latter we perceive to be the Lord's programme [*sic*]; and *promptly in August*, 1914, the Gentile kingdoms referred to in the prophecy began the present great struggle, which, according to the Bible, will culminate in the complete overthrow of all human government, opening the way for the full establishment of the Kingdom of God's dear Son.... The author acknowledges that in this book he presents the thought that the Lord's saints might expect to be with Him in glory at the ending of the Gentile Times. This was a natural mistake to fall into, but the Lord overruled it for the blessing of His people. The thought that the Church would all be gathered to glory before October, 1914, certainly did have a very *stimulating* and sanctifying effect upon thousands, all of whom accordingly can praise the Lord—*even for the mistake*. Many, indeed, can express themselves as being thankful to the Lord that the culmination of the Church's hopes was not reached at the time we expected; and that we, as the Lord's people, have further opportunities of perfecting holiness and of being participators with our Master in the further presentation of His, Message to His people" (Foreword to *Studies* 2, 1917 (1889); italics are mine).

It is hard to say whether Russell still believed in his own prophecies or, as already demonstrated, he was making plans for the future growth and continuance of his organization (as the final sentences in the above quote seem to indicate), far beyond the point suggested by the words "not long after." There is much evidence to indicate he had been outlining his plans for the future for a long time, even prior to 1914, and this—seen in relation to what he presented to his dispirited followers—makes him, at least to me, a somewhat disputable prophet, a man that cynically went further than any honest-minded individual should allow himself to go.

In whatever way we view Russell as a leader and prophet, we must remember: In the area of apocalyptic-cultish groups, anything goes, as long as it can be justified with Bible passages plucked out of context.

A Self-Centered, Power-Hungry Individual

It puzzles me that for so many years Russell lived with manipulating the almost endless faith and trust of his followers. He must have had a "super ego;" an ego unable to function properly without seeing his image reflected in the eyes of his followers—his *self-objects*. If he changed his views, his followers would be obligated to do the same. Russell and the membership were interdependent: Almost a "fascist master-slave-complex," as we know from many historical contexts, both before and after 1914.[122]

Russell was a man obsessed with an idea that robbed him of his senses and his self-control, and required all his energy and *libido*. From 1876 until around 1904, he immodestly brushed aside all potential doubt in his own abilities, and could not stand the slightest criticism. His judicial realism reveals a man with a hunger for power, a self-centered man who would not leave financial concerns to anyone else, not even the Lord. Developmentally, his grandiosity ended probably in its complementary opposite, and his doubts reduced his divine dimension to earthly proportions.

Russell the absolutist—the idealist—underwent a metamorphosis: He had to conclude he had been wrong about everything, a sudden insight he obviously kept to himself. Betrayal by some of his followers further eroded his self-confidence, and this, combined with other difficulties during these years, may have caused a severe depression. Eventually this possible depression, together with his already declining physical health, made short work of him. The *self-objects*—and here I refer to the supporters whose admiration was the precondition for his self-confidence—were left with only weak encouragement that there were ten, twenty-five or perhaps "a hundred years" left—only the Lord knew.

As Russell presumably realized (deep down in his soul) he had been mistaken about everything, he finally bowed his head before God—a little late. But of "that day and hour knoweth no *man*, no, not the angels of heaven, but my Father only."

And to Him, Russell then surrendered.

He Died a Hero

Still, Russell worked and preached with the same intensity as before, and on one of his lecture tours, as he returned from California, he unexpectedly took ill and died near Pampa, Texas. The date: October 31, 1916, a little more than two years after the disastrous turn in his career. The stagnation of the work, the decline in membership, and generally tumultuous recent events no doubt contributed to his death.

The lecture tour which proved to be too much for Russell included, according to *The Tower*, the following cities: Lansing, Michigan; Springfield, Illinois; Wichita, Kansas; Dallas, Galveston, Houston and San Antonio, Texas; San Diego, California; Topeka, Kansas; Tulsa, Oklahoma; and Lincoln, Nebraska. "He was suffering so much at San Antonio that it was necessary for him to leave the platform on three different occasions for a period of from five to ten minutes." He and his travelling-companions continued to California, but they remained in their hotel at Los Angeles, and here he addressed his "last message to the Church."

Russell died as the leader of an organization with an apparently bleak future. The question for them: How to find a successor, someone who could live up to Russell's standards, and help the movement through its crisis? Pastor Russell's work for the movement was "incredible." According to the Bible Students and their successors, the Jehovah's Witnesses, he had travelled more than a million miles, held 30,000 sermons, written 50,000 pages on Biblical interpretation and as many as 1,000 letters a month (by comparison, Alfred Nobel wrote between 20 and 40 letters a day)—in addition to all the organizational work, which Russell personally led. It all seemed to have depended on Russell. He was "the Society," which he had presided over for thirty-two years. (Conley was the first president; *Macmillan*, 1958, p. 72; *Studies* 7, 1917, p. 57, 58; *Divine Purpose,* 1964, p. 62)

It is hard to tell if his followers exaggerated, but there can be no doubt that Russell was an incredibly active and popular leader. Brother Menta Sturgeon, Russell's private secretary who accompanied him on the journey to Texas, sent this telegram to Brooklyn: "He died a hero."

The day before his death, Russell had asked Brother Sturgeon to make a Roman toga for him. After his last appearance, Russell went to the train, where a drawing room was provided for him and Sturgeon to use on the journey east. The following morning, Russell donned the toga, reclined on the couch in the drawing room and closed his eyes. Sturgeon immediately understood that death was near. In the November 13 *Death Letter*, sent to the "dearly beloved co-laborers in the harvest field," a note about the toga was added: "It is interesting to note that the Toga was worn by those who had kept their vows and finished their work in triumph" (*Russell's Death Letter*, November 13, 1916, found on www.watchtowerdocuments.com).

Why Russell would wear a toga on his deathbed one can only conjecture, but I think it was once again his immense grandiosity that prompted him to choose this glorious performance, the hero's death, which reminds me of an archetypical drama from a bygone time. He was hopelessly trapped in his own spin, his own drama. The gentile times were over, the First World War raged, the Kingdom of Heaven was created and all waited only on the millennial blessings to be manifested on the earthly plane. And Russell was, in his exaggerated self-view, entitled to wear a Roman Senator's official dress, a self-invented mark of honor. A rambling drama was nearing its end and lacked only the final curtain.

Sturgeon later described Russell's last hours:

"I called in the Pullman conductor and also the porter and the conductor and said, 'We want you to see how a great man of God can die.' The sight deeply impressed them, especially the porter. I called in the regular conductor, and telegraphed for a physician to board the train at Panhandle [Texas]; and he did. He saw the condition, recognized the correctness of the diagnosis and conclusion, gave me his name, and was off before the train got under headway. / At one o'clock all were dismissed from the room, the door was locked, and we quietly watched over him until he breathed his last … we pressed our lips upon his noble brow, and knew that he had gone to be forever with and like the Lord, whom he loved so well" (*WT*, Dec., 1916; Stroup, 1945, p. 11; WT, 1916, reprints 6006, p. 366-367).

He may have died as a hero, but Mrs. Russell got the last word:

"His life was one continuous round of expensive touring, at tremendous cost to many of his deceived followers. The 'Watch Tower' of the 15th of March, 1911, page 92, to which my attention has been called, tells of a transcontinental tour of himself and company for 7,000 miles, beginning the 9th of June, the special train consisting of compartment, standard Pullman, and tourists' cars, the entire outfit stopping at the principle [*sic*] cities from New York to California, and holding meetings for about a month.… As I look at this pageantry, and consider what it all means, I am so thankful to my Lord who delivered me from the snare, even though it was accomplished through fiery trial.… At a convention he held about a year ago, near Lake Chautauqua, he and his special favourites [*sic*] were settled in palatial quarters apart from the main company. There he held daily receptions, to which five hundred each day were admitted by ticket, all being treated to refreshments, free boat ride, and carfare from the convention grounds to his quarters" (Stroup, 1945, p. 11, 12).[123]

This really harsh and bitter remark from Russell's bereaved wife certainly indicates that she knew what she was talking about. And although she placed that bouquet on Russell's coffin, she apparently never forgave him.

Charles Taze Russell's funeral was held at Rosemont United Cemetery in Allegheny, Pittsburgh. The rising star within the movement, the "Judge" J. F. Rutherford, who we will shortly meet, held a lengthy speech that seemingly exceeded what Russell had wanted as stated in his will: a funeral *without* pomp and circumstance. Regardless of the funeral's grandeur, the headstone they erected shows they were burying an individual of great importance:

Charles T. Russell, "the messenger to the Laodicean Church," who—with a reference to the Revelation of John, 3:14—lived in "the Laodicean period," from "the fall of 1874 to the demise of the last spirit-begotten one," that is, the "rapture," in which the last living members of the congregation would ascend to heaven. (*Studies* 7, 1917, p. 4; 58; 64; see also photograph of Russell's headstone in *Proclaimers*, 1993, p. 64)

A few years later, Russell's successors placed a pyramid near his gravesite to remind visitors that the secrets of the "divine plan of the ages" had been incorporated into the interior of the Cheops pyramid—although Russell had not originated this idea. (*Divine Purpose,* 1959, p. 62)

Engraved on one side of the pyramid is the symbol that had been displayed on the front cover of the *Zion's Watch Tower* from the year 1892 and onwards: A cross piercing a crown. By maintaining this logo and the mysterious pyramid-theory, the Society may have tried to create a sort of *continuity* in an attempt to draw Russell's devoted followers closer to the new leadership. Neither the symbol (which probably served the purpose of attracting other Adventists) nor the pyramid has since appeared in the publications, as the next president of the Society later stated that the pyramids had been built by rulers under the devil's influence. In the voluminous history book of the Watchtower Society of 1993, there is no mention of the miniature pyramid, just a photo of the headstone (p. 64).

The death of Charles Taze Russell was a great loss to the movement, as the followers desperately clung to his ideas; many of them, according to Macmillan, were now almost in a state of shock:

"We did not know what to do. It was so unexpected, and yet Russell had tried to prepare us for it. What would we do? The first shock of our loss of C. T. Russell was the worst. For those first few days our future was a blank wall. Throughout his life Russell had been 'the Society' "—Macmillan wrote in retrospect. (*Proclaimers*, 1993, p. 63-64)

However, this feeling would soon change.

World War Saves the Day

What happened in the Bible Students' collective conscience around the same time the First World War began has since held Russell's successors in a *deadlock*.

After all, some of Russell's predictions, really *did* happen, although the events did not occur as predicted, nor were they subsequently followed by the global (or universal) upheavals the Bible Students had expected. Paradoxically, the war would save the day as the event that brought stability and an opportunity to steam on with the important "work."

Even the most skeptical members must have been struck by the timing of the war beginning in mid-1914, and perhaps Russell and his closest associates were also taken by surprise.

It's perfectly understandable this was a surprising moment—the *one* and only event that would ever get close to seemingly fulfilling Russell's numerous predictions about the imminent Judgment Day. This event consolidated belief in his theory about the end of the so-called time of the Gentiles in 1914.

Russell never acknowledged—at least not officially—that his calculations had been founded on unscholarly, unscientific and speculative ideas, or that he had carelessly adopted these ideas from his predecessors, mainly the Adventists. Russell adhered to this despite suggestion by some of his readers that the chronological point of origin (the first destruction of Jerusalem) be changed to fit what was historically and archaeologically acceptable, as I noted earlier. No matter what happened, no matter how many years passed with no events worth mentioning, Russell could still stubbornly claim that the time of the gentiles had ended in 1914. The world being at war in 1914 "proved" this, and only God knew what would come to pass later. A world-troubling conflict served to offer Russell some measure of credibility while his constant insistence on the "harmony" of the "plan of the ages," pointing to 1914, had long since been forgotten. From this point on, the focus fell on the next hundred years—counting from 2013 that leaves just one year remaining for us.

In April 1916 Russell acknowledged, in somewhat flowery terms, that a long time might pass before all the events he had predicted for 1914 would come true—but like the war, they would happen. The Saints should therefore continue to work like the prophets Elijah and Elisha, and they should not have expectations to a particular moment that was within any "definite point in view" (see the quote in the endnote).[124]

At his death, Charles Taze Russell was effectively removed from the story, and at the Tabernacle in Brooklyn, Society officials began seeking a worthy successor, one who could lead the movement out of its crisis. Although some of Russell's surviving followers stubbornly clung to their old leader and his ideas, an entirely new era was coming within the organization, which of course had to move forward under full steam no matter the cost.

The priority lay in quickly finding a strong, charismatic leader, someone who could reenergize the movement's dynamics and give the followers new hope. Unknown to the officials in Brooklyn, such a player was already scheming from the wings, eagerly planning his *coup d'état* on the movement's stage. Although he in no way resembled the "Pastor" in purpose or method, and later did much to ruin the memory of the once-highly adored founder, the new head of the movement possessed, as did Russell, a dominating personality and character so typical for the "strong leader."

During this difficult process of grieving and leadership change, it was J. F. Rutherford, attorney for Russell and the Society, the dazed and confused Bible Students found themselves following. He was the one that would lead them out of their momentary wilderness. Russell would not, by any means, have suggested Rutherford as his successor. In fact, prior to Russell's death, he did everything he could to separate Rutherford from the Society; he only temporarily succeeded.

PART TWO

The Great Schism

"One fact must be familiar to all those who have any experience of human nature—a sincerely religious man is often an exceedingly bad man. Piety and vice frequently live together in the same dwelling, occupying different chambers, but remaining always on the most amicable terms."

—Winwood Reade (1838–1875):
The Martyrdom of Man, 1872[125]

William W. Reade was a British historian, explorer and philosopher. Quote partially taken from Ibn Warraq's book: *Why I Am Not a Muslim*, Prometheus Books, New York, 1995.

Chapter 11

Power Struggle 1916–1919[126]

On Tuesday, October 31, 1916, or perhaps Wednesday, November 1, J. F. Rutherford boarded a train in Oakland, Maryland, bound for New York. He had suddenly changed travel plans. During a Bible Student convention in Oakland, he had received a telegram from his confidential friend Alexander Hugh Macmillan at Watch Tower headquarters in Brooklyn, New York. The telegram contained a coded message about Russell's death. Evidence suggests that Rutherford almost immediately packed his belongings, and then he took the first and best train connection to New York; if not for the telegram, he would have returned to Los Angeles, where he lived with his family. But fate yielded an alternative. A day or two later Rutherford was in the Bible Students' Brooklyn headquarters where he, apparently without significant resistance, seized control.

As I prepared this chapter, the intense drama of this period in the Bible Students' evolution gradually became clear to me; the movement had reached a turning point. Several times I found it necessary to rework and refine the chapter's substance, which was remarkably difficult to grasp. Only after consulting several internet sources, the original sources from 1917 and literature I possessed—and notably important: contemporary Bible Students and ex-Witnesses, who were well-versed in the material—did it become possible for me to compile the dramatic events that led to Russell's former legal adviser, *Attorney* J. F. Rutherford, determinedly seizing power of Russell's organization.

Through contemplation of the material, it became clear to me that Rutherford's takeover resulted not only in an eventual break with 75% of the Bible Students—who were members on October 31, 1916, when Russell died, and had left the movement by 1930 to 1932—but that Rutherford's takeover, strictly speaking, also meant a new movement was being created. Between 1916 and 1930, the movement greatly changed character compared to C. T. Russell's leadership, becoming more a *sect* or *cult*. Therefore, one understands perfectly well that the majority of the Bible Students—much to their credit—could not support or accept J. F. Rutherford as leader; only the most pliable and adaptive members accepted the changes, and since that time those changes have characterized the movement.

Dominant and Crafty

J. F. Rutherford, who became known worldwide as "the Judge," must have been a striking man, much as Russell was, heavily built and around six feet tall. Rutherford was reportedly dominant and nasty, spoke loudly, and as one journalist wrote of his stature, "more like a senator than most senators." And, "He dressed like a lawyer, with stand-up collar and black bow tie, and carried his eyeglasses on a long black silk ribbon" (Pike). "He was a 'man with a terrifying appearance,'" and against his "powerful personality, there were not many who could resist." Relating to friends, he could act despotic, and against enemies ruthless, hard and sly. (Pike, 1954, p. 22; Penton, 1986, p. 47; Cole, 1955, chapter 6)

In 1959 the Society wrote:

"Judge Rutherford was warm and generous toward his associates but he was also a brusk and direct type of person, and his legal background and experience in early life gave him a directness in his approach to problems in dealing with his brothers that caused some to take offense" (*Divine Purpose*, 1959, p. 68).

Understanding Rutherford is a complex proposition, but for members who saw him only from a respectful distance, he eventually became the subject of an almost hysterical personality cult, despite his initiative "to root out any remnants of creature worship that might be left in the organization" (*Divine Purpose*, 1959, p. 69; *creature worship*: worship of C. T. Russell).

If we judge by the tone of his large literary output, beginning with *The Harp of God* in 1921 and ending with *Children* in 1941—a total of around twenty bound books—his style resembled the Old Testament, hateful and pompous. If we include his booklets, his production approaches 100 publications or more. He suffered, I believe, from a kind of "paranoia" and saw "enemies" everywhere; in fact, this was the name of one of his books from 1937. The first chapter is titled: "Fear."

Christendom's clergymen, and especially the Roman Catholic hierarchy, received his special attention as the most prominent representatives of "Satan's organization"—from 1914–1918, in his view, those representatives did everything possible to destroy the Bible Students, the "only true Christians," on earth. Rutherford seems to have been largely governed by fear. For example, when the US government accused him of treason in 1918, he wilted under the heat and compromised with the authorities' demands, censoring passages in the so-called Seventh Volume—something many contemporary members of the movement do not know. In an apparent attempt to keep himself out of prison, Rutherford even recommended that Bible Students could now buy War Bonds ("Liberty Bonds," *WT*, May 15, June 1, 1918; James Parkinson: "Troubled Years," accessible on the internet; a later endnote also provides more information). We will examine this in more detail in coming pages.

It was probably Rutherford who instigated the new ultra-turgid style that came to characterize the Society's printed matter following Russell's death; the style was a strong contrast to the founder's *relatively friendly* way of expressing himself. Thus the presidential change meant a transformation from faith-nurturing water to all-consuming fire.[127]

The Judge's Background

Joseph Franklin Rutherford was born on November 8, 1869, at a farm in Morgan County, Boonville, Missouri. He had seven siblings, two brothers and five sisters. His parents, James Calvin Rutherford and Lenora Strickland Rutherford, were Baptists. For nearly fifty years, the family lived on a farm near Versailles. When Joseph was sixteen, he secured his father's permission to attend college and study law on condition that Joseph provide funds to train and pay wages to a farmhand to do Joseph's work. Joseph borrowed money from a friend and left home to study. After completing his education, he apprenticed with a judge, E. L. Edwards, for two years. At twenty, Joseph Rutherford was the official court reporter for the Fourteenth Judicial Circuit. In May 1892, he began practicing law in Missouri, following that he served as a public prosecutor in Boonville, Missouri, for four years. (*Freeminds.org*, 2011; Penton, 1986, p. 47; *Proclaimers*, 1993, p. 67)

Rutherford worked as an attorney in Missouri for about fifteen years. During his career, he served as a judge "in several cases" (Penton: "a substitute judge," p. 47), phrasing which may be as close as the Society will ever come to admitting that, in reality, the Judge was really a judge for only a few days, as his critics in the United States have long argued. Still, those few days as a substitute jurist were enough to support his prestigious claim to the office and adorn himself with the title.

Before he became a Bible Student, Rutherford wrote a 128-page textbook with the following, extraordinarily long, title: *Laws Of Missouri. Compilation of the Laws and Legal Forms for the Convenience of Farmers and Mechanics Merchants And Bankers. Business Manual*, printed and published by Stahl & Stahl (publication year not stated). The publisher's preface indicates he was "one of the leading members of the Boonville bar in Boonville," Missouri. (*Freeminds.org*, 2011)[128]

In 2011, I located a treatise by James Parkinson, *The Bible Student Movement in the Days of C. T. Russell* (available on the internet). According to Parkinson, it appears Rutherford sought political office, and thus he may have been active in Democrat William Jennings Bryan's 1896 presidential campaign. Bryan was not elected, but later became foreign minister, under President Woodrow Wilson, from 1913 to 1916. (Penton, p. 47)

With his forceful, fiery ways, I'm convinced Rutherford could have been a brilliant politician.

As a student, Rutherford worked as a bookseller and sold encyclopedias, somewhat unsuccessfully. On one occasion as he traveled between farms, he fell into an icy river and nearly drowned. This prompted him to vow that if a bookseller ever approached him, he would buy his wares. The opportunity came in early 1894 when Bible Student colporteurs sold three of Russell's books to him. After reading the books, Rutherford sent a letter to the head office of the Watchtower Society, in which he wrote:

"My dear wife and myself have read these books with the keenest interest, and we consider it a God-send and a great blessing that we have had the opportunity of coming in contact with them" (*Proclaimers*, 1993, p. 67).

Rutherford decided to be baptized in 1906; in 1907 he was posted as a public speaker and "pilgrim" for the Society. That same year he spoke at a "great convention of truth people" in Niagara Falls with other leading Bible Students. A year later he became Russell's legal adviser. In 1909, through his role as attorney, Rutherford negotiated the relocation of Watch Tower headquarters from Pittsburgh to Brooklyn, New York. In that year he also received—according to the Watchtower Society—his license to practice law in New York State. That same year he was empowered[129] to conduct litigation before the US Supreme Court. In 1913 he advised Russell in his litigation against J. J. Ross, the Canadian Baptist pastor, who sought to have Russell labeled a cheater by all legal means (see Chapter 8).[130] Russell lost his case, and Rutherford's counsel or dearth thereof may have contributed to conflict developing between the two men later in their relationship. If so (and this is only speculation), other and perhaps more-serious reasons could also have contributed to their difficulties. (Pike, 1959, p. 19; *WT*, 1907, p. 293-294; *Proclaimers*, 1993, p. 67; see also *Qualified*, 1955, p. 312-317; *Divine Purpose*, 1959, p. 65-66, and Martin and Klann, 1959, p. 18)

Rutherford was one of the executive committee members of the Watch Tower Society from 1912 until 1916, when he seized power of the association.

Rutherford's private life is not especially well-known. We do know that his wife, Mary Rutherford, did not actively participate in the movement's service. H. H. Stroup—who released *The Jehovah's Witnesses* (The Columbia Press, New York, 1945), which is considered a pioneer work—tells that some vagueness concerning the Judge's marriage prevailed among Bible Students; it seems the marriage had come to a kind of tacit agreement so it could officially continue. Undoubtedly, Russell's separation from Maria played a role. A recent historical production by the Watchtower Society indicated in a footnote that "sister" Mary Rutherford and their son Malcolm had permanent residence in Los Angeles and Monrovia, California, due to her poor health. She died in 1962, at age ninety-three. The *Proclaimers* cites a local newspaper, *Daily News-Post*, from Monrovia, which stated: "Until poor health confined her to her home, she took an active part in the ministerial work of Jehovah's Witnesses." The Rutherfords' only child, Malcolm Cameron Rutherford, must have been a "full-time servant" at some time. However, he does not seem to have held any position of importance, except for working as one of Russell's secretaries. Later, he became an "apostate." (*Proclaimers*, 1993, p. 89; Penton, 1986, p. 72; Stroup, 1945, p. 16; Pike, 1954, p. 23; Brian Kutscher, USA)

Penton argues that the Rutherfords' divorce was conducted quietly; the split was not so much because of her partial disability, but more because of the Judge's choleric temperament—and his alcoholism. Although the Society must have tried to hide it, his drinking habit was well known among headquarters staff. Reportedly, he excused himself, stating the liquor helped ease the lung disease incurred during his imprisonment in Atlanta, 1918–1919; more about this later.

The *Sixth* of Five Substitutes

At this point, I feel it's important to present what is perhaps the most dramatic period in the Watchtower Society's history, when Attorney J. F. Rutherford, using tactical, coup-like methods, took control of the Society from November 1916 to January 1917. There are many details and names involved, as if it were a giant Russian novel from the 1870s, but behind them there are the faces and souls of real human beings with ambitions, faith and hopes, with ideals and personal integrity, most of them (in their own opinions) conscientious Christians who wanted something for the movement they supported, and which they led as directors.

However, Rutherford would destroy their illusions for shaping the movement's future.

The choice of J. F. Rutherford as president of the Watch Tower Society on January 6, 1917, was not without difficulties. Many of those who worked with him at headquarters weren't particularly enamored by him. Partly because of his dominant behavior, partly because he wouldn't tolerate anyone hindering his plans to take over management of the Society. Was Rutherford, strictly speaking, an impostor and usurper, as his opponents accused, or was he the only possible heir to C. T. Russell's empire?

Russell's sudden death on October 31 briefly paralyzed the bereaved workers.[131] Russell, however, had foreseen this situation and sought to ensure the Society's future business by arranging for changes to the editing and publishing of *The Watch Tower and Herald of Christ's Presence* (as the magazine was called at that time), which would commence immediately after his death. In his will Russell provided directives for a five-member editorial committee to edit the magazine.

According to *The Watch Tower* of December 1916, the five-member committee was: W. E. Page, W. E. VanAmburgh, H. C. Rockwell, E. W. Brenneisen and F. H. Robison. Any vacancies were to be filled from among *five* alternates:

A. E. Burgess, R. H. Hirsh, Isaac Hoskins, G. H. Fisher and John Edgar—and a *sixth member*, J. F. Rutherford, who had drawn up the testament in 1907 and mysteriously had his name included on the alternate list.[132]

Since Russell compiled his list in 1907 a few things had changed, and three of the original ten committee members and alternates were unable to serve. Dr. John Edgar (alternate) from Scotland passed away in June 1910; and Page and Brenneisen promptly withdrew from the committee because of residential and commercial reasons—and possibly due to pressure from Rutherford.

Although J. F. Rutherford was only mentioned as an alternate member of the group, as shown in Russell's will and testament as it was published in the December issue, Rutherford is nevertheless *already* listed in that same issue as an equal member of the Editorial Committee. Of course there may have been a *force majeure* situation in which the Society's New York board simply chose someone from management who seemed the best and strongest candidate.

The editorial members named in the magazine's colophon were: 1. W. E. VanAmburgh; 2. J. F. Rutherford; 3. H. C. Rockwell; 4. F. H. Robison and 5. R. H. Hirsh (in that order).

What can we conclude from this? It seems the new editorial board acted quickly after Russell's death and Rutherford, probably within a few days, fortified his position in the management of the Society. Society history shows that sitting on the magazine's editorial committee conferred great prestige. It is thus clear that Rutherford, undoubtedly in his usual forthright manner, rapidly put himself forward to a position and in a manner that likely would not have had Russell's approval. Rutherford's dominant presence at headquarters a few days after the founder's death affected nearly everyone negatively, but nobody on the Society's executive committee or on the editorial team openly speaks against him at this early stage. All were scared and unsure who they should support.

One must understand that everyone in the association was shocked to near paralysis by Russell's sudden demise. He was their founder, their rallying point, the authority of their identity and now he was, according to his will and testament, *transformed*, "changed from glory unto glory." Macmillan put it this way: "We are happy and sad, confused and perplexed; yet the way is clear—and we are glad!…" (*WT*, December 1916).[133]

Just after Russell's death, six men sat on the Pennsylvania Society's board: Alfred I. Ritchie, vice president; William E. VanAmburgh, secretary and treasurer; Isaac F. Hoskins; Henry Clay Rockwell; Joseph F. Rutherford; and James D. Wright. All had been appointed by Russell after moving from Pittsburgh to New York in 1909. Andrew N. Pierson was elected to the board two days after Russell's death; in January, Pierson was elected vice president. When H. C. Rockwell became ill, Bible Student Robert H. Hirsh replaced him in March 1917. Hirsh had served as a proofreader for Russell, reviewing the typeset proofs of the *Watch Tower* before printing. (Cole, 1955, chapter 6)

In his biography, A. H. Macmillan notes that immediately after Russell's death the Executive Committee formed a working committee with Rutherford as legal adviser; W. E. VanAmburgh, treasurer; A. I. Ritchie, vice president; and Macmillan, secretary. The working committee was not formed to meet Russell's testamentary directives, but to keep the work going until a new president could be elected. This would happen in January 1917. (*Divine Purpose*, 1959, p. 64-73; *Proclaimers*, 1993, p. 64-71)

With Rutherford's return to the Brooklyn office, panic over Russell's loss seemed to subside under the attorney's firm hand—possibly a little too firm by the opinion of some.

Rutherford Sacked by Russell

Before I examine Rutherford's leadership of the Society, I'd like to step back to perhaps a year or two before Russell's death. It seems Russell must have planned several changes within the "Bethel family" in Brooklyn, but had not had enough time to realize all these changes. According to Marley Cole (p. 90), it included a plan for staff reduction, including removing the vice president, A. I. Ritchie.[134] Whether those plans included Rutherford's dismissal is not known with certainty, but source material suggests Russell, apparently on the quiet, must have dismissed his legal counsel in 1914 or early 1915, and provided him with sufficient money (possibly a loan/gift of about $1,000 to 1,500, a significant sum in 1915) so he could begin anew in California. Emma White-house and Laura M. Whitehouse, sisters who worked at headquarters during this time, and others have confirmed this information (L. M. Whitehouse was one of the sisters who signed Russell's will in 1907).[135]

At the time of Russell's death, Rutherford appears to have been living in Los Angeles, California, where he worked as a lawyer for a department store, possibly Bullock's (another source states Rutherford was not the store's attorney, but rather a floorwalker or clerk who helped customers locate goods in the store). Several "old-timers" among the Bible Students in Los Angeles, including Edward G. Lorenz, have reported that they had seen Rutherford at Bullock's around 1916. (Source: email from James Parkinson and Jerry Leslie, May 2011)[136]

A. H. Macmillan, who had managed the workers at the Bethel home, must have intercepted a telegram from Menta Sturgeon to his wife shortly after Russell' death; Sturgeon was Russell's last-journey secretary. Afterwards Macmillan telegraphed the following message to Rutherford: "The old man is dead," which might have been a kind of coded message—or perhaps more a disrespectful remark about a person he wanted long gone![137] At this time, Rutherford was attending the Bible Student convention in Oakland, Maryland, but when informed about Russell's death, he immediately telegraphed the Brooklyn Office: "Do nothing until I come." I would guess simply that it was A. H. Macmillan, one of Rutherford's few confidants on the board, who received his telegram. It's understandable, if Rutherford had laid plans for leading the Society after Russell's death, he hastily departed for New York so he could arrive in time to dominate any struggle to be Russell's successor.

Macmillan had baptized Rutherford in 1906 and this may have led to a special personal relationship between the two men, which subsequent developments confirmed. In 1917, it was Macmillan—during Rutherford's absence—who removed four opposing members from headquarters, members who could threaten his friend's position. If it was Macmillan Rutherford telegraphed from Maryland, it alerted Macmillan to *hold the fort* until Rutherford arrived.

There are conflicting stories about why Russell may have booted Rutherford from the leadership team. Russell must have become aware of Rutherford's less-desirable traits, possibly related to his behavior toward some "sisters" at Bethel in Brooklyn, after which Russell probably asked him to leave headquarters. James Parkinson, a current Bible Student, does not believe, however, that Rutherford was asked to leave because of the 1915 expense reduction where seventy office-staff members were laid off. Whatever the reason, Russell dismissed Rutherford, and I assume Russell had *not* mentioned Rutherford as a member or alternate member of the Editorial Committee for this reason, although Rutherford still sat on the board. If Rutherford's name was written into Russell's will (in his handwriting), it is remarkable that he, as a prominent member of the Executive Committee, is only mentioned as a *possible* alternate, for which there was no allowance in the text itself that, as we now know, lists the *specific* number of committee members and alternates, only *five of each*.

One wonders then if Russell, in his testament, should have mentioned Rutherford "amongst the most suitable" from which to fill vacancies on the editorial board if he had been critical enough of Rutherford to dismiss him. James Parkinson thinks Rutherford may have added his name to the alternates list because Dr. John Edgar had died in 1910. Nobody can prove this hypothesis, which relies on anecdotal evidence—evidence that appears to *support* the sixth man is a contradiction to Russell's published testament for *five* alternates to the editorial committee in case of resignation or death. Since the will was signed in 1907, it is clear that by Russell's death nine years later things may have changed.[138] On the website *Jehovah-Witness.net*, where one can find criticism of the 1916 electoral process, the debate around the *sixth* member is lively.[139] [140]

The situation suggests Rutherford, in the days after Russell's death, *may have* added his name to the will, a suspicion corroborated by Rutherford reportedly not wanting to show the will to other board members, apart from VanAmburgh and maybe Macmillan. If this is correct, he begins to appear as a usurper, who with co-conspirators Macmillan and VanAmburgh, and the use of unfair practices and legal technicalities, manipulated himself into the heart of events, maneuvering around his competitors, to assume power. This may be an excellent time to note that Russell's last will and testament, drawn up by

Rutherford, was in front of three witnesses: Mae F. Land, M. Almeta Nation and Laura M. Whitehouse. Afterward, the will was presumably locked safely in Russell's office until it was to be opened for further study or execution by the correct person.

It is possible the will was rewritten in 1911. James Parkinson informed me via email that an earlier worker at the Society's headquarters, Annie Reed, later showed a copy of the 1911 testament to two Bible Students, Kenneth Fernets and Carmelita Fernets, and that J. F. Rutherford's name was not mentioned at that time, except perhaps as signatory of the will. One cannot dismiss the possibility that Macmillan played a crucial role as one of Russell's former secretaries. Immediately after Rutherford's arrival at headquarters he appointed Macmillan as his aide-de-camp or secretary, placing Macmillan in a position of confidence under both old and new leadership. Macmillan was less than popular among the other workers at headquarters in Brooklyn, who probably considered him opportunistic, so clearly Rutherford did not choose him for his popularity. Cole calls Macmillan "the bone of contention" in relation to Rutherford's critics; so there were many reasons for unrest and dissatisfaction smoldering among the "brothers" at Bethel. (Cole, p. 86)

It ought to be stressed that even though Russell may have dismissed Rutherford in 1914 or 1915, Rutherford—according to *Watch Tower* editions I have reviewed—continued to play a particularly important role within the Bible Students leading up to Russell's death, partly as lecturer and partly as a prominent member of the Society's Executive Committee. The members, however, do not seem to have noticed Rutherford's demotion, allowing him to emerge as the natural heir to Russell's *earthly Kingdom*.

Chapter 12

Elected for *Life!*

The election of a new Society president occurred on January 6, 1917, in Pittsburgh, where the main corporation still had offices. A crowd of 600 attended the meeting; the delegates controlled about 150,000 votes, and Rutherford, upon being declared President, apparently assumed voting authority over Russell's shares—a majority by a wide margin. Rutherford was the only nominee, and thereby, elected unanimously as the new president of the Watch Tower Bible and Tract Society of Pennsylvania. He automatically became president of all the subsidiaries, including the New York Corporation, the Peoples Pulpit Association (now the Watch Tower Bible and Tract Society of New York, Inc.), and presumably the International Bible Student's Association in England.

Before the annual meeting on January 6, Rutherford, according to Robert H. Hirsh who replaced H. C. Rockwell (who had been ill) on the board, prepared new statutes that he wanted the board to accept at the annual meeting. The approval of these quite new statutes, previously unknown to the board, would—if approved—give Rutherford almost *total control* over the parent corporation in Pittsburgh and the subsidiaries, particularly the New York society, which had been Russell's main base after he moved to New York in 1909.

According to Russell's will, he did not intend that a single individual should assume management of the Society after his demise. He wanted the Society's interests to be managed *entirely* by the central, seven-member board, including a chairman and president whose role would be one of formal character and, when appropriate, could be dismissed by a majority vote of the board. It seems this is also what the most vital board members considered right. Rutherford knew he had to avoid this situation at all costs, because he seemed intent on assuming Russell's former dominant role. During the meeting in January 1917, Rutherford pushed the board members and annual-meeting delegates to accept his new by-laws without informed consent.

The final word on this situation comes from Robert H. Hirsh, who was elected to the executive committee in March 1917 and over the next few months experienced the dramatic developments that changed him from a "Rutherford man" to perhaps the strongest critic of the new president. In a pamphlet from September 1917, *Light After Darkness*,[141] an indignant response to Rutherford's pamphlet *Harvest Siftings* (August 1917), Hirsh writes:

134

"One of these pseudo-writings may be found in a document recently published and mailed to the friends all over the world, entitled 'Harvest Siftings,' which is an imitation and counterfeit of our dear Brother Russell's Harvest Siftings, but a careful examination of the two writings bearing the same title will reveal the fact that they are entirely different. Brother Russell's Siftings was a real thing; the latter is a deception" (September 1, 1917, p. 1–2).

About Rutherford's new statutes, or by-laws, Hirsh writes:

"The trouble really had its beginning before the election in Pittsburgh last January. Realizing that he [Rutherford] would be elected President of the Society [he had the majority of the votes], and knowing that the Charter places the control of the Society's interests in the hands of the Board of Directors, Brother Rutherford, before he started for the election at Pittsburgh, prepared some by-laws to be placed before the shareholders' meeting. In this connection it would be well to quote a part of the Charter of the Society respecting the only body authorized to make by-laws. Section VII reads: 'The Corporation, by its Board of Directors [not the voting shareholders], a majority of whom shall constitute a quorum for the transaction of business, shall have full power and authority to make and enact by-laws, rules and ordinances, which shall be deemed and taken to be the law of said corporation, and do any and everything useful for the good government and support of the affairs of said corporation'" (*Light After Darkness*, 1917; internet source without the original pagination located in 2011; search with a quote in the document).

Robert Hirsh says further, notwithstanding this provision of the charter, that specifically the board approved the statutes, a committee was appointed to assess the new by-laws instituted at the annual meeting, and after the committee debated them at length, the committee agreed to present them to the annual meeting participants. Rutherford had, according to Hirsh, stubbornly delayed things behind the scenes while he tried to force the directors to accept his new by-laws. At the same time he must have threatened the members of the committee with open struggle from the pulpit if they didn't comply. "Little did the conventioners know of what was going on behind the curtain," says Hirsh, "and little did they realize why the Convention was delayed so long…"

Hirsh says further that the committee "held out courageously against Rutherford," but "fearing the threatened fight and consequent disturbance in the Convention if Brother Rutherford did not have his own way, they finally reported the by-laws as originally prepared by him" (*Light After Darkness*, 1917).

The most extensive new by-law Rutherford pushed through was that "whoever is elected president of the Peoples' Pulpit Association (the subsidiary corporation in New York State) is elected for life."[142] Another of the new by-laws the members of the committee, according to Hirsh, especially opposed, was the president's authority to appoint an *advisory three-man committee,* where the Society's secretary and treasurer, VanAmburgh, would be a "permanent member." Hirsh also notes: "These by-laws and such a Committee would naturally be thought by some to supplant the Directors in their advisory and executive capacity."

At this point of the event maelstrom and on through August and September 1917, Hirsh experienced the consequences of adopting Rutherford's new by-laws and discovered how those by-laws were being used for the promotion of Rutherford's own narrow interests.

After Rutherford's "coup" a proliferation of pamphlets rained on the membership. In October Rutherford followed up on Hirsh's comprehensive and weighty critique with his *Harvest Siftings No. 2*, in order to silence Hirsh and others and then, Paul S. L. Johnson followed up with two pamphlets in November 1917 and August 1918, which we will examine below. (*Divine Purpose*, 1959, p. 69-71; Penton, 1986, note 23, p. 319)

Rutherford Consolidates His Position

Perhaps it is naive to think the elitist and one-man-owned publishing house Russell had founded, and largely funded, could operate with a collective, democratically elected leadership and an honorary equalitarian figurehead as president. Many members continued to need an awe-inspiring leader figure who could strengthen their identities, create peace and progress, and work collectively until the Lord made short shrift of Babylon and world governments during Armageddon. The obvious solution was selecting a strong charismatic-leader personality, capable of extending Russell's inheritance and continuing the organization's work. Who might have taken this role if Rutherford had lost the power struggle, is not easy to know, but we can speculate that the best qualified board member may have been Robert H. Hirsh, a journalist by training. Rutherford, Macmillan and VanAmburgh must have seen his potential too and kept close watch on him, but not for good, as later developments illustrate.

The board's reluctant acceptance of the new by-laws, which henceforth insured Rutherford's personal power base in both New York and Pittsburgh and basically aligned with Russell's management of the International Bible Students, probably contributed to the New York Society being seen as the leading society. The members came to consider this the "leading subsidiary," the movement's highest authority, or *the* Society, whose word became law, until about 1972. However, this contradicted the Pennsylvania Corporation being the ultimate and legal authority—a fact Russell had conveniently ignored before his death and that ultimately formed the basis of Rutherford's dubious legal maneuvers. Rutherford's legal conclusions highlight that circumstance, so at that point he might *formally* have been right.

Rutherford's actions carried consequences for many years. Thanks to the extraordinary authority granted him during that January 1917 meeting, his successor, N. H. Knorr, would use the same Rutherford by-laws to release a new Bible translation in 1950, the *New World Translation*, reportedly without consulting the parent corporation in Pittsburgh. It seems this practice of unopposed presidential decision-making was still the precedent in 1950, and apparently not an easy power to dispel, possibly in part because it sustained the presidential powerbase in New York (internet resource: *Bible Students Fragments*, 1917-1967; first section).[143]

In 1993, *Proclaimers* recounted how the new vice president, Andrew N. Pierson, in panegyrical style recommended Rutherford's election, but one must take note that he later seems to vacillate between supporting the board majority and Rutherford—although the following quote indicates Pierson was in "full sympathy" with the election. By all accounts, Pierson was critical of events, but found it hard to express his dissatisfaction. This may be why the *Proclaimers* article paints him in full sympathy with the election. It's more likely he was not, either during or after the annual meeting. Pierson was simply torn between what he knew in his heart and his loyalty to the presidency, but despite his supposed sympathy, it seems in 1918 Rutherford manipulated matters and had Pierson cast out of his post. In fact, Rutherford amended the by-laws in 1918 so he could surreptitiously cast votes for someone else to replace Pierson, without the replacement being formally nominated. In this case C. H. Anderson, already a board member, replaced Pierson as vice president.

In 1917 the following ran in *The Watch Tower*:

"As the time for the election approached, the question remained Who would succeed Russell as president? *The Watch Tower* of January 15, 1917, reported the outcome of the annual meeting, explaining: 'Brother Pierson, with very appropriate remarks and expressions of appreciation and love for Brother Russell, stated that he had received word as proxy-holder from friends all over the land to the effect that he cast their votes for Brother J. F. Rutherford for President, and he further stated that he was in full sympathy with this.' After Rutherford's name was placed in nomination and seconded, there were no further nominations, so 'the Secretary cast the ballot as directed, and Brother Rutherford was declared the unanimous choice of the Convention as President'" (*Proclaimers*, 1993, p. 65).

In the course of the research, my American contact, James Parkinson, informed me that the report continued in *The Watch Tower* from January 15, 1917. The above quotation comes from *Proclaimers*, but the following, which appeared in the later *Watch Tower* issue, was omitted from the reprint. Why? Careful examination of the content makes it clear: "There being no further nominations, a motion was made that the rule of balloting be suspended, and that the Secretary of the convention be directed to cast the entire vote for Brother J. F. Rutherford. Thereupon the Secretary cast the ballot as directed, and Brother Rutherford was declared the unanimous choice of the convention as President of the Society for the ensuing year" (*WT*, Jan. 15, 1917; reprint 6033).[144]

Initially, I had to overcome some misunderstandings about the above quotations, due at least in part to my linguistic challenges dealing with English.

Once I untangled the threads, it was clear to me why the nomination of other presidential candidates was suspended—or as it says in *Proclaimers*: "[T]here [were] not made several proposals" (p. 65). At first I thought it was because Rutherford would try to prevent Pierson from standing up as a candidate, but eventually I became aware that this was totally wrong. The reason was logical: Had Pierson not been Rutherford's ally at the time, and this he was, then Rutherford would never have accepted Pierson as vice president. Therefore, Pierson stood at Rutherford's side and recommended his election to, at least in part, secure his own position in the hierarchy. What was carefully omitted from *The Watch Tower* report of January 15, 1917, hid the fact that Rutherford's ally, A. H. Macmillan, chairman of the business meeting, refused to recognize shareholders who wanted to nominate someone other than Rutherford.

J. F. Rutherford and his co-conspirators, among them Macmillan and VanAmburgh, were concerned that Menta Sturgeon and Paul S. L. Johnson might be nominated. This would have been an embarrassment, since newspapers around the country had *already received a record of events* at the annual meeting *eight days before it occurred*! More on this shortly.

The annual meeting on January 6, 1917, ended according to Rutherford's plan and full satisfaction. He had not only been elected without rival candidates, but he had also insured he would never be deprived his new, privileged position. It gave him not only virtually unlimited power over *The Watch Tower*, and eventually the International Bible Students, but also over the Society's financial resources.[145] It's understandable that he was full of praise for the annual meeting attendees:

"My heart is full to overflowing. You will bear witness that I have not in any way sought the office of President of this Society. Up to this hour I have not discussed it with anyone. I have purposely avoided doing so, believing that the Lord would accomplish his purpose. What has been done here today I feel that the Lord has directed, and I humbly submit to his will. To him alone is due honor and glory" (Stroup, 1945, p. 14).

Rutherford's statement that he had "not in any way sought the office of President" is probably a testimony to the abhorrence most Bible Students felt for politics of any kind at that time (James Parkinson). However, I think he at least discussed it with his aide-de-camp, A. H. Macmillan. And why not? All politicians entrust plans to their lieutenants or immediate assistants, then and now.

Election events shut out other candidates before any real opposition to Rutherford could manifest itself. Anyone who would have wished to become a candidate never had a chance. The election seems, as far as I can see, almost a caricature of the democratic process, because most of the convention activities, as I said before, apparently had been preplanned down to the smallest detail. Rutherford and his people did not want any other candidate listed; J. F. Rutherford was to be the *only* option,[146] suggesting that the exclusion of opposition was a quiet maneuver in advance of a mighty storm. Throughout the following months, Rutherford defied the Society's board and his critics, including Russell's former close associate, Paul S. L. Johnson, requiring that Rutherford undertake further steps to consolidate his position. (*Divine Purpose*, 1959, p. 64-65; Cole, 1955, p. 80-90; *Qualified*, 1955, p. 313)

Paul Johnson subsequently wrote:

"After my return from Europe I learned that Bros. Rutherford, VanAmburgh and Macmillan conspired to gain for the first Bro. Russell's full power and authority in the work and business of the Society. They began this conspiracy before the election. They prearranged every detail of the voting shareholders' meeting Jan. 6 [1917] … A week before the election Bro. Rutherford furnished a brother with an account of the proceedings of the voting shareholders' meeting for publication in the press of the country, telling of his election by the Secretary casting the ballot of the convention and of the unanimity of his election, and giving some of his speech of acceptance. The Editor of the *New York Herald* [one of many who were given the advance copy] commented on the prophetic gifts of 'those Bethel people' in being able to foretell just what would happen at the election!"[147] (The citation continues in the endnote below, which is quoted from P. S. L. Johnson's original version, *Harvest Siftings Reviewed*, 1917[148]; see also Charles F. Redeker, *Pastor C. T. Russell: Messenger of Millennial Hope*, 2006, p. 277.)[149]

It seems to me that there is not much difference between secular politics and that of religious associations. Politics and religion seem to be two sides of same coin. But this is, of course, an old novelty!

Legal Technicalities

At the Brooklyn offices, a number of workers and other members began to resist the Judge immediately after the election. Four board members who, as it was later revealed, were not elected in Pittsburgh, but in New York according to Russell's procedure—Robert H. Hirsh, Isaac F. Hoskins, Alfred I. Ritchie and James Dennis Wright[150]—demanded (after the January elections) a reorganization that in principle would weaken the president's power and return it to the board members. Clearly, this change would comply with Russell's testamentary wishes. In 1993 the Society recounted these events from a more negative perspective:

"A few, especially at headquarters, actually resented Brother Rutherford. The fact that the work was moving ahead and that he was making every effort to follow the arrangements that had been put in place by Russell did not seem to impress them. Opposition soon mounted. Four members of the board of directors of the Society went so far as to endeavor to wrest administrative control from Rutherford's hands. The situation came to a head in the summer of 1917 with the release of *The Finished Mystery*, the seventh volume of *Studies in the Scriptures*" (*Proclaimers*, 1993, p. 66; Penton, 1986, p. 50).

This is obviously a beautification of the facts by Rutherford's *steadfast* successors, and it does not depict the real essence of the matter, specifically that Rutherford was not trying to "follow the arrangements that had been put in place by Russell," but rather directly flout them.

After Russell's death, apart from Rutherford, who as Russell's former legal counsel knew the rules very well, there was apparently no one on the board responsible for insuring election procedures were followed, including where the elections were to occur to be legally binding—in Pittsburgh or New York. Rutherford seemed to withhold that knowledge, quite deliberately, until the summer of 1917 when it played a crucial role in his persistent efforts to conquer the Society through the adoption of the new by-laws and sneaky tactics regarding critical board members. In fact, Rutherford reveals this in his *Harvest Siftings* pamphlet, published in August, and which Hirsh reacted sharply against. In *Harvest Siftings* Rutherford refers to a conversation with Russell in 1909:

"Brother Russell asked me to see if the WATCH TOWER BIBLE AND TRACT SOCIETY could be registered as a corporation in the State of New York. After a thorough examination of the matter I told him it could not be done, because it is a non-stock corporation organized under the laws of Pennsylvania and there is no provision in the law of the State of New York for registering such a foreign corporation" (*Harvest Siftings*, 1917).[151]

In fact, already in 1909, Russell knew board elections in New York were illegal.

Was the Board Elected Illegally?

Watch Tower Bible & Tract Society of Pennsylvania, which is the Society's registered name since 1884, had its headquarters in Pittsburgh, Pennsylvania, but from 1909 Russell controlled the main corporation's business and elections from its subsidiary, the People's Pulpit Association, in New York. The dual locations and legal subtleties make it difficult to determine what was going on as we look back on it today, and not least of this is *where events happened*, as well as what *legal consequences* this represents, then and now. It appears the board minority of Pierson, VanAmburgh and Rutherford was elected correctly in Pittsburgh in January 1917, according to the by-laws (if they were already members of the board), but not all commentators agree this was the case. (e.g., Hirsh and Penton; Cole, p. 92)

The other four board members were not selected in that January election but had been personally appointed by Russell in New York, a practice Russell used and one said to have been a "time-honored practice." Everyone in the association had, in one way or another, accepted Russell's total control of the Society, which was based on his holding the majority stake, and they had never questioned the procedures—only those who had long since departed the movement may have questioned them.

Robert Hirsh discussed the time-honored practice in his pamphlet from September 1917:

"Little did we then think that those who would undertake to manage the affairs of the Society after Brother Russell's death would attempt to pervert and change *the time-honored customs* and usages left us by our dear Pastor, or that there would be introduced such flagrant and sweeping departures from the form of government as outlined in Brother Russell's Will and in the Charter of the Watch Tower Bible and Tract Society, written by his own hand" (*Light After Darkness*; italics are mine).

In 1955, Macmillan wrote about this too, but his views are more subdued as he presents the facts more favorably:

"Rutherford was elected president. There is no doubt in our minds that the Lord's will was done in this choice. It is certain that Rutherford himself had nothing to do with it. W. E. VanAmburgh was elected secretary-treasurer and A. N. Pierson vice-president. Directors were not elected, as these had been *elected by Russell for life*. This he could do because he held the majority of votes although, according to the charter, they should have been reelected to that office every year as we learned later. J. F. Rutherford was warmly welcomed in his new capacity as manager of the Society's affairs by the majority of those associated with the organization at that time. But from the outset it became apparent that a few, especially at headquarters, resented him" (Macmillan: *Faith on the March*, 1957, p. 71-72; italics are mine).

Of course replacements were made. When a seat became vacant on the main board, for example due to a death, the remaining members had to decide who would succeed the lost member. No more than thirty days after the election of a new member, the original statues dictated the election must be approved by the Pittsburgh Corporation, but that approval was normally done by Russell in New York. For example, two days after Russell's death A. N. Pierson was elected to fill a vacancy.[152]

However, Rutherford could not abide such developments at the Brooklyn headquarters where he had not yet gained full control. His "secret" agenda, where only VanAmburgh and Macmillan were inaugurated, needed to move forward as quickly as possible to have the four dissenting members ejected from Bethel and the Tabernacle (as it was called) in Brooklyn—a legal maneuver based on the statutes of the Pittsburgh Society.

Evidence makes it very clear Rutherford calculated every move. It was not only "the Lord's will" that he "humbly" undertook to perform, but rather his own stalwart determination and goals. He had been the Society's lawyer and was more than familiar with its laws. Rutherford consulted with a secular colleague, Mr. H. M. MacCaughey, who was a well-known corporate lawyer from Philadelphia, in preparation for dismissing the four "troublemakers" (Macmillan, 1957, p. 170; Cole, 1955, p. 90-92; *Harvest Siftings*, 1917).

Among other things, MacCaughey wrote the following in his opinion:

"Therefore, the conclusion is irresistible that Messrs. Wright, Hoskins, and Ritchie are in no sense of the word legally members of the Board of Directors and any acts performed by them in that capacity would be void and of no legal effect…"

As for Robert H. Hirsh, who had been elected in March 1917, Mr. Mac-Caughey noted he was duly elected:

"With respect to Mr. Hirsh, the facts show that he was elected by the board of directors after H. C. Rockwell, whom he succeeded, had resigned. Rockwell himself under the facts, was never legally a member of the Board" (*Harvest Siftings*, August 1917).

Nothing suggests, however, that MacCaughey's opinion could be construed as an objective assessment in a courtroom, and it was never challenged in a lawsuit. Rather, the opinion was a legal contribution, requested and financed by Rutherford!

Regarding his motives for choosing a lawyer to evaluate whether he could dismiss his critics, Rutherford wrote in *Harvest Siftings*:

"Their purpose was to discredit me before as many friends as possible, and then pass a resolution depriving me of the management of the Society. They had told me they were consulting lawyers. I submit that it can hardly be said that I have acted from any selfish or ulterior motive. I was advised by one of the best corporation lawyers in Philadelphia that these four men were not legal members of the Board, and that I had the legal authority to appoint a new board. I appointed this Board not for a selfish purpose, but to protect the interests of the Society" (*Harvest Siftings*, 1917).

Harvest Siftings was a very long legal and personal self-defense, not without rationale or nuances, very self-centered and subjective—and sometimes seductively friendly to his opponents on the Board and at Bethel.

F. H. McGee,[153] a Bible Student and attorney, was an assistant to the Attorney General of New Jersey in 1917; McGee supported the opposition's criticism of Rutherford. This is evidenced by the pamphlet, *Light After Darkness*, in which Hirsh, among others, writes concerning Rutherford's consultation with his Philadelphia attorney:

"During his [Rutherford's] absence he heard of the disturbance at the Tabernacle re the policeman and telegraphed Brother McGee of Trenton that if he were advising us, to tell us to wait until his return, when all would be adjusted. / Little did we realize how the adjustment would be made. His design was that upon the advice of his Philadelphia lawyer he would declare illegal the Board of Directors through whom Brother Russell had been doing illegal (?) business for so many years. On his homeward journey he visited Pittsburgh and appointed brethren to take our places, whom no doubt he felt certain would never attempt to rescind his by-laws, as this was his only cause for complaint against us. /At the noonday meal in the Bethel Dining Room on July 17, Brother Rutherford made the startling announcement to all gathered there that the Directors of the Society had never been legally elected, and that he had declared the offices of four of them vacant and appointed new ones in their places. All the old Directors were present and the Brethren he had appointed were also present" (*Light After Darkness*, 1917).

Robert Hirsh concludes in his pamphlet against Rutherford:

"Upon the best legal advice we can obtain, and concurred in by Attorney Brother McGee, assistant to the Attorney General of New Jersey, it appears that Brother Rutherford's interpretation of these technicalities is erroneous, and we are still the legal Directors of the Society."

The said legal advice that *the four* had been given was probably delivered by A. N. Pierson, Russell's successor on the Board, who was elected vice president in January 1917; during the whole controversy he seemed unsure whose side to take (*Light After Darkness*, 1917).

Chapter 13

The Bomb!

The first edition of the Seventh Volume in the series *Studies in the Scriptures* was presented to the Bethel "family" on July 17, 1917. On this occasion the management also announced the dismissal of four board members—whose names are repeated here for good measure: Alfred I. Ritchie (vice president under Russell), Robert H. Hirsh, Isaac F. Hoskins and James D. Wright. (Haugland: *The Successor Problem*, 2000; Cole, p. 93)

In 1993, the Watchtower Society wrote:

"It was as if a bombshell had exploded! The four ousted directors seized upon the occasion and stirred up a five-hour controversy before the Bethel family over the administration of the Society's affairs. A number of the Bethel family sympathized with the opposers. The opposition continued for several weeks, with the disturbers threatening to 'overthrow the existing tyranny,' as they put it" (*Proclaimers*, 1993, p. 67).

As noted in the previous chapter, Hirsh was a central figure in the explosive events of July 17 and described the events of the day in his pamphlet *Light After Darkness*.

Following the event summary, Hirsh notes, a few lines down, that "Pierson in his letter to Brother Ritchie has taken his stand with the majority members of the old Board, giving us a majority – five to two." That there was a *majority of five* may be due to the fact that Pierson was still unsure whom he should join; Rutherford or the board majority, but he joined finally to the first mentioned. The four newly appointed directors, as Rutherford had appointed on July 12 in Pittsburgh, were: Dr. W. E. Spill, J. A. Bohnet, George H. Fisher and the "controversial" A. Hugh Macmillan. (*Light After Darkness*, September 1917; italics are mine; there are no page numbers listed in the Hirsh document located on the internet; Cole, p. 93)

It seemed a "bomb had exploded" among Society management, or more appropriately a bit of a *coup* had occurred. Heated debates followed, wherein the four dismissed directors accused Rutherford of dictatorial methods and questioned his competence. Rutherford claimed the opposite: The four directors had formed a conspiracy to take control of the Society—perhaps a projection of his own motives toward his "enemies." In reality, the four dismissed directors seemingly sought to maintain Russell's testamentary intentions, and of course, promote their objective that all decisions had to be approved by the board.

In the Society's 1993 history of the movement, the authors obstinately maintained Rutherford's arguments from 1917 (and the leaders still do today, nearly a century later):

"It turned out that although the four opposing directors had been appointed by Brother Russell, these appointments had never been confirmed by vote of the corporation members at the annual meeting of the Society. Therefore, the four of them were not legal members of the board of directors at all! Rutherford had been aware of this but had not mentioned it at first. Why not? He had wanted to avoid giving the impression that he was going against Brother Russell's wishes. However, when it became evident that they would not discontinue their opposition, Rutherford acted within his authority and responsibility as president to replace them with four others whose appointments were to be confirmed at the next annual meeting, to be held in January 1918" (*Proclaimers*, 1993, p. 67, 68).

Vice President Andrew N. Pierson—who initially advocated on behalf of the four expelled board members and who vacillated between the two warring groups—noted that "if the directors were not legally elected, neither were the Society's three officers: Rutherford, Pierson, and VanAmburgh. In order to have been chosen officers in January 1917, they would have had to have been legally elected directors. Yet they had not been, and hence, by Rutherford's own logic, did not hold office "legally." Penton observes that if the case had come to trial, Rutherford would have lost. (Penton, 1986, p. 52)[154]

Eventually, it seems the sacked directors procured a legal opinion that stated Rutherford's dispositions had been "completely illegal." This was probably the four opponents' last attempt to rally members. Still, even before Rutherford sought legal advice from MacCaughey, the opposition chose not to sue the new president, and it's distinctly possible they could have won the case.[155] Their reasoning against bringing suit involved their loyalty to the Society and the opinion that disagreements in management should preferably be settled between the brothers, a quite idealistic and very naive decision that may have glossed over other motives—lawsuits could be costly and lengthy! In James Parkinson's article, *Troubled Years*, he states the ousted board members decided not to prosecute on the basis of 1 Corinthians 6:7[156] where Paul writes: "It is altogether a defect in you, that ye have lawsuits one with another. Why not rather take wrong? Why not rather be defrauded?" (ASV) The leading critics and "troublemakers" apparently accepted expulsion from the board rather than create discord among brethren.

In any event, however, the battle was already lost—Rutherford had seen to that—and within a few years their worst fears were fully confirmed. The member democracy within the Bible Students was overrun by the new president and his policies, and replaced by his new convention, a "theocratic organization," which could be rephrased as: God's rule *through* Rutherford. The establishment of this so-called *theocratic government* led to Rutherford's gaining total power within a few years, and not just at Bethel but over the whole movement. The development in the Pittsburgh Society and the movement as a whole from 1917 through the late 1930s was central to further development toward an organization where leaders at all levels expel any who disagree with their course. (*Proclaimers*, 1993, p. 68; Watch Tower Society presidency dispute (1917), *Wikipedia*, 2011; *Harvest Siftings*, 1917; J. Parkinson: *Troubled Years (1916-1918)*, April 2009)

Paul S. L. Johnson

Shortly before his death, Russell planned to send Paul S. L. Johnson to England to encourage supporters. The November issue of *The Watch Tower* carried an announcement, perhaps out of respect for Russell's wish (and perhaps to otherwise occupy Johnson during the 1917 annual meeting and election), that Rutherford was sending Johnson to London at the end of 1916. Due to the London movement's internal turmoil, Johnson immediately used his authority to dismiss two of the leaders, encouraged by British Bible Student leader Jesse Hemery; afterward, Johnson must have assumed control of the department and frozen its funds. His motive may have been to gain control over the department's financial resources, which could cripple the new president's power in Brooklyn. Or since Johnson may have been overly ambitious, his real goal was more likely to overthrow Rutherford and assume the presidency. On the same occasion Johnson would then step into the prophetic role as the "steward" suggested in Matthew 20:8, which was Johnson's grandiose dream (just one of many, as it turned out).[157]

Paul Samuel Leo (formerly Levitsky) Johnson (1873–1950) was born of Jewish parents who later converted to the Methodist Church. Johnson was educated at the Theological Seminary in Ohio, where he received a master's degree in 1898. He then pastored several Lutheran churches. In 1903 he left the Lutheran Church to join the Watch Tower Society. A year later he was appointed "pilgrim" by C. T. Russell and became one of his three secretaries. Eventually Johnson became Russell's trusted friend and advisor, making his position in headquarters almost untouchable, and he was undoubtedly the object of envy and jealousy among some of the brothers.

As C. T. Russell's confidante, Johnson was a prominent Bible Student, and it naturally fell to him to write a special article honoring Russell. The feature appeared in the December 1916 issue of *The Watch Tower* and seems to be a transcript of the speech he gave at Russell's bier. Other articles are by VanAmburgh, Macmillan and Sturgeon, Ritchie and Woodworth, and of course J. F. Rutherford—who also organized the funeral instead of Russell's relatives.

Johnson's motives may not have been entirely altruistic. It seems he too was something of a schemer. He was partly responsible for the controversy surrounding the "New Covenant," which in 1908–1909 resulted in some Bible Students leaving the movement to form The New Covenant Believers, a group that spread to Australia as the New Covenant Fellowship.

Rutherford, who thought Johnson was unpredictable ("Brother Johnson was of unsound mind"),[158] undoubtedly both a realistic and a political assessment, managed to neutralize the trouble in London, and in April 1917 instructed Johnson to return to New York. According to the Society's historical representation of these events, Johnson had some support within headquarters, making him a bane to the new president. However, the accusation that Johnson pulled the strings and got the majority of the directors to side against Rutherford and the others is untrue, according to Robert Hirsh. Johnson returned from England in April, and the turmoil at the top had begun in January. (Penton, 1986, p. 49; Cole, 1957, p. 93; *Light After Darkness*, 1917)

Since the 1917 controversy in Brooklyn, the Society has more than hinted that the four critics colluded with Johnson, but Robert Hirsh strongly denied this:

"From what we have said foregoing in these pages, we believe that all can see that the coupling of Brother Johnson's affairs with the Board of Directors is an attempt to becloud the real issue and the real trouble, which existed before the return of Brother Johnson to America. Since self-exaltation began before there was any trouble about the English case, and since objections to the President's course were made from January to March, it is manifest that Brother Johnson had nothing to do with our affair. It is absolutely untrue that Brother Johnson became in any sense a leader of the Directors.... At no time did we ever contemplate deposing Brother Rutherford and making Brother Johnson President, as Brother Rutherford well knew. He and those with him also well know that we did not plot against him to oust him and seize control, to exalt ourselves and humiliate him. Since we frequently thus assured him, we cannot understand how he could believe and publish the contrary. All we wished to do was to cooperate with him for the good of the work; and we were well pleased that he act as President and presiding officer. But we were not prepared to quietly allow him to set aside our Pastor's Will and Charter and 'lord it over God's heritage' without a protest. That protest is the cause of all the trouble, even as St. Paul preaching the Truth at Ephesus was mobbed, and then charged with being a disturber of the peace" (*Light After Darkness*, 1917).

In fact, the Watchtower management admitted many years later that Paul Johnson only later joined the critics, and was not an instigator, as Rutherford suggested. The authors of the book *Jehovah's Witnesses in the Divine Purpose* (1959), one of the Society's first major historical representations, note the following about the dramatic dining room meeting on July 17:

"They [the critics] opposed the move because they had not been consulted. But now the book [the Seventh Volume] had been completed and released. In the five-hour debate that ensued the four contentious members of the board of directors were joined by P. S. L. Johnson. All voiced their grievances in the open before the entire headquarters staff. This controversy showed a number of the Bethel family were in sympathy with this opposition to the Society's administration under Brother Rutherford. If allowed to continue, it would disrupt the entire operation of Bethel; so Brother Rutherford took steps to correct it" (*Divine Purpose*, 1959, p.70, 71).

The "steps to correct it" meant that Rutherford had appointed four new members to the board on July 12 in Pittsburgh, five days *before* the dining-room coup. Rutherford told the four board members the change was a *fait accompli*, but graciously offered them the position of "front runners" or pilgrims for the Society, an offer they could only refuse:

"Brother Rutherford did not summarily dismiss them, however. He offered them prominent positions as pilgrims, but they refused and voluntarily chose to leave Bethel. Unfortunately, and as was to be expected, their withdrawal from service at headquarters did not reconcile them to Jehovah's organization. Instead, they began to spread their opposition outside of Bethel in an extensive speaking and letter writing campaign throughout the United States, Canada and Europe. As a result, after the summer of 1917, *many of the congregations all over the world were composed of two parties.* The spiritual drowsiness that had been settling on many during this period made them an easy prey for *the smooth talk of these opposers,* and they refused to co-operate with the awakening spirit of the revitalized work in preaching the Kingdom good news at that time" (*Divine Purpose*, 1959, p. 71; italics are mine).

Johnson did not surrender so easily. In November 1917 he released another pamphlet, *Harvest Siftings Reviewed.* In it he opines that he was destined to be Russell's *successor* as the "steward." [159] [160] [161] As we see here:

"It seemed to me that my experiences in Britain were pictured by those of Nehemiah, Ezra and Mordecai. (Brother Hemery believed that he antityped Eliashib and Hanani in Nehemiah); that my credentials were referred to in Ezra 7:11-26 and Neh. 2:7. From what is said in Ezra 7:11-26 and symbolized in Es [Esther] 8:2, 15, I concluded that I was privileged to become the Steward and Brother Russell's successor."

(Apparently, Johnson was a bit mad!)

In a subsequent pamphlet *Another Harvest Siftings Reviewed* (August 22, 1918), which was a lengthy apology, Johnson uses a new concept coined by one of the rebel board members. During a heated discussion with Johnson regarding Rutherford's takeover of the organization, I. F. Hoskins introduced something he called "Rutherfordism." [162] Johnson immediately grasped the critical-ideological dimensions of it, and wrote about the incident in his 1918 pamphlet. The action came too late, of course. Johnson and the other rebels were forever ousted, shut out of the organization, and although Johnson would reappear later, it was *Rutherfordism* that triumphed and assumed Russell's life's work.

When you look beneath Johnson's flowery, peculiar and allegorical rhetoric, at its simplest it is probably about the power struggle and the ensuing grandiosity that Johnson lost. As the loser, Johnson endured all sorts of accusations right through to his death in 1950. Today, some 100 years later, these accusations about Johnson are maintained by the Watchtower Society. It must be emphasized that Johnson, Russell's former friend and secretary, was *never* considered as Russell's successor.

The Lord Supported the Seventh Volume

In *The Watchtower* of 1916, the Seventh Volume is mentioned several times, and it is highly conceivable that Russell intended the Seventh Volume in his series *Studies in the Scriptures* would eventually be written and published. Some even think Russell had written a rough draft. I doubt this is the case, since the draft notes have never been revealed, and the finished book, released on July 17, 1917, in no way resembled Russell's previous work. If Russell started a draft, it would have undoubtedly been rough and probably not used. Yet it is possible Russell had compiled materials for the Seventh Volume, since Rutherford was able to publish it so soon after Russell's death. No matter what, it is said the preparation and production was realized by two of Russell's trusted co-workers, Clayton J. Woodworth and George H. Fisher,[163] both from Scranton, Pennsylvania.

The preface states:

"While both residing in the same city, they have worked separate and apart from each other, not even comparing notes. The reader will be able to judge how fully the work of each harmonizes with that of the other and with the Divine Plan, thus giving further evidence of the Lord's direction in this matter" (Publisher's Preface, *Studies* 7, 1917, p. 6).

History shows that one of these two "miraculous writers," George H. Fisher, who wrote much of the Seventh Volume, later left Rutherford's Bible Students. In 1926, Fisher advocated that Rutherford had to be disfellowshipped. Woodworth continued to edit *The Golden Age* and the subsequent periodical *Consolations*. Woodworth was born in 1870, and he died on November 18, 1951, on Staten Island. According to my source, Clayton was married twice, with one child by each marriage.[164]

My research revealed C. J. Woodworth was obsessed with religious "purity" and other somewhat unusual topics. He became a leading advocate for the Watchtower Society's blood policy, among others.[165] Lee Elder writes that Woodworth suffered from *dissociative disorders*, which may have affected his perception of reality and personal identity.

A rather strange story about Woodworth was revealed in an article I located on the internet.[166] The article claims Woodworth, in a period when he was critical of Russell, was "completely under demonical control." Woodworth penned a 36-page manuscript criticizing Russell, which Woodworth must have later burned. He continued within the movement until 1951.

Now that we know something of the authors, what about the Seventh Volume's content? The book offers commentary on Revelation (written by Woodworth), the Song of Solomon and Ezekiel's book (written by Fisher), and was reported to be a summary of Russell's views. In reality, it reflected a diffuse perplexity, as its authors indulged themselves in a wild verse-by-verse interpretation of Revelation and the other books, according to the Bible Student's history. It was supplemented by further comments on church history, and an alleged summary of Russell's chronological considerations, predictions and guesswork about the near future. The Seventh Volume looks at Paul, Martin Luther, William Miller and Charles Russell with sympathy.

The book's harsh tone against established Christian groups, the Catholic Church and the American Protestant denominations (representing the despicable and soon-to-fall Babylon), was an important instrument to play for Rutherford and *his kind* of Bible Students, who used it to fulfill Russell's prophetic expectations. Apparently, through the Seventh Volume's rhetoric, Rutherford sought direct confrontation with the many churches in the United States. Since the Bible Students, according to Russell's predictions, already awaited a swift and concerted attack from Babylon, as another necessary event heralding Judgment Day, Rutherford seems all too happy to nudge things forward. Anticipation among the members for the Lord's *intervention* and *attacks* against the churches and the secular governments, the subsequent uptake of the elect to heavenly life, and the governments' collapse in the great apocalyptic battle, Armageddon, could only aid Rutherford's cause.

The authors' nebulous speculations probably helped unite and retain the *old* Bible Students who remained in the movement, still comprising about 70% of the membership in 1917. They waited anxiously on the governments' and the churches' coordinated attacks against the Society; it would assure them that they were on the right path.

The attack was to come with swiftness and in a manner even Russell could not have imagined.

Violent Persecution

In 1918, the so-called "harvest work" ended, and a violent persecution of the Bible Students began in Canada and spread across the United States. The attacks corresponded perfectly to the Bible Students' expectations. As Norwegian writer Jan S. Haugland noted, the wildness of the persecution "fit nicely into the Bible Student's expectations, but its sheer ferocity may have surprised even them."[167]

The period from 1918 to 1925 was to be a time of incredible events with Jehovah, Christ and Satan participating, as well as their angel flocks and demon hordes. It would have an almost apocalyptic and universal quality. The whole world, the earth, sun and moon, plus space and the evil spirits' realm, as well as wonders and forces of nature, would manifest in the Bible Students' Judgment Day. Around October 1925, the "Kingdom" people had anticipated for more than 2,000 years would be restored on the earth (p. 128).

The Seventh Volume, based on Revelation 7:3, says:

"No doubt Satan *believed* the Millennial Kingdom was due to be set up in 1915; and no doubt, also, he knew that seven years prior to the time of the setting up of that kingdom the restraints upon the evil spirits would be lifted. Be that as it may, there is evidence that the establishment of the Kingdom in Palestine will probably be in 1925, ten years later than we once calculated. The 70 jubilees, reckoned as 50 years each, expire October, 1925..." (p. 128; see also "jubilee years" in the next chapter).

The Seventh Volume also indicates the Russellites confusion at the time. The authors embraced the view that only a few years remained until Judgment Day, anticipating it would arrive in 1925 (p. 128), but simultaneously prepared readers that the world's end might not come until a somewhat more distant date.

Their reasoning is complex, leading up to the following:

"The awakening of the sleeping saints, AD 1878, was just half way (three and one-half years each way) between the beginning of the Times of Restitution in 1874 and the close of the High Calling in 1881. Our proposition is that the glorification of the Little Flock in the Spring of 1918 AD will be half way (three and one-half years each way) between the close of the Gentile Times and the close of the Heavenly Way, AD 1921. The three days' (three years—1918–1921) fruitless search for Elijah (2 Kings 2:17-18) is a confirmation of this view. We shall wait to see; but we shall not be indifferent while we wait, lest peradventure another, more zealous, take the crown we have. The time is not long: but if we have to go on for fifty years, why should we care? We are the Lord's. Let Him do as He will with His own" (*Studies* 7, p. 64-65, 1917).

Brother Hatred

Even as the Seventh Volume was labored over, dramatic developments were afoot in Brooklyn:

While Rutherford was traveling, Macmillan summoned a policeman to remove Hirsh, Hoskins, Ritchie (who had been replaced by Pierson in January 1917) and Wright from Society headquarters on Hicks Street. Macmillan accused them of creating unrest. Macmillan needed to prevent the four critics from holding a Board meeting, since Rutherford was not present and they constituted a quorum. According to Macmillan, they were escorted to the door by a baton-swinging police officer. The four men claimed the policeman ceased attempts to expel them, yet all four were evicted from the Brooklyn Bethel home at Columbia Heights 124. (Penton, 1986, p. 54 and 320; *Light After Darkness*, 1917)

Reports of the expulsions show the drama within the movement—drama that particularly lacked "brotherly" spirit, even though the men greeted each other as *brother this* and *brother that*. For example: Brother Johnson wanted to read a letter from Brother Pierson, who at the time was loyal to the old leadership. Brother Rutherford refused this and accused Brother Johnson of having misinformed Brother Pierson. When Brother Johnson protested, Brother Rutherford assaulted Johnson so that he nearly fell, and Rutherford said: "You have to leave this house before night; if you do not go, you will be put out!" Brother Johnson's personal belongings were literally removed and placed in front of the Bethel home, while guards monitored the property to be sure Brother Johnson did not return. Vice president Pierson, who initially supported Rutherford, found it difficult to decide where to place his loyalty, but in the end chose to follow Brother Rutherford. (See also, Penton, p. 53)

I admit, in our era, it is difficult to clearly comprehend what really happened, but it seems to me that it is Russell himself who, through his fundamentally *authoritarian* leadership, condoned the bad habits that now enabled Rutherford to consolidate his position—assisted by his most loyal supporters, William VanAmburgh and A. H. Macmillan, the former being responsible for finances and the latter for office workers.

In 1955, Marley Cole published the book *The Jehovah's Witnesses—The New World Society* in cooperation with the Watchtower Society in New York. The book was probably a response to Brooklyn-based professor Herbert H. Stroup's book from 1945. Unlike Stroup's work, Cole had access to inside knowledge because he was a member of the Jehovah's Witnesses,[168] ensuring it would be a big seller, as it was recommended reading for the Witnesses. I even bought the book when it was published in 1955.[169]

Cole attempted to explain Rutherford's actions:

"Rutherford made no bones about 'going ahead.' The Pastor before him had worked that way. The Pastor made decisions. The Pastor issued administrative orders without the Board's prior sanction. They had not challenged the Pastor. But Rutherford was not Pastor Russell" (Cole, 1955, p. 87).

This quote from Cole also suggests that Russell's management had been rather arbitrary and despotic, insights the Society apparently found interesting in the 1950s. His words also seem to imply there was little difference between the two leaders—except regarding approachability. Among workers in Brooklyn, however, for some time a hidden dissatisfaction had been simmering due to organizational practices, displeasure with coworkers and other conditions, grievances the workers could not express because "the Steward" and the "faithful servant" blocked the criticism. From Cole's statement, one can conclude that people were afraid to speak up while Russell lived, but after his death resentments exploded, and Rutherford's manner exacerbated the situation. The Bible Students' New York congregation felt that there was fault on both sides; 150 members (of about 1,000) signed a letter requesting an independent hearing of the two sides. Rutherford refused, saying, "There are to be no neutrals."

It is also my impression—and I can very well understand why—some members, such as Pierson, vacillated between factions. For, though Rutherford was often swaggering and ruthless, he could be equally kind and considerate and seems to have been when expedience prompted it, as the P. S. L. Johnson problem indicates. (*Harvest Siftings*, August 1917)

Rutherford's critics planned to address the attendees at a convention in Boston in August 1917, a period when they thought they were still the rightful directors of the Society—as they probably were—but Rutherford controlled the speaker schedule with an iron fist and spirit, and none of them got the opportunity to speak. In *Jehovah's Witnesses in the Divine Purpose*, published in 1959, is an interesting and revealing passage about this incident:

"The opposition group thought they could take control of this convention, but Brother Rutherford was determined that they would not do so. To forestall any move on their part in this regard, Rutherford himself, as the Society's president, served as permanent chairman of the convention. In this way he was able to control every session, and those in opposition were not permitted at any time to address the assembly. As a result, the convention was a complete success to Jehovah's praise and a complete failure to those seeking to interrupt the Kingdom work" (*Divine Purpose*, 1959, p. 72).

Straw Poll of December 1917

Rutherford's opponents reportedly now concentrated all their attention on the annual meeting of the parent corporation scheduled for January 1918 in Pittsburgh. The victorious party saw events this way:

"The next move on the part of the ambitious opponents of the Society was an effort to get control of the corporation meeting scheduled for January, 1918, in Pittsburgh. At this annual corporation meeting it was proposed that the new directors appointed by Brother Rutherford would be elected as a legal confirmation of his appointment of them. Brother Rutherford knew that this meeting would furnish the last desperate chance for these opposers of the Society to get control. He was reasonably certain that the majority of the brothers were not in favor of such a move. But the majority would not have an opportunity to express themselves at the election, since it was a corporation matter and must be handled by only those who were members of the legally constituted Watch Tower Bible and Tract Society" (*Divine Purpose*, 1959, p. 72).

Rutherford played his cards cleverly. Before the annual meeting he launched a sort of *test voting* (or a straw poll) in all congregations in the United States. If this was just one of the rules of the game, I honestly do not know—I think not. On December 13, 1917, ballots from the 813 American congregations were counted, and 10,869 out of 11,421 voted in favor of Rutherford as president. (Cole, 1955, p. 87-90; *Divine Purpose*, 1959, p. 72)

The outcome says more than words, illustrating how power and prestige influenced the members and top executives, as the election figures show Rutherford would be the winner of the coming election. Whether the election, viewed objectively, was a success is probably a matter of taste. It was a personal success for Rutherford, and it was the most important for him.

Nineteen candidates presented themselves for the board positions of director, president, vice president and secretary-treasurer. Here, we are concerned with only the most prominent, those who battled for board procedures and membership. It is remarkable that Hirsh, Hoskins, Johnson, Ritchie, Rockwell, Wright and many other critics of Rutherford may still have participated on this occasion—even after their expulsion in the summer of 1917.

Rutherford received the highest number of votes for board membership in the straw poll with 10,990. VanAmburgh was second with 10,909. The other candidates were as follows:

G. H. Fisher (10,333), J. A. Bohnet (10,323), A. H. Macmillan (10,204); W. E. Spill (9,880); A. N. Pierson (8,888); C. J. Woodworth (1,776); Sturgeon (680); Ritchie, opponent (543); Hirsh, opponent (469); Hoskins, opponent (459); Wright, opponent (444;); and Rockwell (342). Paul Johnson was thirteenth with 126 votes. Had the straw poll been binding, Rutherford would have been elected both as president and board member with the highest number of votes cast, respectively 10,869 and 10,990. As a presidential candidate, P. S. L. Johnson got just twenty votes, largely due to the great Philadelphia congregation not participating in the voting. Discussion about the *straw poll* erased any doubt about the outcome of the actual election. The critics had been unable to establish a realistic alternative to Rutherford, who had won the battle for the general members' loyalty almost immediately. (*WT*, Dec. 15, 1917; Cole, 1955, p. 89-90; figures above are according to the Society)

The *Watch Tower* of December 15, 1917, concedes some misgivings about the straw poll: "Some of the classes [congregations] laboring under a misapprehension, as we are advised, neglected to take that vote.... Fifty-five classes reported that they were unable or unwilling to vote."

The first seven "elected" in the straw vote made up the new board of the Watch Tower Society; among them were the four new board members Rutherford appointed in July 1917. Not one of the four critics—Hirsh, Hoskins, Ritchie and Wright—who had all been nominated were elected, not even A. I. Ritchie, the former vice president who Rutherford had pushed out. After this, the voting members of the Pennsylvania Corporation knew which way the wind blew—like a gale in Rutherford's direction. By the annual meeting in January 1918 the opposition would have to acknowledge the game was lost forever. Thirty-one workers at Bethel would be excluded, including P. S. L. Johnson and the "big four"—as Rutherford mockingly called them in *Harvest Siftings.* (*Divine Purpose*, 1959, p. 71-73)

In truth, the straw poll was basically absurd. It was not legally binding and a number of classes had not participated. Rutherford likely used this straw poll to determine where his opposition was concentrated and which candidates still threatened his position, even though he had been *elected for life.*

The annual meeting commenced on Saturday, January 5, 1918. Approximately 163,300 shares were voted, or around nine percent more than the previous year. The Society's report says J. F. Rutherford received 194,106 votes as director of the Society—about 30,000 more than the total shares voting! Add to that the discrepancy of the 23,000+/- shares cast for each of the following: Hirsh, Hoskins, Ritchie and Wright, who all surely would not have voted for Rutherford, nor Macmillan and VanAmburgh. It's been said that the proxy form Rutherford issued to the shareholders was so cleverly worded that it gave the proxy holders attending the meeting the authority to use the votes as they saw fit, despite any reservations the shareholders may have indicated in writing. There were to be seven directors elected; each shareholder could vote for seven candidates. It could be that Rutherford used cumulative voting (sorting)—assigning seven votes to fewer than seven persons, even if all seven votes were to just one person—for more than 8,000 shares (presumably Russell's shares), even if the shareholders had not been made aware of such a possibility. James Parkinson and Jerry Leslie conclude that the total number of votes cast from Russell's shares may have been 100,000 (±20,000). One can only speculate how the election results might have been different if the five trustees—Sister E. Louise Hamilton, Sister Almeta M. Nation Robison, Sister J. G. Herr, Sister C. Tomlin and Sister Alice G. James—had voted Russell's shares as he had dictated in his 1907 testament. (Email from James Parkinson)

After the meeting, *The Watch Tower* published the following results:

J. F. Rutherford, 194,106; A. H. Macmillan, 161,871; W. E. VanAmburgh, 160,215; W. E. Spill, 118,259; J. A. Bohnet, 113,422; C. H. Anderson, 107,175; G. H. Fisher, 83,260; A. N. Pierson, 57,721; Menta Sturgeon, 27,261; R. H. Hirsh, 23,198; I. F. Hoskins, 22,660; A. I. Ritchie, 22,631; J. D. Wright, 22,623; H. C. Rockwell, 18,178; P. S. L. Johnson, 6,469; W. J. Hollister, 3,931.

Note that Robert Hirsh, despite massive opposition from Rutherford, still got 23,198 votes.

Poly Russellism

According to *The Watch Tower* (1918, p. 23), shortly after the annual meeting the opposition formed an independent association ruled by a Committee of Seven and celebrated an annual memorial commemoration on March 26, 1918. This marked the final break, and any sense of spiritual solidarity with *Rutherford's Bible Students* was completely lost. At the new association's convention in the summer of 1918, however, the opposition further divided. The result was a series of new associations and small sects, of which the largest and most enduring was the Associated Bible Students[170] (with no central leadership, the group has cooperated with the Pastoral Bible Institute since 1918), while in later years the Dawn Bible Students Association became the most prominent publishing house. (Established circa 1930; source: James Parkinson and Jerry Leslie)

In 1919, Paul Johnson founded yet another association, the Layman's Home Missionary Movement, and he subsequently published seventeen titles under the umbrella *Epiphany Studies in the Scriptures* (the last two posthumously), plus he produced two magazines from 1918 until his death in 1950: *The Present Truth* (for believers) and another magazine called *The Bible Standard* (for the public). Two former directors of the Bible Student movement, R. G. Jolly and journalist Robert Hirsh supported Johnson. Rutherford's opponents suffered disagreements, and soon one group after another emerged from the morass following Russell's death. Apart from those already mentioned, there were: The Stand Fast Bible Students Association, 1918 (more than 1,000 members); The Elijah Voice Society, 1923 (nearly 300; a splinter from the Stand-Fast movement); The Christian Millennial Fellowship, 1928; and the strangest of them all, The Servants of Yah, which was led by one C. H. Zook, who believed that Satan's name was Jehovah, so Jehovah's Witnesses in reality were Satan's Witnesses. The latter group gradually slipped into oblivion. Three other groups also worth mentioning: Concordant Publishing Concern,[171] Assemblies of Yahweh and Free Bible Students.

The largest group to come out of the Watchtower Society was the Philanthropic Association, or Man's Friends. This group was led by Alexander Freytag, manager of the Swiss branch of the Watch Tower Society beginning in 1898. In 1917 he began publishing his views (using the Society's presses and resources) in *The Message of Laodicea* (*Le Message de Laodicée*), in which he claimed that he was Russell's only legitimate heir. Rutherford ousted Freytag in 1919. Freytag founded a group he named the Angel of the Lord (inspired by a verse of the Apocalypse), and then changed it to Angel of Jehovah Bible and Tract Society, and finally Church of the Kingdom of God or the Philanthropic Assembly of the Friends of Man. This group worked particularly in France and Switzerland. At its peak it had 50,000 members, who all hoped for an earthly paradise. Freytag published a four-volume work in French, later translated into English, Spanish, German, Italian, Portuguese and Dutch. He also published a songbook, penning both lyrics and music, and a devotional book. He wrote innumerable pamphlets and tracts, published two magazines, *The Monitor of the Reign of Justice*, a monthly, and the weekly *Paper For All*. Freytag's model was clearly C. T. Russell, whose role as publisher set an example with an incredible trickle-down effect to his bereaved disciples. In 1951, the movement turned increasingly to philanthropy: help for disadvantaged, relief for the disaster-stricken and material to aid farmers. (*Wikipedia*, 2011; *Proclaimers*, 1993, p. 628; Bible Student Ministries, Daughters of the Tower and A Brief History of the Bible Students since 1917, all located on the internet, 2011)[172] [173]

The strongest motivation for fracturing the Bible Student movement, which I have tried to portray, seems to have been individual desire for power over the good of the movement after the founder's death. When it became clear that their options were exhausted within the original Bible Student movement, the dissenters started their own associations and maintained claim to Russell's legacy. I am tempted to call the resulting collection of movements *Poly Russellism.*

Today, the various Bible Student groups count only about 70,000 members. Most groups are apparently not as tightly organized as the Watch Tower Movement, which really increases the suspicion that strong leadership and the tight structure of the organization are what appealed to so many. Rutherford's desire for power played into the members' need for an authoritarian leader who could stabilize members' sense of identity and their expectations for the near future.

Perhaps another Bible Student could have put himself forward and assumed leadership of the Watch Tower Society—for example, Pierson or Hirsh. It's probably unrealistic to think either of them would have been adequate, because Russell's remaining followers needed a solid and strong beacon to lead them and the movement into the future. Had one of them stepped in, the movement probably would not be the size it is today; it probably would have fractured even more because of prominent members desiring to inherit Russell's dominance and power. Maybe that is why Rutherford came to lead, taking Russell's project even wider into the world. Rutherford also seems to have inherited Russell's dark side: absolute power over an organization and unquestionable influence over an association that seemed perhaps close to dissolution in 1917.

There is bitter irony in the fact that Rutherford's innermost desire was not to continue the founder's ideas, but rather, as it eventually turned out, to consolidate and build his own "earthly paradise" where he could reign unchallenged without risking dismissal.

Astoundingly, this goal eventually succeeded in full for him.

Chapter 14

Prelude to the Trial

The date July 17, 1917, was a milestone in the history of the Watchtower Society and the Bible Students. On that day Rutherford not only threw his critics out of headquarters, but later he announced the release of the Seventh Volume or *The Finished Mystery*, as it was named. Although not destined to make any *bestseller list*, the book became a bestseller in its own right with sure sales within the movement and subsequent distribution in huge quantities. While not a bestseller as we think of the description today, *The Finished Mystery* still had impressive sales. The book, which members had long hoped Russell would write and already, long before its release, referred to as the Seventh Volume, would be the final book in the *Studies in Scriptures* series. The book arrived with the impact of a bomb, surprising and unexpected, but contrary to the anticipated reception, it contributed to disunity in the movement and a looming conflict with the US government.

The Judge was a man of action and he undoubtedly knew that to rescue the movement from crumbling he had to sustain a kind of frenzied environment among the supporters. He fulfilled this through large-scale propaganda campaigns—apparently beginning with the release of the Seventh Volume. He was in "full harmony with Russell's view that the Witnesses must be busy..." (*Divine Purpose*, 1959, p. 66).

Still, for all Rutherford's determination and planning, the difficulties following Russell's death in 1916 soon aligned to more or less paralyze the movement's activities for a time.

In 1917, the admittedly incomplete report of the members' participation in the Memorial showed that 21,274 members had been present. At the Memorial celebration in 1919 the number had dropped to 17,961; the Watch Tower Society estimates less than 4,000 had left the organization. This trend would develop more strikingly the following years until the early 1930s, when most of the original Bible Students had left the movement. In 1917 it seems that the majority of members received the Seventh Volume with great enthusiasm, if one can believe the Watchtower publishers, and during the following seven months 850,000 copies sold. *The Watch Tower* from March 1918 stated:

"The sale of the Seventh Volume is unparalleled by the sale of any other book known, in the same length of time, excepting the Bible" (*Divine Purpose*, 1959, p. 73).

In Australia, the reactions apparently were different than in America. When leaders at Watch Tower headquarters in Melbourne and congregations throughout the country read the Seventh Volume, most workers and members withdrew *en masse* from the movement.

Rutherford and his associates had bet on a success. They had worked feverishly for months to get the book proofread and printed as quickly as possible, so that it could be published *before* the war ended. The timing seems to have been crucial for the sales. However, the publication led to a prohibition in Canada in early 1918, while opposition to the Bible Students' activities also increased in the US. The book also became important evidence in the US government's case against the leaders of the Society from March to June 1918. The trial will be explored in the next chapter, but I will mention here that when one of the book's authors, Clayton J. Woodworth, was cross-examined in 1918 he was asked whether he believed *The Finished Mystery* would achieve higher sales if it was completed and published *before* the war ended.

Woodworth said: "I judged if the end of the war would follow shortly after its publication that it would attract the attention of Bible students everywhere as being a correct interpretation of the Book of Revelation." It was clearly an evasive answer! The government's attorney then asked: "Your thought was to get it on the market *before* the war was over?" Woodworth: "Yes, sir." The government's lawyer: "That that would enhance its sales?" Woodworth: "Yes, sir" (*Divine Purpose*, 1959, p. 70-73; *Qualified*, 1955, p. 314; Etavot, 1959, p. 291; *Proclaimers*, 1993, p. 69; Jim Whitney's documentary article on the trial in 1918, see endnote 179).

The pattern seen here was and is typical of management's approach to solving problems. While they warred for supremacy in the Society, the Seventh Volume was written, proofread, ordered from the printer (W. A. Conkey of Hammond, Indiana),[174] and then produced in the greatest haste. The preparation and anticipation was part of yet another campaign with a powerful theme to direct the members' energy and attention away from problems within the organization toward something new and exciting that could fill the void left by the doomsday debacle of 1914 and by the significant changes in management after C. T. Russell's death. Again, it is Revelation, the last book in the Bible that, as usual, was interpreted as actual and applied to contemporary events, and with it the claim that Russell had been the last of the brilliant reformers. Typically, the Society moved to focus on the traditional enemy, Christendom's clergy, which rather obviously had tired of the Bible Students' incessant smear campaigns. The ordinary Bible Students were simply "drowned" in campaign after campaign.

From autumn 1914 until 1917, the Bible Students had little to be proud of, according to the 1959 history book. Today the Society interprets it as the members being in mourning,[175] which they believed was foretold in Revelation 11:3: "And I will grant my two witnesses power to prophesy for one thousand two hundred and sixty days, clothed in sackcloth." And, yes, they actually had a lot to be ashamed of in connection with the Judgment Day hysteria in 1914 when so few of the predicted events came to pass, and the supporters were left to struggle along in the same old evil and familiar world.

That proceedings within the Bible Students' movement between 1914 and 1918 could have been described in the Bible several thousand years in advance is a bit hard to believe. Still, the allegorical and symbolic interpretation of the books of Daniel and Revelation gave the Bible Students a prophetical and grandiose framework within which they could find new strength. Although they were persecuted by Satan's henchmen, they just needed to stay the course, for soon the Lord would intervene and lift them up to heavenly glory. And, though the Day of Judgment was apparently delayed, there were still just a few years before everything in the existing world would be turned upside down. Either 3-1/2 years from October 1914 to 1918, or—since 1918 ended in failure—eleven years from 1914 to 1925, when again incredible things between heaven and earth *had* to happen. (RSV, 1971; *Daniel's Prophecy*, 1999, p. 286; *Divine Purpose*, 1959, p. 79)[176]

New Provocative Tracts

As the power struggle of 1917–1918 continued within the Bible Students, even after the dismissal of the four illegally elected board members and the release of the Seventh Volume, new initiatives had to be taken to break the deadlock. For this purpose, concurrent with the straw poll discussed earlier, the Watch Tower Society and its sympathizers began mass distribution of a tabloid-sized, four-page tract, *The Bible Student's Monthly*, on December 30, 1917. Production numbered 10 million copies. (No, it's no mistake: 10,000,000 copies!) In this new highly provocative tract it was once more proclaimed that various churches were the modern Babylon, but now with even stronger language. *The Fall of Babylon* was declared on the front page, and on the back was a provocative drawing of the priests from "Romanism" and "Protestantism" climbing through the ruins of Christendom. The masthead of *The Bible Students Monthly* stated it was "An Independent, Unsectarian Religious Newspaper, Specially Devoted to the Forwarding of the Laymen's Home Missionary Movement," though obviously, as demonstrated by the tract itself, was closely associated with IBSA, the official name of the Bible Students International Association.[177] The contents included extracts from the Seventh Volume.

Page two of the tract states: "Through the press and through leaflets the story is being widely circulated that Kaiser Wilhelm is the Antichrist. This is not the Bible view, however. There Antichrist is set forth as a system, not as an individual. According to the Reformers the real Antichrist is the Papacy. The effort to make the people believe that the Kaiser is Antichrist is doubtless a deception—dust throwing—Papal camouflage, to divert attention from the real Antichrist-Papacy. Everyone knows that the Kaiser is an instrument of the Devil. To accomplish his purpose, Satan appears as an angel of light. (2 Cor. 11:14) To prevent people from seeing the real Antichrist, he directs attention to a lesser instrument of his. / The Apostles prophesied that Antichrist would arise in the Church. Afterwards many recognized the Papacy as Antichrist" (*The Bible Students Monthly*, "The Fall of Babylon," no. 9, 1917, p. 2; hereinafter only indicated by the page number).

Whether it is just this passage that agitated church leaders throughout the US to a degree that they helped move the government against the Bible Students, I do not know, but the churches reacted strongly. It's especially likely Catholic circles were behind attacks on the movement, which apparently was done in the shadow of the US entering World War I in April 1918. The sensation in this tract was, in fact, not very sensational, because the Protestant reformers of centuries past, which the tract also notes, had similar views on the Catholic Church's role as the Antichrist, only now, in a war situation that kind of expression was improper—the US needed to unite against the common *German* enemy.

Finally, this tract states:

"What joy will pervade the earth when Babylon [Christianity] is completely annihilated! It will be followed by the glorious Kingdom of Messiah. Long have honest, order-loving Christian people prayed for the coming of that Kingdom. It will be the desire of all nations. Then universal peace will prevail and they will learn war no more forever" ("The Fall of Babylon," p. 4).

An advertisement in the tract promotes Russell's six-volume work, *Studies in the Scriptures*, plus the Seventh Volume, *The Finished Mystery*: "NOW ONLY $4.60, POSTPAID." If anyone was in doubt about who produced this tract, the advertisement for the Seventh Volume dispelled it.

The reactions that followed, reactions which may have had roots in the long-standing hatred of the Bible Students, now came to full expression.

Chapter 15

The Traitors!

According to the Society's official explanation, the Seventh Volume drew a strong response from US authorities, resulting in sensational charges of treason and other things against Society executives. This book and other publications distributed to the public in huge editions from December 1917 onward seemed designed to escalate conflict with other church leaders, and this exacerbated tensions leading to the arrest and imprisonment of Bible Students' leaders. According to the government, the actions of Society leadership were much more egregious than simply taunting the Christian denominations, however. In response, the Society released several tabloid-sized pamphlets.

On March 15, 1918, the Society issued a tract, *Kingdom News No. 1*. It treated such subjects as: "Religious Intolerance—Pastor Russell's Followers Persecuted Because They Tell the People the Truth—Treatment of Bible Students Smacks of the 'Dark Ages'."

Persecution of the Bible Students occurred primarily in the US and Canada, and the Society put the blame on leaders from various Christian denominations. In all likelihood, the conspiracy against the Bible Students probably did come from the suspected circles, and it seems those same sources wished, once and for all, to take the lives of Russellites in one manner or another. As we look back on the situation, the latter suggestion seems like a harsh exaggeration, although the animosity certainly ran deep.

At this point I don't believe Rutherford, VanAmburgh, Macmillan and the other Bible Student leaders were aware of the degree of danger. They stayed their course, undaunted, hurling wild accusations against the clergy and Babylon, and propagandizing descriptions of the dire prospects for the world's future.

Proclaimers wrote in 1993 concerning the release of *Kingdom News No. 1*:

"To expose this clergy-inspired pressure, on March 15, 1918, the Watch Tower Society released the tract *Kingdom News* No. 1. Its message? The six-column-wide headline read: 'Religious Intolerance—Pastor Russell's Followers Persecuted Because They Tell the People the Truth.' Below the heading 'Treatment of Bible Students Smacks of the "Dark Ages"' were set forth the facts of the persecution and the ban that had begun in Canada. The instigators? The tract pulled no punches in pointing to the clergy, who were described as 'a bigoted class of men who have systematically endeavored to prevent the people from understanding the Bible and to throttle all Bible teaching unless it comes through them.' What a hard-hitting message!" (*Proclaimers*, 1993, p. 69–70; Kingdom News, Watchtower Archive at http://wtarchive.svhelden.info/english/kingdom-news/)

The contents of *Kingdom News No. 1* also expressed the Bible Students' thoughts about war. The tract also featured a report about the Seventh Volume, as well as a little about the churches' opposition to this book. An advertisement invited people to a lecture by J. F. Rutherford: "The World Has Ended, Millions Now living May Never Die!… A free lecture by Hon. J. F. Rutherford, member New York state bar" (*Divine Purpose*, 1959, p. 77).

The tract also commented on the United States' right to declare war and register men for compulsory service in the armed forces:

"We recognize that the United States government, being a political and economic institution, has the power and authority, under its fundamental law, to declare war and to draft its citizens into military service. We have no disposition to interfere with the draft or the war in any manner. The fact that some of our members have sought to take advantage of the protection of the law, has been used as another means of persecution" (*Divine Purpose*, 1959, p. 77).

Clearly, Rutherford and his close associates were getting nervous. Had they passed a point of no return?

Kingdom News No. 2 was no better when it was released on April 15, 1918; it "contained an even stronger message against the religious-political conspiracy that was aimed at destroying the Society." According to the Society's 1959 history book, the clergy encouraged the "government agencies to harass the Society, to make arrests, to object to *The Finished Mystery* and cause the brothers to cut out certain pages from the book, which really was a compromise…" (*Divine Purpose*, 1959, p. 78).

And: "This issue of *Kingdom News* repeated the stand the Witnesses had taken on war and explained their belief as to what constituted the true church." And to substantiate that said conspiracy was international, the *Kingdom News* included a quotation from a Danish newspaper:

"The Consistory of Kiel (Holstein, Germany) is calling the attention of the (Lutheran) priests to the activities carried on by the Millennium sect, which calls itself 'Watch Tower Bible and Tract Society,' and also 'Bible Students Association.' The imperial war department has recently requested us to keep a watchful eye on the activities of this sect, which consist in selling the writings of its founder, the lately deceased Pastor Russell, of Brooklyn, North America, in untiring propaganda work, accomplished with American money. The Consistory does, therefore, call the priests' attention to this sect and requests that they take action against it and report to the Consistory their observations of its dangerous activities" (*Divine Purpose*, 1959, p. 78; no source is specified, but the quote may be from about 1917–1918).

The rhetoric and proposed actions from Protestant churches in Europe and North America are strong indeed and seem to carry much weight, but we must remember this was an era where churches and their pastors had an entirely different status than today. One doesn't need to agree with the Witnesses' radical position and their view of these events in order to see the Bible Students were victims of religious and secular intolerance.

One might have expected Rutherford and his associates to act less boldly in the face of such powerful and widespread opposition. However, instead of holding back the smear campaign and propaganda in this very tense domestic political situation, the Bible Students continued their hostile rhetoric against the churches, Babylon, and the secular authorities. Moreover, it was at a time when Rutherford and his henchmen probably understood—or at least sensed—that something more serious was afoot and that the government was preparing legal initiatives and possible actions against them. Although the published indictment indicated the charges stemmed from *certain passages* in the Seventh Volume—and this is what the Society still claims today—there were probably far more serious reasons, as I will below try to illustrate.

As if things weren't boiling enough already, *Kingdom News No. 3* appeared on May 1, 1918. This edition carried the headline: "Two Great Battles Raging—Fall of Autocracy Certain—Satanic Strategy Doomed to Failure—The Birth of Antichrist." It stated: "Tracing the antichrist from its birth to the current deeds of the apostate hands of the Catholic and Protestant clergy, it revealed that *such agents of the Devil were out now to destroy the remnant of Christ's seed*, the anointed ones who follow in the footsteps of Jesus." Translated, this meant that the Catholic and Protestant clergy were trying to destroy Rutherford's Bible Students, who were—in their own eyes—nothing less than Christ's only true successors. At this point it is highly conceivable that Society executives, Rutherford, Macmillan and VanAmburgh, were aware of the government's preliminary investigations for a subsequent lawsuit. (*Divine Purpose*, 1959, p. 78; italics are mine)

Rutherford's intensified rhetoric, garnished with hatred and intransigence, was manifested then. He attuned himself to this rhetoric, his propaganda tool, to present engaging ideas and speculative theories to the members, reinforcing their critical attitude toward the surrounding community and the world, while creating enthusiasm and renewed commitment to the movement. The sharp new rhetoric stirred the membership, which probably was also the intent. It sold the message. Though it was a widespread view among Bible Students that the Day of Judgment was imminent and the sign of the Lord's intervention against Babylon and "Satan's system" would be the destruction of the Christian churches ("the annihilation"), I am not certain Rutherford believed this in his core. He was, after all, too well educated, and a lawyer, accustomed to thinking in concrete, analytical paths. He was what one must *not* become within the movement today: the product of a higher education. Still, he had fought for power over the group; it was his "life's coup" and its program was a crazy, metaphysical message, based on the Seventh Volume's wild interpretations of Revelation, which he needed to embrace. Rutherford had little choice but to accept the consequences and remain on his chosen path. In the process, he might be able to deliver a program to create enthusiasm for the crazed apocalyptic fantasies prophesying that God's Kingdom would soon be established on earth, at the latest in 1925! Rutherford and the Bible Students' criticism of the churches resonated among groups who could be recruited to the movement. Internally, the course served to spur members' imaginations and create unity within the movement. The press willingly pounced on every morsel.

To promote that an unofficial *coordinated action* was in progress against the Bible Students, Rutherford later reported—still according to Witnesses' contemporary history—the opinion of General James Franklin Bell, commander of Camp Upton on Long Island, New York. Bell had told Rutherford that in 1917 a group of priests sent a committee to Washington, DC, to deliver an amendment to the Espionage Law. From the Society's history book (1959): "If passed, all cases against the Espionage Law would have been tried before a military court with the death penalty imposed as punishment."

Bell finished by saying, in an excited tone: "This bill did not pass, because Wilson vetoed it; but we know how to get you and we are going to do it!" (*Divine Purpose*, 1959, p. 79)

Woodrow Wilson was apparently a president with his heart at the right place.[178] Still, according to the somewhat one-sided Catholic periodical *The Tablet*, Brooklyn wrote on May 11, 1918: "*Kingdom News* spread around—Some may

In 1918 eight leaders of the Watch Tower Society in Brooklyn, NY, were sentenced to harsh prison sentences following a government indictment and trial. Seated, left to right: A. H. Macmillan, J. F. Rutherford, W. E. VanAmburgh; standing, G. H. Fisher, R. J. Martin, G. De-Cecca, F. H. Robinson and C. J. Woodworth (retouched by Brian Kutscher).

go to jail" (*Divine Purpose*, 1959, p. 79). This Catholic weekly also stated: "Joseph F. Rutherford and some of his colleagues are likely to pass their summer months in a villa where they will be protected from mobs who insult them by asking them to buy liberty bonds..." (*Divine Purpose*, 1959, p. 80).

Around the United States, Rutherford's Bible Students were attacked by mobs, and in many cases exposed to the most terrible humiliation, such as being tarred and feathered.

Clearly, at this time, fervor against the Bible Students reigned in many corners; members were regarded as unpatriotic enemies of the state. A trial soon followed.

American Jim Whitney has performed a thorough investigation of events, and discloses that the government's accusations against the Bible Student leaders may have had much more serious grounds than previously known. The documents also show that Rutherford and his accused co-conspirators were aware of the serious consequences they faced, especially when one considers the climate wherein the events unfolded—one of national mobilization.

The Indictment

A week after the *Kingdom News No. 3* was released, on May 7, 1918, the United States District Court for the Eastern District of New York issued arrest warrants against eight Society executives including Rutherford, VanAmburgh and Macmillan. The Society consistently writes about *eight* accused, but there were actually *nine*. Robert H. Hirsh was the ninth. For a short time in 1917, as a named alternate, he sat on the Society's board of directors until he was among those expelled in July 1917. On May 8, government prosecutor US Marshal Power received the warrant and the eight principal officials were brought to Federal Court, Judge Garvin presiding. The men were accused of subversive activities—*treason*—a very serious accusation. The charges were partly motivated by the members' attitude toward military service, certain sections of the Seventh Volume, and various anti-patriotic and anti-ecclesiastical publications (the tabloid tracts) released by the Society between 1917 and 1918 (allegedly mentioned in the indictment) as discussed above. Today, we have the advantage of viewing the larger context and it seems as if the Seventh Volume and the highly provocative tracts of late 1917 and early 1918 were only the foundation for the very serious allegations to come during the spring and the summer of 1918.

The indictment stated (I quote partly from the book *Jehovah's Witnesses in the Divine Purpose*, 1959, and partly from the original indictment) the eight "unlawfully and feloniously did conspire, combine, confederate and agree together, and with divers other persons to the said Grand Jurors unknown, to commit a certain offense against the United States of America, to wit: the offense of unlawfully, feloniously and willfully causing insubordination, disloyalty and refusal of duty in the military and naval forces of the United States of America when the United States was at war, *to the injury of the military and naval forces of the United States of America, and to the injury of America, in, through and* [portion in italics is found in the indictment but omitted in *Divine Purpose*] by personal solicitations, letters, public speeches, distributing and publicly circulating throughout the United States of America a certain book called 'Volume VII, Bible Studies, The Finished Mystery,' and distributing and publicly throughout the United States certain articles printed in pamphlets called 'Bible Student's Monthly,' 'Watch Tower,' 'Kingdom News' and other pamphlets not named," [*Divine Purpose*'s quote ends here with a full stop.] "*... which said book and pamphlets were to be published and distributed throughout the Eastern District of New York, and throughout other sections of refusal of duty in the said military and naval forces of the United States of America, and which said solicitations, letters, speeches, articles, books and pamphlets would and should persistently urge insubordination, disloyalty* [*, mutiny and the refusal of duty in the military and naval forces of the United States of America*] ... [etc.]" (*Divine Purpose*, 1959, p. 79, the sections indicated by *italics* were omitted when the indictment was reprinted in *Divine Purpose*; Jim Whitney, Part 5;[179] Etavot, 1959, p. 292; *Proclaimers*, 1993, p. 650–656).[180]

Note the charge of incitement to "insubordination" (the italicized part of the quote) was omitted from the history book *Jehovah's Witnesses in the Divine Purpose*. Also note how the quote was altered when the Society's publishers put a full stop after the phrase, "not named," concealing the continuation of the text. In this way, the 1959 reprint in official Society literature, in my opinion, blurs the main reason the government took action.

When viewed in retrospect, it seems as if the government sought out ways to attack the Society's leaders who, from Russell's early days in the 1870s, had been rather anti-militarist and anti-clerical. Everyone knew the Bible Students were conscientious objectors. Most also felt the members were "crazy" and hostile to surrounding communities, which they believed to be in league with Babylon, Antichrist and the Devil. To me, it seems the government accusations against the Bible Student leaders served a *domestic purpose* in a mobilization situation—as an example to US servicemen. It would only undermine the government's authority if it showed weakness toward the anti-militarist propaganda as it mobilized for the war effort. The government needed to exemplify that such anti-military attitudes were either an expression of cowardice or anti-patriotic.

Provided that this is a reasonable analysis, the highly charged atmosphere caused by the United States' entry into World War I in April undoubtedly incited patriotic Americans who were then tempted to run smear campaigns against the Bible Students. And the membership, almost too willingly, had set itself up as a target and scapegoat, existing for so long as a thorny nuisance to those they provoked with their harsh Babylon-talk. There is little doubt the government and the arch-conservative influential forces supporting action against the Bible Students had decided to make an example of them, a warning to other religious minorities who also opposed participation in the World War.

In the end, it was the anti-militarism, conscientious objection and anti-patriotism,[181] and especially the alleged encouragement that conscripts refuse to answer the call to duty, which were interpreted as treason. This was the government's central point of attack against Bible Student leaders, and it explains why, according to Jim Whitney, the Society has since tried to make it look as though the trial only concerned the Seventh Volume and the tracts.

Pre-trial Events

The following represents the major events leading up to the trial:

1. The United States Congress declared war on Germany April 6, 1917.
2. The Society was under investigation for several months before the federal grand jury met from April 3 to May 6, 1918, to assess evidence and decide whether to indict for subversive activities. The indictment was issued on May 6, 1918, and arrests occurred the same day.
3. The eight defendants and their counsel, Sparks, possibly knew of the government's proceedings before May 6, 1918.
4. A search warrant was issued prior to the search of the Society's headquarters in New York and Pittsburgh. The removal of books, documents and correspondence occurred at both locations.
5. The Seventh Volume supposedly was not a key element of the evidence at the preliminary investigation and before the indictment was brought against the Society's president and board. The main evidence consisted of the seized correspondence between the Society and individuals serving in the US Army and Navy. This material must have given government prosecutors reasonable cause to conclude Rutherford and his colleagues actively contributed to obstruct the registration and call for servicemen to active service in the US Army and Navy.

The Trial Begins

Trial preparations probably began in March 1918, but the trial did not start until June 3, 1918. Judge E. L. Garvin[182] was the first to preside over the trial, but had to recuse himself due to bias. Next, Judge T. I. Chatfield, a New York district judge, was chosen but he too was deemed unsuitable to preside over the case. Finally, District Judge Harlan B. Howe of Vermont was selected. Howe was old school and probably skeptical of the Bible Students' propaganda, but nevertheless he handled the case reasonably and conducted the trial to its end. It was also Howe who, one year later, appealed to the government for acquittal of the eight prisoners. The trial itself lasted fifteen days, and it was later determined that mistakes had been made—according to the Society, 125 in all (*Divine Purpose*, 1959, p. 80). The case attracted much publicity, and on June 20, the jury brought back a guilty verdict. Subsequently seven directors were each sentenced to twenty years imprisonment; one director, Giovanni DeCecca, got only ten years. The penalties would be served in the United States' federal prison in Atlanta, Georgia.

Throughout preparing this chapter and the previous one, Robert Hirsh particularly interested me, but it has been difficult to uncover his role or disposition in regards to the trial. Hirsh was the ninth man accused, but even before the trial began, the government sought to abandon the case against him. During the trial, Rutherford's lawyers argued that Hirsh was not a suitable witness for the government. Fred Sparks, Rutherford's attorney, protested Hirsh's testimony because as the indictment alleged—as did the prosecutors—Hirsh was considered a conspirator. Sparks felt that the proposal to abandon the case against Hirsh would free him to become a witness for the government. Judge Howe accepted this objection and made a compromise with Rutherford's lawyers: Despite the dismissal of the Hirsh indictment, they would not bring him forth as a witness against the accused. In fact, it's clear Sparks and his clients feared what Hirsh, a former board member and someone deeply involved in the rebellion against Rutherford, might reveal about Rutherford and his co-defendants.

According to Jim Whitney's assessment, Judge Howe seems to have been fairly reasonable, as he openly admitted the government could have been wrong in the whole affair; he conducted the trial fairly and gave the defenders ample time to make their arguments. Hirsh's exemption from further indictments suggests the government wanted to be as equitable as possible and may have even worked to conclude the case in a way that would make it easier to abolish the sentences after the war was over. Regarding the allegation that the Society's executives were subjected to a hasty and unfair trial—or were *railroaded*, as the Society claims—Jim Whitney concludes this has been greatly exaggerated.[183]

It is shocking to learn that the eight defendants were willing to go to great lengths to escape imprisonment. During the trail on June 4, 1918, Fred Sparks suggested removing certain passages in the literature that the government wanted to censor. Sparks requested the following before Judge Howe:

"We will now make a motion to your Honor for a continuance in this case, on the ground that we have not had sufficient time to sufficiently prepare this case for trial, and in support of that motion we state that on the 8th of May, this indictment was found against these defendants; that I believe on the 12th of May I went down to Washington [DC] and had a conference with the Attorney-General, the purpose of which was to see whether a general agreement on ... all the works ... of this Association could not be reached with a view of eliminating the publication of any matters the Government considered seditious" (Part 4 of Jim Whitney's articles).

Sparks continued:

"We supposed we could dispose of the entire proposition. We were looking at it from a Government proposition. The Government wanted to accomplish a certain thing. It wanted to eliminate what it designated as religious propaganda, and we were trying to get the Government to state how they wanted us to act in the elimination of that religious propaganda. We assured the Government there was no intent on the part of any member of this Association to impede the draft law, and that we would do certain things without prejudice."

Jim Whitney concludes about this part of the trial (JFR in the citation is Rutherford): "The bigger issue I also see, is that Sparks & his Clients, JFR & Company were willing to cut a deal with the Government to not publish certain things, preach certain things, or engage in certain acts that violated the law … if the Government would only drop the case. So, JFR was not concerned about publishing 'Truth' but cutting deals through his lawyer to curb what he said in exchange for staying out of the Gray-Bar Hotel" (Jim Whitney's comments at the end of Part 4).

Jim Whitney notes another important point (at the beginning of paragraph five of his study): The Society gives its members the impression that the indictment against Rutherford and his colleagues was only about the Seventh Volume or *The Finished Mystery*—which the excluded passage of the quote from *Jehovah's Witnesses in the Divine Purpose*, p. 79, also might suggest. But the Seventh Volume, continues Whitney, was not an important part of the evidence, as the Society prefers to suggest. It was rather the correspondence between the Society's executives and people who were in active service in the United States Army and Navy that was the focal point. The government representatives had seized the materials during their search of the Society's offices in Pennsylvania and New York.

With Whitney's help, we see the indictment had two main concerns: distribution of *The Finished Mystery* to certain people and correspondence to individuals who had been conscripted or were to be summoned to serve in the United States armed forces.

The fourth part of the indictment (abbreviated) states: "…intending and attempting to cause and influence various persons available for military duty to fail to register and to refuse to submit to registration and draft for service in said military and naval forces and to fail and to refuse to enlist for services therein and by inciting others so to do, notwithstanding the requirements of said laws in that behalf and notwithstanding the patriotic duty of such persons and others to so register and submit to registration and draft … and notwithstanding the cowardice involved in such failure and refusal, all of which was to be accomplished by the use of all means and methods aforesaid as a protest against and as a forcible means of preventing, interfering with, hindering, and delaying the execution of said laws of the United States and also to interfere with hinder and delay the Government of the United States in its lawful efforts to build up and maintain an Army for the carrying on of said war…" (Jim Whitney, Fourth Count).

Jim Whitney also notes the indictment does not specifically refer to the Bible Students' conscientious objection, because they did not belong to an *organized* and *recognized* religion which, on the basis of a doctrine, could require such a status. The issue in the indictment was about the Society and its officers actively encouraging servicemen to disobedience, refusal of official duty, lack of loyalty and mutiny. The *defense* sought to make this accusation into a question of *conscientious objection*.

Judge Howe asked the jurors whether they would treat the accused "fairly and impartially" and grant them the rights which the law enjoins.[184] The majority of the jurors replied in the affirmative, and that being the case, Judge Howe proclaimed them "good jurymen." In this Judge Howe showed great understanding and flexibility toward the accused (Jim Whitney, Part 4b).

It is impossible to review every aspect of the trial in this space, but I hope this discussion illustrates the seriousness of these proceedings for both the accused and the government. I still maintain that by the summer of 1918, government officials, prosecutors and court officers felt, on a very deep level, that they had gone too far and they now only wanted to imprison the Society's leaders until the war ended. Meanwhile, the sentencing of the Bible Student leaders apparently could serve to reinforce discipline within the armed forces—not to mention setting an example for other religious groups with similar leanings.

After Judge Howe pronounced the sentences, periodicals were quick to publish the results of the trial. The *New-York Evening Post* wrote the following in its lead article, which, although taken from the movement's own account of the legal proceedings, is important to relate here:

"It was necessary, he [Howe] said, to make an example of those who sincerely taught this religion, which, like that of the Mennonites and the Quakers and many other sects, forbids the taking up of arms. They were guilty, plainly, of having urged men to follow what they considered the teachings of the Lord, and to apply literally the commandment, 'Thou shalt not kill.' So the jury could do nothing less than find them guilty of having violated the statutes of the country, whatever may be the correctness or incorrectness of their attitude toward the moral and religious law. We trust that teachers of religion everywhere will take notice of this judge's opinion that teaching any religion save that which is absolutely in accord with statute laws is a grave crime ... There is no doubt that Judge Howe made his sentences severe enough..." (*Divine Purpose*, 1959, p. 80; *The Case of the International Bible Students Association*, p. 4).

Looking back, it seems a fair assessment that the government representatives and judges were not impartial and may have had a hidden agenda against Rutherford, the Society and IBSA (International Bible Students Association). For example, when the eight men asked for release on bail from the prison in Brooklyn, their requests were rejected, first by Judge Howe, and then by Judge Martin T. Manton, a Catholic.

Rutherford's Worst Nightmare

While Rutherford wrestled with legal matters, more challenges arose from another direction: the movement's members. In a letter from prison, Rutherford warned them against "seven, who opposed the Society and its work during the past year, attended the trial and lent aid to our prosecutors. We warn you, beloved, against the subtle efforts of some of them to fawn upon you now in an attempt to get hold of the Society" (*Divine Purpose*, 1959, p. 81).

It's probably safe to say that Rutherford's worst nightmare was that someone would deprive him of his recently captured control of the Society in New York and Pittsburgh. This conquest represented his biggest success to date. In January 1919, at the Society's annual meeting and simultaneous convention in Pittsburgh, there was much discussion and doubt among the remaining participants concerning future management of the Society—participants with some sympathy for the opposition may have had their own concerns as well. Rutherford was especially worried the opposition's supporters would use the opportunity to elect new leaders (this actually came up for debate at the convention) and then take control of the Society. Yet, when one of the leading participants recommended the attendees re-elect the prisoners as an expression of loyalty, this was adopted with strong support. (*Divine Purpose*, 1959, p. 84, 85)

Rutherford had faced strong opposition on multiple fronts, fighting both external and internal enemies. The court records and legal proceedings illustrate that Rutherford also struggled against his inner demons, something reflected in his only partially unknown willingness to compromise with the representatives of the anti-Bible-Student conspiracy: the government, the judges and prosecutors and the church leaders—"Satan's wicked system."

The fairness of the district court's indictment and the sentences of the eight defendants is certainly debatable today, but the perspective is clearer when events are at least partly viewed in the context of the time: United States' involvement in World War I and the Bible Students' attitude toward military service, and in part, the Christian churches' hostility to the movement, which the Society spent many years fomenting, especially through highly provocative publications released between 1917 and 1918. These publications surely contributed to a sensational atmosphere around the Society's activities that certainly, after Judgment Day was postponed, spurred them to increase members and book production. The Society's hateful campaigns against the Catholic Church and the Protestant denominations were undoubtedly part of a deliberate attempt to provoke the churches and enhance a monstrous image of the movement's enemies, and their deliberate actions had born fruit. Call it self-fulfilling, but they successfully incited the persecution the Bible Students expected during this period. It was, therefore, not surprising that the churches' rhetoric and opposition was strident and reached unprecedented heights. This rhetoric equaled the Bible Students' extreme attacks on the churches, many of whom still fanatically demanded the imprisonment and even execution of the Watch Tower leaders. Thus, after the arrest and imprisonment of the Bible Student executives, the Catholic magazine *Truth* wrote—and I quote here again from the Watchtower Society's 1993 account of events: "The literature of this association fairly reeks with virulent attacks on the Catholic Church and her priesthood" (*Proclaimers*, 1993, p. 655).

As I suggested earlier, context is important. These events occurred a century ago when things were markedly different in many ways and at a time when war—and suspicion—troubled everyone.

Chapter 16

Twenty Years Behind Bars to *The Holy Ones*[185]

The Watchtower Society's perspective of the trial, it seems to me, is that it was a traumatic event the management (perhaps deliberately) finds impossible to hurdle (even today), and perhaps has no interest in ever doing so. They keep it in the fore, almost a kind of *collective inherited mental ulceration*—an event of the movement's history, which despite all common sense, gives the members a historically associated identity (even though I doubt that members today consider this old trial something they need to specifically deal with). Thus far, no new angle, self-knowledge or any kind of admission has manifested itself in the Society's publications.

One can suppose that maybe Rutherford and the Society's "biblical" explanation for the trial and imprisonment was the result of Rutherford's own emotional resentment—a resentment grown out of the government's accusations and his subsequent attempts to avoid prison by entering into a compromise on certain passages in the Seventh Volume. Rutherford did not hesitate to take action about the latter issue either. He sent a hasty telegram to the printer to stop production, and simultaneously, he sent a representative to US Army intelligence services to get details of the government's objections. When he learned pages 247–253 in the English version were the central issue, the portion the government and court absolutely disliked, the Society ordered those pages be removed before the book was offered to the public. When the Government notified the district attorneys that further distribution would be a violation of the Espionage Act, the Society decided that all public distribution of the Seventh Volume had to be suspended. However, some copies of the 1917-circulation distributed by the colporteurs had found their way to the public. Just prior to or shortly after this, Rutherford called on the "brothers" to *buy War bonds*. These events and requests were at odds with the Bible Students' ideas about steadfastly refusing to compromise with Satan's government on earth. (*Proclaimers*, 1993, p. 652)

In *The Watch Tower* the readers found this commendation:

"The people of our Association are not against the Government, nor against the Liberty Loan. Our thought is that the Liberty Loan is not a religious question, but purely one pertaining to the affairs of the Government; and that each person should be left to the free exercise of his individual conscience as to whether he will or will not purchase Liberty Bonds" (*WT*, 1918, May 15).

This article infuriated Charlie Heard (Vancouver, BC) and other members so much that they withdrew to form the StandFast Bible Students Association. They were further incensed by a statement published by Society leaders in June 1918, as follows:

"A Christian, unwilling to kill, may have been conscientiously unable to buy government bonds; later he considers what great blessings he has received under his government, and realizes that the nation is in trouble and facing dangers to its liberty, and he feels himself conscientiously able to lend some money to the country, just as he would lend to a friend in distress" (*WT*, June 1, 1918, p. 168).

One can easily imagine how this hit the Canadians, whose conscientious-objector youth had been going to prison for three years. Still, with his reputation on the line and his credibility at risk, Rutherford made a 180-degree turn and tried to justify the purchase of government bonds! (Source: Jerry Leslie)

"One has a point of view, until one takes a new one," said the former prime minister of Denmark, the late Jens Otto Krag, in November 1966. He was asked how he could change position from one moment to another with regard to the Danish government's reluctance to cooperate with a socialist party. His response could have been uttered by J. F. Rutherford, who dramatically changed his position on the issue of War Bonds.

Everyone can probably be allowed to become wiser.

Events in Brooklyn Predicted in the Book of Daniel

In an old photo, reproduced in the book *Jehovah's Witnesses—Proclaimers of God's Kingdom* from 1993, page 653, we see from left a line-up from tallest to shortest of the "holy ones of the Supreme One"[186] [*sic*]: W. E. VanAmburgh, J. F. Rutherford, A. H. Macmillan, R. J. Martin, F. H. Robison, C. J. Woodworth, G. H. Fisher and G. DeCecca (the first approximately six-feet-three-inches tall and the last just over five feet). Note the photo includes only the eight defendants; Robert H. Hirsh is missing. He was the *ninth* accused, but the government did not pursue his prosecution—a fact which compounded the stress of the defendants and Attorney Sparks.[187] Looking back, it seems clear, Sparks was concerned about preventing Hirsh from testifying against the other defendants, making the Society's contention that the eight men were railroaded seem ludicrous to Jim Whitney. Whitney notes polemically that conferences held in the judge's chambers reveal how fair Judge Howe was and what "an idiot JFR [Rutherford] was in hiring Sparks to defend him...." Personally I think the Society's claims about the unfairness of the verdicts are both correct and incorrect. The real problem was that Rutherford and his colleagues had not fully understood the seriousness of the situation or its implications in regard to America's entry into the war.

The objective view is that the trial was fundamentally fair. Judge Howe was obliging to Rutherford and his people in a way not normally given to state enemies or traitors (Cole). Howe also conceded, as noted earlier, that the government could have been wrong, which President Woodrow Wilson must have recognized, as evidenced by his later statement about the matter. Nonetheless, the Society takes every opportunity to revisit the possible injustice of the arrest and trial. (*Proclaimers*, p. 652)

As my research took me through the Watch Tower materials, I had trouble finding anything of substance about Robert Hirsh. His significant role during the showdown with Rutherford in 1917 led to my writing about him at some length, but beyond his official presence in Society events, there seemed to be little known about him. I found him, finally, in a footnote in the *Proclaimers* book. He was real after all! By the preliminary proceedings in 1918, Hirsh had probably long ago had enough of the situation with Rutherford, and the government's representatives were undoubtedly informed about his moving away from the group. I also learned that he later joined one of the new, alternative Bible Student associations, which had grown out of the power struggle between "the big four" and Rutherford. I've tried to find Hirsh's name in Macmillan's book, *Faith on the March*, but without success. Hirsh seems to have been destroyed to some degree, cast aside or at least ignored. One can well understand why this is so from the information found in the 1917 pamphlet, *Light After Darkness*, in which he and his "accomplices" sharply distanced themselves from Rutherford and his co-conspirators' methods. (*Bible Students Fragments*, 1917–1967; A. H. Macmillan: *Faith on the March*, 1957)[188]

The arrest and imprisonment of Society executives was undoubtedly an experience with negative and positive implications—Rutherford considered the arrest one of the "greatest privileges a man could have"; if there was any way to spin the events in a positive way, Rutherford would find it. Certainly what had come to pass was significant, and thus of such a large scale it had to have been foretold in the Book of Daniel—even though it had been written more than 2,000 years earlier! *It was a "prophetic" book*, with the author claiming to have written it during the Babylonian captivity, centuries earlier, but which, in fact, *probably* had been written during the time the prophecy concerned, around 164 BC. At that time the Jews led a war of liberation against the Macedonian Antiochus IV Epiphanes, who had attacked Jerusalem and executed many inhabitants. Antiochus lost his battle and died that year. But the phrase suggesting a *distant future* ("for it *shall be* for many days") in Daniel 8:26 was a *gefundenes Fressen* (Godsend!) for Rutherford's Bible Students, and likewise for today's Jehovah's Witnesses. The prophecies in Daniel have been ascribed to many events by numerous interpreters, more specifically the first Christians who, around AD 70, made the Roman siege of Jerusalem the object of Daniel's predictions. (*Divine Purpose*, 1959, p. 80; Luke 21)

By way of example, I cite three instances of the unrestrained interpretation (from the same book, same chapter—and note the quotation marks) of the Society leaders' arrest and imprisonment from Daniel and Revelation. I apologize for the sketchy form of the quotations, but the presentation only serves as an example of the Society's abuse of Daniel's book in our time:

"A TINY, defenseless group of people come under vicious attack by a mighty world power ... Daniel chapter 7 foretold these events, which occurred in the early part of the 20th century...." The directors of the Watchtower Society are identified as "the holy ones of the Supreme One," (Daniel 7:22; NW), there was a "spiritual revival," as in the Society's directors resuming religious activities after their release in 1919: "It is a historical reality that in 1918 a small remnant of faithful Christians were subjected to an extraordinary attack that disrupted their organized public ministry. Then, against all likelihood, in 1919 they returned to life in a spiritual sense. These facts fit the description of the resurrection foretold at Daniel 12:2. Some did 'wake up' spiritually at that time and thereafter. Sadly, though, not all remained in a spiritually alive state..." (*Daniel's Prophecy*, 1999, p. 286; 291).

And further:

"The prophecy is quite explicit as to when the 1,260 days would *end*—when there is 'a finishing of the dashing of the power of the holy people to pieces.' In the middle of 1918, leading members of the Watch Tower Bible and Tract Society, including its president, J.F. Rutherford, were convicted on false charges, sentenced to long terms of confinement, and imprisoned. God's holy ones did indeed see their work 'dashed to pieces,' their power broken. Counting back three and a half years from mid-1918 brings us to the end of 1914. At that time the little band of anointed ones were bracing themselves for the onslaught of persecution. World War I had broken out, and opposition to their work was mounting.... As predicted at Revelation 11:3, the 1,260-day period that ensued was a mournful time for the anointed—it was as if they were prophesying in sackcloth. Persecution worsened..." (*Daniel's Prophecy*, 1999, p. 296).

And yet another angle:

"Daniel was told: 'From the time that the constant feature has been removed and there has been a placing of the disgusting thing that is causing desolation, there will be one thousand two hundred and ninety days.' So this time period would begin when certain conditions had been brought about. 'The constant feature'—or 'the continual sacrifice'—had to be removed [p. 297] ... So this first condition of the prophecy—the removing of 'the constant feature'—was brought about in mid-1918 when the preaching work was virtually suspended [p. 298].... By the end of the foretold 1,290 days, the holy ones were well on the way to a cleansed and restored standing. In September 1922, right about the time when this period ended, they held a landmark convention at Cedar Point,

Ohio, U.S.A. [p. 300] … At that time, there was a widely held view that pointed to 1925 as the year for the resurrection to begin and for Paradise to be restored to the earth. Thus, many were serving with a fixed date in mind…" (*Daniel's Prophecy*, 1999, p. 297-303).

The assertion that the arrest and imprisonment of the Society's executives fits the description in the Book of Daniel and John's Revelation, has time and again been repeated in the Society's literature. In particular, the assertions are found in *Jehovah's Witnesses in the Divine Purpose* from 1959, which I include here as source material (p. 79), and in two other books published by the Society: *Your Will be Done on Earth* (1958) and *Pay Attention to Daniel's Prophecy* from 1999 (pages 186–305).

Let us not forget that before 1916 Charles Russell had been expecting and had even written about an upcoming development where the Bible Students would be persecuted, and we know their actions served to stimulate animosity toward the movement. The onset of World War One, the persecutions and mob assaults, arrest and imprisonment of the Watch Tower Society's executives all undoubtedly honed the Bible Students' belief in the nearness of the Judgment Day and the relevance of the apocalyptic events. That these events did not occur with an escalated pace *after* World War One, as the Bible Students had dreamed about (and maybe also had nightmares about), was probably a surprise, as they had already expected other significant events in 1918. Still, they looked forward to 1925, a year that the Seventh Volume had highlighted and that Rutherford would soon feature in a big public relations campaign. It is highly doubtful he believed in these prophesies and predictions himself.

Society's Executives Sentenced

As an attorney, Rutherford may have benefited from a measure of goodwill by the court. Nevertheless, he and six defendants were each sentenced to twenty years in prison and DeCecca to ten years. They began their sentences immediately in a federal facility in Atlanta, Georgia. On November 1, 1918, the First World War ended and on March 25, 1919, the eight Watchtower leaders, by order of the United States Supreme Court were released on bail. Previously, they had been refused bail. The case was heard in appellate court on May 14, 1919. The Federal Court of Appeals reversed the judgment of the original trial, and the following year the eight, according to the Watchtower Society, were completely cleared of the accusations. (*Qualified*, 1955, p. 312-317; *Divine Purpose*, 1959, p. 84-87)

The *Brooklyn Eagle*, which a few years before had scandalized Russell (causing him humiliation), reversed its opinion, saying the case had been unfair:

"Russellite verdict reversed by appeal; 'Trial was unfair.' Judges Ward, Rogers and Manton of the United States Circuit Court of Appeals for the New York Federal District today reversed the convictions of the leaders of Russellism, who were found guilty last June before Judge Harlan B. Howe of Vermont, sitting in Brooklyn, of conspiring to obstruct the draft, discourage enlistment and foment insurrection and insubordination among the armed forces of the Nation. / The decision holds that the attitude of Judge Howe was unfair in his treatment of the [three] Witnesses" (*Divine Purpose*, 1959, p. 86; *Brooklyn Daily Eagle*, May 15, 1920).

The three appellate judges noted above formed a majority and found the Bible Students' conscientious objection in accordance with the law, since the Bible Students organization "forbids members to kill" (Ibid., p. 87). The law presupposed that one could be released on bail, which the Bible Student leaders had been denied.

Judge Martin T. Manton, a Catholic, had refused the defendants' request for release on bail during the 1918 trial. In 1939—still according to the Watchtower's history book from 1959—Manton was sentenced to two years in prison for receiving "bribes of $186,000 for six decisions."[189] The Catholics' lingering animosity toward Rutherford is made clear later in a Catholic publication where he is referred to as a "former convict." A denial of this claim—according to the Witnesses' leadership (which I can neither prove nor disprove)—may be seen in the fact that Rutherford subsequently presented cases in the United States Supreme Court. (*Divine Purpose*, 1959, p. 87: *Proclaimers*, 1993, p. 650–654, where Manton is mentioned in a footnote)

Rutherford Re-elected in January 1919

While Rutherford, VanAmburgh, Macmillan and the other board members sat in prison, the annual meeting commenced in January 1919; Judge Rutherford was reappointed, probably as an expression of loyalty. Before the election, Rutherford was anxious about the outcome and confided so to Macmillan. Rutherford explained that for the first time since Russell's death they would know "whom Jehovah wants as president." To me, this means the elections were the first *truly democratic* within the Society, as Russell had always favored nominating his own people. Perhaps, it was also an indirect admission that elections in Russell's time had not been particularly fair. Macmillan writes in his book:

"I mean that Brother Russell had a controlling vote and he appointed the different officers." This is an interesting angle from one of Russell's highly trusted secretaries (Russell usually had three secretaries), who must have been privy to most, if not all, of Russell's decisions. It is certainly the impression he wants to give his readers. But Macmillan was now Rutherford's man, and Rutherford won the election. Macmillan noted later that Rutherford was happy because he knew now "that Jehovah was running the Society" (*Proclaimers*, 1993, p. 73–74).

The convention in Pittsburgh was marred by confusion, inconsistencies and many discussions, and I sense there were factions who wanted to elect new leaders. When Ernest D. Sexton of Los Angeles, who had been elected to chair a nomination committee and who strongly backed Rutherford in those first few years, spoke to the assembly, he invited them to reappoint Rutherford as president as an expression of loyalty. The resulting election results were as follows: J. F. Rutherford, president; C. A. Wise, vice president (he was new to the board); and W. E. VanAmburgh, secretary and treasurer. Sexton may have backed Rutherford in this instance, but his loyalty was not eternal. In 1930 Sexton left the movement, after writing a resignation letter to Rutherford, because he strongly disagreed with the president's methods and management. In 1931 Sexton published his letter in the *Herald of Christ's Kingdom,* the February 15 issue; the periodical was published by a group of Bible Students who had broken away around 1918. (*Proclaimers,* 1993, p. 72–75)[190]

Beyond the annual meeting's events, the Bible Students' activities were reportedly paralyzed during the imprisonment:

"Shortly after this, members of the Society's administrative staff were arrested, and on June 21, 1918, they were sentenced to 20-year prison terms. The preaching of the good news came to a virtual standstill. Was this the time when they would at last be united with the Lord in heavenly glory? / A few months later, the war ended. The following year the officials of the Society were released. They were still in the flesh. It was not what they had expected, but they concluded that God must *still have work for them to do here on earth*" (*Proclaimers,* 1993, p. 211; italics are mine).

There was plenty to do. With the tensions easing following the war's end, a few years remained until 1925, when great events on earth would transpire, if one could count on Rutherford's apocalyptic calculations. Some members readily placed their trust in him; others took a wait-and-see attitude.

The Judge's main task after his release was, in the tradition of past apocalyptic failures, to put every effort and energy into the Society's activities. In 1919, they held a seven-day convention in Cedar Point, Ohio; 6,000 participated, 200 were baptized and 7,500 attended the public meeting. In the spring of 1919 there were 150 colporteurs (pioneers) and by autumn the figure had risen to 507. The Society writes in 1955: "Truly the stormy years of crisis had been weathered. Yes, 1919 saw the once dead witness work quickly revived by God's great active force, to become an amazement to the nations.—Rev. 11:11" (*Qualified,* 1955, p. 317).

At the convention in Cedar Point, the Judge announced a new magazine, *The Golden Age,* would be released October 1, 1919. Its publication is often described as a turning point. The ordinary members of the movement were invited to participate in the new "house-to-house work" as *class workers* (derived from the Greek *ecclesia,* meaning class or congregation). They were to promote the magazine and if they could not sell a subscription, a copy was to be left in the hope of getting them into every home. Another twist to these operations was that the ordinary members now had to "report" the time they spent in the work with *The Golden Age*. Thus, 8,052 class workers and 350 pioneers reported their hours in 1920—the first reporting year. (*Divine Purpose*, 1959, p. 94-96; *Qualified*, 1955, p. 319)

The-Golden-Age work was a first step in controlling the local *ecclesias* (congregations), and eventually the entire association worldwide. Reporting hours and sales of magazines, books, etc., became a fixture in the Bible Student's everyday life. The reporting became, in one respect, the organization's key to controlling supporters' involvement, and in another, the members' security, for if one was a "mature preacher," he or she was worthy to survive the coming battle of Armageddon, which was still said to be very close—even though the preliminary time *dragged on*.

Chapter 17

Cleaning Up the Teachings

J. F. Rutherford built the "Jehovah's Witnesses" on the rubble of the Bible Student movement. It was no small achievement *if one doesn't consider his methods*. Perhaps I should summarize events:

- During the emergency situation after Russell's death, Rutherford virtually seized power in Russell's bereaved Watchtower Society.
- After the intense power struggle from 1916–1918, we can only speculate who Russell had selected as his true heirs.
- Rutherford stole Russell's international project and decisively changed the preconditions for it.
- He gradually built a new teaching atop Russell's old foundation.

In organizational terms it was probably Rutherford's model that won within the Bible Students, but doctrinally it seems the largest of the opposition Bible Student associations—the by-products of Rutherford's brutality—carried on Russell's ideas, however, they did so less successfully than Russell's earlier project. The offshoots' dedication to him is reflected by the fact that Russell's six-volume work, *Studies in the Scriptures*, is still published by these associations. They have dutifully passed the books to subsequent generations, almost as if they were sacred writings. It seems that Charles Taze Russell's "gold watch" not only stalled, but it's as if time stood still for his doctrinal successors.

At this point, I must stop for a moment and confess that I, to some extent, wrong the Bible Student groups who departed *Rutherfordism*. They should be more distinguished as groups, both in 1917–1919 and today. While Russell lived, and later when Rutherford took control, there were obviously diverging opinions among the Bible Students. This is why we cannot lump them all together as apocalyptic zealots. Not everyone had the perception, as A. H. Macmillan did, that on a certain date (October 1, 1914) the Day of Judgment would come and the saints would be retrieved home. Russell did not strictly adhere to this date-setting, as he clearly tried at the last moment (from 1911 onward) to retract elements of this teaching, but he was captured by his previous statements, leaving little doubt among the members that the world would be shocked and greatly altered around 1914 or shortly thereafter. In fact, a significant change would come to pass, but not quite in the way Russell had portrayed. Many in the movement were skeptical of exaggerations, something probably reflected in *The Watch Tower*. It was very likely these more level-headed members gradually drifted away from Rutherford's new project and did so because they could not identify with it.

A comprehensive study of those groups would undoubtedly fill another volume or more, but for us, it is now time to focus on *Rutherford's* Bible Students.

1914, 1918 and 1925—New Central Years

Rutherford now initiated a gradual cleanup of the doctrines of Christ's Second coming and the world's end, and especially Christ's *invisible arrival time* which was substantially revised. These revisions, however, took some years to complete (into the late 1930s), because the opposition from the Russellites still lingered noticeably. This resistance lasted until 1931–1932, by which time about 75% of the original Bible Students had left the movement.

Rutherford had to proceed slowly and carefully.

As late as 1930 Rutherford seems to suggest that Christ's second coming, as implied by and according to Russell's old schedule for the end-time, started with an invisible "presence" from "about 1879," as stated in the book *Light 1* from 1930.[191] This suggests that Rutherford placed his bets on two horses: 1874–1879 and 1914–1918. In fact, Rutherford wrote "about 1879" (p. 12), but that year was supposedly only mentioned because Russell's magazine, *Zion's Watch Tower*, was first published that year.[192]

Further into the book Rutherford's main point becomes more evident, for example, on page seventy where the prophetic years 1874, 1914, 1918 and 1922 are treated. The old Russellites must have had a hard time accepting that the second coming of Christ, in some strange way, had been moved from 1874–1879 to 1914–1918. Russell had given very strong assurances that he had arrived at 1874 as the year of the Second Coming with "mathematical precision"—with the year 1914 as the conclusion of Christ's forty years of *invisible presence*. (*Studies* 3, 1919 (1889), p. 129)

Rutherford discarded all that:

"It can now be seen that the events pictured in the first five seals were fulfilled from 1914 to 1918, but the meaning thereof man could not understand until after the coming of the Lord to his temple, in 1918. Prior thereto the church had been applying the prophecy of Matthew twenty-four to the events that came to pass from 1874 to 1914. Not until after 1918 was it understood by the church that these events apply after 1914; and hence the seals were not open to or discerned by the John class, that is to say, the remnant, until after 1918, and, in fact, very little until after 1922" (*Light* 1, 1930, p. 70).

Around 1940, Rutherford's advanced and revised arrival schedule for Christ's invisible presence was finally in place, and the official end time, as demonstrated in his book *Religion*, meant Jesus Christ "was enthroned as King in the year 1914, and he came to the temple of God in 1918 and there began the assembling and judging of the consecrated ones" (*Religion*, 1940, p. 12).

In other words: Christ's invisible return was to be counted *from* 1914.

Yet, the year 1914 was and is still maintained as the *central year* in the chronology. In 1914 the gentile times ended, just as in Russell's old teachings, but the year 1874 lost its meaning *because Christ did not return until 1914* to sit on his heavenly throne and monitor the subsequent collection of the selected ones. And although it was not directly stated that Christ's second coming was 1914, *a 40-year leap forward from 1874*, this was the general conclusion. (*Religion*, 1940, p. 12; 109, 110)

If one constructed a timeline, it would show Rutherford moved the entire end-times template forward during the 1930–1940 period so that, for example, what had previously ended in 1914 now started that year. It seems the Society's leadership even then may have had the idea that their new chronology should run *at least* forty years into the future. Thus, when *1954* also passed, a *new year of interest* would emerge: *1974* (and later, *1975*). And on and on, the chronology leapt forward as the leadership needed.

The movement's traditional assumption held the length of King David's reign as the model for Christ's heavenly kingdom in the end times; they assumed Christ's presence or governing period would last at least forty years (under Russell from 1874 to 1914). Therefore, I conclude that all the talk about impending apocalyptic events during those years may have been deliberate speculation of the Society, since as we have seen, they already had plans for the Society's function forty or fifty years on or maybe even longer. (*Studies* 7, 1926 (1917), p. 61, 62)

Before the reorganization of the doctrines concerning Christ's second presence, the main leadership clearly made no attempt to dispel the ordinary Bible Student's expectations of a speedy ascension to heaven (1925), instead the leadership seems to have deliberately played on them while planning new campaign promotions aimed at the organization's long-term survival. (*Divine Purpose*, 1959, p. 61)

To support this conclusion, I offer the following from the Seventh Volume: "The year 1914 brought the end of the Times of the Gentiles, but not the end of the Harvest work." From here it follows that parallel events in the first and second centuries AD could point to "1980"[193]—it's unclear exactly if the harvest work itself would last that long or if it implies other aspects of the prophesies. The year 1980 is mentioned in connection with a future re-establishing of the "fleshly Israel," but in a context that seems both absurd and confusing. Remember the re-establishment of the Jews was one event needed to be fulfilled in the course of "the great trouble" *before* the climax at Armageddon in 1914. (*Studies* 7, p. 67)

As noted earlier, Barbour and Russell had expected the re-establishment of a Jewish state in Palestine shortly after 1881, an idea not completely without merit, because the press indeed wrote daily columns on the matter. So, Barbour and Russell were quite abreast of current events, so to speak. Around 1880 the Jews sought to colonize Palestine because they dreamed of a Jewish state under Turkish sovereignty. Shortly after, in 1897, the Zionists were also organized. Russell was very well informed about what happened in his time, and he fully understood the need to connect to the Jewish cause, and it was incorporated into his predictions regarding events during the "great trouble" between 1874 and 1914.

Millennium in 1925

In spite of this long-term strategy surrounding 1980 (see above), which I think was a slip-up by the two authors of the Seventh Volume, in 1920 Rutherford launched a new large-scale campaign with the book: *Millions Now Living Will Never Die*. This book's timeline looked forward but only a few years. The "Million Book," as it has been dubbed, was only 107 pages and published in Danish-Norwegian, Finnish, Swedish, French, German, Dutch, Yiddish, Greek, Arabic, Russian, Polish, Malay, Burmese and English, of course. It gave 1925 as the new disaster year. (*Divine Purpose*, 1959, p. 98)

In the Million Book the Judge writes "that the old world legally ended in 1914" and "that 1914 marked the beginning of the end of the world" (p. 12). He further suggested that "the great jubilee" and the "restoration of all things" would have their beginning in 1925, meaning the Millennium would begin in that year. (*Millions Die,* 1920, p. 18, 19; p. 87, 88)

Rutherford determined the year 1925 through "a simple calculation" (p. 88), based on a number of texts in the Old Testament—texts taken totally out of context. The "great jubilee cycle" (p. 89) began, according to Rutherford, in the year 1575 BC, and in accordance with Genesis 25:1–12, Israel celebrated a Jubilee every fiftieth year, and in all, they kept seventy years of Jubilee. (Jer. 25:11 and 2 Chronicles 36:17-21) In the Million Book Rutherford shows that seventy of those Jubilees multiplies to a period of 3,500 years. Starting from 1575 BC, this period "of necessity would end in the fall of the year 1925." In 1925, a "full restoration" would then take place or the Kingdom of God would be fully implemented on Earth:

"The chief thing to be restored is the human race to life; and since other Scriptures definitely fix the fact that there will be a resurrection of Abraham, Isaac, Jacob and other faithful ones of old, and that these will have the first favor, we may expect 1925 to witness the return of these faithful men of Israel from the condition of death, being resurrected and fully restored to perfect humanity and made the visible, legal representatives of the new order of things on earth" (*Millions Die*, 1920, p. 88,89 and 106, 107).

And at the end of the Million Book, Rutherford put forward the captivating idea that millions of the living would never die:

"No one can gainsay this positive and conclusive promise that under the Messiah's reign death shall be destroyed, and sorrow, sighing and crying shall cease, and that all who are obedient shall be restored to life, liberty and happiness. And since the old order is passing away and the new is coming in, we can with confidence proclaim the glad message that millions now living on the earth will be granted the opportunity for life everlasting and those who obey shall never die, but shall be restored and live in happiness, joy and peace upon the earth forever" (Ibid., p. 106).

Great as that seems, not everyone gets to live forever:

"Of course, it does not mean that everyone will live; for some will refuse to obey the divine law" (Ibid., p. 97, 98).

Before the Kingdom of happiness could be fully established, there would come a period of great trouble, beginning with the First World War in 1914. Many would perish in this time of trouble, but God would also save "some," perhaps approximately one-third of the population (Zechariah 13:8–9), and those "peoples living on earth at the end of the trouble will be the first ones to be offered the blessings of restoration" (Ibid., p. 68–69). Rutherford's ideas offered certain consistencies and expectations about what had to happen and how the Millennium would gradually be introduced from around 1925, and "those accepting the offer as made and rendering themselves in obedience to it shall be restored to that which was lost in Adam, viz., life, liberty and happiness" (p. 93). They would be young again: "Thus, when restoration begins, a man of seventy years of age will gradually be restored to a condition of physical health and mental balance" (Ibid., p. 100).

"And since the old order is passing away and the new is coming in, we can with confidence proclaim the glad message that millions now living on the earth will be granted the opportunity for life everlasting and those who obey shall never die, but shall be restored and live in happiness, joy and peace upon the earth forever" (Ibid., p. 106, 107).

Who among them was not interested in eternal youth, especially after the war! Remember, Rutherford trumpeted his startling message following the First World Wars' multi-million casualty rate, and one can very well imagine that those who had lost a family member might find consolation in Rutherford's message:

"Many a good mother has spent sleepless nights and wept tears of bitterness because of her loved one that died upon the battlefield. Many a sweetheart, many a father, many a child, has likewise been bowed down in sorrow because of the great suffering that the war, trouble and death entailed upon the people" (*Millions Die*, 1920, p. 101).

Still, Rutherford maintained that in 1925 everything would be almost miraculously changed for the better.

The members were overwhelmingly enthusiastic, and the Million Book was embraced as part of a renewed campaign, and the new message—*the only one so far has survived*—was advertised everywhere on posters, in newspapers, etc.

An article in *The Watch Tower* of July 1, 1920, shows a new short-term road-map suggested in a commentary on Jesus' words from Matthew 24:14 where he encourages his followers to preach the gospel. This gospel must be seen in the context of the "old order of things and end the establishments of Messiah's kingdom…"; the article states: "It will be observed that in the order named this message must be delivered between the time of the great world war and the time of the 'great tribulation' mentioned by the Master in Matthew 24:21, 23.… And the fact that he said that for the elect's sake the time of trouble would be shortened and much flesh saved warrants us beyond doubt in announcing now to the world the message, 'Millions Now Living Will Never Die'. / Therefore it seems that now is the time for the Church to proclaim far and wide in Christendom this good news" (*WT*, July 1, 1920; *Divine Purpose*, 1959, p. 100).

In 1920, Judge Rutherford sailed to Europe to tour with his support staff, including Alexander Macmillan. On October 21, Macmillan landed in Esbjerg, Denmark, and proceeded to the Palace Hotel for the "Million Talk." The event was repeated in Odense, Copenhagen, Aalborg and Randers. (*YB*, 1993)

Macmillan was very engaged in Rutherford's 1925 ideas, and had apparently learned nothing from Society events leading up to 1914. However, in Macmillan's old age he admitted that sometimes "our expectations for a certain date were more than what the Scriptures warranted" (*Proclaimers*, 1993, p. 637).

This quote certainly cannot be repeated too often.

New Disappointments and New Programs

The Bible Students—as they still called themselves—now looked forward to being transformed to heaven in 1925 in connection with the "great trouble"; this is approximately an eleven-year delay from the earlier date in October 1914. Past, faithful patriarchs—Abraham, Isaac, Jacob and others—would also rise from the dead around the same time. They would not be transferred to heaven, but live forever on earth as perfect humans.

It was somewhat a fantastic novelty.

In 1922 Bible Students again held a convention in Cedar Point, an amusement park located on a small island in Lake Erie near Sandusky, Ohio. The event was filled with great expectations. Brother Rutherford delivered a lecture "The Kingdom," and the participants were highly enthusiastic: "Each one present was thoroughly impressed with the fact that the obligation is laid upon every one of the consecrated from this time forward to act as a publicity agent for the King and the kingdom" (*Proclaimers*, 1993, p. 77, 78).

I suppose it was at Cedar Point in 1922 that the concept of Kingdom Publisher ("publicity agent") arose for the first time. A colporteur expressed it enthusiastically: "We were aroused to 'advertise, advertise, advertise the King and his kingdom'—Yes, with more zeal and love in our hearts than ever before" (*Proclaimers*, 1993, p. 77-78).

Rutherford and his team must have realized the importance of launching new programs and ideas *well before* 1925, because they had to expect great disappointment among members and rallying enthusiasm was a good way to dispel previous disappointments while they awaited what was sure to be the next one. The meaning was clear, for gradually as "the spiritual light of understanding grew brighter, the Bible Students began to perceive some thrilling Bible truths," and understanding of these "precious truths gave a powerful impetus to their work of proclaiming God's Kingdom. At the same time, they had to adjust their thinking—and for some this was a real test." The "sifting"—the *code word* to explain why dissatisfied members left the organization—also weeded out those elements within the Bible Students that caused divisiveness around Rutherford's leadership. Now the Society was about to be busy with "spreading books" on a really large scale. (*Proclaimers*, 1993, p. 78; p. 621)

In 1956, William J. Schnell's biography, *Thirty Years a Watch Tower Slave*, was published. As a former senior in the organization, Schnell had seen the truth from inside. His revelations were a severe blow to Society leadership, and the leaders completely ignored the book. Schnell says anticipation for the 1925 events "was fanned by every publication of the Organization of that time and it left a deep imprint upon our minds. In fact, it virtually made irrational crackpots out of many of us. For example, I well remember that in the fall of 1924 my father offered to buy me a much needed suit of clothes. I asked him not to do it since it was only a few months to 1925, and with it would come the Kingdom. This now seems utterly ridiculous to me. Even if the Kingdom as expected had come, I meanwhile very badly needed new clothes" (Schnell, 1956, p. 33).

The members waited anxiously for the big events of 1925, but it came to be quite the opposite and not at all dramatic. Rutherford soon concluded that no old patriarch's legacy could ever assume management of the Society so long as he stood at the helm. Therefore he had to replace the past's *patriarchal bones* with something equally exciting—and frantic!

Presumably, this realization led Rutherford to proclaim the "Birth of the Nation" in *The Watch Tower* of March 1, 1925. Note the timing. In the article Rutherford makes it clear that the battle was now between "Satan's organization" and "God's organization." He describes his Witnesses as "valiant warriors" who would swing their *sword of Jehovah*.[194] (*Divine Purpose*, 1959, p. 107–109; p. 104–109)[195]

The article in *The Watch Tower* was built over a new allegorical (metaphorical) interpretation of Revelation 12, and is said to have contained an *enlightened understanding*—an "understanding of Revelation chapter 12 that some found difficult to accept" (*Proclaimers*, p. 78). Specifically, *Proclaimers* offers this incredibly difficult explanation:

"The symbolic characters mentioned in this chapter of Revelation were identified as follows: the 'woman' that gives birth (vss. 1, 2) as 'God's [heavenly] organization'; the 'dragon' (vs. 3) as 'the devil's organization'; and the 'man child' (vs. 5, KJ) as 'the new kingdom, or new government.' On the basis of this, something was clearly explained for the first time: There are two distinct and opposing organizations—Jehovah's and Satan's. And following the 'war in heaven' (vs. 7, KJ), Satan and his demon supporters were cast out of heaven and hurled down to the earth" (*Proclaimers*, 1993, p. 78, 79).

Earl E. Newell, a reader of *The Watch Tower,* noted how when he and his friends had trouble understanding the *new truths,* "they sat down and studied it all night until they could understand it very well." But others were highly disturbed and upset by this break with Russell's interpretation of Revelation, and they could not accept the new explanations; this caused yet another sifting of members. (*Proclaimers*, 1993, p. 78, 79)

A Society director under Rutherford and a staff member in Russell's time, J. A. Bohnet was now a pilgrim, and he noted that, according to *Proclaimers*, "this interpretation may prove a sifting medium, but the really earnest and sincere ones of the faith will stand firm and rejoice." *Proclaimers* continued: "Indeed, the really earnest and sincere ones did rejoice over the new explanation. It was now so clear to them: everyone belongs either to Jehovah's organization or to Satan's" (*Proclaimers*, 1993, p. 79).

Rutherford's new truths, however, could not alter the facts, and the "year 1925 especially proved to be a year of great trial too many." Among the anointed members a widespread perception prevailed, specifically "the remaining members of the body of Christ would be changed to heavenly glory that year." As before, the disappointments among the Bible Students were great, but even though some left the Watchtower Society, a great majority remained under the protecting wings of the organization. In 1925 Rutherford told the headquarters staff in Germany, among them W. J. Schnell, that "we should not selfishly anticipate going to heaven now in 1925, when there was so much work to be done on earth" (*Divine Purpose*, 1959, p. 107-110; *Proclaimers*, 1993, p. 78; Schnell, 1956, p. 52).

Following 1925, meeting attendance fell off sharply in France and Switzerland. A member from Switzerland, Jules Feller, shared his thoughts about the erroneous predictions: "Those who had set their confidence in Jehovah remained steadfast and continued their preaching activity" (*Proclaimers*, 1993, p. 633).

And by 1931, Rutherford had this to say:

"There was a measure of disappointment on the part of Jehovah's faithful ones on earth concerning the years 1914, 1918 and 1925, which disappointment lasted for a time. Later the faithful learned that these dates were *definitely fixed* in the Scriptures; and they also learned to *quit fixing dates* for the future and predicting what would come to pass on a certain date, but to rely (and they do rely) upon the Word of God as to the events that must come to pass" (*Vindication*, Book 1, 1931, p. 338, 339; italics are mine).

Beth Sarim

Despite set-backs and the loss of members, Rutherford had not totally (or publically) abandoned the hope Abraham, Isaac and Jacob being resurrected. In 1929 a large villa was built for Rutherford in San Diego, California; he named it *Beth Sarim*, House of the Princes. This villa was to be prepared for the men of old time, *the Princes*, when they arose from the dead. Meanwhile, Rutherford lived in the villa, particularly in the winter because of his poor health—he suffered a severe case of pneumonia after his release from prison in 1919. The villa's deed, as published in *The Golden Age* of March 19, 1930, conveyed the property to J. F. Rutherford; after his death ownership would revert to the Watch Tower Society.

Another version of the story says that Beth Sarim was built for $75,000 in materials, using volunteer labor. As the building was finished in 1930, Robert J. Martin (at Bethel in Brooklyn) deeded the property to Rutherford for ten dollars. The property included approximately 100 acres.[196]

Rumors about what was happening on the building site flourished. Jacob Blank from the Highland Park Kingdom Hall (a JW "church" is known as a Kingdom Hall) in northeast Los Angeles was the contractor who built Beth Sarim with volunteers. Blank used to boast that after a day's work, he and the Judge would sit down in the living room and have a drink together. This seems a totally banal, everyday story hardly worth repeating, but it shows "JFR" (as Rutherford is known among Bible Students in the US today) was not a teetotaler. This bit of truth about his character undoubtedly aroused some indignation among Bible Students at that time.

Ernest D. Sexton, the former loyal Rutherford supporter, who for many years was the most prominent member of the Los Angeles Bible Students ecclesia, began moving away from Rutherford's ideas around 1930. As more rumors about Beth Sarim stirred among the members, Sexton and Edward G. Lamel, another Bible Student who had been secretary for the Los Angeles congregation and who broke with Rutherford around 1938, went to San Diego to investigate. They noticed, allegedly, that the employed brothers, among others, were engaged in carrying beverages from the basement into the house. In my opinion this is a minor thing. Sexton, it seems, had already planned to break with Rutherford and in such a situation everything and anything could be used against the enemy. (Source: J. Parkinson, USA)

Around 1948 the Society sold Beth Sarim because the magnificent villa "had fully served its purpose and was now only serving as a monument quite expensive to keep" (*Salvation*, 1939, p. 289; *Proclaimers*, 1993, p. 76).[197]

Even so, controversy and rumors remained regarding the villa. In 1966, Richard E. Abrahamson, the Society's former chief in Denmark (and by his death in 2002, secretary-treasurer of the Watch Tower Bible and Tract Society of Pennsylvania), informed me the Society had not financed Beth Sarim; the funds had come from two individuals who wanted J. F. Rutherford to use the house in wintertime because of his health. As I recall, Abrahamson also mentioned Rutherford had amassed a private fortune from his time practicing law and he also contributed financially to the construction.

Though the Society's leaders had distanced themselves from the notorious villa in California by its sale in 1948, the press continued to mention it in critical articles. Perhaps the press should have been more interested in *who and how many* lived in the house and what their functions were in relation to the Society. According to my research, the residents of the villa were: J. F. Rutherford; his personal secretary Bonnie Boyd (mentioned in Moyle's letter; see Olin R. Moyle's open letter to Rutherford in Appendix); Donald Haslett, who presumably served as a kind of butler; Bonnie Boyd's friend Berta Peale and later, her mother also moved in. Bonnie Boyd and Donald Haslett were each registered as "servants" in the 1930 US census. August H. and Blanch P. Balko were also listed as servants in 1930, and they had an infant daughter. And, it seems, that Rutherford's personal dietician, Matthew Howlett, who had studied medicine in England and taken some postgraduate courses in the United States, also joined the staff later. The total number inhabiting the villa must have been about six to eight people, including Rutherford. (Source: James Parkinson, USA, and "Rutherford Exposed: The Story of Berta and Bonnie," and an email from James Parkinson, September 2011)

Bonnie Boyd came to Bethel with her mother in 1923, and worked as a stenographer for W. E. VanAmburgh. That same year she became Rutherford's stenographer, and around 1931, his personal secretary. According to her testimony, in the *Moyle v. Franz* trial (page 1,367), she took dictation for all books and *Watch Tower* articles authored by Rutherford. (See Moyle's letter to Rutherford in Appendix.)

Imagination sets no limits, but the facts do. Nevertheless, I must mention the detailed reports available via internet search, discussing Rutherford's relationships with the aforementioned female employees. Bonnie Boyd, besides a secretary and trusted traveling companion during luxurious, international lecture tours, must also have had a particularly close relationship with Rutherford. On February 18, 1942, a few weeks after Rutherford's death, the *San Diego Union* quoted her as saying that she was the "adopted daughter" of Judge Rutherford, as she continuously had been with him since she was sixteen. Bonnie Boyd referred to him as her "adopted father."[198] This *could be* an explanation for the close nature of their relationship. Anything further one might uncover or conclude perhaps belongs in the sphere of their private lives and not to a study of the evolution of a religious movement. However, it is obvious that information about the real relationship is of interest to posterity, and not least for historians.

Berta Peale, a young female *Bethelite* who in 1934 also quickly rose to some prominence within the organization, must have had a very close relationship with the Judge as well. Apparently the "closeness" consisted of her serving as Rutherford's dietician and nurse, writes an anonymous "Earnest" in a comment about the story of Bonnie and Berta. The Judge's former dietician, Matthew Howlett, left headquarters in July 1938 in favor of so-called "zone work" (circuit work) in Cleveland, Ohio; this would have been about the time Berta arrived and became the dietician. Howlett returned to Bethel in 1939 and resumed his work as a nurse and dietician for Rutherford.

Berta reportedly made a well-known and careless pronouncement that she had a close relationship with Rutherford—"he [Rutherford] was like a husband to me in every way"; this may be taken to mean something extraordinary but we cannot know for certain. Words alone can be deceptive or subject to interpretation and Berta is no longer living and cannot provide more information. Until proven otherwise, the words cannot objectively prove the character of the relationship, other than that it was very personal and very close.

So much about these stories sounds like gossip, and I have difficulty believing them. Still in the context that Rutherford's Witnesses apparently had a more relaxed attitude towards sexual matters than they did later during the time when N. H. Knorr was Society president—he was a hardliner about such matters—there may be some truth in them. I invite you to read "Rutherford Exposed: The Story of Berta and Bonnie," which is available on the internet, and draw your own conclusions. In the discussion thread associated with the article, Master Member, an anonymous debater (and perhaps a Witness) from California, writes:[199]

"In looking over some of my field notes I found an entry regarding a conversation that I had back in 1960 with an elderly JW by the name of Arthur Mingo. Arthur was in his eighties at the time and had joined the Bible Students in 1906. He was, therefore, an eyewitness to the many changes forced upon those who stayed in the Watch Tower movement.... Arthur also felt joy for those getting married, but then he told us how simple things were back in the 1930s when Judge Rutherford ran the organization. Basically Arthur said that the JWs of that era didn't need government or religious approval to get married. Arthur said: 'If a brother and sister wanted to get married, all they had to do was to inform the Company Servant of their intentions and then they would live together as husband and wife.' It was that simple. Apparently Rutherford did the same with Berta and Bonnie."[200]

Perhaps these conditions within the movement, which apparently evolved after Rutherford's seizure of power, were in fact a *projection* of Rutherford's own private attitude on the subject. Current Bible Students tell me that relationships of the aforementioned character would have been utterly unacceptable in C. T. Russell's days.

Such revelations are new to me, but I accept the rationality of this point of view without making myself an advocate for adultery, loose relationships or promiscuity. Nothing surprises me. In this context I am reminded of a quote from *The Brothers Karamazov* by Fyodor Mikhailovich Dostoevsky, which I note here out of its original context: *"If one tried for a bet to invent the most unlikely story, one could hardly find anything more incredible."* The truth often appears, as a matter of fact, *too* improbable, but that doesn't make it impossible.

As far as I can judge from the circumstantial evidence, Knorr's administration, which assumed management after Rutherford's death in 1942, had wished the Judge "over all the hills" long before his death. But Rutherford could not be fired or dismissed or otherwise removed. According to the new by-laws for the governance of the New York Society adopted on January 6, 1917, he had been elected for life. Therefore, he may have been a "dead man walking"—a done man, even though he was still highly valued among the ordinary members— for some time before his death, but he still held the top post in the organization. Knorr's subsequent administration was marked by moral rearmament, which may have been a reaction to the alleged frolic of the Rutherford period.

Chapter 18

"Theocracy" Implemented by Voluntary Coercion

Russell's old elder system—the very one which elected the Judge—naturally became an obstacle to the Judge's plans for the organization. To counteract it, he began an action against the democratically elected elders. Through intense campaigns, he encouraged the members to discard the principle of democratic elections, which he claimed were contrary to the universal principles of Jehovah. This effort took several years, wherein Rutherford outmaneuvered men "whose hair had grown gray in the Lord's service" so only the hard core of the "Watch Tower Society boys" were left. (Schnell, 1956, p. 55–61; 116)

With the launch of the new magazine *The Golden Age* in December 1919, the Society undertook a reorganization of the congregation structure so that congregations, now charged with disseminating the new magazine, would have to register as "service organizations." A Service Director, who was not subject to the annual election in the congregation, was now appointed in each congregation. This Director, who from now on was the local representative of the Society, had to organize and manage the work; and he was also to encourage local Bible Students to participate in the new service work among ordinary people. I wouldn't be surprised to learn that the elected elders up to that time viewed this new apparatus with some suspicion. However, it really was beyond their control and it discarded and outranked the old, proven system. Rutherford's desire to completely dominate the organization could not be halted, and an elite "theocratic" (God-led) regime was now gradually introduced. (*Proclaimers*, 1993, p. 207–213)

The Society's history book from 1959 reads:

"Those congregations desiring to participate in this new field of service opening up in 1919 were asked to register as a service organization with the Society. When the Society received these requests, the brothers at headquarters *theocratically* appointed one of the local number in the congregation to serve as the Society's appointee, to be known as the 'director.' He was not subject to local yearly election. This meant that for the first time authority was being taken away from the democratically controlled congregations under their 'elective elders,' and direction was to reside now, specifically, under the Society's international supervision" (*Divine Purpose*, 1959, p. 95).

The "visible theocratic organization" began with a gradual takeover program that ultimately ended with removal of all elected elders. Working Directors and the elders shared supervision of members and congregational functions in a transitional period.

I have already mentioned it, but wish to note again that *Society* is written with a capital S. This comes from the 1993 history book, explaining that "the Society" stood for "the faithful and wise servant"[201] and the "Governing Body," that is, specially elected members from the Board of Directors of the Pennsylvania Society.[202] Not quite an ordinary company. (*Proclaimers*, 1993, p. 219 and 639)

The new theocratic organization—Jehovah's direct leadership through the organization, and the way it was introduced—caused some unrest and trouble for the elders: "In the advanced conceptions of the new witness work and the more centralized organization necessary to weld the witnesses together into one solid working force, considerable resistance was encountered from unprogressive 'elective elders' in the local congregations. Many of these insisted on living in the past, in the time of Pastor Russell, who was claimed by them to be the sole channel of Scriptural enlightenment, whom they called 'the servant' of Matthew 24:45" (*Qualified*, 1955, p. 318).

Proclaimers further states that there were constantly "certain 'elective elders' who manifested themselves as opposition to the new, divinely provided leadership. They failed to see that Jehovah's holy spirit or active force was working organizationally in bringing about a governmental transformation leading to a theocratic, God-directed New World society" (*Qualified*, 1955, p. 320).

Note here the introduction of the concept, "the New World society," which from then on came up more and more often. The new world still had not arrived, so one had to be content with a kind of *foretaste*.

Schnell, who experienced this whole process from within, wrote in *Thirty Years a Watch Tower Slave*: "In this manner, and to my everlasting shame, I was used in a middle German town where there was a congregation of one hundred seventy-five Bible Students who would not accept a Service Director, nor would report time or carry out Watch Tower Society instructions. I was sent there from Magdeburg, a mere stripling of twenty-one years of age, with the full backing of the Watch Tower Society to make that congregation toe the line, and with specific instructions to split them up if they would not come around./ Confronting me were men whose hair had grown gray in the Lord's service, fine Christian Elders; and I, a mere youth, over-rode their objections peremptorily by asking the congregation after an hour's discourse, 'Who is in favor of the Watch Tower Society?' Upon receiving no answer I took it upon myself to brand the members of that congregation as 'Evil Servants,' and asked all in favor of the Watch Tower Society to rise and follow me out of the hall. Eight of the one hundred seventy-five assembled followed me out and we repaired to the home of one of the brothers and there organized a new congregation. I, of course, became the Service Director" (Schnell, 1955, p. 56; repaired, as used above is an old fashioned usage meaning to transfer to another place).

From the Top Down

The ultimate blow against the relatively democratic election principle in the congregations came in *The Watch Tower* from 1932; a two-part article, "Jehovah's Organization," showed "the system of 'elective elders' was an unclean practice of this world and not according to the principles of the great Theocrat, who rules his sanctuary from the top down" (*Divine Purpose*, 1959, p. 127).

"Take it or leave it" seems to have been Rutherford and the Society's unspoken motto of this campaign. The Society's ideal congregation publisher (preacher) apparently was a conformed individual, who possessed no personal opinion, and who allowed the leaders of the organization to decide what he should think and believe about everything.

All congregations throughout the world were now invited to send the Rutherford-drafted resolution to Society headquarters in New York, as evidence that they had adopted all the Judge wanted:

"Therefore be it resolved that there is no Scriptural authority for the existence of the elective office of elders in the church and that henceforth we will not elect any person to the office of elder; that all of the anointed of God are elders, as the term is defined by the Scriptures, and all are servants of the Most High."

The resolution further states:

"That, to the end that our service may be orderly, we will select certain ones of our company to perform specific service that may be necessary, including the following, to wit: A service director who shall be nominated by us and confirmed by the Society's executive or manager, and which service director shall be a member of the service committee of this company" (*Divine Purpose*, 1959, p. 127).

In order to give this adoption process "biblical" legitimacy—since all congregations throughout the world had *voluntarily* confirmed the resolution—it was established that the 2,300 days mentioned by the prophet Daniel in the Old Testament expired on adoption day in 1932 "at the exact end of the time period mentioned in Daniel's prophecy"—this of course was *pure invention*. Still, the resolution was interpreted as "the official notification made by Jehovah through his visible channel of communication that his sanctuary had been cleansed and had been restored to its rightful state as regards the elimination of this democratic procedure in electing elders" (*Divine Purpose*, 1959, p. 127). The 2,300 evenings and mornings is mentioned in Daniel 8:14. However, these

"2,300 days" were not whole days, since the Jews practiced both morning and evening sacrifices. In reality, the passage means about 1,150 days.

This coarse abuse of the words about the 2,300 evenings and mornings from Daniel's book was not an anomaly. The Adventists, as previously noted, used this same text from Daniel's Book in connection with the alleged second coming of Christ in 1844. One can easily understand why so many of Russell's elected elders stepped back. It was probably quite a deliberate deception of people who lacked any qualification to understand what the figure 2,300 truly meant. (*Divine Purpose*, 1959, p. 127; *Qualified*, 1955, p. 317-322)

With the purging of the "unclean," democratically elected elders, Rutherford's "sanctuary" was temporarily freed from further opposition, and the working directors could now begin to realize the Judge's vision of top-down rule. Rutherford created "the theocratic man," who was blindly willing to accept anything, if it simply came from "Jehovah through his visible channel of communication" in New York. (*Divine Purpose*, p. 127)

At that time, the visible channel was *the Society*.

Schnell described the 1930 situation as follows:

"The Watch Tower leaders had now perfected the means for a rigid, top-down control of the entire Organization. Through their books, booklets and the Watchtower magazines, they had forged a doctrinal straight jacket. This generated inversely a kind of thinking called 'Organization Mindedness,' a new intellectual lever which we in Germany, back in 1926, had called *gleichschaltung*.... Besides, they had been thoroughly brain washed by the use of stereotyped textbooks published by the Watch Tower Society, and any concept of individual study and individual thinking as a Christian which might have been present had been supplanted by a new set of values, new precepts for thinking, and new motives for doing.... Their own thoughts were thus replaced by a narrow sphere or circumscribed area of thoughts, or as the Watch Tower put it, a 'channel.' " (*Schnell*, 1963, p. 99–106)

Moyle Case—Another Sifting

There seems to be some doubt about whether the "Great Theocrat" governing his shrine "from the top down," was Jehovah or Rutherford, and rightly so. A former, highly trusted employee at headquarters in Brooklyn, who wanted to remain anonymous, wrote the following to H. H. Stroup, former professor of sociology at Brooklyn College:

"Rutherford controls the organization completely. Directors and members meetings are a formality. The Judge sends a note stating whom he wants elected, or rejected, or what he wants done, and that is immediately done unanimously. Woe be unto that one who opposes. Anyone that opposes slightly gets a tongue lashing at the dinner table, and if the opposition is serious, or such one has too much independence of mind he is liquidated from the organization" (*Stroup*, 1945, p. 22; the letter is dated 1941).

Olin Richmond Moyle, who had been a member of the Society's board of directors and legal counsel for the Society, heading its newly formed Legal Department starting in 1935[203], was expelled from the Watchtower organization on August 8, 1939. In a letter to the entire staff at headquarters, Moyle criticized a number of factors that did not agree with the official principles. According to the criticism, Rutherford had discriminated to his own advantage, and owned several properties and generally lived in luxury. Moyle also drew attention to Rutherford's excessive use of alcohol and that vulgar talk was general at the headquarters. Moyle himself was a teetotaler. (Stroup, 45, p. 25; Penton, 1986, p. 80-83; see also, Olin R. Moyle at *Wikipedia*)

Moyle wrote:

"Conditions at Bethel are a matter of concern to all of the Lord's people. Nowhere among imperfect men can there be perfect freedom from oppression, discrimination and unfair treatment, but at the Lord's headquarters on earth conditions should be such that injustice would be reduced to the minimum. That is not the case here at Bethel and a protest should be made against it."

Moyle continued:

"How can we consistently condemn religionists for being intolerant when you exercise intolerance against those who work with you? Doesn't this prove that the only freedom permitted at Bethel is freedom to do and say that which you wish to be said and done? The Lord certainly never authorized you to exercise such high handed authority over your fellow servants."

And on drinking habits at Bethel, Moyle noted:

"Under your tutelage there has grown up a glorification of alcohol and condemnation of total abstinence which is unseemly.... There appears to be a definite policy of breaking in new comers into the use of liquor, and resentment is shown against those who do not join them. The claim is made, 'One can't be a real Bethelite without drinking beer' " (Moyle's letter is dated July 21, 1939; the entire letter can be found in Appendix).[204]

The response from the Society was violent. Since Moyle's letter concerned all at Bethel, the Society's answer was presented to the whole "family" at headquarters. Leadership said Moyle's letter contained, "false, slanderous and libelous statements," and it was "vigorously condemned by the board, and all the members of the Bethel family." The Society's management, the Pennsylvania corporation and the New York department, released a resolution on August 8, 1939, quoting from the second half:

"For four years past the writer of that letter has been entrusted with the confidential matters of the Society. It now appears that the writer of that letter, without excuse, libels the family of God at Bethel, and identifies himself as one who speaks evil against the Lord's organization, and who is a murmurer and complainer, even as the Scriptures have foretold (Jude 4:16; 1 Cor. 4:3; Rom.

14:4). / The members of the board of directors hereby resent the criticism appearing in that letter, disapprove of the writer and his actions, and recommend that the president of the Society immediately terminate the relationship of O. R. Moyle to the Society as legal counsel and as member of the Bethel family."

Further it was stated that "every paragraph of that letter is false, filled with lies, and is a wicked slander and libel not only against the president but against the entire family, and for that reason the letter has been published by the Society.... His only possible purpose in further publishing is to justify himself and to 'cause division among the brethren,' both of which are condemned by the Word of God (Luke 16:15; Rom. 16:17, 18). For this reason the brethren should be warned.... By inducing others to join with him in the circulation and publication of his slanderous letter among the consecrated he makes others party to his wrong. The slanderous paper, being in opposition and against the interest of the Theocratic government, is pleasing only to the Devil and his earthly agents." The resolution was undersigned by everyone in the Society's top leadership. (*WT*, Oct. 15, 1939, p. 316, 317; Penton, 1986, p. 81-82)

In *The Watchtower* Moyle was even compared to Judas: "Judas was entrusted by Christ Jesus with confidential matters, and Judas proved his unfaithfulness by furnishing to the enemy that which they could use and did use against the Lord" (*WT*, October 15, 1939, p. 317).

Moyle had done the one thing a Jehovah's Witness should never do under any circumstance: He publicly criticized the leaders. Consequently, he was immediately excluded from all board meetings. In 1939 he brought a lawsuit against Rutherford and the other directors for defamatory statements and won the case in 1944, two years after the Judge's death. The Society was ordered to pay him a total of $25,000 in damages. (Stroup, 1945, p. 26; Martin and Klann, 1959, p. 27)[205]

The Moyle affair was a relatively important event in the history of the Watch Tower Society, which is why I mention it here. Whether Moyle was right in all his accusations is today difficult to judge. However, he won the trial, which shows that there was truth in his accusations.

Subsequently, many former high-ranking members noted that developments within the movement went from bad to worse. Thus Schnell writes succinctly about Rutherford, who was iconically the "uncompromising foe of organized Christendom," beginning to establish an organization that was "far more absolute and far more rigidly organized than was the Catholic Church," which Rutherford bitterly opposed. (Schnell, 1963, p. 39)

As one would expect in a movement like Jehovah's Witnesses, members always went to extremes in the evaluation of the head. For many of the individualistic elders, Rutherford (like Russell) was the "pope" of a new hierarchy, which strikingly recalled church regimes of the past. Yet, for most of the regular members, he was the unapproachable, elevated "commander." For example, a female member or sister from Rhode Island, who had heard Rutherford on the radio, wrote concerning the Judge's health:

"Dear Judge Rutherford: I hope that your cold is better soon. Your voice seemed so tired. I could hear you sigh and cough a few times on Sunday. We cannot afford to have you sick; so you want a little rest" (Rutherford could be heard at the Society's radio station, WBBR, established in 1921; *WT*, March 1932; Stroup 1945, p. 19).

Conventions—An Important Part of Regimentation

Rutherford soon realized the importance of holding national and international conventions, a practice introduced by Russell in 1893. At the first convention immersion baptism was introduced; for example dunking the member in a swimming pool or lake, as the Witnesses still famously do today. Beginning in the 1950s, the rallies became huge mass meetings held at the world's largest sporting fields, facilitating large attendance and melding together the movement's members. These rallies are where the Witnesses have energetic religious experiences, roughly equating with the euphoric "revivals" in other religious communities.

It is also at these rallies or conventions that new supporters, deeply influenced by the massive presence of thousands of like-minded people, often decide to be baptized, which implies an *unconditional inauguration* and surrender to Jehovah, and in practice, the Watchtower Society.[206] Here then is the eternally binding coalescence between individual and totalitarian authority. The baptized person should henceforth be a devoted Witness of Jehovah, who is said to convey his wishes through his visible organization on earth: The Watchtower Bible and Tract Society in Brooklyn.

During the baptismal discourse at the international convention in Copenhagen, Denmark, in 2003, which I attended to take pictures and make observations, I heard the speaker tell the baptismal candidates that they now had to consider themselves the "property of Jehovah." The words gave me a shiver.

For outsiders, it is clear these mass gatherings meld the participants, so that it is nearly impossible for them to separate their personal thoughts from those of the organization. To put it plainly, the sweeping propaganda reduces or *exterminates* the individual, so that the *self* can no longer withstand the massive influence to which it is exposed. This practice and condition were not so pronounced in 1919 when some individualists still remained in the organization.

The first convention under Rutherford's leadership was held at Cedar Point, Ohio, in September 1919 and aimed to reunite the Bible Students. The atmosphere at this convention was tense and characterized by inconsistencies and discussions that were actually very positive and promising for the time. The next convention was held at the same place in September 1922, and during one of Rutherford's talks a huge banner with the urgent words, "Advertise the

King and Kingdom," was unfolded before the audience. At the last meeting of the convention a resolution against Satan the Devil and the world rulers—"the statesmen, financiers and the clergy" and the League of Nations, which was the "visible part of Satan's empire or organization"—was enthusiastically and "unanimously" adopted by the 18,000 in attendance. And "in the course of weeks 35,000,000 copies of this stinging judgment message expressing Jehovah's anger were distributed throughout Christendom" (*Divine Purpose*, 1959, p. 103; *Qualified*, 1955, p. 321; *Proclaimers*, 1993, p. 77, 260; "Modern History of Jehovah's Witnesses," *WT*, June 1, 1955, p. 334).

At an assembly in Los Angeles, California, in 1923, one more of Rutherford's "new truths" was launched. "The sheep and goats" (a motif from Matthew 25) were identified respectively as a "group of persons of good will" and "that class who claim to be Christians" or so-called Christians. Yet another resolution—Proclamation, A Warning to All Christians...—was adopted by 30,000 enthusiastic supporters, and 50,000,000 printed copies of it were distributed throughout the world. (*Divine Purpose*, 1959, p. 104-105)

Again, at an assembly in Columbus, Ohio, in 1924, Rutherford accused Satan and the clergy of having joined in a "conspiracy for the purpose of keeping the peoples in ignorance of God's provision for blessing them with life," and that "unscrupulous politicians" have "entered into said conspiracy.... We present and charge that the clergy have yielded to the temptations presented to them by Satan ... have joined in said conspiracy.... That they have failed and refused to preach to the people the message of Messiah's kingdom and to point them to the evidences relating to his second coming ... have endorsed the League of Nations and declared it to be 'the political expression of God's kingdom on earth,' thereby breaking their alliance to the Lord Jesus Christ and declaring their alliance to the devil, the god of evil."

Such accusations, which were highly provocative to the various Christian communities, were in fact partly deliberate attempt at confrontation, partly to lure people who did not feel at home in the churches into the Society. This pompous and bombastic accusation was adopted by 20,000 assembly participants. The tract *Ecclesiastics Indicted* was later produced with millions of copies distributed. (*Divine Purpose*, 1959, p. 106; *WT*, 1924, p. 259-264; see also the article: "Delivering Satan's Death Notice," *WT*, Aug. 1, 1956, p. 462)

In 1925, when Abraham, Isaac and Jacob were to arise from the dead, a major assembly in Indianapolis, Indiana, was held with 10,000 delegates; they adopted a resolution addressed "To All People of Good Will," and about 50 million copies were distributed during the following months. (*Divine Purpose*, 1959, p. 109)

At an international assembly in London in 1926, Rutherford revealed the League of Nations was the "abomination that makes desolate" (Matt. 24:15).[207] The League was also exposed as the "eighth king" described in the Revelation of John 17:11. London was identified and branded as the "seat of the beast"

(Rev. 16:10). A resolution, titled "A Testimony to the Rulers of the World," was adopted and distributed in the amount of 50 million copies. (*Divine Purpose*, 1959, p. 110, 111)

By the way, the "abomination that makes desolate" and Rutherford and the Society's interpretation of this concept is yet another blatant example of the totally arbitrary interpretation method the leaders of the movement employed. Like so many other elements they removed from the biblical context, this concept and its application referred to a totally different time in the distant past.

The words in Daniel's book in the Old Testament, where the concept appears for the first time, allude to the Zeus altar that *Antiochus* IV *Epifanes* (175–163 BC), had built in the Temple of Jahve (Jehovah) in Jerusalem around 168 BC. The concept has since been freely used on many ancient and contemporary institutions and events, even by the Christians in the first century, who applied it to the Roman troops' siege of Jerusalem in AD 66 and 70. The Bible Students' methods of interpretation, the allegorical and the *ever-actualizing*, was therefore nothing new but had already been used among Jews and Christians long ago. Old prophetic writings intended for specific periods or events, even as they become increasingly outdated, are applied to new contemporary and seemingly suitable phenomena—such as the League of Nations and the UN.

But now, back to the assemblies:

At yet another international assembly in Toronto, Canada, in 1927, Rutherford had his public lecture broadcast over 53 radio stations—according to the leaders the largest chain of broadcasting stations, and without precedent. A resolution addressed "To the Peoples of 'Christendom' " was adopted, and later distributed in millions as a booklet, 1,898,796 copies to be exact. (*Divine Purpose*, 1959, p. 117)

The following year, at an assembly in Detroit, Michigan, 12,000 enthusiastic members adopted a resolution with unbelievable content, "A Declaration Against Satan and for Jehovah." This meeting was also broadcast using a chain of 106 radio stations. The resolution stated, among other things:

"[Because] Satan will not surrender his wicked rule over the nations and peoples of the earth, Jehovah of hosts with his anointed executive officer Christ Jesus will press the conflict against Satan and all of his forces of evil, and henceforth our battle-cry shall be, THE SWORD OF JEHOVAH AND OF HIS ANOINTED; that the great battle of Armageddon soon to begin will result in the full restraint of Satan and the complete overthrow of his evil organization, and that Jehovah will establish righteousness in the earth by and through Christ the new ruler and will emancipate mankind from evil and bring everlasting blessings to all nations of the earth…" (*Divine Purpose*, 1959, p. 118, 119).

These conventions, seven in total held from 1922 to 1928, were—according to Rutherford and the Society—a fulfillment of the prophetic statements in the Revelation of John. Thus, the imprisonment of Rutherford in 1918 marked the beginning of the 1,260 days, as mentioned in Revelation 12:6. In the past, many others had also tried to use the 1,260 days; again, I pause to mention the Adventists. With the assembly in Cedar Point on September 7, 1922, these 1,260 days ended; this could be considered impressively accurate, if it otherwise could be trusted. Most of the attendees swallowed everything they were fed—perhaps because they felt that they were very important individuals, being mentioned in the Bible and all. This convention and the subsequent six up to 1928 were interpreted as the "seven trumpets" and the "seven bowls of the anger of God" from the Revelation, which were poured down over "Satan's organization" (Rev. 8:2; 16:1).

It seems the Judge was a speculative and spectacular organizer. (*Qualified*, 1955, p. 320; *Divine Purpose*, 1959, p. 108)

The Jehovah's Witnesses

Another landmark event was held in Columbus, Ohio, in 1931.

At this pivotal gathering, 15,000 delegates adopted a resolution giving the movement a new name: Jehovah's Witnesses. Until that time, the movement, understandably, had not adopted names coined by outsiders, including: Russellites, Millennial Dawn people, Watch Tower people, etc. Internally they referred to themselves as Christians, Bible Students and the friends. Since the break-aways had formed their own associations beginning in 1918, all making claims on Russell's legacy, Rutherford felt the time had come to break with the past—the time of *creature worship*—and thus Russell. The new, official name was justified by Isaiah 43:10–12, which among other things states:

"Ye are my witnesses, saith the LORD." (*The LORD* is a transliteration of God's name: JHVH, Jahve or Jehovah.)

Most Jehovah's Witnesses are unaware that Rutherford chose the name "Jehovah's Witnesses" not because of "new light," but because he wanted to distinguish *his* group from those that broke away around 1918. Around 1930–1931, Rutherford must have repeatedly attacked the new independent Bible Student associations in *The Watchtower* and *The Golden Age*, hoping to discourage any association with them.

The relatively high level of activity from holding large assemblies to mass distribution of resolutions and brochures, book sales, etc., resulted in increased membership. The environment Rutherford created seemed to be one of large everything: crowds, editions, distribution. Still, membership did not increase significantly from 1918 to 1930, but from 1931 to 1939 the number of members more than doubled, as the table on the next page illustrates.

Within the movement 1938 is considered the year when the Theocracy was finally completed. Theocracy, God's management from the top-down meant many things including reorganization so that regions with approximately twenty congregations were united in zones. Each Zone was led by a *Zone Servant*, "the eyes and ears" of the Society (per Schnell), to oversee and supervise

Period	Books and brochures distributed/sold	Maximum number of members
1874–1892	1,535,600	400
1893–1918	9,737,224	21,274
1919–1930	93,500,000	3,988
1931–1939	215,984,991	73,469
1940–1945	158,315,308	141,606

(*Qualified*, 1955, p. 311)

each congregation. (Zones later became known as Circuits.) The Zone Servant spent a week in each congregation where he had to cooperate with the leaders and monitor the members' preaching work. A biannual Zone Assembly was held with approximately twenty congregations participating. (*Qualified*, 1955, p. 328; *Divine Purpose*, 1959, p. 148)

That same year, the Brothers were invited to submit resolutions, prepared by Society management in New York, where they confirmed Rutherford's abolition of the elected-elders system. The resolution stated, in part:

"We, the company of God's people taken out for his name, and now at _____ [a named congregation], recognize that God's government is a pure theocracy and that Christ Jesus is at the temple and in full charge and control of the visible organization of Jehovah, as well as the invisible, and that 'THE SOCIETY' is the visible representative of the Lord on earth, and we therefore request 'The Society' to organize this company for service and to appoint the various servants thereof, so that all of us may work together in peace, righteousness, harmony and complete unity" (*Divine Purpose*, 1959, p. 148, 149).

This resolution must have been a nasty bite for the oppressed opposition and the "elective elders"[208] and I assume a sifting of disgruntled elements also occurred at this time. Generally, the local congregations surrendered, one after another, to the great Theocrat's earthly representatives, the Judge and his obedient instrument, the Watch Tower Society in New York, which was now completely under his control: "This amounted to surrender of democratic power or presbyter style of church control that had existed in the congregations for sixty years. Most congregations readily adopted this resolution, and the few that did not have since lost their vision and privileges of Kingdom service" (*Divine Purpose*, 1959, p. 149).

The Witnesses also adopted unconventional and spectacular preaching methods during these years. For example, gramophone testimonies were introduced in 1933 as a new work instrument. These recorded lectures literally assured preaching was completely homogenous. Whether the Judge was more comfortable with this approach is not known, however, it allowed his voice to be heard widely in the US and Europe. Outside the United States, his earnest voice was translated into the local languages: "In 1937 there were 10,368,569 persons reported as having heard these recorded lectures either publicly or privately, whereas for 1938 this number had grown to 13,070,426. By 1938, too, there were 430,000 recorded lectures in sixteen languages besides English in use on 19,676 sound machines" (*Divine Purpose*, 1959, p. 139).

In practice, the Witnesses greeted whoever answered the door, and then played a gramophone record with a speech by Rutherford, afterward the colporteur attempted to sell one of the Judge's many books (published in incredible print runs). Not surprising, in these years the Witnesses also had to use prepared testimonies, which were printed cards called *canvasses*.

The Witnesses also used a rather nontraditional method of preaching: In 1936 they began marching in processions wearing sandwich signs, walking up to six miles per session. Such a spectacular event or style of evangelizing was called "information marching" (*Divine Purpose*, 1959, p. 145, 152).

In 1940 they added "street work" for distributing the magazines *The Watchtower* and *Awake!*—the most remarkable canvassing and advertising method the movement has used to date.

The Great Multitude, the "Jonadabs," are Designated

One of the notable messages of the Rutherford period was that a *large crowd*, numbering in the millions, would survive Armageddon and this crowd[209] would constitute the bulk of the population in the New World following Armageddon. The discovery—or perhaps I should say the *invention*—of *the great crowd* or *other sheep*, was almost done out of *necessity*, because when the *anointed* or *little flock* was in heaven, who would inhabit earth besides the millions to be raised from the dead who never had the chance to hear the message of the Jehovah's Witnesses?

Originally Russell assumed that millions of people living in his time would survive the culmination in 1914—in other words, would get through the last *great tribulation*, after which they would live forever on an earth free of the old institutions. From the beginning in the mid-1870s Russell believed the Adventists' insistence that the earth would burn up at the Second Coming of Christ was nonsense. It was only this world's institutions that would be destroyed, and above all Babylon, the world empire of false religion, including pagandom and all of Christendom. However, until 1932, the Witnesses had no real notions about the identity of the large crowd or "multitude" mentioned in the Revelation of John 7:9-17. Rutherford obliged with a definition. He and his revisionists were convinced the large crowd was not a secondary, heavenly crowd, or class of bridesmaids consisting of less-zealous members as they had once thought; it was a new, large group of people who had to live forever on earth.

Proclaimers clarifies it this way:

"In 1932 it was explained that Jehonadab (Jonadab), King Jehu's associate, prefigured a class of persons who would enjoy everlasting life on earth. (2 Kings 10:15-28) The Jonadabs, as they came to be known, counted it a privilege to be associated with Jehovah's anointed servants and to have some share with them in advertising the Kingdom. But at that time, there was no special effort to gather and organize these individuals with an earthly hope" (*Proclaimers*, 1993, p. 83).

The *Jonadabs* were now encouraged to join the anointed and be baptized, like the members of the *little flock* had long ago done. At the convention of Jehovah's Witnesses and Jonadabs in Washington, DC, in 1935, Judge Rutherford held a lecture on the "great multitude" wherein he called new members to engage in the preaching work with "the anointed." They knew now that there were far more Jonadabs in the world than members of the little flock; there were, in fact, millions and millions of Jonadabs, who could be collected before Armageddon. At the end of the lecture, in typical fashion, Rutherford asked the Jonadabs to stand:

"At the speaker's request, the Jonadabs arose. 'There was at first a hush,' recalled Mildred Cobb, who had been baptized in the summer of 1908, 'then a gladsome cry, and the cheering was loud and long'" (*Proclaimers*, 1993, p. 84).

With these prospects, the anointed Jehovah's Witnesses and the new Jonadabs had again, in a theocratic way, confirmed their commitment to the Watchtower managers' advancing agenda to increase membership to new, large-scale numbers. A lot of work lay ahead for the members, a job with almost infinite prospects and opportunities.

The driving force for this big recruitment campaign was, as always, the warning that the war of Armageddon was about to erupt.

Chapter 19

See You in the Kingdom of God

Judge Rutherford's provocative attacks on the churches led to a lot of trouble with Catholic priests and action groups. As far as I can judge, the Witnesses' information on the extensive harassment aimed at them in the US and around the world is to some extent correct, although the persecution may also have been exaggerated. These persecutions were not just of great value for publicity, but they were also one of the signs indicating the *end times*:

"Then they will deliver you up to tribulation, and put you to death. ... But he who endures to the end will be saved" (Matthew 24:9–13 RSV). So, the persecution was a *requirement* if the prophesies were to be fulfilled.

William Schnell takes the following angle on their tactics:

"In order to gain attention it was necessary to create a condition of war through the creation of issues, coupled with an appearance of being persecuted. The point had been reached where everything that had been written in the books Preparation and Religion, was to be put into practice. / It now became the studied policy of the Watch Tower Society to make Jehovah's Witnesses hated of all men—by their way of preaching, by the methods of their preaching, and by what they were preaching. They hoped thus to put themselves in the position where they appeared to be martyrs for the sake of religion" (Schnell, 1963, p. 101).

Later, Schnell notes how they focused on a specific urban area, for example, New Jersey near Brooklyn, which was equivalent to being "thrown to the lions" (p. 101). If Schnell's observation is credible, the intention was to provoke the local populace so they would complain to the authorities. The police then demanded the Witnesses secure permits to sell their publications door-to-door, which they refused. The police "were stepping into the trap which the Watch Tower had cleverly baited" (p. 102). Organized leagues of Witnesses were put into action supporting the urban offensive, and soon the police began to arrest them. The legal authorities held that the Witnesses were not being denied freedom of religion, their meetings were not being disturbed and they could even sell their literature, if they obtained the necessary permission. (p. 102, 106)

The Witnesses had, according to Schnell, a "history of rough and tumble attack on religion. Therefore, by their very audacity they irritated the courts to a point where they gave them their desired martyrdom in the form of fines and jail sentences" (p. 102, 103).

"We knew all along that we had a right to distribute our books, booklets and pamphlets without censorship under the freedom of the press section of the Bill of Rights. So far we had refrained from using it, because our present methods were drawing fire and were giving us the desired martyrdom. This had tremendous advertising value and was creating sympathy for us" (p. 103).

In those years, Rutherford took advantage of radio to spread the message, and this may explain why the attacked churches of Babylon reportedly worked to remove Rutherford from the airwaves. There are indications that the Catholics in particular tried to silence Rutherford's radio broadcast; since the release of the Seventh Volume in 1917 they had coordinated their actions against the "Kingdom Proclaimers."

According to the Society's history books, the Catholics must have also applied pressure to the owners of the stations broadcasting the Judge's sermons; apparently, the owners could not withstand this pressure.

The Watchtower's propaganda was something of an ideological crusade against the churches. The terminology and the hateful rhetoric had certainly

Awake, ye drunkards, and howl

Archetype of a Jehovah's Witness in the 1930s: "Awake, ye drunkards [Catholics and Protestants], and howl" (J. F. Rutherford: *Religion*, 1940, p. 121).

affected the Catholics deeply, because the Witnesses, in an extreme form, continued the original Protestant showdown with the Roman church. Adventists, Bible Students and Jehovah's Witnesses inherited the Protestant hatred of the Catholic "Babel," and they now continued the religious war with every indelicate method that could be devised. (*Divine Purpose*, 1959, p. 134–140; Schnell, 1963, p. 99–103)

Still, this was nothing compared to what was developing.

Rutherford Angers Adolf Hitler

From 1933 to 1945 was a time of martyrdom for the movement. In April 1933 the Nazis seized the Witnesses' headquarters in Magdeburg, Germany, but the Gestapo found nothing to prove the charge of subversive activities. When Rutherford was told about the Nazi seizure, he hinted to the headquarters' staff in Brooklyn, "that if this be the end of the work in Germany, this might indicate that the great final fight between Jehovah God and Satan the Devil's organization was then near." Not long before, he'd learned it was important to challenge everything, even if you had to walk directly into the lion's jaws. (*Sanctified*, 1961, p. 330)

The Judge had a real sense of drama and staging.

On June 25, 1933, the Society held a protest assembly in Berlin; both Rutherford and future Society president N. H. Knorr participated. Seven thousand participants adopted a resolution, "Declaration of Facts," which was immediately sent to all senior government officials in the Third Reich; 2,500,000 copies of the resolution were distributed to the public. (*Divine Purpose*, 1959, p. 130; *Qualified*, 1955, chapter (Study) 83)

Rutherford was a rude man, and the publications of the *Bibelforscher*'s (German name for Jehovah's Witnesses) contained coarse and political attacks on National Socialism in text and illustrations already by 1929. Rutherford's "grasshopper troops" did not hesitate, but rushed forward as if they *alone* could defeat the Nazi monster. In retrospect, Rutherford's actions seem to be pure suicide. Still, the rank and file members lined up, for this was now the battle to be fought: Martyrdom and the Kingdom of God were very near. Rutherford and his locusts were aware their rhetoric was disruptive, as seen in the "Declaration":

"*The language* in our books or literature concerning the League of Nations has been seized upon as a *reason for prohibiting our work* and the distribution of our books. Let us remind the government and the people of Germany that it was the League of Nations compact that laid upon the shoulders of the German people the great unjust and unbearable burdens. That League of Nations compact was not brought forth by the friends of Germany" ("Declaration of Facts," see the section "League of Nations," internet 2009; italics are mine). Penton emphasizes that the "Declaration of Facts" was the Society's attempt to placate Hitler. The 1974 *Yearbook* cites a letter that came with the declaration, sent to Hitler and his government, and among other things stated:

"The Brooklyn presidency of the Watch Tower Society is and always has been *exceedingly friendly to Germany*. In 1918 the president of the Society and seven members of the Board of Directors in America were sentenced to 80 years' imprisonment for the reason that the *president refused to let two magazines* in America, which he edited, *be used in war propaganda against Germany*" (Penton, 1986, p. 147-148; *YB*, 1974, p. 111; italics found in *Yearbook*).

The country manager for Jehovah's Witnesses in Germany at that time, Paul Balzereit, must have been responsible for trying to reach a compromise with the Nazis. In the 1974 *Yearbook*, the Society also writes that the ordinary member participants in Berlin had wanted a much stronger anti-Nazi statement:

"Many in attendance were disappointed in the 'declaration,' since in many points it failed to be as strong as the brothers had hoped. Brother Mütze from Dresden, who had worked closely with Brother Balzereit up until that time, accused him later of having weakened the original text. It was not the first time that Brother Balzereit had watered down the clear and unmistakable language of the Society's publications so as to avoid difficulties with governmental agencies. / *A large number of brothers refused to adopt it just for this reason.* In fact, a former pilgrim brother by the name of Kipper refused to offer it for adoption and another brother substituted. It could not be rightfully said that the declaration was unanimously adopted, even though Brother Balzereit later notified Brother Rutherford that it had been" (*YB*, 1974, p. 111; italics are mine).

What the Society tried to tell the *Yearbook* readers was probably that, rather than Rutherford, it was Balzereit who tried to compromise with the Nazis. It appeared to be an attempt to explain away *just the Facts*, for in the following year the compromise line of the 1934 *Yearbook* was confirmed.

It has been impossible for me to find the entire text of the Declaration in the more-recent history books released by the Society other than a citation in *Awake!* from August 1995, where they quote a few lines: "Our organization is not political in any sense. We only insist on teaching the Word of Jehovah God to the people, and that without hindrance" (*Awake!,* August 22, 1995).

This incredibly short and meaningless quote from an incredibly *long* statement filling five densely written pages that I eventually found on the internet in 2004,[210] by no means conveys the full weight of the famous declaration text, which presumably is linked to the declaration text from 1933 and does not entirely support the image of uncompromising Witnesses the Society tried to paint at the time.

In the Declaration published in the 1934 *Yearbook,* which came as an official opinion of the Watchtower Society and its president, the Society's directors denied the Jehovah's Witnesses had received "financial support for our work from the Jews." It further stressed that "the Jews entirely reject Jesus Christ and emphatically deny that he is the Savior," and that this proved the accusa-

Locusts attack demonism

"He [the Witnesses] realizes that he is small in himself but strong in the Lord and, like the description of the locusts, he is little, but wise; and like a band of locusts all such go forward as one united band of warriors: 'There be four things which are little upon the earth, but they are exceeding wise; ...The locusts have no king, yet go they forth all of them by bands.' Proverbs 30: 24, 27." (J. F. Rutherford, *Religion*, 1940, p. 176; 190)

tions against the Witnesses were "maliciously false and could proceed only from Satan, our great enemy" (from the section: "Jews").

The Declaration continued:

"The greatest and most oppressive empire on earth is the Anglo-American empire. By that is meant the British Empire, of which the United States of America forms a part. It has been the *commercial Jews* of the British-American empire that have built up and carried on Big Business as a means of exploiting and oppressing the peoples of many nations. This fact particularly applies to the cities of London and New York, the stronghold of Big Business. This fact is so manifest in America that there is a proverb concerning the city of New York which says: '*The Jews own it*, the Irish Catholics rule it, and the Americans pay the bills'..." (section: "Jews;" italics are mine).[211]

The Declaration also stated:

"The present government of Germany has declared emphatically against Big Business oppressors and in opposition to the wrongful religious influence in the political affairs of the nation. Such is exactly our position..." (section: "Our Literature").

Finally, it noted:

"Instead of being against the principles advocated by the government of Germany, we stand squarely for such principles, and point out that Jehovah God through Christ Jesus will bring about the full realization of these principles and will give to the people peace and prosperity and the greatest desire of every honest heart" (section: "Our Literature"; plus Penton, 1986, p. 147–149; 1934 *Yearbook* can be found at www.aggelia.be/yb1934.pdf).

The movement's agitation and preaching activity was immediately banned, effective June 28, 1933, three days after the convention. What had been an attempt to appease Hitler led to exactly the opposite; the signal was given for the Nazis to begin their cruel persecution of the Witnesses.

One can rightly ask whether the Jehovah's Witnesses' top managers just did exactly what they claim they do *not* do: meddle in politics. The result of their actions would soon reveal the truth.

In 1934, via a campaign orchestrated from Brooklyn, all Jehovah's Witnesses' congregations throughout the world sent the following protest telegram to Hitler:

"Hitler Government, Berlin, Germany. Your ill-treatment of Jehovah's witnesses shocks all good people of earth and dishonors God's name. Refrain from any further persecuting Jehovah's witnesses; otherwise God will destroy you and your national party" (*Divine Purpose*, 1959, p. 142).

It sounded heroic and magnificent. But wasn't Rutherford's sharp rhetoric really just exposing the lives of ordinary Witnesses to extreme danger?

Hitler must have taken note of this flood of cablegrams and telegrams:

"This brood will be exterminated in Germany!"

In the following years, 10,000 Witnesses—half of those in Germany—were arrested for subversive activities because they refused to do military service and salute with an enthusiastic *Heil, Hitler*. Two thousand Witnesses died in Nazi concentration camps. (*WT*, Aug. 1, 1955)

Rudolf Hoess, a Nazi later tried for war crimes, offers a firsthand testimony of the Witnesses' martyrdom in Nazi death camps. In his appalling autobiography, *Commandant of Auschwitz*, Hoess wrote:

"There were many Jehovah's Witnesses in Sachsenhausen. A great number of them refused to undertake military service and because of this the Reichsführer SS condemned them to death.... I have met many religious fanatics in my time; on pilgrimages, in monasteries, in Palestine, on the Hejaz road in Iraq, and in Armenia. They were Catholics, both Roman and Orthodox, Moslems, Shiites and Semites. But the Witnesses in Sachsenhausen, and particularly two of them, surpassed anything that I had previously seen. These two especially fanatical Witnesses refused to do any work that had any connection whatever with military matters. They would not stand at attention, or drill in time with the rest, or lay their hands along the seam of their trousers, or remove their caps. They said that such marks of respect were due only to Jehovah and not to man. They recognized only one lord and master, Jehovah. Both of them had to be taken from the block set aside for Jehovah's Witnesses and put in cells, since they constantly urged on the other Witnesses to behave in a similar manner."

And Hoess continued:

"Eicke had frequently sentenced them to be flogged because of their anti-disciplinarian behavior. They underwent this punishment with a joyous fervor that amounted almost to a perversion. They begged the commandant to increase their punishment, so that they might the better be able to testify to Jehovah. After they had been ordered to report for military service, which, needless to say, they flatly refused, indeed they refused even to put their signature to a military document, they too were condemned to death by the Reichsführer SS. When told of this in their cells, they went almost mad for joy and ecstasy, and could hardly wait for the day of execution.... When their time came, they almost ran to the place of execution. They wished on no account to be bound, for they desired to be able to raise their hands to Jehovah. Transformed by ecstasy, they stood in front of the wooden wall of the rifle-range, seemingly no longer of this world. Thus do I imagine that the first Christian martyrs must have appeared as they waited in the circus for the wild beasts to tear them in pieces. Their faces completely transformed, their eyes raised to heaven, and their hands clasped and lifted in prayer, they went to their death. / All who saw them die were deeply moved, and even the execution squad itself was affected."

Interestingly, Hoess added that the Witnesses should be an example for the SS men:

"On many occasions Himmler, as well as Eicke, used the fanatical faith of Jehovah's Witnesses as an example. / SS-men must have the same fanatical and unshakeable faith in the National Socialist ideal and in Adolf Hitler that the Witnesses had in Jehovah. Only when all SS-men believed as fanatically in their own philosophy would Adolf Hitler's State be permanently secure. / A *Weltanschauung* [literally: attitude towards the world] could only be established and permanently maintained by fanatics utterly prepared to sacrifice their egos for their ideals" (Rudolf Hoess: *Commandant of Auschwitz*, (1959) 2000, p. 88–91).[212]

For Jehovah's Witnesses in Nazi Germany, the end of the world had started. World War II was seen by many members as the introduction to Armageddon, and when they succumbed to these executions, they were confident this way of dying guaranteed resurrection to eternal life on the new earth; a martyr's death was only a liberation and a short sleep. Soon they had to awake, not in Hitler's Millennium, but in Jehovah's new kingdom.

One Witness or *Bibelforscher*, Franc Drozg, was arrested in 1942 because he refused to join *Wehrmannschaft*—a German paramilitary branch of the German-occupied Slovenia. Just before his execution he wrote:

"Dear Friend! Rupert, today I was sentenced to death. Do not mourn for me. I send my love to you and to everyone in the house. See you in God's Kingdom." (Reverse of an advertisement in *WT*, Nov. 15, 2001. According to this issue, Franc Drozg penned these words minutes before being shot by Nazi soldiers. Franc Drozg's letter is stored in the Photo Archive Museum of National Liberation Maribor, Slovenia.)

We must in the end honestly say that with the movement's teachings and ideas aside Jehovah's Witnesses truly proved themselves in the harshest, most-hostile situations and they acquired their martyrs. The fanatical religious fervor and zeal they showed in the face of Hitler's Nazi empire inevitably reminds us of the suffering endured by the earliest Christians.

Between Resistance and Martyrdom

From 1998 to 2001 the Watchtower Society sent out a spectacular touring exhibition focused on the movement's suffering under the Nazi regime. The theme came from Dr. Detlef Garber's book *Zwischen Widerstand und martyrdom—Die Zeugen Jehovah im "Dritten Reich"* (Watchtower pamphlet from 1998: *Between Resistance and Martyrdom: Jehovah's Witnesses in the Third Reich*). The exhibition traveled worldwide, but it was particularly shown in Europe, including the Nordic countries, plus Russia and England and some places in the US. In Denmark alone, 55,000 must have viewed the exhibition, tells Erik Joergensen, information manager at Jehovah's Witnesses' headquarters in Denmark.

I visited this exhibition myself in the Odd Fellow Palace in Copenhagen in 1998, and it made a great impression on me. The interview with Erik Joergensen also made some impression on me, because during the conversation he suddenly claimed it was "a problem" that I was ostracized. For this reason, they could not deliver the pictures or other material I had requested. However, he stressed the situation "was not personal," and with that, the conversation ended. (December 15, 2004)

Perhaps I had over-tightened the bowstring during our phone conversation because I held and referenced a special issue of *Awake!* magazine that showed examples of illustrations from Rutherford-era *Watchtower* magazines, illustrations that exposed the church's cooperation with the Nazis. The illustrations were harsh caricatures of evil in the 1930s, and the tone of the accompanying commentary mirrored the illustrations' frankness. Thus, the Nazi leaders reading the magazine *Consolation* (forerunner of *Awake!*) found the following challenge:

"Hitler is such a perfect child of the Devil that these speeches and decisions flow through him like water through a well-built sewer" (*Awake!,* August 22, 1995; this issue of *Consolation* from May 15, 1940, was re-published in 1998 at the time of the exhibition).

I assumed this reprint of *Consolation* with the anti-Hitler tirade was cited as an example of Jehovah's Witnesses uncompromising struggle against the Nazis. I noted to the chief public relations man for the Witnesses in Denmark that it might not have been wise to use such rhetoric against Hitler at a time when the movement's members in Germany were almost the *führer's hostages.*

Rutherford's Alcoholism and a New Rebellion

There are several causes for Jehovah's Witnesses to be excommunicated or disfellowshipped; alcoholism is among them. The practice of disfellowshipping means the ostracized persons are deprived of all contact with family, parents, siblings and friends. It is a serious and thorough process. With this in mind, it's shocking to learn that Rutherford, by all accounts, was an alcoholic and none of his closest friends and associates at the New York headquarters intervened against his bad habits. (Penton, 1986, p. 72–74)

Walter Salter, Rutherford's long-time friend and former director of the Canadian Watchtower Society, was the one exception. In 1936, Salter broke with the Judge over teaching issues; Salter was ostracized. In 1937 he published an open letter personally condemning Rutherford; in a broad way, this must have been shocking to the Society. He accused Rutherford of purchasing whiskey at $60 a case and other beverages such as brandy, spirits and beer, all with the Society's money. Salter wrote: "A bottle of liquor or two would not do; it was for the PRESIDENT and nothing was too good for the PRESIDENT."

After describing Rutherford's ostentatious lifestyle, Salter continued with bitter irony:

"And, oh Lord, he [Rutherford] is so courageous and his faith in Thee so great that he gets behind four walls, and surrounds himself literally with an armed bodyguard and bellows away his dreams ... and sends us from door to door to face the enemy while he goes from 'drink to drink' and tells us if we don't we are going to be destroyed" (Penton, 1986, p. 73). Whether all these accusations were solid is hard to say, however, it illustrates some of the violent hatred directed at Rutherford by former employees. (Penton, 1986, pp.72-74)

Children

In the latter half of 1941, Rutherford and his anonymous clique dispensed unfortunate advice to the younger members. Being a youth myself at that time, I experienced some of the repercussions of this Society-serving pronouncement.

The *Proclaimers* recounts that, while World War II raged in Europe but before the Japanese attacked Pearl Harbor, the Society arranged a large theocratic convention in St. Louis, Missouri, in August 1941. A Witness noted: "In 1941 … we all felt we were in for some critical days ahead with the war now going on in Europe. So everyone wanted to go to St. Louis." And, not surprisingly, *everyone* came, spurred because the Witnesses fairly buzzed with rumors about the nearness of Armageddon. The convention facilities were filled to overflowing. According to a police estimate, a peak of 115,000 persons attended. (*Proclaimers*, 1993, p. 86)

However, instead of the distressing warning that the big battle would come in a few months, the convention turned its focus to the participants' children. Approximately 15,000 between ages five and eighteen were called to gather in front of the podium where Rutherford, after waving to the many children with his handkerchief, spoke on the theme "Children of the King." He preached to the full crowd for more than an hour, and then he focused on the children in front of the podium. I quote from an eyewitness account printed in *Proclaimers*:

"'All of you … children,' he said, fixing his attention on the young beaming faces before him, 'who have agreed to do the will of God and have taken your stand on the side of his Theocratic Government by Christ Jesus and who have agreed to obey God and his King, please stand up.' The children rose as one body. 'Behold,' exclaimed the enthusiastic speaker, 'more than 15,000 new witnesses to the Kingdom!' There was a burst of applause. 'All of you who will do what you can to tell others about God's kingdom and its attending blessings, please say Aye.' A thunderous cry, 'Aye!' / To climax it all, Brother Rutherford announced the release of the new book *Children,* which was received with shouts of joy and tremendous applause. Afterward, the speaker, a tall man, shared in distributing free copies of the book as a long line of children walked up on the platform and filed past him. Many wept at the sight" (*Proclaimers*, 1993, p. 86–89).

What the above account fails to address is the book's content: incentives for young people *not to marry*, since there was *such a short time until Armageddon.* It was a ruthless exploitation of young people's emotions and idealism. The book, received as a god-sent gift, would eventually become an intolerable burden for them, since many refrained from marriage so that they could accomplish more in the service of Jehovah's organization.

The main characters of the book were Eunice and John—for many years the pair was a fascinating theocratic example for all ambitious young people within the movement, including me. In the story, the couple makes a very crucial decision:

"'My choice, Eunice dear, is to serve Jehovah and his THEOCRATIC GOVERNMENT, and I now declare aloud that I make this my choice. Will you choose to go with me?'/'Dear John, I would choose nothing else....' / 'Some sweet day, Eunice, we shall have some children and they will be greatly blessed. The prospect set before us is glorious.… Armageddon is surely near, and during that time the Lord will clean off the earth everything that offends and is disagreeable. Then, by His grace, we shall begin our life.… Our hope is that within a few years our marriage may be consummated and, by the Lord's grace, we shall have sweet children that will be an honor to the Lord. We can well defer our marriage until lasting peace comes to the earth. Now we must add nothing to our burdens, but be free and equipped to serve the Lord. When THE THEOCRACY is in full sway it will not be burdensome to have a family.' " (*Children*, 1941, p. 346–367)

As it turned out, they had an extremely long wait.

"I was then nineteen," says Raymond Franz, author of the book *Crisis of Conscience*, "and today at sixty-one I can still remember the inner emotional stirrings, a strange mixture of agitation and depression, those expressions generated in me. At my age, to be confronted with statements of that kind that, in essence, called upon me make a decision and set aside interest in marriage for an indefinite time, had an unsettling effect.… Of course, the force of the Watch Tower president's urgings lay in the shortness of time till Armageddon…" (*Conscience*, 1983, p. 14).

In short, the young and unmarried in the 1940s were to commit all their energy, even their sexual *libido*, to the work of Jehovah and the Society. Even the married were charged with practicing *self-restraint* and instructed to refrain from having children. By waiting until after Armageddon, they could in the future—without restrictions and for many hundreds of years—bring children into the world *in the new world*!

Few of those who followed the call for oppression of sexual instincts in favor of selling books and causing mass agitation ever imagined the sales work would last so long; many served more than fifty years, and if alive today range in age from eighty to ninety years old.

Since the Society's policies regarding marriage and intercourse have changed several times, it has been common for many years that young Witnesses now marry *too early*, due to the movement's unduly restrictive sexual politics. This policy implied—and continues to imply—that unmarried people's sexual relationships in the strictest sense are condemned. (See next section and *Proclaimers*, 1993, p. 86–87; see also *Pay Attention*, 1991, p. 92–94, available on the internet.)

In addition to the Society's recommendation that its members not have children before Armageddon, Rutherford also put forth a number of ridiculous prohibitions. The first of these concerned private social events such as Christmas and birthdays; secondly, he dictated members develop a hostile attitude, almost a martyrdom, toward the national anthem in schools, flag salutes and the Pledge of Allegiance (especially in the US), and participation in democratic elections. Christenings and confirmations had been dropped previous to this, so the membership was removed from the ways of Babylon and all its alleged *paganism.* Even the Christian cross was discarded in favor of a stake. The result was the membership became totally isolated from all social normality.[213]

Unjustified Pedophilia Allegations

Perhaps the recent rise in cases of pedophilia and incest within the Jehovah's Witnesses is an indirect, long-term consequence of the Society's past and present attitude toward sexual matters. The news at the turn of the 21st century has certainly been burdened with reports of these incidents. The Society management's *pedophilia* politics has been viewed by journalists as an attempt to *save the violator,* and make the victim the penitent one. The intention in such cases was probably, first and foremost, to protect the reputation of the organization. That this policy was standard practice for many years indicates "Brooklyn"[214] was too slow to recognize how it spared the perpetrator and punished the victim, twice, because in order to halt the abusers behavior—as I understand it—there had to be *witnesses* to the infringement.

Still, the Watchtower management in no way tolerates abuse of children. This is clearly apparent from the elder's handbook, *Pay Attention to Yourselves and to All the Flock*[215]. An elder tells me the book instructs them in the attitude to adopt for various forms of sexual *sins,* including the concept of *pornei'a* (fornication, sexual relationships between unmarried individuals, homosexuality, etc.) The book makes reference to pedophilia and incest (child abuse within the family), and encourages the elders to do everything to ensure the sexual-abuse victims are treated with great thoughtfulness.

I feel it's important to stress here that *today* we cannot assume the Jehovah's Witnesses organization generally protects pedophiles among its members—not to mention that the movement must be a place where pedophiles can operate unhindered. Rather, the alarming number of cases mentioned in the media worldwide brought much attention to the movement's hitherto negative attitude to the alleged abuses of minors within its own ranks. This seems to have spurred the New York managers to develop a different view, realizing they may have treated these cases inappropriately. In December 2005, an elder told me the Society abandoned the old, *unfortunate* policy and now invites members to report any violations to the secular authorities.

Probably as a result of the press coverage of pedophilia the Society now speaks more directly in a brand new children's book:

"Do you know what they may do to get pleasure of themselves?—Well, they may try to rub your sex organs. Or they will even rub their sex organs against yours. But you should never let anybody play with your penis or vulva. Not even your own brother or sister or your mother or father. These parts of your body are private.... If someone tries to do this, say firmly in a loud voice: 'Stop that! I'm going to tell on you!' " (*Learn From the Great Teacher,* 2003, p. 171)

That's putting it quite forthrightly!

In a tabooed environment where members are prohibited sexual contact before marriage—in the strongest terms, members are discouraged from even completely innocent private situations with the opposite sex, such as *touching of breasts*—we must necessarily expect deviations and perversions will arise. However, the Society's matrix is, after all, essentially the same as society as a whole. When elders are informed of deviations, they reportedly take action. If it is only a *minor impurity*, one or two elders deal with the matter.

Today masturbation is apparently no longer considered *pornei'a*, as it was when I was young, but it is still described as dangerous.[216] In order to define *pornei'a*, *The Watchtower* says "the term *porneia* embraces the various kinds of sexual activity that might take place in a house of prostitution"—so, it isn't the small matters at issue! A former member of the movement tells me that, in the 1990s, leaders spoke to the congregations suggesting strongly that excessive and inveterate masturbation was a form of "loose conduct" and could be cause for disfellowshipping. (*WT*, March 15, 1983; see also under *porneia* in index of the elder's handbook, 1991, p. 92, 93; 178)

It is entirely possible these failed views on sex and the Witnesses' enclosed and sectarian environment facilitates these secretive, *deviant* sexual behaviors (pedophilia within the Witnesses is examined more thoroughly in chapter 32).

The Judge's Death

After the convention in St. Louis, where Rutherford spoke to an assembly of 115,000, the now 72-year-old president's health faltered, and after colostomy surgery due to colon cancer, he died on January 8, 1942, during his winter recreation in Beth Sarim, the house of the Patriarchs. In accordance with his last wish, he was buried in a crypt on the grounds. Some months later, however, his remains were transferred to the Society's grave site at Rossville, New York, because the municipal authorities of San Diego would not allow interment at Beth Sarim.[217]

Jehovah's Witnesses in general viewed Rutherford as a great and dear leader who had gone away. Nobody can deny that the Judge as a person, to an incredible degree, represented the organization during his time as president. Yet, just as Russell had done, Rutherford indicated before his death—perhaps as a kind of belated penance—that future work should be managed collectively. The time of "creation worship" was over—*again*; maybe this was the new power clique's penitent admission to the members in a transitional period.

In a notice in *The Watchtower*, February 1, 1942, it was stated:

"TO ALL LOVERS OF THE THEOCRACY: On January 8, 1942, our beloved brother, J. F. Rutherford, faithfully finished his earthly course.... To him it was a joy and comfort to see and know that all the witnesses of the Lord are following, not any man, but the King Christ Jesus as their Leader, and that they will move on in the work in complete unity of action" *(Proclaimers*, 1993, p. 90).

Perhaps the truth lies somewhere between this excerpt from *The Watchtower* and the words from an individual identified only as "Farkel"[218]—the somewhat-famous anonymous author of "Rutherford Exposed: The Story of Berta and Bonnie" an internet-published article. Farkel writes (perhaps with a touch of humor): "He was so disliked by his fellow Bethelites that only four of them attended his funeral."

A local newspaper ran the following under the headline "Judge Rutherford Death Revealed":

"San Diego, Calif., Jan. 10,—(UP)—Judge Joseph Franklin Rutherford, founder and leader of an estimated 2,000,000 Jehovah's Witnesses, died at his palatial 'King David's mansion' here yesterday, Mortician Harvey Lewis, Jr., revealed today. / News of Judge Rutherford's death did not leak out until today when Lewis revealed that the body was being held at the funeral parlors awaiting instructions for burial. / Rutherford was 72 years old and leader of one of the largest sects in the world. He claimed a following of more than 2,000,000 in 36 different countries. / Death occurred in the 20-room Spanish mansion which Judge Rutherford had built less than 10 years ago as a home for King David 'when he returns to earth.' The judge has been occupying the house since its completion as a 'caretaker.' "[219]

Whether the Judge died friendless, as the above quotes suggest, is uncertain. What is not subject to doubt is that it was the human being J. F. Rutherford, the man who put his strong stamp on the movement for years, who had died. And I am pretty sure that more than four people mourned his passing.

With his passing the survival of the organization was again placed in the seat of honor. In the Brooklyn complex's corridors, the heirs to the throne, Watchtower officials Knorr, Franz and Covington, awaited unfolding events. Rutherford's successor would come from among these three men. Franz and Knorr belonged to the *anointed*, while Covington, a lawyer, was a Jonadab. Covington was soon eliminated from consideration. The time of the Jonadabs had *not yet come*.

With the scope and nature of his work for the organization, Rutherford had almost challenged God's position. Clearly, he had placed his imprint on "God's theocratic organization," ruled from the top down, and in Rutherford's time no one doubted who had the final say—probably not even Jehovah.

Chapter 20

Battle of Armageddon
Gets Ever Closer[220]

During my work with the Jehovah's Witnesses' history I gradually realized my suspicion that the movement's members are victims of systematic and organized cheating by Watchtower managers, and that speculative dates more or less seem to have been ongoing since Russell and Barbour joined their respective groups in 1876. Even before Russell, these encouraging preaching methods were regarded as legitimate since their application promoted the interests of God.

I found a suspicious coincidence between apparently organized "highlights" linked to apocalyptic events predicted for specific years, and the launch of new campaigns in the same years the events were to occur. The launch of a *new truth*, or a new organizational goal, would intentionally create great enthusiasm among the members that would erase the disappointments over the failure of the Society's previous predictions. Typically the leaders realized afterwards that Armageddon would not arrive for a few more years and much work was still to be done, since those who shall survive must be collected everywhere on Earth, and then the end will come suddenly with much disruption—and very, very quickly!

Could there be a deliberate strategy behind it? Could one produce an outline, resting on the Witnesses' published statistics, which could show that Watchtower leaders are deliberately cheating the members?

My investigations indicated exactly that.

Shortly before the Judge's death, Society member Raymond Franz—who in time became an important member of the Jehovah's Witnesses' Governing Council, and subsequently wrote a highly critical book about the movement—attended a meeting where his uncle, Fred W. Franz, one of Rutherford's close associates, lectured against the widespread view that the Witnesses' work approached its end. Fred Franz stressed that if someone wanted to subscribe to *The Watchtower* magazine, he "needn't send it in for just six months—he could send it in for a full year or for two years if he wanted!" (*Conscience*, 1983, p. 12). The new management in Brooklyn didn't expect this.

Raymond was shocked by his uncle's opinion, which did not correspond with either official policy or perception among members; Raymond feared his uncle could be accused of disloyalty if his opinions were known in Brooklyn.

It seems Fred Franz, who became vice president and later president, already at this time might have had another date in mind, one *more than a few years* into the future.

A Quick and Unanimous Election

Some weeks before his death, the mortally ill Rutherford met with four of his executive members at Beth Sarim, and they decided the election of a new president should happen as soon as possible. On January 13, 1942, five days after Rutherford's death, the executive members of the Pennsylvania and New York corporations held a meeting to select the new president.

The choice posed no difficulty, as any opposition no longer existed within the Jehovah's Witnesses. The old semi-democratic organizational structure of elected elders had been completely replaced by the theocratic organization— governance *from the top down.*

N. H. Knorr—vice president under Rutherford since 1940—had suggested to the board members a few days earlier that they earnestly seek "divine wisdom by prayer and meditation," to identify who should be Rutherford's successor. After this, the 36-year-old Knorr was unanimously chosen as president, and the 30-year-old H. C. Covington, the Society's lawyer, became vice president. (*Divine Purpose*, 1959, p. 195; Pike, 1954, p. 24; *Proclaimers*, 1993, p. 90, 91)

In a letter dated January 14, 1942, the day after the election, a member of the Bethel family expressed the unanimous support behind Knorr:

"His [Rutherford's] change shall not slow us up in the performance of the task the Lord has assigned to us. We are determined to keep close to the Lord and to one another, firmly pushing the battle to the gate, fighting shoulder to shoulder.... Our intimate association with Brother Knorr for approximately twenty years ... enables us to appreciate the Lord's direction in the choice of Brother Knorr as president" (*Proclaimers*, 1993, p. 91-92).

The word "change" in the quote alludes to Rutherford's immediate admission into heaven and his re-creation into a spirit being, where he then—presumably with C. T. Russell—was included in Christ Jesus' heavenly government. I assume, however, that the Judge also received a serious warning with his inclusion in the heavenly government that now had to restructure God's earthly organization after his dubious presidential period.

Nathan Homer Knorr was born in Pennsylvania in 1905, and in 1921 at age sixteen, he joined the Bible Students in Allentown. Knorr resigned from the Reformed Church in 1922, and in 1923 he attended a baptismal lecture given by Fred Franz from Brooklyn. Afterwards Knorr was baptized in the Little Lehigh River in Eastern Pennsylvania. Shortly thereafter Knorr became an assistant at the Society's headquarters in Brooklyn. In 1932 he was appointed as the head of the printing and publishing department, and in 1934 he was elected director of the Peoples Pulpit Association (now Watchtower Bible and Tract Society of New York, Inc.), also called the New York Corporation. The following year he became its vice president. In 1940 he advanced to vice president of the Pennsylvania corporation, the second highest position within the Jehovah's Witnesses' organization. Knorr lived with his wife at the Society's headquarters in Brooklyn. (Pike, 1954, p. 24; *Proclaimers*, 1993, p. 91)

A former employee of the Society's Denmark headquarters told me the restrictions against hiring married men at Bethel (headquarters) was alleviated following Knorr's marriage. The invitation to avoid marriage before Armageddon, as Rutherford had recommended in *Children,* was forgotten for some years. In 1966, however, the restrictions were tightened again: "One who is married may not be able to serve at a Bethel home of the Watch Tower Society, whereas a single person may be so blessed." However, Mrs. Knorr's stay at the headquarters in Brooklyn was secured. (*WT,* Sept. 15, 1965)

In 1945, Watch Tower Society management weathered another slight change when H. C. Covington, at his own request, resigned as vice president. He belonged to the Society as a Jonadab not as one of the "little flock," as we already know; he continued as a director and legal counselor for the Society after his resignation. F. W. Franz was elected as his successor.

Frederick William Franz was born in Kentucky in 1893. He was baptized in November 1913. He had studied at the University of Cincinnati but interrupted his studies in 1914 and entered full-time ministry as a colporteur. In 1920 he moved to headquarters in New York, where Rutherford employed him as an editorial assistant. Franz reportedly spoke fluent Spanish, Portuguese, German and French. He had studied Greek in college for less than two years, and he was self-studied in Hebrew, Syrian and Latin (in terms of the *dead* languages, it emerged later during a trial, known as the "Walsh trial,"[221] that he was not at all a master in these languages). According to A. H. Macmillan, Franz was nevertheless an invaluable traveling companion. He was Rutherford's top adviser in religious matters, a role he continued under Knorr's management. While Nathan Knorr was responsible for organizing Society activities and expanding preaching, Franz took charge of the editorial work, and apparently it was Franz who authored many normative articles in *The Watchtower.* He was unmarried. As the Society's *gray eminence* and senior dogmatist, Franz was the natural choice to be president when Knorr's life term ended. (Cole, 1955; Macmillan, 1957, p. 180–182)

The seemingly well-educated Fred Franz has proven to be an extremely complex man.

Reorganization, Regimentation and Expansion

With Knorr at the helm and Franz overseeing the dogmatic line, the movement entered a period of more pronounced regimentation. *The new theocratic man*, who bore certain resemblance to the political regimentation of authoritarian regimes (such as under Communism), was now under further development.

Knorr's regime was characterized by an inane organizational and business mentality. In studying Rutherford's books we find grotesque drawings of the nefarious trinity—church, big business and politics—often portrayed as caricatured, symbol-charged characters, trampling around in blood. (*Light* 1 and 2, 1930) With Knorr the illustration style changed again toward a more bloodless, anonymous and *socially realistic* (similarities with the Communist or Socialist realism art of the Stalin era are striking), a development that has since accelerated. If the idea of *art* can even be used here, *theocratic art* is *today* completely without nerve and spirit. The textual content and form in the Society's publications also significantly changed under Knorr. Where previous books such as *Creation* (1927) were written in a *certain* personable style, the management changes brought a rigid, template-like and impersonal form.

Rutherford had been worshiped as a divine idol, but with his passing the days of "creation worship" ended. Knorr initiated a much stricter, almost-puritan structure that was introduced gradually. The change not only put greater demands on members' activities, but also strained their personal lives. A stricter structure required a "clean organization" and rigid discipline among the members; the hunt for heretics followed, always looking for those who did not fit into the system.

J. F. Rutherford flanked by N. H. Knorr and H. C. Covington, both members of the Adam Street clique. Photo likely taken in the 1940s. Image from *Jehovah of the Watchtower*, Zondervan Publishing House, 1950 (pp. 14–15). Used with permission; retouched by Brian Kutscher.

Due to illness Rutherford had been a somewhat absentee leader for some time before his death. The vice president, Knorr—a member of the new "Adam Street clique" (an expression Schnell used to describe Knorr and his people who stood ready in the wings to take over after Rutherford)—had acquired extended authority and powers and hence more opportunity to organize the future work while Rutherford was still alive. There are indications that Knorr and his staff had already planned major changes in the organization—changes to be realized as soon as the Judge was out of the picture. According to Schnell, there was an unseen internal power struggle between Knorr's Adam Street clique and Rutherford's old guard. (Schnell, 1963, p. 168) Thus, the transition to the new Knorr administration was not quite as smooth as the Society otherwise portrays. On the surface everything seemed to have been happening in a properly "theocratic" manner and in accordance with the statutes of the main corporation.

Shortly after Knorr ascended to leadership, a thorough reorganization and streamlining of the work began. The US would certainly come out of World War II victorious, so the new management had to prepare an effective organizational device to implement when the war was over.

At a large convention in Cleveland in September 1942, it was made clear to the Witnesses that the world's end would *not immediately* follow the end of World War II, but the "international security 'beast,' formerly the League of Nations, would be revived" and after the war "a period would follow in which the good news had to be preached before the end at Armageddon" (*Divine Purpose*, 1959, p. 200). Society vice president Fred Franz "rousingly declared" that Jehovah's Witnesses received *the signal* to continue the preaching work: "'Here, then, is the "Go ahead" signal from the Highest Authority to keep going on in his [work] of witness no matter what happens before Armageddon comes.' … It was no time to slack the hand and relax" (*Proclaimers*, 1993, p. 92, 93).

"There is further work to be done; much work," Knorr said in his lecture, which followed Franz's speech. Presumably then, Fred Franz's conspirator had been Knorr when Franz shocked his nephew Raymond by stating Armageddon was still somewhere in the future during his earlier lecture when Rutherford was still alive. The Adam Street clique had high ambitions for the expansion of the organization, so Armageddon had to wait a little longer.

During a lecture on the last day of the assembly, Knorr offered, also in contradiction with Rutherford's views, the idea that World War II, which raged at the time, "would not lead into Armageddon, as some thought, but that the war would end and a period of peace would set in. There was still work to be done in proclaiming God's Kingdom" (Ibid., p. 93). That "some thought" the opposite was probably a cloaked allusion to Rutherford's conviction that World War II would go *directly* into Armageddon. (Penton, 1986, p. 74; *Proclaimers*, 1993, p. 93)

After the end of World War II a new training program was launched. "Course in Theocratic Ministry" had already begun among New York's headquarters staff just a month after Rutherford's death. At a convention labeled "Call to Action," which was held in the US in 1943, leadership announced that all Jehovah's Witnesses' congregations worldwide would have a Theocratic Ministry School. The general members were encouraged to join so they could learn voice techniques aimed at public lectures and door-to-door service work. The Watchtower leaders hoped ordinary members would improve speaking skills so they could replace the ten-year-old service campaign using gramophones. As part of the Witness training program they had to learn to present "three- to eight-minute sermons" to people at their doors. These in-person testimonies did not deviate much from the gramophone record testimonies. The pupils of this new theocratic school, who so far were simply brothers in the organization, would be led by an instructor or *School servant*. In 1944 the local congregations were also encouraged to establish theocratic ministry school libraries in their Kingdom Halls. (*Divine Purpose*, 1959, p. 213–216)

In 1958 at a large convention, Knorr proclaimed the sisters in the congregations would be privileged to join the weekly theocratic school beginning with 1959. (Ibid., p. 289) Throughout the movement's history the sisters had played a certain role, especially as pioneers, and in this regard, Knorr showed wisdom and foresight when one considers how women remained part of the general labor market even post-war. Now, women also had an important role in Knorr's global expansion.

The regular inspections of local congregations conducted by the zone servants were also reorganized, and the title Zone Servant was replaced by Servant to the Brethren, and then renamed Circuit Servant (today known as a Circuit Overseer).[222] The Servants to the Brethren personally monitored the members' Publisher Record cards which were kept in each congregation's Publisher Record card index (this report card contained a member's monthly work data and results: hours, return visits, home Bible studies and the quantity of literature sold). Also a new guide was published and distributed to the servants: *Organization Instructions.* The booklet was designed to make the managers more effective. (See footnote, *Proclaimers*, 1993, p. 223.)

In brief: All were charged to exert themselves more, because the Witnesses "were determined to plow right on through opposition and persecution, declaring the good news without letup" (*Proclaimers*, 1993, p. 93; p. 223). Nobody needed to believe everything would grind to a halt because Rutherford had waited for an imminent outbreak of apocalyptic events, and then left the arena before they came to pass. The answer was, as usual, create *new initiatives* to excite and occupy everyone's attention—and to conveniently displace the disappointments and frustrations, as all these people must have felt in their innermost being.

The views of the clique, which Fred Franz expressed shortly before the Judge's death, had once seemed unfair to Rutherford, but in light of all the new tones, Franz and his words seemed a *vanguard*. Saying that he walked "ahead of the organization"—something the ordinary members would see as a risky action—was out of the question. Yet, as the *Oracle* of the organization, as Raymond Franz might have called his uncle, Franz was of course at the absolute top, and he *should* "go ahead."

The message from the new team in Brooklyn was now: "Forward!"

The School of Gilead

As part of the global expansion, in 1943 the new management created the School of Gilead, a kind of theocratic university, to train specially selected Jehovah's Witnesses from many countries. When World War II was over, they would be sent out as missionaries around the world. In 1953, the Watch Tower Bible School of Gilead, according to the movement's own data, was officially recognized by the US Department of Education as an institute of higher learning.

Even today it is a great honor and privilege to attend Gilead; it is seen as a great "success inside the New World society" for those fortunate to attend. Only those who are pioneers (full-time servants) for at least two years can be considered. From 1943 to 2012, thousands of students called *Gileadites* participated in the school's training courses, and afterwards they dispersed throughout the world as missionaries. This often proved to be a "double blessing," as stated in the 2011 *Yearbook*, because some of the young missionaries later found wives among their teammates. (*Qualified*, 1955, p. 333; *Proclaimers*, 1993, p. 524; 2011 *Yearbook*, p. 118)

Blood Transfusion

As with the other medical advances developed during World War II, blood transfusions soon became a widely used lifesaving technique in civilian hospitals. Articles in *The Watchtower* from November 1945 and February 1946 strengthened the Society's anti-blood-transfusion doctrine from a biblically fundamentalist view regarding the sacredness of blood. The Society forbade members to receive blood transfusions. The edict was justified by the apostolic decree given early Christians in the Acts of the Apostles in the *New Testament*, which, among other things, forbade the eating of idol-sacrificial flesh, blood, and meat of strangled animals. (Acts 15:28, 29)

In the February 15 *Watchtower* article, it was pointed out that "the only use of the blood, [God] gave orders for raising human lives, was its use as a means of reconciliation…" (Danish *WT*, Feb. 15, 1946, p. 63; see also *Proclaimers*, 1993, p. 183, where it states that contempt for the requirement that Christians abstain from blood, "would be an evidence of *gross disrespect for the ransom sacrifice of Jesus Christ…*"; italics are mine).

The 1946 article explains how the requirement of the "sanctity of blood" applied to Christians, and refers to the Book of Acts: "For it seemed good to the

Holy Spirit, and to us, to lay upon you no greater burden than these necessary things: that ye abstain from things sacrificed to idols, and from blood, and from things strangled, and from fornication; from which if ye keep yourselves, it shall be well with you. Fare ye well" (Acts 15:28-29; ASV, 1901).

This opinion originated with a conflict within the early Christian church wherein fanatical Jewish members of the Christian church council in Jerusalem demanded that non-Jews who converted to the new Christian faith had to observe Mosaic Law with all its rules, including circumcision. The apostle Paul vehemently objected, and at the apostles' meeting in Jerusalem in AD 48 or 49, with church elders and members attending, the above compromise was adopted. Simply put: The non-Jewish Christians were only required to comply with the four minimum requirements, equivalent to those previously applied to foreigners in Israel.

There is no doubt that the Christians of those first centuries took the Apostolic Council's ban on blood seriously. During the Roman persecutions, Christians were subjected to a sort of *eat test*, where they had to consume blood sausage, for example. If the defendant agreed to eat blood-containing food, he or she would pass the test and not be condemned as a Christian.

In the booklet *Blood, Medicine and the Law of God,* published in 1961, the Society reinforced the ban on consuming blood: "You might obtain an immediate and temporary extension of life, but for the consecrated Christians this is achieved at the expense of eternal life" (p. 57). And there was no hedging on this for "whether it's whole blood or a blood fraction, God's law is the same" (p. 14; both quotes translated from the Danish edition, 1962).

For the devout, it was all or nothing.

The Adventists, whose doctrines are closest to the Jehovah's Witnesses, were never so zealous about blood, but they did observe the eating ban.

By all appearances, however, the first Christians' ban on eating blood was a temporary injunction to unify the Jewish and non-Jewish Christians. The blood ban died step by step as Augustine (354 to 430) put his imprint on the church, teaching that the decrees of the Apostolic Council were intended to guide Christians at a time when gentile Christianity was not yet fully established.

The Society's decision to prohibit members from receiving blood transfusions was spectacular and found its way to many a newspaper's front page. It seems as if the Watchtower management may have planned to extend the Jehovah's Witnesses' martyr status, acquired during years of Nazi persecution, with this controversial and widely publicized counterpart. What they discovered was the ban caused them major problems with authorities everywhere. The movement, already very unpopular, eventually became even more unpopular because of this latest example of fanaticism. Often this blood policy affects the very young most of all. For instance, 15-year-old Witness Joshua McAuley refused a transfusion in 2010 and died despite the doctors' attempts to save him.[223]

As I write this, it is possible changes are underway in the Society's blood policy. But Brooklyn has time on its side. They know it takes time to win souls, and steadfastness to keep them, and in this case, change must develop slowly, patiently, and quietly. Over several years there will probably be full clarity about some of these issues, and only then will Jehovah's Witnesses perhaps discard one of their biggest doctrinal errors to date—one which biblical texts in no way support. (See Appendix: Brooklyn's double-tongued signals about blood policy.)[224]

Of note here is the Society's loosening its prohibitions to allow some blood transfusions. In a 1998 agreement with Bulgarian officials, as the Society attempted to be accepted in the newly freed Bulgaria, they stopped expelling members in that country if they used blood, although the JWs in Bulgaria will privately, and unofficially, still shun those who take blood. (See endnote regarding Jehovah's Witnesses and blood transfusion in Bulgaria; source: Jim Whitney.)[225]

Giant Assemblies Blessed with New Light

Knorr's program for global expansion included gigantic international conventions, first held after World War II ended. The members became immensely engaged in these milestone events. Outside the United States, Witnesses planned their participation in these mammoth assemblies because they were required to have them in their experience registers. Attending also afforded some higher status in the local congregation. They became persons of *importance* when they returned home from the long journey and reported the magnificent experiences and blessings they received.

At about this same time, I applied myself to studying English, which would prove advantageous in time.

The colossal convention events, which afforded the Witnesses much publicity and goodwill (because the New World Society gathered in silence and order), began in Cleveland, Ohio, in 1946 where 80,000 attended the first meeting. It was at this convention that the Witnesses' most important textbook of the period, *Let God Be True*, was released; by 1958 this textbook was available in fifty-one languages and 17,854,273 copies were produced.

District Assemblies were introduced in 1948. These assemblies were regional events rather than national or international. Each *zone* (later known as *circuit*) was comprised of multiple congregations (about twenty) and each *district* contained a number of zones. For example, a country such as the United States would be divided into several districts, and each district held its own assembly. These conventions were conducted under the direction of a district servant (known today as a district overseer), who inspected the supervisory work of the zone servants or the servant to the brethren in each zone. Any organizational efforts were met with much enthusiasm, and there were always many changes. The intention was probably to create a climate of constant renewal which would engage and inspire the members.

The first significantly large convention was held in 1950. This international event—attended by 10,000 delegates from Europe, Africa, Australia, Latin America and Canada—was called "Theocracy's Increase Assembly of Jehovah's Witnesses." It was held at New York's Yankee Stadium and lasted eight days, and at the Sunday meeting, 123,707 attended Knorr's public lecture.

As I try to imagine how the delegates must have felt during these huge assemblies, I can only think to compare the experience to attending an international Olympic event. The spectators and participants packed into a large stadium—tens of thousands of like-minded individuals from all countries joined together—must experience intense enthusiasm, strong feelings of community and camaraderie, captivated by an intense, collective mood and perhaps moved to tears during the closing ceremony, where they—and now I am talking about the Witnesses only—make solemn promises and identify themselves with the leaders and their common purpose. The sheer feeling of mass convergence with the thousands and thousands of other convention participants often puts the individuals in a state of personal annihilation (in a purely psychological way), which in itself becomes an irrefutable argument with great conviction. Of course the individual participants' excitement varies, and there are certainly some who, despite the collective pressure, manage to keep their wits intact.

However, an individual's experience may look somewhat different when viewed retrospectively. A former sister (disfellowshipped in 1994) told me, in her eyes, a convention was just something to be overcome. Outwardly, it was a positive experience—or it *should* have been—but deep down she hated it. All participants had to dress perfectly. No practical clothes were allowed in the rain (although I have seen rally participants with raincoats more than once!), and the lectures were often long and boring. Children attended too, and it was almost unbearable for toddlers when they grew restless and couldn't cope anymore. They had to sit quietly, of course, for days beside the adults, listening to the lectures and sermons. Not surprisingly, the assemblies were a great challenge for families with young children.

The Princes, Again

At the 1950 assembly an additional *new light* on the somewhat obscure question about the Old Testament princes or heroes of faith arose. The old heroes' resurrection had been expected around 1925, or at least, when the battle of Armageddon erupted. Rutherford's Beth Sarim was to be ready for the princes when they arrived. However, after Rutherford died, the Watchtower Society sold the complex in 1947–48. So then, where would these princes live? The Society's charismatic vice president Fred W. Franz asked the following questions to the emotionally electrified and impressionable crowd in Yankee Stadium:

"Would this international assembly be happy to know that HERE, TO-NIGHT, in our midst, there are a number of prospective PRINCES OF THE NEW EARTH?"And the crowd responded: "A tremendous and sustained clapping of hands and shouting for joy assured the speaker that nothing at the moment interested them more. A hushed and profound silence then settled over Yankee Stadium. Every ear strained in order not to lose a syllable as Brother Franz began a discussion of some very important facts concerning Psalm 45:16…" (*Divine Purpose,* 1959, p. 252; capitalization is by the WT publishers).

In his interpretation, the vice president now emphasized that the word *prince* in the above reference was not a title, but merely designated as *an office of a servant,* implying *a servant inside the New World Society organization.*

The majority of the throng applauded, but certainly some were disappointed because for many years they had looked forward to witnessing the resurrection of the old Patriarchs: Noah, Moses, Abraham, Isaac and Jacob, King David, Solomon and others. Now they reeled from another setback, surely feeling they had been duped once again. The pattern was all too familiar. Throughout its history the movement has disappointed hundreds of thousands who blindly believed in the sophisticated and *cunning fables*, and became angry when they discovered all their efforts had been in vain. By 1950, they can hardly have been aware of the inevitable disappointment. Yet, the disappointed members were there, the future, inevitable victims of Watchtower tactics. Unfortunately, thousands of new converts stood ready to join the apocalyptic circus.

At the assembly at Yankee Stadium, many new brochures and books premiered. These were seen as gifts from Jehovah, given through his visible organization. The convention participants threw themselves at the new books, which could be bought for practically nothing. They quickly leafed through the pages, and if they couldn't find anything about the proximity of Armageddon, their interest lapsed immediately.

Jehovah's Witnesses' Bible

The most notable of the publications released at the New York assembly was a newly developed version of the New Testament, translated by the New World Bible Translation Committee. The translation was apparently based on the standard Greek text published by Britons, Westcott and Hort in 1881, and D. Eberhard Nestle's translation, *Novum Testamentum Graece* (developed by Nestle and published in 1948). Fred Franz, who was the *gray eminence* of teaching issues, was probably the driving force behind or within the translation committee. They called their new version: *New World Translation of the Christian Greek Scriptures*; this was eventually followed by *New World Translation of the Hebrew Scriptures*. Both were just as dogmatic and pseudo-scholarly as the other publications from the Watchtower Society. It was and is truly Jehovah's Witnesses' *own* bible. Often it is translated into an artificially and constructed

English, and at crucial points its content is adapted to the doctrines of the Watchtower leaders (especially in terms of the translation of the New Testament). For that reason it was and is *quite useless* in any reasonable way—but *apparently* very skillfully done. (*Divine Purpose*, 1959, p. 257; *Proclaimers*, 1993, p. 111; p. 603–615)

The Watchtower Publishers contended in 1993 that a professor of Hebrew, Benjamin Kedar of Israel, held a positive view of the translation—especially the *New World Translation of the Hebrew Scriptures*. According to *Proclaimers*, he was reported to have said: "I have never discovered in the 'New World Translation' any biased intent to read something into the text that it does not contain" (*Proclaimers*, 1993, p. 611; original source unknown). After a brief search on the internet, it became clear to me that Kedar is an absolute exception because most researchers who have been interested in the quality of this translation deem it unreliable. Thus, Robert M. Bowman Jr. of the Christian Research Institute in California said there is "evidence of a pervasive doctrinal bias in the NWT [New World Translation]" (Bowman: *Jehovah's Witnesses*, 1995, p. 65, 66; regarding B. Kedar, see footnote in *Proclaimers*, 1993, p. 611).[226]

Dr. Bruce Metzger, a highly respected professor of New Testament language and literature at Princeton University, notes "the Jehovah's Witnesses have incorporated in their translation of the New Testament several quite erroneous renderings of the Greek."[227]

Dr. Julius Mantey, one of the best ancient-Greek experts in the United States, gave his clear perspective of the Watchtower Society's translation of the New Testament. In his 1974 letter to the Society[228] he calls it a "mistranslation" and a "perversion" of God's Word. Mantey also noted that no part of his book, *Manual Grammar of the Greek New Testament*, "may be reproduced in any form without permission in writing from the publisher," and required the Watchtower Society cease quoting from his work. He also stated *The Watchtower* magazine must publish an apology. "If you have such permission," he concludes the letter, "please send me a photo-copy of it. / If you do not heed these requests you will suffer the consequences." Perhaps he was a bit academically pompous, but one can see why he didn't want his name or work associated with the Society's. (See internet sources for Julius Robert Mantey; see also: Jehovah's Witness: *Dr. Mantey*, Greek scriptures, linear translation / Jehovah's Witness/ Dr. Mantey; *WT*, Aug. 15, 1961: Oct. 1, 1962; June 15, 1974)

About the *New World Translation* H. H. Rowley, a scholar specializing in Old Testament Hebrew at Manchester University, England, said: "The translators have their own views on Hebrew tenses.… They profess to offer a rendering into modern English which is as faithful as possible. In fact, the jargon which they use is often scarcely English at all … the translation is marked by a wooden literalism which will only exasperate an intelligent reader.… From beginning to end this volume is a shining example of how the Bible should not be translated."[229]

Typical of most Witness literature, in the new Bible translation, the name Jehovah was introduced everywhere we read "the LORD," for example in Deuteronomy 18:14. Wherever the Tetragrammaton JHVH or YHWH (Hebrew has no consonants) appeared, more than 6,800 times, it was translated to Jehovah. The name Jehovah was already known before the English King James translation was produced, but the Hebrew letters could just as rightly be translated *Jahve* or *Yahweh*. In the Society's *New World* version of the New Testament (the Christian scriptures), the Watchtower translators did something *absolutely new*: They introduced an unprecedented number of occurrences of the divine name. First-century Christians did not use God's name in its original Hebrew form in their writings, but replaced it with Lord, *Kyrios*. Yet the JW-version publisher defies the theological and historical traditions connected with the name. The new book featured the word *Jehovah* in all 237 places in the New Testament, a *blatant* break with the earliest Christian traditions.

Although the translators' names do not appear in the *New World Translation*, their names are well known: William Cetnar, who worked at the Society's international headquarters in Brooklyn (he later left the movement and revealed the other translators' names); President N. H. Knorr; F. W. Franz, vice-president; A. D. Schroeder; G. D. Gangas; and M. G. Henschel. At the time, all were high-ranking Society officials. Franz alone possessed adequate education to work as critical translator, and his skills were not impressive, as shown in a Scottish courtroom in November 1954 when Franz was unable to read a Hebrew text. He was the only member of the translation committee who had any schooling in Koine Greek. According to the professor Bruce Metzger, Benjamin Wilson, author and translator of the *Emphatic Diaglott* (1864), was the real ancestor of the *New World Translation* of the New Testament. (See the internet locations listed in endnotes 225–228; and Benjamin Wilson section of Chapter 4.)[230]

Everything points to the sweeping and extensive work titled *New World Translation* being the work of non-professional translators. *The Watchtower* of December 15, 1974, under the "Questions From Readers" section, addresses why the authors of the New World translation were not credited: "These translators were not seeking prominence; they did not desire to draw attention to themselves. In the spirit of 'doing all things for God's glory,' they wanted the reader to base his faith on God's Word, not on their worldly 'qualifications'" (p. 768). Possibly these men were that humble; more likely, the Watch Tower Society held back the names because the authors' lack of credentials and linguistic skills was not publicly known. Therefore, presumably, anonymity had distinct advantages.[231]

But let me return to our previous topic, the New York assembly.

Another part of the Society's grandiose plans revealed at the assembly involved expansion of the headquarters in Brooklyn. A new administration building had been constructed, and the printing works at 117 Adams Street were greatly enlarged. Convention participants were invited to visit the new Bethel headquarters and during several days, thousands of convention attendees toured the two centers for theocratic ministry. (*Qualified*, 1955, p. 322–340)

The New World Society

An even greater international assembly, the New World Society Assembly of Jehovah's Witnesses, was held in 1953, again at Yankee Stadium in New York. At Knorr's Sunday lecture, 165,829 listened to his presentation: "After Armageddon—God's New World." When everything was done, 125,040 attendees had voted to adopt a resolution whereby the membership identified itself with a new *extended* name: Jehovah's Witnesses—the New World Society. The Witnesses had now, so to speak, set their feet inside the New World, which also implied a major organizational conformity, a uniformity of social conventions and moral relationships, and a lot of restrictions and rules in several areas—including gender rules—as a foretaste of community relations in the coming earthly paradise. Coincidentally, these large events were the Witnesses' equivalent of dating clubs or singles bars because those seeking love could meet others and maybe find a future spouse.

The Society even tackled the issue of fashion, dictating the "theocratic" Witnesses' appearance, dress and hairstyle. Even today, outsiders who attend their conventions quickly notice this totally unique style, and it is a striking identifier of the movement's members, whether they're from Greenland, Australia, the United States or Africa. This theocratic respectability allows Witnesses to quickly sort out less-theocratic, suspicious elements.

A former American elder within the movement, David A. Reed, did notice that Watchtower editors had manipulated an illustration from 1981 so it reflected *new truths* about theocratic hair style. The picture showed a father and son. Their hair was shortened considerably in the 1982 version. Reed writes, the "altered illustration could easily have come from the desk of Winston Smith in Orwell's novel [*Nineteen Eighty-Four*], since he had the job of altering periodicals and illustrations to bring them into line with Party policy under Big Brother" (D. A. Reed: *The Author's Testimony*, located on the internet in 2010).[232]

From the gigantic assembly in 1953 forward, I worked with even more of the Society's books and publications—up until 1959 when I finally broke away from the Witnesses.

The "Fortieth Year"

In 1942, Knorr and his "Watchtower Boys" needed some time until the battle of Armageddon; if it was *too close* there would be no time for the global expansion. At the Cleveland gathering in 1942, they stated the "beast" in Revelation 17:8—previously interpreted as the League of Nations—would be reanimated after the war, and a peaceful period, in which the Jehovah's Witnesses' message of the "new world" was to be proclaimed, would follow before the arrival of Armageddon. (Divine Purpose 1959, p. 200)

By 1950 eight years of this peaceful period had passed and a large number of ordinary members earnestly believed Armageddon would come in 1954. This view, very common among the membership, was constantly encouraged by the Watchtower managers' ambiguous statements about the nearness of the battle of Armageddon. Everyone knew 1954 would be the "fortieth year" under the rule of the Kingdom—the Kingdom reign with Christ Jesus as King from 1914. (*Children*, 1941)[233]

The general view among the members, almost a tradition even, was that the fortieth year played a special role in Jehovah's schedules. As the reader may recall, Russell had fixed the Second Coming of Christ in 1874, and partly from his Adventist contacts, he determined a harvest of forty years would follow with the present world coming to its sad end around October 1914. Following this the Bible Students would be admitted to heaven to govern as Christ's fellow kings. However, Rutherford gradually changed the roadmap so that now the *invisible* Second Coming *had* happened in 1914 and that a period similar to Russell's harvest, wherein the warning message would be preached worldwide, would follow before the final battle at Armageddon.

As a result, Witnesses throughout the world saw 1954 as the year for Armageddon, because the Kingdom of God had ruled and the warning message had been spread for forty years. The contemporary generation would survive Armageddon, and millions of the then-living would never die! Yet, as we know, this propaganda could backfire. Still, the time could be closer in 1950 than in 1914 or 1925, those other world-end dates. Convenient to their own purposes, officials of the Watchtower Society in New York found it apparently unnecessary to clearly and unequivocally deny the doomsday rumors among adherents, or to stress that there was no reason for alarm—or even that there was no reason to expect anything special in 1954.

As I clearly recall, the Watchtower officials stoked the fire with their ambiguous statements, for they knew quite well how common it was for members to anticipate and speculate about the approaching disaster year, 1954.

Again, it's clearly indicated, that the Society used the threat of approaching Armageddon to stimulate the members' commitment, and with such a threat of *the* total, universal war looming—one far worse than any third, fourth or fifth World War—it is not surprising that the ordinary members became "virtually irrational crack-pots," as Schnell expressed it.[234]

The Attack by "Gog of Magog"

Wednesday, July 22, 1953, during the huge assembly at Yankee Stadium and after President Knorr presented the *New World Translation of the Old Tes-*

tament, Society vice president Fred Franz captivated the great assembly of breathless delegates with his discourse: "New World Society Attacked from the Far North."

There could not be any doubt: Franz spoke of an *imminent threat*, based on yet another allegorical interpretation of an ancient Bible text, the Book of the Prophet Ezekiel, chapters 38 and 39, where the figure "Gog" from "the land of Magog" is interpreted as Satan and his demons. From a "limited spiritual realm near earth's vicinity following their expulsion from heaven by 1918" they will initiate a "global conspiracy" against "Jehovah's New World society here on earth." Satan is jealous of Jehovah's Witnesses' "prosperity, unity and security," which provokes a desire in "Satan's hordes to eliminate Jehovah's people once and for all" (*Divine Purpose*, 1959, p. 265).

Excuse me: That's sheer nonsense! Another slanted, subjective interpretation for the usual purpose.

So, Fred Franz announced an impending attack on Jehovah's Witnesses, and said, among other things in his lecture—and please excuse me the long quote, but it illustrates how the Watchtower leaders availed themselves of every tool in their need to intimidate and retain the members:

"The prophecy must apply in this 'time of the end,' particularly since 1919.... The attack would therefore be timed by Jehovah God to fall at the close of the years of the 'time of the end.' This would be when Armageddon ... would be scheduled to begin. Since the 'time of the end' began at the birth of God's Messianic kingdom in 1914, we can appreciate that we are well along in the 'last days' of prince Gog's world organization. How we need to fortify ourselves against the impending attack, which we ourselves are now commissioned to announce in obedience to Jehovah God! ... Gog schemes the final, do-or-die attack on the only part of Jehovah's theocratic organization that he can get at, now that he has been permanently excluded from heaven ... Gog's visible allies on earth have no faith in Jehovah's purpose to step in behalf of his spiritual Israel. So they are willing and ready to put him to the test just once more, not realizing that this time it may be tempting Jehovah too far.... As for their invisible sovereign prince, Gog of Magog, he painfully knows he has but a short period of time ... and he is now itching to begin his final attack upon the New World society. Let him now have his wish, for Jehovah's time to lead the condemned criminal out to his execution has come, to show Gog His power.... The hour of execution arrives!" (*WT*, Oct. 1, 1953; abridged)

These urgent words supercharged the huge crowd's emotions, and no one had the slightest doubt that the time of Satan and his demons' worldwide attacks were extremely close. The assembly participants were gripped by fear and the strong and serious sense that impending persecutions, on a gigantic, worldwide scale, would come just before the battle of Armageddon:

"Be from now on never relaxing guard," said Franz with his usual electrifying manner. "Jehovah's Witnesses have to know of Armageddon in advance" that they may be "forewarned and forearmed." And Franz concluded: "Let us not be careless in our great prosperity" (*Divine Purpose*, 1959, p. 265).

When I think back to that intense atmosphere—which spread to congregations worldwide during the 1950s—and when I consider their assorted, ever-changing positions and actions concerning the time and nearness of Armageddon, and leadership's urgent cries that much work "remains to be done,"[235] my suspicion deepens that this dramatic discourse was merely a *strategic part* of the methods (to put it kindly!) Watchtower leaders used to stoke their "global expansion" to run full steam.

The Witnesses Anticipated Major Events in 1954

On the last day of the 1953 assembly, Knorr held a serious, admonitory and urgent talk in which he, among other things, said:

"The sign of the nearer approach of the battle of Armageddon is now before our eyes. When this adulterous, religio-political combine finally cracks up and the symbolic beast and its ten horns turn against the harlot system of organized religion it will denote that the 'war of the great day of God the Almighty' has begun by which he will execute all the foes of his Messianic kingdom. That war will end when Jesus Christ the King together with his angel executioners will destroy all the 'disgusting thing' and all other elements of this old world that line up in opposition to his rule.... There is now no time for delay. It is high time to flee for safety" (*Divine Purpose*, 1959, p. 266).

That Sunday, Knorr also said "that Armageddon is so near at hand it will strike the generation now living" (*Survive Armageddon*, 1955, p. 11).

In the evening the big assembly ended with a last urgent note from Knorr, who said "no matter how small the unit or how great the assembly, the New World society will travel right on through the battle of Armageddon under Jehovah's protection. So let us all bless Jehovah by our returning to our homes and carrying on faithfully in our service."

Afterward, the great crowd was invited to sing song No. 41, "Sing Triumphal Praise!" After a prayer to Jehovah the "greatest assembly of our Christian era came to a happy ending" (*1953 Report of the New World Society Assembly of Jehovah's Witnesses*, July 28, 1953, p. 75).

Knorr and Franz's inciting and appealing warnings were played to and fueled the members' already tense imaginations. Large events were in store; for this reason the world should now have the last warning.

In January 1954, the *Watchtower* magazine featured an article titled "In its fortieth year":

"Since 1914 we have been living under the rule of this kingdom. Today we live in the fortieth year of its irresistible reign. What does that year mean to us? We cannot say. It will be much better for us to wait until this fortieth year is completely past and then look back to see whether that fortieth year of the Kingdom had some special significance…" (*WT*, Jan. 1, 1954).

I wonder: What did the Witnesses who looked at 1954 with backward glances think the impact of the year had been? The answer is reflected to some extent in an opinion penned by a former Witness and quoted in an article on Jehovah's Witnesses in a Danish tabloid from February 1957:

"I and many, many other Witnesses looked at each other when we entered the year 1955, and nothing had happened, but the elderly in the congregation admonished us to be patient, because, as they said, remember, brothers, Christ purified the temple for three and a half years while he lived here on earth. These years, we attach to 1954, and then around 1958, the great war of Jehovah will come. The servants of the congregation let us all understand that it was best when we talked to people at the doors, not to mention a special year…" (*B.T.*, Feb. 1, 1957).

Personally, I know that many Witnesses were very disappointed by the absence of the battle of Armageddon in 1954, and as before, many members left the movement for the same reason. Still, a large majority endured because the time was quite close, and perhaps Jehovah was only testing the patience of his Witnesses. Only those who endured until "the end" would survive the impending battle. (Matthew 24:13)

There were always plenty of excuses. At the big assembly in New York in 1953 Knorr said they would hold many smaller conventions in 1954, and for 1955 they planned a series of global assemblies in the United States, Canada, England, France, Germany and other European countries. So no matter what the leaders said one year, they always had a backup plan for the next. Whenever Armageddon would come, and it was always *pretty soon*, the responsible leaders of the organization would make plans for the future until Jehovah said "stop" through his visible organization.

About this same time, rumors buzzed among the Witnesses, stirred by an article in the *Watchtower* magazine, "Freedom from fear in 1955." An excerpt:

"What this psalm in its seventh verse says of this collective 'man' or class of persons will be true during 1955, yes, true until the victorious end of the battle of Armageddon…. He faces the new year *fearlessly*…. In 1955 Jehovah's witnesses want to have *the biggest distribution of literature* yet in any one year, because the time shortens to get out the lifesaving message, now that the world destruction at the battle of Armageddon *gets ever closer*" (*WT*, Dec. 15, 1954; italics are mine).

In late 1956, the movement's members were alarmed by Watchtower management's steady hints that perhaps now there was only a year or so before the Armageddon-war would begin. This feeling of alarm was fairly common among the Witnesses, at least in Scandinavia. It originated with an article in *The Watchtower* that included the following:

"No doubt a great multitude of other people of good will must yet hear and flee to safety as this proclamation continues a little longer. / The urgency of the times cannot be emphasized too strongly. The time is short, much shorter than when this proclamation began, and there is no time to lose. Armageddon draws on apace. *It is now almost forty years since Satan was cast out of heaven down to this earth.* The climax of all ages is fast approaching" (*WT*, Aug. 1, 1956; italics are mine).

Quite simply, that statement is an ideal example of the totally irresponsible misinformation campaign conducted between 1954 and 1958. The Society leaders knew what rumors stirred among the members, since those leaders so deliberately played on the members' credulity and fear by planting the rumors' seeds to begin with. With the release of the 1956 article, ordinary Witnesses thought it likely the battle of Armageddon could come in 1958: Around March–April 1918 Satan was thrown down to earth—3-1/2 years after October 1914—making 1958 the "fortieth" year. From 1954 to March–April 1958 had to be the "critical last days before Armageddon," the ultimate end-stage. (*WT*, Feb. 15, 1958)

Note the speculative and deliberate strategy top management uses. They maintain the widespread atmosphere of fear, but without providing a *definite* prediction or date because they could be held responsible. Previously 1954 was the fortieth year; now, the leadership pushed it out to 1958, making it the *new* important year, where the members could expect something special.

Perhaps the scientific project identifying 1957 to 1958 as the "geophysical year"[236]—the year when mankind would try to penetrate beyond the Earth's atmosphere and beyond the borders that Jehovah had put up for humankind—was an important sign. Perhaps the artificial satellites would ignite an electrical storm that would facilitate the rage of the Armageddon war? Ordinary Witnesses engaged in this kind of speculation; anything could be viewed as a viable flashpoint to bring on Armageddon.

In 1958 an apostate Witness told to a Danish newspaper:

"Of course I was suspicious, because I soon discovered how they month after months changed what was previously said as unchangeable facts. As you know, humanity perished not in 1954, therefore, the big showdown in 1958 or 1959 was postponed, and now they have been wiser; now say simply: 'Can you endure?' After 1954, there were many elderly people who looked at each other without daring to say anything, because ordinary Witnesses must not 'murmur' " (*Berlingske Tidende*, Oct. 5, 1959, p. 32).

This testimony is of course subjective, but it nevertheless reflects, very reliably, the rumors surrounding Armageddon's arrival that circulated among the Witnesses throughout the world during these years.

Chapter 21

The *Last* Giant Convention Before Armageddon

With Armageddon looming, the leaders chose to hold the hitherto biggest international convention of the Jehovah's Witnesses in 1958; this one was much bigger than even the 1953 gathering. Yankee Stadium and the nearby Polo Grounds, the two largest baseball stadiums in New York, were rented for eight days (July 27 to August 3).

The Society advertised in advance about this tremendous convention arrangement: "This may probably be the largest convention ever arranged for by the Watch Tower Society *before* Armageddon" (*WT*, Dec. 15, 1958; italics are mine).

Watchtower Society plans included, presumably, that there would be no more assemblies of this magnitude, which seems to explain why it *had to be the last one*. And as I write this in the second decade of the 21st century, it is still, as far as I know, the last giant assembly. I can only say this must be a long-term strategy. Not until 2003 did the Society resume major international conventions around the world, but not of the magnitude of the 1953 and 1958 events (in fact, between 1970 and 2003, the Society held a few international conventions).

The 1958 convention was called The Divine Will International Assembly of Jehovah's Witnesses, and it lacked nothing in organizational respects. Everybody *had* to come. It was a mass gathering, a multitude of joyful faces and seemingly happy people who applauded almost on cue.

I was just twenty-two at the time and could not afford to attend, nor did I want to. Already at that time I found myself beginning to break with the movement.

In the eight days of meetings, daily attendance exceeded 145,000. At Orchard Beach, 7,136 were baptized—as the Watchtower leaders said this "was 4,136 more than were baptized that day of Pentecost long ago" (*Proclaimers*, 1959, p. 289).

Again, the Society launched many new books during the convention.

The fourth volume (of five) of the *New World Translation of the Hebrew Scriptures* (from Isaiah to the Lamentations, published from 1953 to 1960) was released, and tens of thousands of copies were sold. At this time, the leaders also released the complexly illustrated *From Paradise Lost to Paradise Regained*—an allegedly terrible book. The book, with its orange-red cover and large fonts and, true to say, appalling drawings across its 256 pages, was specially designed for propaganda in developing countries. Gilead missionaries in Thailand had asked if the Society could produce a book presenting only the "true biblical" teachings. (*WT*, Feb. 15, 1959)

Although this book was initially conceived for missionary use abroad, it was later determined to be a suitable tool for teaching the Witnesses' children. In an upcoming chapter on Armageddon I will return to the *Paradise* book, which today's educators and child psychologists would undoubtedly find inappropriate for children of any age.

A considerable part of the title of the new book was almost certainly borrowed from John Milton's *Paradise Lost*. This famous English work was first published in 1667; it was followed some years later by *Paradise Regained*. Milton's epic poem in blank verse is about man's fall, Adam and Eve's temptation by the fallen angel, Satan, and the human couple's expulsion from Eden that became the "lost paradise." There is a kind of shamelessness in copying the title of one of history's great literary works, especially considering the Watchtower Society's new book was no kind of poetic achievement; actually it was a diametric opposite. (Milton's poem is available to read on the internet.)

As I said, we will return to this issue later.

The Book of Daniel Re-interpreted

The book *Your Will Be Done on Earth* was released on the penultimate day of the assembly; within days, 228,000 copies had been sold. The first printing ran one million copies.

In 1965, as I began writing my first book on the movement, *Your Will Be Done on Earth* seemed to be one of the worst I had ever seen from the Watchtower Society. Yet the publishers considered it one of the Society's most outstanding books. Primarily, it was an interpretation of the Old Testament book of Daniel. Its interpretations—and this must be stressed—were written by people with access to *all* the necessary scholarly literature on the subject, yet with a certain (but crippled) insight into things, they seem dangerously close to being pure fraud. Still the book's completely wild speculations show how things at the Society were moving along in their typically easy manner. Its reasoning technique consists of deliberate misinformation, in which fiction and historical facts are interlinked so the average, common reader cannot discern one from the other, leaving the impressions it's all fact.

A brief example:

In the book of Daniel 11:30 we read: "For the ships of Chittim shall come against him: therefore he shall be grieved, and return, and have indignation against the holy covenant: so shall he do; he shall even return, and have intelligence with them that forsake the holy covenant" (KJ).

The Watchtower writers interpret this verse in an extremely arbitrary way. The "ships of Chittim" became the great British and American fleet, which in 1917 fought "against him"—that is, Emperor Wilhelm. But when the same verse says that he "will rage against the holy covenant," it's another *he* altogether; in this case, it's Adolf Hitler's anger that flares against the Jehovah's Witnesses in 1933. Those who "forsake the holy covenant" are the Christian clergy, particularly the Catholic.

The following quotes demonstrate how judicious and interpretative this disinformation is:

"More 'ships of Kittim' came from the west later, after the German submarine, U-20, sank the British Cunard Liner Lusitania off Ireland on May 7, 1915, and 124 American lives were lost."

And even World War I *tanks* rolled through the book of Daniel:

"In September, 1916, however, the British had introduced a strange kind of armor-clad land battleship against the king of the north, in the form of the tractored 'tanks' " (*Your Will Be Done*, 1958, p. 271–273; the small quotations here from Daniel 11:30 are taken from Jehovah's Witnesses' *New World Translation*).

The concept of *ships of Kittim* (or Chittim) in Daniel's book is probably in reality an allusion to the Romans, and in the Dead Sea scriptures (e.g., *The Habakkuk Commentary*) the word *Chittims* has been used in the same manner.[237]

The fact that you could get someone to seriously believe in such blatant misinterpretation of old texts, which deal exclusively with specifically defined religious and war history—the Maccabees' rebellion against Antiochus IV Epiphanes[238] and their takeover of power in Judaea around 165 BC—is incomprehensible and the acceptance of this practice must be viewed in the context of the ordinary Witnesses' lack of higher education.

The Divine Will International Assembly of
JEHOVAH'S WITNESSES
invites you to hear the
PUBLIC LECTURE

GOD'S KINGDOM RULES—IS THE WORLD'S END NEAR?

by
N. H. KNORR
President of Watch Tower Society

YANKEE STADIUM AND **POLO GROUNDS**

3 PM SUNDAY AUG. 3

Seats Free   *No Collection*

This flyer was distributed to New York City residents inviting them to attend President Knorr's public lecture at Yankee Stadium and Polo Grounds, Sunday, August 3, 1958.

During my research, I searched for this book's title on the Society's literature CD, but oddly enough it could not be found! I suppose this book has finally been put among those that nobody talks about today.

Now, let's return our focus to The Divine Will International Assembly of Jehovah's Witnesses, New York, 1958:

Among the various speeches, Knorr presented "God's Kingdom Rules—Is the World's End Near?" in which he said:

"Since the close of World War I in 1918, the Gentile nations led by the god of this world, Satan the Devil, have been on the march to Armageddon for their final, showdown fight against God's kingdom. That means that by the year 1958 they have been on the march *for forty years.… How much longer* will the march go on before the "war of the great day of God the Almighty" begins? / This generation of humankind is nearing its normal end. Jesus prophesied that this generation, which saw the Gentile times end amid World War I and the beginning of world sorrows, would also see the end of those sorrows in the world's destruction at Armageddon.… We know not the day or hour, but the world's end is near" (*WT*, Oct. 15, 1958; italics are mine).

A crowd of 253,922 heard the lecture; about 60,000 New York City residents were among them.

At the assembly Brother Knorr also announced a new training program would be introduced in 1961: "So if it be the divine will that we continue in this great work of preaching the good news of the Kingdom for a number of years, then the Society is prepared to train all of its overseers over a period of time."

This training program would be conducted at the Society's headquarters in the United States, Canada, England, Germany and France, as well as many other countries. First and foremost the branch servants and circuit servants would undergo a ten-month course, and then thousands of ordinary congregation servants would come to school. This course was called "Kingdom Ministry School" and consisted of twenty-four school days with ninety-six classroom sessions and twenty instructional lectures. To undergo this course, the Society recommended congregation servants take a month-long leave from their secular work. (*1958 Report of the Divine Will International Assembly of Jehovah's Witnesses*, 1958, p. 97; *Divine Purpose*, 1959, p. 292-294)

Apostasy, Exclusions and Stagnation

All of this regimentation, rigid discipline and authoritarianism—plus years of failed predictions—overburdened some of the members of the movement. When you more or less force people to express things beyond what they feel in their hearts, frustrations arise that can cause them to become passive robots, mechanically fulfilling commands without being mentally or emotionally engaged in them. Outwardly, as they knock on doors and talk to the interested people they encounter, the members appear happy, but within (unconsciously) they are increasingly self-conflicted. They begin to doubt, often suffering great guilt, and not infrequently they suffer under the delusion that their secret thoughts and doubts are the influence of Satan, going around as the biblical "roaring lion" to entice them. I characterize this as a struggle between the "Watchtower Superego" and a member's true, repressed ego attempting to break through the impersonal layers of rhetoric, false axioms and banalities, indoctrinated by the *engineers* of the "true" faith over many years. To codify this, a popular mental health term used among former members is *cognitive dissonance.*[239]

Today more and more Jehovah's Witnesses are successfully breaking out and leaving the movement, perhaps because the Watchtower leaders' excuses have become too transparent. The so-called "demon-occupied" members feel disconnected from their fellow believers in The New World Society, and thus they avoid them. And so their ability to endure any longer ends with an abrupt bump. They can no longer suffer the cliché-embossed insipidity of the Jehovah's Witnesses. They are aware that they themselves have an identity, a right to be respected, and they may experience (as I did) an amazing liberation. It happens when the scales fall from the eyes and the proper context of the cause unfolds.

At best, they definitely and demonstratively break with the movement. In the next-best scenario they go their way, silent and unnoticed. Often it depends on family relationships and what is suitable for an individual. Of course, if one has family within the movement, wife and children, or parents and siblings, etc., it might be wise to keep a low profile for some time, since a break with the Witnesses can easily end tragically for anyone who publicly shouts his views from the rooftops.

If one chooses to speak with his former fellow believers, in order to raise awareness that things are not as they should be, it can quickly lead to disastrous events. No time is wasted. The rebel is quickly engaged in a conversation with the "judicial committee of the Christian congregation," as if he was a heretic or a criminal. After a short process the rebellious member is disfellowshipped, and this is announced with deep seriousness before the congregation at a subsequent service meeting. Thereafter, the excluded person can actually consider himself sentenced to death by Jehovah through his visible organization. After this ceremonial act of expulsion, no one is to maintain friendly relations or even greet the expelled, who is considered nonexistent by the congregation.

The number of former members marginalized in this way from 1952 to 1957 appears in an exclusion report,[240] but this report includes only US statistics. During this period, 2,500 members were expelled or disfellowshipped, and from April 1957 to April 1958 the figure was at 1,334. There is no data from countries outside the US, so far as I know, but to all appearances, the figures were just as high. I would guess that exclusion figures for Denmark, from 1955 to 1965, ranged between 300 and 600. (*WT*, March 15, 1959)[241]

The baptismal figures were not listed among Watchtower statistics in the early 1950s, so it is difficult to accurately calculate the number of dropouts later in that decade without knowing how many people came into the movement, but we can be certain the number baptized then—as now—was somewhat inflated compared to the actual growth the *Year Book* reports every year.[242]

One thing seems certain: Many left the movement from 1954 to 1958, presumably either as rebels because the big battle didn't happen as predicted, or as outcasts who committed some sort of sin (according to the Society). An incipient stagnation seemed to advance in 1956, probably due to Armageddon failing to manifest in 1954. Yet, while the movement lost members, partly because of the battle of Armageddon and partly because of its intolerant policy towards dissidents, many thousands more signed up.

In 1958, Knorr said, "70,000 new people come into the organization every year." The Watchtower leaders seem to have been incapable of subtraction, since they disclose nothing about how the number of deceased and renegade members affected this growth. They do not bother to look at statistical growth versus statistical losses and reconcile their numbers. There is talk about a so-called "revolving door" situation: "What you put on the merry-go-rounds, you win on the swings" (*Divine Purpose*, 1959, p. 293; see also *Conscience,* 1983, p. 31).

The "Jehovists" in the Soviet System

Much has happened since 1966 when I published my first book about Jehovah's Witnesses; some of it even concerned the now-dissolved Soviet Union. In the years before the great doors of the East and West were flung open, Jehovah's Witnesses had a difficult time. Yet, in spite of powerful resistance, they made progress, even as the Soviet authorities tried (unsuccessfully) to prevent it. An emerging religion is a difficult thing to stop, especially the always-active and belligerent type like the Witnesses. It spreads despite national boundaries and national interests. It is global, and no matter where members are located, it is surrounded by *enemies*—oddly enough, this provides special growth conditions under totalitarian regimes. The Jehovah's Witnesses planted firm roots in Russia, where the Communists—just like the Nazis—were unable to prevent their intrusion. In the vast Soviet empire, which was so well-equipped for sectarianism, the Witnesses' gradually branching and banned organization, together with other illegal groups, helped facilitate greater freedom and democracy. At first this seems to be a paradox, but that doesn't negate the truth of it.

Knorr's global expansion slowly crept beyond the Iron Curtain, seemingly taking a route through Poland. According to the Watchtower Society's own data, some Gilead-trained missionaries went to Poland in 1947, and in 1950 there were 18,116 active Jehovah's Witnesses there. That same year, however, the Witnesses' business was prohibited in Poland, and most of the "servants" were arrested and sent to labor camps. The same happened in other Eastern European countries: Czechoslovakia in 1948 (in 1951 the local movement had 3,705 members) followed in succession by Yugoslavia, Bulgaria, Hungary, Romania and East Germany.

In 1956, the Watchtower leaders sent a request to Prime Minister N. A. Bulganin of the USSR. According to the request, it appears the Soviets had sent more than 2,000 Jehovah's Witnesses to the penal camp at Vorkuta, and more than 7,000 Jehovah's Witnesses had been arrested in the Baltic states at *Bessarabia* (earlier part of Romania), and then transported by freight trains to remote areas between Tomsk and Irkutsk and near the Bajkal Lake in Siberia. (*Divine Purpose*, 1959, p. 277–279)

In 1959 Jehovah's Witnesses' problems in the Soviet Union were treated in a headline article in the *Washington Post* (March 21, 1959). Excerpts of the article are found in the Witness history book, *Jehovah's Witnesses in the Divine Purpose*, from 1959, where it states:

"It is interesting to learn, by way of an extended denunciation in *Pravda* [the Communist Party's main news organ in Moscow], that the sect of Jehovah's Witnesses has become almost as much of a headache to the rulers of Communist Russia as it was to the rulers of Nazi Germany. It seems that the Witnesses have been making converts all over the Soviet Union, even in such distant places as Siberia and Kurgan, and that they now constitute a formidable movement of underground resistance to the regime."

And the *Washington Post* article continued:

"The editors of *Pravda* affect to believe that the whole movement is being subsidized by 'the most reactionary elements of American capitalism' and that its purpose is to infect the Soviet masses with a spirit of meekness and resignation that will frustrate or delay the world-wide triumph of the revolutionary proletariat. The organizers of the movement are described as 'former war criminals, Fascist collaborators and Gestapo informers' who were indoctrinated and trained for the work in German concentration camps.... At any rate the chiliastic doctrine of the Witnesses ... has had an immense appeal to people who live under the more totalitarian and tyrannous forms of government. Thus one can readily accept the estimate of the Witnesses themselves that the number of their converts beyond the Iron Curtain is more than 100,000..." (*Divine Purpose*, 1959, p. 280).

Author Walter Kolarz thoroughly dealt with the Witnesses' enterprise in Russia during these years in his book, *Religion in the Soviet Union*. He notes that a sect worshipping Jehovah (and using that name) existed in Russia even before Jehovah's Witnesses arrived. This sect arose in the 1840s, and the members were referred to as *Yegovisty (Jehovists)*; a name which the Witnesses have now inherited. Kolarz's very credible account confirms both what the Witnesses reported about their fellow believers' conditions under Soviet despotism and whatever else is known about the case. Kolarz wrote:

"In deporting them the Soviet Government could have done nothing better for the dissemination of their faith.... With the proclamation of the Soviet amnesty in 1955, both the 'Witnesses' of long standing and their new converts either returned to their homes or remained as free labourers [*sic*] in their places of banishment. In this way the Jehovists spread like the Pentecostalists to many parts of the Soviet Union. They reappeared in all Western Soviet Republics. They established new organisations [*sic* all] in the former forced labour [*sic* all] areas such as the Far East and the Komi Republic, where there are Jehovist branches along the ill-famed Pechora Railway line with its terminus at Vorcuta. The Jehovists also 'invaded' Siberia and Kazakhstan, where they are particularly numerous. Organizations of 'Witnesses' are to be found in many parts of the vast country—in Ust-Kamenogorsk, in the mining towns of Karaganda and Dzhezgan and in Tekeli in the Taldy-Kurgan Province which borders on China.... / In short, the Russian branch of the Jehovah's Witnesses may be regarded as one of the strongest in the world, and there is certainly no branch anywhere which receives so much adverse publicity from the secular power. / Experience has shown the Soviet authorities that the Jehovah's Witnesses are not just another sect with strange beliefs, but are first and foremost an organisation. Organisational and propaganda work is far more important to the 'Witnesses' than the observance of a religious cult. They believe that their organisation was set up by Jehovah himself. Membership of it is in itself a guarantee of salvation. All Jehovists will survive the battle of Armageddon, foretold in the Book of Revelation, which the 'Witnesses' believe will precede the end of the world. It is these beliefs which give the 'Witnesses' their moral and ideological strength and which have enabled them to form the most efficient and widespread illegal organisation that has ever existed under Soviet rule.... Indeed, no other group in Soviet Russia, whether of religious or political inspiration, has ever thought of embarking on such an extensive and illegal propaganda and publishing work. The fervor and courage of the Jehovah's Witnesses in propagating their faith has likewise its roots in their strange theology.... Contact is maintained with the help of letters in which a simple but highly characteristic code language is used. 'Family' stands for the Jehovist branch organization, 'mother' for the organization as a whole, 'food' for Jehovist literature and 'harvesters' for those who receive this literature.... The Soviet authorities are given the Biblical name of 'Ammonites'" (W. Kolarz: *Religion in the Soviet Union*, Macmillan & Co. Ltd., London 1961, pp. 338-344; see also *WT*, Sept. 1, 1965).[243]

No better testimony to the Jehovah's Witnesses' unity and sacrifice, which prevailed when they had to go underground, could hardly be given. And Kolarz's testimony is no less striking when one considers that the Witnesses and the Communist organizational structure were similar in many key areas, with one major difference: While the Communists secured and held power over the masses by coercion, the Jehovists were converted souls who *voluntarily* succumbed to a similar compulsion. In this lay the strength of the Witnesses in relation to the Soviet people who, by joining the *Yegovisty*, benefitted in two ways. They could satiate part of their craving for opposition to the Soviet system and vent repressed religious needs. Though they then slid straight into the grasp of another equally totalitarian system they seemed able to ignore in passing.

Other extremist religious groups were also active and experienced severe hardship in the Soviet Union, among them the Seventh-day Adventists, whose experience mirrors the Jehovah's Witnesses to some degree. Apparently, the Seventh-day Adventists did better than the Witnesses, but they were also exposed to the Soviet authorities' harassment, particularly because of their observance of the Sabbath (held on Saturdays). They practiced something of a survival policy, consisting of a relatively positive attitude towards the Soviet authorities; however, this was only considered a cunning maneuver. (Kolarz, 1961, p. 327)

After the Soviet Union collapsed in 1990, Jehovah's Witnesses realized freedom of their own, and they have since, according to internet resources and the *2008 Yearbook of Jehovah's Witnesses*, won a fair amount of popularity and spread further in the large country. In 2007, they had approximately 150,056 reporting members, which is the peak figure for the reporting year 2007. By 2010, the number of Witnesses in Russia was 162,182 (the highest number of preachers), representing an increase of two percent compared to 2009, with a peak Memorial attendance of 278,813, including non-member participants who were favorably inclined to the movement. Still, in accordance with their long tradition, twenty years of religious freedom and the right to meet and assemble were replaced by new restrictions at the start of the current century. This is mainly due to the movement's attitude on blood transfusion and military service, as well as the Russians' traditionally negative attitude toward the movement. ("Will Jehovah's Witnesses be banned in Russia?" internet resource page: RT, *Russia Today*, Dec. 12, 2009: *YB*, 2008, p. 230 (approx.) and *YB*, 2011, p. 44)[244]

Just before Christmas Eve 2009, I read the *2008 Yearbook of Jehovah's Witnesses* cover to cover, and I must confess (as I did with the Nazi persecution of the movement) that individual Witnesses' moving reports from the Soviet-era repression, deportation and forced labor, led me to draw parallels with the earliest Christians under the Roman Empire. The Russian Witnesses' often-fanatical devotion and perseverance seem impressive and terrifying, especially in light of the Watchtower Leaders' years of manipulation.

What Next?

As I sit looking back today, I find the Jehovah's Witnesses of the early 1960s were at a crossroads. The collective disappointments shared, more or less, by all members in 1954, 1955, 1956 and 1958 created a *vacuum of disappoint-*

ment in the movement—although, since no one could say the Society's leaders spoke clearly on these matters, they could hardly be vilified for their erroneous predictions.

The disappointments following the lack of Armageddon in 1954 are illustrated indirectly by the fact that the highest number of serving members throughout the world in 1956 indicates a loss of 2,582 compared to 1955. However, the small decline was quickly recovered the following year, as management redirected focus to 1958, where the month of March would mark 3-1/2 years after the fortieth year ended in October 1954.

It's no surprise to us that 1958 came and went, and the Society had to continue the program, because if Knorr's global expansion could be injected with new energy, something special had to happen. And it's pretty obvious what was coming: the old trick with a *new date* for the world's end.

Armageddon, as it evolved from Russell's relatively "soft" version, became the Watchtower Society's *new hell doctrine*; it was still the *crucial element* to stimulate the organization's activities and push its members to recommit to the Watchtower's worldwide campaigns.

Apocalypticism, belief in the world's near end, was still the means to encourage the members' efforts. And if the Watchtower leaders' expansion dreams were to be realized, something only achieved by stimulating members' dedication and enthusiasm, it was necessary to reapply the gradually abused doomsday scenario.

If you wanted to survive, you had to hurry. It was all or *nothing*, and there was no time to lose.

Armageddon was approaching very quickly!

PART THREE:

Human Destinies

"We know from modern as well as from ancient history that such ideas are often so strange, indeed so bizarre, that they fly in the face of reason. The fascination which is almost invariably connected with ideas of this sort produces a fanatical obsession, with the result that all dissenters, no matter how well meaning or reasonable they are, get burnt alive or have their heads cut off or are disposed of in masses by the more modern machine-gun. We cannot even console ourselves with the thought that such things belong to the remote past."

"But if people crowd together and form a mob, then the dynamisms of the collective man are let loose beast or demons that lie dormant in every person until he is part of a mob. Man in the mass sinks unconsciously to an inferior moral and intellectual level, to that level which is always there, below the threshold of consciousness, ready to break forth as soon it is activated by the formation of a mass."
—Carl Gustav Jung (1875–1961): *Psychology and Religion*,
Bollingen Foundation, New York, 1958, first chapter

Chapter 22

The Breakaway, Summer of 1959

When my parents were recruited by the Jehovah's Witnesses around 1938, they withdrew from the Danish National Church. From then on, most family events were concentrated around the activities of the "Friends." Both of my parents were adult-christened and participated actively in the agitation. As a result, for some years I stood by my mother's side when she campaigned "from door to door." So I was thoroughly trained as a seller of the Watchtower Society's publications.

Much later in life, around 1990, I became aware, to my surprise, that my mother's grandfather, my great-grandfather, had been pastor of the Apostolic Catholic Church in Copenhagen, a small church affiliated with *Irwingianism* in England. Therefore, the microbe (or seed or perhaps some genetic component) to be so devoted and passionate had seized my ancestors, and apparently was transferred to my mother's family. Still, most of them had distanced themselves from the church, and I understand my great-grandfather died a disappointed man.

His son, the famous Greenland painter Emanuel A. Petersen, had the virus as well, but his passion followed an artistic path. I realized, in one way or another, I too was infected with the family tendency, because I am not only a painter, but also—at a time when I had no knowledge of Emanuel—had been passionately captivated by mountain scenes in Norway. When I visited an exhibition of Emanuel's paintings a few years before writing this book, I was deeply moved by the many wonderful landscapes of Greenland. They went straight to my soul. Today, Emanuel's works hang in Christiansborg Castle, where the Danish Parliament is housed.

My father, also an artistic soul, was a talented painter and carver; he often sat in our kitchen producing the most beautiful, hand-carved frames. In 1951, he broke with the Jehovah's Witnesses movement. The congregation ostracized him, as one would expect, and my parents separated. Then, everything went black. In 1954, my mother died of a serious cancer, after she had refused blood transfusions for some time. To the end, she maintained hope of seeing *the end* as persistent rumors hinted Armageddon would arrive around October 1954. If she could live until then, she hoped to survive both the disease and Jehovah's doomsday war, so she might get to live forever in God's new world.

After her death, my father returned to our home, and I had to move because of the conflicts created by his exclusion and subsequent return. For some years our little family was scattered to the winds.

Around 1951, I had already met my wife, Birgit; she also grew up within the movement. We married in 1956 at age nineteen. In 1959, we broke with the Witnesses. Despite the fact that Christmas had not been celebrated in our childhood homes, in 1959 the small remnant of our family met in our former home in the little village of Dollerup near the beautiful Lake Hald and Dollerup hills in central Jutland to celebrate Christmas on December 24. The family was restored. In 1964, I too became ostracized, which led to my immediate exclusion from my wife's family. Today, most of them are dead—all those who were to live eternally.

When I published my first book on the Witnesses in 1966, Birgit and I could both put the past behind us. Not until 2003, thirty-seven years later, did I decide to write a new book on my old topic. Not because I wasn't done with the topic, but because I wanted to delve deeper into the substance. The topic fascinated me even after so many years. Another reason was that several people had approached me with requests to update my old book.

Now that you know something of my history and situation, let's go back to the years 1954–1964 to see what transpired:

Armageddon, Right Around the Corner

Sometime around 1957, members of congregations all over the world were regularly bombarded with requests to be pioneers or full-time publishers. As part of this campaign, the Society composed a number of letters, signed by the "governing body,"[245] wherein young Witnesses in particular were invited to engage themselves in the pioneer service.

The tone of the letters went far beyond common decency. They left no room for doubt concerning a baptized Jehovah's Witness's responsibilities in relation to his God, Jehovah. If one had the "opportunity" to serve as a pioneer, but neglected to do so, one would certainly have a tough time defending oneself in the eyes of Jehovah—and at Armageddon.

At the time, I was a very young man, and decided to devote all my spare time to the ministry work. I became a JW pioneer.

In January 1954—the year many Jehovah's Witnesses believed Armageddon would come and this included my mother—the organization stressed, yet again, the importance of the ministry work: "It is a serious matter to be a pioneer.... Perhaps, it is a more serious matter not to be, if you have the opportunity" (translated from the Danish *WT*, Jan. 15, 1954).[246]

Members who did not work as pioneers suffered from a persistent feeling of guilt. After all, Armageddon was "right around the corner," and one could never know *exactly* when that would be.

An article in *The Watchtower* from 1956 states:

"This obedience and willingness to serve are what Jehovah God expects of those who accept the treasure of full-time service. Persons who are stubborn and self-willed are of no value to him. He wants servants who delight to do his will and gladly obey whatever instructions are given them through the theocratic organization.... When engaging in the full-time service as a pioneer, a person has little time for personal pursuits" (*WT*, March 15, 1956).

The stiff-necked and self-willed Jehovah's Witnesses, all those who decided what was good for them despite the Society telling them otherwise, were obvious candidates for the same fate as the world's *bad people*. Such Witnesses went to their destruction in meeting. So a monstrous pressure was placed on young people who may have started an advanced education, or who had very different and more realistic plans. The independent-minded were scared witless into making a special effort in the service of not less than 100 hours a month.

One of my young friends from that time, Carl Johan, was strongly influenced by this tremendous pressure. He gave up his apprenticeship as a lithographer at a well-known weekly publication to serve as a pioneer in the last few years before Armageddon. He died shortly afterwards in a car accident.

"Success" for young people primarily meant success "within The New World Society of Jehovah's Witnesses." And if you wanted to be successful you had to start in the pioneer service. For the idealists it was either/or, and a matter of "do or die." In those years young people obviously could have "success," because the Society selected "Special Pioneers" from among the ordinary pioneers, and later those were selected to attend the School of Gilead in the United States. From there, those considered the most successful could be circulated as missionaries in foreign countries. It was almost the highest position one could achieve in the time before Armageddon. To come within this success framework was like stepping into an inner sanctum. You could play an important role, gain influence within the organization and even reach the top in the Watchtower headquarters in Brooklyn, New York.

That a pioneer was considered a certain kind of *elite* within the movement is evident from the fact that, and I quote: "[If] the Society removes a pioneer because of wrongdoing and the Society is the only agency that knows about the wrongdoing of the individual, there is no reason for the Society then to notify the company and have that company disfellowship that person, not if that person has confessed his sin and asked for forgiveness from the Society. Then that one can go on his way. The Society would probably put restrictions or bounds around that individual because of the course of action he has taken. By way of punishment it may take him off the pioneer list for six months or maybe a year" (*WT*, Marsh 1, 1952).

This self-appointed role of the Society is highly thought-provoking. We have already heard about a religious society, the Society of Jesus (*Societa Jesu*) or Jesuits, that had the power to grant forgiveness and condemn to death on God's behalf long before the Watchtower Society appeared. So, although all the publishers of the Kingdom stood on equal footing, the pioneers of the time around 1952 were clearly considered to have been *more equal than others.*[247]

Today, however, I imagine that this policy has been tightened.

"... while there is still time"

Year in and year out, the Watch Tower Society rumbled on with its aggressive recommendations:

"Of the 10,000 publishers in Denmark there are for the moment only about 200 in the full-time service, besides the staff who work at the Betel home and in the printing works. Many more want to engage in the full-time ministry. Why do they hesitate? ... You must not think that a personal goal of hours ... can replace ... the pioneer service. All you who can achieve to be a pioneer ought not to set a personal goal under 100 hours per month. It would not agree with your consecration promise.... You should not hesitate. Engage in the full-time service while there is still time" (translated from the Danish KM, *Rigets Tjeneste*, Oct. 1961, p. 3).

At this time, a pioneer's duties involved no less than 100 monthly hours of field service (canvassing door to door). A Special Pioneer was obligated to spend at least 150 hours per month and in return received a small monthly income. Of course, many were forced to take a normal job on the side to meet living expenses.

Gilead-educated missionaries had additional conditions placed on them. Their tasks included "theocratic challenges" on several continents—Europe, Africa, Asia and South America. The organization expected the missionaries to travel abroad at the end of their education. They acted as branch overseers, zone servants (circuit overseers) or held other high-ranking positions within the organization, giving them huge prestige.

With just a few years left before Armageddon, I naturally took up the challenge. Who would not want to strive for higher goals and *be successful* through new challenges—to be something in the eyes of the organization? *And survive.* It was this dual-pronged theme the leaders played on so strongly. Consequently, I quit my job as a lithographer for I. Christian Soerensen in Copenhagen (lithography and offset printing), and started as a pioneer in Thy, the northern part of Jutland. My wife and I stayed with her parents for no cost, using our savings for any other expenses. The situation didn't last long. It was a nonstarter, doomed from the beginning. In part, the circumstances put my faith to the test to such a degree I could hardly push the pedals on my bicycle; also, a pregnancy complicated things further. We joyfully welcomed this new development in our lives and moved to Aarhus, the biggest town in Jutland, where I again got jobs in lithography.

A Risky Theological Question

Around 1957–1958, I attended a circuit assembly in Ringkøbing, a borough in northwest Jutland, and it was at this convention I first had a falling out with the organization. During these years, my critical attitude to everything the Watchtower organization taught had been awakened. In my head, a fierce debate ensued. Not a single issue was left untouched, for it was as if I was driven by something deep in the core of my being. I quested for truth. One day at the convention, I encountered the district overseer. I decided to ask him a question regarding one of the issues that had been causing me distress.

The Gospel of John 3:16, reads:

"For God so loved the world that he gave his only Son, that whoever believes in him should not perish but have eternal life" (RSV 1971).

For years, Watchtower leadership had taught us that "the world" that God loved was not "this world," but the "world to come" after Armageddon. I had problems accepting this, and there I was, standing before the charismatic and always impeccably dressed district overseer. Or was he a zone servant? Right now, I don't remember exactly, but he was at least a very important man. So, I decided to tempt destiny, with a perfectly reasonable question (at least in my opinion):

"The world that God loves, which is referred to in the Gospel of John, is it not more plausible that the world in reference is *this* world and its people, rather than what the Society says, the *coming* new world?"

Clearly, my question was deemed highly inappropriate, and the reply consisted of the following tirade, accompanied by a rather disapproving stare:

"There are some brothers who prefer to go *ahead* of the Organization, brothers who believe they always know what is right. Then there are those who patiently wait for Jehovah and his organization, the 'faithful and discreet slave.'[248] And these are the ones who will receive meat in due season" (quoted from memory).

What he said struck me, and of course, I knew perfectly well the old cliché of *not going ahead of the organization*, but it was more the *way* he said it that affected me. It was an unpleasant experience. For a split second I experienced the whole narrow-minded, authoritarian mentality within the organization, and that aside, I remained in no less disagreement with him regarding the issue I had asked about. After all, I could read and knew very well what was written in the Gospel. So from a theological point of view, there was no room for discussion as far as I was concerned. Thus, the case was, from my theological view, completely clear. Paradoxically, yes. But God loved the world so, for that reason, he would save it.

Eventually, however, I learned I truly had been "ahead of the organization"—far, far ahead—as the Society would later change its opinion regarding this particular doctrine. For this, I received no praise, for it was not of importance *that I had understood the scriptures better* than Jehovah's company in Brooklyn, New York, but rather that I had not been humble enough to keep my mouth shut.

I was just twenty-one, and the experience had disheartened me. Still, I stuck to my opinion, and in hindsight, I truly believe this was my *moment of clarity*. From that point on, my "theocratic attitude" went downhill fast.

While I was still pioneering, a circuit overseer came to stay with us at our congregation in Thy as part of his service. I seized this opportunity to ask him a few questions—questions that would reveal my doubts about almost every aspect of the religion. I was told Satan and his demons were the cause of my loss of faith. However, my belief in Satan and his demons was far from enough, and after much thought, not to mention an all-out loss of faith, it became increasingly clear to me that my *inner voice* was neither Satan nor his demons; *it was my own.*

The Problem of Conscientious Objector's Service

As early as 1957, I was on a collision course with the organization. Reviewing my letters to my wife, I can see that in September that year, I left Aarhus, the biggest city in Jutland where we lived at the time, and traveled to the Watchtower's national headquarters in Virum, a suburb north of Copenhagen, to meet with the branch overseer in Denmark, Richard E. Abrahamson. The purpose of this meeting was a discussion regarding how I—due to the pressure placed on me by the organization—felt literally coerced into not attending the camp for conscientious objectors.

At this time, almost all the young men within the movement refused to attend the camp. Civil service was considered to be just another way of contributing to a potential war effort. As goes the mantra: It was "a matter of conscience." The truth was these overzealous conscientious objectors refused all and any service because they were instructed—directly or indirectly—to do so by the organization. Only a few "spiritually immature" chose to show up at the camp, and *fortunately*, I would be one of those *few*. However, I would first undergo great trials.

The meeting with Abrahamson clarified the situation: I was not to attend the camp, and I would be incarcerated for two years. This was nothing compared to France, where one would be imprisoned up to twelve years, or the United States or South Africa, where one would get five years. Later, I would discover that in Denmark, one would usually be released for good behavior after fourteen months. Still, it was a high price to pay for a cause I no longer believed in.

In 1958, the authorities caught up with me. After having refused to report to the conscientious objectors' camp in Kompedal plantation in Jutland, I walked the long mile to the jail in Aarhus, where I spent forty days weaving horse halters of twine. Our first son had just been born, and I believe he was only nine or ten days old when I left. The pressure I had been subjected to by my wife's family, the local congregation and the headquarters at Virum had been too much to withstand. I was terribly divided, as I constantly pictured myself lying down on the endless battlefield of Armageddon along with the five or six billion clean-picked skeletons. The organization's dogma still filled my head.

Following my stay at the jail in Aarhus, I was again called up for the conscientious objectors' camp; although the authorities tried to help me by finding grounds for my dismissal, I was eventually sentenced to twenty-two months.

When I once again had to terminate my job, we moved from Aarhus and returned to live with my in-laws where we took up residence on the first floor. I then began serving my prison sentence at the juvenile detention center in South Jutland. There were around ten young Jehovah's Witnesses there, living in a kind of collective and arranging meetings five times a week. I even fulfilled my "hours of service" while still in prison. After all, it reminded me more of a theocratic forced labor camp than a prison.

After meeting first with the leading teacher and then the prison-inspector, I proceeded to apply for a pardon through the ministry of internal affairs; one month later, I was released. I had revealed my plan to just one of my fellow prisoner-brothers. One day, after the others had been sent off to work, I packed my few belongings, and proceeded to the camp at Kompedal, halfway between the towns Viborg and Silkeborg. The transition was a great upheaval and quite overwhelming. The conscientious objectors' camp became my first "university," where I learned a number of new things and met idealists of all sorts. In fact, I had arrived at quite a madhouse. Still, I managed to get through it, and I'm glad to have had this experience, although living among conscientious objectors, pacifists and communists was no easy thing. Pacifists were not as peaceful as I had expected.

At this time, I was still not so much outside the organization that I had completely detached myself. This process was a sensitive one, in which I would slowly reclaim my individualism. Reestablishing one's own personality is not done overnight—although I initially saw it that way. It takes time. Years! The *theocratic super-ego*, the result of years of indoctrination and brain-washing, had to be broken down first, and while going through this, I had only myself and my wife for support. My in-laws failed me completely. No one understood the *essence* of Christianity. To them, it was all about Armageddon and the organization.

And what about my father, you may ask? He would have supported me during this process, but he was completely cut off, ostracized.

Still a member of the Jehovah's Witnesses, but as a "less-mature brother," I accepted that I could not hold positions in the organization for three years after completing conscientious objector camp. However, this didn't worry me. We were on our way out of the organization, and what had simply been an unthinkable consideration a few months earlier, was now quietly taking over the lead.

In May, I wrote to my wife's brother-in law, as he was going to serve a prison sentence due to his refusal to serve as a conscientious objector:

"Are you doing this for Jehovah, or because you do not dare trust your own judgment.… I know that you are only willing to go to prison because you want to remain loyal to the Society, but remember that you also owe your wife loyalty. Can't you see that you are just following other peoples' norms, norms you even, by your own admission, are unable to comprehend? … If you do not act out of what's in your heart there is no point."

I wrote letters to my in-laws as well, but they neither could nor would try to understand me. The first time I was on leave from the conscientious objectors' camp, I met my father-in-law at the front door. He just looked at me briefly without greeting me, and then retired to another part of the house.

Shortly thereafter, my wife, our one-year-old son and I moved to a small apartment in the village of Dollerup. Here we lived for about a year while I attended the conscientious objectors' camp in Kompedal plantation where we performed various types of forestry work.

The Final Break

Even though I was considered a less-mature brother, I was still expected to complete the minimum hours of service, meaning house-to-house work, selling magazines and other literature. At the last service meeting my wife and I attended, we were handed our report cards from the congregation's ministry files to see if we had been regular Kingdom proclaimers during the last year. Only the industrious who completed a minimum ten hours per month could feel confident they would be safe at the end. When the service meeting was over, Birgit and I decided to keep our report cards and hoped no one would notice. The congregational servant later tried to convince us to return them, but the attempts were in vain.

I can vividly remember the last time we participated in field service.

We were canvassing in the outskirts of Dollerup, and as we approached the last house in a row, we decided that it would be our *last house*. Astonishing, isn't it?

The next morning, we were out of the organization. My subconscious (Satan, according to the organization) must have at last processed all my thoughts, feelings and questions, for overnight, the seesaw tipped. Suddenly, my feet rested firmly on the earth, while the organization seemed to be floating in thin air. Things had been turned completely around, and what had previously been *the Truth* became *systematic falsehood*. Birgit followed me without hesitating.

As we failed to appear at the meeting hall over a period of time, we were called upon by the circuit overseer Joergen Larsen—later appointed as branch overseer of Jehovah's Witnesses in Denmark, and now deceased. As Joergen gazed upon my bearded face—at that time considered unacceptable among the Jehovah's Witnesses—he gestured disapprovingly, hiding his eyes as if he would relieve himself of a terrible sight. What he saw was my independence of the organization. Birgit and I had regained our individual selves. They had lost power over us. The fact that he now met the *true us* did not change anything; I believe we were proud to be so distinguished.

I let my beard grow so no one could be mistaken. Reportedly it is now acceptable to grow a full beard, but it was absolutely not the case back then. Shortly before Joergen Larsen's visit with us, I had attended a convention in Randers, another city in the middle of Jutland, during which I was accosted by a sister who thought that I should not wear a full beard, for in "the sweat of thy face shalt thou eat bread, till thou return unto the ground." The beard symbolized the verdict passed onto Adam from Jehovah.

In short, my full beard symbolized an inappropriate lack of correct, theocratic behavior; I knew this, of course, and from my perspective, the beard was an outward signal of the rebellion that was to come. A representative of the movement was not supposed to resemble a revolutionary. On the contrary: We should rather resemble a *vacuum cleaner salesman*.

Our second son was just born, and we now needed a proper income and better housing. While traveling to Copenhagen, I found an available apartment in a tenement house north of the city. In April 1960, we moved in. Following our move, I was transferred to another camp in a forest (Gribskov) on the Isle of Zealand (the island where Copenhagen is located) and here I served my remaining time as a conscientious objector.

We had now fallen away and were as out of the Jehovah's Witnesses as one could possibly be in such a short time. Before we left Dollerup, Birgit burned all her theocratic books in the stove while I hid mine in a cardboard box. At this time, I was already entertaining the idea of writing a book.

Our break with the organization had happily been made complete and our experiences with the outside world were merely a continuance of our liberation. I can imagine how the people of Eastern Europe must have felt when they rid themselves of their communist dictators. We were happy in our new life, even if it was somewhat uncertain. We were in a sort of no-man's land: "the old, wicked world outside." They had brainwashed us into believing it was a horrid place. Eventually, it turned out to be the opposite. Just like, as I recall, in George Orwell's novel *Nineteen Eighty-Four*. Julia and Winston, the novel's main characters, realized their physical and emotional yearnings during their excursions in the humble proletarian milieu of London's outskirts. Here they

262 Judgment Day Must Wait

experienced paradise, a sliver of freedom, albeit temporary. For a small sum, they rented a room at Mr. Charrington's store; the room, not surprisingly, had hidden electronic monitoring equipment. Eventually, Big Brother's omnipresent police arrested them. It's a wonderful but terrible and tragic love story about forbidden love in a hellish society.

Birgit's family had not broken ties with us, for we had not been formally disfellowshipped. Of course, it was just a matter of time.

In the introduction to this chapter, I spoke of my reunion with my family, my father, sister and others who would eventually support us—my family members who were not part of the movement. And this was the time, before we moved to Copenhagen, that we began to celebrate Christmas together, exchanging presents and smoking fat cigars—something as forbidden as my new beard!

In 1963, I suffered unpleasant psychological symptoms. The upheavals and stresses in my life had proven to be too dramatic and profound. After a couple of months, I had recovered and with it came an intense need to get everything out in the open, to talk and understand my parent's divorce, my mother's death in 1954, the breach with my excommunicated father. To sum it up: All the problems my little family and I had been through—all of which I had been unable to face for a time. At this point, everything revolved around the short life that would, from then on, be lived solely on our own terms. Eternity, which had always been our comfort, was gone forever.

"Who, that keeps silent, dies!"

So, I talked and wrote my way through the traumas, with the aid of a psychiatrist and a series of conversations. It was exactly what I needed. It was the self-awareness, the self-confidence, which had to be cemented.

Shortly thereafter, I launched my own, private campaign against the Jehovah's Witnesses in Denmark, one that would be fought in newspapers willing to print my contributions. Later, I also wrote feature articles. I even took steps to establish an association to inform the public on the activities of the Jehovah's Witnesses, but alas, this particular part of my effort was a bit premature. (*Politiken*, April 4, 1964; *Ekstra Bladet*, April 10, 1964; and *Kristeligt Dagblad*, April 4, 1964)

Summoned to a Meeting

It was, of course, inevitable. The organization came calling.

My recent activities had finally come to the attention of the branch headquarters in Denmark and caused a certain amount of concern for my old friend, the branch overseer, R. E. Abrahamson. Presumably it was Abrahamson who began the process of disfellowshipping me. After all, my writings were being read by the members, and an expulsion action was, at least theoretically, a way to prevent them from reading my published articles.

Apparently, our peaceful departure from the organization was just that: apparent. One day in early 1964—five years following our departure—the local congregation servant T. H. Christensen visited to request my presence at the Kingdom Hall. Naturally, I knew what was going to happen.

Since I would not be allowed to bring a witness to the proceedings, I arranged to borrow a portable tape recorder from a radio shop near my home, Riedel Radio; I carried the recorder concealed in my old leather briefcase saved from canvassing days. And so armed, I appeared at the scheduled meeting.

Three men I had never seen before, probably members of the judicial committee, or the committee of three, awaited me, silent gentlemen who sat on the opposite side of a long table. They remained quiet during the proceeding. The meeting chairman, a vice congregational overseer, began by mentioning that the zone servant (or was it the circuit overseer?) had initiated the meeting, which the chairman proceeded to refer to as a trial (the tape, my only witness, attested to it!). At that point, I knew what was about to happen. The Bible study servant, one of the members of the committee, then asked me the following question:

"From what I understand, your attitude towards the almighty God is in contradiction with what you once said yes to, because you have inaugurated by water baptism and said 'yes' to the questions that were put there, and according to that I think we can say that you are really going against the spirit of God." (Literally, according to the tape recording.)

Of course, this seemed absurd beyond my grasp. My family and I had long been freed from the power-sphere of the Watchtower organization. So I bided my time and argued against this primitive, fundamentalist God-concept, as I did not think modern people could believe in a God who was all-powerful and omniscient, and hence able to see into a person's future. That is, the Jehovah's Witnesses believed in a person's freedom to choose, and they believed at the same time that nothing was impossible for God. This theological enigma—the idea of an omniscient god who could see into the future of a person but chose to let it be—was something beyond my comprehension. It might be God and his earthly representatives who had a problem. I believed I had a relatively free will and had used it in my discussions with the Witnesses, although I didn't fully realize the concept that freedom was an inherent right. Of course, I was presumptuous and cocksure, which was necessary for me to survive. But I was after all only twenty-eight—and it was only five years earlier we had left the movement. Five years after the year "zero."

When I subsequently expressed knowing the conversation I was summoned to marked the beginning of an exclusion process, Christiansen replied: "I can say this generally that you can never talk about an exclusion before the file is known."

All my words were lost on these three committee members, who, I believe, did not want me to have a long life—and certainly not a life *forever*.

The meeting was more than forty-seven years ago.

Part-way into the trial I revealed I had brought a mechanical witness with me into the courtroom without asking permission, and that it recorded everything said. I was not sure the microphone had optimal working conditions, of course.

The room fell deathly silent!

The committee members were dumbfounded, and then they leapt from their seats and assigned one member to remain with me. The other two went into an adjacent room and conferred with another brother by phone—Abrahamson at Danish headquarters. The meeting was adjourned shortly after.

Afterwards, I sent a letter, dated February 16, stating the committee could resume the interrupted hearing, but only if I would be allowed to bring my own witnesses. The proposal was one the committee members were predisposed to reject. I subsequently received a letter notifying me the witnesses would not be permitted.

The letter I received from Christiansen a few days after having proposed a resumption of the meeting, said:

"I have received your letter the sixteenth of this month and just want to say that we salute freedom and tolerance, and we have nothing against that you believe in another God than the God we believe in, we just want to clarify what you yourself have confirmed that you no longer are among the Jehovah's Witnesses" (Dated February 20, 1964).

Since the exclusion was not communicated with particular clarity, I wanted to know what would be publicly pronounced in the Kingdom Hall near my home. Therefore, I wrote two letters, one to Christiansen and one to Abrahamson on February 23. In these letters I asked for elaboration. Was it a formal exclusion, and would the exclusion be announced publicly in a Kingdom Hall? I reiterated my offer to resume the trial, if they would permit the presence of my witnesses. In late February, I received a reply from Abrahamson:

"We have received your letter which shows that you have understood the decision of the congregation of Bagsvaerd, a decision you appeal to us. The committee has from yourself heard what you expressed and also have written, and what also is clear from your letter to us, that you no longer have the same belief as we have, but propagate another teaching. We find no reason to hold a new meeting of that reason" (Dated February 29, 1964).

As a result of the public exclusion, which had disastrous consequences with my wife's family, I again appealed the decision directly to Abrahamson, as I simply would not accept this ill treatment. Abrahamson knew beyond any doubt what he did, and how it would affect our family. I slowly realized it was a severe intimidation. In the letter I explained that I considered going to court:

"I have relatives among the Jehovah's Witnesses, my wife's parents, sisters, etc. If you don't understand what this means to me, I must—if you do not give me a clear message—consider legal counsel" (Dated March 2, 1964).

In the letter, I also pointed out the possible irregular aspects in relation to the Danish Constitution, but I knew already that there was no more to do. I was not dealing with normal, civilized people. These were primitive, possessive fundamentalists, modern Jesuits who had washed their hands of personal responsibility. They were mentally quite in line with the organization, respectively, in Denmark and in Brooklyn.

However, I took steps to initiate legal proceedings and made an enquiry directed to a High Court lawyer, who initially arranged a contact with the well-known newspaper *Politiken*. Subsequently the whole story appeared on the front page. (*Politiken*, April 9, 1964)

It was also important for me to learn on what grounds the ruling had been handed down at the public meeting, where notice of my exclusion was published as a warning to the members. In previous cases they had published offensive details of the excluded's behavior, especially if there had been charges of so-called impure sexual behavior. With no appeal process or anything to refute their claims, an excluded's reputation could be ruined in any way they saw fit. The nature of the information given at the meeting, where the exclusion was announced, could be crucial for an upcoming trial.

Since I had never been connected with the congregation in Bagsvaerd, where I lived, I didn't know my prosecutors in advance, nor did I remember their faces after the trial, and I never expected the community members would not greet me, which they were not allowed to do, when they encountered me in public.

Since there was little prospect that I would win a court case, I quickly relented. I could not achieve anything useful in this diffuse conflict. The battle was obviously lost beforehand, but my response served to draw attention to the Jehovah's Witnesses' ungodly and inhumane methods toward anyone who dared move on.

From an article published in *The Watchtower* in November 2003, it appeared that R. E. Abrahamson came to Denmark specifically to clean up at the former headquarters. A group that "did not want to follow all instructions from headquarters in Brooklyn," as it is so tastefully worded, was forced away, including the former translator of the magazine *The Watchtower* into Danish, Svend Joergensen.[249] Abrahamson continued, presumably willingly, in this hunting for dissenters in the Danish congregations, until in 1980 he was called for a special job in Brooklyn. He and his wife professed they "did not dwell on where we preferred to be but tried to focus on our current assignments and whatever challenges they posed," as it was piously noted in his biographical article. (*WT*, Nov. 1, 2003)

Later on, Abrahamson was assigned to the so-called Writing Department of the Watchtower Society in New York, and in 1992 he was assigned to assist the Governing Body. Since then he has advanced to a high position within the parent company, Watch Tower Bible and Tract Society of Pennsylvania, where he was secretary and director. Whether his new management tasks included acting as the Society's *eyes and ears*, I do not know, as I have not been able to uncover anything to support or deny it. I did learn he died a few years ago. Whether this highly adaptable Brooklyn official felt guilt about his actions, one can never know, but former members know the extent of unhappiness and personal misery he inflicted on the excluded. Some of them, reportedly, took their own lives. Particularly outrageous is the fact that his long arm reached those who wanted to quietly leave the Witnesses, to depart unnoticed. If we were to gather the individual stories of all the disfellowshipped in Denmark, they might add as much as 200 pages to this book—exclusively for Denmark.

The exclusion action meant the relationship with my wife's family was forever destroyed, even though my father-in-law told a journalist conducting the interview for a tabloid paper that he speaks with "people who are not Jehovah's Witnesses.... Why may I then not be allowed to talk to my son-in-law?" (*Ekstra Bladet*, April 10, 1964)

But it was not true. They would not talk to us, or at least not with me. They would not visit us. When they phoned Birgit and I answered the phone, they explained very briefly that they were not allowed to talk to me. All contact ceased. And they fanatically obeyed, to their death, the directives from the Governing Body in Brooklyn. The Society was more important than family.

Strangely enough, Birgit was not excluded, despite her solidarity and public support of my decision; she even sent a written resignation to the Danish headquarters. Still, she and the children could go home to her parents. Presumably, she was not expelled because the Watchtower leaders felt I had pressured her to resign. This was not the case. It was *her* reaction and *her* response to the family cruelty forced upon us.

Surprisingly, we saw Birgit's family some years later, but it was obviously because the Watchtower Organization had recently eased the unpleasant atmosphere within the movement. This was around 1978, three years after the apocalyptic year 1975. The organization had been forced to relax discipline, since Armageddon and the New World had failed to come, *again*. The members' frustrations provoked discussions and caused a stir within the top management in New York; this was quite unusual. Due to this, the chains were loosened for a short time.

In his book *Crisis of Conscience*, Raymond Franz mentions a brief "conditional" moment of joy and relaxation or "pleasant moments" as he names it. This subject will resurface in more detail as I later address developments in the years following 1975.

Persona Non Grata

I was now *persona non grata*, not wanted, sentenced to death *in absentia*; a death sentence postponed until Armageddon, where I would be one of the bare skeletons on the Judgment Day battlefield. Luckily, Birgit and I had no doubts about leaving the movement together and returning to the old world. Otherwise it would, as other exclusion stories show, probably have destroyed our marriage.

In revisiting this period of my life and reading the *Ekstra Bladet* article, I'm reminded of the time we were expecting a visit from my parents-in-law at Easter, but as the journalist wrote "instead a letter came stating that it was probably better that their daughter and the children visited them this summer. There was not as much as a greeting to the son-in-law. This is also forbidden."

Pardon me for a moment as I again express my opinions of the time, but revisiting the old interview helped to remember:

" 'A normal family life cannot continue if a member is excluded,' says Bregninge, 'and this I find unacceptable. There are no limits to the human tragedies these rules cause, and therefore I would like to pursue a principle lawsuit against the organization' " (Lizi Bundgaard, *Ekstra Bladet*, April 4, 1964).

Not only had I saved the old article, but I also found letters from other outcasts, which I received after the article was published. It was the same sad story, of how the excluded were isolated from the closest family members as part of the leaders' attempt to demolish the exhausted ex-members' psyches. Since that time, nothing has changed. They still use this practice to bind members to the organization, so they know what awaits them, if they abandon the organization.

Still, after all, life in Bagsvaerd went on happily without the announced trial, and I decided to write my first book on the Witnesses. It was released in September 1966 and became the method whereby the Bregninge family finally distanced itself from all the Jehovah Witnesses represented.

The future opened to us and we looked on a free horizon. Quite frankly, once we reached that point, we thought very little of Jehovah's Witnesses again until around 1990. At that time, we came in contact with new defectors, victims of the accelerating exclusion policy in the 1990s.

They had harrowing reports to tell.

For now, I'd like to take events back to the movement's expectations around the year 1975, and how this disastrous year played a vital role in many members' choice to leave the movement.

Chapter 23

What about 1975?

In 1966, the Watchtower Society published a bestseller which stood the whole movement on end, and which up until the turn of the 21st century still gave cause for some concern.

The English title of this book was: *Life Everlasting—in Freedom of the Sons of God*. The opening lines read:

"You enjoy being free. Naturally so, for man was created to be free. Man has a built-in love of freedom. Appreciating his own freedom, the man who is unselfish likes to see other—his equals—free. If a man is made to feel that he is not free, he longs to become free; he makes an effort to gain his freedom. Never will he be satisfied with anything less than freedom" (*Life Everlasting*, 1966, p. 5).

Surprisingly, I can attest to this need for freedom, for it was exactly what I experienced some years earlier during my struggle to free myself from "God's visible organization." Yet the Witnesses were not done. They had much more to say. The next line from the book explains the real intent of this high-flown speech: "That is why today man's heart rejoices at the news that a day of liberation is coming, or, better still, that that day is at hand!"

Despite this book's undeniable historical role, it seems to have been excluded from the Watchtower library—certainly from the CD I obtained with digital versions of the publications—and has ended up in a sort of unofficial Watch Tower Index (*Index librorum prohibitorum*), which in reality probably means it has been shelved by the Watchtower Society. Maybe this is due to the fact that the book's long-term effect was not adequately calculated since it gave rise to a prolonged crisis of confidence among the members, beginning after 1975, and ongoing repercussions for the Society leadership. One might also locate a copy of this book on the shelves in front of a vintage bookseller's, perhaps one on a little-traveled side street—if you're lucky.

New Timetable

Between 1954 and 1959, a time many ordinary members associated with the approach of Armageddon, some of the disappointed left the movement. Of those that remained, many wondered what year would be the next target.

Once a disappointment was forgotten, a new future-scenario was needed to keep the mechanism perpetually running. Since the release of *The Truth Shall Make You Free* in 1944 with its brand-new chronological calculation, the Witnesses had been aware that something important might happen in the mid-1970s. In the new "*Truth*" book from 1944, the leaders of the Society taught that the first 6,000 years of the "seventh day of Creation" would expire around 1972. In 1944 then, Society leaders believed that 5,972 of the 6,000 years had passed. The missing twenty-eight years were added to 1944 to arrive at the year 1972. About this time schedule the aforementioned book noted: "We are therefore near the end of six thousand years of human history, with conditions upon us and tremendous events at hand foreshadowed by those of Noah's day.—Luke 17:26-30" (*The Truth Shall Make You Free*, 1943, p. 152).

Note that when I write "the seventh day of creation," six days of creation (each of which lasted 7,000 years for a total of 42,000 years) have already passed prior to the start of the seventh day. According to the Watchtower Society, Adam and Eve were created at the end of the sixth creation day. When all creation days, plus the Millennium, are combined (again according to the Watchtower Society), it equals 49,000 years. This is all about the first 6,000 years of the seventh creation day. It's somewhat complicated perhaps!

When reading the text in Genesis chapter one, you quickly discover that the Witnesses' ideas do not work with the Genesis text. In Genesis, the author or authors are probably really talking about six ordinary days of creation, where everything—including the stars, moon, sun, all animals and finally man—was created. God rested then on the seventh day. And it is only now that the fall occurs in the Biblical account.

Because of additional corrections to the earlier schedule, which the Watchtower Society undertook later, they concluded 1975 was the year the first 6,000 years of the "seventh day" of creation would end rather than 1972.

Since the *Truth* book's publication in 1944, not much more was written about 1972 in the Watchtower literature, but it was enough for the Witnesses—including the former Scottish country manager in Denmark, William Dey[250], who sometimes considered 1974 as the possible deadline for the establishment of the Millennium. According to a morning newspaper, Dey mentioned 1974 in a letter which they quoted as follows: "The great fulfillment thereof will take place in Christendom between now (1952) and 1974, when Christ in the battle at Armageddon will kill anyone who are not marked on the forehead" (*B.T.*, Feb. 9, 1957). So, the soil was fertilized with speculations about 1972, 1974 and 1975.

Birgit's brother-in-law decided around 1958 that Armageddon would come *at the latest* in 1975. So he biked around in his district to save as many people as possible—and himself—and now he's gone, worn out, possibly, by his fanatical behavior, and still Armageddon has not come.

The disappointments surrounding 1954 to 1959 probably contributed to the stagnation tendency that gained traction at this time, first appearing in 1956, but especially from 1961 to 1966, when a notable number of Witnesses left the movement. About this, the *Watchtower* wrote:

"It is evident from the year's report that a number of persons who used to be Jehovah's witnesses found reasons sufficient to convince themselves that they need no longer worship and serve Jehovah and attend meetings at the house of their God. Such ones drifted away. However, there is still an opportunity before one dies to ask for forgiveness and share in God's goodness by returning to the ministry.... While the annual report shows there were 1,058,675 regular Kingdom publishers engaging in the field ministry each month of the past service year, still this is an increase of only 24,407 over last year. But 58,904 were baptized. Where were the other 34,497 that cannot be accounted for? Allowing for one percent of the population dying in a year's time would mean a drop of about 10,000 persons. But where are the others? Has materialism attracted them? Has the loose living and immoral conduct of the world ensnared some of them? Where is that love for Jehovah's organization and his service that they once had? / As we analyze the report for the world, as set forth in the chart on pages 24–27, you will see that some countries had no increase at all" (*WT*, Jan. 1, 1967).

While the Watchtower Society registered progress in some developing countries, there were slight signs of stagnation in the Western countries. Therefore, something had to be done, and what was more natural than to push out Armageddon's proximity a little. The obvious next choice was 1975.

1974 to 1975?

For some years, ordinary Witnesses had speculated that 1974 would be *the year*, and on this basis, in 1965 I dared—when I worked on the manuscript of my first book on the Witnesses—predict that the next year assigned for Armageddon's arrival would be 1974. At the time I was not aware of the time/calendar problems surrounding 1 BC and AD 1: There is only one year from 1 BC to AD 1, not two. The year *zero* does not exist in the chronology. The Watchtower leaders had also discovered this and that's why the 6,000 years (of the seventh day) would not end in 1974 and had to be changed to 1975. To my great surprise it was just—in principle—this revised date that was designated in the new book, *Life Everlasting—In Freedom of the Sons of God*, published in the summer of 1966, the same year my first book was published in September.

In 1993, the Society wrote retrospectively about the 1966 book:

"The Witnesses had long shared the belief that the Thousand Year Reign of Christ would follow after 6,000 years of human history. But when would 6,000 years of human existence end? The book *Life Everlasting—In Freedom of the Sons of God*, released at a series of district conventions held in 1966, pointed to 1975. Right at the convention, as the brothers examined the contents, the new book triggered much discussion about 1975" (*Proclaimers*, 1993, p. 104).

The end result of this *new book* was a disastrous influence on the movement's future.

I actually thought Brooklyn had finally learned. But their actions make it clear that this date-setting was integral to the movement's existence and method. Time calculations, choosing specified years and year-guesswork seemed to have a stimulatory effect on the ordinary members' commitment, and this whole complex apparatus was in their blood. It had become an imperative, an inner necessity for most, except perhaps for the highest-ranked senior commanders, and of course, those in the ranks who murmured their misgivings. I strongly doubt the Society's managers, Knorr and Franz, were convinced their theological and apocalyptical project had credibility. But it was prudent to guard against all eventualities. By making the nearly definitive statements about the proximity of *the* day ambiguous, they assured both statements would be encouraging *and* used later as evidence that the Society had indeed expressed some *reservations* about what would happen in 1975—with appropriate references to Jesus' words that no one but God would know the exact day and hour of Jesus' return. Personally, I am certain they had planned their previous "mistakes" in *advance*. So why not this one?

When *Life Everlasting—In Freedom of the Sons of God* was released at conventions around the world it was greeted with massive enthusiasm. The first printing numbered 2,000,000 copies, and the conventioneers bought them ea-

CHART OF SIGNIFICANT DATES FROM MAN'S CREATION TO 7000 A.M.

DATE B.C.E.	DATE ANNO MUNDI	EVENT	REFERENCE
1945	5970	The Watchtower (July 1) exposes blood transfusion—Ps. 16:4 (September) World War II ends; (October) United Nations Organization ratified	
1957	5982	(October) Russia sends up first satellite; causes world to fear	
1962	5987	(October 11) Pope John XXIII opens Vatican Council II	
1963	5988	Pope John XXIII, at Council, publishes encyclical "Pacem in Terris" in which he praises United Nations Organization. June 3, he dies despite blood transfusions	
1964	5989	(May) "Spy satellites" and astronauts increase world tension	
1965	5990	(October 4) Pope Paul VI visits United Nations Headquarters in New York city, endorses United Nations and confers with president of U.S.A. December 8, he closes Ecumenical Council Vatican II	
1966	5991	Threat of World War III grows more ominous as between "king of the north" and the "king of the south." (Dan. 11:5-7, 40) Expansion of organization of Jehovah's Christian witnesses continues, and international series of "God's Sons of Liberty" District Assemblies are scheduled to begin on June 22, in Toronto, Ontario, Canada. Book Life Everlasting—In Freedom of the Sons of God to be released Saturday, June 25, 1966	
1975	6000	End of 6th 1,000-year day of man's existence (in early autumn)	
2975	7000	End of 7th 1,000-year day of man's existence (in early autumn)	

Since the 1975 book, *Life Everlasting in Freedom of the Sons of God*, was published in 1966 speculations accelerated among members. The schedule shown above made a deep impression. Members were extremely attentive to disaster-year 1975, as shown by the table's next-to-last line (*Life Everlasting*, 1966, pp. 31–37).

gerly. They hoped to find sensational news in this book, news to dispel their despondency over the delayed Armageddon. Usually the Witnesses were quickly disappointed when they first read a new piece of literature, but not in this case, as exemplified by the Watchtower managers' joyous report:

"At all assembly points where it was released, the book was received enthusiastically. Crowds gathered around stands and soon supplies of the book were depleted. Immediately its contents were examined. It did not take the brothers very long to find the chart beginning on page 31, showing that 6,000 years of man's existence end in 1975. Discussion of 1975 overshadowed about everything else. 'The new book compels us to realize that Armageddon is, in fact, very close indeed,' said a conventioner. Surely it was one of the outstanding blessings to be carried home!" (*WT*, Oct. 15, 1966)

Brother Franz, the Society vice president, said in regard to the new book:

"You have noticed the chart [on pages 31–35, which included a chronological table].... It shows that 6,000 years of human experience will end in 1975, about nine years from now. What does that mean? Does it mean that God's rest day [the *seventh* 7000-year-old creation day] began 4026 BCE? It could have. The *Life Everlasting* book does not say it did not. The book merely presents the chronology. You can accept it or reject it. If that is the case, what does that mean to us?

"What about the year 1975? What is it going to mean, dear friends?

"Does it mean that Armageddon is going to be finished, with Satan bound, by 1975? It could! It could! All things are possible with God. Does it mean that Babylon the Great is going to go down by 1975? It could. Does it mean that the attack of Gog of Magog is going to be made on Jehovah's witnesses to wipe them out, then Gog himself will be put out of action? It could. But we are not saying. All things are possible with God. But we are not saying. And don't any of you be specific in saying anything that is going to happen between now and 1975. But the big point of it all is this, dear friends: Time is short. Time is running out, no question about that.... *So we know that as we come to 1975 our deliverance is that much nearer.* / Let us make the most of the time and get in all the good hard work to Jehovah while the opportunity affords..." (*WT*, Oct. 15, 1966; italics are mine).

Note the coupling between the apocalyptic expectations and the work to be done before the world's end. In this manner, the Watchtower leaders probably expected to prevent stagnation and in turn boost enterprise. What risk was there, after all, that the managers and the average Witnesses would actually be *that much nearer* to Armageddon and the establishment of the new world in 1975? The Society's leaders are masters of safeguarding themselves behind double-speak, indirectly indicating that they very well know, in advance, what the outcome will be.

In Denmark, the new year of the world's end garnered much attention. At an assembly held simultaneously at Aarhus Stadium in late July 1966—part of a worldwide series of conventions where *Life Everlasting* was released—the branch servant for Denmark, my "old friend" Richard E. Abrahamson, expressed himself in a way that could not be misunderstood. According to eyewitness Poul Dal, Abrahamson came out from behind the podium and right up on stage with the new book in hand and spoke enthusiastically about the calculations and theories detailed in its pages.

Ambro, a well-known Danish journalist of the period also witnessed the event and wrote an article for *Ekstra Bladet*:

"It looks, according to the book, that 6000 years from the creation of Adam will come in 1975, and then says the book already in the first chapter that it could be very interesting and possibly in line with God's intentions and not a coincidence that Jesus Christ's millennial Kingdom will be in parallel with human existence here on earth." Ambro writes further that Abrahamson did not want to say that there was 100% proof that the Judgment Day would come in 1975.

Continuing with Abrahamson's convention remarks:

"We know that the world situation is complicated today, and we know that the kings of the North and the South are about to come pretty close to attacking each other—or perhaps at least to get started with a trial of strength, and we know that our service activities are also spread throughout the earth, and that many people have had the opportunity to take their stand. We also know that the generation that lived here in 1914 ... the generation that had grown enough to observe these events [in 1914], is becoming quite old now in 1966 [note this]. And we know that there aren't many of that generation left. So also in the light of this, we believe that there is not a long time before the world reaches its end. We must all live each day as if it were the last" (*Ekstra Bladet*, August 1, 1966; translation is mine).

Note the surprising accordance of all the Jehovah's Witnesses' opinions at this time. All delegates subjected themselves, almost as one entity, parroting the statements coming out of Brooklyn, because if something went wrong, they could claim they had said nothing more than they had been ordered to do.

Ambro captured the situation *very well*.

When the *Watchtower* magazine published Richard Abrahamson's biography in 2003, they completely ignored the period from 1975 to 1980. It was functionally non-existent. This is, I believe, what is called *selective memory*. (*WT*, Nov. 1, 2003)

Zigzag Course

In Raymond Franz's book from 1983 he comments on the wave of expectations unleashed by the "1975 book," as *Life Everlasting* was later called, that arose everywhere among the Jehovah's Witnesses:

"Not for many decades had there been such a sense of excitement among Jehovah's Witnesses as these statements generated. A tremendous surge of expectation developed, far surpassing the feeling of the end's nearness that I and others had experienced in the early 1940's" (*Conscience*, 1983, p. 61).

Still, after previous failures, did the ordinary Witnesses really expect the Millennium would be established in 1975? Yes. They could hardly expect anything else. And although the Watchtower managers expressed themselves somewhat ambiguously, they wrote so much about the newly designated year they left no doubt about what they wanted the ordinary Witnesses to believe— or at least be left in fearful uncertainty about—in the late 1960s. Armageddon *would* or *could* come in 1975, and the Millennium shortly thereafter, and they best keep their spiritual houses in order to be prepared just in case. I located and noted the following quotes back in 1966–1967, but they are worth a quick look here as they may offer some clarity on the managers' hint strategy.

October 1966:

"In what year, then, would the first 6,000 years of man's existence and also the first 6,000 years of God's rest day come to an end? The year, 1975. This is worthy of notice, particularly in view of the fact that the 'last days' began in 1914, and that the physical facts of our day in fulfillment of prophecy mark this as the last generation of this wicked world. So we can expect the immediate future to be filled with thrilling events for those who rest their faith in God and his promises. It means that within relatively few years we will witness the fulfillment of the remaining prophecies that have to do with the 'time of the end.' … What cataclysmic times are fast approaching! A climax in man's history is at the door!… So how much longer will it be? The answer is: 'Not long, for the end of wickedness is near.' " (*Awake!*, Oct. 8, 1966)

The scare campaign ran for years without interruption, so it is nothing to say that many of the members were horror-stricken. The message and clichés were repeated until they became unbearable, so it was not surprising members finally found themselves in a state of *conscious unconsciousness*.

And further on, in January 1967:

"But, without a doubt, nothing has created more interest in this textbook than the first chapter with its chart and fine information regarding the 7,000 years of God's rest day. The observation that 1975 may well mark the beginning of mankind's great Jubilee has intrigued many" (*WT*, Jan. 1, 1967).

Note the term "mankind's great Jubilee" was also used in connection with the year 1925; in Rutherford's publication, *Millions Now Living Will Never Die* (1920), he designated 1925 as the year the Millennium would be established. And before 1925, new initiatives and campaigns were presumably already planned for that year and beyond and were aimed at the organization's future growth.

That the Millennium would be set up in 1975 was officially considered a reality in 1967:

"According to a more recent calculation of the Bible timetable, six thousand years of man's existence will end in the latter half of the year 1975, which is well within this century. The Bible millennium is ahead of us, and, according to the count of time and the events of world history, it is approaching" (*WT*, April 15, 1967).

In an article in the May issue of *The Watchtower*, "Where Are We According to God's Timetable?" it notes in relation to 1975:

"What will that year mean for humankind? Will it be the time when God executes the wicked and starts off the thousand-year reign of his Son Jesus Christ? It very well could, but we will have to wait to see" (*WT*, May 1, 1967, p. 262).

However, Brooklyn held to a zigzag course, ducking and weaving. One moment they were categorical, the next reserved. In 1967 *The Watchtower* magazine printed the article "Why Are You Looking Forward to 1975?" (p. 494). In this article a certain reservation was expressed, as if they were worried about what the whole hullabaloo around 1975 could lead to. The article said:

"What about all this talk concerning the year 1975? Lively discussions, some based on speculation, have burst into flame during recent months among serious students of the Bible. Their interest has been kindled by the belief that 1975 will mark the end of 6,000 years of human history since Adam's creation. The nearness of such an important date indeed fires the imagination and presents unlimited possibilities for discussion" (*WT*, Aug. 15, 1968).

Then it was explained, among other things, why Bishop James Ussher's (1581–1656) old calculation of the date of Adam's creation was not accurate enough, and why it is important to study the genealogy records that exist in the Bible:

"Well, for one thing, if 4,026 is added to 1,968 (allowing for the lack of a zero year between CE and BCE) one gets a total of 5,993 years, come this autumn, since Adam's creation. That means, in the fall of the year 1975, a little over seven years from now (and not in 1997 as would be the case if Ussher's figures were correct), it will be 6,000 years since the creation of Adam, the father of all mankind! ... *Are we to assume from this study that the battle of Armageddon will be all over by the autumn of 1975*, and the long-looked-for thousand-year reign of Christ will begin by then? Possibly, but we wait to see how closely the seventh thousand-year period of man's existence coincides with the sabbathlike thousand-year reign of Christ. If these two periods run parallel with each other as to the calendar year, it will not be by mere chance or accident but will be according to Jehovah's loving and timely purposes. Our chronology, however, which is reasonably accurate (but admittedly not infallible), at the best only points to the autumn of 1975 as the end of 6,000 years of man's existence on earth. It does not necessarily mean that 1975 marks the end of the first 6,000 years of Jehovah's seventh creative 'day.' "

The cunning explanation follows:

"Why not? Because after his creation Adam lived some time during the 'sixth day,' which unknown amount of time would need to be subtracted from

Adam's 930 years, to determine when the sixth seven-thousand-year period or 'day' ended, and how long Adam lived into the 'seventh day.' And yet the end of that sixth creative 'day' could end within the same Gregorian calendar year of Adam's creation. It may involve only a difference of weeks or months, not years" (*WT*, August 15, 1968; italics are mine).

The article concludes:

"One thing is absolutely certain, Bible chronology reinforced with fulfilled Bible prophecy shows that six thousand years of man's existence will soon be up, yes, within this generation! (Matt. 24:34) This is, therefore, no time to be indifferent and complacent. This is not the time to be toying with the words of Jesus that 'concerning that day and hour *nobody* knows, neither the angels of the heavens nor the Son, but only the Father.' (Matt. 24:36) To the contrary, it is a time when one should be keenly aware that the end of this system of things is rapidly coming to its violent end. Make no mistake, it is sufficient that the Father himself *knows* both the 'day and hour'! / Even if one cannot see beyond 1975, is this any reason to be less active? The apostles could not see even this far; they knew nothing about 1975. All they could see was a short time ahead in which to finish the work assigned to them. (1 Pet. 4:7) Hence, there was a ring of alarm and a cry of urgency in all their writings.... So too with Jehovah's faithful witnesses in this latter half of the twentieth century. They have the true Christian point of view. Their strenuous evangelistic activity is not something peculiar to this present decade. *They have not dedicated their lives to serve Jehovah only until 1975....* Those who will flee Babylon the Great and this Satanic system of things are now running for their lives, headed for God's kingdom, and *they will not stop at 1975.* O no! They will keep on in this glorious way that leads to everlasting life, praising and serving Jehovah for ever and ever!" (*WT*, Aug. 15, 1968; italics are mine)

I must admit that such statements confuse me with regard to Brooklyn's sincerity. The words support what I would characterize as a *relative apocalyptic accountability*—if such is possible, and the conclusion is that Brooklyn is actually expressing some uncertainty. They do not know *what will happen after 1975*. Yet all the members must remain active, because the apostles similarly could not know there was a long future before them. So it must be noted that Brooklyn is suggesting the "nearness" is *relative*, including the period after 1975: "They have not dedicated their lives to serve Jehovah only until 1975," and "they will not stop at 1975." Some have undoubtedly noticed these cunning nuances.

And what of 1997?

It's only mentioned in passing, but what if Bishop Ussher's (1581–1656) calculations are right? (We have known for no less than 150 years that they were not!) Do not be surprised, but even this reference may have been a hint that the leaders were hedging—again. I believe the professional apocalypticians at the top of the Society very well knew the direction things were going.

It's important to note there was an obvious uncertainty about Adam's creation in play as well, and it certainly proves the apocalypticians perhaps kept an ace or two up their sleeves at all times, which they could later use to explain to their members why Armageddon and the Millennium did not come in 1975.

Of course, *they* knew it already.

Via Raymond Franz's book, we are introduced to the big, pressurized machinery operating in Brooklyn. Franz notes that *Watchtower* articles are written by different people, and therefore—despite their anonymity—may have different styles and individual approaches to the treatment of a subject and task. The task here might have been: Write a *Watchtower* article which will prepare the readers for the fact that further work will be needed after 1975.

Overall, the tone between 1968 and 1975 was not so restrained, as in the above article from the 1968 *Watchtower*, but the articles became more and more hysterical—as we later will see—the closer they came to 1975.

Misrepresentation of the Paddock Brothers

In a new book *The Truth That Leads to Eternal Life* (also called The Truth Book) published by the Society in 1968, and subsequently released in large numbers worldwide, it was indirectly suggested that 1975 was of *particular importance*. Within The Truth Book (on pages 88 and 89) another book authored by brothers W. and P. Paddock, *Famine—1975!* [251], is quoted. In their book, published in 1967, the Paddocks stated:

"By 1975 civil disorder, anarchy, military dictatorships, runaway inflation, transportation breakdowns and chaotic unrest will be the order of the day in many of the hungry nations."

There can be little doubt this quotation was used by the Society as an indirect allusion to events predicted for *1975*, and thereby designed to further excite the Witnesses about the next apocalyptic prediction. This has since been confirmed, because the allusion was *not included* in the revised edition of The Truth Book from *1981*.

The Truth Book was used for a recruiting campaign in 1968; its starting point was a six-month curriculum designed to lead students to attend the movement's meetings. "If," and I quote, "at the end of six months of intensive study and conscientious efforts to get them to meetings, they are not yet associating with the congregation, then it may be best to use your time to study with someone else who really wants to learn the truth and make progress. Make it your goal to present the good news on Bible studies in such a way that interested ones will act within six months! / And act they did! In a short period of time, the six-month Bible study program had astounding success. For the three service years beginning September 1, 1968, and ending August 31, 1971, a total of 434,906 persons were baptized—more than double the number baptized during the previous three service years! Coming as it did at a time when there was a feeling of expectancy and urgency among Jehovah's Witnesses, the *Truth* book and the six-month Bible study campaign greatly aided in speeding up the disciple-making work..." (*Proclaimers*, 1993, p. 105).

In the 1990 edition of *The Guinness Book of World Records,* The Truth Book is listed under "Highest Printing." In 1997, 107 million copies were either sold or given out in 117 languages (see also Truth Book in the List of Publications).

Several issues of *The Watchtower* and *Awake!* magazines clearly show that use of the Paddock brothers' book was part of an intimidation campaign orchestrated for 1975; the issues bear dates from 1970, 1972, 1973,[252] 1974[253] and 1975. In February 1975, one finds the following, still indirect, reference: "What do the authors say now, in 1975? 'Everything is so much worse than when we wrote that book,' says William Paddock. 'You have a couple of hundred million more people to worry about, you've got the energy crisis, you've got inflation" (*Awake!,* Feb. 22, 1975, p. 29).

Beyond 1976 the Watchtower Society's publications no longer mention the Paddocks' book. Thus, in searching the Watchtower literature there is not a single hit on the name Paddock *after* 1975. Their book had apparently, in the eyes of the Watchtower Society, served its purpose.

Impact on the Annual Reports

How did the ordinary Witnesses see the 1975 campaign? Did they begin more "service from door to door?" Did they attract more people to the movement in the years up to 1975? In other words: Could one trace the results of the campaign in the annual reports, and discover if the leaders managed to reverse the trend of stagnation?

As already noted, Society leadership had long been aware of the decline in new-member intake numbers. The "global expansion" threatened to shrink somewhat. However, we must conclude that when the *Life Everlasting,* the 1975 Book, was released back in 1966, the Society's managers understood the problems, and the new book's release must have been viewed in relation to reduced figures from the apocalyptic depression of the 1950s and early 1960s. In 1967, tallies showed 323,986 persons had been baptized during the previous five years, yet there was an increase of "*only* 174,088 ministers. What happened to the other 149,898?" (*WT*, March 1, 1967; italics are mine)[254]

If my assumption holds true, the renewed stimulation from the 1975 Book and the intensified scare campaign produced gradually strong results in the statistics from 1966 up to and including 1975. After 1975, one would expect an abysmal decrease in the members' commitment; in fact, the rising membership curve makes a distinct downward turn. The ambiguous apocalyptic strategy worked for a time, at least.

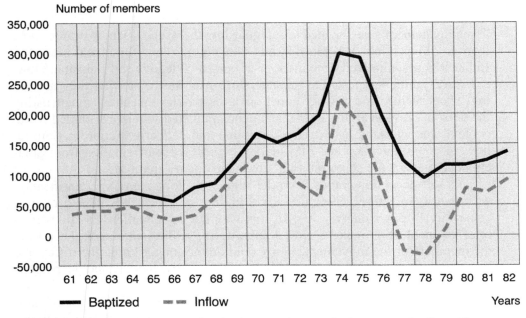

Number of members

350,000	
300,000	
250,000	
200,000	
150,000	
100,000	
50,000	
0	
-50,000	

61 62 63 64 65 66 67 68 69 70 71 72 73 74 75 76 77 78 79 80 81 82

━━ Baptized ▬ ▬ Inflow   Years

Note that, throughout, the curve for the baptized exceeds the curve of inflow. This is partially due to a certain percentage of deceased members per year. Since the organization tightened the exclusion policy in 1972, the graph shows a sharp dive in the inflow in the years immediately thereafter, although the number of baptized, after a slight decline, rose nicely again. The reason was the large number of exclusions. After the 1975 fiasco, we see a similar trend, because many left the organization after the disappointment. (The above graph is prepared by Jette Svane on the basis of the statistical figures of Jehovah's Witnesses' Yearbooks.)[255]

The annual reports show membership increased from 1966 to 1975, however, they also hide the number of members who left the movement.

The graph illustrates the waxing and waning membership numbers surrounding an apocalyptic depression. It is evident how inflow increases markedly the closer we come to 1975, while the corresponding figures fall sharply afterward—note 1978 and 1979.

Looking at the figures, I note how a strong frustration manifested itself among the membership between 1975 and 1980. There is a clear increase of activity in the apocalyptic years 1974 and 1975, when approximately 600,000 were "inaugurated to Jehovah" by adult baptism. The number who subsequently became less committed or left the organization must be extracted from the statistics. Still, the numbers constructing the curves tell something about the *volatile* base on which the Watchtower organization builds its worldwide activities. However, if more and more likewise enter the fold, it seems reasonably valid to say the Jehovah's Witnesses' membership moves through a *revolving door*.

Organized Self-delusion

Top management's persistence in safeguarding themselves demonstrates, more than anything, their dual-plotting and—in my opinion—unethical practices. Either it is systematized deception, or at best, a collective self-delusion. However, everything suggests the managers are well aware of what they are doing. The structure and practice construct a master-slave mechanism entrusting the personal responsibility to management conducted within a secluded social context characterized by extreme discipline and collective subordination; all lines of communication and information beyond those originating from Society headquarters are shuttered tight, excluded and discredited.

This self-deception comes from the Witnesses' long-standing identification with the organization's literature and thinking, in which they have grown as one entity through many years. In this way the organization functions as a reinforcement of a weak "I" and a submissive, willing character. Therefore, the members of the movement, in my opinion, no longer know the difference between right and wrong, truth and untruth. The individual "I" and the perception of truth belongs to the organization.

The welfare of the organization, its growth and dissemination, is the main objective for the Watchtower officials, whose thinking and actions are under the constant influence of the mutually controlling group mentality—where all watch all—while they are simultaneously practicing a creepy "self-censorship." The organization is in fact their real "god," and for the *organization* they must be willing to sacrifice everything—even "the Truth" (Raymond Franz). There exists a genuine member-fear for the organization, and to allay this anxiety and ensure that one is not designated as "victim" in the heretic-hunting atmosphere which subsequently develops, Witnesses inform on former friends and even members of their own families.

The members, of course, will clearly deny this. They would quite honestly argue that this is not a characteristic of their religious community. They can't see it. It's as if their intellectual abilities are stunted, switched off; yes, it even seems reasonable to deduce they have suffered distinct psychological damage by decades of profound Society influence.

One should not "be swept up by dates."

That the statements from before 1975 could later be used for explaining away earlier unfortunate pronouncements after that year is shown in the Society's 1993 history book. Armed with hindsight of what really happened in the "prophetic year" 1975, we read (with minor repetition from the previous quote):

"At the convention held in Baltimore, Maryland, F. W. Franz gave the concluding talk. He began by saying: 'Just before I got on the platform a young man came to me and said, 'Say, what does this 1975 mean?' Brother Franz then referred to the many questions that had arisen as to whether the material in the new book meant that by 1975 Armageddon would be finished, and Satan would be bound. He stated, in essence: 'It could. But we are not saying. All things are possible with God. But we are not saying. And don't any of you be specific in saying anything that is going to happen between now and 1975. But the big point of it all is this, dear friends: Time is short. Time is running out, no question about that.'" (*Proclaimers,* 1993, p. 104)

Note how, after 1975, the doomsday writers used deceased-president Franz's opinions (he died in 1992) just as one could expect. What he said and wrote from 1966 and forward could be used to stir up, stimulate and incite *before* 1975, *and* to explain away *after* 1975. And don't anyone tell me these apocalyptic professionals were unaware of how this double-talk policy could be used later.

Note that what follows the above quotation, which despite everything has a bit of a confession, is still not decisive because these people perpetually represented irresponsible and unreliable assertions, which were completely disingenuous:

"In the years following 1966, many of Jehovah's Witnesses acted in harmony with the spirit of that counsel. However, other statements were published on this subject, and some were likely *more definite than advisable*. This was acknowledged in *The Watchtower* of March 15, 1980 (page 17). But Jehovah's Witnesses were also cautioned to concentrate mainly on doing Jehovah's will and *not to be swept up by dates* and expectations of an early salvation" (*Proclaimers,* 1993, p. 104; italics are mine).

Now, let's investigate what a "middle manager" in Denmark in 1969 could get out of the Society's "definite" suggestions.

Chapter 24

Jacobsen's
Circumstantial Evidences

Around 1969 a well-known leader of the Jehovah's Witnesses in Denmark, Egon Jacobsen, held a lecture for a small group of members—possibly this was an invitation-only event—where he discussed a topic of utmost urgency for all members around the world at that time.

The lecture was part of the nine-year, worldwide campaign designed to culminate in 1975—the year the New York leadership identified as the probable time for the establishment of the Millennium during a number of huge international conventions in 1966. Consequently this was also the year of the Armageddon war, since they had calculated the first 6,000 years of mankind's existence would most likely terminate in the autumn of 1975.

In his lecture, Jacobsen firmly declared 1975 would be the year for this terrible war of judgment, something the members had been looking forward to for several generations with fear and trepidation—but also with hope. This year would finally fulfill the expectations of the Millennium, the period immediately following the battle of Armageddon, a quiet new world where select people would live

This illustration can be found in *Awake!*, October 8, 1968. Text beneath the illustration included the following: "The fact that fifty-four years of the period called the 'last days' have already gone by is highly significant. It means that only a few years, at most, remain before the corrupt system of things dominating the earth is destroyed by God. How can we be so certain of this?" (p. 13)

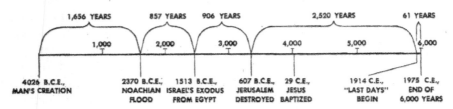

The Watchtower Society hammered constantly on the year 1975; for example, in this table (like Russell's) from *Awake!*, 1968, which shows that the 6,000 years would end in 1975 (*Awake!*, Oct. 8, 1968).

forever, and the peace of paradise once and for all would descend on everything and everyone. This would be the realization of Judge Rutherford's propaganda slogan of the 1920s *that millions of now living people would never die.*

Criticism is unthinkable in this audience; the members listen with breathless tension and only ask questions aligned with the Society's established positions. The lecturer, Jacobsen, who is incredibly cocksure in his views, is talking with borrowed authority. His lecture and its contents are dictated by headquarters in New York and subsequently from the Danish department where he is employed. He has, however, to some extent shaped his speech with his own words, and there is also room for humorous comments between the earnest words.

The lecturer holds his audience rapt; each listener devours every word, and no one is in doubt about what the battle of Armageddon will entail.

All are listening with great seriousness. They live in the most important time ever, and there is probably only a short time (again).

The lecture was recorded and made available on tape. I obtained a copy and listened to Jacobsen's pitch; it appears he had great authority within the movement at that time, which may be due to his earlier time as a zone servant,[256] as the Society's travelling inspectors were called at that time.

Of course, forty-three years after Egon Jacobsen's lecture his grotesque opinions can be quite amusing, but for his audience all was deep, deep seriousness. And just as the Adventists did before 1844, between 1966 and 1975 many members of the Jehovah's Witnesses believed so strongly in the nearness of Judgment Day they sold everything they owned because they wanted to serve the movement as full-time publishers to spread the final, worldwide warning. If you were a Witness at that time, you *had* to be on the bandwagon, tooting your horn loud and long. The *gospel* about the battle of Armageddon and the subsequent new world had to be proclaimed more intensively than ever, now, with only a few years left.

To be exact: Only four, five, six or seven years. Exactly.

Having established the importance of the year 1975, Jacobsen said:

"Does this mean then that we can go out and knock on the doors and honestly say: 'Hello, I come from the Jehovah's Witnesses. In 1975, it is finished!' No! It's not the idea, but on the other hand, we can of course not say it, because we do not know the day and the hour, and it could be it came much earlier—or a little before! Because when that date is passed in October, in the autumn of 1975, there is much to happen before that time. 'The woman'[257] [the Christian churches] must be 'undressed' [revealed], Armageddon will come, and we do not know how many months or years the battle of Armageddon might take, so therefore we cannot go out and say so. Well, must we be totally quiet, has someone asked, or is it just something we have to whisper about?"

And Jacobsen continued:

"Can you remember the campaign we had last year in April with the magazines: 'Why God permits evil.' Can you remember the article: 'How much longer will it last?' And there was the headline here: '6,000 years ending in 1975,' and the magazines were distributed in millions and millions throughout the world. And it was not said in a parentheses that 'you must not say it to somebody' [laughter]; the aim was just to get it [the message] out around."[258]

Then Jacobsen referred to a conversation he had had with a brother who was "completely finished" with Armageddon-year guesswork because nothing at all happened in 1954. Jacobsen notes that the Jehovah's Witnesses' main leadership in New York said nothing in particular about 1954, but this time the Society was specific in relation to 1975, "and it might be that there is a difference, right?"

Only 10,981 Anointed Left

In his speech, Jacobsen refers to a special kind of evidence which he describes as "circumstantial evidence,"[259]—this, as most will know, is indirect evidence—and all should support the deduction that Armageddon would come in "early autumn" of 1975. (*Life Everlasting*, 1966)

Some of this circumstantial evidence—as Jacobsen seriously stressed—was that only 10,981 "anointed" remained who had also been members in the years around 1914, the year the invisible coming of Christ occurred. The anointed belonged to the "little flock" of members who hoped to ascend to heaven with Christ to rule as kings over the world for 1,000 years.

Furthermore: Their numbers diminished very quickly year by year; so in the course of just a few years there would only be a minority left. The dwindling number itself was another piece of circumstantial evidence that the time for Armageddon was very, very close.

Jacobsen justified his arguments with the statistical evidence taken from the *Yearbook*, published annually and featuring the statistics of living members in the movement:

"The Bible says clearly that some of the 'little flock' will survive Armageddon and lead the 'great crowd'[260] into the cleansed earth, and numerically ... the *Yearbook* of 1965 shows, that there were 11,550 who demonstrated that they had this hope [by taking the emblems, the bread and wine]. In 1966 the figure had dropped down to 11,179, in 1967 to 11,039, and the *Yearbook* of 1969 shows the figure to be 10,981 [the figure for 1968]. Many of these are obviously high up in years, and statistically their life cycle will be completed even faster, according to where we are—isn't it true?"

Jacobsen was right, of course—the elderly members were going to die before long. If one draws a graph showing the number of anointed as a line traversing marked years, there will be a declining curve that will reach zero in the near future.[261]

So it seemed the audience had to handle some very weighty evidence. In any case, it was evidence that all members ought to carefully consider any major decision. For example, money spent to start their own businesses or to invest in homes or cars might be better spent on Kingdom interests.

By way of example, Jacobsen mentions a spiritual brother who, at one of the Kingdom Ministry School meetings, asked Jacobsen whether it was a good idea to withdraw the 200,000 Danish crowns he had invested in a company and live on the money until Armageddon so he could do more for the Kingdom— even though he could not exactly be a pioneer. This idea seemed acceptable to Jacobsen, although he noted that of course it was not something "we say."

I don't have the slightest doubt that Jacobsen's circumstantial evidence had made a particularly strong impression on the audience.

Chapter 25

Culmination of Hysteria

Between 1966 and 1975, thousands and thousands joined the Watchtower organization, and new initiatives from Brooklyn began to streamline the organization and ensure greater control by congregation leaders. This would prepare the entire movement for the outrageous disappointment that would spread like a silent, heart-rending undercurrent among members when it became clear to them the predictions about 1975 were "more definite than advisable" (*Proclaimers*, 1993, p. 104).

Due to the pre-1975 propaganda and campaigns, membership rose considerably, a new plan for Bible studies was implemented, targeting all the new members. Part of this plan was the Truth Book—*The Truth That Leads to Eternal Life*. After a short time, the publication motivated the baptisms of 434,906 believers from September 1968 to August 1971, "more than double the number baptized during the previous three service years!" (*WT*, Jan.15, 1997)

Obviously, Watchtower leaders deliberately organized these campaigns to take advantage of the apocalyptic hysteria that had gradually developed in the local congregations, as shown by the following quote (borrowed from a previous quote in Chapter 23):

"Coming as it did at a time when there was a *feeling of expectancy and urgency* among Jehovah's Witnesses, the *Truth* book and the six-month Bible study campaign greatly aided in speeding up the disciple-making work" (*Proclaimers*, 1993, p. 105; *WT*, Jan. 15, 1997; italics are mine).

The Watchtower leaders are here insincerely modest, for they were the ones putting incredible pressure on the general members, and it was something of a misrepresentation when in 1993 these leaders wrote that the members before 1975 "were cautioned to concentrate mainly on doing Jehovah's will and not to be swept up by dates and expectations of an early salvation" (*Proclaimers*, 1993, p. 104). Yet, they had all but flogged their members to do more field service in one campaign after another, especially in connection with the pre-1975 campaign to mobilize those who "hold back." In the internal *Kingdom Ministry* (today, *Our Kingdom Ministry*), one finds the following request:

"Most of us know of interested persons in our territory who have responded favorably to the Kingdom message. We have studied with some through the Truth book and, in some cases, other publications as well. They attend meetings from time to time, show a willingness to be identified with Jehovah's witnesses and profess to accept most of the fundamental teachings of God's Word. Yet, they do not join us in the preaching work. They hold back from 'disowning themselves' and getting baptized.... If they have learned, for example, the identifying traits of the true religion, can they honestly say that their former religion is the true one? If not, then it must be a false one and part of the empire of false religion for which God's Word clearly foretells destruction in the near future.... Time grows short and the need for a definite stand becomes increasingly urgent..." (*KM*, January 1974, p. 3).

One senses that, by that point, the articles are *pure routine*.

Concerning the conventions of 1974, the *Watch Tower* had this to say: "Looking forward in faith, Jehovah's Witnesses have planned similar—though small—assemblies to begin in June 1974, *if Jehovah wills*" (*WT*, April 1, 1974, p. 206; italics are mine).

And in an addition to the *Kingdom Ministry* of May 1974, they presented these words of encouragement:

"Yes, the end of this system is so very near! Is that not reason to increase our activity? In this regard we can learn something from a runner who puts on a final burst of speed near the finish of a race. Look at Jesus, who apparently stepped up his activity during his final days on earth.... By carefully and prayerfully examining our own circumstances, we also may find that we can spend more time and energy in preaching during this final period before the present system ends. Many of our brothers and sisters are doing just that. This is evident from the rapidly increasing number of pioneers.... Yes, since the summer of 1973 there have been new peaks in pioneers every month. Now there are 20,394 regular and special pioneers in the United States, an all-time peak. That is 5,190 more than there were in February 1973! A 34-percent increase! Does that not warm our hearts? *Reports are heard of brothers selling their homes and property and planning to finish out the rest of their days in this old system in the pioneer service. Certainly this is a fine way to spend the short time remaining before the wicked world's end*" (*KM*, May, 1974, p. 3-6; italics are mine).

The July issue of *Rigets Tjeneste*, the Danish issue of the *Kingdom Ministry*, notes a slight decline in the number of pioneers and special pioneers in Denmark. People were encouraged to re-read the internal newsletter's June supplement. A little financial encouragement was also offered to the special pioneers the month they attended the circuit convention; if they achieved their 130 hours, they were eligible for a bonus and could apply for full reimbursement. (*RT*, July 1974, p. 3)

Generally speaking, however, territory was gained across the entire front, and the combined effect of the expected *end of the world*, increased Witness-activity and the enlisting campaigns reaching astonishing levels was right on track with leadership's plans. There was just a little more than a year to "the end," which most Witnesses now anxiously awaited.

Everything was well-oiled and running smoothly.

In Brooklyn, however, they probably long before began an action plan for movement rescue operations to be initiated in 1976, 1977, 1978, 1979 and 1980. Something tells me that on the top floor of Brooklyn headquarters, they were quite cool about the situation, while the members were sweating and wringing their hands in the summer heat, putting every extra effort into recruiting new supporters before it was too late.

Aggressive Exploitation of the Situation

Another new book, *God's Kingdom of a Thousand Years has Approached*, was published in 1973, but it did not stir up the same enthusiasm as the 1975 Book did at its release in 1966; that one ignited a whole series of apocalyptic expectations. Still, the new book stuck to the doctrine established in 1943 and presented in one of the Society's bestselling books, *The Truth Shall Make You Free*: The 6,000 years of human existence would end sometime around the 1970s.[262] In the 1973 book, 1975 is not directly mentioned anymore. Instead, the claim is made that the "the end of six thousand years of human existence on earth and the beginning of mankind's seventh millennium of existence may come many years sooner than the year 2000 CE," and the focus is put on "the decade of the 1970s;" perhaps as opposed to the previously specified year, 1975. That could resemble the prelude for a "smooth landing." (*Approached,* 1973, chapter 1, § 17, p. 14; and chapter 11, § 55. p. 209)

The tone of the latest book was slightly subdued in contrast to the more contemporary-oriented internal monthly publication, the *Kingdom Ministry*, which continuously focused on the short remaining time until the first few months of the year 1975. For this reason special meetings were organized:

"Why has this special meeting been arranged? Because the time in which we are living makes it urgent that you give careful and prayerful consideration to your standing before Jehovah God.... The fast-approaching execution of God's judgment is referred to in the Bible as a 'great tribulation.'... All who refuse to come to know God as his devoted servants and who persist in disobeying the 'good news about our Lord Jesus' will then perish everlastingly.... While not knowing the exact time, we do know that God's judgment is to be executed within the lifetime of the generation that saw the beginning of the 'last days.' ... *Already nearly sixty years have passed. Those persons who were at an age of understanding in 1914 are diminishing in numbers.* Clearly, then, the time for Jehovah God to act is near at hand" (*KM*, August 1974, p. 3-4; italics are mine).

The special meeting had only one aim: to involve the many "interested ones" the Witnesses had contacted during the door-to-door agitation, and who maybe could be enlisted as tomorrow's new "regular publishers":

"In view of the evident nearness of the 'great tribulation,' we want to appeal to you not to delay in choosing life as an approved servant of God.... But you may be fearful about sharing with Jehovah's witnesses in their door-to-door preaching. Have you progressed to the point where you could dedicate yourself to Jehovah God? Then, do not allow selfish considerations to cause you to delay.... Regardless of your state in spiritual growth, we urge you to continue working toward coming into an approved relationship with Jehovah God before it is too late" (Ibid.).

The pressure increased in the following issues of the *Kingdom Ministry*:

"As we enter the new service year, we have a feeling of keen anticipation. We are well aware *that we are now nearly sixty years into the* 'conclusion of the system of things,' and that the time remaining is short. None of us know exactly when the 'great tribulation' will strike, but we have full confidence that it will come at precisely the time fixed in advance by Jehovah.—Hab. 2:3; Matt. 24:36.... But before that time arrives, we have work to do—lots of it! This is evident from the numbers of interested persons that show up at our Kingdom Halls. It is shown in reports that during the past year, in one country after another, record numbers of persons presented themselves for baptism as dedicated servants of Jehovah. It is also evident from the number of persons who accept our literature when we call at their homes, and from the worldwide increase in the number of home Bible studies.... Right from the start, urge them to attend meetings at the Kingdom Hall. *There is no time to lose*" (*KM*, September 1974; italics are mine).

Take note of the reference to Habakkuk 2:3, the Biblical passage also frequently referred to by the Adventists of the 19th century when they had to explain why nothing ever happened. After 1975 this would also be misused by the Society to explain why time dragged on. The passage in full:

"For still the vision awaits its time; it hastens to the end—it will not lie. If it seem slow, wait for it; it will surely come, it will not delay" (RSV).[263]

A perfect Bible text for the Jehovah's Witnesses: Though it *hesitates* (KJ: "it tarries"), it's still not *delayed*! That Habakkuk, a so-called minor prophet of the Old Testament, somehow was relevant in the 20th century is more than the old text may bear.

Already by 1974, Brooklyn had gradually started preparing the Witnesses for the inevitable excuses that would follow without fail, because in *The Watchtower* for June 15, 1974, they stated:

"[The] most accurate Bible chronology available indicates that 6,000 years of human existence will end in the mid-1970s. So these Christians are intensely interested to see if that will coincide with the outbreak of the 'great tribulation' of our day that will eliminate all wicked ones on earth. It could. But they are not *even attempting to predict exactly* when the destruction of Satan's wicked system of things will occur. They are content to wait and see, realizing that no human on earth knows the date.—Matt. 24:36" (p. 375-380; italics are mine).

This sounds fairly harmless.

However, only the fewest members at the congregation level registered this kind of *preparatory* statement—or accepted what it really meant—for at the very same time the leadership was constantly telling them how dangerously close they were to the end of the world.

It is harrowing reading.

Internal Doubts Concerning 1975

At last, the year in which the thousand-year reign would *probably* be established came.

Raymond Franz—nephew of Society vice president Fred Franz and author of *Crisis of Conscience*—reported he was becoming uneasy. In a lecture Raymond held at the time he warned his audience about "becoming unduly excited over 1975," but when his uncle heard this he said: "And why shouldn't they get excited? It's something to be excited about."

At the time, Fred Franz was an old man of eighty-three, so he—in the same manner as Rutherford—may have been driven by a sincere wish to see something happen in his own lifetime; at least, this is one view of him from the most positive side. Therefore, it indicates this man *might* have believed in his own half-hearted statements, although I also have my strong, justified doubts. However, he had certainly covered himself very well through his ambiguities. And it is these that ultimately identify him as what he was, a false prophet.

Fred Franz was a charismatic personality who apparently had a strong need to electrify his audience, by which he, psychologically speaking, assumed a role that may have given him a strong sense of significance (interaction in full flower!).[264] Franz was the center of fiery attention—at this time possibly directed against him. At the entrance to the prophetic year 1975, he seemed willing to "walk the plank" by putting himself forward in the preparations; during the worldwide tour he and Knorr completed on behalf of the New Year 1974–75, it was reported Franz delivered speeches everywhere with electrifying effect. In his 1983 book, Raymond Franz described his uncle's style:

"Earlier, toward the start of 1975, President Knorr had made a trip around the world, taking Vice President Franz with him. The vice president's speeches in all countries visited centered on 1975. Upon their return, the other members of the Governing Body, having heard reports from many countries of the stirring effect of the vice president's talk, asked to hear a tape recording of it, made in Australia." This request to hear the recording, according to the Danish version of *Conscience*, occurred during a meeting of the Governing Body on February 19, 1975; the information was not found in Raymond Franz's American edition (*Conscience*, 1983, p. 208).

In his speech, the vice president characterized 1975 as a "year of great possibilities, tremendous probabilities"; a statement that, in my view, truly reveals him as an *unrestrained charlatan*, who fully exploited the situation with no regard to his followers. The members of the so-called Governing Body apparently had a critical view of Fred Franz when they asked to hear a recording of the speech. If the speech effectively caused Knorr and Franz to lose power and prestige between 1972 and 1976, I do not know for sure. Franz had gone to extremes in his speech. He had stated more than once that they already found themselves in "the fifth lunar month of 1975," and that the Hebrew year would end with Rosh Hashanah, the Jewish New Year, on September 5, 1975. (*Conscience*, 1983, p. 208) A strong echo from William Miller's days!

Franz had *Watch-Tower-typically* also suggested that, because of the time lapse between Adam and Eve's creations, there were some uncertainties about how long events would last (previously there was talk about *some weeks or months, not years*). Many things had to be done in the autumn if all was to be accomplished. In Franz's speech, he referred to both previously failed expectations and that the organization had learned not to make extreme predictions. Yet he warned the audience against believing that doomsday could be "years away." There was no reason to marry, build a business or study at a college. (*Conscience*, 1983, p. 208; *VT*, Dec. 12, 1968, p. 543)

Raymond Franz's book clearly shows that the Governing Body was critical, to put it mildly, of the ambiguous outpourings of the vice president. Still, they took no responsible action. Nobody it seemed could prevent Fred Franz from persevering, for in March 1975 the vice president again offered statements equal to those quoted above (Ibid., p. 208) to an outgoing class of missionaries in the Society's Gilead school. Later, Fred Franz was elected by the same critics as the new president of the whole company. So one must conclude their criticisms had no impact—or they lacked the courage to give them with any vehemence and instead chose to pussyfoot.

Clearly, the propaganda strongly contributed to the growth of the movement, and this then justified the entire insanity, and apparently, none of the *divine-guided* Governing Body in Brooklyn ever saw it appropriate to raise a responsible objection. I guess this is not unexpected in consideration of the history of obvious doubts concerning 1975, which they themselves mutually and confidentially had aired. Although there was one exception: Raymond Franz, who we now know publicly warned against the apocalyptic hysteria. His leading position and opinion of developments undoubtedly set him on a collision course with the all-important, and maybe most-important, Watchtower injunction that no one should "move ahead of the Society." After all, Raymond was not Fred. By this time Raymond's file probably contained enough bad reports for the Society to step in on a suitable occasion and act against him with disciplinary measures.

Still, "pleasant [liberal] moments" were on the horizon as substitutes for the promised thousand-year reign that still "tarried." So any potential action would have to wait. However, there is no reason to assume that the "pleasant moments" were implemented as a result of a deliberate plan. On the contrary, this new and surprising wave of "liberalism" seems to be the development's "admission" to the members of the organization, who within a couple of years, surprisingly enough, found the reins loosened on account of Brooklyn's weakened state. (*Conscience,* 1983, p. 82)

This was yet another *tactical* decision, as we shall see later.

New Campaigns, Expansion and Real Estate Development

In the *Kingdom Ministry* of January 1974, management announced that the need for new books and magazines was so great it had been necessary to buy more printing presses and "the night shift in the factory has been expanded to increase book production."

I wonder what the Jehovah's Witnesses around the world thought when the *Kingdom Ministry*'s messages regarding first one project and then another clearly implied the Society in no way expected a doomsday just yet?

For example, the following message appeared in the internal member magazine of March 1975:

"Have you heard the latest news? Remember, back in July your congregation received a letter about the possibility of the Society's buying much-needed property to house more members of the Bethel family. Well, the Society bought this property—the Towers Hotel building—on January 17. A picture of this large building appears on the first endsheet of the 1975 Yearbook. Eventually it may house some 1,000 members of the Bethel family."

Eventually...ha!

Did that mean they'd all be waiting longer than the autumn of 1975?

Yes, much suggested that the Watchtower Society in Brooklyn had extensive plans for the future. Most likely they had already been studying the lessons learned in the aftermath of 1914 when the disgruntled Bible Student's had been persuaded to continue their labors again and again.

While the average Witnesses were still advised to refrain from getting married, starting businesses or attending university, the leadership of the Society seemed to have plenty of time for all sorts of projects—among others, a new and unexpected building enterprise:

"In Germany, excavation has begun on a new Bethel home, and a recently purchased factory building is being cleaned and remodeled. Arrangements were made to enlarge the branches in Switzerland and Italy. And a new Bethel home, factory and office are being planned for Greece.... During zone visits in January, the Chile branch dedicated a new printery, and the Ecuador branch dedicated a new two-story addition. Indeed, marvelous things are happening" (*KM*, March 1975).

It was even announced that brothers Knorr and Franz, while on their worldwide tour, had established a branch office in Tahiti. (Ibid.)

So, during the spring and summer of 1975 the inflammatory remarks of the imminent end of all things were scarce and far between. Instead, the focus was now put on special campaigns. For instance the new edition of the *New World Translation* was presented in June as the "deal of the month":

"During June we will be featuring the *New World Translation* and the book *Is This Life All There Is?* on a contribution of $1.25.... And remember to demonstrate faithfulness by making definite arrangements to return where interest is shown in an effort to start a Bible study" (*KM*, June 1975).

Apparently, the members did as instructed. In the July issue, leadership deemed it appropriate to praise their loyal followers:

"Once again during a month when we were distributing tracts, we reached a fine new peak of publishers. The report for May showed 560,897 sharing in the field service. That is 6,640 more than our previous peak, and 114,167 more than reported field service just two years previous! Truly delightful!... Brother Knorr has just returned from Europe, where he visited six branches. He told the Bethel family about the wonderful progress that the brothers are making in France, with a new peak of 64,091 publishers.... During May, Germany was sharing in tract distribution, and they reached a new peak of 100,351 publishers. New peaks were also reported from Switzerland (10,060), Italy (50,488), Spain (30,679) and Portugal (16,183)" (*KM*, July 1975).

In the Danish edition of the *Kingdom Ministry* one can read another version of the article above, adapted to the members in Denmark, here I present the most important parts:

"We live in a very critical time and we certainly want to continue the publishing work with unabated fervor and zeal.... In early June Brother Knorr and Brother Larson from the headquarters met in Brooklyn with eighteen branch overseers and other brothers from thirteen European countries.... They discussed, among other things, the substantial rise in paper prices" (*Rigets Tjeneste*, the Danish issue of *Our Kingdom Ministry*, July 1975, p. 1; my translation).

Could rising paper prices *be* a problem in the six-thousandth year?

Habakkuk, Again...

A particular article printed in the May edition of *The Watchtower* may be related to the leadership's efforts to reduce the anticipation and urgency about September-October 1975. This must have seemed like a cold shower to the most ardent and hopeful of the Witnesses. Suddenly they were presented with *this*:

"It is only natural for us to want relief as soon as possible from the world's mounting problems, the day-to-day struggle of trying to make a living, as well as sickness, old age and death. But what if that relief were not to come as soon as you personally might expect? How would that affect your heart? Might you be tempted to forget about the importance of a proper relationship with Jehovah God and see what pleasures you might still find in the world? *If you truly love Jehovah, your service to God is not limited by any date.... /* Never should we conclude that what is here said means that the 'great tribulation' is far off and allow ourselves to slip into a pattern of thinking like that of the world alienated from God. As long as people are still responding to God's warm appeal, this should encourage us. It is in harmony with Jehovah's desire that none be destroyed but that all attain to repentance. (2 Pet. 3:9) Our sharing God's viewpoint toward mankind will cause us to rejoice that the way is still open for others to take their stand on Jehovah's side, with the prospect of eternal life in view. And our continuing to see an obvious fulfillment of Jehovah's purpose that as many as possible gain an approved standing before him should certainly strengthen our conviction that his 'day and hour' for executing judgment will come, for this, too, is part of his unchangeable purpose.... / From a human standpoint, it may, to some persons, appear that it has delayed. Nevertheless, it is just as was revealed to the Hebrew prophet Habakkuk: 'The vision is yet for the appointed time, and it keeps panting on to the end, and it will not tell a lie. Even if it should delay, keep in expectation of it; for it will without fail come true. It will not be late.' (Hab. 2:3)" (*WT*, May 1, 1974; italics are mine; the Habakkuk quotation is from the New World Translation)

That Habakkuk's words were again trotted out must or *should have set off alarms* in the minds of the Witnesses, and left them in *wild* frustration.

Would nothing happen after all?

Autumn 1975

A note on the back of the *Kingdom Ministry* reports that "on June 29 Brother Knorr was in Toronto, Ontario, Canada, to share in the dedication of the expanded branch facilities and the new Kingdom Hall that has been built on the Society's property there" (*KM*, August 1975).

At this time, it is as if the leadership in Brooklyn had decided to completely ignore the emotions and expectations they had been stirring up for almost a decade (since 1966); the numbers now overshadowed everything. Under the headline "How Did We Do in June?" these developments were presented:

"For many of us June was the month for attending the 'Divine Sovereignty' district assembly program, and what a delightful time we had! Also, it was good to see that the 510,947 who shared in publishing the good news placed 822,358 books and made over 3,000,000 return visits. This is excellent indeed. Incidentally, from September through June, 7,359,773 books were placed in the field service, and as we all make more return visits and cultivate interest in the good news, surely this will result in opening the way for many more Bible studies" (*KM*, September 1975).

In the Branch Letter of the same issue, it is stated:

"We thought you would be interested in the theocratic progress in New York city [*sic,* all appearances] these days and we are happy to share some thoughts with you in this regard. Some thrilling developments are taking place. For example, there are now 266 congregations, with a total of 26,285 publishers, including 878 pioneers. With 63,813 persons at the Memorial this March, this means that one out of every 124 persons in New York city attended the Memorial. The Bethel family contributes much to the activity of the New York city congregations, and there are currently 346 members of the Bethel family who serve as elders in the various congregations" (*KM,* September 1975; "New York city" was the form used by the publisher).

But as early as in the September, a calmer tone had been adopted. Two articles in the *Kingdom Ministry* for August and September told members indirectly to *calm down* and referred thereafter to "the 1976 service year," namely the *new service year.* For example in the article "Choose Life—Follow God's Way?":

"As we enter *the 1976 service year* all of us are filled with anticipation for the near future, for our generation. Of course, *we cannot set a date* as to when the old system is going to end, can we? Jesus plainly said that we do not know the day or the hour when the 'great tribulation' is to begin, but obviously we can see that the hour is late" (italics are mine).

A *new* service year?

A new service year, so I am told, begins in September—therefore maybe only four months remained of the old year and maybe the *old system* at the very beginning of the new service year. But this doesn't work either, because as stated in the quote above, the Society could not set a date. (*KM,* September 1975)

Leadership uttered not one word to counter the frustration such a sentence would spark. No, the focus now lay on "finding new interested ones" who—as some might have astutely reasoned—could be cultivated when both old and new Witnesses reacted to the absence of dramatic events in 1975.

Not to be remiss in their fear-mongering, in the October issue the drums of doom are banged again, perhaps merely to remind "Jehovah's people on earth" that they are not yet forgotten by the "brothers" at Brooklyn. And maybe to counter some of the tensions and frustrations growing among the Witnesses.

Under the headline "Jehovah's day is near," headquarters states:

"We must keep wide awake spiritually, appreciating that Jehovah's day is now immediately ahead. / Since we are interested in the lives of people, it is important that we urgently warn all whom we can, awakening them to the imminent presence of Jehovah's day. What a fine aid the *Awake!* magazine is for doing this excellent work. For 56 years now, *Awake!* has been used to carry a lifesaving message to the people to alert them to the times in which we live. Every two weeks more than nine million copies in 31 languages currently are put into the hands of the people world wide [*sic*]. It will be a pleasure to feature *Awake!* again during October. Since most people identify *Awake!* as a companion to *The Watchtower*, why not offer both subscriptions, with six booklets, for $3.00? / Much good is also accomplished by the distribution of individual copies of the magazines. During October we have outstanding issues of both magazines to use. The special *Awake!* of October 8 will be titled 'A Sound Guide for Modern Living,' and the October 22 issue will also be most interesting on the subject 'Does It All End Here?'... / Jehovah is certainly blessing the efforts of his people with marvelous expansion..." (*KM*, October 1975).

In this the Society has revealed the tactics and thought behind the Armageddon-propaganda but probably not willingly. Anyway, there is no doubt the members were encouraged by the constant droning drums of doom. From eyewitnesses, I know emotions were simmering near to boiling. Thus, a great deal of ingenuity arises for keeping track of the "remaining time." Many measuring tapes were used as calendars, so you could get a daily sense of how long it would last.

New campaigns emerged in November with encouragement to engage in more house-to-house service:

"Maybe in 1976 all of us can pay a little more attention to budgeting our time.... Another thought-provoking point was the drop of 10,000 in the number of home Bible studies conducted weekly. Interestingly, there were also 10,000 fewer persons baptized. Bible study activity is something that we are going to try to improve by use of the three new study booklets during the *Watchtower* campaign. These will provide a good basis for return visits. So we hope and pray that the first four months of the 1976 calendar year will see a fine increase in this activity.... By the way, Brother Knorr recently visited five branches in Europe. He spoke to 3,075 in a packed-out new assembly hall in the Netherlands on September 19. Then, on the 23rd, he shared in the dedication of a new Bethel home and remodeled factory in Wiesbaden, Germany.... It has been a good year, and all of our brothers are joyful, full of faith, working hard" (*KM*, November 1975).

"Maybe in 1976 all of us..."

The "Theocratic News" section included this inflammatory information in November:

"The new service year began with a total of 7,117 congregations in the USA—575 more than the previous year! Over one third of all congregations in the country were formed within the past five years" (*KM*, November 1975).

Worldwide, more than a million new Jehovah's Witnesses were baptized in less than six years. In the *Kingdom Ministry* of September 1975, there is also information about the "special deals" of September and October and then a suggestion concerning the *following year*, 1976:

While some "brothers" are selling their businesses and houses, surgeries and medical treatments are cancelled (Penton, 1986, p. 95), and others *alleg-*

edly took up loans—which, of course, would *never* have to be repaid—the Society engaged itself in building projects and other measures *with the future in mind.*

Rosh Hashanah, the Jewish New Year, on September 5 in 1975, was the date Fred Franz had implied, with some exaltation, for establishment of the thousand-year reign; it had passed with no attention or comment from either the vice president or other figures of authority at "the Tower" (Concerning "Rosh Hashanah," see p. 301; *Conscience,* 1983, p. 208).

October had passed, and the Witnesses found themselves facing November-December; this required a new but quite-familiar theme. Under the headline "The Door is Still Open," the internal newsletter now proclaimed:

"At our recent district assemblies one of the dramas reminded us that, in the days of Noah, Jehovah made it very clear when the opportunity for others to gain salvation in the ark had ended. It was not Noah who shut the door. After Noah and his family, along with specimens of the birds and animals, had gone into the ark at the appointed time, then, as the Bible says, 'Jehovah shut the door behind him.'—Gen. 7:16. / What about our own day? Now it is the spiritual paradise that is the antitypical ark, Jehovah's provision for survival.... During just the past service year, right here in the United States, 71,300 persons were baptized in symbol of their dedication to Jehovah through Jesus Christ, the Greater Noah. Obviously, the door is still open! / *How inappropriate it would be for any of us to endeavor in effect to pull that door shut prematurely by letting up in the preaching of the good news*! God's will is that 'all sorts of men should be saved and come to an accurate knowledge of truth.' (1 Tim. 2:3, 4) The ingathering of recent months is an indication that *there is work yet to be done.* Blessings come to us when we harmonize our lives with God's will. And we have opportunity to do that during November by offering in the field service a book that discusses at length the spiritual paradise and how to get into it. The book also points to the delightful prospects for the future that await persons who take the necessary steps now to be numbered among the survivors of the 'great tribulation.' This is the new book *Man's Salvation out of World Distress at Hand!* Let's be enthusiastic about offering it to others" (*KM,* November 1975; italics are mine).

Enthusiastic, indeed!

The above quotation is inevitably associated with the Adventists in the aftermath of 1844. In that year the Adventists' worldwide recruitment campaign ended and the "door" to the heavenly residences was closed. Some other Adventists said the door would remain open, meaning the missionary work should be resumed despite the failure and "the Great Disappointment."

Many Adventist churches are still going strong, although more than 168 or more years have passed since the fiasco of 1844, and they still promote the opinion that the end of the world will soon be upon us.

One Year After the Fiasco

The post-1975 years would show that even Jehovah's Witnesses would have "something to do" after their "Great Disappointment." Not just something, but a lot! *The Watchtower* tells them so, thoughtfully, in September 1976, a year after the disaster year:

"On how much greater a scale the witnessing work is yet to be done, we simply do not know. We should not overlook the fact that Jehovah is responsible for this work and is *using angels in heaven to oversee it.* (Rev. 14:6, 7)... Since we are assured that our all-powerful and righteous God will decide when the preaching is done to the extent he purposes, we can with singleness of mind concentrate on what we have to do. He has not told us to determine when sufficient preaching has been done, but has told us to keep on declaring the good news. Lives are involved" (*WT*, June 1, 1976; italics are mine).

Anyone should be able to see how this is a theme with unlimited and indefinite possibilities for exploitation. As long as there is growth, the door is not closed; it is open wide!

Knorr's "global expansion" had been extremely successful. Thousands joined the organization annually. But would it be possible to keep all these new followers? And would the *old-timers* allow themselves to be systematically *let down* and *deceived* in the years ahead, swallowing lies, hook, line and sinker, with occasional reference to Habakkuk, when they were wrong again? Add to this the new excuse that it was Jehovah (and—tacitly implied—*not* the organization) who was *responsible.* And all the while, the zealous, loyal followers in congregations around the world had believed that the Watchtower Society of New York was Jehovah's *sole channel of communication* to mankind.

Many Witnesses may simply have felt this latest deception was the last straw.

Chapter 26

The Long Road to an Apology

In Raymond Franz's 1983 book he says that in 1976, a year after the catastrophic date, a few Governing Body members in Brooklyn "began urging that some statement should be made acknowledging that the organization had been in error," and that it "had stimulated false expectations." However, they were reluctant to do so, because it would "just give ammunition to opposers."

Milton Henschel, who became Watch Tower Society president in 1993, opined that they should ignore the whole matter and "that the wise course would be simply not to bring the matter up and that in time the brothers would stop talking about it" (*Conscience,* 1983, p. 209).

This would prove to be a disastrous error in judgment.

After all, thousands had set *everything aside* to sacrifice themselves for the great cause. They sold their houses. They quit their jobs. They refrained from getting married, and thereby missed the opportunity to have children. How on earth could Henschel and the so-called Governing Body in Brooklyn—which constantly insisted on being God's "visible channel of communication"—believe such enthusiasm, such senseless, insane apocalyptic obsession, which they seemingly systematically and effectively had unleashed among their gullible followers, could simply be brushed aside and forgotten, as if nothing had ever happened? (*WT,* May 1, 1957; Jan. 15, 1969; Sept. 1, 1991[265])

Naturally, a reaction was imminent, one reflective of the enormous disappointment among the lower-level Witnesses. From previous experience, Henschel and the other Society leaders had to know many were likely to leave the organization in the years to come, whether it be by drifting, fading quietly away, or by slamming the door behind them. Perhaps Henschel and the other top executives anticipated the possibility of re-enlisting some of these disgruntled ones after a few years.

However, by their irresponsible indifference to these previously enthusiastic Witnesses, the old men at the top of the Watchtower hierarchy demonstrated, yet again, that the destinies of their individual followers were of little or no concern to them. They were merely statistics. The primary concern was, and always would be, the survival of the organization. Of course, this should, in itself, have caused worry for the leaders in Brooklyn. A significant dropout rate would undermine the great enlistment achievements of the late 1960s and early 1970s that represented the deeper meaning of the preaching work and the only justification for still quoting Habakkuk 2:3 and II Peter 3:9, rightly or wrongly. If growth figures stagnated, then clearly time had run out, the "door" was shut, and the "hour and the day" had come. The growth was, seemingly, still the most important aspect to the leaders of the movement. And for God knows how long, old Storrs proved to be right again:

It all culminated in pure Babel!

In October 1975, *The Watchtower* commented on the "great crowd" that joined the "anointed remnant of Jehovah's Kingdom" after 1935:

"*For forty years* the ingathering of this 'great crowd' has proceeded. Now more than two million of these servants of God look forward to passing through the fast-approaching 'great tribulation' into a cleansed earth, where a literal paradise will be restored throughout this globe, and for all eternity! In some 35,000 Christian congregations, in 207 lands of the earth, God's zealous people are being prepared for survival…" (*WT*, Oct. 1, 1975; italics are mine).

As has been previously shown, the *forty-years* symbolism again became significant. The above passage is another modest example of how leadership recycled this old trick, still it was probably strong enough to set the imaginations of the common Witnesses in motion yet again: The "nearness of such an important date indeed fires the imagination and presents unlimited possibilities for discussion," as it was said in 1968 under the title "Why are you looking forward to 1975?" (*WT*, Aug. 15, 1968)

Although nothing happened in 1975, the level of expectation had to be maintained. Anyone could add the two figures and come up with the correct sum— 1935 + 40 = 1975—and although 1976 rapidly approached, clearly, one still needed to "prepare for survival." The expectation meter had been pushed to its limit, until the current flowing among the members fairly crackled for "the Tower guards."

The Vice President Runs from his Responsibilities

In 1976, Fred Franz, Society vice president, spoke to a large audience in Toronto, Canada, and asked a rhetorical question:

" 'Do you know why nothing happened in 1975?' Then, pointing at his audience, he shouted: 'It was because *you* expected something to happen' " (*Apocalypse Delayed*, Penton, 1986, p. 100).

As Penton observes, Franz lays the blame for the fiasco on the general-member Witnesses, acting as if he bore no responsibility for the whole mess whatsoever. At the same meeting, Franz presented an argument for the "delaying" of Armageddon: The last day of creation (Genesis 1), which, according to the Jehovah's Witnesses, was to last for a full 7,000 years, commenced *after* the creation of Eve, and the exact date for the creation of Adam's companion in paradise was not known. Concerning this, Penton argues in this context that Franz ignored this same fact a few years earlier. *The Watchtower* from May 1, 1968, included: "According to reliable Bible chronology Adam and Eve were created in 4026 BC" (*WT*, May 1, p. 271, 1968; Penton, 1986, p. 100; footnote p. 327 where the source is apparently wrongly noted as *Awake!*, Oct. 8, 1968).

In a 1976 *Watchtower* article this explaining-away approach deepens, showing the Society's managers maintaining their 1975-chronology in principle. However, this "explanation" was age-old,[266] and it may have seemed strained for the older Witnesses who had been presented with this argument before:

"How much time elapsed between the creation of the man and that of the woman? The Bible does not reveal this. It could have been a relatively short time.... We do not know whether it was a brief time *such as a month or a few months, a year or even more*. But whatever time elapsed would have to be added to the time that has passed since Adam's creation in order for us to know how far along we are within God's seventh 'day,' his grand day of rest. So our having advanced six thousand years from the start of human existence is one thing. Advancing six thousand years into God's seventh creative 'day' is quite another. And we do not know just how far along in the stream of time we are in this regard.... This does not mean, however, that chronology is of no concern to us..." (*WT*, July 15, 1976; italics are mine).

Previously, the Witnesses had been told it wasn't a matter of years, but *weeks* or *months* at the most.

In a subsequent article in the same magazine it says:

"Are we serving Jehovah God because we love him, trust him and have full confidence in what he says? Or are we 'becoming weary in well-doing,' looking for a certain date primarily as bringing a relief to ourselves, with little concern for the lives of other people?... It may be that some who have been serving God have planned their lives according to a mistaken view of just what was to happen on a certain date or in a certain year. They may have, for this reason, put off or neglected things that they otherwise would have cared for. But they have missed the point of the Bible's warnings concerning the end of this system of things, thinking that Bible chronology reveals the specific date" (*WT*, July 15, 1976).

So it was clearly *the ordinary Witnesses' fault*; they had believed too much in the so-called "definite" suggestions, which among other things the vice president personally, and on behalf of the organization, represented prior to 1975. Yet those same faithful members who had obviously botched things with their date-specific faithfulness could be excommunicated from said organization if they dared spread their private thoughts and doubts within the congregation. (Concerning "definite," see *Proclaimers*, 1993, chapter 8, p. 104.)

It further states in the same article:

"Did Jesus mean that we should adjust our financial and secular affairs so that our resources would just carry us to a certain date that we might think marks the end? If our house is suffering serious deterioration, should we let it go, on the assumption that we would need it only a few months longer? Or, if someone in the family possibly needs special medical care, should we say, 'Well, we'll put it off because the time is so near for this system of things to go'? This is not the kind of thinking that Jesus advised" (*WT*, July 15, 1976).

This begs the question: Was it not the internal monthly magazine, the *Kingdom Ministry* that had in 1974 encouraged the Witnesses to commit themselves 100% to the preaching work in the short remaining days of this old world? Jesus may not have advised this kind of thinking, but the Society's leaders did:

"Reports are heard of brothers selling their homes and property and planning to finish out the rest of their days in this old system in the pioneer service. *Certainly this is a fine way to spend the short time remaining before the wicked world's end*" (*KM*, May 1974; italics are mine).

Yet, in 1976, the leadership states:

"But it is not advisable for us to set our sights on a certain date, neglecting everyday things we would ordinarily care for as Christians, such as things that we and our families really need. We may be forgetting that, when the 'day' comes, it will not change the principle that Christians must at all times take care of all their responsibilities. If anyone has been disappointed through not following this line of thought, he should now concentrate on adjusting his viewpoint, seeing that it was not the word of God that failed or deceived him and brought disappointment, but that his own understanding was based on wrong premises.... However, say that you are one who counted heavily on a date, and, commendably, set your attention more strictly on the urgency of the times and the need of the people to hear. And say you now, temporarily, feel somewhat disappointed; are you really the loser? Are you really hurt? We believe you can say that you have gained and profited by taking this conscientious course. Also, you have been enabled to get a really mature, more reasonable viewpoint.—Eph. 5:1-17" (*WT*, July 15, 1976).

And last, they finished off with this amazing exhibition of word acrobatics:

"The chronology in the Bible is not there without good purpose. That chronology indicates that we are at the close of six thousand years of human history. While not revealing when God's day of adverse judgment upon this wicked system of things will begin, this chronological fact does add one more reason to the many, many other reasons we already have for being confident that the remaining time is very short" (*WT*, July 15, 1976).

I hardly think this explanation, at this time, did much more than increase the frustration of approximately two million reporting Jehovah's Witnesses worldwide. Their sole mistake lay in having allowed themselves to be spiritually raped by the leaders of the Watchtower Society in the first place, leaders who would clearly embrace any means to achieve the "global expansion" they desired.

And beyond the continuing double-talk about dates, they now refused to take any responsibility *at all* for the entire 1975 fiasco.

The Credibility Gap

Raymond Franz recounts how the question of whether to release another official statement on the 1975 mistake resurfaced in 1977; the Governing Body adopted a proposal stating Counselor Lloyd Barry had to insert a statement in a convention speech he was preparing. After the proposal was approved, Lloyd Barry was apparently confronted in one of the many hallways at headquarters by Milton Henschel and Ted Jaracz, members of the Governing Body, who persuaded him to drop the declaration. When Raymond Franz asked Lloyd why the declaration had not been inserted in his speech, he answered that he had simply not been able to accommodate it. Therefore, the explanation and the apology to the masses had to wait for another opportunity. (*Conscience*, 1983, p. 210; Theodora Jaracz died in June 2010)

The pus-filled abscess would not be punctured until 1979.

Robert Wallen, secretary for the Governing Body, wrote the following internal memo:

"I have been associated as a baptized Witness well over 39 years and with Jehovah's help I will continue to be a loyal servant. But to say I am not disappointed would be untruthful, for, when I know my feelings regarding 1975 were fostered because of what I read in various publications, and then I am told in effect that I reached false conclusions on my own, that, I feel, is not being fair and honest. Knowing that we are not working with infallibility, to me it is but proper that when errors are made by imperfect, but God-fearing men, then corrections will be made when errors are found" (*Conscience*, 1983, p. 209, 210).

It sounded, for once, like honest discourse.

In Brooklyn, others also decided to break the silence, surprisingly without being excommunicated. The *liberal tendencies* in these few years from 1976 to 1978 acted as a safety valve, relieving some of the pressure and creating the impression that freedom and honesty would now prevail. The following quotes from internal memos to the Governing Body are all taken from Raymond Franz's book, *Crisis of Conscience*, which gives an intense and up-close description of this era.

Fred Rusk of the editor's office:

"Despite any qualifying statements that might have been made along the way to admonish the brothers not to say that Armageddon would come in 1975, the fact is there were a number of articles in magazines and other publications that more than hinted that the old system would be replaced by Jehovah's new system in mid-1970's" (*Conscience*, 1983, p. 210).

Harold Jackson of the Service Department wrote:

"What is needed now is not a statement to the effect that we were wrong about 1975 but rather a statement as to why the whole matter has been ignored so long in view of the fact that so many lives have been affected. Now it is a credibility gap we are faced with and that can prove to be disastrous" (*Conscience*, 1983, p. 211).

If anyone has been disappointed...

Then in 1980 came a declaration that seemed to be the closest the Watchtower leaders in those years—probably under the impression of a growing opposition within the movement—could come to openly admitting they had made a disastrous mistake about 1975. The opinion was vague, but still remarkable.

With reference to the second letter to the Thessalonians (2:1-3), wherein the Christians are warned they should not by any means let themselves be "deceived," the editors of *The Watchtower* wrote:

"In modern times such eagerness, commendable in itself, has led to attempts at setting dates for the desired liberation from the suffering and troubles that are the lot of persons throughout the earth. With the appearance of the book *Life Everlasting—in Freedom of the Sons of God*, and its comments as to how appropriate it would be for the millennial reign of Christ to parallel the seventh millennium of man's existence, considerable expectation was aroused regarding the year 1975. There were statements made then, and thereafter, stressing that this was only a possibility. Unfortunately, however, along with such cautionary information, there were other statements published that implied that such realization of hopes by that year was more of a probability than a mere possibility. It is to be regretted that these latter statements apparently overshadowed the cautionary ones and contributed to a buildup of the expectation already initiated" (*WT*, March 15, 1980).

In this unusual statement, the author of the article referred directly to the *Watchtower* article quoted a few pages earlier in this book, but now it was addressed from a more humble, self-critical angle.

It continued:

"In its issue of July 15, 1976, *The Watchtower*, commenting on the inadvisability of setting our sights on a certain date, stated: 'If anyone has been disappointed through not following this line of thought, he should now concentrate on adjusting his viewpoint, seeing that it was not the word of God that failed or deceived him and brought disappointment, but that his own understanding was based on wrong premises.' In saying 'anyone,' The *Watchtower* included all disappointed ones of Jehovah's Witnesses, hence *including persons having to do with the publication of the information* that contributed to the buildup of hopes centered on that date" (italics by *The Watchtower*).

There is no doubt here—according the Society's own standards—they had gone very far. Yet, after this, the leaders put forth statements that could only increase frustration for members:

"Nevertheless, there is no reason for us to be shaken in faith in God's promises. Rather, as a consequence, we are all moved to make a closer examination of the Scriptures regarding this matter of a day of judgment. In doing so, we find that the important thing is not the date. What is important is our keeping ever in mind that *there is such a day*—and it is getting closer and it will require an accounting on the part of all of us.... It is not a certain date ahead; it is *day-to-day living* on the part of the Christian that is important.... It is impossible for us to figure out the world's end in advance" (*WT*, March 15, 1980; italics by *The Watchtower*).

This was what millions in the movement had been waiting for, but it was *too late*. Many had long since left the organization.

The whole mess surrounding 1975 would not easily be forgotten. It was the signal for an uprising that slowly but surely spread worldwide. The result was a relatively large dropout rate, a growing number of exclusion cases and steadily increasing resistance from the apostates. They had tasted blood—or fear—in the Governing Body and wanted more. The leaders of the Watchtower had, by their utter irresponsibility, fed this new tendency in the so-called "newer history" of the Jehovah's Witnesses.

Something had to happen, but what?

Chapter 27

Growth, Regimentation and Rebellion

The widespread disappointment and frustration among members around the world after 1975 and its subsequent events left an indelible mark on the movement.

Development is always a combination of many factors, some relatively random and chaotic, others very planned and deliberate. I've consistently held the thesis that the Society's leaders, the president, vice president and entire Brooklyn staff, deliberately exploited the apocalyptic expectation—the heart of the organization's recruitment mechanisms since its origins in the 1870s. The practice was in the officers' blood. They could recite it all by heart, and as we have seen, there was almost a *total collective interconnection* across every level of the organization—drone bees following a committee of kings.

While reviewing the period from 1966 to the present, I have the feeling the top-level leadership team in Brooklyn (and here I am thinking in particular of the presidents and their confidential employees) must have had an overall, comprehensive plan that went far forward beyond 1975, perhaps even up to the first third of the 21st century—something to be explored in a later chapter.

When one considers the many building and enlargement projects initiated throughout the world before 1975, it demonstrates with frightening clarity how warnings about 1975 were merely fuel for the machinery. And the various campaigns, dislocated and disjointed as they sometimes were, kept the enthusiastic Witnesses employed, so when one campaign ended, a new one—running beyond 1975—was already fully engaged. The newly converted, attracted by the 1975 campaign, were incorporated into the organization, trained and made ready to sell Watchtower teachings to yet more potential recruits. No one in the organization ever got a quiet moment. All were instructed to work in field service and sell literature, drawing them deeper and deeper into a whirling apocalyptic roundabout.

The table on the next page illustrates my *overlapping-strategy-hypothesis*.

I freely admit that sometimes it's difficult to judge whether the Society's senior executives believe what they write for their publications—for the whole

306

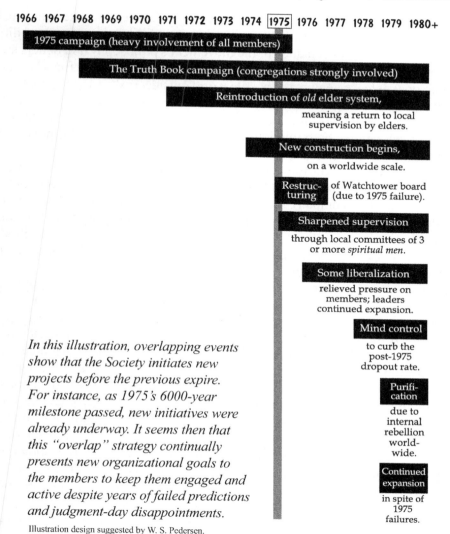

1966 1967 1968 1969 1970 1971 1972 1973 1974 [1975] 1976 1977 1978 1979 1980+

1975 campaign (heavy involvement of all members)

The Truth Book campaign (congregations strongly involved)

Reintroduction of *old* elder system,

meaning a return to local supervision by elders.

New construction begins,

on a worldwide scale.

Restruc-turing of Watchtower board (due to 1975 failure).

Sharpened supervision

through local committees of 3 or more *spiritual* men.

Some liberalization

relieved pressure on members; leaders continued expansion.

Mind control

to curb the post-1975 dropout rate.

Purifi-cation

due to internal rebellion world-wide.

Continued expansion

in spite of 1975 failures.

In this illustration, overlapping events show that the Society initiates new projects before the previous expire. For instance, as 1975's 6000-year milestone passed, new initiatives were already underway. It seems then that this "overlap" strategy continually presents new organizational goals to the members to keep them engaged and active despite years of failed predictions and judgment-day disappointments.

Illustration design suggested by W. S. Pedersen.

project is still, I believe, a part of them and their identities. They have completely lost touch with their own inner selves and souls.

Both new converts and Witnesses who grew up in the movement's sectarian and very limited, restrictive environment have largely grown together with the organization. It is this "embodied" organizational dependency that gives them strength and meaning. If they would continue to feel like whole individuals they must approach *total* accord with the organization. Not only on the surface as a matter of practice but also deep within their souls. A system of resistances (psychological) are at work, implanted in their very fragile souls and immediately activated when confronted with ideas they've been forbidden to even acknowledge, let alone ponder. Only a sustained and highly effective influence conducted over months and years, also called *brainwashing*, can lead to this mental condition.

The converts' acceptance of the movement's philosophy and beliefs and mutual acceptance of them within the movement's closed world, function partly as personal defense against the hostile world outside, and partly as a highly effective, long-working deterrent to prevent individuals from leaving the movement. This mechanism is, I think, universal and can be seen operating in many different organizations, both religious and political. Still, within this movement, the mechanism operates optimally.

Members of the movement belong to all kinds of professions, and they will naturally and stubbornly refute they are brainwashed and unidirectional. But if you are in their company for even a short time, you have absolutely no doubt. They spiritually cling to and don a manner of thinking, making them largely unable to assess anything objectively. And who can oppose such blindness? The only way out comes from within, because no one from outside the organization can penetrate their armor.

The Jehovah's Witnesses' movement is one relatively limited example of how strangely and adversely things can evolve. As such, this movement is worth exploring for a broader perspective of extremist and fundamentalist groups increasingly setting agendas throughout the world in this century. Actually, it is the fundamental social mechanisms for these heterogeneous groups that hold so much interest. Still, what can single individuals gain by joining these groups where their personal and innermost self is overridden by surrender to a higher purpose? Although it sounds harsh, I have trouble seeing any outcome other than the individual's spiritual destruction. On the other hand, humans function empirically in social contexts that are synonymous with social acceptance from our immediate environment and present certain advantages for us. This affiliation is a vital necessity, and therefore, overrides individual attitudes in the interest of those of the closed community; however, we may go on *secretly* maintaining opinions and beliefs until one day when they will become more permissible.

While I am writing this, I'm reminded of a large flock of birds I observed in late summer at the seaside. The flock contains perhaps as many as tens of thousands of individuals—and possibly many more. Yet they behave collectively during flight, where the smallest hint and movement by the leader causes the entire flock to turn as one, twisting up and down, back and forth. The flock seems guided by a single brain. It is both fascinating and frightening to look at, for all the birds are subject to instincts and laws that they as individuals have little influence on or resistance to. They are completely dominated by their flock instinct, their *social* determination. Their life purpose is to follow their innate behavior standards which presuppose this sky-high formation flying. By following as they do, they afford themselves the greatest chance of survival.

Those who are attracted to the Jehovah's Witnesses have, as far as I can see, a clear need for authoritarian leadership, someone to stand above them who must *tell them* what is right and wrong, or what to do to be accepted, so they can feel safe and complete. To take responsibility for one's own decisions is almost perceived as *painful*, and for them it's a relief and liberation to be governed and monitored by a higher authority which also carries their burdens. Yet, if taken to the extreme where they are too much trouble and not dependent enough to satisfy the organization—or even themselves—then they're *out, disfellowshipped, expelled*.

And here we reach what is probably at the innermost core of all religions: The liberation from the heavy burden of personal responsibility. Life's pain and all the existential problems must be seen in the context of an objective (or a *solution* that only serves an *immediate* or *temporary* substitute for an *everlasting* religious security) which consists of the permanent ownership and maintenance of "the Truth" and of the reward, eternal life in a New World. This in turn requires the belief that we are living just before the old world's end, and therefore, must perform acts or live a certain kind of life to make survival possible. Translated into the various religions' ritual languages, each of their truths is, of course, *universal* and applies to everyone on this planet.

Therefore, management must always deliver a product which causes agitation, enthusiasm and hope (and now I focus again on the subject of this book). If these conditions are met, the whole organization works smoothly from top to bottom. Disturbance in this pattern creates unrest, insecurity and collective depression, threatening the very meaning and function of the concept. It is clearly not primarily about compassion, or Christian charity, even though the leaders say it is; rather, it's particularly about figures, statistics and increase compared to the previous year's "peak figure of publishers" or simplified: The continued growth and expansion of the organization.

All those who stand in the way of this growth must be guided back to understanding or eliminated. It's like a military dictatorship, a communist organization or an insect community. The individual means nothing; the organization, everything.

If a subject's change of view ends with exclusion or disfellowshipping, his life can go in any direction, from a fantastic feeling of liberation as the most positive experience to despair and suicide as a last resort. The root of the problem is that when the excluded is left alone and "naked," he is deprived of his past and his *artificially enlarged* "organization-I" (the super-ego), and therefore his completeness. What remains is the original, vulnerable "I," which now must go out into the world and test its strength against all it has been sheltered against. It is here that professional help is often required, help that many different kinds of therapists—psychologists and psycho-analysts, but also self-appointed professionals in a sort of post-cult recovery—willingly offer.

This recovery process can in many ways become rather expensive if one seeks or requires help beyond that of a good friend or even a small group, for it is through conversation and openness with others that one can lighten the burden of being alone in a somewhat alien world.

The "Theocratic Organization" Restructured

Based on the original organizational structure of the early Christian Church—as the Watchtower leadership defined its structure—in 1971 the Society took steps to restructure the congregation-organization along with an increasingly exaggerated, apocalyptic-doom mood; this was an opportune time when everyone's attention was on 1975. One year later, in September 1972, the organization initiated power-sharing among the leadership of the local congregations across the globe:

"The following year, in September 1972, the first shifting of responsibilities in the congregations began, and by October 1 the rotation in most congregations was completed. During the next three years, Jehovah's Witnesses experienced impressive growth—over three quarters of a million persons getting baptized. But now they were facing the autumn of 1975. *If all the expectations concerning 1975 were not realized*, how would this affect their zeal for the global preaching activity as well as their worldwide unity?" (*Proclaimers,* 1993, p. 107; italics are mine)

Indeed, a true statement *if* it is given in the 1990s and retrospective of what actually *did not happen* in 1975.

In any case, the organization restructured and was now equipped for the large crowds which were expected to join in the coming years. With the re-organization of the elder-buffer system, they introduced a method to manage the fuss that would inevitably follow the anticipated 1975 failure. This would consequently, and with some certainty, lead to a higher level of activity among the "judicial committees" throughout the organization as they persecuted any who showed signs of straying.

During a number of conventions in 1971, the vice president presented the changes in a speech "Theocratic Organization Amidst Democracies and Communism." Fred W. Franz noted that the Christian congregations in the first century had more than one man as *overseer*. A "body of elders" formed the supervision, in which all were "equal, having the same official status, and none of them was the most important, most prominent, most powerful member in the congregation" (*WT,* Nov. 15, 1971).

Later N. H. Knorr, the Society's president, stated every congregation had to elect a "body of elders" during 1972 and one of the elders was to be appointed chairman, yet everyone was to share responsibility for decisions. Consequently, all members—except *sisters*—"as were qualified could now 'reach out' and be appointed to the 'office of overseer'" (*Proclaimers,* 1993, p. 105-107; *YB,* 1975, p. 248).

Today, when I read *Proclaimers,* it is clear that the overall perspective before 1975 was: *work, work and more work.* Because of the insane 1975-obsession, a lot of so-called "new ones" came into the organization, but there soon came a day when all these people had to live with an uneventful 1975 and the many years that followed. So again, I can only surmise, the reorganization of the Society was part of a well-planned and well-prepared survival strategy.

At about the same time, in October 1971, the Society's senior management announced it too was changing: The board-leader's position, from then on, would rotate to a different board member each year, moving in alphabetical order. Fred Franz was the first—probably not exactly in line with the alphabetical-progression rule. Maybe he was still a little more "equal" than the others.

These changes, which indicated a new method of power-sharing among top managers in Brooklyn, may have reflected a power struggle at the Society's top level.

The introduction of the *new* elder system at the bottom of the organization had a natural consequence of new principles also needing to be introduced at the top level. However, at the same time, there were efforts underway to decentralize the power of the organization. The answer was the reintroduction of the *old* elder system, which was superficially similar to the elder system from Russell's time, abolished in the 1930s by the bombastic and dictatorial Rutherford because it threatened his discretionary power. Therefore, in the midst of the despotism of the 1970s, there could, theoretically, have been *some genuine democratic actions*. Though, it seems undeniable that even in the new "democratic" developments there was strategic planning for what would come after.

I will pause here briefly to clarify that the apparent restoration of the elder system, from my point of view, was only a hollow speech about a new form of organizational supervision and control. Subsequent developments soon showed this was the case. The elder system was simply a new variant of the *Inquisition*, and this is no exaggeration. From 1980 onwards, the hunt for heretics increased, which we shall learn more about in later chapters.

Back, now, to the power struggle at the top of the organization:

Raymond Franz, Fred's nephew, who was once a very prominent member of the Governing Body (from 1971) and was excluded in 1980 after a cleansing action at the highest level, confirmed that in these years a power struggle limited presidential powers and gave greater influence to the members of the board of directors, who thus far had been fairly anonymous.[267]

The Society had largely seen the corporation board as a dispatch office designed to simply rubberstamp what was agreed upon in advance. It had a purely formal function. This was shown by the production of the Jehovah's Witnesses' Bible, *New World Translation*, in 1949–1950. The new statutes, pushed through by Rutherford in January 1917 in Pittsburgh, gave the New York company extended authority in certain cases, for example about new books that had to be published. The corporation board was not informed of this translation's undertaking, until it was finished and ready for printing. (*Proclaimers*, 1993, p. 607; *Conscience*, 1983, p. 62–64)

If the board had rejected any material of any kind, the president could still consider publishing it without board approval. This happened in 1975 in connection with a new book. The book didn't get the necessary two-thirds approval by the board, but the president still drove it through the system. (*Conscience,* 1983, p. 62-66)

The leadership's actions continued even after the formal changes in the New York society, with the president and vice president at the head as leaders. It was really they who were the Society. So, there arose gradually increasing tensions between the president and the board—the Watch Tower Bible and Tract Society of Pennsylvania which gradually became known as the Governing Body after 1975, written with initial capitals compared to previous references that spelled it in all lower case. (*Paradise on Earth,* 1982, approximately p. 195)

In a 1972 speech, Fred Franz expressed the view that *a governing body* existed that would be the direct heir to the first-century apostle council in Jerusalem. The truth was, however, that there really was no Society governing body, just an arbitrary president, a *monarchial authority.* It had been that way since 1879, and by Franz's speech in 1972, amazingly, nothing changed. (*Conscience,* 1983, p. 66) Yet, after the speech, a little movement was made toward resolution of the old conflict issue. The new roles could be implemented because, among other things, there had been a *Watchtower* article stating the Governing Body always existed and simultaneously stated this council—unlike the Society's board of directors—did not have a president. However, this seemed at odds with the realities in Brooklyn. (see *WT,* Dec. 15, 1971)

Thus far, the Governing Body handled only routine, less-important matters, especially exclusion or disfellowshipping cases, while the Society handled everything important. However, in 1975 two Bethel elders wrote to the Governing Body complaining about unacceptable conditions among the Brooklyn headquarters staff. An atmosphere of fear, discouragement and discontent reigned in the Brooklyn enclave, and by April 2, 1975, the problems were addressed in a hearing with the Governing Body. The result was that governing practices up until that time were abandoned and the Governing Body took control of leadership and the Society's future. In the protocol published by Raymond Franz we find:

"The corporations should recognize that the Governing Body of seventeen members has the responsibility to administer the work in the congregations throughout the world. There has been a delay of putting the arrangement into effect at Bethel as compared to the congregations. There has been confusion. We do not want a dual organization" (*Conscience,* 1983, p. 69-71).

Such an announcement indicates, despite everything else said publicly, that after 1971 there was movement towards greater openness, suggesting the management allowed a broader view of differing opinions, which previously (and later, it appears) were untenable because of deep conflict with the psychological need for leadership and an authoritarian regime—a characteristic feature for the majority of the members of the movement. True to say, we see here the normal phenomena to some extent prevalent in all forms of human society, yet within which the totalitarian organization develops as a *caricature* of normality.

Throughout the process, beginning in 1976, both Knorr and Fred Franz probably were against the new era of the organization. Knorr apparently adapted to the new situation, while Franz—as the *prima donna* in the power game—seemed to have been sitting on the fence, waiting and watching for better times.

The result was the rise of a more collective-style leadership, where both the president and vice president and the new, powerful board—the Governing Body—reached a power balance that maybe, for a time, even paralyzed it. The unfortunate aspect of this development was that responsibility now became *collective* with the most unfortunate characteristics of *collectivism*, where nobody stepped up to take responsibility and where decisions often happened as part of a corridor policy. The "strong man" was missing. The easily insulted Fred Franz had obviously waited for the favorable moment, where he, as the old sly patriarch, could strike and restore the glorious, old-established modes.

With the introduction of the elder system in 1972—which initially may have looked like a democratic decentralization—the Watchtower management was in fact, paradoxically, strengthened significantly. The predominant impression is the reintroduction of the elder system soon implemented a *church discipline*, often resulting in a pure inquisitorial-like process. Something that probably never could have happened in Russell's time, although his methods formed the prerequisite for this development.

Stagnation and a New President

The credibility gap following the 1975 fiasco stood in the way of continued growth, and the movement experienced stagnation for a few years after 1975. The organization had to survive some turbulent years before it again could find its balance.

Knorr, who more than anyone else had been responsible for the growth or expansion ideology, became ill in 1976. The diagnosis? An incurable brain tumor. He died in 1977. He was seventy-two.

Two weeks later, 83-year-old Fred Franz was elected president of the Watchtower Society. He had long been the *gray eminence* in the Brooklyn headquarters, supreme commander of education materials and issues until the power was shared among the president, vice president and Governing Body during the 1975–1976 period. In the following years, the power he wielded was not as strong as previous presidents', but despite his advanced age, it appears he was able to bide his time. He was at his post until age ninety-nine.

Knorr and Franz had not been zealous advocates of the management-level changes. Yet, the developments required they come into a new era, one where a new brotherly spirit, greater moderation and flexibility apparently held sway (*Conscience*, 1983, p. 228). From 1971 to 1976, the board was expanded to seventeen members, eventually creating greatly increased prestige under its new title of Governing Body (like the old apostle council, if there was any real comparison at all). Raymond Franz wrote about the period following the introduction of the elder system and the changes in top management:

"The years of 1976 and 1977 brought some *pleasant moments*. A very different climate seemed to be in evidence at the international headquarters, a spirit of greater brotherliness, openness and equality. Some compared it to the 'window' that Pope John XXIII had opened in the Catholic Church to 'let a breath of fresh air in' " (*Conscience*, 1983, p. 92; italics are mine).

It was during this period that all of my wife's family, my parents-in-law, my wife's siblings and their children, suddenly announced their entirely unexpected arrival for a Witness convention in Copenhagen. Until then a visit by them had been completely unthinkable. We were astounded and nearly panicked. We bought extra chairs, Norwegian chairs of pine, and the dining table was prepared for a real family gathering which, despite our differences, boded well for the future. Sadly, the pleasant moments were brief, and soon the theocratic rules again prevailed.

This event was 34–35 years ago, and apart from my wife's continued contact with her mother (now deceased) and her oldest sister, any communication with our family was mercilessly disrupted. It was as if memories of relationships were switched off in their brains. It was in any case effective—and frightening.

After the Pleasant Moments Comes the Bad

The short-term liberalization seen from 1976 to 1978, somewhat similar to the Soviet thaw but in Lilliputian-scale, must have relieved some of the accumulated discontent, the result of the millennial *absentia* in 1975. In retrospect, this matched the tactical thaw so well in the situation that the short term apparently facilitated the aforementioned pleasant moments. Maybe even as a *foretaste* of the Millennium.

Overall, however, I find it hard to identify anything pleasant at all. It was only a momentary release of the excessively totalitarian grip on the movement's members, an all-too-brief manifestation of the management's post-1975 crisis. The previous hard line persisted beneath the pleasant moments, for example in regard to the practice of smoking tobacco. Much is revealed in how the 1993 history book retrospectively describes this period:

"As a further forward step in consistent application of that Bible counsel, none who were still smoking were accepted for baptism from 1973 onward. During the following months, those who were actively involved in tobacco production or in promoting the sale of tobacco were helped to realize that they could not continue to do that and be accepted as Jehovah's Witnesses. The counsel of God's Word must be applied consistently in every aspect of life.

Such application of Bible principles to the use of tobacco, marijuana, and the so-called hard drugs has protected the Witnesses. With the use of the Scriptures, they have also been able to help many thousands of persons whose lives were being ruined by drug abuse" (*Proclaimers,* 1993, p. 180,181).

Baptized members who smoked could still be excluded. So the new liberalism was spotty at best, especially when you add in the tobacco ban's presumed proprieties for Society representation and sales opportunities: The publishers could not smell of tobacco or have nicotine fingers when they canvassed as booksellers. The ban seemed yet another grim encroachment on individual freedom (also the tobacco prohibition was, as you presumably remember, an inheritance from the Adventists).

Raymond Franz, who still sat comfortably at the destabilized top, was tasked with writing articles for *The Watchtower* in 1974–1975. The articles were intended to mitigate the situation for members who had contact with excluded family. The articles encouraged the Witnesses, elders and judicial committees, to "manifest a more merciful attitude in many areas of their contacts with disfellowshipped persons," and soften the rigid policies governing dealings with disfellowshipped family members. (*Conscience*, 1983, p. 308)

From February 1976, another change moved through the Society's branch offices around the world. A branch office's leadership was now subject to a committee of elders consisting of three or more "mature men" with one as a permanent Branch Committee coordinator. The scheme adopted by the Governing Body was intended to prevent certain unfortunate tendencies around the world, as some Branch Servants in foreign countries had developed prima donna complexes.

The new system shared power within a country among committee members, so any unauthorized actions could be prevented. This tightening of control, which between 1976 and 1980 was experienced as liberalization in some places, soon led to an intensified hunt for the "liberal" elements in Brooklyn, particularly starting in 1980, and resulted in a broader purge directed by the highest level of the Society.

Brooklyn was moving toward a *complete regimentation.*

New Executive Committees

In 1971, the Pennsylvania corporation board consisted of eight members, but it expanded to seventeen in 1975. Part of the effort to restrict the power of the presidents, vice presidents and the societies (previously the president and vice president had actually been "the Society") was to make a fundamental change in top management. The designation of the Pennsylvania-based board as the "Governing Body" was part of that change and uplifted the previously rather *pale* board with a growing prestige. Sitting on this council became almost synonymous with a divine status among the common membership, a development the early leadership would not have particularly favored.

The council's influence was further strengthened through a system introduced in 1976. All activities conducted by the Watchtower Society worldwide were now subject to six newly formed Executive Committees. The committees consisted of different ranking members of the Governing Body, who thereby controlled everything.

By 1993, these changes are seen as epoch-making:

"Jehovah's Witnesses were well fed spiritually before 1976. But an examination of what has taken place since then under the direction of the Governing Body and its Writing Committee reveals that the waters of truth have flowed out in ever greater quantities and in more diversified forms" (*Proclaimers,* 1993, p. 110).

However, there is also room for a small admission on the same page of *Proclaimers*: "At times, specific needs of Jehovah's people have been addressed by means of timely counsel in the pages of *The Watchtower.* For example, the worldwide report of the activity of Jehovah's Witnesses for 1977/78 reflected a *decrease* in the number sharing in the preaching work. Was the decrease at least partly due to disappointed expectations concerning 1975? Perhaps. But there were other influencing factors. What could be done?" (*Proclaimers,* 1993, p. 110)

Of course the answer was: *More work.*

"The Governing Body took steps to strengthen the conviction among Jehovah's Witnesses that *there was a need to continue zealously proclaiming* the Kingdom from house to house" (Ibid., 1993, p. 111; italics are mine).

The theme is almost the same today.

When was Eve Created?

In 1993, the Watchtower leader's looked back at events, and in the softening light of post-rationalization seemed to forget all the negative aspects which were anyway overshadowed by the Watchtower Society's many new activities. Thus, the speculation about the length of time between Adam's creation and Eve's was also apparently forgotten. For instance, if Eve was created a year after Adam, it would upset the establishment of the Millennium from 1975 to 1976. But how much time elapsed? How many weeks, months or years? In 1993 it appears the answer may have been years!

Adam must have been a bachelor quite a long time.

As I sought to clarify earlier, Watchtower management must have had an overall plan reaching far into the future—yes, perhaps well into the 21st century! And we know now, thanks to Raymond Franz's disclosures, that the leaders even discussed the possibility of revising the entire schedule because top-level management's members increasingly lost confidence in the previous timeline.

The fateful year 1914, marking the end of the so called *gentile times* and the beginning of the *time of the end*, played a key role in the context of "this generation," as some of them would survive until Armageddon. In 1980 a reportedly imaginative presentation by some Society members led the council to discuss whether the starting point of the "generation" could be calculated from 1957, the year the space age began and the first Russian *Sputnik* was launched. However, they chose not to alter 1914 as the final year of the gentile times. The high-ranking Watchtower officers, Albert Schroeder, Karl Klein and Grant Suites, stood behind the 1957 proposal. The fact that they were not dismissed from the council shows, as Raymond Franz wrote indirectly, that other board members were also uncertain about the whole issue. That the space dog Laika and the first man in space Cosmonaut Gagarin had indirectly found places in the Jehovah's Witnesses' teaching system was very ingenious, but the idea was met with skepticism.

The three prominent members of the council, Schroeder, Klein and Suites, had submitted their emergency solution in a document featuring a presumption drawn from various Bible commentaries originating with other denominations: The "generation" (Matt. 24:34) "mostly denotes the sense of contemporaries." Further, all "these things" (Matt. 24:33) are not specifically aimed at 1914, but perhaps may refer to "the space age 1957 onward." Why? Because Matthew 24:29–30 talks about "powers of heaven" which "shall be shaken." Therefore, 1957!

The council members' document, as Raymond Franz notes in his book, says: "In that case it would then be the contemporary generation of mankind living since 1957." This was a bold assertion, and the majority of the board members obviously sensed it put them on shaky ground.

Again according to Raymond Franz, the proposal was rejected. Still, the presentation and rejection shows the serious consideration applied to the interpretation of the phrase, "this generation" (KJ); later, in 1995, it was partly accepted when this new aspect again gave rise to some debate. Likely it will rise again in the future and cause even more members to flee the movement. We'll examine this in more detail later; it was obviously not the last time this teaching point was adjusted. It happened again in *The Watch Tower* of April 15, 2010. (See *Conscience*, 1983, p. 219-222; *WT*, April 15, 2010, p. 10)

Internal insecurities, including upheavals in the organization that led to a more pleasant atmosphere of liberation for a few years and alleviated some of the frustration over the missing Millennium in 1975, likely had a backlash that led to a tightening at the Society's top. This would have culminated around 1980. The Society had to strike back. The *Proclaimers* explains this indirectly:

"Another situation also needed attention. By 1980, a number of persons who had shared in the activities of Jehovah's Witnesses for some years, including some who had served prominently in the organization, had been in various ways trying to cause division and oppose the work Jehovah's Witnesses were doing. To fortify Jehovah's people against such apostate influence, *The Watch-*

tower carried such articles as 'Remain "Solid in the Faith" ' (August 1, 1980), 'Quietly Bringing in Destructive Sects' (September 15, 1983) and 'Reject Apostasy, Cling to the Truth' (April 1, 1983), while the book *'Let Your Kingdom Come'* (1981) emphasized the claim that the Kingdom is at hand, having been established in the heavens in 1914. The Governing Body did not allow the efforts of opposers to distract it from the primary objective of Jehovah's Witnesses—proclaiming God's Kingdom!" (*Proclaimers*, 1993, p. 111)

However, it was not only a question of a few *prominent* individuals, but actually a *movement within the movement*. Several members of the Brooklyn staff were removed from their posts during this clean-up campaign, including Raymond Franz and Gilead School superintendent Edward A. Dunlap. In his book, *Crisis of Conscience*, published for the first time in English in 1983, and later in new editions, Franz detailed this process. By eliminating all those who "murmured,"[268] the Society hoped to eliminate the rebel threat, so growth could continue undisturbed.

Yet, outside the United States, unrest fermented and bubbled. I will offer some harrowing examples later in this volume.

Growth Eastern and Southern

Proclaimers states that, since 1976, "the waters of truth" under the direction of the Governing Body "have flowed out in ever greater quantities" and ever faster from "God's visible organization" in New York. This means a turnover of enormous quantities of books, magazines and publications in one uninterrupted stream in every language. (*Proclaimers*, p. 110)

The customers were, among other interested persons, the growing number of new converts, who through the newly established, private "home Bible studies" were gradually brought into the organization's routines:

Stage 1: The interested one is found by house-to-house work.
Stage 2: The establishment of a home Bible study.
Stage 3: Invitation to come to the meetings in the Kingdom Hall.
Stage 4: Request to participate in house-to-house work.

Thus the circle was closed, and the new, quickly incubated publishers could go forth and find even more new candidates for future work in the field. In this way, each member became a *regular publisher*, who could *almost be sure* of admission into the New World after Armageddon.

Society statistics show that, after some years of declining activity, levels rose again around the world—so dramatically even, that the movement has been called the "fastest growing religious movement in the world" since the late 1950s. (*WT*, Feb. 1, 1958; *WT*, Dec. 22, 1978; *WT*, April 1, 2001)

And the growth continued indeed, although it later revealed to be a qualified truth, which I will discuss in coming pages.

Looking at the published, simplified graphical representations of growth found in the 1993 history book, there is only a membership drop in the years just after 1975. The growth curves start to rise again, as if 1975 and its disappointments were completely nonexistent. (*Proclaimers*, 1993, p. 108-117)

The Society saw strong growth in the number of pioneers, the number of volunteer Bethel staff members, literature sales, new congregations, and finally, an impressive increase in new members, who like those before them were convinced to look forward to imminent deliverance. At this time no new date was offered, although 1984, according to Raymond Franz, was mentioned unofficially. *The Watchtower* often assured its subscribers, however, that Armageddon was very, very close. (*Conscience*, 1983, p. 218)

From 1984 to 1989 the Society was booming in all areas.

With 1989 came unprecedented opportunities through the fall of Communism. Jehovah's Witnesses almost invaded the once tightly controlled countries to the east, spreading the movement with broad, aggressive strokes. Thus in these years, there was growth and more growth.

The Society's top elite were extremely proud of the results, which conveniently confirmed for them that the 1975 mistake—as seen in the statistics and perspectives of the growth curves—had been a good investment. The management's not-particularly well-intentioned regret over the great misfortune they had caused among the generally disappointed members was to be overlooked. Now everyone had to pitch in. It was the "time of trouble"[269] or the period that began in 1914 and would end before "this generation" was gone. The climax at Armageddon could come at any time, so one had to be on the safe side.

There appeared, however, to be some *unexpected* growth problems:

In recent decades, the movement experienced difficulties with youth members—including the pleasures of tobacco, alcohol and pre-marital sex—and in response put a firmer stamp on Jehovah's Witnesses' own children and adolescents. Many young people within the organization could no longer live with the many "moral" prohibitions. They began to experiment with all that was banned, which often led them to depart the movement. This was unfortunate, since retention of children and young adults was key to consistent membership growth.

The Watchtower quoted a theology professor who said "churches today grow usually by *biological growth* ... or by *transfer* growth (when a newcomer transfers his or her membership from another local church)" (*WT*, Jan. 1, 2004; italics by *WT*). But this obviously applied just as much to the Jehovah's Witnesses' movement. Therefore, a number of new books were soon published, bound in wild, vibrant colors with gold lettering, to influence the young members who had grown up within the organization and contributed to the admirable growth rates. The books encouraged them to adhere to the Watchtower Society's perceptions of moral behavior.

Some of these titles were: *Your Youth—Getting the Best Out Of It* (1976), *Questions Young People Ask—Answers That Work* (1989) and an illustrated

Bible, *My Book of Bible Stories*, published in 1978. Another publication was aimed at the family unit, *Making Your Family Life Happy* (1978); this was also brightly colored and eye-catching. (*Proclaimers,* 1993, p. 110)

The Society's increasing investment in children and young people within the movement is reflected in publication of the illustrated book *Learn from the Great Teacher* and by the number of international conventions held in 2003. The first English edition of the book had five million copies produced. While significant growth occurred throughout the world, the closer members came to the year 2000 the clearer it became that new growth was mainly in eastern countries in Africa and South America while stagnation trends appeared in Europe, the United States and Canada. In Denmark for example, there were apparent signs of decline.

The Society's Vast Property Holdings

The decrease in the influx of new members, particularly in the Western hemisphere has not, however, characterized the Society's property acquisition and construction activity. Rather the opposite. Since the 1970s, the Society's operations in this field remained in a constant "boom." As recently as 1996, according to the *Watchtower* article "Expansions—With Jehovah's Blessing" illustrated with eleven photographs of the Society's properties in New York, they justified their monumental efforts:

"In 1969, when the last Brooklyn Bethel residence building was dedicated, there was a peak of 1,336,112 Witnesses preaching the good news of God's Kingdom worldwide. But in 1995 there were 5,199,895 doing so, more than three-and-a-half times as many. Thus, to keep pace with the growing demand for Bible literature, the Brooklyn Bethel family has increased from 1,042 regular members in 1969 to more than 3,360, who now live in 22 residences" (*WT*, April, 15, 1996).

Since 1969, the Society's leadership acquired many residences to use as housing for staff; in all they had bought and renovated seventeen residential structures and two other buildings. They had also rented several floors of the nearby Towers Hotel until December 1973 when President Knorr wrote a letter to the hotel's board of directors informing them "that the Society planned to 'move out of the Towers Hotel at October 1, 1974.' " This seems to be a somewhat suspicious coincidence of *prophetic dates*—especially one of *October 1*, and just a year before the greatly anticipated *October 1975!* (Ibid., p. 26)

Presumably this threat to vacate centered on the rather obvious proposition that Brooklyn just wanted to *encourage* the owners of Towers Hotel to sell the building to the Watchtower Society so they could easily resolve accommodation shortages for the staff. However, there was a problem, because the other tenants needed to receive notice. "We'll empty the building for you," the Towers Hotel's management promised, after suggesting they'd sell it to the Society. Afterwards, Watchtower management bought the property at a fair price. From what I am told, Towers Hotel's managers or owners were members of the Jehovah's Witnesses, which seems evident, though indirectly, from a story in *The Watchtower*, April 1996.[270]

At an inauguration program, September 18, 1995, where Brother Couch informed the participants of the almost *miraculous* details regarding the purchase of the Towers Hotel, it was officially noted that "Jehovah God has truly blessed the expansion of his Witnesses at the location of their world headquarters in Brooklyn, New York." About the acquisition of these properties, Couch posed the following in an address:

"'Why did Brother Knorr write that letter?' Couch asked his fascinated audience. 'He probably didn't know himself, but that is the thing that sold the Towers Hotel to the Watch Tower Society.' "

The location in Brooklyn was ideal because the Witness management had linked the whole complex with tunnels between the buildings and under the street. Couch remarked on the many building acquisitions in mid-Brooklyn, noting that virtually every one had "an interesting story behind it that would point to one thing—that Jehovah God is the one *who directed the visible organization to acquire that particular building*" (p. 27; italics are mine).

This huge construction and expansion activity surprised some members, as is indirectly reflected in an article in *The Watchtower* January 1, 1986, with the heading, "Building for an Eternal Future":

"'But why,' someone may ask, 'are there so many expansion projects when we stand face-to-face with Armageddon?' The answer is that Jehovah's organization does not 'close up shop' with the approach of Armageddon. That is 'closing time' only for Satan's organization. Jehovah's organization is building for an eternal future. Whether or not man-made structures weather the storm of Armageddon, we know that God's organization will survive as a going concern and that Jehovah will use it and those who loyally support it, establishing eternal peace and security in the glorious earthly Paradise of God's promise."

On the pages 352 to 401 of *Proclaimers*, we see the colorful and flamboyant presentation of the Society's worldwide property holdings. And, naturally, as one comes to understand the magnitude of the activities, he or she will inevitably ask: "How can this multinational company finance such a gigantic construction project?"

The answer? Member donations, wills and gifts, where the Watchtower Society receives a *substantial portion* of the donated funds.

Beyond this, many Witnesses also commit themselves with others in the congregation to a form of tithing, where they pay regular, fixed, monthly contributions for example, reportedly as a declaration of commitment. Even *renegades,* or members existing on the fringe, can maintain such a commitment through a transition period. The Witnesses themselves also pay for the literature they need for canvassing and soliciting new members, making large literature purchases so they can spread publications around and in some cases give them away; in this way they help pay the publishing bills, even if the funds come from their own pockets.

The worldwide preaching and education work was able to continue unabated, which seems to have been the plan from the outset.

Problems Ahead

As always, more problems loomed ominously ahead. During the next few years the very foundation of Jehovah's Witnesses' existence would be called into question by the movement's interior critics: the unfortunate who put their hopes on *1975*, and were *left adrift* by the Jehovah's Witnesses' own Great Disappointment. The Society took steps to quickly neutralize these members. Or those who preferred simply abandoned the perceived sinking ship. Unfortunately, the questions that drove them out came only after they had become renegades, and then it was too late for them to influence their previous theocratic family. Nobody dared listen to them anymore.

Still, one member made his voice heard, and that member's voice came to reverberate in the ears of all, whether they wanted to hear or not.

Chapter 28

"Brooklyn"
Shaken to its Foundations

Carl Olof Jonsson was a Swedish Jehovah's Witness whose research and conclusions upset the Jehovah's Witnesses' central organization in New York down to its footings.

Jonsson was a pioneer, a full-time evangelist or publisher. One day a person in one of his home Bible study meetings challenged Jonsson to prove that the year the Society set as the year for the destruction of the city of Jerusalem by Babylon was correct. The man drew Jonsson's attention to the fact that all historians believed the destruction happened approximately twenty years later than the Society teaches (607 BC), in 587 or 586 BC.

Jonsson reported:

"I was well aware of this, but the man wanted to know the reasons why historians preferred the latter date. I indicated that their dating surely was nothing but a guess, based on defective ancient sources and records. Like other Witnesses, I assumed that the Society's dating of the desolation of Jerusalem to 607 BCE was based on the Bible and therefore could not be upset by those secular sources. However, I promised the man I would look into the matter. / As a result, I undertook a research that turned out to be far more extensive and thoroughgoing than I had expected. It continued periodically for several years, from 1968 until the end of 1975. By then the growing burden of evidence against the 607 BCE date forced me reluctantly to conclude that the Watch Tower Society was wrong" (*The Gentile Times Reconsidered*, 2004, p. 7; the following citations also refer to Jonsson's publication).

Jonsson discussed the discrepancy with some close friends, and they could not refute his findings. Thereafter, he began to prepare a systematic treatise on the subject, which he eventually sent to Brooklyn in 1977. The treatise was later expanded and published in 1983. In 2004 the fourth revised edition of his remarkable book, *The Gentile Times Reconsidered*, appeared.

Before Jonsson arrived at his conclusion, much had changed in his life. Also in 1977, he tried to initiate correspondence with the Governing Body regarding the matter, and it soon became clear that New York management was unable to refute his arguments. Before 1980 they did not even attempt to discuss his inquiry. Meanwhile, however, Jonsson was repeatedly warned against discussing his findings with others. A letter from headquarters dated January 17, 1978, warned him in clear terms:

"However, no matter how strong the argumentation may be in support of those views, they must, for the present, be regarded as your personal viewpoint. *It is not something that you should talk about or try to advance among other members of the congregation*" (p. 8; italics are mine).

From the time the Society's officials received Jonsson's first letter (dated May 20, 1977), they realized that wide-spread knowledge and perhaps even publication of his investigation could cause a real disaster in the movement. Their warning letter continued:

"We are sure that you can appreciate that if changes of importance are made they should be made in an orderly way.... We are also sure that you appreciate that for individuals to advance and advocate such changes would have, not a unifying effect, but a divisive one producing confusion.... It is hoped that you will observe the counseling supplied above. In due course we hope to look into your treatise and evaluate what is contained therein" (p. 8, 9).

The letter was not signed, but the initials under the letterhead (GEA: ESB) seemed to point to Lloyd Barry, one of the members of the Governing Body, who in this case was a hardliner.[271]

Headquarters gave Jonsson the impression it needed more time to investigate the whole matter, however, by May 1980, Jonsson was again asked not to publicize or discuss his discoveries, as they could "raise serious questions and problems among the brothers" (p. 8).

At a meeting for European branch office managers in August 1978, Albert D. Schroeder, a member of the Governing Body, claimed "that there was a campaign going on both inside the movement and from outside to have the Society's 607 BCE–1914 CE chronology overthrown" (p. 10).

In September Jonsson was summoned to a hearing with two representatives of the Watch Tower Society in Sweden, Rolf Svensson, a district overseer, and Hasse Hulth, a circuit overseer. They had been authorized by Society headquarters to arrange this hearing because the brothers in Brooklyn had become "deeply concerned" about Jonsson's investigation. Jonsson was once again warned against spreading the information he had gathered. The Society did not need nor wish individual Jehovah's Witnesses to become involved in investigations of this type. That sort of thing should be done exclusively by the Governing Body. A perfectly normal start to an *inquisitorial process*!

Subsequently, Jonsson gave up his post as an elder in his congregation and also resigned from other tasks and assignments within the organization. Soon, word spread that he rejected the Society's chronology.

A hue and cry, initiated by top management in Sweden, went out against Jonsson and his accomplices, and all sorts of invectives of the worst kind flew madly about: rebellious, presumptuous, false prophets, small prophets who worked out their own little chronology, evil servants, blasphemers, immoral, lawless ones and demon-possessed. (p. 10)

It is obvious that Jonsson's impressive study, which had fully pierced the marrow of the Brooklyn leaders, had left them short of arguments and probably quite fearful. The slanderous words aimed at Jonsson show the leaders were struck deep in their souls; all they could offer was abusive language in response to Jonsson's very fine scholarly study. Doubtless their whole campaign was aimed at minimizing and repairing the damage Jonsson caused among the members who heard of his study, while there was still time to stem the spread of his views. The ordinary members had to be protected from Jonsson's influence, and this was best accomplished by expelling the critic. And that is exactly what they set out to do.

At the highest level of Brooklyn they had been aware for some time that Jonsson's thesis might eventually be published. Therefore, before this could happen, Jonsson and his supporters had to be stigmatized and expelled as quickly as possible.

Condemnations also appeared in *The Watchtower* magazine, which alluded to Jonsson and his Witness supporters with these words:

"Lawless persons have even tried to penetrate the true Christian congregation, arguing that the 'promised presence' of our Lord is not in this day. They ridicule the elders and dispute the Master's appointment of 'the faithful and discreet slave' to care for his Kingdom interests on earth. (2 Pet. 3:3, 4; Matt. 24:45-47) Persons of this kind are included in Jesus' warning recorded at Matthew 7:15-23: 'Be on the watch for the false prophets...'" (*WT*, July 15, 1979, p. 13).

In December 1978, Jonsson wrote to Albert Schroeder:

"How tragic, then, to observe how a situation develops, where the attention is drawn away from the question raised—the validity of the 607 BCE date—and directed to the person who raised it, and he—not the question—is regarded as the problem! How is it possible that a situation of this kind develops in our movement?" (p. 11)

Jonsson received a reply, but his questions were left unanswered.

Finally, late in 1979, something happened in the case. Bengt Hanson, who was the branch coordinator in Sweden, visited Jonsson to discuss the matter. Subsequently, early in 1980, he wrote to the Governing Body to press for a response to Jonsson's inquiries. Hanson acknowledged that it was not Jonsson who was the problem, but his research results, which until then had not been addressed or challenged. Hanson's answer arrived in March 1980 and was a rehash of previous positions. The top leaders clearly demonstrated they did not have the courage to face the facts because the consequence would be invalidation of the Society's entire timeline and chronological system. Thus, the very foundation of the Society's gospel—in view of the world's alleged imminent end—had to be reinforced without delay until Armageddon arrived. The Society's whole structure was, so to speak, pierced in the heart. If the leaders made concessions to false prophets, they would risk having everything collapse. (p. 12)

Jonsson replied to the letter and added more reasons for his thesis; the Society remained silent about the added evidence until they published a new book, *Let Your Kingdom Come*, in 1981, wherein they tried to assuage some of the criticism's bite.

It would be futile here to repeat the meandering argumentation of this book, which did not contribute anything new but merely maintained the prior unsustainable dogmatic arguments. The book reiterated yet again the old, hackneyed positions around the 1914 date, claiming the 2,520 years that had elapsed since 607 BC ended in 1914, and that the events surrounding the First World War had been predicted by founder Charles Taze Russell:

"Thirty-four years before 1914, the magazine Zion's Watch Tower and Herald of Christ's Presence, in its issues of December 1879 and March 1880, was pointing to 1914 as a marked date in Bible prophecy. An article in its issue of June 1880 called attention to the approaching end of 'the Times of the Gentiles (Luke xxi. 24).' Though the writer at the time did not understand the full implication of events about to take place, he showed from Bible chronology that a period of 'seven times,' or 2,520 years, of domination in government by godless nations, starting from the first desolating of ancient Jerusalem, was due to end in 'AD 1914' " (*Let Your Kingdom Come*, 1981, p. 127).

As I have pointed out, initially Russell was only sure of one thing after 1914: The gentile times had ended in 1914. Of course, this would always be just an unverifiable claim. In addition, it was not Russell that had originally calculated 1914 as the period-ending year, but the Adventist Barbour and others before him.

In *Let Your Kingdom Come* the Watchtower Society attempted to refute Jonsson, but the readers were not able to see the issues around the Society's chronology. The Watchtower directors in New York knew this only too well. The members had long ago left that kind of complex and also hopelessly uninteresting doctrine to the faithful and wise servant in Brooklyn (or in Pittsburgh, Pennsylvania), where these matters were actually settled.

Anyway, the events were leading to Jonsson's being ostracized by his local congregation, as it also has happened to scores of other members as far back as I can remember. Jonsson prepared himself for the rapidly approaching break with the organization. This development was meant to hang over him as a threat because the organization would tear his connection with family and friends and shatter the life he had lived as a sincere Jehovah's Witness.

After twenty-six years as an active Witness, as Jonsson wrote, he prepared to leave the Watchtower organization in 1982:

"It was quite clear to me that this would mean a complete break with the whole social world I had been part of during all those years. The rules of the

Watch Tower Society require Jehovah's Witnesses to cut off all contacts with those who break with the organization, whether this break occurs by excommunication or by voluntary resignation. I knew that I would not only lose virtually all my friends, but also all my relatives within the organization (of which there were over seventy, including a brother and two sisters with their families, cousins and their families, and so on). I would be regarded and treated as 'dead,' even if my physical 'execution' would have to be postponed until the imminent 'battle of Armageddon,' a battle in which the Witnesses expect Jehovah God to annihilate forever all who are not associated with their organization" (p. 16, 17).

Everything that now happened to Jonsson followed the prescription for dealing with a "wolf in sheep's clothing"; first came a friendly opening maneuver, and then the vehement strike. The man who least of all deserved such hateful and unfair treatment was attacked insidiously and entirely for the purpose of cleansing the organization of dangerous infections, as discussion and criticism are considered to be.

Throughout the process, Jonsson behaved with theocratic correctness, as the record says, showing all possible respect for the leadership, who he still saw as his spiritual brethren. Brooklyn dismissed him with the excuse that they had not had time to look into his treatise, probably a dodge for them to gain more time. The battle was to be prepared, and above all, the fortifications had to be consolidated before the news began to leak out.

Jonsson's plan was now to publish his entire treatise in book form as soon as possible. But when he was almost finished with the manuscript he received a letter from the Swedish branch office, dated May 4, 1982. It contained a call for an investigation, as a judicial committee—or a "court of inquisition" as Jonsson called it—consisting of specially appointed representatives from the Society, who would undertake to "find out about your attitude toward our belief and the organization" (p. 17). Jonsson wanted to have the meeting postponed. He believed it was appropriate for the committee members, as a precondition for reaching an informed decision, should be given the opportunity to make a thorough investigation of his extensive, bullet-proof material. After this, he argued, they could be better prepared for a discussion of the matter.

Neither the branch office nor the judicial committee members wanted such a discussion, and in a new letter, the original summons was maintained. It was clear to Jonsson that his sentence had already been handed down, and when, in light of that condition, he refused to appear before the committee, the committee members decided without further discussion to expel Jonsson on June 9, 1982.

Jonsson appealed the decision, hoping to gain more time for a proper review of his material. He still—as a condition for his appearance before a judicial committee—wanted its members to give his thesis a thorough investigation. Without addressing his appeal the Swedish branch leaders appointed an appeal committee, and on July 7, 1982, without further delay, they upheld the earlier decision. Subsequently, Jonsson was effectively cut off from the Jehovah's Witnesses in Sweden.

This case was solely undertaken because Jonsson's research and thesis showed he did not fully agree with the Society's doctrines. The very heart of the matter, the thesis and its arguments and substance, was of no interest to the leadership in New York or in Sweden, for that matter; there only concern was for his act of dissention.

Brooklyn Had No Choice

What on earth was so disrespectful to the Watch Tower Society in Brooklyn that it would cause such drastic reactions?

Jonsson had, in his comprehensive study, demonstrated that Brooklyn was *deliberately lying* about the basis for the calculation that the gentile times had ended in 1914 (if you at all accept their speculative way of thinking).[272] His study simply showed that Jerusalem's destruction did not happen in 607 BC, as the Society claims, but in 587 or 586. But the leaders could not, of course, either in 1982 nor in the 21st century as I summarize the order of events, accept the fact that twenty years were unaccounted for. Instead they have ensconced themselves behind *thick walls of ignorance.* By extensive expulsion actions against anyone who proposed to have an opinion different from the leaders at headquarters, they now tried to make it a criminal offence to disagree with the Society.

The core problem was, of course, that if Jonsson was right about the missing twenty years, the destruction of Jerusalem did not happen in the year 607 BC but in *587* causing 1914, the fundamental basis for the Watchtower's apocalyptic chronology, to be incorrect. They would need to revise calculations, making 1934 the important year. Did anything special happen in that year? No! And although 1934—which might have given the organization more time to craft a solution—had been suggested by some Brooklyn and Pittsburgh leaders (one of Russell's readers had realized this deferment option even before 1914), they could not accept this model in the 1980s. The year 1914 was too *cemented* and *sacred.* It could not be touched without risking the collapse of the entire teaching, or at least creating problems that could halt the organization's progress, inhibit the sale of literature, cause membership growth to stagnate and the expansion program to shrink. Such a development was a truly horrific scenario for the leaders in New York. They knew deep down that Armageddon predictions were *just bluff and rhetoric*; but the prospect of seeing the growth stop was the *worst of all.* It was simply too dangerous to alter anything about 1914.

So the policy of the organization *post-Jonsson*:

Nothing was to be touched. No changes were to be made. All had to be left as it was.

We have Jonsson's report about events to study, but fortunately, for this incident, we also have corroborating information from an inside source: Raymond Franz. Raymond's history is linked with Jonsson's, because Raymond worked at the very top of the "Tower" and had great authority as a very trusted member of the Governing Body during this time.

Raymond reported that as he edited a major Society publication, *Aid to Bible Understanding*, released in 1969–1971 by the Watch Tower Society, he discovered that "the Society's date of 607 BCE for Jerusalem's destruction by Babylon was contradicted by all known, historical evidence." Raymond and his team consulted various secular researchers, and found *no* support for the Society's dating the destruction of Jerusalem to 607 BC. (*Conscience,* 1983, p. 140)

Like everyone else at the top of the organization, Raymond, despite sustainable argument from non-Society scholars, still preferred to rely on the Watchtower Society's "Bible chronology," since he was sure it was the historians' reasoning that was flawed.

Raymond maintained this view until 1977 when he saw how Carl Olof Jonsson's thesis was received in the Watch Tower hierarchy.

In 1979, Raymond made copies of the first twenty pages of Jonsson's thesis. Each member of the Governing Body received one, however, it appears they were not prepared to even discuss it let alone render an opinion. One of the members, Lyman Swingle, who was head of the editorial staff of the Governing Body, drew the council's attention to the Society's earlier dogmatic statements, explaining that he—in the context of what had happened in 1975—did not want to be "misled" again. (Ibid., p. 215)

Raymond pointed out that not only was 607 BC not supported among historians, but the members who had experienced 1914 as adults and potential witnesses to Armageddon were now quite elderly. For example, those who were twenty years old in 1914 were eighty-five by 1979; those who were thirty now ninety-five, etc. Lloyd Barry, however, did not see any problems with this, as in the Soviet Union "there are regions where people live to be 130 years old" (Ibid., p. 216).

The discussion ended with the decision to continue on the old path. Raymond, however, urged that the whole issue should be examined in minute detail. Naturally, the majority did not see any need for this. They determined to adhere to the 1914 dogma and the doctrine that "this generation" would not die before the outbreak of Armageddon (p. 184). At this point, according to Raymond Franz, editorial coordinator Lyman Swingle expressed the following sharp opinion about their decision:

"All right, if that is what you want to do. But at least you know that as far as 1914 is concerned, Jehovah's Witnesses got the whole thing—lock, stock and barrel—from the Second Adventists" (Ibid, p. 216).

Sufficient evidence exists to indicate the council members did not agree on the year 1914 at that time. There were strong conflicting views. Even President

Knorr had been in doubt before his death in 1977, as he stated during a meeting of the Governing Body on February 19, 1975, the same year many members of the movement expected the end of the world:

"There are some things I know—I know Jehovah is God, that Christ Jesus is his son, that he gave his life as a ransom for us, that there is a resurrection. Other things I'm not so certain about. 1914—I don't know. We have talked about 1914 for a long time. We may be right and I hope we are" (Ibid., p. 217).

At the time of the 1979 meeting, Raymond was concerned because the organization called on members to uphold the 1914 dogma; while doubts expressed about the date could be a criterion for possible expulsion, the top management internally expressed doubts about the dogma yet never took action against themselves.

During the Writing Committee's meeting before the Governing Body's full board meeting on November 14, 1979, the committee discussed whether they had to continue to use the year 1914. They managed to agree that, in any case, they should not advertise or promote the date. Karl Klein, one of the old men at the top, had even suggested reinstating a past practice: If one wanted something changed, for example a certain teaching, the old information would not be mentioned for some time. Then, if any change came, the previous teaching would have faded and the change "would not make such a strong impression" (Ibid., p. 217).

Various aspects of the 1914 calculation and teachings were discussed by top management. Lloyd Barry, considered to be Knorr's successor after his death, thought they should remain firm in asserting 1914. Just two months later, Schroeder, Klein and Grant Suiter stated the 1914-teaching was one of the key doctrines that members had to believe if they wanted to avoid being expelled.

Unfortunately, Raymond Franz gave no further information about management's handling of Jonsson's treatise, but I believe I am not entirely wrong when I assume that the thesis was discussed in the corridors and the subterranean tunnels of the Watch Tower buildings, and that it partly was there and partly during council meetings that they ultimately, to curb further infections, decided to maintain the hard line against Jonsson and the like-minded.

In fact, there was nothing else to do. Either they said yes to Jonsson, and then they could probably pack up the whole movement, or they could insist on 1914 and expel Jonsson.

They eagerly showed him the way out!

Chapter 29

Jette Studies Babylonian List of Kings and Loses her Children

In the early 1980s Jette Svane lived in the town of Randers on the Jutland peninsula, where Denmark connects with Germany. Jette once ran a small fashion business in central Randers, but following exclusion and divorce, she sold her business and applied herself to designing websites. As the incidents of her disfellowshipping unfolded, she was hit by a series of family related disasters, and it is these that this chapter is about.

Before all these calamities, and before her exclusion and divorce, Jette and others wondered what occurred within the movement during the late 1970s and early 1980s. For some time, the mood in the movement had been quite promising with the more-liberal spirit circulating in the congregations. For example, in the Jehovah's Witnesses' assembly hall in Silkeborg, another town in Jutland, several Witnesses began gathering once a month to sing *Kingdom songs*. This also occurred elsewhere in the country; a kind of *alsang*[273] (a patriotic singing), as during the German occupation of Denmark from 1939 to 1945. All who took part were apparently exhilarated and more or less uplifted by the new spirit.

But perhaps it was, in fact, an "evil spirit," perhaps a kind of *demon obsession*, because soon the Denmark headquarters intervened in the fun and prohibited the singing. *Theocracy* meant divine top management by God's visible organization on earth, the Watch Tower Bible and Tract Society, located at 117 Adams Street, Brooklyn, New York, to be exact. A *very visible* organization. The rationale was that the Governing Body did not initiate or support the practice of gathering to sing; therefore, it was totally wrong because it had originated with the ordinary members.

The ban meant no more live orchestral music at the assemblies. Perhaps a tape recorder could be used to supply music but only at the big conventions. At small assemblies with about 900 present, they had to be content with singing to piano accompaniment performed by an attending member.

About this same time, a story emerged about how a member who enjoyed playing the violin, and meeting privately and regularly with four or five other Witnesses to practice, was suddenly banned from meeting in this way. She wrote to Brooklyn to ask why gathering to play violin had been banned; she was told to simply accept that this was the case.

Even the management in Denmark had been carried away with the exhilarating sense of freedom during this period. In the late seventies, after convention-closing time at a gathering in Aarhus, Jutland, the participants enjoyed Danish manager Richard E. Abrahamson serving as a song conductor. In January 1981, Abrahamson was called to headquarters in New York. Whether it was because of the common singing and directing with his baton is not easy to say. It was probably not—but certainly the singing and music situation was interpreted as alarming because it came from the bottom of the movement, and had even, as I am told, led to an ominous spreading of the disturbing new habit to brothers south of the Danish border.

Contemporary with these events, the headquarters reportedly began to warn families and young people against gathering in groups, even if it was, in all innocence, for studying *The Watchtower* magazine. A traveling circuit overseer said from the rostrum at an assembly that everyone had to be obedient in all things and accept anything which came from the Governing Body. They were clearly afraid even the most innocuous social gatherings could lead to too much gossiping in corners.

Returning to Jette, my source on this issue, she learned later that as all these things were happening in Denmark there had been a cleansing of the Society in New York. Employees at headquarters had been meeting for weekly Bible study, and this had led to some differing doctrinal views. Though nothing indicated a conspiracy was afoot, management reportedly had a tantrum about the situation and began a wave of cleansing, which among other things drew the presidential nephew, Raymond Franz, into the melee.

Reportedly, in 1980 fifty people left Brooklyn headquarters over this.

Printing-factory headman Tom Cabeen, former overseer of the Watchtower Printing and Pressroom, friend of Raymond Franz and a later (in 2006, according to research[274]) defector who joined the Catholic Church, had borrowed Carl Olof Jonsson's study of the gentile times, to read in secret—in the restroom. In time, eighteen of the fifty workers in the editorial department were so shaken by the Swede's evidence that they packed their suitcases. Tom Cabeen was one of them.

A city overseer (a leader who coordinates the local activities in larger cities) from Canada, John Poole, who was also an elder, had been given—with Jonsson's agreement—the *confidential* task of checking the English translation of Jonsson's manuscript. The Society had no idea Poole was the manuscript's proofreader, even though he was officially still a Witness. He locked himself up to carefully review the manuscript in private. Three days later he emerged and said, very seriously: "We have been deceived!"

John Poole, who was highly educated, moved in a circle that included Professor James Penton of Lethbridge, Canada. James Penton authored the book *Apocalypse Delayed;* when Penton was ostracized for his criticism of the organization in 1981, about fifty people—including Poole—left the movement (ref. letter from C. O. Jonsson, February 19, 2004).

Initially, these events circulated as unconfirmed rumors that Jette Svane knew nothing about, but she and others felt something was afoot in Brooklyn.

The spreading spirit of independence was increasingly invoked by the Society as a negatively charged concept and members soon realized that independent, personal opinions differing from the Society's were considered sinful, a sign of arrogance and lack of humility for Jehovah's visible organization.

Still, this was nothing compared to what was coming.

Exclusion Moves Closer

About 1984, Jette's brother, who had only been in "the Truth" for three to four years, was ostracized for apostasy. At the time, he lived in Odense, the main town on the island of Fyn in central Denmark. The rationale was foolish and merely highlighted how the exclusion frenzy had seized hold in the elder councils.

At their uncle's funeral, Jette's brother stood while the priest asked for blessings over the coffin. An elder in Odense was informed and her brother was called to a conversation. However, he had previously indicated a lack of interest in the movement by failing to appear at meetings. Likewise, he did not appear for the conversation but called an elder and said that he, under no circumstances, required being registered as a Jehovah's Witness. Shortly thereafter, the brother's good friend in Randers, where Jette lived, informed the elders that he too did not wish to be a member anymore. This happened after he had been reprimanded from the platform because he had criticized some of the elders, and because he maintained contact with Jette's brother. In this way, he also caused himself to be cut off and subsequently treated as disfellowshipped.

One cannot just withdraw from the Jehovah's Witnesses; they must have the final word on the situation.

Jette shrugged it off because she imagined worse things had emerged during the conversation, and she simply had not been informed about them. The hearings always happened behind closed doors, and the elders practiced professional secrecy. Jette remained a Witness and later resumed contact with her brother.

Ten years later, it was Jette's turn.

Although Raymond Franz's book *Crisis of Conscience* was published in the US in 1983, the book was not published in Danish until 1991. It caused quite a stir.

Jette became aware of Franz's book when it was mentioned during a Danish television program in the autumn of 1992—a program the Society's leadership expected would have great promotional value. The broadcast was even mentioned during the Witnesses' summer meetings that year, increasing its members' expectations. Not surprisingly, the broadcast organizers had their own agenda, and therefore, no intention of ignoring Raymond Franz's book. After the television broadcast, the Witnesses were strongly warned against reading the book; Jette was one of many who could not accept the warning:

"If the book were substandard and lying, I would as an adult individual presumably be able to assess it. We lived not any more in the Middle Ages," she said.

Unacceptable Costs

Jette bought the book, read it and was deeply shaken.

She set it aside for her husband, one day he surprised her by reading it. Afterward he went to the elders in the local congregation. This, of course, was his duty. Otherwise, he might be accused of complicity and excluded. So it was actually a *kind* of thoughtfulness, for he clearly intended to *save* his wife from the influence of the renegades.

Shortly after, she was visited by two elders; one of them was a presiding overseer. He declared her "spiritually weak," as evidenced by her poor hour report, and she was also told not to read apostate literature. The truth was Jette had spent many hours and much money to visit an "interested" person who was in jail in another city. And by her own statements, she naively reported only the conversation hours and no travel time, resulting in her report showing four paltry hours a month!

"I must admit that from then on I was really afraid of being ostracized for being a renegade, because I had lost my faith. Everything I read in the book, I already 'knew' was true. It lay just under the surface of the consciousness, and now suddenly had been broken free. It was felt as a great liberation, but it was also scary, because how did I come out of it? What about my friends? It was not easy. It was obvious to me that this religion could not be abandoned without huge costs. *The Watchtower* had written the following (November 15, 1981, p. 23): 'Persons who show that they are "not of our kind," by deliberately rejecting the faith and beliefs of Jehovah's Witnesses, should appropriately be viewed and treated as those who have been disfellowshipped for wrongdoing.' At the same time I could, among other things, read in *The Watchtower* that if you do not believe that Jesus was installed as King in 1914, you could be excluded for apostate thinking" (Letter from Jette, February 10, 2004).

Jette was now in a very difficult situation, as her marriage slowly deteriorated, and her major concern was that if she were ostracized, she could lose her entire social network. She therefore had to shut up, be sweet and beautiful, and obey orders!

That Fateful Day

Jette calls *that day* she first attended a meeting of Jehovah's Witnesses at Kingdom Hall, "the fateful day." She met nothing but kindness but was bored bravely.

Some of the Witnesses invited her for coffee and cake in their home after the meeting. Jette began to feel a certain friendliness with them and soon she and her boyfriend were pulled into the movement. The Witnesses could answer everything.

Quickly she and her boyfriend discovered it probably would be best if they got married, and did so a year after they were baptized. Still, Jette's nature was to question everything, and it went even beyond much of what Jehovah's Witnesses believed. She wondered about the unique fashions worn by those within the movement, that they should not touch glasses and make toasts, as well as the obvious suppression of women. She recounts that she slowly lost confidence in her own reasoning, which was seen as a positive development because it showed that one owned the "noble characteristic humility." But then Jette thought God was chastising her.

Gradually, she was pulled deeper and deeper into the movement's way of thinking, until her "I" seemed to step completely into the background. She thought she had received answers to her questions about the meaning of life, had consolidated her belief that a new just world soon would appear, and she comforted herself with believing that if the so-called Governing Body was wrong, then the Society would "change it along the way." The Society was the only "channel" Jehovah used to communicate to mankind. If she disagreed, she was told she rejected the channel; this idea was emphasized in every meeting, one after another, three times a week, year in and year out.

Yet, even though Jette was more and more critical of the teachings and practices, she was very busy as a housewife. She had three children who also had to be brought up to be good Jehovah's Witnesses and later represent the Watchtower Society at doors and from house-to-house, and with three meetings to attend every week, there was plenty to keep her busy.

"For my part, the burden that was placed on my shoulders through my children's upbringing felt almost insurmountable. Particularly difficult was the work of getting the children ready for the meetings while they were small, and not least to get them to sit quietly without disturbing proceedings! The meetings took place usually at a time after their normal bedtime, so that any reasonable person who had a little knowledge of the children would realize that this cannot be demanded of parents, and even less so of small children. But this is not understood by the Jehovah's Witnesses' Governing Body. This council is only composed of elderly men who never have had children.... Through the years, I was so broken down after each session that I often cried when we came home, and it would take some hours to calm down, because I was in a constant conflict between what, on the one hand, I felt deep down was too much to ask of a child, and what, on the other hand, I thought was God's direct guidance to parents through the channel…"

What finally penetrated Jette's miasmic state was the Society's exclusion policy:

"But when you could read reports in various newspapers about young people, who were raised inside the Jehovah's Witnesses and just wanted to live their own lives like other young people, being deprived of their entire social network, and you had to face the fact that the price they would pay to be themselves was losing their family and friends, yes, it made an impression on me. These young people really had *no choice*."

Earlier, Jette would have said it was all not so bad, but since she became acquainted with Raymond Franz's book, which was strongly forbidden reading, the full truth about the exclusion policy came to her. Since 1981, the Society had strengthened the position against renegades, and began to ostracize them for nothing.

Something Wrong with the Society's Calculations

Jette had not just read the forbidden book, but she also carefully considered and evaluated its allegations. She noticed quickly that the key-year 1914 was uncertain. And she also noted that an elder in Sweden (Carl Olof Jonsson) had sent a larger thesis to Brooklyn that included an attack on the movement's chronology. I would like to emphasize here that Jette did not know details of this Swedish Elder's study; she only knew there was something wrong with the chronology. On this basis she began her own investigation.

In October 1994 Jette presented her very thorough investigation to the Watchtower Society, six A4-size sheets in total; her study broadly aligned with others' archaeological and historical-scientific conclusions. Jette's study also largely agreed with Jonsson's thesis.[275]

What is vital here is the fact that two independent studies function as an *objective experience*. The more scholars basing their studies on identical conditions and reaching the same conclusions, the more likely those conclusions are objective, and therefore, reliable.

Jette's small treatise of six pages, which was a slow-fused bomb, concluded with these words: "I hope you understand that this is something I have thought much about, and I am obviously aware that it may affect our understanding of the 'Gentile times' … I have presented this to the elders in my congregation, and they have advised me to write to the Society. I look forward to hearing your reply."

The answer—which ultimately said that a copy had been sent to the elder's council in her congregation—was, as expected, meaningless.

Under the heading "50 years or 70 years" Jette wrote:

"The whole 1914-doctrine of the Watchtower Society depends on whether the period from the first destruction of Jerusalem to the Jew's return to Jerusalem after the Babylonian captivity lasted 50 years, as the experts say, or 70 years as the Watchtower Society claims."

And after a long, thorough argument—where Jette completely repudiated the Society's doomsday chronology as derived from Barbour and Russell's original calculations (which had designated 1914 as the year when the 2520 years or gentile times would end)—she wrote:

"The Watchtower pulls the world history twenty years backwards by putting twenty extra years in between the kings who reigned in Babylon from Nebukadnezar's death until the fall of the last king, Nabonids."

Therefore, there is a divergence or difference of twenty years between the scholarly accepted time of the *first destruction* of Jerusalem and the time which the leaders of the Jehovah's Witnesses advocated. And believe me: The Watchtower leaders knew it. They were completely aware of the situation, but thought they could deny their members this knowledge, because members wouldn't dare draw the necessary conclusions. This knowledge originated from the banned books written by renegades that the Society, at any cost, had advised their members against reading.

But it is unreasonable to expect such things of human nature. Forbidden knowledge seeps in quietly and will gradually penetrate a movement. The curious read secretly in bathrooms, libraries and wherever they can study in peace, away from spying spouses and scheming elders.

The Children, the Real Victims

Sometime after Jette forwarded her chronology study to the Society, her world fell apart. Decline of her marriage accelerated because of the impossible life she lived, and because she had acted in response to the desperation she felt.

She threw herself into a relationship with a boyfriend from her youth she became reacquainted with during this time. Jette's Witness-related life crumbled, for now they had all they needed to censure her: reading forbidden literature, adultery and a looming rebellion against the organization. Her husband was now free to possibly marry again, the congregation's judicial committee had a new exclusion case to use for tightening discipline, and the Society could shut down the criticism of the chronology.

Initially, Jette chose to be silent about her digression because the pressures and consequences were incalculable. When she informed her children she planned to divorce they were unhappy, due partly to her married life being upset by conflicts, partly because she would leave the movement. During this process the children were the real victims of the elders' zealous fault-finding.

Jette's husband sought help from the elders who tried to convince Jette to stay in the marriage; they asked her directly whether she had been unfaithful and she denied it. Her life was none of their business! The frightening thing about the whole situation was that she now felt her children were hostages. Still, she held hope that a divorce might allow her to quietly get custody of her children. The problem was the children were under the excessive influence of the organization. They were raised in its shadow, marked by its limiting social life within the congregation and primarily influenced by their member-parents.

And now their mother was on the way out of the organization.

When Jette revealed she had been unfaithful, all hell broke loose, as Americans are fond of saying. The elders were informed and the situation reversed. Now Jette's husband sought the divorce, and Jette's young daughter was in shock, forced to deal with her mother being someone rejected by Jehovah.

At this point, things began to move rapidly.

Jette was summoned to a committee meeting, but since she didn't want to be humiliated further, she wrote a letter in which she explained the reasons for her actions. She also asked them to leave her in peace, because she wanted time to think everything through. In the letter to the elders, Jette honestly placed all the cards on the table. She turned everything out, and nobody, not even the *holiest people on earth* could be in doubt that an entire family's future depended on the ruling elders. Jette practically begged for time and understanding:

"I must apologize that this had to happen by letter, but I can best keep track of my thoughts when I write them down. And being quite emotional, I cannot at present cope with a confrontation" (March 3, 1995).

But the elders would not grant her peace and time to collect herself. Soon, she was thrust into her most difficult life crisis yet.

In her next letter of March 17, 1995, as rawly honest as the previous, Jette explained her position on a number of key teaching points. Among other things, she wrote:

"I can learn Jehovah's Witnesses' interpretation of, for example, the Book of Daniel and the Book of Revelation by heart. I can raise my hand in the book study group and answer that the resurrection to heavenly life began in 1918 (3-1/2 years after 1914) because it took three and a half years from Jesus' baptism and his death.... But I cannot force myself to believe it. And this is just one of many examples.... I often have the feeling that it doesn't really matter whether everything we make a cocksure statement about is true, as long as we merely preach it!"

And in her last letter to the elders she wrote:

"If the Governing Body is really the only channel that Jehovah uses, we must necessarily expect them to be honest (even if they are imperfect human beings with faults)."

With the suggestion that Jehovah's Witnesses' so-called Governing Body could *possibly* be *dishonest*, Jette had aired the unspeakable and sealed her fate. Initially the elders had conducted things in secret and could have arranged for a peaceful, private severance from the movement, but they did it not.

Before her disfellowshipping, Jette had been firmly pressured by the elders; they had even suggested an elder and his wife had to study with Jette and her husband once a week since Jette was considered weak in the faith. Another elder once tried to convince Jette she was mistaken about 1914. But this too was ineffective, because when Jette presented evidence for her allegations, he folded. They watched her closely at this time, but no one could catch her telling others about her discoveries.

Jette attended another committee meeting, but only after the third and final call to appear, since she would be automatically excluded if she continued to refuse. Her only motive was to avoid exclusion so she could keep her children. She was blindsided when her youngest son, in the middle of it all, said:

"Mom, if you are excluded, I cannot stay with you because you're 'bad company!' "[276]

She felt the children were about to slip completely away. Would she ever be with them again? She began to feel as if they were dead to her. She sat there, opposite the three elders, feeling paralyzed and humiliated, and unable to express all she felt. The children were pawns in the movement's game. Nobody in the movement cared for her children's welfare; the elders had the power to destroy her children's relationship with their renegade mother and they did not care about the long-term costs.

It surprised Jette at the time that the elders did not offer to mediate between her and her husband; she told them that she could not cope with losing the children and that she was willing to stay with her husband for their sake. "I interpreted it at that time as a sign that they knew it was impossible. But today, I am not quite sure," says Jette.

"This was just about condemnation," she said, "a condemnation that was so hard-hearted they [the elders] afterwards with clear consciences told the children they could no longer pray for or with their mother or discuss anything with her related to the faith of the Jehovah's Witnesses."

The situation dominated Jette's relationship with the children for several years thereafter. Jette noticed the children were trapped and all conversations went silent if she raised an issue that was considered sensitive by the Witnesses.

Jette was now so far down emotionally that she "just fell and fell into a deep dark hole." People turned away from her; she was a plague. And her children would be subject to numerous social restrictions against her when they grew to adulthood or became baptized.

She could not think how it all would end, and of course, the elders' judicial committee chose the most vicious and ungodly solution they could imagine.

Jette was excluded for: 1. Lying; 2. Adultery; 3. Because she had accused the Governing Body of dishonesty.

Her treatment resembled historic inquisitions and punishments for heretics, sans only the flaming pyre.

Looking back on that time, Jette reports her reaction to the exclusions this way:

"Larger grief thrust on me by Jehovah's Witnesses' 'elders' because of what happened could hardly be heavier for a mother to bear. It felt to me as if they had killed my children! Of course it would also have been difficult to endure a 'normal' divorce, but certainly not on such a scale. The blame for it, I am quite conscious about, and it hurts, because I am my own judge."

The elder committee would not expel Jette as a dropout since "she had not spread her private thoughts in the congregation"—*that* they had carefully studied—rather they expelled her for being *critical* of the Jehovah's Witnesses Governing Body. However, the elders were not willing to even discuss the criticisms leveled in her letter to the Society or demonstrate where she had been mistaken.

Jette continued in her letter to me:

"It seems to me that we have to deal with people who easily turn a blind eye to an organization's senior management that takes advantage of direct dishonesty and thus—in the name of God—misleads millions of members while they simultaneously condemn one individual who, as a result of a desperate situation, lies to prevent 'losing' her children and tells the truth only a week later. If this is not hypocrisy, what is?"

Jette's eldest son was soon told that he could no longer socialize with his mother, but could only be with her in connection with necessary, practical things. As the two youngest were minors and unbaptized, "they were allowed to be together with me," says Jette, "but only to that day they were baptized. At that time they would get the same message as the oldest one."

Not only was she eventually divorced, but she also partially lost contact with her eldest son, and then later on, completely lost contact with her daughter when she was baptized.

"Mom, you know I may not visit you," her daughter tells her now when Jette telephones.

Another Tragedy

Jette was pleased when her son Ruben left the organization in 2000. They had a close relationship until 2007, and could talk quite openly about everything the family had been through over the years. "It is infinitely difficult," continues Jette, "if family members may not engage with each other, and when you cannot talk and discuss problems, how can you reach out to each other?"

Ruben, who had been disfellowshipped from the local congregation and subsequently lost contact with his siblings, as they had been forbidden any social contact with him or to even talk to him, now opted to complete his neglected education. He decided to train to be an optician. Sadly, his plan was thwarted when he developed Tourette's syndrome and became unable to get an apprenticeship. In his despair, he took his own life. What had seemed promising for both him and Jette became only more grief and despair.

Rubens's death, however, had not gone without notice by Jette's other children, and Jette secretly hopes a change is still possible and that the two other children have inherited a little of her independent spirit, the very one the Watchtower Society warns against.

One day her children may dare to ask critical questions about all the terrible things their families have endured as victims of the Society. Jette's greatest desire is to reunite with her two other children one day, despite the enormous pressure they're under, and talk about the devastating events that crushed their family.

Chapter 30

Gangrene in the Congregation

In the early 1990s, I came into contact with several former Jehovah's Witnesses who had been recently excluded.

They questioned the whole basis of their faith. All had read the Danish translation of Raymond Franz's *Crisis of Conscience*. As you may recall, this book created a great stir among Witnesses worldwide; that it had been translated to Danish, in addition to other languages, was quite monumental. For the first time non-English-speaking members could read about what actually occurred within the top level of the Watchtower hierarchy in Brooklyn.

Franz's book played more or less a central role in all exclusion cases, as it was considered reason for exclusion to have read the book or even talked to others about it. Those who found themselves under the scrutiny of the Exclusion Committees simply had to relinquish their books to the judiciary committee members, who then had the forbidden books destroyed.

That is, *if* the wrongdoer would deliver his copy!

The Case against Poul Dal

One of those who came to the attention of the Exclusion Committee was professional photographer Poul Dal of Viborg; his family had been involved in the movement's work for several generations.

The background is as follows:

Poul Dal's great-grandfather, Poulsen Dal, had been an employee of high-school teacher Christen Kold and started Galtrup College of Mors,[277] an island in the Limfjord[278] in the northern part of the Jutland Peninsula. Following some strife with the Free Church he had joined, Poulsen Dal and his wife and eight children immigrated to America in 1883.

Eight years later they returned to Mors, but one of their sons, Niels Ebbesen Dal, remained in the United States. One day Niels discovered one of Russell's books, *The Divine Plan of the Ages*, which completely changed his life.

In 1918, he returned home to Mors, and converted first his brother Frode, and sometime after, some of Frode's sons and daughters. Niels had returned to Mors as a colporteur to spread Russellism on the island. Frode's sons, Kristian and Knud, were converted around 1920 and they also became colporteurs. Knud was Poul Dal's father. Apart from Knud and Kristian, virtually all of Poulsen Dal's descendants left the Bible Students, a fact the Danish headquarters of Jehovah's Witnesses failed to explain in the 1993 *Yearbook*, in which among others the Dals' history and the movement's development in Denmark are treated (Asger Højmark and Uffe Hansen: *De Grundtvigske Fri-og Valgmenigheder*, A. C. Normans Forlag A / S, Odense 1944; *JW Yearbook*, 1993, p. 79).

Poulsen's great-grandson Poul had, in some way, the dissident microbe in his blood. The Exclusion Committee took interest in him because he resigned his post as elder and later aired his innermost thoughts to another elder.

The committee sent a two-man delegation to an elder who lived fifty kilometers south of Viborg to obtain damning statements about Poul Dal's dissenting views. Later, the two envoys turned up at Poul Dal's home to summon him to a meeting. "There are no charges," they explained, "but we have some questions regarding your resignation as elder."

Poul Dal had resigned as elder because personal circumstances hindered his ability to continue the task. In his resignation letter he wrote certain things that apparently brought him under scrutiny, having mentioned he found it difficult to handle "certain findings and calculations regarding the fulfillment of the promises." However, he also stated anticipating that if there were "matters of dispute," as he put it, "these could be resolved when the time is ripe for it. The ideas of Kor. 1:13, verses 8-13 gives me comfort in this respect" (dated December 2, 1993).

Whatever impression he gave on the surface, Dal must have known what he was doing would bring him trouble.

Dal told the two envoys he would think about the matter and later that evening he phoned back and said that he—in addition to the reasons he had already given in his letter—did not want to explain his position further. As with so many others, the festering abscess of inquisition broke when the person at the other end of the receiver revealed they actually had an "indictment" against him.

The previously mentioned elder who had been Poul's confidante—and whose mission was to provide damning evidence against Poul Dal—had, under the mask of friendship and the guarantee of strict confidentiality, pressed Poul to discuss sensitive (restricted) topics that happened to be the background of an article in *Awake!* titled: "Does the Bible Discourage Freedom of Thought?" (*Awake!*, June 8, 1994)

Christians had to be able to speak freely, the elder told Poul, but of course one should not spread one's "deviant" views to everyone in the congregation. Feeling he had the other man's confidence, Poul Dal trusted he could continue their conversation in good faith. The content of these was reported to the elders in Viborg and, hence, Poul was summoned and indicted. Yet, when Poul repeatedly refused to appear, the case was suspended.

Sufficient Material

In December, however, the matter escalated again, and for the second time he was visited by two representatives from Viborg West congregation. They wanted Poul Dal to attend another meeting, since they now had sufficient evidence against him. But Poul was prepared for confrontation, although he had wanted to leave the organization quietly.

At the meeting with the Exclusion Committee, the elders confronted him with several absurd allegations:

1. He wanted to defend himself when his former fellow believers went to see him.
2. He did not believe that Jehovah's Witnesses' exclusion rules were based on a biblical basis.
3. He read apostate literature and did not want to get rid of it.
4. He doubted that the organization is the only true one.
5. He had rejected offers of help.

The elders now engaged in a discussion with the accused, who thought it was unacceptable that he should get rid of "certain books" and remarked how the situation reminded him of the Nazi terror regime.

"Why can't we leave the Jehovah's Witnesses' organization, without sanctions immediately being taken against us?" Poul asked. "We come not literally into prison, but there is created a spiritual prison around the person in question, so that the former co-religionists do not mix with the apostates."

Poul went on to point out that there is only one foundation "we can build on: Jesus Christ." And, "since the Watchtower Society often states that for currently living people there is virtually no possibility of salvation in the biblical sense—without having to align themselves with Jehovah's Witnesses' organization—one could naturally ask, whether it is because the Watchtower Society is beginning to build on another foundation than Jesus Christ?" (*Kristen Frihed* or *Christian Freedom*, December 1995, p. 1-2)

After the meeting, Poul remarked that things were done better before, and the presiding overseer replied, as by a slip of the tongue: "Yes, but we are bound hand and foot by the Society!" And, after a short pause, he added: "We can also say we want to be loyal to the Society." (Ibid.)

Poul was headed for prompt exclusion!

Incalculable Consequences

When Poul Dal realized the seriousness of his situation, he appealed the decision. His wife and children were still members, and it was totally incalculable what impact a possible exclusion would have on the family's continued unity. In January 1994 Poul sent an appeal to the committee in which he responded to the five allegations:

"I find it very worrying that you seek to justify your decision on exclusion with background from the Bible. In God's Word, doubt is certainly described as something that had to be treated with compassion, and fault-finding is discouraged."

A new meeting was scheduled, and Dal, being quick-witted, suggested they celebrate this last meeting with a sip of coffee; this commemorative action seemed quite inappropriate to the committee members. His joke would not change the case, which undoubtedly had been determined in advance of the meeting.

Also of note: The meeting did not begin with a customary prayer. Devout members do not pray together with an excluded! Chief Elder Freddie Rasmussen stated that, overall, the number of indictments gave reason for exclusion. At this time, Poul played a tape of country director Joergen Larsen's statements to a well-known Danish television program, *Lorry*, where among other things he firmly denied that Jehovah's Witnesses' rules could lead to exclusion because of *doubts*. Rasmussen replied: "But you doubt on the 'faithful and discreet slave!'[279] And that is a very dangerous doubt, because then you doubt also God's organization, which Jehovah has installed to do his will here at the time of the end" (Ibid., p. 3).

Since the elders were entirely beyond their pedagogical scope, in Poul Dal's opinion, he wrote a six-page letter to the Watchtower headquarters in Denmark, in which he, among other things, outlined his views:

"If this community [Jehovah's Witnesses] cannot tolerate that a member is unsure about some calculations and assumptions, which have proved to be unsustainable, I think Christian patience, charity and mercy within this community is not on a high level."

He concluded with:

"I would finally urge you to reconsider the matter for reassessment and not succumb to the same repression of otherwise-thinking Christian dissidents' faith as Jehovah's Witnesses have been subjected to, both by political and religious authorities, who also often claimed they were doing God's will with their persecutions. 'For judgment is without mercy to one who has shown no mercy; yet mercy triumphs over judgment' (James 2:13; RSV)."

After two days he received this response from the Watchtower Society: "You have not been ostracized for having doubts, or because you've asked questions, but because you have refused to follow the biblical guidance applicable to those who will be Jehovah's Witnesses."

Poul Dal was stubborn and wrote yet another letter in which he asked for further clarification:

"What kind of guidance have I refused to follow? Is it about managing a behavior the Bible condemns and which I will not give up? Or do I advocate a teaching that is not grounded in Christianity, which is evident from the Holy Greek Scriptures? In that case, I would like to know exactly where I can read it."

A few days later, Poul Dal received a final letter from the Society:

"We have received your letter of January 21 and just want to inform you that we have no further comments. Since we have been told that you still have not delivered the mentioned book [the *Elder Manual*] in our letter of January 16, which you wrongfully retain, we will ask you to immediately do so" (signed: Watch Tower Bible and Tract Society). Among his other transgressions, Poul had refused to return his *Elder Manual* when he resigned as elder.

This is a typical example of a letter wherein officers of the Watchtower Society terminate the excluded's longstanding membership of Jehovah's Witnesses' congregations; it is administrative, cold and unkind. No reprieve or appeal. It is over. The excluded is now regarded as dead, and his fate will be decided in the flames of Armageddon.

Poul Dal retained the *secret,* internal-use-only *Elder Manual*[280] that contained a large amount of *inflamed* opinions; apparently the leaders were afraid it would be exposed to the public. No further demands were made for return of the *manual*; the books seem to have been issued exclusively to elders.

Strangely, most of the *secret* text in the manual is actually reprinted from earlier issues of the Society's publications, including articles from the magazine *The Watchtower.* Therefore, if one wants to quote from this book, which seems to be forbidden, one can simply refer to the exact article in *The Watchtower.*

The case against Poul Dal ended then. He was divorced from his wife and lost all contact with his former family; he does not communicate with his now-adult children aged thirty-one and thirty-eight at the time of our communication, and does not speak with his former wife. Poul Dal tried to contact his son, and succeeded a few years ago, but now: "*Keine* contact," as he says showing his quick wit. No one doubts the development hit him hard, but Poul survives chiefly because of his humorous outlook. He is active in an Ex-JW Support Group and he has plenty to do. He likes to help others who find themselves in a similar situation. Poul has also remarried one of his fellow excludeds: Jette, who we have already met (Chapter 29).

Poul Dal believes today that Jehovah's Witnesses, through their exclusion policy, muzzles dissent and takes hostages within families. "In this way the Jehovah's Witnesses have created thousands of meaningless family tragedies."

Five members were excluded from the Viborg congregations during a short time. Long after the exclusions, unrest fermented in the congregations there.

Many could not comprehend why these old "honorable" members, who had "been in the truth" for twenty to thirty years with proud family traditions in the movement, could no longer be tolerated.

Finally, the Viborg West congregation held a special service session in the Kingdom Hall on February 16, 1995, at which the elders tried to justify their actions. At the meeting it was said that they had found a "gangrene in the congregation, and that it was necessary to cut it in order that the gangrene would not spread."[281] Subsequently, one of the exclusion committee's members was nicknamed "the butcher of Randers."

Chapter 31

Eve's Choice

Over several years, as I prepared this book, I tried to contact apostates who might contribute stories of their experiences as they broke with the Witnesses. In January 2005 I received a letter from a woman I shall call Eve who very much wanted to contribute to my book but on the condition that she be anonymous. We agreed to obscure or alter geographical details, so no one within the Jehovah's Witnesses could identify her. This chapter is devoted entirely to her story, told in her own words.

Eve's Story: "I was unlike any other."

The following is Eve's own rendering of her experiences:

When I was born, my parents were members of Jehovah's Witnesses, and they still are. I was never in daycare or in a kindergarten, and thus I was protected from "harmful influences" until school time. Therefore, I also grew up as a Jehovah's Witness, brought up to go from door to door and witness.

I had only sporadic contact with "worldly people" and for the most part played only with children of my parents' friends. We met at the meetings Sunday, Tuesday and Thursday, and on Saturday we were in "field service," that is, out and ringing the doorbells. Those guests who came into our home were all members of the Jehovah's Witnesses, and they brought their children along with them, with whom I also played.

Both my parents were well-rooted in the movement, and my father functioned as an "elder" in the congregation. Their friends were good Jehovah's Witnesses, and we talked from time to time that we should take care not to deal with those members who were "bad company." There were both "good" and "bad" Witnesses. I would eventually become *bad company*, but that was much later.

In principle, I asked no questions about religion. Not until I went to school did it dawn on me that I was not like everyone else. During the first school years I felt it was a shame that my schoolmates had to die. And I tried to convince them of the "Truth" because I would like to have them with me in the new world. I remember that I thought about how unfair it was that they were to die, for I had some sweet school friends.

Simultaneously, I was warned that it could not be useful to have strong friendships with these school friends, because I would regret it when they died in Armageddon. So I tried to keep to myself and not involve myself too much with them, and therefore, I was a bit of an outsider. I was also different when my friends went to birthday parties. And when my schoolmates followed each other along home, I walked alone. I held my head high, because I had learned that it was my school friends who were to be pitied, not me.

Fortunately, my schoolmates did not tease me about being different. There were two girls in the class who were overweight, and were subject to teasing, so I went unnoticed. I think I managed myself pretty well, and I fit into the class well. But I remember that in fourth grade, a new boy from out of town thought I had to be mobbed. It was not too bad because no one supported his teasing. Later I was told that his mother had actually gone out of the Jehovah's Witnesses and perhaps he had heard a thing or two at home, and therefore felt I was to be teased.

"Should you not soon be baptized?"

Many of my friends were baptized in the teen years, many already when they were twelve, thirteen and fourteen years old, and their fathers soon began asking me about when it was my turn. I was supported at home, however, in that it was my own decision and not just something I did because the others did. After all, I thought it would have been nice to be baptized when others in the class were confirmed in the church. Then I had to talk about it. But I would not, of course, have a party—it was not something that was celebrated, "because, then it was something we did for the sake of the party, like the conformation candidates." So, we didn't celebrate my baptism at all.

I was now fourteen years old, and they started to push me a little more. "Should you not soon be baptized?"; "Is it not, what you want?"; "What would you do then?"; "What is your affiliation?"; "If you choose not to choose, Jehovah will not choose you!" However, I was never under pressure at home, because my parents were "late" baptized after the standards of the Jehovah's Witnesses, and therefore, they knew I had good time. They knew that I probably would make the "right decision." But it was all the others who tried to pressure me.

When I was fifteen, I was baptized and finally became a "true" Witness. I actually got more attention from the other young people than I got at home. But I felt it was the right decision. All said "congratulations" on the big day, and I felt comfortable and got a bit of attention.[282]

I was an "auxiliary pioneer"[283] within a month together with my girlfriend. However, the purpose of our work was mainly in two districts which were fairly far apart. We would make a visit in the first place, and then ride our bicycles out to the other district and make a visit there. Then we would ride back again and make a visit in the first district. Moreover, it was accepted that we began and ended in a place other than where we served from door to door, because we also had hours of driving, and then suddenly three hours would have passed, and they could be included in the report. [284]

"On the subject of boyfriends"

As a 16-year-old I met Andreas, a really sweet guy. He and I were together for a long period. He was also a Jehovah's Witness. His parents were well into "the truth" and he was approved by my parents. I think he was "the dream of every mother-in-law;" at least my mother was very sorry when we broke up. She had visions of a wedding about a year away. I broke up with him because I had not (yet) accepted the side of Jehovah's Witnesses that he represented.

Andreas was eighteen, therefore of legal age, and went to parties. If he went to these festivities with his friends inside the Witnesses, the parents would have no concern about either drinking or otherwise behaving like any other young person. And then, he had a school sweetheart.

It was, at that time, just too heavy for me to deal with. Subsequently, I began to participate in all these *blessings*. If I went out with other young Jehovah's Witnesses, the world stood open for me, and there were no restrictions. All of us exploited our parents' belief that we policed each other. I wonder if our parents did the same in their youth.

"Higher learning unwelcome"

After primary school, I decided to start at the Commercial School. I got support from my father, who himself had studied and was very inquisitive. The Witnesses did not welcome that we continued our education. However, it was okay within the congregation that I completed the first year in HG.[285] This was necessary for me to get an apprenticeship of some sort, but then they preferred that I not continue in school. Nonetheless, I chose to pursue HH[286] and graduate. Funny enough, my father supported me still, despite the recommendation from the Society that we ought to pursue as short an education as possible and try to provide for ourselves haphazardly until Armageddon.

At the Commercial School, as fate would have it, I got to go to class with a very sweet young man, Peter. He and I became really good friends, and yes, over time, more than that. I knew well that sexual relationships were strictly forbidden, so I saw him on the sly. We played truant from school and drove off to the beach and went for long walks; we met when I was at work, too. I rode my bicycle far to get to a phone booth (this was before everyone had mobile phones), so we could talk. I spent fortunes on phone cards, even from abroad, and when we were on holiday alone, I bought talk-time cards rather than souvenirs.

"On a short leash"

We went together for more than a year before I put the cards on the table. To cut a long story short, I informed my parents by letter that I had met Peter, and that it was serious. My announcement fell absolutely on barren ground. I had thought that honesty about our relationship would resolve the problem, but it seemed exactly the opposite. Actually, I had imagined that I'd get free rein, if my parents just knew where I was and what I did.

First, they would not talk to me for several weeks. After this, a family council was convened. I was presented with the demand that I change school because, as my mother said, if it was serious, Peter would wait for me one year until I was finished with school, and then we could resume our relationship. (Of course, she and I both knew if Peter and I were separated for a year, then he might give up on me.)

I refused and said I would finish my school year at the same school as Peter. I was then banned from using the phone, and not allowed to write to him, talk to him or do anything extra when staying at the school. The phone was locked when my mother was not home. And when my parents went on holiday, I was cared for by other family because I could not be alone at home, despite the fact that I was eighteen years of age. Naturally, all this was impossible for an 18-year-old girl in love to endure, so eventually I had to leave home. Peter and I were absent from school as much as possible and saw each other as often as we could—still secretly.

Also, I was monitored and kept on a very short leash by my family. If I had been at a party (of course, along with other Witnesses), it was reported to my parents what time I had left the party, and they calculated how long the transport home would take, and combined it all to see if it matched with the time I returned home. Therefore, I was often in hot water, because the two times did not always match precisely, and how could I then explain that?

Despite the fact that I was almost nineteen now, I had great respect for the house rules and I dared only behave properly—or move. I got a room in another town where I now lived pro forma. That is to say, it was my official address, but actually I lived with my boyfriend.

"And then monitoring and exclusion"

My parents began to wonder why I never answered the phone, and they watched my apartment to see when I was home, and whether Peter's car was also parked outside. They also began to sneak around at night to see how long Peter's car stayed parked near my residence. From this, they tried to determine if we slept together or not.

Soon, I was summoned to a meeting in the Kingdom Hall.

I felt Peter should participate because it was us and our situation that would be discussed, not just me. I prepared myself for all possible outcomes: ending our relationship, being required to marry, or that I would be ostracized. But I quickly learned it was not possible, under any circumstances, for Peter to participate; what they were afraid of, I don't know. However, the elders came up to visit in our apartment, where Peter was also present, because I had insisted that he be included. They came, however, just to greet us, and nothing was talked about much other than weather and other generalities.

I went to the meeting in the Kingdom Hall, because I knew that if I not did show up, I would be excluded simply because of absence. During the meeting they prayed with me to Jehovah, and they told me that I had stepped on a terribly slippery slope. They read aloud numerous passages from the Bible. I was informed I had to immediately stop sleeping with Peter, or I would get an "official warning" regarding my situation. This meant that at a meeting of the congregation they would announce someone had been given a warning and say my name, and they would ask an elder to prepare a talk explaining how terrible that or another sin is. Otherwise, you are assured that the contents of the warning are secret when they proclaim the "public reprimand" and warning, as it only concerns the accused and the three elders who participated in the "conversation" in the Kingdom Hall.[287]

And regarding the secrecy of the content of the warning, you can take it with a pinch of salt, including the content of the lecture that is associated with the meeting at which the warning is given. And yes, "little I" actually sat there along with three fully grown "gentleman," who interviewed me about everything. And they really have a right, according to the Society, to examine *EVERYTHING*. And they do! They pry into everything that could offend them! Today they would not have had much response from me, but I was young and naive and brought up to behave and accept tactless questions.

Following the meeting at the Kingdom Hall, my boyfriend declared that he would sleep alone, if it would help. But I lacked self-confidence and asked him to sleep with me. It was against the recommendations, and I was called in a few days later. I can still remember the horrible feeling in my stomach when the phone rang and one of the elders, without identifying himself, said:

"Well, have you got a car? I've noticed that Peter's car has remained in the parking lot over by the school until six o'clock every morning in the last week."

And it was so. Afterwards one could only wonder what he did in that parking lot every morning at six o'clock! Peter and I are today amazed we did not think to park at various places in the city every night!

After that phone call, a few days went by, and then two elders rang at my door, after which I was excluded.

I had no strength to call my parents and tell them the news, and therefore, I asked the two elders if they would share the news with them. I have not talked to my parents since that day. I have only indirectly heard that my father was very disappointed I did not even phone and tell them about the exclusion. But what can parents expect from a 19-year-old young woman who knows her parents' world would collapse when such a message comes out of her mouth? I could not tell them.

When I was ostracized, I was overwhelmed by anxiety. But as time went by, I felt I had to step back to rejoin the congregation. I was really sorry that I had lost my siblings. My little brother was quite small, so it was almost like losing my own child, except that I still knew he was safe and sound and in good hands. I wept much the first year. Besides, I was very afraid of Armageddon, and every time there was talk of "war" or "peace" in the television news, I was sure I would die the same night.

But fortunately I did nothing about rejoining. I could not go back and say I still lived with my boyfriend. We would not marry by order but only if we wanted it ourselves. We continued living together, and I remained excluded.

"My new life"

My good school friend, the only friend from my old life as a Witness, contacted the Danish support group for former Jehovah's Witnesses. Thus I obtained some materials to read and found the opportunity to share my story with others in the same situation, and I could get advice and support. It was really nice to be able to discuss ideas, which were previously banned, and feel that these ideas were shared with others.

My former Witness-boyfriend, Andreas, was ostracized almost simultaneously with me and for the same reasons, so we had ample opportunity to discuss a lot. Indeed, we were better friends after the exclusion than when we were lovers. Andreas also had a little brother, who was not too old, and he missed him very much. We talked very much about our little brothers and our feelings about needing to see them.

Unfortunately, Andreas could not remain excluded. He missed his family, understandably enough. He lived for a time with a girl in Copenhagen, but left her. Afterward he settled in a major provincial town in Denmark where he gradually was resumed. Subsequently, I know he returned to living with the same girlfriend in the capital. So now he can visit his parents without restrictions, while he can take care of his life in Copenhagen with his girlfriend, without someone raising an eyebrow.

I spoke with him after he had been resumed and had moved back to Copenhagen. He told me that he had not contacted me in a long time (in the resuming period) because he knew my position and knew that I thought he was a hypocrite, living his life on a false basis. But he agreed with me. He knew perfectly well it was hypocritical, but he took care of his own hide and used the holes in the system, which still exist.

"Entering therapy"

To feel peace again, a psychologist, who had experience helping former members of Jehovah's Witnesses, was recommended to me. But it wasn't just a psychologist I needed most. I have always been good at talking about my situation and have never been afraid to open up. Now I still talked about my situation but had to pay for the conversation. So my thoughts had a price per minute while sitting in that chair.

After the psychologist, I was referred to a psychotherapist. However, we weren't compatible, so I went there only three times.

Finally, I saw a kinesiologist. The therapy was really something, pulling the fear and grief out of my stomach. I found out that it was not in my brain alone (at first, I needed something more than talk-therapy) where something was amiss, but in the stomach where my feelings had been penned up. I attended treatment eight times, and found out there were blockages in my body, sadness and anxiety, remnants from the Witness-time. These I was happily freed from, and so I am now (almost) free of the fear.

I still experience grief, but it has been reduced significantly, and I have gained distance from it, so I can cope with it.

I was married in 2002, and I have now a little son that I must be a good mother to. This is why it was important for me to resolve the old repressed sentiments. And yes, it is Peter, my old school sweetheart who is my son's father. We were finally married, but only because we felt it was what we wanted.

Today, I have it really good. I believe in the future along with my family, which I have chosen and have struggled to retain. And I have gradually built up a great friendship circle, and my husband's family has now become my new family.

Eve

A Bit More Regarding Eve

Since I corresponded with Eve about her very personal experiences inside the Jehovah's Witnesses, she also told me about an older, baptized member's inappropriate advances toward her and other girls in the congregation. Eve was only twelve years old at the time. The person in question was summoned to a meeting with the elders, but it lead to nothing. Eve and I decided we would not include this incident in her material. Why should the Jehovah's Witnesses become the gathering place where pedophiles—without being prosecuted—could conduct their miscreant behaviors?

However, in December 2005, I came to a realization.

My change of mind was encouraged through contact with Barbara Anderson of the United States; she was once a highly trusted employee at Watchtower headquarters in New York. Barbara's story made it clear to me that there was more to the matter of secret abuses than I initially had imagined.

Chapter 32

Barbara Anderson's Discoveries

To call Barbara Anderson's discoveries startling and important would be appropriate. She made them while researching for a new Jehovah's Witnesses' history book from 1989 to 1991. Barbara found, by mere chance, some old association documents from 1881 that revealed Charles Taze Russell had not been the first president of the Watch Tower Society. This was but one eye-opening aspect of what she uncovered.

In December 2005, I contacted Barbara Anderson to learn about her life since she discontinued her association with the Jehovah's Witnesses, and to ask her whether she would be interested in presenting her story in my book. She sent me thirteen pages, which I—with her permission—have abbreviated to include here. The main issue of importance, which I soon realized, was the fight against pedophilia within the Jehovah's Witnesses organization as it was waged by Barbara and another former member, Bill Bowen. After reading Barbara's story, I was forced to revise my attitude regarding this sensitive matter because now it seemed to be an important part of the "newer history" of the Jehovah's Witnesses—regardless of the number of cases or my desire to not advertise how closely guarded this secret was within the Society.

In September 2009, I contacted Barbara and asked her to proofread this chapter which resulted in some important additions; I received them with gratitude.

I am sure the issue concerning pedophiles inside the Witness organization is a *very complex one* in which the Jehovah's Witnesses, as a movement, may have been *singled out* by pedophiles or groups because of the organization's patriarchal and fundamentalist structure. However, all along, the Witnesses' child abuse policies seemed to have been a problem, and even though the organization's leaders apparently now have a changed attitude and *decided to reform their policies*, many difficulties and concerns remain—not unlike the Roman Catholic Church in this regard, which is a remarkable irony.

Barbara's Story: A Disastrous Choice

I was born in Long Island, New York, to Polish-Catholic parents. When I was an inexperienced, discontented 14-year-old, I made a choice that, in effect, narrowed my opportunities to make choices—I joined one of the most aggressive, controversial religious groups, the Jehovah's Witnesses, which became the center of my life. I put aside my heart's desire, the study of archaeology, because of the religion's criticism and ban of higher education. Hence, evangelistic activities took priority over education.

At nineteen, I married Joe Anderson, who I met the year before when he worked at the world headquarters of the Watch Tower organization. Joe operated one of the printing presses there from 1956–1959. We pioneered until our son was born in 1961. My husband was an authority figure in whatever congregation we belonged to—most of the time he was presiding overseer. He also spent over twenty-five years in the full time volunteer ministry work. Hence, most years, we both worked part time to support the family. Over the years we converted over eighty people to our faith because we were zealous believers. From the very beginning, I put faith in the Watchtower Society's theology and influence because they appeared to have Biblical answers to age-old questions about life, death, war and peace, during a time of intense instability and insecurity in the 1950s bomb-shelter and cold-war years. Although the 1975 date set by Jehovah's Witnesses for the coming Apocalypse came and went, I was not deterred; after all, I had too much invested in the religion to throw in the towel.

Volunteer Work

In 1982 the Watchtower Society invited Joe and me to become volunteer staff members at their headquarters, named Bethel, in Brooklyn, New York. The year before, at age nineteen, our son Lance volunteered to work at the headquarters and was accepted. He was assigned to work in one of the Watchtower Society's many factories, tending one of their many high-speed printing presses that turned out literally millions of pieces of Watchtower religious literature annually.

My husband was the reason we were invited to Brooklyn Bethel. When visiting our son in March 1982, Joe was talking to Richard Wheelock, one of the factory overseers, and when Richard found out Joe was by occupation a plumber, Richard started the ball rolling to have us come to live at headquarters.

Sometime later we found out why Richard was so interested in Joe's trade. Negotiations were underway to purchase an old Brooklyn factory located right next to the East River on Furman Street. This neglected building was huge— over a million square feet of space—armored artillery tanks were built there during WWII. In addition, the rundown 12-story Bossert Hotel (opened in 1909) on Montegue Street in downtown Brooklyn Heights, was secretly under consideration for purchase. With all these purchases and the need for experienced plumbers in mind, Richard arranged interviews with Watchtower officials, and by the end of the morning we were invited to become members of the then over 2,000-member Watchtower headquarters' staff.

We returned home, put our affairs in order, and returned to New York in June 1982 eagerly anticipating our new adventure. Eventually, I would be assigned as secretary to one of the architects, a former missionary, who was designing a new residence building.

Since the Heights section of Brooklyn is deemed an historic area, all new or renovated buildings must meet certain architectural requirements. In time, an important part of my work assignment included researching local historical and architectural questions so we could meet those requirements. Consequently, because of this research experience, in 1989 I was transferred to the Writing Department to do research work under the direction of senior staff writer Karl Adams. He was writing the history of our religion that eventually became a 750-page chronicle titled, *Jehovah's Witnesses Proclaimers of God's Kingdom,* published in 1993.

Surprising Discoveries

Working in the Writing Department was interesting and challenging. Each week Karl would give me a list of questions he wanted researched regarding the early history of the Watchtower Bible and Tract Society. I learned a great deal about my own religion, as I discovered archival material that had long ago been placed in cabinets and forgotten.

One thing I discovered was that William H. Conley, an Allegheny, Pennsylvania, banker, not Charles Taze Russell, was the first president of the Watch Tower Association formed in 1881. Russell's father, Joseph, was vice president and Charles Taze was secretary-treasurer. The appointment was based on shares purchased at $10 per share. The information was noted in a small, red cardboard-covered notebook where the handwritten organizational charter was folded with one side of the paper pasted to the inside cover. Through handwriting comparison, I found that Maria Russell penned this first charter.

This was a thrilling find, for no one at headquarters knew about Conley being the first president. I found the little notebook in an old paper file folder inside of a file cabinet, which was located in a huge concrete vault in the middle of the Watch Tower Treasury Department at 25 Columbia Heights.

At one point I was asked to establish the "faithful and discreet slave"[288] links from the death of the last Christian apostle up until Charles Taze Russell and his group. For six months the Writing Department spared no expense to bring in books from Oxford University in the UK and from libraries all across Europe and the United States. I had access to translations into English of important foreign-language books discussing the break-away, nonconformist religious groups. I examined groups formed during the Reformation and also during what is known as the Radical Reformation period. I studied every word attributed to the many early Arian groups. I looked at the Lollards, the Waldenses, Socinians and Anabaptists with a critical eye. My examination was based upon four points or standards which the "sons of the kingdom" had to have in common—the rejection of the doctrines, Trinity, hellfire and the immortal soul. The fourth standard was the most difficult. There had to be acceptance of the ransom sacrifice of Christ.

I subsequently proved to Karl that there was not "one generation of the slave-class that fed the succeeding generation" as one 1975 Watchtower magazine claimed, and he promised me that he would make sure that claim was never again made in Watchtower literature. On page forty-four of the book, *Jehovah's Witnesses, Proclaimers of God's Kingdom,* the best Karl could say in answer to this question, after he hemmed and hawed, was that, "Throughout the centuries there have always been TRUTH LOVERS."

At one time, while I was researching another question for Karl, I read the divorce trial cross-examination transcript of Charles Taze Russell. The transcript of Maria Russell's cross-examination was not given to me to read. At that time, I did not question why Mrs. Russell's cross-examination was not made available to me. Only years later, out of curiosity, I read it and was amazed at how Mrs. Russell's problems with Pastor Russell were misrepresented to Jehovah's Witnesses in Witness literature.

During another assignment Karl gave me, I examined the entire 1917–1918 period to see what led up to the federal indictments of Rutherford and his associates by the government of the United States for basically obstructing the recruiting and enlistment service of the United States during WWI. When Rutherford learned that the government objected to pages 247–253 in the seventh volume of the *Studies in the Scriptures* book series, *The Finished Mystery,* Rutherford directed that those pages be cut out of all copies. Later, when it was learned that distribution of the books would be in violation of the Espionage Act, Rutherford directed that distribution be suspended. Reading Rutherford's words in the trial transcript was quite surprising. During the trial of Rutherford et al. v. United States, Rutherford told the court he did everything he could to placate the authorities and couldn't understand why they were dealing so harshly with him. Karl commented privately to me how amazed he was reading Rutherford's conciliatory statements of how he tried to appease the government. To Karl it was clear Rutherford definitely compromised his integrity. Karl added that Rutherford's guilt had to be the reason why he vowed, when he came out of prison, to go full speed ahead to announce the Kingdom no matter how severe the persecution. One thing was plain from my research: Rutherford had a knack for deliberately stirring up trouble by attacking and baiting religions, the clergy and governments. This would incite acts of retribution, the victims of such being the Bible Students, whose leader, Rutherford, would then claim persecution.

As a committed believer, my research revealed many surprises, good and bad, about the organization. The negative discoveries did not influence me in any way to doubt the rightness of my beliefs. I was disappointed in behavior that brought reproach on the organization, but I believed objectionable behavior of believers was just "people junk," not in any way a reflection of the correctness of the religion.

Another interesting discovery was reading material which indicated that in the early 1950s, the reason exclusion of "sinners" became policy throughout all of Jehovah's Witnesses' congregations was primarily because of the discovery of wife swapping between some Brooklyn headquarters' personnel and local Witnesses. [289]

Harry

Among my most cherished memories was of my friendship with Harry Peloyan, a senior staff writer and coordinator (editor) of the *Awake!* journal. Harry was firmly convinced that he had the *truth*. However, from our conversations, I saw that some of his theological beliefs weren't set in stone, and he was quick to opt for a change in viewpoint if he believed a teaching was not scriptural.

Contemporary women's issues intrigued Harry. I perceived him to be an advocate against the domination and tyranny of women and children by men in the faith who used Bible teachings as a whip. Part of the *Awake!* magazine format then was to feature articles that would show how applying Bible counsel made for better lives. Consequently, when our son wrote us a letter of appreciation for his upbringing, Harry had it reproduced on the back page of the April 8, 1993, *Awake!*

Toward the end of my two years as researcher on the Watchtower's then forth-coming history book, Harry slowly began to share with me what he saw as some serious problems within the Watchtower organization. Of major concern were accusations of child sexual abuse committed by perpetrators who were Jehovah's Witnesses. From what I was told, such reports came in by letter or phone call and were too numerous to ignore. In the mid-90s, my inside-Bethel sources told me that recordkeeping of such conduct reported by the congregations began to be compiled at Bethel in the Service Department as far back as 1969.

To notify the authorities about an abuse accusation within the Witness organization was an exception to the rule. Rather, the majority of such accusations were handled secretly by judicial committees within the congregation. If victims were unhappy with the results of such hearings—because they were not believed or because the pedophile was never disciplined—they kept quiet, believing that to go to the authorities would blemish the reputation of Jehovah's Witnesses. Some became embittered but remained silent believing their abuse was an exception.

The abuse of women by domineering, patriarchal men in the organization also concerned Harry. Both of us knew that many Witness husbands misused their authority as head of the house. Busy with my work, I buried my anxiety, thinking that men such as Harry had everything under control.

The Clumsy Policies of the Watchtower

As 1992 progressed, I learned more about the serious problems involving sexual molestation of children within the congregations of Jehovah's Witnesses throughout the United States. Furthermore, I can say without any hesitation that I learned the problem extended around the world.

Shortly before I was fully aware of the evidence of inept handling of child abuse by the Watchtower organization, an article, "Healing the Wounds of Child Abuse," which was meant to help abuse victims, was published in the October 8, 1991, *Awake!*. I believed it to be an excellent article that would most assuredly help mitigate the lasting effects of this heinous crime. It was after the publishing of that particular *Awake!* I learned that it was Harry, a caring and perceptive man, who recognized the devastating trauma child abuse caused to the victims, and as chief coordinator of *Awake!*, and later as editor, was the one who influenced Lloyd Barry to authorize staff writer, Lee Waters Jr., a man known to be especially sensitive to the needs of minorities, woman and children, to write the article.

Up to this time, the Governing Body, especially one leading member, was dead set against the flock seeking out mental health advisers or therapists, believing that their counsel came from Satan's world. This even included marriage counselors. These men were convinced that applying Bible examples, statements, rules and principles could restore a person's psychological stability, even if suffering from depression. The common response from so-called "mature" Jehovah's Witnesses was to point out that reading the Bible, going to Bible meetings and participating in the door-to-door ministry to propagate Jehovah's Witnesses' religious message would cure whatever ails you, i.e., an unhappy marriage, family problems and without exception, depression. With attitudes like this, a collision course was likely to occur from events the headlines blasted forth during the late 1980s and early 1990s.

Did anyone see it coming? Without a doubt, reports of molestation within the organization were reaching the Watchtower. One young woman I worked with in the Construction Engineering Department at Bethel was shocked to learn a prominent elder in her home congregation had been arrested and convicted for pedophilia in the early 1980s. He molested four or more girls in his congregation, including his own daughter. At the time, I thought this behavior was an aberration, not a frequent occurrence, but I learned later from a Writing Department staff member that it was because of too many cases like this one that were being reported to the Service Department that an eight-page article titled, "Child Molesting, Every Mother's Nightmare," appeared in *Awake!* on January 22, 1985. The article did not admit to a problem within the organization but warned parents how to protect their children from sexual molestation. Parents were also alerted to signs of molestation.

Prominent in the 1980s were accusations of molestation by priests in the Catholic Church. I assumed that the Watchtower organization was immune to this type of problem, but I was told letters and reports were being received during those years containing similar accusations within the congregations. From Harry I learned that there were many individuals within the Watchtower organization coming forth claiming they had been abused. Further, I was told some cases were so scandalous that appalled circuit representatives, who knew prominent Jehovah's Witnesses were guilty of molestation, were reporting the situation in letters to headquarters, yet most accusations were not reported to the authorities.

Bad Advisers

Headquarters' Service Department told elders who inquired about these unusual circumstances to advise victims to "get over it, read the Bible more and look forward to the new world." This was construed by more liberal members to be taking the hard line. When victims called and talked to personnel in Writing Correspondence they were treated compassionately and advised with up-to-date information about their condition. There was a mass of contradiction going on between departments with the victims being re-victimized. That is why, to right this situation and clear the air, Lloyd Barry, the head of the Writing Department, authorized the 1991 *Awake!* article, "Healing the Wounds of Child Abuse."

At the end of 1991, elders attended the Kingdom Ministry Schools in convenient locations. Soon after, the March 23, 1992, letter to all Bodies of Elders arrived in all US congregations reiterating the problems experienced by victims of child abuse, as discussed at the elders' school, with advice as to how elders could help victims of child abuse. Professional therapy was not condemned as in the past, but the letter reminded elders that seeking treatment from professional therapists was a personal decision, and cautions were given.

By the time the March letter was received by the elders, hundreds of letters and phone calls had come into the Watchtower Society regarding the timely *Awake!* article in October 1991. To the victims, the article was like a breath of fresh air blowing through the organization, but in reality, nothing changed. Within the inner sanctums of the congregations, the dirty little secrets continued and the pressure on the victims to remain silent continued so as not to bring reproach on the religion. For the same reason, abusers were still protected.

Soon, Lloyd Barry authorized another article on child abuse for the *Awake!* of April 8, 1992. It was titled, "I Wept for Joy." This article featured quotes from the hundreds of letters received in which victims and their friends and families expressed deep appreciation to the Governing Body for the helpful October 8, 1991, article series.

Sometime during the early part of August 1992, I decided to terminate my stay at the Watchtower facility in Brooklyn, leaving there at the end of the year. Deploring what I found to be lack of desire on the part of the Watchtower organization to really address their serious child-sexual- and domestic-abuse problems, and the Society's refusal to assist the victims by advising elders of the legal and moral thing to do—and sometimes protecting perpetrators—I decided this was no place for me, although I kept my opinions to myself, expressing them only to my husband.

However, before I left, I spent time on one more research project. Harry authorized me to put together a package of information alerting and proving to the Governing Body that we had a serious problem with sexual child abuse within the organization. One week after I left headquarters, Harry Peloyan forwarded the huge packet of documented information I had gathered to each one of the Governing Body members in early January 1993.

When I returned to my home in Tennessee, I continued to do research for the Writing Department. I studied the breadth and scope of the sexual child abuse problem in other religions and across society at large. In this way, I thought I could be of some use to those at Watchtower headquarters who desired a change in child abuse policies.

I was greatly relieved when another letter was received by all Bodies of Elders in the United States. It was dated, February 3, 1993. I saw that the work I had done had reaped results as the letter actually discussed information I included in the package for the Governing Body. In the letter the elders were instructed how to help individuals who had recently started having memories of abuse. Further, both the seeking of professional help and the reporting of abuse to the authorities was not to be spoken of disparagingly by elders.

However, much to my horror, after being home only a few months, I learned that within the congregations in our area there were a number of molestation accusations. It was disturbing to know these cases were dealt with secretly by untrained elders.

New Clumsy Policies

I sent a general letter about the situation to the Watchtower Society, and also a personal, beseeching letter on July 21, 1993, to Governing Body member Lloyd Barry, now deceased. In my home congregation there was a confessed molester who used the Witnesses' house-to-house ministry program to make friends with women and their children with the intention of molesting the children. This was one of the reasons I wrote the letter to Lloyd Barry asking him to forbid confessed molesters from engaging in the house-to-house religious activity. I also expressed my concern that, within the congregations, too often predators who expressed repentance over their acts were eventually put back into their position of authority after a certain amount of years, their acts never made public. Consequently, they were in a position to molest more children, which many of them did. Lloyd Barry never acknowledged my letter although I talked to him briefly when I visited Watchtower headquarters in 1994.

Additionally, friends at the Writing Department told me certain members of the Governing Body were backing away from what was stated at the 1991 elders' school and the two excellent letters sent to the elders.

Nothing was done about this situation until January 1997 when the Watchtower Society announced in the January 1, 1997, Watchtower article, "Abhor What Is Wicked," that they would not allow anybody who had a history of molestation to hold a position of authority or responsibility within a congregation. The announcement also said they would not protect a child abuser. However, I was deeply disturbed to read these words, "If he [molester] seems to be repentant, he will be encouraged to make spiritual progress, share in the field service..."—exactly the opposite of my request to restrict their religious field service activity.

In addition to this, there was a loophole in that policy statement. The article stated that "no known molester could hold a position of authority in the organization." The key word "known"[290] was the way molesters stayed in positions of authority. If they weren't "known" as molesters to the congregation or to the community, they were not removed. This information is found in the March 14, 1997, letter "To All Bodies of Elders." In that same letter another problem emerged. It stated that "Others may have been guilty of child molestation before they were baptized. The bodies of elders should not query these individuals."

If that wasn't enough, I had a huge problem with the two-witness to child abuse[291] rule because it was basically the reason elders gave victims to explain why they (the elders) wouldn't believe the accusation or report the abuse to the authorities.

When I first became aware of sexual child abuse in the Watchtower organization, I didn't comprehend the scope or harm of the "two-witness" Bible teaching as applied to molestation. It was only after 1997 when I discovered that the requirement of needing two witnesses to the molestation protected molesters, and this was a larger threat to all the children in the congregations. And the confidentiality rule, if the victim couldn't back up their accusation, and the accused person denied the allegation, was the trap that kept molesters hidden and children open game. The two-witness rule most certainly needed to be reformed.

The World Outside

I officially left the organization in the beginning of 1998. Putting my anxiety aside, I went to a local community college to take some tests, whereupon I received a scholarship, and that gift gave me the strength to go on without my Jehovah's Witnesses' friends from all over the world. (I knew for a certainty that they would shun me when they realized that I was no longer one of them.) While attending college I discovered there was life outside of the Watchtower. At that time my husband and I had been married thirty-nine years. We never kept secrets from one another. Trust and respect was the backbone to our very successful marriage. Therefore, Joe accepted my exiting of our religion, and he was aware that I could not accept the sexual child abuse policies. Further, he knew I was convinced that I should not extend my right hand in friendship to anybody breaking God's laws because that principle was taught to all Jehovah's Witnesses. I believed the Witnesses' leaders were encouraging elders to break Caesar's law by not reporting the crime of child abuse and not encouraging parents and/or victims to go directly to the authorities.

My immediate Witness family did not forsake me then. In the beginning, they were okay with my leaving the organization. In fact, two of them also left the organization, and those who remained Witnesses, including my husband, just did not talk to me about religion, so we continued to have a good relationship. My son, an elder in another state, and daughter-in-law along with their new baby, continued to associate with me because I was not disfellowshipped. My husband was still an elder and the other elders did not have any idea why I left the religion and were, it seemed, reluctant to ask my husband. Also, I did not say anything negative to anyone about the Witness organization, so I was not perceived as a threat.

Bill Bowen

Towards the end of 2000 a friend of mine saw, on a Jehovah's-Witness-related internet discussion group, a post written by an elder asking if any other elders had a problem as he had just encountered when he discovered the presiding overseer in his congregation had admitted to molestation some years prior. Since the congregation had no knowledge of the crime, the man remained in his position.

My friend corresponded with this elder and within a few months so did I. What I told this man about the serious problem of molestation and how it was dealt with within the organization was quite a revelation to him. We knew that the Watchtower organization was internationally guilty of concealing the *crime* of child abuse and they had to change their ways. Soon the elder, Bill Bowen, decided to resign his position and go public over this issue. This happened on January 1, 2001. The media coverage in Bill's home state of Kentucky about his resignation as an elder over the child abuse issue was tremendous. In addition, Bill and I came up with an idea for a website which Bill established and named *Silentlambs*. There, Jehovah's Witnesses who were victims of sexual child molestation by Witness perpetrators could tell their stories. Within weeks there were 1,000 posted. After four years, there were nearly 6,000 (2009).

Publicity and Excommunication

Although I did not reveal myself publicly when Bill did, within weeks, Bill and I were on a plane going to New York City to be interviewed by national television network NBC about the Watchtower's child abuse problem for their documentary program *Dateline*. After the producer did extensive research, which established our claims were true, he scheduled us for taping interviews. The producer also discussed the accusations with the Watchtower Society, which they denied. The program was set to air on May 28, 2002, and the Watchtower organization was informed of this. They then quickly notified the local elders to schedule judicial hearings for us. In early May, I proved to them that I was not guilty of the charges brought against me. One of the charges was "causing divisions within the organization." I disproved that charge because I had not as yet caused any divisions. Within days the local elders scheduled another judicial hearing with new charges concocted. I declined to attend that meeting because it seemed futile—if I disproved those charges, it was obvious they would just come up with different charges. So, I was subsequently disfellowshipped on May 19, 2002. I asked for an appeal hearing, but declined to go because it was going to be held in an area motel with six men and me, and my attorney was not allowed to attend.

Bill Bowen was disfellowshipped around the same time. It was obvious to us that we were disfellowshipped shortly before *Dateline* was broadcast so any viewers, who were Jehovah's Witnesses, would not believe our story because former members are viewed as disgruntled, and disfellowshipped members are construed as being unrepentant sinners and not to be believed, so this was a cunning move for the Watchtower.

Then something else happened that really stunned me. Because of a letter the Watchtower sent to all US congregations in the week before *Dateline* was broadcast, which my husband Joe believed was filled with half-truths about the issues, he handed the presiding elder his keys to the Kingdom Hall after the letter was read to the congregation, and told the elder he was resigning. Joe was asked to submit a letter of resignation which he did, giving each elder a copy and sending copies to two Governing Body members, along with one copy to a friend in the Service Department at headquarters. Joe was subsequently disfellowshipped in July 2002 because he defended me in his resignation letter. He also expressed his own views about the child-abuse situation, which were not the same as the Watchtower's views. Like Bill Bowen and me, Joe's major complaint was that child sexual abuse was a crime and should be reported to the authorities and not to the elders.

In trying to defend itself, the Watchtower publicly libeled Bill and me to reporters, saying the judicial hearing was called because we were sinners, not because we were going to be on *Dateline*, even stating that they did not know who was going to appear on the program. When asked by reporters what scripture did the religion use to disfellowship, Watchtower spokespersons were quoted as saying the scripture was 1 Corinthians 5:11,12 which commands that congregations remove the wicked man who was greedy, a fornicator, an idolater, a reviler, a drunkard, or an extortionist. Since I did not commit any of these gross sins, in November of 2002, I filed a defamation lawsuit against the Watchtower which is slowly winding itself through the judiciary system. Since that time, Bill Bowen and I have been interviewed many times by the press as we continue to try to make the public aware of the Watchtower's protection of pedophiles.

In the August 8, 1993, *Awake!*, our son's beautiful letter appeared extolling our parental virtues,[292] yet not even ten years later, he completely changed his mind and decided to totally shun us after we were disfellowshipped for speaking out about the hidden child-sexual-abuse problem within the organization. He told the press I did a "noble" thing trying to protect the Witnesses' children, however, he did not believe I did the right thing by going public. (Apparently, I broke the eleventh commandment, the most important one to Jehovah's Witnesses: *You must not commit publicity.*) He was told that I misunderstood the Society's policies, and by my actions, caused thousands of people to leave the organization, leave the Bible and leave God. Hence, these walk-away Jehovah's Witnesses were going to die at Armageddon and I was responsible for their deaths. He chose to believe what he was told and this is the reason he has never spoken to me again. It has been over seven years since we have seen our son, daughter-in-law and their small child, our grandchild. If we send any mail to them, it is always returned unopened.

When I look back over my life from the time I was baptized as one of Jehovah's Witnesses at the age of fourteen, it simply amazes me where that first step led. My only desire as a woman in the Watchtower organization was to help people to understand the spiritual mysteries of life, of course, in line with the Watchtower's interpretation. Soon after leaving the Watchtower organization, my goal was still to help people, but I have concluded that I'll never be able to unravel the mysteries of life, let alone help others to understand them. However, in my opinion, what I can do best is to share my experiences to help people understand the mysteries of the Watchtower Society. In that way I am making known the truth and the truth as I experienced it might even set Jehovah's Witnesses free.

Barbara Anderson,
Sept. 11, 2009

Conclusion

The efforts of Barbara Anderson and Bill Bowen have, without a doubt, contributed to a change in the Watchtower's policies regarding pedophiles within the organization. As of October 2003, when the Bodies of Elders received a letter in which this problematic issue was addressed, the elders are now advised to report all sexual abuse within the congregations to the authorities.

Still, it puzzles me that even in this letter the fundamentalist "two-witness" rule was upheld. Victims of abuse are still required to produce two witnesses to the alleged crime. Referring to the *two-witness rule* of Deuteronomy 19:15, the letter concludes that only if "two persons individually have witnessed an incident of ... abuse, the statements of these two witnesses are sufficient for action to be taken." ("Letter to all elders," October 2003; translated from the Danish edition.)

Apparently, the leaders of the Watchtower Society still prefer to solve cases involving sexual abuse behind closed doors. And, only if the problems can't be solved internally and the victim insists, the authorities *may* be involved.

By the above-mentioned letter to the Bodies of Elders, it appears the accusation is to be reported to the Jehovah's Witnesses branch office and the elders have to follow the law of the country when that requires that they must report such a case, and then report the matter to the authorities, even in the absence of a confession or an indictment not being confirmed by other witnesses. Furthermore, it appears from the letter that if the victim wants to address the authorities, the person concerned is in his full right to do this. In autumn 2011, I learned, however, that the published "Letter to all elders," at the request of the Watchtower Society in Denmark, has now been removed from the site.

In the least, the leaders of the Watchtower Society are now seemingly doing more to expose the pedophiles within the movement. However, I will still sadly be forced to conclude that many, both elders and victims, will still often choose silence over speaking out for a number of reasons: the elders for fear of being perceived as being critical towards the organization, the victims for fear of bringing reproach on their religion and their families. The result being that not only will the victims have to deal with the psychological effects of their traumatic experiences but also run the risk of losing the social ties to their religious community, which, in itself, can cause a severe personal crisis.

On January 22, 2006, I received an email from Barbara, in which she wrote:
"When I returned home from Bethel, I quietly interviewed three elders who were close friends. Each of the men went to different neighboring congregations. I asked them how many child abuse molestations among Jehovah's Witnesses were of common knowledge in their area and happened in the ten year period from 1984–1994. The total was about eighteen. That's an average of six per congregation which were known to the community. I wrote to Governing Body member Lloyd Barry and told him about my findings, begging him

to take a second look at the Society's policies and change what needed to be changed to better protect the children. But, nothing happened."

In February 2007, the corporate heads of Jehovah's Witnesses, the Watch Tower Bible and Tract Society of Pennsylvania, secretly reached out-of-court settlements for nine lawsuits brought by sixteen victims of molestation. Surreptitiously informed of the settlement, Barbara Anderson then purchased all of the court records from the nine lawsuits, nearly 5,000 pages, and put them on a CD, along with a 100-page commentary titled, *Secrets of Pedophilia in an American Religion, Jehovah's Witnesses in Crisis.*

On November 21, 2007, in a segment of the NBC *Nightly News* program, the out-of-court settlement along with an interview with Barbara was broadcast on television. NBC also published a lengthy MSNBC article on the internet which discussed facts found in the documents about three notorious JW-molesters who were never reported to the authorities by the Witnesses, even after many complaints by Witness victims to church elders. One of the pedophiles, Rick McLean, is still on *America's Most Wanted* list. Furthermore, included in the article was the settlement figure for one victim that amounted to nearly a million dollars. (For further study, see http://www.youtube.com/watch?v=QLAC9kS_EqM and http://www.msnbc.msn.com/id/21917798.)

Sexual abuse of children is a global occurrence within all layers of society and all religious communities, and Jehovah's Witnesses are no exception to this. However, in the US, investigations have confirmed that insular patriarchal religions such as the Mormons, Jehovah's Witnesses and Amish have a higher incidence of molestation than mainstream religions. (Reference Barbara's email of Jan. 22, 2006.)

However, it should also be noted here that the Catholic Church, as of early 2010, has been the subject of a worldwide criticism because of reported assaults on minors, which must have occurred during a long period of time, and where the church is accused of protecting the involved priests. Church celibacy has been identified as the reason for the infringements, but this is disputed by the church, which believes the crux of the problem is homosexuality. In any case, this latest development shows that Jehovah's Witnesses by no means are alone in this type of violation. Despite the fact that Jehovah's Witnesses do not practice an institutionalized form of celibacy, although young people within the movement are recommended to practice celibate-like restraint for a number of years so they are better able to engage in service work, violations still take place. This may be due to two factors:

1. That the movement may attract pedophiles
2. That the movement's hostile attitudes toward sex through the decades have created a collective complex in relation to sex, which therefore, at some point can be released in assaults on minors.

Barbara Anderson and Bill Bowen have, by approaching the media, done a commendable pioneering work and today their efforts are recognized as an *important part* of the history of the Jehovah's Witnesses. They have, no matter how many or few the victims, given the *silent children* or "silent lambs" within the movement a voice and a forum in which they might speak out about what happened to them, and the trauma that was inflicted upon them.

Barbara Anderson's report and discoveries inspired another former member who had been an elder for over thirty years. He lives in a European city considered historically important in many regards—including Christian church history—Geneva. Like Barbara's story, my book would be incomplete without this one.

Chapter 33

The *Human Rights* Aspect

In 2009, I visited the former JW elder I mentioned at the end of the previous chapter. At the time, he was sixty-five, yet energetic beyond the ordinary. His name is Roberto di Stefano. An Italian, born in Egypt, he lived in a large house in France just across the border from Switzerland. From his home, we crossed the border into Switzerland to visit Geneva.

Roberto took me on a sightseeing tour of the famous old city. We looked, among other things, at the large statues of the four Protestant church fathers, including Jean (John) Calvin from around AD 1541. By that year the Middle Ages had ended, and a new era, the Renaissance, had just started to ignite the world. Calvin was a terrible "idealist" and fanatic who became notorious for his "theocratic" church regime in Geneva.[293]

The following account may perhaps be perceived by my readers as a trivial story about a man who had to break away from a religious community he had been part of since his childhood, meaning what happened was simply his own fault, end of story.

However, as is often the case with these situations, there is much more to his story than initially meets the eye.

Roberto di Stefano had lived in Geneva with his family most of his life, but due to his professional activities and, at that time, his heavy commitment as a Jehovah's Witness, he never had the time to really explore the city he lived in. However, after he took early retirement, he was able to play the tourist for the first time. Naturally, it was not the first time he visited the Old Town, but the first time he saw it with new eyes.

Roberto had "inherited" his faith in the Jehovah's Witnesses through his parents, who originally lived in the Italian community of Alexandria in Egypt, where he grew up. Because of this he is fluent in Italian and French, speaks some Arabic, Spanish and German, but particularly knows English very well.

The Triggering Factor

Because of Roberto's commitment, first in Geneva in the Italian-speaking Witness congregations, and then, regularly, all over Switzerland as a public speaker, he was well-known; he and his family had always been appreciated and seen as a model for the religious community. Still, after serving for almost thirty years as an elder, Roberto suddenly found himself in conflict with the area's circuit overseer and the elders of his former congregation.

Roberto di Stefano was not only the presiding overseer, that is, a leader of a local congregation, but also a so-called *circuit assembly overseer*. This position gave him responsibility for and management of a larger number of elders from various departments of the entire Swiss-French organization. In his role, it was not infrequent to have to deal with interpersonal issues. Unfortunately, one of these had to do with one of his best friends, the circuit overseer. The list of complaints about the way many members felt they were treated by the circuit overseer became longer and longer. Therefore, Roberto decided to take up the matter personally with his friend. Contrary to Roberto's expectations, his friend did not appreciate his initiative and started a subtle backbiting campaign through other elders against Roberto.

"Wait on Jehovah"

Roberto resigned as elder. He appealed to the Swiss branch of the Watchtower Society in Thun, but without success. They gave the impression they wanted to settle the issue, but in reality never did so, trying to cover up the whole issue by asking Roberto to "wait on Jehovah."

For five years he waited for the branch to resolve the situation. Seeing no signs of progress, he finally concluded that "this organization, which pretended to be God's only representative on Earth, was not trustworthy." He began to wonder why he had always accepted this for so long, and began investigating their credentials and biblical claims, which he had taken for granted all his life. By examining the teachings and the history of the movement compared to its claims, Roberto concluded the movement could have never been chosen to be God's *only* organization on Earth. Towards the end of 2004, he finally decided to simply abandon the movement without any public demonstration of his newly acquired personal freedom.

For the next five years he continued to investigate the history and teachings of the movement, only to find more and more confirmation of his previous findings. Still, Roberto knew that due to his reputation in Switzerland and abroad, the organization would soon look at his situation and push to change it.

He expected that, one day or another, the organization would expel him. In this way, they would prevent him from having contact with any acquaintances in the movement: "I was not to pollute them with my views," Roberto said. He added with a smile, "Even a simple 'hello' is forbidden." It seemed like the first time he realized how it all was, when the truth dawned on him in this new way.

For him, the roles had been reversed, and then the truth hit twice as hard. Roberto had at one time participated in expelling members of the movement that would not behave. So he really knew it all from within. And it had been thus as long as he could remember. Little surprise, then, that it took him years to come to his senses. The movement was deeply etched in his soul, and its marks could not just be wiped away overnight.

Not that he personally cared too much about it, since his good friends continued to see him. "But the very thought that an organization teaches this level of discrimination in our century, when human rights are claimed everywhere, was unacceptable," Roberto said with a strength that comes from allowing the truth into his mind.

What I found most interesting in Roberto's story, however, was the way he had tackled his new situation. And I was very impressed by his action-oriented approach or proactive behavior. The situation required him to act. He could not help it. It was simply not in his nature just to shut up and go quietly. Why should he? Basically, I think the choice suited him well. He would have control over what happened to him next.

Knowing very well how the situation would evolve, he devised an action plan that would publicly expose the Watchtower organization at the right moment.

Roberto Fights Back

Roberto has recently accepted an early retirement option from Du Pont de Nemours, the world-renowned, multi-national petro-chemical company that had employed him for almost forty years. Therefore, he had time and means to engage in an information campaign against the Jehovah's Witnesses:

"The first thing I did was to develop a website critical of Jehovah's Witnesses' teachings. The website would go live at the same time the right moment would materialize," Roberto said.

"The next thing I did was write a letter to my former fellow believers explaining the reasons for my resignation as an elder. But also why I now no longer shared the beliefs I held for the past fifty years, in particular why the Watchtower could not be God's organization. Three hundred copies of the six-page letter were prepared and placed in their respective envelops, ready to be sent at the right moment."

This came some months later when the Body of Elders in Geneva summoned him, via registered letter, to appear on May 20, 2009, in front of an internal judicial committee. During the trial, they would inquire about his critical attitude towards the teachings of the Watchtower Society. In the course of our discussion, I queried him about the events and he answered as follows:

Did everything happen as you had planned? I asked.

"I never showed up at the judicial committee meeting I was summoned to attend. That same day about 300 people received my letter—and another 100 received an email with the letter that I had prepared many months before and which gave the reasons for having left the cult. Of course only a few replied, some angrily, but many more gave me their support. And some even left the movement. So, it was not a bad idea after all."

Did you receive a written notice of your exclusion?

"No, I have not received any notice, neither a letter nor a phone call. I was informed *verbally* by someone who attended the meeting of June 4, 2009, where they announced I was *no longer a Jehovah's Witness*. In fact, the situation was even worse. According to the internal rules of the movement, when someone does not appear at the judicial committee meeting, he is summoned a *second time* and only if he then does not attend is he judged *in absentia*," Roberto said.

"In my case," Roberto continued, "I have to say that things went differently; in fact violating their own internal procedures, I was declared "expelled" without even knowing about the second summons. I was traveling abroad at that time and upon returning home on June 3 found a post office notice for a registered letter addressed to me. This means that they proceeded with the disfellowshipping [excommunication] process and announced it publicly to the congregation, even before I had a chance to discover the content of the second registered letter."

Roberto knows about the rules of order in such situations. He was chairman for about thirty judiciary committees. And although the decisions of the committees were not his responsibility solely (they are, after all, three-man committees), he nevertheless comforts himself that only one-third of the accused were ostracized. In retrospect, that number seems to him to be too many.

European Conferences in 2009

Also in anticipation of his expulsion, Roberto invited Barbara Anderson to attend the European conferences in June–July of 2009. The same Barbara Anderson who maintains an active presence within the X-JWs worldwide and was instrumental in uncovering the pedophilia issue.

Roberto had translated her speeches into French and Italian to publicly expose the Society's pedophilia issues in different European cities, including Rome, Paris, Barcelona, Edinburgh and Geneva. Hundreds of people attended the conferences and heard about the pedophilia cover up by the Watchtower Society and its internal policies.

"I had been an elder for almost three decades but knew nothing about the problem," Roberto said. "Neither the branch nor the traveling overseers ever informed us, the Body of Elders, about it. At that time, I was not yet using the internet to do research. Therefore, I did not know that there were several legal cases involving the Watchtower Society which had to pay millions of dollars to settle a number of these cases.

Grandir avec Jéhovah

Expecting to be expelled one day or another, Roberto had made prior contact with Swiss Television Channel TSR1, to promote a program exposing the methods of the Watchtower Society. He contacted the same journalist who had been instrumental in the French broadcast of a Swedish program on Jehovah's Witnesses concerning the pedophilia issue on July 14, 2005.

The new program was centered on the way children are brought up in the organization, with all the fears and restrictions. The program was titled "*Grandir avec Jéhovah*" (Brought-up by Jehovah). It aired on November 11, 2010, in the series *Temps Présent* and later a dozen more times on several francophone TV stations around the world (TV5). It showed the effects of being raised as a Jehovah's Witness, in a world apart, alienated from the society in which they take little or no part. Roberto elaborates:

"I was told by the journalists who conducted the program that it had been a real success, since it captured 41% of the audience that night, one of the highest ever reached by the series *Temps Présent*. The second success the same TV channel obtained involved a number of related posts on the *Temps Present* blog forum. Over 900 messages were received in only four days! This also seems to have been a record for the Swiss TV program, according to the journalists."

Human Rights Defense

Roberto is not short of ideas. He participated in organizing a demonstration against the Watchtower Society in front of the Italian Parliament on December 1, 2010. Although the crowd was small, it was the very first time that such demonstrations were held in Italy. The cause of the demonstration was the exclusion policy the Watch Tower Society applied to members who leave the movement. In particular, in relation to an Italian law proposal which, if enforced by the Italian Parliament, would give the local Witnesses *more privileges*, despite the fact that their internal regulations, unknown to the Italian senators, violate the Charter of the Human Rights because of the ostracism practice. Roberto added, gravely:

"For almost ten years the Italian branch office of the Jehovah's Witnesses in Rome actively sought the Italian government's recognition similar to the Catholic Church's. In 1986, the branch had been granted the status of legal entity, but they wanted more privileges as a religious movement, such as the right to collect income taxes for their movement through the state's income tax mechanism. Very awkward from an organization who condemns governments to their destruction by God, but who, in the meantime, wants to take advantage of government-sanctioned opportunities."

These agreements between some recognized churches and the Italian government are called *intesa*, or simply, agreement.

Due to the historical failure of succeeding Italian governments, the Jehovah's Witnesses' claim was never debated in front of the parliament. This time, however, a law proposal made its way through and the government presented it to the Italian Parliament on June 8, 2010.

Roberto continued:

"In the past, to stop such an initiative from being processed by Parliament, a petition signed by over 20,000 people was sent to the authorities. This time, in 2010, in addition to hundreds of letters sent by former Jehovah's Witnesses to members of Parliament, we decided to organize a demonstration in front of the Italian Parliament. The issue we wanted to expose was the discriminatory policies of the Watchtower Society, unknown to the general public and, in particular, to secular authorities. These are the policies imposed by the leadership of the movement, against those who decide to use their freedom of religion to quietly quit the Jehovah's Witnesses. The ostracism is such that it corresponds, basically, to the *social death* of the outcast.

"I therefore participated in the organization of the manifestation and took part, as speaker, along with another long-time dissident and whistleblower, Doctor Achille Aveta."

Human Rights Violations

The growing opposition to the Watchtower Society all over the world is an important part of the history of Jehovah's Witnesses. The opposition is not so much about the beliefs, but particularly about the destructive internal regulations damaging the lives of hundreds of thousands of individuals both within the organization and without. A more strident opposition began years ago with the life-threatening ban on blood transfusion, a doctrine that has already killed too many people, including defenseless children. Recently, the pedophilia issue has highlighted the irrational policy requiring *two witnesses* to the crime before it will be internally condemned. If this continues, it will surely become as large a thorn in the organization's reputation as has happened for the Catholic Church.

Now the opposition issue pivots on the human rights violation of the internal policies that deny members their right to hold personal religious opinions, to share their ideas with others, and even the right to change religion altogether. The internal regulations call for a complete discrimination against anyone in the organization who chooses to recognize and act upon these rights.[294]

Still, this issue is difficult to assess because it clashes with claims of freedom of religion which any religious movement can claim to embrace, including Jehovah's Witnesses. This freedom is about beliefs, true, but it should not be a shield used to hide internal practices and regulations that violate dissenters' human rights and intimidate their personal relationships.

Regarding the future, Roberto di Stefano said:

"I will use all my available resources and take advantage of the freedom given to me by the law, the Constitution and the Declaration of Human Rights, to expose the hidden and dangerous side of the Watchtower organization and teachings by organizing and participating in any event which would help the cause."

(To read more, please visit Roberto di Stefano's website: http://www.testi-moni-di-geova.info/)

PART FOUR

Evasive Acrobatics

To harmonize their views with the 'New Testament,' church theologians must indulge in what amounts to theological acrobatics: juggling, twisting, or even ignoring critical Bible texts.
—Awake! June 22, 1991, p. 6

The Churches of Christendom and their ministers, instead of copying the fine example of Jesus in giving clear, straightforward answers from God's Word, have resorted to long-winded and evasive explanations that caused one of the advertising experts to remark: 'The Church is an interference factor between God and man.'
—Awake! September 8, 1981, p. 19

Chapter 34

Problems Arising for the "Little Flock"

Throughout the 1970s, Brooklyn debated whether 1914 should be disregarded. Even the supreme leader of the Witnesses at the time, President Nathan H. Knorr, expressed doubts about 1914 to a closed circle at the top of the organization. He was—according to Raymond Franz—not very sure of this crucial year, stressing the fundamental Christian doctrines as the basis for this. Knorr was primarily an organization man, which is why he entrusted education matters to the Society's *gray eminence*, Fred Franz—the man who succeeded Knorr as president in 1977.

In the 1970s they mainly discussed if 1914's significance could be applied to 1934; this would give them space in the timeline, but subsequently create other problematic discrepancies. The whole teaching system had come under fierce criticism—partly from Raymond Franz (*Crisis of Conscience,* 1983), partly from the congregational base (Carl Olof Jonsson and others)—even though relatively few individuals fostered this development. Still, it invited a violent reaction from Brooklyn that was reflected in the many purge trials.

A veritable cleansing virus attacked all across the entire organization. Yet, if the leaders denied 1914 as a pivotal year, then everything in the doctrine system must also be carefully examined. And then, they necessarily had to ask: What about growth? Would they be able to continue with the same growth rate, if they no longer set Armageddon as the boogeyman just around the corner? Would this not affect the members' commitment and enthusiasm, and thus, burden the movement's international growth? To reject Armageddon's immediate approach would be throwing away the *main motivation* for the movement's seven million members. I think these were the issues the Brooklyn leaders discussed and debated at length.

Stuck in the 1914 Lies

The management needed to act quickly. After Jonsson's published investigation about the Society's chronology, with the gentile times as fulcrum, and

Raymond Franz's 1983 book (both available in the United States in new additions) the leaders were compelled to stem the criticisms. Based on the reactions of the Governing Body, one can conclude the members of the council have been managing an ongoing emergency situation since 1980. They were stigmatized and totally paralyzed because of the 1914 dogma. As we have seen in the context of exclusions worldwide, when the accused placed emphasis on basic Christian values, leadership's role was dictated partly by *loyalty* to the Society's 1914 dogma, partly by *obedience* to the Organization—with a large *O*—and these factors ultimately decided whether the accused could continue to be members.

Rather than respond to the critics, the Society did the exact opposite. They shut down, shut out, turned off. They made it clear to members that not believing in or even questioning the 1914 teachings was, henceforth, cause for exclusion. Of course, the 1914 doctrine eventually proved to be built on quicksand. Neither archaeological scholars nor Bible critics could justify an untenable theory founded on amateur-like speculations from the 18th century—and even earlier.

In *The Watchtower* feature "Questions from Readers" in the April 1, 1986, issue, someone asked why Jehovah's Witnesses had "disfellowshipped (excommunicated) for apostasy some who still profess belief in God, the Bible, and Jesus Christ?" As we have seen in previous chapters, it is precisely the type of argument common among apostates. If someone still believes in basic Christian values, why are they expelled?

This oft-repeated query was apparently such a big problem for the Brooklyn leaders that they now brought it up in the magazines' reader box. At the same time it was indirectly an indication of what direction the opposition within the movement had taken. The critics focused on fundamental Christian values—Knorr's simple values. About these simple doctrines, *The Watchtower* wrote:

"Obviously, a basis for approved fellowship with Jehovah's Witnesses cannot rest merely on a belief in God, in the Bible, in Jesus Christ, and so forth. The Roman Catholic pope, as well as the Anglican Archbishop of Canterbury, professes such beliefs, yet their church memberships are exclusive of each other. Likewise, simply professing to have such beliefs would not authorize one to be known as one of Jehovah's Witnesses" (Ibid.).

In the response from *The Watchtower*, the editor enumerated various points of the doctrines, in particular including those "Scriptural beliefs that are unique to Jehovah's Witnesses." Actually, this was a reasonable point of view, when the movement wanted to be identified by its exceptional positions initially based on its origin in the 1870s. (Ibid.)

Having established Jehovah's sovereign rule, it was explained that "Jesus Christ had a *prehuman existence* and is *subordinate* to his heavenly Father" (which in fact is *Arianism*[295]), that there is a "faithful and discreet slave," who has received all of Jesus' earthly interests entrusted, and that this "slave is associated with the Governing Body of Jehovah's Witnesses," the 1914 dogma is listed fourth:

"That 1914 marked the end of the Gentile Times and the establishment of the Kingdom of God in the heavens, as well as the time for Christ's foretold presence..." (Ibid.).

Other doctrines were also strongly emphasized, for example: only 144,000 Christians will receive the heavenly reward; Armageddon, the battle of the great day of God the Almighty, is near; the battle will be followed by Christ's Millennial Reign, which will restore an earth-wide paradise; and the first to enjoy it will be the present "great crowd" of Jesus' "other sheep" (Ibid.).

If the accused did not believe in the above teachings, they were considered as diseased limbs attacked by gangrene and needing to be removed. A veritable campaign against the apostates appears to have been initiated in March 1986. *The Watchtower* of that month included a comment about the dreadful disease mentioned above:

"Like gangrene, apostate reasoning is nothing but quick-spreading spiritual death. And since the members of the congregation are like one body, there is a danger that others may be infected. If the one spreading apostate teachings cannot be restored to spiritual health by loving but firm application of the balm of God's Word, amputation of this member (disfellowshipping) may be the only alternative for the protection of other members of the body" (*WT*, March 15, 1986).[296]

The organization addressed the growing doubts among the members with extreme seriousness in those years, as seen in a campaign against the apostates from the beginning of the 1990s, which I must characterize as decidedly hateful. *The Watchtower* of October 1, 1993, reads:

"Apostates are included among those who show their hatred of Jehovah by revolting against him. Apostasy is, in reality, a rebellion against Jehovah. Some apostates profess to know and serve God, but they reject teachings or requirements set out in his Word. Others claim to believe the Bible, but they reject Jehovah's organization and actively try to hinder its work. When they deliberately choose such badness after knowing what is right, when the bad becomes so ingrained that it is an inseparable part of their makeup, then a Christian must hate (in the Biblical sense of the word) those who have inseparably attached themselves to the badness" (*WT*, Oct. 1, 1993).

The 1914 doctrine was gravely wounded, and Brooklyn knew it.

The "Composite Sign" Fall

Clearly the problem was greater than Jonsson's first thesis showed, because the Jehovah's Witnesses' whole eschatological and apocalyptic teaching threatened to crumble.

If 1914's significance had to be discarded, they also needed to question the doctrine of *the end*, which was also rooted in 1914. But that still was not all! The fulfillment of the signs—consisting of world wars, earthquakes, widespread famine, persecution of the "only true Christians"[297] (the Jehovah's Witnesses), emergence of false prophets, immorality, the layout of the "abomination of desolation"[298] (UN), Jehovah's Witnesses preaching of the gospel of the new world and much more called "the composite sign" by Watchtower leaders— would collapse with a resounding thud.

Brooklyn was totally shocked at the possible domino effect of discarding 1914.

Carl Olof Jonsson also discussed the fulfillment of these signs in the book, *The "Sign" of the Last Days—When?,* which he and Wolfgang Herbst (his friend Rud Persson, who was forced to write under a pseudonym because he was still an active elder at the time) published together in 1987.

This book was written because of readers' reactions to the Swedish edition of Jonsson's first publication, *Slutade hedningarnas tider i 1914?,*[299] published in 1984. Jonsson soon learned the Society rejected his book with the response: "Yes, the chronology of the Watchtower might be mistaken, but it is not so important, because we have the 'composite sign' that has been proven since 1914" (letter from Jonsson, February 20, 2004).

In the book, Jonsson and Herbst documented that Jehovah's Witnesses' teachings on the so-called composite sign were a house of cards ready to crumble at the slightest touch. Not surprising, the Watchtower leaders discouraged reading *renegade literature* because members studying those books would quickly make the sad discovery that they had been duped for years. Or rather that they had, perhaps, fooled themselves.

The risk of exposure to undesirable material is small when the members, to great extent, are constantly held behind a barrier of fear that effectively discourages them from even daring to read that kind of "bad" literature. So it's still *the loner*, the Adam-like maverick, who is willing to take the decisive step further toward the fruits that hang on the Tree of Knowledge, which simply must be plucked—one by one.

"1914—The Generation That Will Not Pass Away"

The above headline is from an article in *The Watchtower* of May 15, 1984. The title refers to Matthew 24:34, as found in the Jehovah's Witnesses own Bible translation, *New World Translation*. The verse reads: "Truly I say to YOU that this generation will by no means pass away until all these things occur." And the same verse in the *King James Version*: "Verily I say unto you, this generation shall not pass, till all these things be fulfilled."

On the front page of that *Watchtower* issue is the image of a bunch of elderly, grey-haired people who look toward the imaginary horizons of liberation. The Witnesses' NW-translation is obviously adapted to the dogmatic needs of the time of publication; some of the people living in 1984, who were born prior to

1914, still had to witness the end in Armageddon. That is, within a generation's lifetime.

The article asks what Jesus meant by the term "a generation" and the answer, in part:

"*Some have* interpreted 'generation' to mean a period of 30, 40, 70 or *even 120 years*. However, a generation is really related to people and events, rather than to a fixed number of years." And after a reference to various dictionary definitions, they come to the conclusion that these "definitions embrace both those born around the time of a historic event and all those alive at that time" (p. 5; italics are mine; notice the subtle accusation: "some have"; and also: "even 120 years").

It's of interest that Brooklyn here—eleven years before 1995 when the doctrine of "the generation" was at last rejected—begins offering conflicting arguments. These are almost literally repeated in 1995, where the conclusion is quite the opposite of that in 1984. In 1984 the generation who experienced 1914 could still be alive when Armageddon began.

To illustrate the contrast between 1984's discussion and 1995's, *The Watchtower* gives us this for comparison:

"Rather than provide a rule for measuring time, the term 'generation' as used by Jesus refers principally to contemporary people of a certain historical period, with their identifying characteristics" (*WT*, Nov. 1, 1995).

In the article from 1984 the Society wrote:

"If Jesus used 'generation' in that sense and we apply it to 1914, then the babies of that generation are now 70 years old or older. And others alive in 1914 are in their 80's or 90's, a few even having reached a hundred. There are still many millions of that generation alive. Some of them 'will by no means pass away until all things occur'" (this quote from Luke 21:32 is from NW-1963; *WT*, May 15, 1984, p. 5).

A little later in the article one finds the headline and accompanying article:

"Is There Enough Time?"

"From a purely human viewpoint, it could appear that these developments could hardly take place before the generation of 1914 disappears from the scene. But fulfillment of all the foretold events affecting the generation of 1914 does not depend on comparatively slow human action. Jehovah's prophetic word through Christ Jesus is: 'This generation [of 1914] will by no means pass away until all things occur.' (Luke 21:32) And Jehovah, who is the source of inspired and unfailing prophecy, will bring about the fulfillment of his Son's words in a relatively short time..." (*WT*, May 15, 1984, p. 4).

They could not possibly explain the 1914 generation's situation with any more conviction.

[Of important note is the occurrence of the words "this generation," with slight variations, in all three gospels in the New Testament. These three gospel chapters are known as the "small apocalypses" (Matthew 24, Mark 13 and Luke 21).]

In 1984 the Governing Body interpreted that particular generation as all people who were alive in 1914—from infants to elderly. Carried through then, some of these people *must* also be alive at the time of the battle of Armageddon.

Consequently, we see in 1984 Brooklyn is already preparing the ground for later modifying the generation idea by employing "a more accurate understanding"; this provides leaders the chance to postpone Armageddon sufficiently in the longer term, buying time to adapt the entire speculative, apocalyptic-chronology thinking.

The otherwise broadly accepted Witnesses' dogma that the generation who experienced the onset of World War I would also witness Armageddon was about to fall. Surprisingly, this was probably not noted among *The Watchtower* readers. Or, if they did notice, they kept—mentally bound to the movement as they were—their thoughts to themselves.

The Watchtower Society's tactic is often to present certain news in a complex linguistic, cryptic context with conflicting messages. If the article needed to suggest Armageddon could be some way off in the future ("is there enough time?"), the message was so cleverly embedded that only the reader's subconscious received the meaning.

With the new signals, Brooklyn began building a bridge to an *endless future* with *unceasing literature production*; of course all these publications had to be sold to the growing number of members, who probably were—and still are—the most frequent and prized customers because they also purchase the literature they give away during canvassing.

Armageddon Postponed

Over numerous years, the members of the "great crowd" were repeatedly told that they, as a group, would survive the battle of Armageddon. Throughout the period, beginning with the start of WWI in 1914, this battle had to come several times. Armageddon would arrive within their lifetime, during the time of *their generation*, meaning their generation would never die. The Watchtower Society has reiterated this doctrine so often in their literature that it has been integrated into the members' doctrinal and personal identities.

How then to toss this vital thing overboard to prevent the ship inevitably sinking?

The answer was a crucial change in the perception of what the word "generation" meant. The evolution began via two articles in *The Watchtower* in November 1995. At this time there were only about ten years left in the lifetime of the 1914 generation. Witnesses who noted the official teachings back in the 1970s—teachings not previously denied and which assumed one had to be ten to twenty years old in 1914 to belong to the "generation"—were taken aback when the 1995 article arrived with a new idea just in the nick of time. In the article the meaning of the Greek word *genea'* is examined (Matthew 24, 34); this must have been shocking reading for the members.

In 1995, the readers of *The Watchtower* were first presented with a *more accurate understanding* of what "this generation" meant, and it's not the least surprising that the presentation contained so many contradictory and indirect elements one had to be up to date about the movement's concepts, fluctuating editorial style and strategy to sense that Brooklyn was suggesting that, perhaps, a *lot more years* would pass before the battle of Armageddon erupted.

Quoting the article:

"Therefore, in the final fulfillment of Jesus' prophecy today, 'this generation' apparently refers to the peoples of earth who see the sign of Christ's presence but fail to mend their ways. In contrast, we as Jesus' disciples refuse to be molded by the life-style of 'this generation'.... No human can say when that end will be, but we know that the end of 'this generation' of wicked people will come once the witness has been given to God's satisfaction 'to the most distant part of the earth' " (p. 19–20).

And then, the explanation for changing the ultimate truth about *who* and *when*:

"Does our *more precise viewpoint* on 'this generation' mean that Armageddon is *further away* than we had thought? Not at all! Though we at no time have known the 'day and hour,' Jehovah God has always known it, and he does not change. (Malachi 3:6) Obviously, the world is sinking further and further toward terminal ruination. The need to keep awake is more critical than it has ever been. Jehovah has revealed to us 'the things that must shortly take place,' and we should respond with an absorbing sense of urgency..." (*WT*, Nov. 1, 1995, p. 20; italics are mine).

This ended the specific talk about the pivotal generation of Jehovah's Witnesses, and people in general, who saw and recognized the signs of the time of the end in 1914 would also survive until Armageddon. Now it was about the Witnesses' contemporaries, the world's people "who see the sign of Christ's presence but fail to mend their ways" (*WT*, Nov. 1, 1995, p.19; p. 30). When the new viewpoint was presented in 1995, it offered a *certain* time limit—in reality a *postponing* of doomsday—and sustained a (fantastic, remote) chance the 1914-born members, the 81-year-old, white-haired frontline members who for a time drew their strength from anticipation, would live to see Armageddon erupt in their lifetime.

Yet again, the announcements from the Society are confusing and ambiguous, for simultaneously with the *implied*, actual postponement, the near proximity of Armageddon was continually stressed: "That time is short, indeed, compared with the thousands of years of Satan's rulership. The Kingdom is at hand, and so is Jehovah's day and hour for executing judgment on this wicked generation!" (*WT*, Nov. 1, 1995, p. 19)

With this article in *The Watchtower* came a considerable leap away from the doctrine of "this generation"; this was further compounded when the mission statement in *Awake!* was crucially changed in the same month.

Prior to November 1995, its closing words were:

"Most important, this magazine builds confidence in the Creator's promise of a peaceful and secure new world before the generation that saw the events of 1914 passes away."

In *Awake!* November 8, 1995, however, the text was dramatically changed:

"Most important, this magazine builds confidence in the Creator's promise of a peaceful and secure new world that is about to replace the present wicked, lawless system of things" (p. 4).

The phrase "before the generation that saw the events of 1914 passes away" was removed from the statement. This change was obviously not accidental, but at least partly a result of *The Watchtower's* November article, and partly a probable first step toward a new apocalyptic chronology following a long-term strategy devised by Brooklyn. The change is likely to have been sensational for the Witnesses, because for the first time they're given the chance to live a fairly normal life *completely to its end.*

This grand turn in thinking led to the title of this book's fourth section: *Evasive Acrobatics!*

Many Feel Relieved

In 1996 at a small restaurant in Roskilde (the town where the Danish kings are buried), I met with the branch overseer of the Jehovah's Witnesses in Denmark, Joergen Larsen (now deceased). He brought with him an odd, indirect admission regarding the Society's deferral of Armageddon.

Hoping to spring a sort of sly trap, I asked the overseer whether the Jehovah's Witnesses were disappointed that Armageddon—as a result of the November 1995 articles in *The Watchtower*—had been postponed. To this question he simply replied:

"No, quite the contrary, many feel relieved!"

It was an interesting admission. On the surface it appeared to be a *slip of the tongue*, because he had admitted the postponing of Armageddon was perhaps the *real message* of the November article—and I have no doubt he did not intend to make any kind of admission. Still, Armageddon was postponed indefinitely and the members seemed glad.

This conversation with a high-ranking overseer came about only because the relaxed restraints at that time allowed Witnesses to make a "return visit" to an expelled on a *yearly basis*. He was, in fact, free to meet with me openly and not fear condemnation by other Witnesses. I found the overseer's opinion quite important, because it supported my feeling that the Jehovah's Witnesses' teachings regarding apocalyptic issues will undergo certain changes follow-ing the arrival of the 21st century and without needing to abandon cautions of Armageddon's proximity.

This shows something not particularly remarkable in theological and escha-tological ways, since all Christians *in principle* await the second coming of Christ as a future event. In fact, most churches have placed the reappearance of Christ on the shelf, probably offering nothing more than an indulgent shrug for those who still *literally* see this event as a real, near-future possibility. That is apart from fundamentalist Christians who still tout a literal belief that Christ's return is approaching.

Jehovah's Witnesses' postponement of Armageddon conveniently solves several problems related to growth, as the Witnesses—not surprisingly—were by no means done with proclaiming their message about the quickly approach-ing new world. Jehovah and his Witnesses wish of course that *all*—or as many as possible—"should come to repentance" and be converted, as stated in 2 Peter 3:9. At least, they believe everyone should have the chance before it's too late. And this "last chance" gets Earth's population, by virtue of worldwide canvassing by Jehovah's Witnesses' printed materials, through the next ten, twenty, thirty or maybe *100 years* (as Russell suggested more than a hundred years ago!).

A one-hundred-year period, however, is not specifically called out in the latest Watchtower literature. Unofficially, it is suggested that it seems *unlikely* it will take a long time. They have *hinted at 2034* as a possibility (120 years calculated from 1914), which I will explore later. I am, as always, compelled to note again how the movement's leadership drifts purposefully in a sea of contradictions—or evasive explanations.

The World's Complete Destruction is Fast Approaching

The 1995 *Watchtower* article deserves a second closer look, because in it Brooklyn warns against new speculations regarding the longevity of the period defined by the lifetime of the generation.

As follows:

"Yes, the complete triumph of the Messianic Kingdom is at hand! Is any-thing to be gained, then, by looking for dates or by speculating about the lit-eral lifetime of a 'generation'? Far from it! Habakkuk 2:3 clearly states: 'The vision is yet for the appointed time, and it keeps panting on to the end, and it will not tell a lie. Even if it should delay, keep in expectation of it; for it will without fail come true. It will not be late.' Jehovah's day of accounting hastens ever closer..." (p. 19; the quotation from Habakkuk comes from Jehovah's Wit-nesses' *New World Translation*).

In conclusion, the article states:

" 'The time left is reduced,' said the apostle Paul. It is time, therefore, to keep ever awake and busy in Jehovah's work, as we endure trials and hatreds imposed by a *wicked generation of mankind*" (p. 21; italics are mine).

Regardless of the alleged "more accurate understanding" of the term of "the generation," it is still *now* however and whenever it comes, although it may even drag on. So it's really about preaching the message before it is too late. Nobody knows the day and hour of its arrival. The fulfillment of "the signs" proves with *unswerving surety* the urgency. If one wishes to survive the battle at Armageddon, there is still time, but probably not much. Be prepared!

When the fog cleared, Brooklyn's message of the postponement appeared to be somewhat complicated and toothless for, although the Witnesses had been indirectly told they could no longer expect Armageddon to arrive before the last members of the 1914 generation were deceased, the leaders kept pounding the doomsday drum. The result? The two messages about both the *postponement* and the *nearness* didn't harmonize.[300]

An article series about *sheep* and *goats* appeared in *The Watchtower* beginning October 15, 1995; it seemed to fire speculations about Armageddon's (and the Judgment Day's) postponement. An earlier chairman of a support group for former Jehovah's Witnesses in Denmark, S. B. Henriksen, considered the matter in an article in *Den Nye Dialog* (The New Dialogue, DK), an anti-cult association, and expressed that these *Watchtower* articles could be interpreted as meaning the *air* had been let out of the "dynamic that had been the members' motivation to preach."

Something indicated, then, that members might be a bit more relaxed now, whether the reason for that relaxed attitude lies in the two *Watchtower* articles is difficult to say. Beroea (not his real name), a highly critical elder I have been in contact with since 2000, says the magazine's messages were "completely meaningless and almost incomprehensible" and the articles may have left members somewhat bewildered and in a state of helplessness. On the one hand, Armageddon and doomsday were postponed into a future where the anointed generation is extinct (which the Society wisely neglects to discuss just now), while simultaneously, the Watchtower managers constantly pressure members with fiery arguments that it is more *urgent* than ever to serve out at the doors. Still, the dual message, despite *The Watchtower's* relentless drumbeating for the latter element, presumably leached into some of the members' consciousness.

The end's approach was urgent enough, but it was not so urgent either!

Using statistics and percentages, I sought to quantify what this meant to the movement. Would the trend be reflected in the figures from the annual reports?

Annual Reports Sustain Theory of Relaxed Trend

For decades the members of the movement accepted that if they hoped to survive Armageddon, they had to be regular publishers. The number of "hours spent in field service" informed the organization whether they were "mature" and therefore (implicitly) worthy to survive. Since all members were required to make a monthly hours report, Brooklyn received tallies every year from the branch offices all over the world; when totaled, the results are tremendous.

In 2011, well over *one and one-half billion* hours were spent in the field. On the table below, the left side shows reported hours from 1991 to 2012, the middle rows list the record (peak) and average numbers of publishers in the same years, and the right column shows the percentage increase of members in relation to previous years (the Watchtower Society's annual statistics in the *Yearbook* list both the *average* number of publishers and a *record* number of publishers, the so-called *peak publishers*; in the table below I have listed both the record (peak) numbers and the average numbers):

Year	Year of release	Total Hours (by year)	Record Hours (peak pub.)	Average Hours	% increase over previous year's avg
1991	(1992 YB)	951,870,021	4,278,820	4,071,954	5.9
1992	(1993 YB)	1,024,910,434	4,472,787	4,289,737	5.3
1993	(1994 YB)	1,057,341,972	4,709,889	4,483,900	4.5
1994	(1995 YB)	1,096,065,354	4,914,094	4,695,111	5.0
1995	(1996 YB)	1,150,353,444	5,199,895	4,950,344	5.0
1996	(1997 YB)	1,140,621,714	5,413,769	5,167,258	4.4
1997	(1998 YB)	1,179,735,841	5,599,931	5,353,078	3.6
1998	(1999 YB)	1,186,666,708	5,888,650	5,544,059	3.6
1999	(2000 YB)	1,144,566,849	5,912,492	5,653,987	2.0
2000	(2001 YB)	1,171,270,425	6,035,564	5,783,003	2.3
2001	(2002 YB)	1,169,082,225	6,117,666	5,881,776	1.7
2002	(2003 YB)	1,202,381,302	6,304,645	6,048,600	2.8
2003	(2004 YB)	1,234,796,477	6,429,351	6,184,046	2.2
2004	(2005 YB)	1,282,234,887	6,513,132	6,308,341	2.0
2005	(2006 YB)	1,278,201,985	6,613,829	6,390,016	1.3
2006	(2007 YB)	1,333,966,199	6,741,444	6,491,775	1.6
2007	(2008 YB)	1,431,761,554	6,957,854	6,691,790	3.1
2008	(2009 YB)	1,488,658,249	7,124,443	6,829,455	2.1
2009	(2010 YB)	1,557,788,344	7,313,173	7,046,419	3.2
2010	(2011 YB)[301]	1,604,764.248	7,508,050	7,224,930	2.5
2011	(2012 YB)	1,707,094,710	7,659,019	7,395,672	2.4
2012	(2013 YB)	1,748,697,447	7,782,346	7,538,994	1.9

As seen in the right-hand column (percentage increase) of the table on the previous page, there has been a tendency toward decline in the annual intake of adherents. All figures in the four columns are taken from Jehovah's Witnesses' yearbooks and other accessible statistics. Years on the far left refer to the actual year of accumulation; the next column is the reporting year; the last column is percentage change over the previous accumulation year. That is the 2006 Yearbook of Jehovah's Witnesses lists results from 2005, and the percentage of increase in that row indicates growth or decline over the 2004 average, etc.

The figures suggest that hour-engagement stagnated slightly during the 1991 to 2006 period, while the number of members rose slightly (perhaps because the per-publisher hour requirement is somewhat lower today than previously). From 2007 to 2010, however, the percentages become more consistent. Thus, it seems difficult to draw any definitive conclusions from the figures. Yet, I believe that the development period could imply that members, generally, may have become frustrated at the movement's doctrinal and organizational progress approaching the turn of the 21st century. Experiences from 1975 are perhaps weighty in their memories, or maybe just unconsciously, yet the potent cocktail of the strong religious and social relationships, family bonds and the Society's strict discipline trapped everyone. The drums of doomsday still echo in members' minds. The vast majority then, though pondering their own doubts, remain in the organization, without clearly recognizing that perhaps they are no longer as engaged and enthusiastic as before.

Web-based sources of Jehovah's Witnesses' statistics are surprisingly plentiful. Even *Wikipedia* features a graph showing growth within the movement from 1931 to 2006, and it demonstrates that the movement, in spite of the various downturns—as in the years after 1975—is steadily growing. However, the growth in 2011, as shown above, slipped again to a modest 2.4% over 2010. Thus we find growth fluctuates an average of approximately two to three percent. (See http://en.wikipedia.org/wiki/Jehovah%27s_Witnesses, 5. "Demographics of Jehovah's Witnesses"; author viewed this article in September 2011.)

Note that, when there is zero growth or even decline in a country or region's reported numbers, as seen in the 2011 annual report, the editors often leave an empty field rather than listing the unflattering percentage. When studying the figures for 2011 as found in the 2012 *Yearbook*, I could deduce the empty field meant either stagnation or decline. By exclusively studying the omissions and their corresponding data I could see which countries had less-than-desirable outcomes. My results are summarized as follows:

Austria, zero growth; Belgium, zero; Croatia, zero; Denmark, slight decrease; Estonia, zero; Finland, zero; Iceland, zero; Ireland, zero; Japan, zero; Holland, zero; Poland, zero; Portugal, zero; Slovakia, zero; and Sweden and Switzerland, zero. The United States showed an unimpressive 2% increase. Many other countries showed modest progress, still others outright decline. For example, Chuuk, located in the Pacific, showed an 11% decline. To think, prior to reading the reports, I didn't even know this island existed (pp. 40-47). In 2011, however, there was a growth of two percent, bringing the number up to forty-three (2011 and 2012 *YB*, both editions pp. 40-51).

A relatively high growth of 3,380,189 adherents from 1991 to 2011, despite a reduction in work effort, can probably be attributed to propagation—the members' own children growing up within the movement, ensuring a steady annual membership increase—in recent years of about 2% annually. Yet, this is precisely where the problems of the movement begin to emerge. The young are less tolerant of the tight restrictions, as reflected in secret behaviors that are condemned by the organization, if discovered.

An overview of annual new member recruiting numbers can be seen in the figures of the third and fourth columns of my chart (average and percent increase), and these also appear to show a decreasing trend overall.

The worldwide total for 2002, or 1,202,381,302 preaching hours (an increase over the previous year) and an increase in member numbers 6,048,600 (2.8 more than 2001), is a deviation from the general view; however, it falls to a more normal level the following year, 2003 (2.2). The above increase in recruits may indicate that both interested outsiders and members responded to events of September 11, 2001. Notable then are the decreases in 2004 (2.0) and 2005 (1.3), where the terrorist danger level is apparently reduced, had passed altogether, or was at least of lesser concern.

In Denmark, however, 2002 membership change was shown at zero, although the exact figures reveal a minute decline. Such has the trend been for several years, as Danish Witness leaders will acknowledge.

Of course, one must consider these statistics and calculations with a cautious eye, but they may inspire one to a deeper study that can only reveal even more enlightening trends.

An elder told me that as long as the charts show an increase in the publisher-hours average—something considered absolutely *essential* for the movement—annually of about 2%, Brooklyn is satisfied. So, I wonder, if the numbers of publishers (preachers) do not increase, or if they even decline, would this be considered very serious? If that happened then the leaders could no longer claim Jehovah's Witnesses are a growing and "blessed" religious community. I must therefore conclude that if growth slows markedly, it will again be time for a new and sensational campaign about the *nearness* of the Judgment Day!

The graph on the next page is based on figures from the *Yearbook*. It reveals the connection among the number baptized, inflow and defection (including dropouts) throughout the world in those years.

The Suspiciously Slowly Dying Anointed Generation

One of the JW's fundamental dogmas, the doctrine of the 144,000 (as found in the Revelation of John 7:4)—also known as the little flock, the anointed or the bride

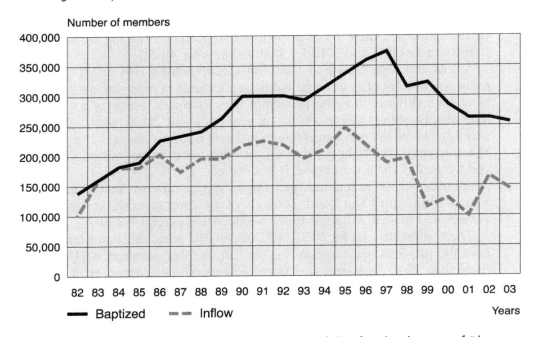

Note the curve for "baptized" and the curve for inflow falls after the doctrine of "the generation" was changed in 1995. The defection is reflected in the difference between the curve for baptized and the curve for inflow. Thus, the defection is greater than the number of new baptized in said period. Note that the defection gradually seems to increase significantly after 1984 (compiled by Jette Svane).

class—is of particular interest here. For the *remaining* members of this flock, "the remnant" or those who yet live on the earth, there was still an opportunity to experience Armageddon's arrival before they would ascend to heaven. For their entire lives this had been the fervent hope that kept them going.

At this point, by way of putting things in perspective, I should probably add (or perhaps repeat!) that the little flock must ascend to heaven and reign with Christ when they die while the "large crowd" will live forever in the New World that comes after Armageddon.

In my childhood I encountered members of this small, select group, white-haired "brothers and sisters in the faith" who, with the spirit of clarity and certainty of salvation in their eyes, firmly believed they would go to heaven and co-rule with Christ. The reality: Most were members of the movement even *before* 1914—the latest recognized as such in 1935—and they died, of course, gradually with their number steadily decreasing as each year passed.

Further, as we know from Egon Jacobsen's pep talk to a small assembly in 1969, this relates to one of the "circumstantial proofs" that the Millennium would come in 1975. Yes, maybe "a little before," or even "something before."

Since some of the little flock would apparently live on to Armageddon, where the last of them—before their ascent to heaven—would lead the members of the great crowd into the new world, and since each year there were fewer and fewer of the 1914 group, mathematics allows one to calculate forward to an approximate time in the near future where Armageddon, in all likelihood, would come. If all members of the little flock died before something conclusive had happened, members might have realized something was quite wrong.

As time has worn on, this group's number has continued to shrink, and though it once formed the backbone of the movement as associated with the fateful year 1914, this group now constitutes a miniscule minority in relation to the total membership of the movement.

Note here the numbers of the remaining 144,000 anointed as they appeared in the Jehovah's Witnesses' yearbooks during the publication years 1973, 1983 and 1993 (p. 31, p. 31 and p. 33, respectively). In 1972 there were 10,350 anointed. In 1982, the number was 9,529, and in 1992 the figure was 8,683.

Over this twenty-year period the numbers diminish, but it appears *too slowly*—almost *suspiciously slowly*—if one takes their advanced ages into account.

This has resulted in a really *irritating* problem for the movement in recent years. The doctrine of the 144,000 anointed has been inextricably linked to the teachings of the Jehovah's Witnesses. In a few years the leaders might be arguing that all members of the little flock are already co-rulers with Christ in heaven. Yet, none would have lived to ring in Armageddon, and this will mean the foundation of the organization's power structure will crumble again—as we shall see later.

It will be interesting to see how one of the most central doctrines of the Jehovah's Witnesses will appear to undergo a radical reconstruction. Obviously, I cannot say with certainty whether the Society's leaders have developed a deliberate strategy to ultimately explain how the last of the 144,000 die by completely natural means. In 1935 only 39,225 anointed remained, so how the Society solves the numbers problem today is not easy to know. Still, looking back on previous resourceful explanations, I have no doubt they can invent something *smart*.

Even as the leaders of the Witnesses are careful accountants of the apocalyptic *days and hours,* they are, at the same time, always able to devise clever long-term strategies to save what can be saved and strive on. And yet, they delude themselves and others into thinking that they *firmly believe* in the core teachings. Perhaps they do believe in these teachings, and for that reason their strategizing can be justified. They do not see the strategy as a way to *explain away embarrassing* things. Rather, they find the appropriate texts in the Bible, and twist and wring the arguments so they fit with their reoriented message and their "new light" on events past and future.

The Little Flock Refuses to Die

Although the Jehovah's Witnesses' international leadership in Brooklyn offered new insights about the 1914-generation in 1995, the leaders failed to explain why so many of the little flock remained on earth.

The "circumstantial evidences," as Egon Jacobsen called them in his 1969 speech, designed to plausibly explain that the Millennium would arrive at the latest in 1975, was among other things based on the small number of the little flock still living in 1969—a number that was rapidly diminishing. If they were about twenty years old in 1935, according to Rutherford the year the gate to heaven was finally closed, they would be quite advanced in years by 2012. Although, I suppose, ninety-six is probably not so advanced an age in a religion where eternity poses no real problem.

Yet the situation needled me, and as I looked deeper I observed something surprising. When I checked the *Yearbook* for 1996's statistics, I noticed the number of members who usually partake of the so-called "Memorial emblems"—the bread and the wine at the annual Memorial meeting reserved for members of the little flock—had *increased* over the 1992 figure of 8,683 persons. In 1996, the number—which statistically should have decreased or at most remained constant—actually *increased* by *seventy-four members.*

Armed with a *reasonable suspicion* that the discrepant numbers indicated a *manipulation* related to the doctrine of the 144,000 and the "remnant" of this crowd, I decided to examine whether the increased number in 1996 was a statistical coincidence or even genuine human error. Or, as my now-suspicious mind considered, could there be an organized attempt to extend the time the little flock had left on earth? Even though the figure 144,000 was reportedly complete in 1935, much exists to suggest that after 1935—from Brooklyn's viewpoint—a convenient transformation of sorts occurred within the heavenly flock: Some members of the heavenly crowd became apostates, and they needed to be replaced by newer, younger members. This allows the deadline to be postponed some years because these younger replacements would likely live longer than the original members.

Were there tactical considerations in the process? Did the number of the little flock need to be stabilized so they could move out the deadline, even into the 21st century? It appeared, once again, they cleverly manipulated things in that direction.

Spurred on, I checked yearbook after yearbook, and the trend was unmistakable as the 21st century approached and beyond (see table, next page).

Conclusion: Looking at 2002 as compared to 1991 (the first year noted in the chart), the size of the little flock diminishes by ninety. The number in 2004 is 8,570, again a minimal loss, as one might anticipate. Yet, in 2006 it again rises to 8,758 anointed, an increase of 188, and this means an increase during the three-year period since 2003! The 2006 number takes on a more normal aspect, but by 2007 the number of the anointed has risen again over the previous year with a remarkable gain of 347. (YB, 2005; 2007; 2008 JW-CD) From 2008 to

Year	Little Flock Tally	Note
1991	8,850	
1992	8,683	Decreased
1993	8,693	Increased
1994	8,617	Decreased
1995	8,645	Increased
1996	8,757	Increased
1997	8,795	Increased
1998	8,756	Decreased by 39
1999	8,755	Decreased by 1
2000	8,661	Decreased by nearly 100
2001	8,730	Increased
2002	8,760	Increased
2003	8,565	Decreased slightly
2004	8,570	Increased
2005	8,524	Decreased
2006	8,758	Increased
2007	9,105	Increased

2012 the number increases further, but I will address this period at a later time. However one compares the numbers, it certainly seems as if the little flock will remain on the earthly scene many years yet.

Members Ask Questions

Questions published in *The Watchtower* show how these small plus/minus variations concern the magazine's readers. Under the heading, "Questions from Readers," the leaders address the questions in 1996:

"The most recent published report is for the year 1995, and it shows 28 more partakers than in the preceding year though the ratio of partakers to those attending did actually drop. On balance, that a few more chose to partake of the emblems is no cause for concern. Over the years some, even ones newly baptized, have suddenly begun to partake. In a number of cases, after a while they acknowledged that this was an error. Some have recognized that they partook as an emotional response to perhaps physical or mental strain. But they came to see that they really were not called to heavenly life. They asked for God's merciful understanding" (*WT*, Aug. 15, 1996).

The editors, however, reassured the questioner with the following words:

"There is every reason to believe that the number of anointed ones will *continue to decline* as advanced age and unforeseen occurrences end their earthly lives. Yet, even as these truly anointed ones prove faithful till death, in line for the crown of life, the other sheep, who have washed their robes in the blood of the Lamb, can look forward to surviving the impending great tribulation" (*WT*, Aug. 15, 1996, p. 30-31; italics are mine).

So, there is hope ahead, at least for members of the large crowd.

The real figures from the annual reports, however, tell another story, perhaps because "false anointed" have *slipped* in, and now, very conveniently, have admitted to being included in the count.

It appears then that the size of the little flock is relatively stable at this time, and I imagine that as long as Brooklyn has not finally resolved what to make of the whole complex problem we will see the numbers officially falling—although they actually seem to grow a little in between.

Now assuming the number will, in time, reduce to zero—as it rightly should if Brooklyn is realistic about the matter—a new issue will emerge:

It is the remnants of the little flock who partake in the Memorial emblems. If they all died the Jehovah's Witnesses would be in a situation where *none of the members* of the movement can participate in Holy Communion—the bread and wine; this is *quite unusual* for a Christian organization.

The Eucharist was, according to *The New Testament,* established by Jesus as a memorial for his coming sacrifice. The bread was a symbol of his body, the wine of his blood, shed "for many for the remission of sins" (Matthew 26:28). How do the Jehovah's Witnesses reconcile this with seeing themselves as the *only true Christians* in our time? A Christian without absolution and no hope of coming into heaven is surely a very unusual type of Christian. And in not too many years, the Jehovah's Witnesses must face the fact that they will run short of members who may participate in the Lord's Evening Meal.

Clearly, the little flock is slowly dying and diminishing—though things suggest the crowd does not have any prior plans to completely leave the scene. Still, it's obvious that inevitable events at the turn of the 21st century have driven changes in the management of the Jehovah's Witnesses' organization worldwide.

They have begun to fill many positions in the organization with members from the great crowd, the average members, and this development has resulted in increasing pressure on the anointed, whose work inevitably shrinks every year again due to illness, disability and death. Not only are they slowly dying out (in theory, at least), but they are probably so old now that they have largely left the arena of active service or should have. Yet they are there anyway, counted among the active, as shown by the halted decline in their number, almost abruptly, in the early 1990s.

How can this be? Has Brooklyn called up *reserves* to sustain the team?

This seems to be the case; either that or the remaining members of the 144,000 living on earth refuse to die. At the time I compiled this research, June

2012, I learned from the 2012 *Yearbook* (see the official "2011 Service Report of Jehovah's Witnesses Worldwide") that the number of anointed had *increased* to 11,824 (*YB*, 2012); compared to 1978 that's an increase of 2,062! Therefore, number of anointed appears to not only have leveled out since a count of 9,762 in 1978 but it seems to actually be vaulting towards heaven! It is somewhat uncertain how to interpret this, but it *could* mean that there is, in Brooklyn's view, *more time* for the arrival of Armageddon than the members expect today. This suggests the average members can relax their anticipation, partly because Brooklyn has given itself more flexibility in the timeline for doomsday (*WT*, January 1, 2000; *YB*, 1996; *YB* 2012; *YB* 2013).

Something Wrong with the Figures

There are indications, then, that allow us to conclude it is these "reservists" who appear in the *Yearbooks'* annual statistics, affecting the numbers of the anointed, and the reservists' number, instead of falling, is about to rise. I asked the accounting-experienced Jette Svane to look at this complicated puzzle, and she had no doubt there was something wrong when she looked at it statistically. Here is her conclusion:

It appears from *The Watchtower* of February 15, 1970, that the figure of those who were partakers and enjoyed the emblems (the bread and wine), had fallen from 39,225 in 1938 to 10,368 in 1969. In other words, if you must take the organization at its word, there were 144,000 minus 10,368, a total of 133,632 anointed in heaven in 1969. It also indicates that the figure during this thirty-one-year period—from 1938 to 1969—had fallen by 73.6%, and in the next thirty-four years—1969 to 2003—fell by only 17.4% to 8,565—despite the average age of the anointed logically being markedly higher in 1969 than it was in 1938.

In the coming years then, the Watchtower Society faces a significant dilemma. How will this society reassure skeptical members who can figure out that, if the 8,565 who enjoyed the emblems in 2003 are "genuine anointed," most of those who enjoyed the emblems in 1969 must be "false anointed"—or apostates.

Conversely: If those who enjoyed the emblems in 1969, and now for the most part have died, were genuine anointed, would those who are enjoying the emblems today, be false anointed—because, new anointed are only added to the 144,000 to replace those who drop out? (*WT*, Feb. 15, 1975)

One may ask if it's really necessary to *dig so deeply* into this issue. I can, being the reasonable person I am, say yes, it is. When the Society provides numbers and statistics, as well as touting "a more accurate understanding" of their claims, they have just legitimized any examination of what they publish! (See also the additional note in Appendix by Jette Svane.)

Chapter 35

2000–2012:
Old Guard Disarmed

On October 7, 2000, the Watch Tower Bible and Tract Society of Pennsylvania held its annual meeting in New Jersey. Toward the end of the meeting, John E. Barr, Society chairman and a member of the Governing Body, made a special announcement that was a follow-up to speeches made earlier in the day by two other members of the Governing Body, Theodore Jaracz and Daniel Sydlik. Barr's announcement seems to have been a serious one, since it concerned the difference between the legal parent company in Pittsburgh and the role of the Governing Body. The Governing Body's authority and responsibilities were not attributable to the legal statutes of the Watch Tower Bible and Tract Society of Pennsylvania, but rather to *God's interest.*

The old men who had been sitting at the very top of the organization since time immemorial were being pensioned off. They departed in favor of younger forces able to more easily relate to the necessarily impending upheavals in the doctrines and the organization.

Some changes in the organizational structure were announced at the same meeting; these were justified by the movement's international growth—by year 2000 they had reached six million worldwide. The changes included the appointment of seven new directors to the Watchtower Bible and Tract Society of New York, Inc. (previously *the Society*), all belonging to the great crowd, plus the creation of new sub-corporations. In the future, the resigned board members, who all belonged to the *anointed* little flock, would deal only with biblical subjects, doctrine issues and the like.

John E. Barr's remarks included:

"In their discourses, Brothers Sydlik and Jaracz had explained that the fact that 'the faithful and discreet slave' has been entrusted with all of the Lord's earthly belongings does not prevent the slave class from allowing qualified men from among the 'other sheep' to care for certain routine administrative responsibilities. (John 10:16) Nor is there any Scriptural reason to insist that all or any of the directors of the legal entities used by Jehovah's Witnesses be anointed Christians" (*WT,* Jan. 15, 2001).

Barr further stated that "recently certain members of the Governing Body of Jehovah's Witnesses who had been serving as directors and officers *voluntarily* stepped aside from the boards of directors of all the corporations used by 'the faithful and discreet slave' in the United States. Responsible brothers of the other sheep class were elected as replacements." So it was "anointed brothers" who had stepped aside in favor of *younger leaders* who belonged to the new class of "other sheep" (*WT*, Jan. 15, 2001; italics are mine).

Note that the anointed leaders had voluntarily withdrawn from the Governing Body. However, I am more inclined to think it has been about voluntary coercion, because if one cannot directly be sacked or dismissed, one can still be promoted in the system! And that is, I think, what happened at this point in the movement's development. In their new roles as ministers, the resigned members of the Governing Body officially now served as the movement's spiritual supervisors while real power was exercised by the administrative, bureaucratic positions within the corporate structure.

Barr went on:

"This decision is beneficial indeed. It allows members of the Governing Body to spend more time in preparing spiritual food and in otherwise caring for the *spiritual needs* of the worldwide brotherhood."[302]

Finally, Barr told the delighted listeners: "While various legal and administrative duties have been assigned to experienced overseers … all of them serve under the spiritual direction of the Governing Body…" (*WT*, Jan. 15, 2001; italics are mine).

The Pennsylvania legal corporation's administrators were now R. Wallen, vice president, and Richard R. Abrahamson (at that time eighty-one and now deceased), former leader of Jehovah's Witnesses in Denmark. Before his death Abrahamson was advanced up through the system and had been appointed secretary and treasurer of the reorganized Pennsylvania legal corporation. Both men belonged to the other-sheep class of members. Also four other persons, who were not members of the little-anointed flock, were added as new board members. Thus, members of the great crowd assumed positions at the organization's top level.

Notable organizational changes also occurred among the approximately 100 registered subsidiaries in the year 2000. These companies were all subject to the Pennsylvania legal corporation. In these endeavors members of the great crowd also replaced some of the time- and service-worn anointed. The former influential members of the little flock who had long-held powerful posts in the organization were now slowly diminishing in number and responsibility.

Also in the year 2000 three new corporations were formed:

1. Christian Congregation of Jehovah's Witnesses to oversee the appointment of elders.
2. Religious Order of Jehovah's Witnesses, which would manage those in full-time service.

3. Kingdom Support Services, Inc., to initiate construction projects and operate as the owner of the Watch Tower Society's properties.
(Among others: *Isaiah's Prophecy* 2, chap. 21, p. 303; *KM,* January, 2002) [303]

Max Larson

Among the resigned seven members of the New York corporation was the aging and anonymous Milton George Henschel. Since Fred Franz's death in 1992 Henschel had been president of both the Pittsburgh and New York companies. Henschel, who was sick and old, served until 2000 when he was replaced by Max H. Larson. For years Larson had been a member of the Bethel *family* and working at the headquarters in New York. However, Max Larson became president of the New York corporation only. Henschel died in 2003.

In 1977, Larson had been appointed vice president of the New York corporation, or the Watch Tower Bible and Tract Society of New York, Inc. Therefore, for some time before his appointment in 2000, he may have been under consideration as a candidate for president of both the subsidiary company in New York and the parent corporation in Pittsburgh.

In 1989, the editors of *The Watchtower* printed a full eight-page biography of Larson, titled, "Making Full-Time Service a Career"; it featured illustrations of the not-exactly beautiful tenant and printing-business buildings the Society had purchased or built in Brooklyn. One can sense how this extraordinarily lengthy presentation in 1989 could predict future advancement within the organization. During Knorr's leadership, Larson had served as his secretary. Therefore, Larson had both high status and great organizational and business experience, qualifications highly valued within the New York headquarters. Larson had also served as factory overseer at headquarters for several years. (*WT*, Sept. 1, 1989, p. 23-30)

Whether Larson—who died in 2011 at age ninety-six—belonged to the little flock is not entirely clear. He was first baptized in 1938, yet the wording of this *Watchtower* biography could well mean Larson was a member of the anointed. At his inclusion in the Bethel family in 1939, he and his friend Bill had to complete a form that asked: "Do you agree to stay at Bethel until the Lord takes you away?" (Ibid.) From the article, it appears Max Larson put his X in the appropriate box. Of course, this may have been about an *older* form. In 2012, my research uncovered a post in a web discussion that stated Max Larson began to receive the symbols of bread and wine late in his life. This *might indicate* a new attitude about membership in the 144,000, which the Society needed to alter if they wanted to prevent the heavenly crowd on earth completely dying out. (Website source: Bro Max Larson died today / jw-archive.org)

Today the president's powers are not nearly as comprehensive as in years past. This dramatic change came after 1972–1976 when responsibilities were officially divided among the Governing Body and the corporations in Pittsburgh and New York. Who currently wields the *real* power within the organization seems unclear to me—especially since Max Larson's death. Those I've contacted tell me the Governing Body (which previously only consisted of anointed or little-flock Witnesses) acts as the chief executive of the organization's top management, while the companies manage all the practical matters. Others have stated the Governing Body no longer plays a major role, so it is clear opinions and understandings differ.

Until the year 2000 a member of the Governing Body—at that time Milton Henschel, one of the anointed—had to be president of both the main limited-liability company in Pittsburgh and the subsidiaries in New York and London. In 2001, the Society established that company executives did not also have to be members of the Governing Body nor did they need to be members of the little flock. This was a crucial decision because it opened up the possibility that *non-anointed* members could now be elected to the Governing Body.

Was Larson involved in purging of the *old* "elders" in 1939?

Max Larson and his close associate, Bill Griffith, attended a public talk given by J.F. Rutherford in 1938 titled "Lovers of Righteousness." At this time Rutherford introduced the concept of pioneer service. Max Larson was quick on the uptake and he and Bill Griffith went to the Field Service Department to get their pioneer applications. Here they met the then secretary-treasurer of the Society, William E. VanAmburgh. He advised them about the pioneer commitment, agreed with their decision and said, "You're doing the right thing, but go into this as if it was your lifetime career." Excitedly, they turned in their applications, and the next day, June 5, 1938, they were baptized. The following day they received their first pioneer assignment. (p. 24, 25)

The next two weeks, Max Larson read Rutherford's books *Enemies* and *Riches*. The third week, the two young men were assigned a pioneer district and sent to Raymond, Washington, where they were given authority to lead a congregation of twenty-seven members, train new preachers (publishers) and set up Bible studies in private homes. Larson and Griffith were each about twenty-three years old.

Shortly afterwards, Max led the congregation's weekly study of *The Watchtower*, in particular he introduced Theocratic management. The newly converted Larson, who probably lacked any prerequisite for understanding what the Bible Student movement was about, presumably initiated the cleansing process that William J. Schnell described in his book, *Thirty Years A Watch Tower Slave*—a process that Max Larson may have later found difficult.

The company servant did not have time to accompany Larson and Griffith in field service to try to start a private Bible study, so they attempted to start one on their own. Max Larson soon understood why he didn't have time to accompany them, because later in the day, when Larson and Griffith arrived at a crossroad after they had been out preaching from house-to-house alone, they encountered the company servant leading a parade for the Veterans Association and American Legion! I can only conclude Max and Bill, acting in the spirit of Theocratic principles set things straight among the old Russellites; the company servant presumably was thrown out of his position as a result. In the end, only three of the congregation's twenty-seven members accepted the new form of government; the rest had had enough.

I can vividly imagine what happened. Those leather-tough, veteran Russellites would not tolerate two green "Watchtower boys," whose only doctrinal luggage was the Judge's aforementioned books, who suddenly arrived and began to dictate a new operating method. It was during this period that Russell's elder system was brutally discarded.

Larson eventually became a highly placed senior *apparatchik* in the Watchtower hierarchy. Through special pioneer service Larson soon moved to Bethel in New York where he was employed in the printing works by factory servant Nathan H. Knorr. Within a short time Larson was promoted and became Knorr's secretary; as already discussed, Knorr succeeded Judge Rutherford as president. Subsequently Larson served Knorr *faithfully,* handling the publishing and construction company activities for the Society. In 1989, the lesson derived from Larson's memoirs was "Bethel is the best place on earth this side of the coming earthly Paradise" (*WT*, Sept. 1, 1989, p. 23-30).

Today, if one asks an ordinary Witness who the real leader of the movement is, the person will probably sidestep the issue, claiming it is *no longer important*. When you consider the role former presidents had, it seems there has been a remarkable break with the past. Neither of the two presidents, of which now only Don Adams (see below) is formally known as president, could have stepped into the previous god's place as held by Russell or Rutherford. Today it is the *anonymous* and *efficient* Watchtower apparatchik [304] that holds the power in Brooklyn. All the real personalities—for example Raymond Franz—have either been expelled for apostasy or have removed themselves.

Don A. Adams

After Max Larson's death in 2011, the 86-year-old and almost-unknown Don Alden Adams continued as the sole president for the two corporations.[305] Don A. Adams replaced Milton G. Henschel in 2000, but like Max Larson was only entrusted with *half* the power, specifically management of the original, limited-liability company in Pittsburgh.

Don Adams came to headquarters in 1944 and became secretary under N. H. Knorr. In the 1960s Adams was a zone overseer, and later he became director of the missionary department. Between 2000 and 2011 the change to split presidential power between two men might suggest that *only one* of the two presidents, Max Larson, was required to be a member of the heavenly flock. Personally, I believe this new power-sharing arrangement was a form of *power-limitation* due to the 1975 scandal, and partly as a sort of *interregnum* in the transition period when the anointed would have forever left the earthly scene.

In a group photo of the members of the Governing Body (*WT*, July 15, p. 26, 2013) one sees D. H. Splane, A. Morris, D. M. Sanderson, G. W. Jackson, M. S. Lett, S. F. Herd, G. Lösh, and G. H. Pierce (all anointed), but Don Adams is not found among them.

When the anointed are finally all gone, or at least when the Society allows the number to finally reach zero, the members will probably witness more changes at the top, where younger people chosen from among the other sheep will fill all the positions of the Governing Body—unless the Body is given *extraordinary transfer ability* to replace the many who left the organization after Rutherford's introduction of "the Theocracy."[306] So far, developments indicate such transfers have already occurred (although this never can be verified, of course), as the number of the anointed is increasing.

Information about Don A. Adams is not easy to find via web search or on the Watchtower Library CD. However, as far as I can see, Don Adams is not a member of the Governing Body. Whether he is a member of the little flock is unclear (he was born in 1925), and information suggests he no longer plays a major role in the power game, even though he, technically speaking, is the current president of the Society. Adams has quite effectively remained outside the media spotlight. Result: He is almost completely unknown, even among the average Witnesses!

From correspondence I received in March 2012 from a previous American Witness, I learned that since Max Larson's death Don Adams seems to be alone at the top as president of the entire dual-corporate structure. He remains—if I can believe my source—subordinate to the Governing Body. Since Don Adams was eighty-seven at the time I wrote this, it will not be long before a new and potentially more significant figure could emerge within the movement. To predict who he is, however, has been impossible to discern at the time I updated this information. Still, it is entirely contrary to the movement's history that they did not, immediately after Max Larson's death, officially appoint a new president of the entire corporate structure.

I think the heart of this matter hides behind this apparent silence about a successor, which could be due to: 1. management in the two corporations does not want to replace Max Larson with the appointment of a new New York president, as the management is moving the entire headquarters out of New York to Warwick, a small town in the upstate New York near the New Jersey state line; or, 2. management will wait until Don Adams dies or retires, and then take a new, clear path for presidential initiatives. However, due to the somewhat surprising stabilization in the little-flock number, the new leader will probably once again be an anointed, perhaps one of those who was recruited after 1938 to replace anointed members that left the movement because of Rutherford's introduction of *the Theocracy.*

Impossible to Identify a Leader

In recent years a power vacuum has gradually occurred at the top of the Watchtower organization where different groups position themselves for a not-too-distant future. However, as they deal with a collective organizational mechanism for making decisions, a structure in which everyone performs subservient, conformist roles while still scouting for the pinnacle of power, it is hard to guess where any changes are leading.

Who then was the real leader, Adams or Larson (or any other person), until September 2011 remains somewhat unclear to me. Formally speaking, it was the Governing Body, the decisive power authority within the movement, and it has been impossible to discern a *true* leader. However, if one takes the latest version of the Witnesses' literature CDs, containing their various texts and histories, and counts the occurrence of the two leaders' names, who until September 2011 helmed the two corporations, one finds eighty-eight occurrences of Larson, but only fifty-nine for Adams. Perhaps it's only a small, suggestive clue, but there it is. On the other hand, if one searches for the term Governing Body, the number of hits far surpasses the presidents'.

The memorial publication (or printed obituary) for Max Larson published by the Watch Tower Society between October 2011 and early 2012 could indirectly imply that the New York subsidiary (and the headquarters there) still *unofficially* plays the main role within the movement.

To review, Russell moved headquarters to New York in 1909 and *in practice* transferred many functions to the New York corporation that the Pennsylvania parent company had otherwise formally and legally handled. For example, elections of board members were held in New York after 1909, but legally they should have been held in Pittsburgh, the stated corporate headquarters. The New York-based election process led to a number of board members being regarded as not legally elected; Rutherford took advantage of this when he purged the board of its most troublesome members. During this time Rutherford also insured that the New York subsidiary could not dismiss him because he secured the president's position for life at the general meeting in Pittsburgh in 1917.[307]

Until his death in 1942, Rutherford had almost unlimited power over the Watchtower movement, including all its companies. As late as 1950, Rutherford's successor, N. H. Knorr, demonstrated he had inherited Rutherford's power over the Society's business when Knorr arranged the release of *New World Translation* of the New Testament by the New York subsidiary. This independence from the Pittsburgh parent company lasted probably until the mid-1970s and possibly beyond.

Moses also had Spiritual Needs

The Governing Body, which has slowly become dominated by members who do not have the *heavenly hope* (are not among the 144,000 anointed), will probably continue to *officially* serve as the chief executive body of the Jehovah's Witnesses worldwide. The members of the council, or the Body, are considered to have been placed there by God. Its members can't be elected through any democratic procedure, since the Council only—under Jehovah's guidance through prayer—can choose new members. The Governing Body has no president today, only a chairman, and members rotate into this position in turn. Theoretically then, no one occupies any special position in this council any longer.

Some anointed members of the Governing Body have been removed from leadership positions in the Society's various subsidiaries. Barr expressed their limited future roles this way: "'The faithful and discreet slave' and its Governing Body have had entrusted to them interests that are higher and far more encompassing than those granted to legal corporations" (*WT* Jan. 15, 2001, p. 31).

One can very well imagine that the aging members of the council are murmuring in the corridors—or the underground tunnels connecting buildings in the Watchtower complex in Brooklyn—but as it is written in the 2003 *Yearbook*, Moses also recognized, even at age eighty and "after being mightily used by Jehovah," that he had "his spiritual need." As I read the various direct and indirect messages pumped out by the Society, particularly those in Brooklyn's press releases and publications beginning in January 2001, the old guard must, like Moses, adapt to new times. (*YB*, 2003, p. 15)

The real reason for these rearrangements is supposed to be because most members of the Governing Body were quite aged by the turn of the 21st century. Frail and sick, they could not be expected to have the same responsibility for the affairs of the organization they'd had previously. By 1999 Lloyd Barry was dead; in 2001 Lyman Swingle died at age ninety-one; and in 2003 Milton Henschel died at age eighty-three.

It is clear then, that by 2000, a number of well-known men at the top were ready for replacement:

Leader Name	Age in 2000	Died
Klein	95	2001
Schroeder	89	2006
Sydlik	81	2006
Barber	95	2007
Barr	87	2010
Jaracz	75	2010

Gerrit Lösch, born in 1941, joined the Governing Body in 1994, and is seventy-one at this writing. The previously discussed Max Larson died in 2011.[308]

The last four members elected in 1999, Samuel Lelt, Gay Pierce (born 1934) and David Splane (1944) among them, according to Jehovah's Witnesses' *Yearbook* for the year 2000, had an average age of fifty-seven (in 2012 the average would be sixty-nine years). In 2010 a website article noted that younger men replaced the aged and dying men at the top of the Watchtower hierarchy; all were born after 1934: Samuel F. Herd, born 1935; Geoffrey W. Jackson, 1949, member of the Governing Body in 2005; M. Stephen Lett, 1949, joined the Body in 1999; Anthony Morris (age unknown, but he trained as a missionary in 1943), admitted in 2005.

It is not known how many of these men today profess to be part of the anointed flock. But for anyone who considers himself a member of this small flock, it seems safe to say (theoretically) that if he was born *circa 1943*—assuming he did not take an elected position before he was around age twenty—then he would have felt drawn to the anointed crowd *around 1963*. Yet, belonging to the anointed probably still gives one status within the movement; thus, it's easy to imagine that in order to increase one's status he may be tempted to profess to be one of the anointed.

During these years management changes were inevitable at Brooklyn and in the parent company in Pittsburgh, changes which inexorably replaced the old anointed-group leaders with younger men. Reportedly, in 2004, the Governing Body was reduced from thirteen members to ten, and in 2010 the number reduced again to around seven.[309] It seems the organization is slowly shrinking the Governing Body. If the number of members is further reduced, it could indicate an intention to dissolve it or at least reduce it to a tertiary function.

What impact these changes will have in the long term is difficult to say at this time, but it might indicate that a new generation will attempt to make changes the very old men at the top would try to block. Will the replacement members institute drastic alterations that could totally transform the dogmatic and organizational structure of the movement? Again, it is too early to say. That they might break with the original dogmatic foundations of the movement—Jehovah's Witnesses' special and *unique* doctrines that one must ardently and publicly embrace to avoid exclusion—is probably too optimistic. Only time will reveal if this evolution in leadership will become a revolution in practices.

The Swedish magazine *Informationer*, published by former members of Jehovah's Witnesses in Sweden, suggests some other reasons for the changes underway in Brooklyn:

"Another important reason the Governing Body has operated outside the boards of the corporations can be as Raymond Franz, a former member of the Governing Body, recently [around the year 2000] said in an interview: 'They seek to find legal ways to protect themselves.... As a legal entity the Watch Tower Society is threatened with various charges, among other things because of the movement's opposition to blood transfusions, and also because of the strict exclusion policy. The purpose of the changes could be to isolate and limit liability. This motive was of course denied by the movement's official spokesman" (*Informationer*, October 2000; my translation).

Power Struggle in Brooklyn

Perhaps a clue about the direction Brooklyn was taking can be found in *The Watchtower* from March 1, 2004, under the title, "A 'Slave' Who Is Both Faithful and Discreet," which emphatically describes the true theocratic teachings today.

The 1914 doctrine is maintained in the strongest terms because "most aspects of Jesus' prophecy have been fulfilled." The collective characteristic of "the servant" or "slave" is emphasized: It is not about a single person but a collective group of Christians who would "supply food at the proper time"—that is, in practice, the Governing Body's anointed members, whose number is not known today. And then, those more and more influential members of the "great crowd" are clearly put in their place:

"The great crowd of other sheep have imitated their anointed brothers. They are aware that their knowledge of God's purposes brings great responsibility.... However, anointed Christians are keenly aware that the talents were placed in their hands. They must render an account for the way the Lord's belongings on earth are administered. Even though they are few in number, they cannot abdicate their responsibility to the great crowd. With this in mind, the faithful and discreet slave continues to take the lead in caring for the King's business, grateful for the support of devoted members of the great crowd. These recognize the responsibility of their anointed brothers and feel privileged to work *under their oversight*" (*WT*, March 1, 2004, p. 18; italics are mine).

The article serves as a powerful political demonstration by the Watchtower's aging leaders. The message hidden in this 2004 article was probably intended to remind the large majority of young, ambitious leaders that they should not think they were *something special* even though they were younger and stronger and slowly but surely would assume leadership throughout the organization apparatus.

However, time had its own reckoning. In 2009, as I understand it, the last devastating message for the elderly who had so long endured appeared in the Society's main organ. The senders were obviously not members of the heavenly flock; they were leading members of the new power elite of the *other sheep*, who by now had fortified their positions within the organization. Under the subheading "The Correct Viewpoint" the editors of *The Watchtower* wrote:

"How should these anointed ones view themselves as they await their heavenly reward? They realize that although they have received a wonderful invitation, it is only that—an invitation. They must remain faithful until death in order to obtain this prize.... However, Christians who have truly received this anointing do not *demand special attention.* They do not believe that their being of the anointed gives them special insights beyond what even some experienced members of the 'great crowd' may have.... They do not believe that they necessarily have more holy spirit than their companions of the 'other sheep' have.... They *do not expect special treatment*; nor do they claim that their partaking of emblems places them *above the appointed elders* in the congregation." (Italics are mine.)

And further on:

"Members of the great crowd appreciate the spiritual food produced under the Governing Body's direction. But at the same time, while respecting the slave as class, members of the great crowd are careful not to *elevate any individuals* who claim to be part of that slave" (*WT*, Study Edition, [310] June 15, 2009, p. 24; italics are mine).

Members of the little flock were finally sacked, fired, shoved aside.

Or were they?

What currently happens in the relationship between members of the small and large crowds, where the anointed are apparently being driven to the fringes, is hard to follow at this time. The governing cadres within the companies in Pittsburgh and New York must struggle with new self-created problems, because, as we now know, new anointed members continue to appear in the statistics as their number still increases, at least it had up to 2012 when the 2011 statistics were published. So it's obviously difficult for the Society to be rid of them. And as long as the old veterans and their replacement new "anointed" still stand at the helm, nothing groundbreakingly new is likely to emerge. The 1914-ideology, in the years after 2000, was sustained as never before. And since Armageddon apparently is not forthcoming, notwithstanding that the members of the Governing Body stubbornly insist that it never has been more urgent than now,[311] they have perhaps, in spite of everything, arrived at a time that, within a couple decades, could prove to be useful as a new chronological focus for propaganda.

The year 2034! This is the *new important* year.

The Society stresses that people in the "days of Noah" were given the entire *120 years* before the deluge came, and the members are well aware that the deluge was a picture of Armageddon. Yet can it really be that Brooklyn has sunk so deeply? It has been said that they have learned much by the 1975 mistake. Or have they?

Chapter 36

Will Armageddon Arrive *Before* 2034?

From the Society's beginning various dates for the world's end have circulated among Jehovah's Witnesses. Some dates were set by Brooklyn and broadcast through the organization; other dates circulated among members, usually initiated by hints planted in *The Watchtower.*

The Watchtower management has had burnt fingers over this date-setting so many times that one would think they had finally learned. The last time nothing happened was in 1975. Since then, there has been speculation about various years, but Brooklyn deflected the date-setting attempts, saying only that God alone knew "that day and hour."

Yet, they did not completely shun the concept.

Some Ninety Years Have Passed

Near the end of 2003 as I routinely browsed *The Watchtower* from December 15, I noted with growing disbelief that Brooklyn seemed to again be giving attention to a particular year that could serve as a future focus point for the battle of Armageddon and the millennial establishment.

Under the heading "Our Watchfulness Takes On Greater Urgency," I found the following:

"Drawing a parallel between then and now, Jesus said: 'Just as the days of Noah were, so the presence of the Son of man will be.'—Matthew 24:37. / It is reasonable to assume that Jehovah feels about the present world as he felt about the pre-Flood world. Since he brought an end to the ungodly world of Noah's day, he will certainly destroy the wicked world of today. Having a clear understanding of the *parallel* between that time and our day should fortify our conviction that the end of the present world is near. What, then, are the *similarities? There are at least five.* The first is that a warning of coming destruction is given in no uncertain terms..." (italics are mine).

Here, it is repeatedly emphasized that it is the *similarities* that count.

The article states further:

"In Noah's day, Jehovah declared: 'My spirit shall not act toward man indefinitely in that he is also flesh. Accordingly his days shall amount to a hundred and twenty years.' (Genesis 6:3) The issuance of this divine decree in 2490 BCE marked the beginning of the end for that ungodly world. Just think what that meant for those then living! *Only 120* years more and Jehovah would bring 'the deluge of waters upon the earth to bring to ruin all flesh in which the force of life is active from under the heavens.'—Genesis 6:17. / Noah received the warning of the upcoming catastrophe decades in advance, and he wisely used the time to prepare for survival. 'After being given divine warning of things not yet beheld,' says the apostle Paul, '[Noah] showed godly fear and constructed an ark for the saving of his household.' (Hebrews 11:7) What about us? *Some 90 years have passed since the last days of this system of things began in 1914.* We are certainly in 'the time of the end.' (Daniel 12:4) How should we respond to warnings we have been given? 'He that does the will of God remains forever,' states the Bible. (1 John 2:17) Now is therefore the time to do Jehovah's will with a keen sense of urgency" (*WT*, Dec. 15, 2003; italics are mine).

As I read that issue of *The Watchtower* in 2003, only thirty-one years remained before 2034 arrived—and perhaps Armageddon.[312]

Are the 120 years a *trial balloon*?

Immediately I became aware that Brooklyn may have been about to launch a new apocalyptic timetable—one based on Jesus' comparing the days of Noah with the "times of the end," stretching from 1914 until Armageddon—wherein similarities between the time before the Flood and the current world order are indicated. This consists of a full *five* points of similarities—the first being "a warning of coming destruction is given in no uncertain terms" (p. 14, 15).

The article is, like any other literature from Brooklyn, written in strange impersonal language, without any nerves, heart or modulation. It is cold, toneless and cliché-filled. It is "Newspeak," as in Orwell's *Nineteen Eighty-Four*: a sexless and inhuman language, free from nuances. The pulse of the language is completely lacking, regardless of the alleged proximity of Armageddon.[313] Except maybe there was a hint of fear's quickened heartbeat.

Please accompany me for a moment as I must make a small digression:

In 2005, while I penned the Danish edition of this book, I had not read David A. Reed's report, "The Author's Testimony," which I first discovered in 2010. Reed made the report, his personal story, available on the internet. It is an interesting chronicle about his journey into and out of the Jehovah's Witnesses, and easily translates into other languages using web-based resources if anyone should wish to pursue reading it. Reed also draws comparisons with Orwell's *Nineteen Eighty-Four* (in Danish, *1984*), especially in regard to the language, Newspeak. I find it interesting that our response to Brooklyn's propaganda ended in the same conclusion.

Returning now to our previous topic, I was only able to surmise the words about the 120 years *were not accidental* but appeared in *The Watchtower* article because they have a particular *function*. The treatment of the topic had to direct, suggest and inspire.

If my assumption is correct, the new article focused on the 120-year span partly so Watchtower leaders could surmount the dilemma of the slowly dying 1914 generation and partly to justify intensifying the warning message again since they implied that *not more than* (approximately) thirty-one years beyond the 2003 publication they would again be at Armageddon's door.

Still, the Society's language is less direct than it was before 1975. The message is delivered more subtly, hint-like, so that afterwards no one can say the "*Watchtower* again was wrong." In this way, they once again leave the responsibility for new date speculation to the average Witnesses at all levels, except top leadership. In connection with the many hints about 1975, Brooklyn used the same trick, for the "nearness of such an important date indeed fires the imagination and presents unlimited possibilities for discussion" (*WT*, Aug. 15, 1968, p. 494). The stimulating and inciting methods are the same as always, giving *authorized permission* to speak about a new speculative topic, this time focused on the new 120th year, 2034. The 120 years mentioned in *The Watchtower* have not been addressed since that article. Yet the members have at least been provided with a hint about a time in the future where Armageddon may have long since passed.

Looking forward from 2012, it appears Brooklyn provided itself with a method to continue the warning work for another twenty-two years. This happens to fit well with *The Watchtower's* teaching somersault in 1995, when the magazine—in addition to the dogma about the "wicked" generation—published the article on the adjusted doomsday understanding. (*WT*, Nov. 1, 1995) Judgment Day was no longer the period from 1914 to 1919 and the subsequent period of tribulation until Armageddon, in which *the sheep and the goats* (NWT) are separated, but a relatively short event in connection with Armageddon that in 1995 still belonged to the future.

The new "more-precise viewpoint" Jehovah's Witnesses gleaned from the 1995 publication gave management time for new campaigns, worldwide construction projects and new growth, however, a new, finite timeframe for the world's end, something to drive continued growth of the organization, was still missing. In 2003 this was remedied. With the new *Watchtower* article's indirect suggestion about the 120 years, the message that "the time is very short" was sustained and broadcast to reach even more people.

Noah has Many Uses

Despite the fact that Brooklyn has, in recent years, put even greater effort toward converting even more people, they still emphasize that only a few will survive. Those select few will have "a privilege similar to that given to the Flood survivors. The survivors may for a time be able to have offspring as a part of the new earthly society" (pp. 14–19); a tempting perspective one must say!

In the same issue of the magazine, one finds the article "Prove Yourself Ready for Jehovah's Day" and it includes this:

"In the last book of the Bible, the glorified Christ Jesus stresses the suddenness of his coming, saying: 'I am coming quickly.' (Revelation 3:11; 22:7, 12, 20)."

Again, the same old techniques are employed. Simultaneous with the new thirty-year perspective Watchtower leaders gave themselves beginning in 2003, they continue speaking about Armageddon's nearness. A disastrous consequence of this event being ever-nearer meant the young people within the movement were again discouraged from pursuing higher education. Why fear such education, unless the leaders know quite well how such an education can provide students with analytical tools that can lead to a break with the movement:

"Granted, a certain level of schooling may be useful to obtain employment. However, the truth is that in the time-consuming pursuit of obtaining advanced education, *some have harmed themselves spiritually.* What a dangerous situation to be in as the day of Jehovah nears!… Time ran out for the world of Noah's day, and it will run out for the present system of things" (*WT*, Dec. 15, 2003, p. 24; italics are mine).

Just as before, the young members are asked to abandon their long-term studies, and they are advised to abandon all worldly "materialistic lifestyle" plans and instead set out in the richly blessed full-time service. Only *now* this is urgent and it is clearly apparent that Jehovah and his organization, the "slave" and the Governing Body, need the manpower. Now is the time to preach, the time to build printing works, branch offices and Kingdom Halls en masse, so global expansion can continue.

Despite resistance created by apostates, especially in Western countries, and despite aftereffects arising since 1975 when many disappointed members left the movement, the growth has been increasing regularly, from 4,472,787 publishers in 1993 to 6,429,351 in 2003; an advance of 43.7% in ten years. Today the growth has stalled, maintained at just +/-2% per year. Although in 2009, worldwide growth suddenly showed a 3.2% increase. The rate declined to 2.5% again the following year; and in 2012 it fell further to 1.9.

"Now, they've done it again!"

Could it really be true: Brooklyn had again launched a new *final deadline* for the end of the world?

I was actually somewhat amazed when I learned their next move.

It defied the alleged reluctance to fabricate new dates for the world's end, something Brooklyn has said since 1975. Nobody knew the day and hour, and yet they presented a new speculative deadline to the membership which seemed to have grown quite apathetic. Now they were inspired by the Society's calculated "similarities" with Noah's days. To me the leadership was deliberate, cynical and incorrigible, playing these new speculations against the fragile and insecure human beings' genuine religious feelings and hopes. Why? Probably to create fertile soil for continued growth and promote increased sales figures.

Beroea, the elder I'd been in contact with, exclaimed simply:

"Now, they have done it again!"

In 2004, the record number of publishers reached 6,513,132, representing a relatively slight increase of 83,781 over the previous year. Thus, Brooklyn still had mounting recruitment problems, and needed to heap coal into the doomsday engine. (*YB*, 2005, p. 38)[314]

Developments from 2004 to 2008/2009 show the same downward trend, and today the movement shows annual growth of only around 2% (1.3% in 2005 to 2.2% in 2006, 3.1% in 2007, 2.1% in 2008, 2.4% in 2011, and 1.9% in 2012). This is almost regarded as stagnant compared to previous, impressive growth curves (for example 3.8% in 1973, 7.1% in 1984 and 5% in 1994). Yet the Jehovah's Witnesses purport to be the world's fastest growing religious movement. Statistics can be manipulated or cleverly told to create an impression, but facts show the Jehovah's Witnesses' growth has been comparable to the Seventh-day Adventists' growth, which today is about twice as much as the Witnesses'. It's important to note in this comparison that the Witnesses do not include their children in growth numbers unless those children are "adult baptized" members. The Witnesses register themselves with the Society during baptism, which is the result of a decision to dedicate oneself to Jehovah. This decision happens, of course, under great pressure from family and the local congregation. Jehovah's Witnesses do not baptize their children; rather the practice is an individual decision and commitment made in adulthood.

Seventh-day Adventists numbered 15,780,719 for 2007-2008. In the same 2008 service year Jehovah's Witnesses claimed 7,124,443 peak publishers, making it clear the Witnesses' growth curve—still increasing, but to a lesser extent—declined compared to the Seventh-day Adventists' (Source: The SDA-Church, Denmark; and *2009 Yearbook of Jehovah's Witnesses*).

The comparison and disparity is revealed in the graph below, respectively showing the Seventh-day Adventists' and Jehovah's Witnesses' growth since the second half of the 19th century (respectively 1864 and 1879). The Seventh-day Adventists, founded in 1864, had a lead of fifteen years. That aside, the Seventh-day Adventists membership increases by about one million members per year, while the Witnesses apparently are in a growth-rate decline (apart

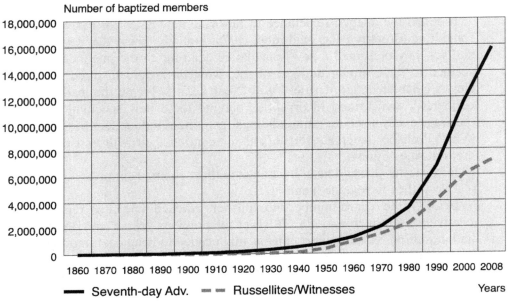

Number of baptized members

Seventh-day Adv. ━━━ Russellites/Witnesses — Years

Despite an approximately 16-year lead, in which the Seventh-day Adventists didn't show a marked increase in the number of baptized members, the basis for the graph comparison shows a similar rate of increase. The two movements have followed similar development rates from 1863/1879 (Russellites founded in 1879) to around 1900. Going forward, the Seventh-day Adventists' growth is more pronounced than the Jehovah's Witnesses. Although both movements had problems in the last quarter of the 20th century affecting growth (Jehovah's Witnesses' failure of 1975, and the Seventh-day Adventists' "The Glacier View" controversy of 1980), it is clear the Seventh-day Adventists took the lead even as the Witnesses' growth curb flattened. (See *Divine Purpose*, 1959, p. 312; graph compiled by Jette Svane.)

from the increase in 2009, which in turn is matched by a slight decline in 2102 with just 1.9%—short of the magic 2%, YB< 2013, p. 178)).

Erik Joergensen's Slip of the Tongue

Now that we've established how easily the Witnesses inflate their own growth and stability, let's return to the main theme of this chapter: the 120 years from 1914 to 2034.

The case was debated in the Danish Christian morning paper *Kristeligt Dagblad* in 2004. Anne Korsholm, a journalist at the newspaper, contacted Erik Joergensen, the Witnesses' Information Manager in Denmark, and according to the newspaper, he said readers who felt the *Watchtower* article indicated Armageddon would come in 2034 were completely wrong:

"2034 is, to the best of my judgment, *too far out in the future*. Only God knows the exact day, and just a few Jehovah's Witnesses imagine that it may be so long" (*Kristeligt Dagblad*, front page, January 7, 2004; italics are mine).

Erik Joergensen's not-very-thoughtful argument is revealing because, apart his statement's obvious contradictions, he says, in effect, he believes Armageddon will come *long before 2034*. Obviously, despite claiming no one knew Armageddon's exact arrival, Erik Joergensen seemed to be privy to God's thoughts about the day and hour.

Two days after the fateful interview, Erik Jorgensen withdrew his statement in a contribution to the Christian newspaper: "There is no case or story. There is not in the above-mentioned material from *The Watchtower* (December 15, 2003) any 'Judgment Day calculation' and we make no expectations concerning any year" (*KD*, January 9, 2004). I'm left wondering if some of his superiors at headquarters prompted Joergensen to disavow his unfortunate statements.

If the global expansion was not maintained, the Watchtower leaders were in a mounting dilemma. The new, unofficial end-time year, which can be derived from the suggestions about the 120 years, clearly could have been planted deliberately. Brooklyn needed a focal point in the relative near future to sustain growth over the next twenty-two years (counted from 2012). This new observation about Noah's time was poised to do just that.

I also asked the former Swedish elder and pioneer Carl Olof Jonsson, author of *The Gentile Times Reconsidered,* what he thought about the matter, and he wrote to me:

"Regarding the article in *The Watchtower* in December 2004 on the 120 years, I believe like you that there is an intention of the declaration. They wrote understandably not very clearly that the end could come 120 years after 1914, but the intention was presumably that some would get the idea. The very essence of the movement's identity from the outset was that there is a time frame for the eschatological period. That 1914 now belongs to the beginning of the last century may leave many Witnesses wondering whether there might be something wrong with the year, particularly since the 1914-generation is about to leave the arena. The intention of creating a period of 120 years from 1914 may be a way to reinforce faith in 1914 as the beginning of the time of the end. The apocalyptic movement is nourished by the feeling that the end is upon us. That feeling must be kept alive if such movements are able to continue to flourish. So I don't think it is a coincidence that they remind the readers of how long 'the time of the end' was in the days of Noah" (email, dated March 7, 2004; translation mine).

One can discuss the significance and supposed similarities between the 120 years in the days of Noah and the same period today at the "time of the end"— begun in October 1914—according to Jehovah's Witnesses. However, it is critical to note these similarities are now discussed inside *and outside* the Jehovah's Witnesses worldwide. A web search on a related term such as "Armageddon in

2034" reveals many articles and discussion boards. In this way, claims about the 120 years fall exactly where they have the strongest effect—in the members' *minds*, reinforced by talk within and without. It reminds me a little of the Society's hints about 1954. It's highly possible the pre-1954 hype may have been the template for what might be called the *hint program* for many years. The design, of course—combined with the theme of the article "Our Watchfulness Takes On Greater Urgency"—is to inspire those who desire to preach, or as Erik Joergensen so movingly said:

"We try to be awake and ready to be accountable to God ... we maintain that more than ever it is important to live god-fearing while we wait for, and in our thoughts accelerate, the coming of the day of God" (*KD*, January 9, 2004).

Spontaneous slips of the tongue can be revealing.[315]

And now we know that at least Jehovah's Witnesses' Denmark information manager, Erik Joergensen, really *did* believe 2034, according to his best estimate, was "too far in the future."

Chapter 37

Armageddon is Here!

Armageddon will be the worst disaster to ever strike our world, except maybe for the Flood or Deluge. In Noah's time this must have covered the entire globe from pole to pole—*if the Witnesses are right*. Almost all humans were destroyed, except Noah and his nearest family. The water must have surpassed the highest mountains: around *fifteen cubits*, as the Bible says, or as the Society notes in one of its recent works: "c. 6.5 m" (*Insight* 1, 1997 p. 609; subject: Deluge).

What follows now is harsh and vividly descriptive. It may be difficult for some to read. If that is the case, one may skip over this chapter and proceed to the next, yet consider returning to this information later once its full and impressive implications are realized. Still, the terror scenario of Armageddon is the prerequisite to understanding why Witnesses remain willing to endure the widespread repression that, in my opinion, they are subject to in the movement, and so, I hope you will read on.

Armageddon Mentioned in One Place

The Revelation of John 16:16 is the only place in the Bible where Armageddon is mentioned. It reads:

"And he gathered them together into a place called in the Hebrew tongue Ar-ma-ged-don" (KJ).

The phrase alludes to a distorted representation of the Hebrew noun *har Megiddo*, meaning "the Mountain of Megiddo." However, the old Canaanite and Israeli city Megiddo was not near any mountain but on the Jezreel plain in northern Palestine, at which several battles had been fought in the past. Among Jews today, the word *har-megiddo* can possibly be related to the place where the Jewish Messiah would destroy his opponents.

Armageddon Around AD 95

The Revelation of John was written circa AD 95 by a man named John[316] who, according to tradition, was the last living apostle of Jesus. It seems he used the old Jewish concept to symbolize the location where the decisive battle in the last times would occur between all the enemies of God and God's Kingdom. John probably assumed this battle was imminent. (Mosbech, 1943, p. 257; 297 DK[317])

The difficult-to-comprehend material in the Revelation of John has, over time, given rise to numerous interpretations, all based on the principle where contemporary events (from the current time) are partly read *into* the text and thereafter interpreted topically *out* of the text. The interpretation history of Revelation shows that down through time there has been a free-for-all, including all kinds of imaginable and unimaginable interpretations, and the Jehovah's Witnesses are no exception to this general behavior of creative interpretation.

The following example fully illustrates this assertion.

Revelation 17:7-8 states:

"But the angel said to me, 'Why marvel? I will tell you the mystery of the woman, and of the beast with seven heads and ten horns that carries her. The beast that you saw was, and is not, and is to ascend from the bottomless pit and go to perdition; and the dwellers on earth whose names have not been written in the book of life from the foundation of the world, will marvel to behold the beast, because it was and is not and is to come." (RSV)

In a fairly recent commentary on this quote, the editorial staff of *The Watchtower* wrote:

"John here sees in vision a combination of such rulerships—'a scarlet-colored wild beast.' This is the man-made League of Nations that appeared on the world scene in 1920 but plunged into an abyss of inactivity when World War II erupted in 1939. What, though, is 'the mystery of the woman and of the wild beast'? / By divine providence, Jehovah's Witnesses received enlightenment on that mystery in 1942. World War II was then raging at its height, and many thought it would escalate into Armageddon. But Jehovah had a different thought! There was still much work for his Witnesses to do! At their New World Theocratic Assembly of September 18–20, 1942, with the key city Cleveland, Ohio, tied in with 51 other locations in the United States, Nathan H. Knorr, president of the Watch Tower Society, gave the public talk, 'Peace—Can It Last?' Therein he reviewed Revelation 17:8, which says of the 'scarlet-colored wild beast' that it 'was, but is not, and yet is about to ascend out of the abyss, and it is to go off into destruction.' He showed how the League of Nations 'was' from 1920 to 1939. Then the 'is not' stage was reached because of the League's demise. But after World War II, this combine of nations would ascend out of the abyss. Was that Bible-based forecast fulfilled? Truly it was! In 1945 the international 'wild beast' emerged from its abyss of inactivity as the United Nations" (*WT*, April 15, 1989).

Can one seriously consider the validity of a "Bible-based forecast" as applied to current events? No, not at all!

The Watchtower leaders are attempting to give themselves credit for an alleged *prediction* that the League of Nations, after the end of the Second World

War, would reappear in a new guise. This is an abuse of the current knowledge of the time, because back in 1941 (on August 14), Churchill and Roosevelt negotiated about the creation of a new peace organization, and the name United Nations was used for the first time in the 26-nation negotiating statement of January 1, 1942, where it was agreed to continue fighting against the Axis Powers. However, the foundation of the United Nations was not laid until a conference held from April 25 to June 2, 1945, in which fifty nations participated. The pact was signed on June 26 the same year.

This knowledge can be extracted from most of the major lexicons about the United Nations published after 1945. (See also the commentary on Matthew 24:15 in Chapter 39, where the "abomination of desolation" and UN are discussed.)

Russell's Armageddon

In 1897, Charles Taze Russell published an entire book about the doomsday battle, *The Day of Vengeance*—later titled *The Battle of Armageddon*. This book was the fourth volume in the *Millennial Dawn* series—also known as *Studies in the Scriptures*, as the series has since been named. Whether Charles Russell or his wife Maria authored this volume is not important in this discussion (the issue of who likely authored the book is discussed in Chapters 6 and 7). In either case, Russell had final editorial responsibility. As recently as the mid-1920s, which is probably the last publication of this edition, the publishers could still embrace Russell's words that proclaimed the culmination of the "Day of Vengeance"—"a period of forty years; that began in October, 1874"—would end in October 1914[318] (*Studies*, 4, 1915 (1897), p. 546, 547; the following page references are also to this edition).

In the publication year it was stated that worldwide troubles "are rapidly culminating"; it was very characteristic of the Society's propaganda that *the* Day was always rapidly approaching. Stating *the* Day will be awful only emphasizes the need for fear if the reader had not already brought himself into safety before the climax of the "time of Trouble" with the small crowd, whose members would ascend to heaven around October 1, 1914. In the eleventh chapter of this Fourth Volume, as it was also called, Russell told his readers that even though the tribulations suffered by Judea and Jerusalem "were terrible in the extreme, they were only on a small scale as compared with the great tribulation, now fast approaching, upon Christendom, and involving the whole world" (p. 529). Here Russell refers to, among other things, Jerusalem's sad end in the year AD 70 when the Romans stormed and occupied the town and burnt down its temple. But Russell also refers to the French Revolution, 1789–1799, using it as an object lesson in what was soon to happen:

"In fact, the French Revolution seems referred to by our Lord in his Revelation to John on Patmos as a prelude to, and an illustration of, the great crisis now approaching" (p. 531). This revolution was only as "the rumbling of distant thunder" that would augur the end of "the present order of affairs" (p. 535). Russell expects that, in 1914, the circumstances responsible for the French revolution "are now operating to produce a similar, but far more extensive revolution, a revolution which will be world wide" (p. 531).

Russell's Millennial Ideology

Russell often expressed somewhat vaguely, compared to the Witnesses of today, his ideas of what lay ahead, and as far as I can determine, there was less talk about the dripping blood bath of the scope Jehovah's Witnesses revel in today:

"That the dark and gloomy day thus described by the prophets is a day of judgment upon mankind socially and nationally—a day of national recompenses—is clear from many scriptures. But while noting these, let the reader bear in mind the difference between national judgment and individual judgment. While the nation is composed of individuals, and individuals are largely responsible for the courses of nations, and must and do suffer greatly in the calamities which befall them, nevertheless, the judgment of the world as individuals will be distinct from its judgment as nations" (p. 11, 12).

We must remember Russell believed the Millennium had already begun in 1874, simultaneous with Jesus' invisible coming in the same year. In the revolutionary inventions of Russell's time he saw further indications of the daybreak of the Millennium. The culmination of this gradual transition to the blessings of the Millennium would manifest itself in 1914, when God's intervention would bring ruin to the world system of governments, but not against humanity as a whole. All humanity still had a chance when Christ finally established his universal government. Only those who stood against him would be eliminated:

"In a secondary sense it will include the earthly ministers or 'princes' who will be its visible representatives among men. In a still wider sense it will include all those who, when they recognize its establishment, will render to it loyal submission and devotion—both Jews and Gentiles. In the widest sense it will gradually include all subjects who obey its laws, while all others will be destroyed" (p. 643).

The "great crowd" (Revelation 7:9), which would live forever on earth, had not yet been invented in its present form. Therefore, it seems Russell expected all those willing to submit themselves to the new heavenly government's representatives in the future, as well as submitting to the new rules and laws that would be dictated to humanity, would be allowed to live until they would be exposed to the ultimate test at the end of the thousand-year realm. Russell is talking about "the supervision and instruction of mankind" (p. 529). In Russell's end-time teachings, which remind me a bit of some sort of an *apocalyptic-*

political-class-struggle ideology, most people still had a second chance. Russell indirectly expressed some sympathy with the contemporary and ordinary people in his own time, and believed that the "cries which preceded the French Revolution were as nothing in comparison to the appeals now going up from the masses all over the world to those in power and influence" (p. 536).

"Such is the order of the Battle of the Great Day of God Almighty. Its general character is that of a struggle of light against darkness, of liberty against oppression, of truth against error. Its extent will be world-wide—peasant against prince, pew against pulpit, labor against capital..." (p. 541).

It is almost like a quotation from the *War Scroll* of the Dead Sea texts.

Following this initial *class-struggle-sounding terminology*, it is not surprising to see that renegades from this movement often sought to join socialist parties where they would find familiar footing on new ground, and vice versa, some left the political-utopian parties to come into Russell's new *millennial ideology*. This phenomenon was also observed in the 20th century, and again often in connection with a transition to or from socialist parties.

Reforms Under the New Conditions

After I read the following astonishing descriptions of the transition after the creation of the new divine kingdom on earth, I realized how much Russell's ideas differ from today's Jehovah's Witnesses':

"Moral reforms will be instituted along all lines; financial, social and religious questions will all be recast in harmony with both Justice and Love. Judgment will be laid to the line, and righteousness to the plummet (Isa. 28:17); all of earth's affairs will be squared and plumbed with righteousness—and will be brought into strict conformity thereto. How much this will signify as regards the suppression of all lines of business which tempt humanity by alluring and seducing through the weaknesses of their fallen natures and the unbalance of mental and moral qualities. The distillery, the brewery, the saloon, the brothel, the poolroom, all time-killing and character-depraving businesses will be stopped; and their servants will be given something to do that will be beneficial to themselves and others. Similarly, the building of war-vessels, the manufacture of munitions of war and defense will cease, and armies will be disbanded. The new Kingdom will have no need of these, but will have abundant power to execute summary justice in the punishment of evil doers, when they have determined to act, but before they have done injury to others;—for none shall injure or destroy in all the holy Kingdom (Isa. 11:9) except as the competent and righteous Judges shall cause the Second death to come upon the incorrigible" (p. 632, 633).

Russell wrote like a businessman with practical, economic insight, and added a *Marxist-sounding rhetoric*, which must have had some appeal among ordinary people and visionaries at this time:

"The banking and brokerage business, and other like employments, very useful under present conditions, will no longer have a place; for under the new conditions the human race will be required to treat each other as members of one family, and private capital and money to loan and to be needed will be things of the past. Landlords and renting agencies will find new employments also, because the new King will not recognize as valid patents and deeds now on record" (p. 633).

Nowhere in Russell's books or other written works do we read highly detailed descriptions of Armageddon's horrors as those found in Watchtower productions today. Anyway, it would have been somewhat strange for Russell to produce such macabre depictions of the Armageddon destruction when he had enough to do with turning the "hose on hell" to "put out the fire."

In this respect, Russell was *friendliness himself* on God's behalf.

When you read Russell's books, it's clear that revolutions and battles between workers and capitalists played a role in his ideas about how the 1914 culmination would be or—shortly thereafter—would proceed. There would be the greatest breakdown of human institutions that ever has been seen. The revolutionary masses had huge expectations for the future, but Russell's Millennial Kingdom would surpass everything else. An ideal society would arise that, for all future time, would be freed from any form of wickedness, and which, exclusively, was dominated by the law of love, the pure *Utopia*:

"But when that which is perfect shall have been attained for mankind, by the Mediatorial Kingdom, they will be all kings as was Adam before he sinned. And to these kings, unitedly, will be delivered the post-Millennial Kingdom of God; and all shall reign harmoniously under the law of Love, and their President will serve and represent them. O Lord, we pray, Thy Kingdom Come! for thy present saints' sake and for the world's sake" (p. 646).

Yet, before the introduction of the new paradisiacal harmony on earth, the churches would in an ultra-short period of time "occupy a prominent place at the side of the governments," that is, a religious-political alliance. This development would be encouraged by the governments. They would use the "so-called churches" through the threat of "hell torture" to "impede the transition to socialism, or anarchy." And further: "The Churches will be happy to take advantage of such an opportunity," but "the Bible declares that the achieved 'queen position' will only be short-lived" and that "Babylon will soon witness a terrible fall, as when a large millstone is thrown into the sea. It is during this short church regime, that the presentation of the present truth for the world will be prevented by force … then will rapidly follow a complete overthrow and destruction of the current governments" (Foreword, p. 7, *DK;* translation is mine).[319]

As everyone knows, Russell died in 1916 without this or any other of his prophecies coming true.

In the following review of events preceding Armageddon and the eternal peace that thereafter would descend upon Russell's ambitious paradise project forever, I need not summarize all the *signs* in the "composite sign," as Russell's heirs believe virtually all must be fulfilled in the time after 1914, but only concentrate on the last two signs. These two will be fulfilled immediately before the end, and their fulfillment will announce Armageddon's all-consuming approach.

After fulfilling these "last signs," things will evolve rapidly and dramatically.

An Installation in the Subconscious

The last two signs are:

1. The "peace-and-security sign," and,
2. The state leaders' coordinated attack on Babylon and then on the Jehovah's Witnesses.

When that happens, it's "Midnight" and Jehovah and his field marshal, Jesus Christ, trigger the Armageddon events.

Regarding the first sign:

The peace-and-security sign means national leaders worldwide will, shortly before the battle breaks out, engage in international peace conferences and sign new peace agreements. This will heighten Jehovah's Witnesses' vigilance, because they know then that it is *just before* Armageddon starts. Therefore, the members of the movement are very observant of any new peace initiatives, such as the "roadmap for peace" in the Middle East—something very topical in 2011–2012.

In the years after 1990, when I slowly began to return to the subject of this book, it struck me, as I talked with the young people inside the movement, that they often referred to the peace-and-security sign. I became aware that this alleged "sign" was an extremely effective psychological oppression tool (as seen in Chapter 31 where Eve discusses it). The sign acts like a kind of "installation"[320] in the subconscious; it sears itself into the mind and destroys all ideas about liberation.

Brooklyn found the "peace-and-security" sign in Paul's epistle to the Thessalonians: "For YOU yourselves know quite well that Jehovah's day is coming exactly as a thief in the night. Whenever it is that they are saying, '*Peace and security!*' then sudden destruction is to be instantly upon them just as pang of distress upon a pregnant woman, and they will by no means escape" (1 Thess. 5, 1-3 in NWT, 1963, p. 3399; italics are mine).

None of the younger members apparently knew anything about current events during the time Paul wrote those words. The sign he refers to, which actually is not a real sign at all (like the "signs" in Matthew 24), dominated the young *indigenous* members so much, they have obviously linked it to the 20th century's many major wars and numerous peace conferences. The formation of the League of Nations, and subsequently the United Nations, which was facetiously called the "peace beast" or the "peace and security beast" in 1981, Brooklyn interpreted as "the beast" in the Revelation of John and linked to the "peace and security" sign in Paul's letter (*Kingdom Come,* 1981, p. 162-174; *WT*, Oct. 1, p. 13-18, 1985).

The peace-and-security sign is a very sophisticated, psychological propaganda invention for, by constantly using it in the movement's literature, members are kept in a more or less *constant state of alert.* And since no one within the movement has been made aware of the specific circumstances when Paul's words were written to the Thessalonians, the members—and especially the young ones—are entirely at the mercy of the Watchtower Society's reckless interpretation of the ancient apostolic writings. The peace-and-security sign has, in fact, almost become a regular *mental syndrome, which is in need of treatment.*

Applying Paul's letter to the Thessalonians on contemporary peace conferences approaches pure and deliberate deception. The ideas of the Second Coming and the world's end belong to the apocalyptic-eschatological events that, beyond any doubt, Christians expected to be fulfilled in the first century AD. If one reads Paul's words in proper context, it is true his warning is aimed to warn Christians that they should always live as if the "Day of the Lord" could come at any time. But it is also quite clear that the wording is a part of that learning-consolidation and congregation-discipline, which after AD 70 would evolve into established Christian congregations (further discussion of this follows in Chapter 39).

State Leaders' Overthrow of Babylon

As for the second sign: Simultaneous with the peace-and-security sign it appears the secular government leaders will overthrow Babylon, which (today) would be *all religions,* including the hated Christian churches. That message was central for Russell and Rutherford and is still very topical in the movement. The churches will have exactly what they deserve, and the Witnesses all over the earth will cheer when Jehovah destroys the hated "fallen" churches.

The churches—in league with US authorities in 1918, detained the Society's leaders, "the holy ones of the Supreme One"—will soon find that "Michael, the Great Prince" (Jesus Christ) will "go into action as the divinely appointed executioner of this system of things" (*Pay Attention to Daniel's Prophecy,* 1999, p. 305).

The Battle of Armageddon Begins

After the peace-and-security signs have been fulfilled, Satan will, as an expression of his desperation, attack the "remaining true Christians," the international community of the Jehovah's Witnesses, and there is no way back:

"The Bible, however, indicates that the world scene will undergo a drastic change. 'Babylon the Great,' the world empire of false religion, will suffer sudden destruction. (Revelation, chapter 18) With this debacle of false religion, the remaining true Christians will seem vulnerable, and Satan, or 'Gog,' will not be able to resist attempting to destroy them. He will see to it that under demonic influence 'the kings of the entire inhabited earth' are gathered together 'to the war of the great day of God the Almighty' at Har–Magedon.—Ezekiel 38:12-16; Revelation 16:14, 16" (*WT*, Jan. 15, 1985).

Even the UN will, as part of Satan's organization, participate in the attack on the Jehovah's Witnesses. In one of the Watchtower Society's books from 1975 one finds the rhetorical and facetious:

"Forward, then, to the attack, you united national members of the world organization for international peace and security! Forward, yes, but not really against the surviving witnesses of the Sovereign Lord Jehovah; rather, against their heavenly Leader, Jesus Christ, the once-sacrificed 'Lamb of God'! For, respecting the political powers that gave their earthly 'power and authority' to the world organization for domination of mankind, it is written: 'These will battle with the Lamb, but, because he is Lord of lords and King of kings, the Lamb will conquer them. Also, those called and chosen and faithful with him will do so.'—Revelation 17:13, 14" (*Man's Salvation,* 1975, Chapter 18).

It was J. F. Rutherford who developed this extreme rhetoric that increasingly came to influence the content of the movement's hate-marked literature. Rutherford's book *Religion* from 1940 states:

"The battle forces of the righteous under the immediate command of Christ Jesus are these: Jehovah, the Almighty God, the Supreme Commander; Christ Jesus, the Field Marshal and Leader of the forces of war against unrighteousness; and all the holy angels of heaven who at all times obey Jehovah God and follow the lead of Christ Jesus. The men and women who are on earth and who are on the side of righteousness, being fully devoted to Jehovah and Christ his King, have a vision of the battle array and witness the battle, but they take no active part therein. They are Jehovah's servants on earth, faithfully attending to the duties assigned to them; which is to sing the praises of God and Christ during the assembly of the warring forces, and while the battle is in progress..." (*Religion,* 1940, p. 339, 340).

The book, *From Paradise Lost to Paradise Regained,* from 1958, says the following about the position of the secular nations in the battle:

"On the Devil's side will be all the nations of the earth. The Bible tells us how the demons are leading 'the kings of the entire inhabited earth, to gather them together to the war of the great day of God the Almighty. And they gathered them together to the place that is called in Hebrew Har-Magedon" (*Paradise Regained,* 1958, p. 203).

Jesus Christ heads the heavenly combat forces:

"Fighting on the side of Jehovah will be Christ Jesus and all the armies in heaven. Christ will lead heavenly armies of powerful angels. The Bible gives us a symbolic picture of Christ on a white horse leading heaven's armies to battle at Armageddon…" (reference to Revelation 19:11-15; Ibid., p. 204, 205).

"Thrilling indeed is this picture of Christ and his armies. Christ is at the very front. This means that the King is certain of victory.… A sword comes out of Christ's mouth. This means that when the King gives the command to his army to destroy, it shall be done. The action then will be sharp and quick, and of the result there will be no doubt. Victory is certain…" (Ibid., p. 204, 205).

That sounds extreme, but it is obviously only *symbolic rhetoric*; still, it primarily serves to stimulate the average Witnesses' involvement in sales and propaganda work.

Worse than Nuclear and Bacteriological War

Armageddon is not a *measly* nuclear war, like one fought between major earth-based powers, but is Jehovah God's universal war on this wicked world:

"Release of all the nations' atomic bombs and hydrogen bombs, disease germ bombs and chemical gas bombs will not compare in magnitude, powerfulness and devastating effect with this 'unwonted act' of the Almighty God, Jehovah. Besides panic-striking physical phenomena in the literal earth and atmosphere, there will be tumbling to ruin of human institutions political, social, commercial and religious that have long stood like mountainous backbones of human society. In the world-wide confusion, when 'every man's sword shall be against his brother,' the Babylonish, religious, womanlike rider of the 'wild beast' of international alliance will have its complete number of deadly horns turn upon her and make her perish with the sword of the state, which she all too often wielded against Jehovah's holy ones and the witnesses of Jesus. Every defensive wall will crash to the ground; and the wild beast of international alliance will be destroyed by the flying apart of the United Nations, despite all the cement applied by the political 'false prophet.' While still operating, those institutions will be flung into a symbolic fiery lake of endless destruction" (*You May Survive,* 1955, p. 340; concerning UN, revisit the treatment of Matthew 24:16 in Chapter 33).

The United Nations still exists, so when the destruction of the world organization will actually occur is lost in the mists (see the story of the Society as NGO-member of the UN from 1991 to 2001 in Chapter 39, under the treatment of Matthew 24:15).

Tongues will Rot in the Mouths of Those Who Laughed

Most of the world's population will be destroyed in the Armageddon War; in today's numbers that's more than 6,700,000,000 (6.7 *billion*) people. The destruction is quite literal, as in: All meat will rot from the lifeless bodies lying anywhere on the battlefield of the war, leaving only tons of bleached skeletons

pain as a woman in travail; they shall look in amazement one at another; their faces shall be faces of flame."—Isaiah 13:6-8, AS.

25 Soul-chilling terror will spread through the masses of people so that they will lose control of themselves; they will begin killing one another. "On that day a great panic from the LORD [Jehovah] shall fall on them, so that each will lay hold on the hand of his fellow, and the hand of the one will be raised against the hand of the other." (Zechariah 14:13, RS) Then "every man's sword shall be against his brother." (Ezekiel 38:21, AS) But their selfish fight to live will be all in vain. Those who escape being killed by their neighbors will be destroyed by God's heavenly armies.

26 Christ's angels will smite all the opposers of God's kingdom and his kingdom witnesses with a terrible destruction. A flesh-eating plague will destroy many. Says Jehovah: "Their flesh shall rot while they are still on their feet, their eyes shall rot in their sockets, and their tongues shall rot in their mouths." (Zechariah 14:12, RS) Eaten up will be the tongues of those who scoffed and laughed at the warning of Armageddon! Eaten up

25. In their fear, what will people do to one another? 26. What kind of plague will Jehovah bring upon those who fight against his people?

"A whole generation of children have grown up fingering the Paradise book, carrying it to meetings with them, sharing it with their little playmates, being able to relate, long before they were old enough to read, a whole series of Bible stories just from the pictures." Pronouncement made by Grace A. Estep, a schoolteacher raised in a small town near Pittsburgh, Pennsylvania (*Proclaimers*, 1993, p. 101).

to show that billions of people who did not want to be converted to the Jehovah's Witnesses had lived in the "old world":

"Christ's angels will smite all the opposers of God's kingdom and his kingdom witnesses with a terrible destruction. A flesh-eating plague will destroy many. Says Jehovah: 'Their flesh shall rot while they are still on their feet, their eyes shall rot in their sockets, and their tongues shall rot in their mouths.' (Zechariah 14:12, RS) Eaten up will be the tongues of those who scoffed and laughed at the warning of Armageddon! Eaten up will be the eyes of those who refused to see the sign of the 'time of the end'! Eaten up will be the flesh of those who would not learn that the living and true God is named Jehovah! Eaten up while they stand on their feet!" (*Paradise Regained*, 1958, p. 208, 209)

Quite a frightening description, particularly considering those words have been given to an entire generation of children and young adults within the movement from 1958 onwards. A Danish psychologist, Tue Toft, said in 1997 to the tabloid *B.T.*, that the children will "come to feel great guilt and are burdened by chronic bad conscience. It is the kind that children grow up with. And it takes many years to shake the guilt from them, if they come out" (*B.T.*, Dec.11, 1997, p. 34; translation mine).

Further it is stated in this so-called children's book:

"Where can people hide from this destruction coming from God? Nowhere! Jehovah says: 'Not one of them shall escape...' (Amos 9:1-3, RS) Closed will be all avenues of escape! Wherever they flee God will find them and destroy them" (*Paradise Regained*, 1958, p. 209).

Even from the outside looking in, this gives a better understanding of why the young members and their parents even today are so horrified at the thought of leaving the movement: No one can escape the destruction in Armageddon. The once-young members grew up with this textbook's horrific descriptions of the end of the world since 1958, and those same people are now parents within the movement. And the cycle continues.

Jehovah's Witnesses would say that these quotes are from "older literature." But the inspiration for fear and warnings is updated regularly, particularly in *The Watchtower*, where leaders stated in 1985: "Yes, blood will run deep under the hand of God's executional forces. The 69 million deaths of two world wars will pale in comparison to those slain in God's war of Armageddon" (*WT*, Feb. 1, 1985, p. 4).

In 1993 the Society made a statement about the 1958 book—without any acknowledgement of the book's, to put it mildly, catastrophic contents:

"To the delight of the 145,488 delegates present on Thursday afternoon, July 31, Brother Knorr announced the release of the new book *From Paradise Lost to Paradise Regained* / Brother Knorr urged all to use the new book in their field ministry. He also suggested that parents would find it helpful in teaching their children Bible truth. Many parents took the suggestion to heart" (*Proclaimers*, 1993, s. 101).

In the children's book, *Learn From the Great Teacher,* published in English in 2003, one finds a very frightening illustration. On page 243 the illustrator depicts how the Battle of Armageddon develops: Jehovah's symbolic horsemen of the Apocalypse pursue fleeing, screaming children on the street while sending arrows down on them from heaven. The illustration also shows glowing comets (or rockets), collapsed buildings, fires and water coursing through the streets (see this and similar illustrations at http://dciscorp.com/qwotes/pictures.htm).

That is pure doomsday science fiction.

Jehovah is the Epitome of Love

In the same article from *The Watchtower* of 1985, the problem of how a loving God could cause worldwide destruction during Armageddon is treated:

" 'GOD IS LOVE.' Not only does God show love, says the apostle John, but he *is* love—the very embodiment of love.—1 John 4:8./ Yet, this same God of love is often portrayed by some as a vindictive god who brings cruel punishment upon those who have fallen from his favor.... Particularly do portions of the book of Revelation come in for censure where God's judgments upon the wicked are described, culminating in the battle of Armageddon.... / Actually, it is *because* of God's love that the battle of Armageddon must be fought. Jehovah God's purpose for the earth is to restore it to its original Paradise state and to have mankind live on it in peace and perfection 'with no one to make them tremble'..." (*WT,* Feb. 1, 1985, p. 4-5).

The White Bones Removed by Antimatter[321]

"As the smoke of Armageddon's battle clears, Jehovah's visible organization will still be here, ready for use in whatever way he directs. And may we be counted worthy, also, to be here individually.... God's people will need to keep organized under the Kingdom government in order to accomplish the monumental work of beautifying the cleansed earth, transforming our globe into a veritable 'garden of God'" (*Kingdom Come,* 1981, p. 176).

Here we must return to the children's book from 1960, where it deals with some more unpleasant aspects of this beautification work:

"Dead bodies will be everywhere—from end to end of the earth. Says Jehovah: 'I will call for a sword upon all the inhabitants of the earth.' Ungathered, unburied, unwept for, the bodies will be like so much fertilizer on the ground, just as the Bible says: 'The slain of Jehovah shall be at that day from one end of the earth even unto the other end of the earth: they shall not be lamented, neither gathered, nor buried; they shall be dung upon the face of the ground.'—Jeremiah 25: 29, 33, AS" (*Paradise Regained,* 1958, p. 210).

For the record, this quote from Jeremiah in the Old Testament describes not a future Armageddon occurring in our time, but the Babylonian armies advancing against Jerusalem *about 2,600 years ago.*

It goes without saying that six billion skeletons will put their fairly special mark on the landscape in the new paradisiac world. To help the survivors really acknowledge the difference between the old secular system and the new theocratic kingdom, they will tidy the scattered bones, effectively, into heaps. In this way the new theocratic community will soon be able to hide the horrific testimony of the many billions of human beings who, for better or worse, lived a kind of life in the wicked old world before Armageddon.

The following macabre and detailed description makes clear the extent of the horrors:

"After Armageddon the surviving sheep of the New World society will go forth to look upon 'the slain of Jehovah.' Says the Bible: 'They shall go forth, and look upon the dead bodies of the men that have transgressed against me: for their worm shall not die, neither shall their fire be quenched; and they shall be an abhorring unto all flesh.' (Isaiah 66:24, AS) To all surviving flesh the dead bodies will be disgusting, hateful things. Worms will not stop swarming over the millions of bodies until the last body is eaten up. Birds and beasts also will eat their fill of human flesh until nothing is left but white bones" (*Paradise Regained*, 1958, p. 210).

The fact that so many billions will be dead must not be seen as an insurmountable funeral task. In a relatively recent piece of literature from 1972 reassurance is provided:

"The fact that Jehovah leaves the bodies of those slain at the defeat of Gog's attack lying exposed on the ground for birds and wild beasts to gorge themselves upon symbolizes that they will not be laid in respected memorial tombs in hope of a resurrection for them. The unburied dead, 'those slain by Jehovah,' will be so enormously many that even the carrion birds and scavenging wild beasts could never take care of their consumption. The burial of even what remains after these lower creatures have their fill would be stupendous. Doubtless the Almighty God will use some highly scientific means, whether including antimatter or not, to dispose of the surplus of decaying bodies in a speedy and sanitary way" (*Nations Shall Know*, 1971, p. 377, par. 22).

Reconnaissance Columns Sent Forth

After Armageddon is done, the time comes for reconnaissance missions to be sent out to mark and bury billions of skeletons. In an article in *The Watchtower* of 1956—in spite of its relative age, the quote offers important insight—the duration of the cleanup work is described in detail:

"In the wake of Armageddon's carnage, disease and pestilence from the rot and decay would plague the survivors were it not for the fact that Jehovah sends forth an invitation to the birds... Ezek. 39:17, 18, *AS.* / With such a glorious feast of victory concluded, only the bones, bones from one end of the earth to the other, will be left for burial. What a task that will be for the survivors, to cleanse the earth of every remaining evidence of Gog's forces! Even with the work well organized it will take seven months, Jehovah says, just to bury the bones. Scouting corps will be sent out on a full-time basis to search the land thoroughly and, when bones are found, markers will be set up for those with the spades and shovels who follow. (Ezek. 39:14, 15) Those privileged to share in that cleanup work will not view it as a revolting and disgusting assignment but will rejoice to be alive when Gog's long and oppressive rule has come to an end and when the wicked are no more. Survivors of Armageddon will be happy and will greatly rejoice to have a share in preparing the earth for a global paradise of beauty and perfection under the reign of the King Christ Jesus. But first, before that happy day, this message against Gog must be delivered in its completeness" (*WT*, Aug. 1, 1956, p. 465, par. 16; see also *Paradise Regained*, 1958, p. 210-211).

I once believed those who survived were vaccinated against—or at least would be made immune to—the filth and pestilence when they stood in the middle of all the mess.

All this merely serves to encourage the members—just to be on the safe side—to do more field service *before* Armageddon.

Not Everyone sees the Work as a Privilege

A former Jehovah's Witness in the US, Michael Pendley has written a kind of science fiction tale about this macabre stage in the cleanup work after the "Big A is over." Even though his fiction is not acknowledged by "God's organization" in Brooklyn it is a brilliant object lesson. Actually, it's a little masterpiece! In a series of diary entries Pendley describes a process that in many ways resembles other attempts to portray life after the big disaster, such as *The Scarlet Plague* (1912) by Jack London.

Pendley reports about how the survivors gathered in the Kingdom Hall, which as might be expected was spared by Jehovah's heavenly armed forces. Here they learned some of the brothers and sisters were missing, about which the presiding overseer, Brother Thorn, noted "that those who were missing should have spent more time in field service" (*The Diary of an Armageddon Survivor*, as found on the internet, 2009). Michael Pendley—who I suppose is the main character in this "theocratic" science fiction—is one of those designated responsible for the unpleasant work:

Day 3: "Brother Thorn has assigned me to the burial detail. It seems that most of us single brothers have been assigned this unpleasant duty. The dead bodies are already starting to get to me. It sickens me to watch the birds and other animals scavenge the corpses. I actually saw a raven pluck out an eyeball today. Disgusting! Rob Johnson got a bulldozer running and has begun to dig a large common grave. My job is to go around collecting bodies and load them into the back of a pickup truck.... This burial work is taking a heavy toll on me. I can't help but feel saddened at the waste of so much human life.... Why couldn't Jehovah have found a way to save more people? The children are the worst, I can't stand to see their little bodies anymore."

Pendley lay sick the following day but was visited by the presiding elder who told him to get to work and that "everyone feels well all the time in the New World." Nevertheless, Pendley eventually tried to flee, but was seized by brothers from the Westview congregation, located nearby, and was escorted home by Thorn and two others, all bearing weapons. Then Pendley was expelled and put on latrine duty. Later he was subjected to re-indoctrination. After a new rebellion attempt, Pendley was again arrested and put into a makeshift jail cell in the Kingdom Hall basement.

Day 125: Pendley is labeled as an "unrepentant apostate" and forced to attend a hearing where he is not allowed counsel and cannot call witnesses. He is sentenced to death by stoning. Before the execution he ponders his situation:

"Well, this is the end. Later today, I will be led out for my execution by stoning. I would rather be shot in the back of the head, but the Society obviously feels that stoning provides a better object lesson. If I get a chance I will throw one of the rocks back at Ed Thorn. The funny thing is that I don't really feel so bad about my impending demise. This New World Society is not my idea of a paradise and I don't want to live with these people for all eternity. From paradise lost to paradise regained to paradise lost again."

On day 126, Pendley was executed.

After this local, fictional incident as one—*in fact still living*—rebel and renegade in the US has reported, the new world can finally begin. The following quote is not from Pendley's little science fiction, as the reader might think, but from the Society's children's book from 1958: "Armageddon is over. Gone now are the invisible troublemakers! Gone are all the nations! Gone are all the goatlike people! Gone is the old world—gone forever! A new world begins" (*Paradise Regained*, 1958, p. 211).

New International Construction Programs after Armageddon

The enormous building program undertaken by the Watchtower Organization worldwide in the period before Armageddon is a necessary part of expansion plans still pursued by Brooklyn leadership, and although Armageddon is "just around the corner," the work continues as if there are many years before the final sentence because "only God knows the day."

Before the expected battle of Armageddon in 1975 it was not uncommon for Jehovah's Witnesses to walk through neighborhoods with single-family houses for "fun" (or was it deadly earnestness?) to select homes that could be theirs after Armageddon. When I visited some ex-Witnesses a few years ago, we went for a walk in their neighborhood. By a large, beautiful house my friends stopped and told me jokingly that before 1975 they had selected it as their post-Armageddon home.

Pendley's story confirms this practice, when he tells us that on day four the group had its first judicial hearing after Armageddon because Larry and Sue Winters had moved into the McRae's mansion: "The problem was that Sister Thorn [the wife of Ed Thorn, the presiding overseer] had already had her eye on the place and, as wife of the presiding overseer, she figured that she should have first choice." Brother and Sister Winter were then ordered to move out of the house, but at the next morning meeting, the Thorn's announced they would be moving into the McRae place, and as Pendley remarks: "Position has privilege, even in the New World."

The livestock in George Orwell's *Animal Farm* had practically the same experience. The obese pigs quickly became "more equal" than all the other livestock on the farm, which soon led to the pure dictatorship.

According to Jehovah's Witnesses' teachings, after Armageddon the survivors will build a lot of new housing for themselves and others, for an enormous devastation has struck the cities of the old world:

"No doubt housing projects will flourish earth wide—not the constructing of ugly city blocks of tenements, but the landscaping of beautiful family residences in paradisiac surroundings. Yes, there will be much work to do, but it will be joyful, interesting work, a rewarding work concerning which King Solomon said, 'There is nothing better' than that 'every man should eat and indeed drink and see good for all his hard work'" (*Kingdom Come* 1981, p. 177).

Billions will Inhabit the New World

The Watch Tower Society has also prepared for the huge population increase to come after Armageddon:

"It is expected that *millions* will find salvation through the 'great tribulation' to enter into the blessings of the 'new earth.' (Revelation 7:9, 14) Yet thousands of millions, *billions,* will ultimately enjoy life here under the Kingdom. Why do we say 'billions'? After the flood of Noah's day, Jehovah gave to the righteous survivors a mandate, saying: 'Be fruitful and become many and fill the earth.' This suggests the joyful prospect of human marriage and the bringing forth of children *in righteousness* for at least a time after Armageddon. (Genesis 9:1, 7; 10:1-32; Matthew 24:37) However, that will not be God's principal way of 'filling the earth' with mankind at that time. How, then, will God populate our globe, thus accomplishing his original purpose? (Genesis 1:28; Isaiah 45:18) It will be by repeating, billions of times over, his great miracle of the resurrection" (Ibid., p. 178; the Bible quotations are from the New World Translation).

Together with the resurrected, the total population of the "new earth" will be tens of billions, a far greater number than those living today. And it will probably disappoint some members that it will only be a "piece of time" in which they will be able to reproduce themselves, but that is because, as mentioned above, many billions of deaths will occur. Among these resurrected from the dead will be the past's faithful princes, and they will get their lives back at a relatively early stage: "It is reasonable to expect that such faithful ones who endured persecution 'that they might attain a better resurrection,' along with integrity-keeping ones of the 'other sheep' who today may die before Armageddon, would experience an early resurrection into the 'new earth.' Perhaps you yourself have lost dear ones in death, even faithful servants of God. What a joy to welcome these back from the dead, and to tell them of Jehovah's great act of vindication…" (Ibid., p. 179).

New History's Largest Educational Program

A university education program, like that known in different cultures in the old world for many thousands of years, will never be considered for Witnesses after Armageddon. The education program in the new world will have completely different purposes:

"Will that be a fearsome time for the resurrected ones? Religious pictures of the Last Judgment notwithstanding, it will be a most joyous time. For those resurrected ones will not be judged according to their wrong deeds of former times, but, rather, according to their willingness to live up to the righteous requirements for life in the realm of God's kingdom. (Compare Romans 6:7.) And every effort will be made to help them along the pathway to complete reconciliation with God. The greatest educational program of all time will be carried forward under the Kingdom organization. / 'Scrolls' will be opened. These will be instructions published to help resurrected humans to perform those 'deeds' that will qualify them for everlasting life. (Revelation 20:12) The educational facilities and programs in the 'new earth,' being directed by Jehovah and his Messianic King, will be far advanced in comparison with anything Satan's world has ever offered" (Ibid., 1981, p. 180-182).

Old cultures will be of no interest because they belong to the past's epochs of the evil world history, and their sole function would then be that they could provoke the now-perfect, theocratic human into *independent thoughts.*

The purpose of the new education program will be to destroy the memory of all past architectural masterpieces: Rome with its Pantheon and Forum Romanum; the pyramids in Egypt; Angkor Vat, the temple complex in Cambodia; and the Taj Mahal in India. All the magnificent monuments built by ambitious rulers in the past, often as temples of "false" gods, will be destroyed.

The survivors will not publish literature on these ancient cultural marvels, and books from before Armageddon that escaped destruction will probably be collected and destroyed. The same will happen with the libraries of the old world, which will go up in smoke. All knowledge of the wicked past will be destroyed forever in the same way. Perhaps someone during the cleanup after Armageddon will find books from the *old times* and hide them in a safe place. Yet it is likely that such good intention will ultimately fail. Millions of spying angels and ubiquitous *elder inspectors*, acting as Jehovah's "eyes and ears" on earth, will undoubtedly discover what is happening, or come to wonder why a member of the new-world community hides away to read old, yellowed books that long ago should have been destroyed in the organized bonfires.

The person concerned will, because of his inappropriate curiosity (maybe he has found Ray Bradbury's *Fahrenheit 451*, a novel set in an imaginary future where reading is banned and firemen conduct book burnings), in the best case be reconvened, or something like that, so universal harmony can be restored. Just one rebellious individual can, however, with his willful thoughts and untheocratic behaviors make Jehovah ashamed. The insurgent will, if he or she does not quickly improve themselves, be removed from the surface of the righteous "New Earth" and go to an eternal death in the meeting. Since all the weapons have been forged into iron plows, the sinner will probably be stoned to death if celestial lightning does not conveniently appear. Stoning, a common-enough biblical method of execution, may well be considered a realistic option—that is if one believes there will be any kind of realism in this ghastly *New World Project*.

The doctrine of Armageddon will, as an example of fear and warning for the new world's inhabitants, form an integral part of school curricula, and become forever read as follows:

"As in the days of Armageddon…!"

The paradisiac peace will gradually descend over everything and everyone, and everyone will receive a new spirit from Jehovah through the representatives of Jehovah's visible organization. An authoritative, directing spirit, with the extremely willing intermediaries of the elder committees, will regale the survivors and tell every human being on earth how one should behave in the New Theocratic World as a "perfect free human being."

The Last Test

Apart from worshipping Jehovah, something the survivors will be busy with forever, there will be time for various other forms of recreation and amusements:

"We can anticipate, too, that there will be relaxation time for happy associations and healthful exercise, the enjoyment of music and other worthwhile arts, and always arrangements for worship of our Grand Creator. All will want to bless Jehovah, as did David in making arrangements for temple worship…" (*Kingdom Come*, 1981, p.183).

So, everything looks quite promising, except that the survivors must once again be tested. The Jehovah's Witnesses expect that Satan will be released from his prison in the "abyss" for a short time at the end of the thousand years, *perhaps for approximately fifteen years*, and in that short time he has the task of trying to entice the new *theocratic human beings* to revolt against Jehovah. This will, to some extent, succeed for him, which in turn may be a further cause of stress for today's Witnesses living *before* Armageddon if they do not fulfill proper service as regular publishers. Therefore, no one can feel any measure of safety about the future:

"For a short season, Satan will be released from the abyss, to test the perfected world of mankind regarding its loyalty to Jehovah's kingship. An indefinite number may choose to follow the Devil, but judgment will be executed swiftly upon them. The 'seed' of God's 'woman,' Christ Jesus, will perform his final act of vindication by crushing the head of the original Serpent, annihilating him and his brood as completely as by fire that lasts 'day and night forever and ever.' The great issue raised in Eden as to Jehovah's rightful sovereignty over his creatures will have been tried and settled for all time!" (*Kingdom Come,* 1981, p. 185)

It must still vex Jehovah a little that an "indefinite number may choose to follow the Devil," because existence of these rebels, who have actually reached the perfect stage, poses another big question about whether Jehovah's new world will be as wonderful as his *visible organization* on earth today claims it will be. These rebellious survivors will apparently prefer eternal death over existing under the management and control of Jehovah's visible organization—represented by the elder committees worldwide.

Should any be so unlucky as to become rebels—people tempted to ask "untheocratic" questions by the end of the Millennium concerning the meaning of this whole unimaginable paradise-project—and subsequently be sentenced to death by a local committee of elders, they can console themselves with the fact that the "eternal extinction" will arrive with merciful quickness.

"Any humans that Satan then succeeds in misleading will then find their rebellion against divine ruler-ship to be ineffective and short-lived. With Satan and his demons these earthly rebels will be obliterated from the realm of the living" (*Approached*, 1973, p. 81).

Still, those less-fortunate survivors will be able to think, in their last moments, that after all they had been able to live a thousand years *extra*. Just a thousand years, and then everything is forgotten. That doesn't seem so bad!

Chapter 38

Beroea's Choice

I met Beroea a few years prior to writing this book, after I had corresponded with him via email for some time. He is currently as elder in a Jehovah's Witnesses congregation. We agreed to meet at a neutral location where we could talk in peace about things. I was the first from the "old world" who came to know his true identity and the problems with which he struggled.

Beroea had posted multiple debates online where he raised an *unprecedented* sharp criticism of Jehovah's Witnesses' leadership and teachings, a criticism that was answered with harsh accusations. He was called a traitor and well pisser, and in a post by one of his opponents the man claimed to know Beroea's real identity and said he would contact him directly. Fortunately, it was impossible to trace Beroea using only his email address.

Beroea's situation was unenviable from my point of view, but I soon discovered that he had a firm grip on things and his Beroea identity gave him a certain brute strength, as well as remorse, because his family knew nothing about his subversive activities.

He had simply exceeded the invisible boundary between the *old* evil world and the good *new* world. But thus far he had been unable to move fully away from the Witnesses; he had many good reasons. He remained calm, but was resolved even to the point of an open confrontation if his identity was revealed. Until then, he preferred to remain a member. He would decide for himself how and when he would leave the movement.

Popular within the congregation, as surprising as it may sound, he thrived among his fellow believers. A church community is more than rigid dogmas, which don't always directly concern the members. The most important aspect for them is often not the content of the teachings, but rather the social community and the feeling that they are part of a large international organization under God's supervision.

If one remains an ordinary member, out of the organization's limelight, one can live a comparatively anonymous life as a Witness for many years, focused on one's duties as a publisher. Thus Beroea, doubts and concerns kept secret, could move about in the congregation as a spiritually mature elder, playing the role of the caring shepherd responsible for the sheep.

I suppose leaders in the Danish headquarters would really like to know his identity so they can remove "the wicked person"[322] from among their midst. However, Jehovah has not provided them with any major hints about his identity. Naturally, this has given Beroea cause for serious reflection on whether the alleged divine direction of the leaders should be taken literally! (1 Corinthians 5:13, KJ)

What does *Beroea* mean?

Beroea adopted this pseudonym because he identified himself with Acts 17:11 where the city Berea is mentioned. Berea lay in the province of Macedonia, about sixty-five kilometers from the city of Thessalonica, as visited by the Apostle Paul around AD 50. The Jews in Berea "received the word with all readiness of mind, and searched the scriptures daily, whether those things were so." Beroea chose his name because he wanted to emphasize that he was putting the Holy Scripture over the doctrines of the Watchtower Society.

When the Society issued its 1995 turnaround concerning the problems associated with the 1914 generation—those aging Witnesses were supposed to survive right up to Armageddon—Beroea became immediately aware that something was very wrong. The Society explained away one of its most important dogmas, and he soon understood that Armageddon, from then on, was only rhetoric that exclusively served to facilitate a minimum "two percent annual growth" in membership. The Society had installed a "cat flap" so the nearness of Armageddon could be pushed into the future as needed.

However, the consequences of being an "apostate" are too serious for Beroea. Although he now hates the system, as an elder he feels enslaved by it, he cares for so many of the ordinary Witnesses, who he considers to be decent people. He said: "But we are poor victims who have got God replaced with a man-made beast."

Strong words published in the Danish tabloid *Ekstra Bladet* on a Sunday in May 2004.[323]

Fear has been Dominant

Perhaps *Ekstra Bladet*'s article didn't attract much attention among its readers, but I am sure the Witnesses at headquarters took quite an interest.

In the article, Beroea said:

"Fear has been dominant. We fear that if we express ourselves in conflict with the official, approved ideas of the organization, then we are no longer accepted in the community. The fear of loneliness; the fear that your wife or your kids look at you with a glance: 'You have betrayed us.' A Witness's self-esteem is synonymous with that of being a Witness. Outside the organization, you are completely naked, without faith and without network."

He continued:

"It is like the old East Germany, where people feared Stasi and were afraid of being denounced. We try with all power to avoid a misstep. Nobody discusses ideas that differ from the official. So the conversations that take place between the Witnesses are often without substance. You can either be like a parrot, repeating everything you have learned. Or on the other hand, the silence spreads suddenly, and the conversation stalls. Everyone knows why. The spoken words had come too close to a forbidden area. Inside the Jehovah's Witnesses, there is a filter between God and the individual. This filter is the Jehovah's Witnesses' organization. Individuals are not able to achieve God's love without going through the filter. To 'go through the filter' implies that you have to comply with the organization's laws and rules to the letter. And by listening to its words through the elders and the magazines, *The Watchtower* and *Awake!*, one follows the word of God. It gives the organization a huge and ghastly power..." (*EB*, May 16, 2004, p. 18).

One day in January 2005, Beroea and I were sitting in a cafe in the center of the old town in Copenhagen. Beroea is a courageous man, for he has faced the facts about his religion. Yet he is disappointed and indignant, which is understandable because it is a difficult process to free oneself from this movement. To be inside is hopeless, and to leave the movement is synonymous with being a skeleton on Armageddon's battlefield. Brainwashing makes almost-indelible marks. However, Beroea uses his sense of humor as a counterweight against the whole of an impossible situation. He was raised within the movement and doesn't know a life without it.

I wonder why he has not already packed his Sunday best and said goodbye. On the other hand, I understand him well and also respect his solution to his problems. Actually, his way seems to closely resemble the way many churchgoers in other religious communities and denominations solve their problems with their communities and churches.

Primarily, It Works

Even though I understood his feelings, I asked Beroea the following questions:
Why do you not take your Sunday best and leave the movement right now?
The answer came promptly:

"Well, it would indeed be the most honest. But first of all, I am just a human being, and I have no illusion that I alone can shake the views of the Watchtower Society. It's a beautiful wasted effort. At the same time leaving would have some personal consequences; I wouldn't have a problem with them but my family would. I'd like to spare them the difficulties. But I am well aware that the situation is untenable, and that there is a risk everything sooner or later can get out of control."

How can you endure it?

"It is also difficult, but primarily it works. There is too much to lose by standing up publicly with my views, because the matter would quickly be forgotten, but my family and I would be isolated from other members and they would not listen to us. If excluded, I could not talk with the members at all. It is simply that situation I would avoid. It's too great a price to pay for so little gain. So better to try to make the best of it. I want to protect my children so they can make their own choices, without threats of retaliation simply because I could not keep my mouth shut. So, especially for the sake of them, I take it calmly and try to teach them to do without the organization."

What binds you except the family?

"There are so many weak members within the Jehovah's Witnesses who need support. In particular, many older people who have been involved in the movement for many years and perhaps now are a little disappointed and resigning. Unfortunately I cannot tell those who remain that the reason for much of their suffering is due to the Watchtower system. They will simply not understand. To them, everything the Society stands for is necessarily true, because they have invested their whole life in it. So rather than dream of something else, we delude ourselves into thinking we still firmly believe in the cause. Many Jehovah's Witnesses are well equipped for this. It is tragic, and it often fills me with indignation, but it is impossible to change. I often think that it is one thing to only deprive people of their delusions, but quite another to also give them something better they can be happy with. Many people within the Jehovah's Witnesses are living very well with their faith in the coming new world, and I don't think I have any right to deprive them of their dreams if I can't give them something better. It is beyond my powers—unfortunately."

Regarding 1914:

What are the consequences, right now, since Armageddon seems to have been pushed thirty years into the future?

"There are no consequences. 'The end' will be preached as if it is 'just around the corner.' How many who are quietly wondering is unknown because nobody in the congregation discusses it. This is a dangerous topic. Some might think their thoughts in an unguarded second, but those thoughts are quickly abandoned, because if they were allowed to develop, the person in question would perhaps lose hope. Remember that for the individual Jehovah's Witness they have a personal investment in the Jehovah's Witnesses organization and teachings, almost a complete identification, and losing this will, for many, mean a personal, emotional collapse."

If the 1914 doctrine is abandoned, I imagine that member's discipline breaks down?

"The discipline is based on the fundamental apocalypticism of the Watch-tower Society, which in varying forms has been reflected in the last 125 years. And *only* Jehovah's Witnesses will survive Judgment Day. If the crucial apocalyptic dogmas are being weakened, it is unlikely it will function. But you must not overlook the importance of one's relationship with 'the friends' in the organization. The congregational community, which the Witness members do not experience or recognize as something negative, despite the pressure of constant meetings and agitation, still binds them together. Remember, members largely have only this form of 'legal' contact with other people, and even if they do not speak confidentially with each other on controversial issues, still the social relations among members of the congregation are a very strong binding factor. It is only when 'the scales fall from our eyes,' and one suddenly sees clearly what is going on, that one experiences the so-called community within 'The New World Society' as burdensome. But even then, one clings to the Society vehicle, for where would we go 'in the old world outside?' And if one becomes an apostate, disowned by all the people that you have shared years of community with—friends and especially family, wife, children, parents-in-law and grandparents—it would be a terrible situation."

The Big Villain:

Has the movement ended up in a terrible state of uniformity?

"For me it is the organization itself that is the big villain. It has quietly, through 125 years, had its own independent life. In its pure youth, we could perhaps connect the activities with a degree of sincerity, but it has since grown too big and strong, and all humility is gone. It has been immensely self-satisfied and even forgotten to serve its supporters. Instead, it sits on a throne, from which it requires unconditional obedience of its often fanatically loyal subjects. Most Jehovah's Witnesses have quietly become accustomed to it, and they do not even see it. I still have a strong belief in God and I am indignant at the fact that an organization has put itself in God's place and can get away with it. It is tragic! You can secretly hope that God will open people's eyes, but he seems sadly silent. Yet the organization is alive and well. There are plenty of members who willingly support it and bring it nourishment; it's really an excellent system in that respect. The Witnesses slave away for it their entire lives, without getting especially much in return, and the organization just shows more and more greed. But as long as its leaders can maintain the illusion that they are installed by God, as Jehovah's "channel," it works, apparently."

Eventually Beroea found a way to manage his relationship with the movement and in April 2010, a subdued Beroea wrote to me in an email:

"I have little contact with 'the system.' I have, in a way, put it behind me, but without bitterness—I only want to keep contact with some old friends, therefore, I show up occasionally. And my faith has been clipped—I am probably an agnostic now."

It was Beroea's choice to tiptoe out rather than run, partly for reasons of old friends who respected him and, partly and most importantly, for the sake of his family, because if "the system" heard of his activities, it could go horribly wrong.

So far, so good, for my friend, Beroea.

The organization that has set itself in God's place—truthfully, something *not-exactly rare* in our old world—appears to be slowly approaching a cross-road. Its tyranny can hardly be much worse, so the point of change and inno-vation is probably only ten to twenty years ahead, if I can be optimistic. But it is difficult to assess what might happen as a result of the accumulated dis-satisfaction among the ordinary members, who, from an unconscious "stock" of repressed and forbidden thoughts, slowly presses against the organization. Members do not like to reveal their frustrations, except when they—like Beroea—can behave anonymously.

The risk is, as we have seen, too dire.

Summary, Conclusion and Outlook

Up to this point, I have tried to portray the extreme development of the Jehovah's Witnesses following the end of original Russellism after C. T. Russell's death in October 1916. The roots of this extremism were deeply hidden in the legacy of the Adventists. The Adventists' shattered expectations about the visible Second Coming in 1844 led to the emergence of the most bizarre and extreme Adventist churches that each developed unique concepts to explain away and supplant the disappointing lack of Judgment Day in 1844. They evolved the strangest doctrines, and in order to codify the most consistent of them the Adventists organized, partly as a step toward preventing the dissolution of the acquired religious community, partly as a replacement for the failed return. Where the foretold "Return" had earlier created the necessary enthusiasm to sustain believers, discipline and order—the "Organization"—now fulfilled this role.

The Adventists' consolidation efforts eventually led to the kind of organization noted Adventist George Storrs, one of Russell's mentors, had warned against, but there was no way back. On the one hand, new, wild doomsday dates continued to be proposed, while on the other hand an organization capable of creating togetherness and fellowship grew. Therefore, out of the confusion around the collapse of the movement, there arose, between 1844 and 1880, a series of Adventist associations or churches, some of which still exist. The biggest of these is the Seventh-day Adventist church, and the next-biggest is the Advent Christian Church—the same church where the young Charles Russell applied for "ministerial credentials" and was rejected. When one tallies all the adherents of the movements, from every major and minor Adventist and fringe-Adventist group, including the Jehovah's Witnesses, all spawned by William Miller's original revival message, the whole movement today numbers about 40 million followers and members.

Right from the start in 1879–1884, C. T. Russell secured himself against any of his supporters, or people from outside, taking over his association. As we have seen, he ran it almost as a one-person business. Therefore, it was with an inner, inexorable logic and consequence that Russell's association degenerated and ended in the extreme dictatorship and regimentation that still characterizes the movement of the Jehovah's Witnesses today.

It should be emphasized, however, that the transition from Russell to J. F. Rutherford in 1916–1918 was a turning point that changed the movement radically:

1. A number of more or less radical Bible Student associations and sects appeared in these years, all claiming to be Russell's heirs. They identified themselves with all the original founder's ideas. Today, however, they play no major role, as they have been standing—so to speak—frozen by those perceptions that characterized Russellism by the time of Russell's death in 1916. Together they now amount to approximately 70,000 members, with no significant leading organization or prominent and well-known leaders. They are also, and increasingly so, a place of refuge for former Witnesses who have either left the movement or were expelled.

2. J. F. Rutherford's takeover of the Society (International Bible Students) led, according to strong criticism from many of Russell's former staff members, to a distinct member dictatorship early in the development; this gradually transformed the original movement into a personality cult surrounding the "usurper" J. F. Rutherford. Historically and quantitatively—from 1916 to 1931—it was actually *Rutherford's Bible Students,* which assumed the new name *Jehovah's Witnesses,* that became the real inheritors of Russell's Bible Student movement. It was clearly this group of Bible Students that further developed the founder's original ideas and organization which eventually degenerated into the extreme organizational dictatorship. The founder of one of the new, competing Bible Student Associations, Paul S. L. Johnson, and another former prominent Bible Student leader, I. F. Hoskins, characterized this perverted dictatorship as "Rutherfordism."

As the driving force for this entire "doomsday machinery" they had the expectation that the absolute destruction of this world's regimes would occur in the large battle at Armageddon in the autumn of 1914, which, as we know, failed to materialize. Since then, Judgment Day and Armageddon have been permanent ingredients in Jehovah's Witnesses' scare propaganda. And the members have faithfully persevered, because *he that shall endure unto the end, the same shall be saved.*[324] Many have left the movement through the years, however, often without subsequently examining the reasons why they allowed themselves to be fooled. They choose instead to displace the personal issues that could have made them vulnerable to the leaders' arguments. The need for confrontation is repressed, yet the unresolved issues continue to pose a danger for the individual.

Irrational Fears

It surprised me to learn how sophisticated the Watchtower Society's practices were. I was obviously well aware that the Watchtower leadership abused the doomsday theme in the Bible, but not so much as I gradually came to realize—even the "abuse" was due to habitual thinking and rhetoric. Since I had written about the Jehovah's Witnesses in 1966, I knew this already. But by systematically exploring the CD-version of the Witnesses' literature using selected keywords and topics, I managed to discover the systematic and suggestive repetition of selected core concepts, as in: A single, relatively short article could reach entirely unreasonable occurrences (thirty to fifty times).

My conclusion was that there could only be talk about a deliberate wish using the *constant repetition principle*, to "brainwash" the general members—and for that matter—the management itself. In summary then, my conclusion is that the Watchtower management *itself is subject* to all these self-staged mechanisms; when observed collectively, these mechanisms manage to enslave all within the organization apparatus, so that the regimentation and control of the individuals can be maintained and expanded. The goal still seems to be an organization which continues to grow, with the always-close Judgment Day as the main sustaining message. So the members are not left in doubt that the Day of Judgment remains extremely close and also that Jehovah's *fervent* love for mankind demands that the *crucial moments* are continually postponed.

Some do succeed in leaving the movement, but they suffer continuously from an underlying, *irrational fear* of Armageddon, with international peace conferences, thunderstorms or earthquake disasters programmed into their minds as mechanisms capable of triggering their return to the Jehovah's Witnesses' doomsday movement.

With this book, I hope I have given these "refugees" protection against relapse, and at the same time a possibility of a psycho-social "repatriation" and reconciliation with the real world they are, after all, a part of.

Nevertheless, for each of them the Judgment Day doom is still dangerously close, and Watchtower management neglects no opportunity to beat the drum:

"A new peak of 7,313,173 publishers joined their voices in preaching to all, as well as teaching those of honest heart who are searching for solutions to the many problems facing them each day. An attendance of 18,168,323 at the Memorial of Christ's death shows promise *that millions more may yet call upon Jehovah's name before the end of this wicked system of things.* / As long as Jehovah permits, we will continue to preach the Kingdom good news with zeal, using every possible means to reach people in our territories. (Matt. 24:14; Mark 13:10) Whether from door to door, on the streets, by letter writing and telephone witnessing.... We have every reason to believe that Jehovah will soon act to sanctify his name. (Ezek. 36:23) The time is fast approaching when all those who defame it will be silenced…" (*YB*, 2010, p.4, 5; italics are mine).

In short: Once more a *postponement*; once more a *deception*!

Stagnation

Whether changes within the Witnesses will gradually result in an outright collapse with new anti-cult initiatives in effect is too early to say anything about, for the majority of the members seem to accept almost anything, as long as it gives meaning, identity and acceptance within the social community they have joined or were raised within. The Watchtower leaders, who continuously have almost free rein over their members, indeed know.

Still, beneath the surface, it is brewing. Over the past twenty-five to thirty-five years, many books by apostates have been written and many recovery and aid organizations formed. All these activities have, however, surprisingly only partly influenced the Society's power base, but they will probably eventually help to reform its teaching foundation and educational level, and thus the tight restriction of the members.

Growth and popularity of the internet has created breathing room to diffuse some of the frustrations. Not surprisingly, Watchtower leaders warn members against exploring this medium. Yet, many different discussion boards operate, allowing an individual, *disobedient* Witness to breathe a little fresh air.

The divergent activities seem to have led to some stagnation within the organization. The last figures from the Jehovah's Witnesses' annual report show that from the reporting years 2004 through 2005, the movement's growth worldwide was approximately halved.[325] However, in 2009 the percentage rose by 3.2% (over 2008), but fell again in 2011 to 2.4% (over 2010)—and in 2012 it fell further to 1.9% (over 2011). Thus growth now appears to be between 2% and 3% annually. (*YB* 2013)

One would think these stagnation tendencies would cause reflection and a certain degree of liberalization in the Watchtower headquarters in New York. But the opposite is the case. Brooklyn continues, as far as I can judge, the almost unconscious walk from bad to worse, a development that seems to have no end. Today there is hardly one other religious movement that defines itself as Christian yet displays a similar intolerance toward its own members. A policy, to an appalling extent, as we have seen, based on *mind control*, *manipulation* and *misinformation*.

What began in the 1870s as an idealistic and ambitious young man's *heaven-defying* project has evolved into its diametrical contrast: An (in my opinion) unholy and heartless repressive apparatus. The Watchtower Organization has become a "giant" without heart or sense. That the members continuously maintain the belief in the Watchtower's *cunningly devised fables* must be partly due to the extensive indoctrination and family and social ties, and partly due to the members' continually fearing the arrival of Judgment Day. But, of course, the members are also sustained by utopian dreams of the future that the movement continuously, after many years of delays, still insists upon: Eternal life in a coming eternal paradise, the so-called New World. This dream has become a sedative, a numbing habit and an incredible luxury they hate to abandon. So it would be a big step to take, saying goodbye to this endless future life with a hand-picked house, beautiful green hills and former predators (lions, tigers and all), who now walk around like *tame pets* among the inhabitants of the New World.

Still, I believe—and must reiterate—that an individual's principal motive for not leaving this *community* undoubtedly lies in the social affiliation and social security, identity and protection membership implies and which you can lose if you abandon the organization. For many members, it eventually becomes too much to bear. Some leave the movement, but they have often ended up in *no-man's land* where no one is able to ask the necessary questions in order to move forward. The apostates repress the critical and religious considerations, or put them on autopilot, perhaps because they, for understandable reasons, are motivated by desire for greater freedom, often for the most fundamental things, such as personal, sexual relationships.

Email from "Ruth"

The "biologically" recruited members, children and adolescents who were born and brought up inside the Jehovah's Witnesses' oppressive atmosphere, are hardest hit. As they grow up and understand there is a completely different world "outside" they struggle with *overwhelming problems*, often related to the incorporated reflexive attitudes, a *robotic programming*, from which it is almost impossible to free themselves.

These ill-treated children and young people, who are indoctrinated right from the moment they could toddle into a Kingdom Hall, often live in *two worlds*[326] between which they roam in and out like zombies without really being involved in either world and without ever completely understanding their lives. Through their upbringing, and because of the extremely staged, regular exposure to the moment's dogma, bordering on suggesting that they suffer every day, year round, they grow in a condition I must characterize as a state of *robot-like unconsciousness,* a life-threatening mental disparity between strictly separate worlds, as the movie *Worlds Apart* portrays.[327]

Of course, Jehovah's Witnesses—considered a limited, closed community— are not alone when it comes to such psycho-social conditions. However, in my view, they constitute a strong, deterrent example, a pinnacle of what *not* to do or accept in any religion.

Religion is okay to me. I have no quarrel with the idea of it or people choosing to follow one, but a religion should not *anaesthetize* the believers until they lose personal responsibility and sovereignty over their life choices.

During the last few years I have tried to contact some of the young former members who experienced a psychologically unstable situation after their break. Suddenly, at the last moment before the finalization of the manuscript, exactly the response that I had hoped for came into my hands. I received an email from "Ruth," who convinced me these environment-burdened young ones have *plenty* of opportunities to pull themselves out and up to new lives, if they just *consistently* start from scratch.

I think the content speaks for itself:

I was expelled in 1999, and I have since moved far away from the Jehovah's Witnesses. I know many who also dropped out, but who still are in doubt. My younger sister has it a little in this way, and although one no longer really believes in Armageddon, it is still worrying us when we hear of wars and disasters. It is something in the sub-consciousness and that is because we are brought up with this way of thinking. It is the same with many other things. But I am now fully aware that no one can basically say that they have the "truth" and certainly not the Jehovah's Witnesses.

I am now studying at a teacher-training college where I have Christianity as one of my main subjects. It has opened many windows in relation to faith, but I have been somewhat bitter about the fact that my upbringing in the Jehovah's Witnesses kept so many good and beautiful things hidden from me. So I have enjoyed my new life in the "old world" to the full, and I am still enjoying it. Also my younger sister and little brother have been excluded, so we help and support each other.

Here is a little story, which in all its cruelty tells a little about the fanaticism that prevails within the Jehovah's Witnesses. My father is a very strict and regular elder. When he said I would be ostracized, I asked if we could just be together once in a while, to which he replied: "Ruth, you do not understand the seriousness of what must happen. What you have done is very serious ("immorality!"). As a parent in the time of Israel, I would be the one who had to throw the first stone, when you would be stoned..."

My mother still has contact with us children, and I am deeply grateful. Now I am over the worst, but it has been terribly hard!

I will end here, since I must return to teaching again; you must have it really good. Many greetings,

Ruth

Today, Ruth is thirty-two, her little sister Hanna is twenty-three, and little brother Jacob is twenty-one. Their names are pseudonyms, of course. Their anonymity is understandable and reveals something about the oppression within the movement. Fear of public exposure typically controls many former members, especially those who attempt to avoid exclusion by moving quietly away. They tread softly, and the consequences are very frightening—as evidenced by interviews with my inside contacts and earlier by now-excluded members. Brooklyn is not to be trifled with!

I have remained in contact with Ruth and Eve, and I happily report they are doing well. Ruth has completed her training as a schoolteacher, and has begun teaching. Eve left her job as a legal secretary and is now studying to be a teacher. Both chose educational courses, which may mitigate some of the long-term harm they experienced due to lack of advanced schooling. Now they have new tools that enable them to understand not just themselves, but also some of the most absurd interpretations of the Bible and the history of religion, of which they were unwitting victims.

There is a *broad difference* between members of Jehovah's Witnesses and "this world's" people. Stepping over the divide is like a panicked jump across a dangerous abyss, where the bottom is covered in dead men's bones. Only very few even dare to think about jumping, and once they do stretch over the threatening abyss, it requires great courage to contact the "apostates" they've been taught to abhor.

Perspective

It is about getting on with life *after* Jehovah's Witnesses. Yet, my experience says this is easier said than done. It's work to throw off the long-standing mental influences, social isolation and psychological and knowledge-related disabilities caused by growing up within the Witnesses.

As I've already noted, the Watchtower leaders, via *steady repetition,* create a mind-controlling condition in the members, an *unconsciously installed program* that the "soul engineers" of the Watchtower Society can put on alert when it suits them. This program, whose function partly is to keep an eye on *the individual host,* partly to maintain the individual's dependence, anxiety and guilt so he feels as if he's under constant prosecution and surveillance, is entirely reliant on ignorance, evasive explanations and manipulation. The name of the program could very well be "the Truth," and it is this demagogic and suggestive *Truth-program* which I believe must be disabled.

And when the *deprogramming* has succeeded, what's left?

Experience shows that many who leave the Jehovah's Witnesses, before breaking, unconsciously have established a "secret" and completely private side, kept hidden from the Witness world, their brothers and sisters, and perhaps also from themselves. After breaking from the Society, it serves as the "core I" and becomes the base to build upon. It is this unconscious potential that lends a positive perspective to the future.

It is crucial that apostates analyze their situations and then find like-minded people with whom they can share their experiences. They must make new social contacts that can replace the now-failed relationships with family and former friends. They must tell people who are willing to listen about the psychological terror inside the Jehovah's Witnesses. Openness and initiative can provide new courage and help redeem psychological potential, *which is present within them*, in order to eventually find themselves and in turn open new doors for *the real world*.

A previous Witness phoned me one day, and in the conversation he stated he believed the brain could suffer physical damage from constant indoctrination. I thought about his theory and later contacted a neurological specialist. He could not provide support for my friend's view, but believed instead that the repercussions the apostates are struggling with perhaps may be described as post-traumatic stress disorder—also known as PTSD.

That there are serious traumas, I have not the slightest doubt. Whether there is physical damage from years of exposure, adaptation and acceptance of extraneous thinking, often characterized by monotonous rhetoric and ever-repeated clichés that members identify with, is doubtful. Yet it is possible the symptoms of PTSD may result from the actual showdown where the outcasts are in open confrontation with members of their former social circle. The rebellious person is deliberately expelled from the community to suffer his own fate, loneliness, isolation and probable depression. It's scary to think that such isolation measures are often applied by people who consider themselves Christians. The apostate man or woman is under an incredible, frightening pressure, which is by no means a new phenomenon in church history. In fact, it seems endemic in Christianity!

No Man's Land

Fear of what might happen if one moves into No Man's Land, an unknown and perilous land lying between Jehovah's Organization and the old normal world, is utterly immeasurable for Witness members. They are—I would claim—still attached to the rhetoric of *the* Organization to a degree an outsider would find very difficult to imagine. The idea of moving into No Man's Land is associated with many dangers, both psychological and social. And without a fighting spirit one doesn't go. It must be something you want, or something you cannot resist, because it eats at you, inexorably, from inside. It is a rebellion that comes directly from a deeper "I" that now aspires to breathe freely.

Recently I received a link to a website I did not know. It came from an American Bible Student I have been in contact with while working on this book. He wanted me to be aware of a movement currently underway inside and outside the Jehovah's Witnesses. People are asking questions about the Watchtower's policies and doctrines. The website carries the headline: "Friends of Jehovah's Witnesses. A Fear-Free Zone."

In a sort of manifesto the site tells visitors:

"You are anonymous here. You can speak to other Jehovah's Witnesses, former Jehovah's Witnesses, Bible Students and other Christians. When posting your comments, you will be able to use a Pen Name. Your email address and website info are completely optional. No one can identify you. No one can report you. You have a home and quiet place to pray and honestly investigate scriptures. It is not our purpose to indoctrinate you, but merely to provide you with resources for further study of Jehovah's word. You are not alone. You have friends."

So, nearly 100 years after Judge Rutherford's coup in Pittsburgh and Brooklyn, where all C. T. Russell stood for was declassed or rejected, there is a movement to steer the organization back to its roots. It resembles a kind of historical justice if the "new" Bible Student Associations that resulted after 1917 as the results of Rutherford's coup, finally get some sort of redress today.

However, I will not judge whether such a move is wise, because my recommendation would take a completely different road: a road where one breaks with fundamentalism rather than flee from one fundamentalism to another, into old fashioned associations. The breakaways ought to leave cleanly, quit cold turkey, to get completely free, if they have the courage to do so. They should delve into the substance of the original historical-theological basis for the Christian apocalypticism, and be shocked by all that they do not know.

This alone could be their key to a new kind of freedom.

When I left, it was almost as if I was a member one day and not one the next. And after I wrote my first book, I did not so much as think of the Witnesses for the next twenty-five years. They were actually non-existent in my mind! I had obviously heard of their message about 1975, but it did not concern me at all. Birgit and I found ourselves in a new-life situation in 1975, and we actually bought our first house that year. To us, that was the most important event in 1975. Then, in 1990, however, several defectors from the movement contacted me; this was very exciting and gave impetus to the idea of updating my old book from 1966. At that time, I realized what I had always known deep down: You cannot run from your past. The past will always be part of you as baggage that accompanies you everywhere you go. But for many of my former co-religionists, it was a still-emerging trauma, a stigma or a plague that could require professional treatment. I learned to use my traumatic past to move on in my own way, a way I hereby recommend to my readers.

Obviously I meet clever people who kindly tell me that when I write such a thick book about my religious past so long after, it is because I'm still preoccupied with the topic. To a certain extent they're right. History, theology and fundamentalism interest me, and they amaze me still. I know the truth may lie somewhere else. I also know large parts of the religious world are ruled by irrational ideas, often causing all sorts of misfortunes because the adherents do not know better. But this book is long enough already, and those matters could be the subjects of several more volumes.

Of course I am like anyone equipped with some form of religious embossing that not only has its basis in childhood teachings by well-meaning parents, but which has its roots far back in my family through generations of comings and goings. I am also, despite all common sense, religious at my core. It is an archaic and archetypical nature all of us share, more or less. This becomes clear in the following story:

Moustiers St. Marie

Some years ago, when my wife and I were on holidays in France, we came into an old chapel in Moustiers Sainte Marie in the southeastern part of the country. It was quite a coincidence that we just ended up there. The town has been a center of pottery production and trade, especially *faience*, for centuries. The chapel, called the Notre-Dame de Beauvoir, is located above the town in a wide cleft between some rocky massifs. An artificial star has been hung on a wire across the cleft and over the chapel. The steep walk up to the chapel has been used for pilgrimages since around the year 470, and one can easily fall on the slippery steps. When we came into the chapel, I did something I never had done before: I took an altar candle and carried it to the designated place, a special display in front of the altar—however, I did it for an "unknown god" as is mentioned in Acts. 17:22, 23.

As we came down from the chapel and back into town, Birgit bought a small book about Moustiers St. Marie. It was good to see pictures of the town and the area, the pilgrim's staircase up to the chapel, and the great star over the cleft.

PART FIVE:

A Closer Look

This generation, circa AD 70

Now learn a parable of the fig tree; When his branch is yet tender, and putteth forth leaves, ye know that summer is nigh: So likewise ye, when ye shall see all these things, know that it is near, even at the doors. Verily I say unto you. This generation shall not pass, till all these things be fulfilled.

—Matthew 24:32-34; written circa AD 70;
King James Version, conformable to the 1611 edition

I am coming soon, circa AD 95

And he said to me, "These words are trustworthy and true. And the Lord, the God of the spirits of the prophets, has sent his angel to show his servants what must soon take place. And behold, I am coming soon."

—The Revelation of John 22:6; written circa AD 95;
Revised Standard Version; New Testament, second edition, 1971

Judgment Day delayed, circa AD 120–140

Note this first: in the last days there will come men who scoff at religion and live self-indulgent lives, and they will say: "Where now is the promise of his coming? Our fathers have been laid to their rest, but still everything continues exactly as it has always been since the world began."

—The Second Letter of Peter, 3:3; written circa AD 120–140;
The New English Bible–New Testament, Great Britain, 1961

Chapter 39

Great Signs and Wonders

"Then if any one says to you, 'Lo, here is Christ!' or 'There he is!' do not believe it. For false Christs and false prophets will arise and show great signs and wonders, so as to lead astray, if possible, even the elect."
—The Gospel According to Matthew 24:23, 24; *RSV*

A review of the eschatology of the Jehovah's Witnesses as it relates to the concepts expressed by the first Christians

A few years after Birgit and I left the Jehovah's Witnesses, I wrote my first book about the movement. The writing process proved to be a form of self-therapy. When the manuscript was finished, it was clear to me that the book was completely unwieldy. Five hundred pages front to back on Jehovah's Witnesses' interpretation of Matthew 24, verse for verse. Who could grasp that? Yet, the work was not entirely wasted, because I had discovered something.

The Watchtower Society's interpretation of the Gospel of Matthew 24 constitutes the engine of the entire movement's apocalyptic concept, and virtually all the arguments for the Witnesses' thesis of the so-called "composite sign" are found in this chapter. The movement stands or falls upon the interpretation of it. My discarded manuscript later formed the basis for the tenth chapter of my 1966 book. It appears that chapter has made a deep impression on many former Witnesses who had difficulty understanding the nature of "the signs" that, according to the Watch Tower Society, had been fulfilled since 1914.

Therefore, it was clear I needed to look beneath the surface of the profound mental influences, perform a kind of detective work to learn when the Gospel of Matthew had originated, to whom it was written, and not least, the time and "future" it referred to. If one could uncover the real story behind the birth of the gospel—and for that matter, the whole New Testament—much could be achieved and better understood. It could become the key to deconstructing the Witnesses' *manufactured* truths.

But of course it is impossible for us to tell "the whole truth and nothing but the truth" about the origin of the New Testament. The truth is, probably no man of our time can quite understand what people back then—in light of their contemporary religious ideas and apocalyptic thinking—imagined about their world and its future, particularly considering Christianity quickly became a tapestry of inseparable Jewish, Christian and pagan ideas.

Still, the history needed exploring, and doing so required an analytical method, as follows:

The Scholarly Method Used

The *Historical-Critical Method* aims to consider and analyze an ancient writing in the context in which it was written. Hence, it must, in my opinion, be understood from its period of origin. Therefore, since the writing occurred in a particular historical period, it must be viewed within the religious, cultural and political situation of that period. When someone receives a letter from a business associate or fellow member of a group or organization, the letter must be evaluated in context of the time it is written, its content and what events it might refer to. Its meaning, sense of urgency, or moment-specific information may even come in a sort of shorthand language understood by writer and receiver that if read years later by strangers would have different or even no meaning. In this way we must also assess Paul's letter to the Thessalonians. It is not addressed to us here at the start of the 21st century, even though we can choose to allow the letter writer to "speak" to us in the present time. Since the letter is written in a particular historical period, it must be understood in light of the ideas of said period.

I have deliberately chosen Thessalonians for this example because it is where the "peace-and-safety" phrase was found by Watchtower leaders. The young members of Jehovah's Witnesses, who have been raised in the movement and experienced years of Watchtower propaganda indoctrination, say this peace-and-security refrain creates an almost insurmountable mental barrier against leaving the Witnesses. (Reference Chapter 31: Eve's Choice)[328]

My aim is to demystify this apocalyptic concept inherited from Judaism, and understand that Paul *wasn't* writing about peace and security conferences on an international scale during the 20th century; he wrote about actual, topical issues occurring between AD 50 and 60. His intention was *not to deliver a prophecy or designate certain signs to be fulfilled in an unthinkably distant future*, but likely designed as a measure to keep his congregations vigilant, for the "day of the Lord cometh as a thief in the night" (1 Thessalonians 5:2). For Paul and those who followed him, they were living at "the time of the end," and it was a matter of death and eternal life to be awake and stay ready.

Nothing could be more eye-opening for former Witnesses—and for that matter, members of other fundamentalist creeds—than reading church history from a *historical-critical* approach. And this is why knowledge and study at university level are the worst enemies of fundamentalists. Probably this is the reason Witness leaders in New York discourage their members from pursuing a higher education. How heartbreaking that many young Witnesses never received the education they dreamt of, and when they finally, after a painful clash with the brainwashing methods of the Watchtower organization, falteringly can stand on their own feet they often discover they are socially and educationally stunted.

My experience from many years of working with the historical-critical method is that it is one of the most effective keys available to unshackle the "engrams"[329] or refrain-like concepts that can maintain and enslave a believer through a lifetime. Once the method has penetrated the oppressive sludge of unceasing repetitions, the historical-critical method seems to be a true eye-opener.

It is useful to study history so we can learn from past mistakes and perhaps understand how useless it is to wait for something in the future, something that invariably belongs to the past and destroys our ability to live the only life we've got to its fullest potential.

The Very Last Days

Ever since the emergence of Christianity, members have imagined they were living in the "last times." Many Christians prepare themselves for it in their daily lives, and these ideas naturally color their view of what Jesus said about these things when he came around and announced his message to the Jews.

More or less unconsciously, they have gradually caused Jesus' biblically recorded words to swing toward the excessive and grandiose. One must, however, bear in mind that, although the Christian message may seem fantastic and unbelievable today, it was more palatable and practical for people living in a different cultural period. Angels were fully accepted. That there were "heavens" on top of each other was also a widely recognized concept. To these ancients, the scholarly discoveries of our time would have been pure heresy, an assessment one can make in our time by studying the fundamentalists' reactions to the same. Their worldviews refer broadly to the cosmic perceptions of an ancient world they have adapted to the facts, where applicable.

In the first century, the Christians lived every day hoping Christ would soon return and fulfill his promises, as delivered to the congregations—largely around the Mediterranean coast—where Christianity had spread. As expected, problems arose in these newly assembled congregations, such as within the congregation of Thessalonians where Paul had to intervene because some members unexpectedly died (1 Thessalonians 4:13-18) and he needed to reduce unrealistic expectations. Much needed to happen before it was over:

"Now concerning the coming of our Lord we beg you, brethren, not to be quickly shaken in mind or excited, either by spirit or by word, or by letter purporting to be from us, to the effect that the day of the Lord has come. Let no one deceive you in any way; for that day will not come, unless the rebellion comes first, and the man of lawlessness is revealed, the son of perdition, who opposes and exalts himself against every so-called god or object of worship, so that he takes his seat in the temple of God, proclaiming himself to be God" (2 Thessalonians 2:1-4; RSV).

The second letter to the Thessalonians indirectly tells us that the Christian congregations in Greece were quite concerned about the Second Coming and the nearness of Judgment Day. However, many were increasingly disappointed about the long wait. Still, the belief that the end was near nevertheless enabled the members of the congregation to endure: "But he who endures to the end will be saved" (Matthew 24:13; RSV). These words were probably said and written because of the congregations' need for them, making it easy to realize the congregations had difficulty controlling their impatience.

Around the year AD 64, Emperor Nero began the first great persecution of Christians who were accused of setting Rome on fire. Between AD 94 and 95, severe persecution of the Christians began again, this time launched by the Roman emperor Domitian. This great persecution was interpreted by the Christians as proof that "the end" was imminent. And because of that impression of the persecution, a new Christian writing, later known as *The Revelation of John*, appeared.

Before I begin a systematic review of the Watchtower Society's interpretation of Matthew 24, I shall explain how this last book in the Bible shows that Christians around the end of the first century AD expected the Second Coming and the world's end *at that time*.

The Beast—a Secret Code

The Revelation of John was written circa AD 95. It depicted the Roman tyranny and the events of the last days in a secret, symbolic and figurative language that only Christians could interpret. The writing is also sometimes called by its Greek title, "The Apocalypse."

The Revelation had a topical focus and is actually understood best using the historical-critical approach. In chapters thirteen and seventeen, "the beast" that would perish in the upcoming battle at Armageddon is mentioned (Revelation 16:16). This beast might be seen as a secret expression of the eighth Roman emperor, Domitian. At that time, many considered Domitian to be the resurrected Nero; this is reflected in Revelation 17:11. The succession of emperors from Augustus to Domitian is as follows: 1. Augustus, 2. Tiberius, 3. Caligula, 4. Claudius, 5. Nero, 6. Vespasian, 7. Titus and 8. Domitian.

In The Revelation of John 17:11 we read about *the eighth*, that is, Emperor Domitian: "As for the beast that was and is not, it is an eighth but it belongs to the seven, and it goes to perdition" (RSV).

This "beast"—Emperor Domitian who "was, and is not"—was, according to the tradition of some, considered to be the arisen Emperor Nero. The beast was then both the "eighth" emperor, Domitian, but is still of the "seven," that is, Nero. This is a scholarly hypothesis, but it seems plausible when considering the time and place of origin.

When we read John's Revelation, we must pretend we live in Rome at the end of the first century when the emperor sentenced Christians to cruel persecutions. The year is *AD 95*. Forget everything you know about the centuries that followed it, because you are a member of a Roman-Christian congregation that expects the imminent return of Christ. This terrible persecution by Rome is one of the signs!

A further indication of the beast's identity derives from Revelation 13:18: "This calls for wisdom: let him who has understanding reckon the number of the beast, for it is a human number, its number is six hundred and sixty-six" (RSV).[330]

In Hebrew, the *Emperor Nero* is written with the consonants: *qsr nrwn*. Taking the Roman numeral value of these letters, one gets the numerical values 100+60+200+50+200+6+50, which together provide a "number of a man"—or 666. Danish New Testament professor Holger Mosbech (1886-1953) writes in his commentary from 1943, *Johannes' Aabenbaring* (Revelation of John):

"That the explanation is correct is confirmed by the fact that there is an old variant: 616 instead of 666; it probably emerged because the copyists, having known the significance of the number, worked from the Latin form 'Nero' instead of the Greek, 'Neron'; in that way, the assembled expression with a missing "n" = 50 less, and the sum of the remaining letters numerical value becomes then only 616" (p. 257–262).

Mosbech also mentions a very illustrative example: Writing a person's name in number values was very common at that time. When excavating Pompeii, south of Rome, the archaeologists found a love declaration engraved on a wall:

"I love her whose number is 545" (Mosbech, p. 258).

The Society's editorial staff members are possibly well informed, even though I actually doubt it. Anyhow they try to ridicule the most serious explanation for what is expressed in Revelation. As recently as April 2004, *The Watchtower* published an article, "666—Not Just a Puzzle." In this, the magazine's editorial office writes that "some believe" 666 can be connected to the Antichrist and the Pope: "Substituting Roman numerals for the letters in a form of the pope's official title, Vicarius Filii Dei (Vicar of the Son of God), and manipulating the figures a little, they come up with 666. It is also claimed that the same number can be calculated from the Latin name of Roman Emperor Diocletian and from the Hebrew version of the name Nero Caesar.... These fanciful and contrived interpretations, however, are very different from what the Bible itself says about the mark of the beast.... The Bible does reveal that those with the mark will experience God's wrath when he brings an end to the present system of things" (*WT*, April 1, 2004, p. 3 and 7).

The argument is typical and one senses the intention. First the article mentions a *later* interpretation, which seems obviously *wrong*. Then it mentions the *wrong* emperor in the *wrong* time, Diocletian, who had nothing to do with the matter (he reigned from 284 to 305).

The relevant emperors, who could be related to the number 666 or 616, all reigned *before the end of the first century.*

"Babylon" is the City of Rome

That the book of Revelation had an exclusively topical aim and was only written to refer to an immediate future, specifically the persecutions around the year AD 95, is abundantly clear from the book's introduction:

"The Revelation of Jesus Christ, which God gave him to show to his servants *what must soon take place*; and he made it known by sending his angel to his servant John, who bore witness to the word of God and to the testimony of Jesus Christ, even to all that he saw" (Revelation 1:1-2; italics are mine; RSV).

The writer, *possibly* the apostle John, but who could also be an unknown elder (the issue of the author is a subject of an ongoing discussion among scholars[331]), thought obviously that the Second Coming (*parousia*) was imminent. Yes, one can possibly even find a calculation of when this would happen. The calculation occurs in chapter thirteen, verse seven, where, among other things, it says only forty-two months will pass before the beast, Domitian, would be destroyed. The author himself is probably one of the many victims of persecution, interned by the Romans on the island of Patmos. In picturesque visions he sees and describes how the existing world order and its emperor succumb to God and Christ's supremacy. Thus, Christians are invited to leave the doomed world-city Rome, code named "Babylon" in the book, for the city *soon falls.* (Rev. 18:1-4)

That it is the city of Rome hidden behind the mysterious name Babylon, is seen in mention of "the woman" (17:9), who also symbolizes Rome, sitting on "seven mountains." These seven mountains are presumably the seven hills on which the city of Rome was built. "The woman" (Rome) is "drunk with the blood of the saints and with the blood of the martyrs of Jesus" (17:6), and it is described how the murdered martyr's souls shout: "O Sovereign Lord, holy and true, how long before thou wilt judge and avenge our blood on those who dwell upon the earth?" (6:10). It would not last long because the living martyrs are comforted that the dead souls shall only "rest a little longer…" (6:11; RSV).

The dead souls screamed, and the living martyrs waited, all while they scrutinized the words: "Surely I am coming soon…" (Revelation 22:20; RSV). But the waiting would take a long time, and none of the then-living would be alive to meet the Lord in the air.

Judgment Day Delayed

It is clear that the Early Church now faced a dilemma. Should it continue to preach Christ's imminent return and the world's impending end, or should the Church prepare itself both internally and outwardly for a longer existence on earth?

The answer seems to be given by the author of 2 Peters' letter, most probably not written by the apostle. It seems to be written about AD 100 to 120 (perhaps as late as 140[332]) and is probably the youngest writing in the New Testament. The letter addresses why the Lord's coming and the Judgment Day dragged on and tries to explain that the Lord Jesus does not hesitate with his coming, but has patience ("longsuffering;" 2 Peter 3:9) with the letter's recipients, people in general and other not-yet converted Gentiles, as he wished all should be rescued. However, the scoffers needed to know that "the day of the Lord" was near and that it could come as a thief in the night—silently and without warning. It predicted that soon the scoffers would perish in the burning earth's foaming flames, when "the elements will be dissolved with fire, and the earth and the works that are upon it will be burned up" (2 Peter 3:10; RSV). Only the Lord's selected few would avoid this terrible fate.

Slowly, early Christianity gave up preaching the gospel's apocalyptic content, the proximity of the Judgment Day and the coming of Christ; the church gradually evolved into a powerful institution where theology partially depended on the State's condition. The Catholic Church was born. This development culminated around AD 312, after Maxentius[333] was defeated by Emperor Constantine the Great during the battle at the Milvian Bridge. Faith in apocalyptic events, the Second Coming and Doomsday, were now merely rhetoric, rudimentary appendages, isolated in the creeds. The church's role was now to support the secular state respectively by guaranteeing its citizens continued life beyond their earthly existence, *above* or *below*, depending on merit. However, the doomsday rhetoric was not totally forgotten. In succeeding centuries it was more or less used to subdue church members, not least because the so-vivid, fearsome rhetoric was found in the New Testament.

Originally, the Christian congregations believed the resurrection would take place at the Second Coming and the Judgment Day, but the church gradually developed a belief in an immediate resurrection after death—a kind of *middle existence* (this is already indicated in John 5:24; 11:25). The Second Coming had, in a way, occurred on Pentecost day, and the coming millennial kingdom was later interpreted as the church's presence and work on Earth.

All these speculations and excuses naturally created dissatisfied members among Christian congregations; they saw the church's new civic situation as an expression of apostasy, and the dissatisfaction gradually crystallized in many sectarian directions.

The eschatological promises belonged to the childhood of the Early Church, and as the church grew and needed to comply with world political powers, it rejected its naïve teachings, those remembered in a sort of isolation via the creeds.

The sects adopted with alacrity what the church no longer used. The church experienced sectarian segregation and opposition to the existing situation: the consolidation and *rapprochement* with the secular powers. The church could not then, and cannot today, regress to the child stage and again become a primitive church, because the Early Church's beliefs and ideas were based on many elements of contemporary religious ideas combined with Jesus' recently delivered revolutionary message. The church simply had to follow history and its development's requirements.

Both the Adventists and the Jehovah's Witnesses experienced development which is a classic repetition of what happened within Christianity in the first and second centuries AD. This regression to the old ways has been seen again and again within Christian sects or groups who have preached virtually identical apocalyptic messages in all the centuries down to our time. Many were swallowed up in the ocean of time but may have left a mark here or there—even in the established churches, which from time to time are carried away by the old ideas.

Whether the absence of those particular apocalyptic and eschatological events, like those identified with the Jehovah's Witnesses for 134 years, will bring about a decline in the movement's activity, is currently difficult to say because it depends on whether the movement can find new ways to maintain momentum. The Christian church did not disintegrate because apocalypticism had to be revalued; it found new guidelines and targets that pointed forward. Apocalypticism, and the accompanying belief in the world's imminent end, was a kind of framework, within which new designs and a new conceptual structure had to be developed.

The Adventists, especially the Seventh-day Adventists, are a good example. Despite their composure under Ellen G. White's leadership in the 1860s, where the Day of Judgment was deferred to the distant future, this church grew more than any other Adventist Church. The particular objects of faith, the special doctrines, didn't matter; the social community of the moment mattered, the individual's membership in a particular community capable of strengthening an individual's self-esteem and identity. If the community remained open to the outside world, it was a sympathetic entity. When the opposite occurred, when a religious community closed itself off from the world, it would be a disaster that would isolate the members and leave them in a fantasy world severed from reality with no lifeline back.

The Gospel of Matthew

The Gospel According to Matthew, the first book in the New Testament, was probably written between approximately AD 80 and 90.[334]

Scholars generally assume it is partly based on the Gospel of Mark, which is estimated to have been written around AD 70 and partly regards a now-lost collection of Jesus' sayings, the hypothetical so-called "Q document," or "logia-source."

In the Watchtower Society's mammoth work, *Insight on the Scriptures,* from 1988 (two volumes containing 2,554 densely printed pages, originally drafted by the subsequently excluded Raymond Franz), AD 41 is given as the approximate year Matthew's gospel originated—i.e., from seven to ten years after Jesus' death. It is pointed out that "*no reference* is made to the fulfillment of Jesus' prophecy respecting Jerusalem's destruction would point to a time of composition prior to 70 BCE...." An interesting consideration, as a similar logic is not applied to the Gospel of Luke, which contains *very clear* references and allusions to the Jewish-Roman War. (*Insight*, 1988, Volume 2, p. 352; see also Luke 21; italics are mine)

It is by no means certain that it is Jesus' apostle Matthew who wrote the gospel carrying his name. It was standard practice at that time that authors "borrowed" a famous person's name to give their writing authority. The author's name is probably added later. The books got their names gradually for many reasons, including making it possible to distinguish one from another. The first to refer to the names of all four gospels is Irenaeus *around the year AD 180.*

Most likely, the Gospel of Matthew is primarily addressed to the Jewish Christians in Syria, since it is keen to prove that Jesus' life and death fulfills the Old Testament prophecies concerning the coming of a Messiah. Some scholars believe, however, that an original gospel from the Apostle Matthew's hand may have consisted of an early collection of transcribed maxims of Jesus. *Another Matthew* subsequently used these maxims to produce the enlarged gospel that has come down to us.

Another argument against the Gospel of Matthew being authored before the year 70, as the Watchtower Society claims, is that Paul—writing his letters long before AD 70—*never* quoted any written gospel; he died around AD 64. The simple explanation could be that they did not yet exist as the widely known collection of Gospel writings we have today.

The Gospel of Matthew originates in the belief of Jesus as the Messiah who would liberate the Jewish people. Therefore, it has a Jewish-Christian character. It is believed by some scholars that it was designed for use in the congregations' services, containing "lessons" for an entire church year (the "Lectionary-hypothesis").[335] This view is based upon, among other things, that some early manuscripts divide the Gospel into sixty-nine sections, the equivalent of one year of Sundays and holidays in a Jewish-Christian congregation.

Matthew's Gospel is a *post-rationalizing* report, where words and situations, without the slightest hesitation, are ascribed to Jesus. The fact that Matthew alludes to Peter as the Church's *future* foundation, also suggests the gospel came into being sometime after AD 70—perhaps as late as AD 80 to 90, when a Catholic Church slowly moved toward the stage. This development is not visible in the Gospel of Mark, and the concept of *the church* does not occur there.

That the Second Coming was imminent and would come in the disciples' lifetime was probably a widespread belief in the Christian congregations before the year 70; this is reflected very distinctly in the gospels.

But after AD 70, second- and third-generation Christians gradually adapted to a longer life on earth. A new situation manifested that, over time, had to be explained. The explanation—God's "longsuffering" (2 Peter 3:9)—was a model argument for all later apocalyptic Christian cults.

Expectation of Impending Apocalyptic Events

Paul understood early, in contrast to the prestigious ones in Jerusalem, Christianity's *internationalism* and he was the main figure in the new religion that, while he was alive, reached out to the entire Mediterranean region. Thus, he made Christianity a religion that addressed all people. In his lifetime it reached almost the entire Mediterranean region. Before Paul's death around AD 64, he had already proclaimed an early return of Jesus Christ, although Paul evidently also thought the gospel of salvation by Christ had to first be preached throughout the world before the end would come. Thus, Paul wrote about this in his first letter to the congregation of Thessalonica because the people there were alarmed by Judgment Day rumors. The members argued about who would be raised first at the Second Coming. To assure the Thessalonians that the deceased would also be raised at the return of Christ, Paul wrote:

"For the Lord himself will descend from heaven with a cry of command, with the archangel's call, and with the sound of the trumpet of God. And the dead in Christ will rise first; then we who are alive, who are left, shall be caught up together with them in the clouds to meet the Lord in the air; and so we shall always be with the Lord. Therefore comfort one another with these words" (1 Thessalonians 4:16–18; RSV).

Time and again Paul suggested that the Second Coming and the end were near. Thus he wrote to the congregation at Corinth: "Now these things happened to them as a warning, but they were written down [what we now call the Old Testament] for our instruction, upon whom the end of the ages has come" (1 Corinthians 10:11; RSV). Elsewhere he writes: "I mean, brethren, the appointed time has grown very short..." (1 Corinthians 7:29; RSV).

The authors of Peter's first epistle and the epistles of John also pronounce rather unequivocally about the nearness of the end of world. For example, the author of the first epistle of Peter says: "The end of all things is at hand; therefore keep sane and sober for your prayers" (1 Peter 4:7; RSV). And the author of 1 John wrote (at the end of the first century): "Children, it is the last hour; and as you have heard that antichrist is coming, so now many antichrists have come; therefore we know that it is the last hour" (1 John 2:18; RSV).

Here it is also interesting to note Jesus' words, as they are reproduced in Matthew's gospel, chapter 24. According to this account, Jesus directly foretold the destruction of Jerusalem. It is done in such a way that the audiences at the Christian services in Syria and in other parts of the Roman Empire could identify the wording with the actual events, although the words in the text appear *as a prophecy* spoken by Jesus. In fact, Jerusalem was already devastated by the Roman armies by that time.

In the edited, post-devastation setup, the disciples asked: "Tell us, when will this be, and what will be the sign of your coming and of the close of the age?" (Matthew 24:3; RSV) The issue arises (in the edited context), because Jesus has just said about Jerusalem:

"But he answered them, 'You see all these, do you not? Truly, I say to you, there will not be left here one stone upon another, that will not be thrown down'" (Matthew 24:2; RSV). Another translation of the New Testament is *The New English Bible* from 1961.[336] This renders Matthew 24:2 as: "He answered, 'You see all these buildings? I tell you this: not one stone will be left upon another; all will be thrown down.' "

In truth, the Romans let some remnants of the temple stand, using it as a shelter for their garrison; this remnant is known today as the Wailing Wall.

Matthew 24—the "Little Apocalypse"

Personally, I have difficulties believing Jesus said what was reported in Matthew 24. I think the sign-prophecies were attributed to Jesus *after* AD 70, because the "fulfillment" of these *signs* would comfort the congregation.

If this assumption is correct, the audience would, during the recitation from the Gospel of Matthew, partly think of the words of "the signs" as an expression of *future events* belonging to the *near* future. The destruction of Jerusalem—which at the time they looked *back* on—was one of those signs. Therefore, the Second Coming could, in principle, be expected anytime.

The apocalyptic idea was crucial to the early Christians. They were convinced the Second Coming might occur in *their lifetime*. Therefore, I also find comprehensible—though naïve—reasons why apocalyptic-informed Christians in *our time* may be tempted to believe that "the time of the end" and the Second Coming are topical events, belonging to their *near* future. They read the Bible every day. The main argument for these people seems to be that since Christ has not yet come and the world still stands, then the "end times" and Christ's return are still to come.

Some of my reviewers have claimed that I am a *preterist*, a believer who thinks Christ came back in AD 70. In a sense it is true, I suppose. I believe teachings about the Second Coming were exclusively aimed at the first century. And since none of that happened the way the Christians originally anticipated, they extended the waiting period, and thus they became "futurists" (placing the return in a distant future). Yet, I also do not believe it. I think simply that the time has passed and this is something that has escaped the attention of Christian congregations and churches—both then and now. Christ will never return in the way the early Christians imagined. Considering the many vain and false predictions and assumptions that Christians have developed over the last 2,000 years, it's probably about time this was said.

A Criticism of the Watchtower Society's Interpretation of Matthew 24

In the following commentary on selected verses in the Gospel of Matthew, I quote from both older and newer books and magazines released by the Watchtower Society. With regard to the most important verses in Matthew 24, I have chosen to examine systematically those dealing with a specific topic. The main themes are divided into sections, and at the beginning of each section, I quote first the *Revised Standard Version* (RSV) second edition of the New Testament, 1971, by The British & Foreign Bible Society; second is the Watchtower Society's *New World Translation of the Holy Scriptures*, published in English in 1984 (NWT 1984). This translation is a revised version of the NWT translations, continuously released from 1950 to 1963, when the first complete edition of the entire Bible was published. In the accompanying endnotes I will continue to comment on the differences between these two versions, the 1963-edition and the 1984-edition, where applicable.[337]

If Bible translations other than NWT or RSV are mentioned, for example ASV (*The American Standard Version*) in quotations from Watchtower publications, this is normally indicated with an (ASV) in connection with the quote.

With regard to recent scholarship, I refer to the comprehensive commentary on Matthew's Gospel by W. D. Davies and Dale Allison: *The Gospel According to Saint Matthew*, vol. 1-3, International Critical Commentary, Edinburgh: T & T Clark, 1988 to 1997, in particular volume three, chapters 19–28, which may be of greatest interest. Concerning my primary Danish sources, see the endnotes.[338] Dr. Donald Guthrie's *New Testament Introduction* (reprinted at InterVarsity Press, England, 1981) is also recommended. Guthrie gives an authentic and careful examination of Matthew on pages 21–52.

As a beginning, I suggest reading the full twenty-fourth chapter of the Gospel of Matthew so you can form your own opinion on the content. And it does not matter whether you read the *Authorized* or *King James Version*, the *American Standard Version*, the *Revised Standard Version* or other translations, because the intention in the old text remains, although the wording may vary.

"Coming" or "Presence"

Under this main theme, the following verses from Matthew 24 are treated: 3, 23, 24, 25, 26, 27 and 30.

VERSE 3
Revised Standard Version of 1971 (The New Testament):
"As he sat on the Mount of Olives, the disciples came to him privately, saying, 'Tell us, when will this be, and what will be the sign of your coming and of the close of the age?'"

NWT 1984 (*New World Translation* of 1984):
"While he was sitting upon the Mount of Olives, the disciples approached him privately, saying: 'Tell us, When will these things be, and what will be the sign of your presence and of the conclusion[339] of the system of things?'"

Comment: As it was pointed out in the chapters on C. T. Russell, the Watchtower Society translates Matthew 24:3 in a misleading way. The word "coming" in the phrase "your coming and of the close of the age" is translated so as to reinforce the Jehovah's Witnesses' special conception of Christ's coming. The word "coming" is translated to "presence" from the Greek *parousia*. But the word can also be translated into *coming, arrival* and, e.g., *presence*. The word must be judged in the context in which it occurs. It is about the Messiah-King coming in triumph on the clouds of heaven.

Jesus had just spoken woe over Jerusalem (23:27-39) and in the introduction to the chapter he points to the temple complex and says: "Truly, I say to you, there will not be left here one stone upon another, that will not be thrown down" (24:2). These words indicate that the content of the verse is influenced by the events in the year 70, when the Romans conquered Jerusalem and the Temple and subsequently destroyed the Jewish capital. But in its editorial and literary *scene setting*, the disciples are interested in knowing when this will happen, and what signs *in advance will show* that the coming of Christ is near. The church needed such signs after AD 70.

Originally, the disciples probably thought that Jesus, before his death, would create a Messiah kingdom, but now after the year 70, at the time the Gospel of Matthew was written, the coming and final establishment of this kingdom interested the congregations (cf. Acts 1:6–7). But if the disciples really asked Jesus what the *preceding signs* of his return would be, it is important to emphasize the disciples in the account were *asking for answers* and not simultaneously in the third verse delivering a *specified cryptic recipe* for the manner of the Second Coming intended for C. T. Russell and Jehovah's Witnesses to use before and after 1914. Russell translated and interpreted based on Benjamin Wilson's *Emphatic Diaglott* and its translation of *parousia* to *presence*, by means of which Russell *read in* the non-original meaning in the disciples' questions that they did not ask about the sign that he *would* come, but rather what the sign was that he *had come*. This is a gross falsification of the original meaning of the text, which clearly shows that the sign comes *before* the Second Coming. In Russell's system, the signs are fulfilled after

1874, in which year Jesus had to have returned "invisible" (as a *presence*). Russell missed the original meaning and the current Witness leaders overlook it; maybe today quite deliberately. The signs are *signals* which *must precede* the Second Coming and the world's end. The signs will tell, like the blooming trees herald summer's arrival, that the coming of Christ is near (Luke 21:29-31; Matthew 24:32-33). [340]

Wherever *parousia* appears in the Greek text, the Watchtower Society, without much concern for the context, translated it as *presence*. The *New World Translation of the Holy Scriptures*, the Watchtower Society's first publication of the entire Bible, released in English in 1963, concludes in the Appendix:

"It is true, as shown by Dr. Adolf Deissmann in his *Light from the Ancient East* on pages 368, 369, that from the Ptolemaic period down into the 2nd century AD one of the Eastern technical meanings of par-ou-si'a was the arrival or visit of a king or emperor. However, this does not deny or disprove that in the Christian Greek Scriptures the word has the meaning of presence where it is used in connection with Jesus Christ and others" (NWT, 1963, p. 3590). In spite of this knowledge, the Watchtower translators preferred, around 1950, to translate the word in a way that supports their interpretation, which is crucial for the Witnesses' understanding of the end-time.

Parousia appears a total of twenty-four times in the New Testament, and the Society translated it exactly the same in all twenty-four cases. Yet, if the Watchtower leaders consistently translated *parousia* to *presence*, surely they know very well the word can also be translated to *come*, which of course gives a somewhat different meaning in verse three. [341]

Other places in the New Testament also show, beyond any doubt, how Matthew 24:3 shall be construed, as the Early Church in its various writings itself explained the problem—without, of course, knowing that a small sect calling themselves Jehovah's Witnesses would claim after 1914 that Christ's coming was invisible. Worth mentioning here is Titus 2:13, which states: "Looking for that blessed hope, and the glorious appearing of the great God and our Savior Jesus Christ..." (KJ).

The word *appearing*, or better *appearance*, is translated from the Greek *epiphaneia*, and refers to Christ's visible coming or manifestation (NWT reads: "[T]he happy hope and glorious manifestation of the great God and of [the] Savior of us, our Christ Jesus..."). Also in 1 Timothy 6:14 we find the word *epiphaneia* used in connection with Christ's visible coming, specifically in the admonition: "I charge you to keep the commandment unstained and free from reproach until the appearing of our Lord Jesus Christ..." (RSV). And the continuation of verse fifteen reads: "and this will be made manifest at the proper time..." (RSV).

In recent years, as previously discussed, the Society has focused more on Christ's *future* coming, which will occur in connection with Judgment Day, where he will separate the sheep from the goats. (see *WT*, Oct. 15, 1995)

The Watchtower of September 15, 1998, stated:

"Although present as King since 1914, Jesus Christ must yet judge systems and individuals before executing judgment on those he finds to be wicked."

In the same issue and the same article, with the headline "Waiting in 'eager expectation,' " we find precisely the formula that aroused my suspicions about a *new understanding* of Christ's coming:

"With all these exciting events ahead of us, should we not exercise faith and eagerly keep on the watch for *Christ's coming*?" (*WT*, Sept. 15, 1998, p. 18; italics are mine)

It seems Christ's *real* coming is now postponed to sometime in the future, an angle which is becoming more and more popular while time passes and nothing happens.

VERSES 23, 24, 25, 26, 27 and 30
Revised Standard Version:

"[23] Then if any one says to you, 'Lo, here is the Christ!' or 'There he is!' do not believe it. [24] For false Christs and false prophets will arise and show great signs and wonders, so as to lead astray, if possible, even the elect. [25] Lo, I have told you beforehand. [26] So, if they say to you, 'Lo, he is in the wilderness,' do not go out; if they say, 'Lo, he is in the inner rooms,' do not believe it. [27] For as the lightning comes from the east and shines as far as the west, so will be the coming of the Son of man... [30] then will appear the sign of the Son of man in heaven, and then all the tribes of the earth will mourn, and they will see the Son of man coming on the clouds of heaven with power and great glory....""

NWT 1984:

"23 Then if anyone says to YOU, 'Look! Here is the Christ,' or, 'There!' do not believe it. 24 For false Christs and false prophets will arise and will give great signs and wonders so as to mislead, if possible, even the chosen ones. 25 Look! I have forewarned YOU. 26 Therefore, if people say to YOU, 'Look! He is in the wilderness,' do not go out; 'Look! He is in the inner chambers,' do not believe it. 27 For just as the lightning comes out of eastern parts and shines over to western parts, so the presence of the Son of man will be... 30 And then the sign of the Son of man will appear in heaven, and then all the tribes of the earth will beat themselves in lamentation, and they will see the Son of man coming on the clouds of heaven with power and great glory."

Comment: These verses say something about "the manner" for the Second Coming. Note the stylistic structure of the verses, which comes from the editing author's hand. It seems striking that verses twenty-three to twenty-six setup for a contrast in verse twenty-seven. It does not happen in the "wilderness," or in the "chambers"—or "here" and "there"—but in such a way that all may see it, just as when lightning flashes from east to west. Christ's *parousia*[342] will be seen by all, (verse thirty) both good and evil. Just as *literally* the Adventists also perceived the words before 1843–1844.

To take the sting out of any self-established Christs or false prophets, which was a problem for congregations after AD 70, the contradiction is clearly drawn so that nobody can be left in doubt. The Second Coming will be a sparkling clear event, not a *secret,* or something that happens in the wilderness or in the chambers. If any false Christs went around confusing the members of the congregations, Jesus' words were good to use against these self-appointed prophets.

Why should the Second Coming be something hidden—in chambers or invisible? Christ's glorious *parousia* meant nothing less than a royal conqueror's march in triumph across the clouds of heaven, bringing the salvation of the selected ones, the punishment of the nations and the world's destruction by fire. These were things very terrible and very wonderful, and such things can't happen *secretly.*

Very well! Perhaps it was very-embellished language they once used, but it was, at least in this way, how the first Christians imagined the second coming of Christ, just as the Adventists would in the 1840s. The Adventists believed what they read in the Bible, and therefore, imagined that Christ's return in 1873–74 would happen just as the early Christians imagined it.

One must also consider how the church leaders after AD 70 could use Matthew 24 during services for the congregations. There was a need to reject false Messiah-pretenders who could not deliver anything even remotely like the gospel's magnificent conceptions of the Second Coming. Therefore, when ambitious imposters attempted to mislead the members of the congregation, the descriptions of the Second Coming worked effectively.

Believing there is a code embedded in the words of the *parousia* is just as unacceptable, for instance when Barbara Thiering in her book, *Jesus the Man* (1993),[343] interpreted the gospels of the New Testament as having hidden, coded information: That Jesus had not died on the cross; that he had a wife and children and that he had died around the year 64. However, Thiering's book is interesting as an example of how much we—if we have the imagination—partly can read *into*, and partly can read *out* of the text.

Based on verses twenty-three to thirty, it would thus be meaningless if there was a *hidden meaning* in Matthew 24:3, specifically, that the glorious return was in fact invisible. Assuming this claim, we must also conclude that as the disciples asked for an answer from Jesus, *they* simultaneously supplied the answer. Then why ask?

The Witnesses (and other fundamentalists) miss something important: throughout, Jesus' words appear in an edited, literary context.

That the Jehovah's Witnesses still adhere to the invisibility theory demonstrates how difficult it is for successors, who *once* assumed a thesis that serves as the *cornerstone* of an extreme teaching system, to confront the original teacher's perceptions. The invisibility theory is perhaps even more central to the Jehovah's Witnesses than the *1914 dogma*, as it is this dogma—*presence* instead of *arrival*—which represents the *cardinal points* of the entire doctrinal construction. Everything rests on this idea.

That the return had to be seen with "the mind's eye" followed logically from the translation of *parousia* to *presence*. The Society's most important textbook reads:

"His return is recognized by the eyes of one's understanding, such eyes being enlightened by God's unfolding Word. Christ's arrival and presence are not discerned because of a visible bodily nearness, but by the light of his acts of judgment and the fulfillment of Bible prophecy. This light spreads from east to west and everywhere. His return is recognized by the eyes of one's understanding, such eyes being enlightened by God's unfolding Word. Christ's arrival and presence are not discerned because of a visible bodily nearness, but by the light of his acts of judgment and the fulfillment of Bible prophecy. This light spreads from east to west and everywhere" (*Be True*, 1952, p. 198).

This explanation, however, does not work because it is stressed in Matthew 24:27 (as opposed to verses 23–26) that the coming of the Son of Man will light up the sky from east to west. And in Matthew 24:30 one finds that "all the tribes of the earth will mourn, and they will see the Son of man coming on the clouds of heaven with power and great glory." Referencing other text in the New Testament, it is evident that "all"—not just the Christians (or Jehovah's Witnesses)—would see his return *literally*.

In John's Revelation we read: "Behold, he is coming with the clouds, and every eye will see him, every one who pierced him; and all tribes of the earth will wail on account of him. Even so. Amen..." (Revelation 1:7; RSV).

In 1955 Thomas J. Sullivan, a senior leader of the Watchtower hierarchy, expressed to author Marley Cole that when the earth is *round*, "everybody" can't see "Christ sitting on a cloud at one spot." I quote (Cole asking, Sullivan answering):

"'But,' I [Cole] insisted, 'doesn't the Bible say that every eye shall see him?'/ 'See him literally,' he [Sullivan] asked, 'or symbolically?'/ 'Well, people in general are looking for him in a visible appearance, I always thought.'/ He [Sullivan] dropped his tone. 'Do you believe that the earth is round?'/ 'I rather think so. Yes.'/ 'And still Christ returns from heaven visibly, on a cloud?'/ The intimation was that if the earth is round and Christ comes on a cloud, how can everybody look up into the sky, all around the globe, and see Christ sitting on a cloud at one spot? After his chuckle Mr. Sullivan started off on a new tack" (Cole 1955, p. 162-164; regarding M. Cole, see Chapter 11).

The original Christians had no idea the earth was round. They thought as everyone else, that it was flat and the Second Coming would be visible from end to end of the world. That Christians may have had such a perception is shown in Matthew 4:8, where it says Satan takes Jesus up on a "very high mountain" to show him "all the kingdoms of the world." Matthew's author obviously did not intend to say anything revealing about the perception of the world of his days, but indirectly we may find a clue about how people of that time saw the world's physical condition.

A deeply strange example of the Society's distortion of the basic text of the original meaning can be found in the book *Make Sure of All Things*, where we find the following text given as evidence that Christ's second coming is "invisible:

"Second presence of Christ proved invisible by his 'sheep' not being able to *see* him with their natural eyes..." And then it quotes Matthew 25:37-40: "Then the righteous ones will answer him with the words: Lord, when did we *see* you hungry.... When did we *see* you a stranger... When did we *see* you sick or in prison?..." (*Make Sure,* 1953, p. 321; italics are mine).

The Signs

Under this main theme I examine the following verses from Matthew 24:6, 7, 9, 14, 15, 16, 22, 29, 31, 32, 33 and 34.

VERSE 6
Revised Standard Version:
"And you will hear of wars and rumors of wars; see that you are not alarmed; for this must take place, but the end is not yet."

NWT 1984:
"YOU are going to hear of wars and reports of wars; see that YOU are not terrified. For these things must take place, but the end is not yet."[344]

Comment: The book *True Peace and Security—How Can You Find It?* will be helpful in examining these verses. It was published in 1986 and is a revised version of the book, *True Peace and Security—From What Source?* published in 1973. Chapter seven of the 1986 version includes a review of all the signs mentioned in Matthew 24 that are interpreted as prophecy for events to be fulfilled before and after 1914 (*True Peace and Security,* 1986, p. 69–70).

Previously the Society interpreted verse six to mean the "wars and rumors," attributed to Jesus in the *edited* evangelical account, referred to all wars fought *before* 1914: "Such wars during the centuries prior to 1914 were mere wars against human nations, human governments" (*New Heavens,* 1953, p. 246).

This had to be apparent from the last words of the verse: "...but the end is not yet." By 1914 this accounts for more than 1,900 years of minor and major wars.

The Society recognized, however, that Jesus' prophecy on war and "rumors of wars" in "this generation" actually meant the *then* generation:

"But the question may be asked: 'Were not some of those prophecies fulfilled before the destruction of Jerusalem by the Romans in the year 70 CE?' Yes, some were. But more was to come, as the prophecies themselves show. True, Jesus was answering a question of immediate concern to his disciples. But he used the opportunity to provide long-range information…" (*True Peace*, 1986, p. 69-85).

A little further along says:

"The fact that some portions of Jesus' prophecy did have a fulfillment in the first century stamped it as truthful, giving sound reason for confidence in everything else Jesus said would happen" (Ibid., p. 76).

The idea is that "some" of the signs, but not all, were "smaller" fulfillments prior to AD 70.

The author of the Gospel of Matthew may have consciously, or unconsciously, adapted the whole sign-prophecy discussion in Matthew 24 in relation to real events up to, around and after AD 70 when Jerusalem fell to Roman forces. Apparently the author knew this, but concluded: "for all these things must come to pass, but the end is not yet," i.e., the Second Coming, the Judgment Day and the world's end. Together with his co-believers the author is now in an *intermediate stage* where the signs appear but he still looks forward to the "end" itself, which will come very soon.

The translators working for the Society translated verse six more emphatically in the first *New World Translation* of 1950: "YOU are going to hear of wars and reports of wars; see that YOU are not terrified. For these things must take place, but the accomplished end is not yet." I guess that the use of the word *accomplished,* even for those translators, seemed a little strange, because *that* time, the first century, was not the "accomplished end" but only, according to the Society, a "minor fulfillment" of the prophecy! So the translators faced a challenge in getting the translation to fit both past and present events.

Earlier (1950–1963) it was presumably important that canvassing publishers explaining the text to those they met in the field could say that only *after* verse six it is the "accomplished end." *There* it was *before* 1914, and *now* it is *after* 1914! Since 1963, the translators have, however, apparently become wiser, for in the recent *New World Translation* of 1984 the "accomplished end" has been replaced with the simpler, "the end."

One can always learn something.

VERSE 7
Revised Standard Version:
"For nation will rise against nation, and kingdom against kingdom, and there will be famines and earthquakes in various places."

NWT 1984:
"For nation will rise against nation and kingdom against kingdom, and there will be food shortages and earthquakes in one place after another."

Comment: In verse seven, according to the Society, a marked change happened, as the *right, true or proper* "end" now begins with the year 1914. The Watchtower leaders are familiar with the widespread belief among scholars that Jesus' prophecy of wars and rumors of wars *only* applies to events in the first century. But this didn't bother Brooklyn, because they found a "greater" and more "complete fulfillment in this 20th century" (*True Peace,* 1986, p. 76; recommend reading chapter seven to understand full quote in context).

The Society has determined *all* the signs Jesus mentioned in Matthew 24 constitute the composite sign. It is the *number* of signs, Jesus said, that makes the difference, for this *composite sign* was not *fully* fulfilled in the first century. So there would be "another larger fulfillment" sometime in the future. Thus, the book, *True Peace and Security—How Can You Find It?* says:

"Have those things occurred? As you examine the accompanying chart headed 'What Will Be the Sign?' you may recall reading about wars of earlier centuries. But World War I stands out from all the others as distinctive, a turning point in history. You may recall, also, that food shortages, pestilences, earthquakes, times of lawlessness, and unusual efforts to promote peace and security have taken place before 1914. Yet, no other time in history has seen all these things come on one generation in such overwhelming measure. In all honesty, if the events since 1914 do not fulfill the sign, what more is required? Without a doubt, we live at the time of Jesus' 'presence' in Kingdom power" (*True Peace,* 1986, p. 76-78).

A schedule on page seventy-eight of the same edition of *True Peace* titled "What Will Be the Sign?" notes the following about the fulfillment of verse seven:

"World War I killed 14 million combatants and civilians; World War II killed 55 million. Since World War II hundreds of coups, rebellions, and wars have taken the lives of some 35 million people. / Thus, since 1914 over 100 million lives have been lost to war!"

The biblical verse seven also calls out famines and earthquakes. Studying how the Watchtower leaders concluded that since 1914 there has been more hunger and more earthquakes than previous centuries would require page after page of discussion. The claims are repeated in their literature in a steady stream from the 1950s through to the 21st century, at least as far I have examined. There is absolutely nothing new and nothing of value in any of it. It is pure self-delusion, and what is worse: The allegations of the increase in famines and earthquakes after 1914 are not based on any kind of credible statistics. They are based only on the dogma of what *must have* happened in 1914, where Satan and his demons were thrown down to earth, and in their fury started the First World War and all the subsequent wars in the 20th century. In the book *Knowledge That Leads to Everlasting Life* from 1995, this repeats what the Witnesses were indoctrinated with during the previous seventy-five years (to study in more detail see Carl Olof Jonsson and Wolfgang Herbst's *The "Sign" of the Last Days—When?*).[345]

For example:

"Since 1914 there have been at least 20 major famines. Afflicted areas include Bangladesh, Burundi, Cambodia, China, Ethiopia, Greece, India, Nigeria, Russia, Rwanda, Somalia, and Sudan" (*Knowledge*, 1995, p. 102). Typically, they use as documentation the quote of *any* scholar that accidentally supports their premise, claiming it is "documentation"; in this case they chose Dr. Abdelgalil Elmekki of the University of Toronto, showing that often famine has political explanation because leaders are more interested in buying weapons than feeding their populations. It's probably true, but not in this context where people's suffering is being misused as a point of evidence, and where such a basis is beyond all reason.

The same book mentions a whole series of "signs" that partly come from Matthew 24 and partly from elsewhere in the New Testament, where the end times are described: plagues in Luke 21:11; increasing lawlessness in Matthew 24:12; destruction of the earth, Revelation 11:18; critical times *and* excessive love of money, 2 Timothy 3:1; disobedience to parents, 2 Timothy 3:2; lack of affection, 2 Timothy 3:3; sensual pleasures greater than friendship with God, 2 Timothy 3:4; lack of self-control *and* lack of love for the good, 2 Timothy 3:3; indifference to the impending danger, Matthew 24:39; scoffers reject signs in the last days, 2 Peter 3:3, 4; the Kingdom of God is proclaimed throughout the whole earth, Matthew 24:14 *(Knowledge,* 1995, p. 102).

The *signs* in Matthew 24 must be viewed in light of the origin of the writing, which must have been marked by reports of the appalling horrors the inhabitants of Jerusalem endured during the siege; that is, unspeakable atrocities ranging from famine to cannibalism. The only reasonable question to ask in relation to the intent of Matthew 24 is: How could the congregation use it for events after AD 70—and before the 90s AD where John's Revelation seems to be right on track. Of course, the members of the congregation have been occupied by the questions the disciples—in the editorially designed version—asked Jesus, and the answers he gave that seem to satisfy what they want to hear.

In other words: The question and answers tell us that Christians, in the years after AD 70, had dealt with the problem of Jesus' triumphant return, during which they would be led to heaven. Anything beyond this is pure speculation.

VERSE 9

Revised Standard Version:

"Then they will deliver you up to tribulation, and put you to death; and you will be hated by all nations for my name's sake."

NWT 1984:

"Then people will deliver YOU up to tribulation and will kill YOU, and YOU will be objects of hatred by all the nations on account of my name."

Comment: The Watchtower Society considers this verse one of the most important of the alleged thirty-nine signs, and verse nine became number five in the composite sign. The Watchtower leaders even think that this sign particularly concerns them in connection with the "larger fulfillment" after 1914, as Satan crashed to the ground he "instigated his seed on earth [Christendom's priesthood] to engage in cruel persecution of the children of the Kingdom's mother, 'the remaining ones of her seed' [the Bible Students]" (*New Heavens*, 1953, p. 251).

The outbreak of the First World War "furnished the opportunity at last for the religious clergy and the principal ones of their flocks to strike at the headquarters of the legal servant of Jehovah's witnesses, the Watch Tower Bible and Tract Society, at Brooklyn, NY. False accusation served the Devil's cause well, and in short order eight officials and prominent members of the headquarters family were railroaded to Federal penitentiary.... While selfish traitors worked within the organization to try to disrupt it, other arrests and imprisonments of Jehovah's witnesses occurred over all the earth, accompanied by mobbing.... The enemies rejoiced and congratulated themselves. (Rev. 11:7-10) All this added to the evidence that the 'time of the end' had begun in 1914 and that the nations were irreversibly doomed. It was all a part of the great 'sign' that Jesus foretold showing the 'consummation of the system of things' and his invisible presence" (*New Heavens*, 1953, p. 251, 252).

This quote is from a 59-year-old Watchtower book, but it makes little difference where the interpretation of verse nine is concerned. Roughly the same arbitrary view is expressed today. The leaders of the Watchtower Society simply can't get over the events following the outbreak of the First World War where, on the matter of internal divisions, they experienced government interference and imprisonment, which to some extent were self-inflicted. (Reference Chapters 11 through 16)

In *Insight*, under the theme "persecution" we find:

"The book of Revelation shows that such persecution continues down to the time of Christ's taking power to reign and even thereafter for a period, for when Satan and his angels are cast down to the earth, the dragon 'persecutes the woman, waging war with the remaining ones of her seed who obey God and bear witness to Jesus.' (Rev. 12:7-17)" (*Insight* 2, 1988, p. 609).

The Watchtower leadership does not restrict this interpretation of verse nine to only the Bible Students/Jehovah's Witnesses; they now admit such persecution is a distinctive condition for Christians for all time. It started with Christ's impalement (Jehovah's Witnesses do not believe Jesus was crucified but impaled on a vertical pole), the stoning of Stephen, and the Roman persecution of the Christians. (*Insight* 1, 1988, p. 610)

But to me it seems there is a serious problem. If verse six concerns everything *before* 1914, and verse seven concerns everything *after* 1914, how can persecutions mentioned in verse nine also belong to the time *before* 1914?

The problem is just another inference to support the fact that all the signs Jesus mentioned in the Matthew text *only* concern the specific "time of the end" for the author of the Gospel of Matthew and his readers during the time they lived—after AD 70. *It was about Jesus' generation and his contemporaries.* It is therefore quite logical to assume that the words of persecution specifically were aimed at Jesus' audience (the disciples and, indirectly, the established Christian congregations) in the edited literary account of Jesus' apocalyptic talk. It was the disciples who—before the "accomplished end" (NWT from 1950-1963)—would be persecuted; the text then refers to only those persecutions familiar to the author. If Matthew's gospel was written after the year 70, the author undoubtedly had knowledge of the horrors around the year 64, as the Christian martyrs endured during Emperor Nero's persecutions in Rome. Hatred and persecution of the Christians were historical realities, still sharp in people's minds, at the time Matthew's gospel was penned, and the Christians had only one consolation to draw, namely "he who endures to the end will be saved" (Matthew 24:13; RSV).

VERSE 14
Revised Standard Version:
"And this gospel of the kingdom will be preached throughout the whole world, as a testimony to all nations; and then the end will come."

NWT 1984:
"And this good news of the kingdom will be preached in all the inhabited earth for a witness to all the nations; and then the end will come." [346]

Comment: In the teachings of the Watchtower Society, the "time of the end"[347] begins in 1914, from which year the invisible presence of Christ shall be calculated. The conclusion of *the end time* or the Day of Judgment—referred to in verse fourteen—the Witnesses still await.

The author of Matthew's gospel knew nothing of a "larger" fulfillment sometime in the future nor did he know that the "end" he wrote about, and probably preached about to the Christian congregations, would not be the "accomplished" end. For him there was only a very specific end: "the end" in *definite form*. The gospel mentioned in verse fourteen was the message of salvation through Jesus Christ, the crucified and resurrected.

Just after AD 70 there was no room to distinguish between 1. Jesus' "presence"; 2. the preaching of the gospel; and 3. the proximity of the end. Christ had been among them, at least among those eye witnesses who could testify to his first coming. They looked now for "signs" of the Second Coming that would happen soon, and in the meantime, they would preach to Jews and Greeks. Therefore, the gospel had to be preached *before* the Second Coming, and not *after*, as the Watchtower Society teaches. By changing the original meaning of the basic text with the translation of *parousia* as *presence*, they rendered it so that the disciples' asked about the sign that Christ *had* come (invisibly). But this violates the original text! The fulfillment of the signs, the terrible events, which probably referred to the destruction of Jerusalem in AD 70, announced the *nearness* of the *visible* Second Coming.

Whoever wrote Matthew presumably knew all that when he edited his text on the basis of the existing gospel of Mark, and oral and written reports of Jesus' ministry. He knew about the demolition of the temple, had seen or heard of the near-total destruction of Jerusalem, and that many Jews had been deported to other parts of the Roman Empire.

Around 1955 the Watchtower Society concluded that the message of the kingdom is *not* the message "of a kingdom yet to come in the far-off, indefinite future, but of God's kingdom born, set up, and with the anointed Jesus in the heavenly throne, invisibly present..." (*New Heavens,* 1953, p. 254).[348] And in the same company's main textbook for many years, *Let God Be True,* one can read: "This is not the good news of a kingdom coming, but the news of one now established. So from and after 1919 the most sustained publicity campaign ever given on earth has been to the effect that 'the kingdom of the heavens has drawn near'" (*Be True,* 1952, p. 141; in the book, *Make Sure of All Things,* from 1953, p. 338, Matthew 24:14 is listed as sign number eleven).

For those who read Matthew 24:14 as a religious writing that came into being a little more than 1,900 years ago, it is clear that "this gospel of the kingdom" was already being preached when the Gospel of Matthew was written. The gospel's testimony of the life of Jesus and his moving about was a part of this preaching, as the writing (the Gospel of Matthew) was intended for Jewish Christians who fled to Syria to prove to them that Jesus really was the long-awaited Messiah-king. And "the glad tidings" were that the kingdom the Jews had longingly awaited for centuries would soon be established; their wait was over.

Concerning the proximity of the kingdom of God, an important subject for Jesus, the Society explained (away!) in 1952 that as long as "Christ Jesus was in the midst of them the disciples likewise proclaimed the presence of the Kingdom.... But there is no record that they continued to do so after his ascension on high. Such an announcement would *not be appropriate* until his return and second presence" (*Be True,* 1952, p. 140; italics are mine).

VERSE 15
Revised Standard Version:
"So when you see the desolating sacrilege spoken of by the prophet Daniel, standing in the holy place (let the reader understand)..."

NWT 1984:
"Therefore, when YOU catch sight of the disgusting thing that causes desolation, as spoken of through Daniel the prophet, standing in a holy place, (let the reader use discernment,)..."

Comment: The "desolating sacrilege" or "abomination of desolation" (KJ) occurs for the first time in Daniel 9:27, and in the apocryphal writing, *The First Book of Maccabees* 1:54. Both places allude to the altar to Zeus built in the temple of Jerusalem around 168 BC by Syrian King Antiochus IV Epiphanes. It was this desecration and Antiochus' ban on the Jewish religion (circumcision, sacrifice, and Sabbath observance) that, under the leadership of Judas Maccabeus, triggered the freedom fight against the Syrians from 166 to 161 BC.

At the time of the origin of the Gospel of Matthew, these difficult-to-understand and cryptic prophecies in the Book of Daniel gave the Christians new meaning. They read Daniel as if it was addressed specifically to them, and the words on "the abomination of desolation" were understood as a prophecy about the temple and the fate of Jerusalem and its destruction in AD 70.

The author of Matthew looked back at the event recorded in Daniel and put the words of warning into the mouth of Jesus.

The words in 24:15 must first and foremost *again* be seen in regard to Jesus' words and the disciples' question in the edited text about the destruction of the temple (24:1-3). "The desolating sacrilege" (RSV), or "the abomination of desolation" (KJ), was something that primarily concerned Jerusalem and its temple. That the Gospel of Matthew was written after AD 70 is further confirmed by verse sixteen in which Christians are told to flee to the mountains. This actually happened during a break in the Roman siege in AD 68 (more on this during the examination of verse sixteen).

In the Watchtower's 1997 two-volume encyclopedic commentary, *Insight on the Scriptures*, it states under "disgusting thing":

"The popular view has generally followed early Jewish tradition in applying this expression to the profanation of Jehovah's temple at Jerusalem in the year 168 BCE by Syrian King Antiochus IV (Epiphanes). Attempting to stamp out the worship of Jehovah, Antiochus built an altar over the great altar of Jehovah and sacrificed upon this a pig to the Olympian Zeus (Jupiter). An expression like that of Daniel (associating disgusting things with desolation) appears in the Apocryphal book of 1 Maccabees (1:54) as applying to this event. / But this was only the Jewish interpretation of matters, not an inspired revelation. Christ Jesus showed this view to be in error when he gave the warning to his disciples: 'Therefore, when you catch sight of the disgusting thing that causes desolation, as spoken of through Daniel the prophet, standing in a holy place, (let the reader use discernment,) then let those in Judea begin fleeing to the mountains.' (Mt 24:15, 16) These words show that 'the disgusting thing that causes desolation' was not then past but future" (*Insight* 1, 1997, p. 635).

Today the Watchtower Society is well aware that the words "desolating sacrilege" and "abomination of desolation"—or, for that matter, "the disgusting thing that causes desolation" (NWT 1984)—*primarily* focused on the destruction of Jerusalem in year 70. But the Society believes that this was only a "minor" fulfillment of Jesus' prophecy, and that a "larger" fulfillment was far off.

Why Jesus did not immediately tell the disciples this is a mystery to me (see also *Insight* 1, 1997, p. 634).

Today we should then see the "parallel" or "major" fulfillment of Jesus' prophecy from Matthew 24:

"Parallelwise, what turning point in history shall we reasonably say is marked by those things that we oldsters of this generation have seen occur on a global scale since 1914 CE, that year which those International Bible Students had been declaring since 1876 CE would seal the end of the 'times of the Gentiles'? / We would be blinding ourselves to the ominous 'sign' if we did not discern that the end of the global system of things is marked by such things occurring since 1914 CE" (*Man's Salvation*, 1975, p. 22, 23).

In the Society's "composite sign" Matthew 24:15 appears as sign number twelve. In 1955 "the abomination of desolation" was interpreted as the League of Nations and the UN, which stands on "a holy place"—meaning it stands in "place of the established Kingdom of God" (*Make Sure*, 1953, p. 338).

About this topic, we find the following from 1953:

"The adoption of the League of Nations after the 'seven times' of the Gentile nations had ended in 1914 was a rejection of Jehovah's universal sovereignty.... On January 10, 1920, the League of Nations began its existence with the signing of the peace treaty, and the 'disgusting thing that causes desolation' began standing in the holy place, as a substitute for God's kingdom by his Son.... It is operating on borrowed time in defiance of the end of the 'appointed times of the nations' in 1914. The idea of it is Babelic, Babylonish, in opposition to Jehovah's kingdom by Christ. It leads its dupes only one way: 'it goes off into destruction' " (*New Heavens*, 1953, p. 275–276).

Following the Second World War, "it" again came out of the "bottomless pit" (Revelation 17:8; NWT: "abyss"), but this time as the United Nations. (Ibid., p. 276-279)

Regarding the League of Nations and the United States, an article in *The Watchtower* in 1999 said under the heading, "Let the Reader Use Discernment":

"Jehovah's Witnesses have long exposed these human peace organizations as disgusting in God's sight" (*WT*, May 1, 1999). But in the above mentioned *Watchtower*, in which the magazine quoted "an electrifying talk," as former vice president F. W. Franz gave in 1969, a 'clearer understanding' of verse fifteen clarifying what 'stand in the holy place' means, was presented:

"In reviewing the previous understanding [that is, the Society's understanding in 1970] of Jesus' prophecy, Brother Franz said: 'The explanation was given that the "great tribulation" had begun in 1914 CE and that it was not allowed to run its full course then but God stopped World War I in November of 1918. From then on God was allowing an interval for the activity of his anointed remnant of elect Christians before he let the final part of the "great tribulation" resume at the battle of Armageddon.' Then a significantly adjusted explanation was offered [Franz again speaking]: 'To correspond with the events of the first century … the antitypical "great tribulation" did not begin in 1914 CE. Rather, what took place upon Jerusalem's modern antitype in 1914–1918 was merely "a beginning of pangs of distress".… The "great tribulation" such as will not occur again is yet ahead, for it means the destruction of the world empire of false religion (including Christendom) followed by the "war of the great day of God the Almighty" at Armageddon.' This meant that the entire great tribulation was yet ahead.… Accordingly, we expect the great tribulation to begin soon, but it will be cut short for the sake of God's chosen ones. Note this key point: In the ancient pattern, 'the disgusting thing standing in a holy place' was linked to the Roman attack under General Gallus in 66 CE. The modern-day parallel to that attack—the outbreak of the great tribulation—is still ahead. So 'the disgusting thing that causes desolation,' which has existed since 1919, apparently is yet to stand in a holy place…" (*WT*, May 1, 1999, p. 16, 17).

It is not easy to understand, I admit, but since it suspiciously reminds one of a method of explaining away, it's more understandable!

The article gradually reached the conclusion that although "the disgusting thing" appeared after the First World War, it would not, until the near future, "take a position in a unique way" and appear in "a holy place." What the article eventually leads to is that "political elements in league with *former Christians*" encourage "hostility against religion in general and *true Christians* in particular" (*WT*, May 1, 1999, p. 17, 18; "former Christians" may refer to critical apostates Raymond Franz, Carl Olof Jonsson and others, while "true Christians" refers to the Jehovah's Witnesses; italics are mine).

What this strange terminology means is that the Society predicts that, just before Armageddon begins, the UN and the world's politicians will attack the false religion, Christianity, which is "drunk with the blood of the holy ones" (Revelation 17:6; NWT):

"When the 'scarlet-colored wild beast' attacks the religious harlot [the false religion], 'the disgusting thing' will be standing in a menacing way in Christendom's so-called holy place. So desolation will begin on faithless Christendom, which portrays itself as holy" (*WT*, May 1, 1999, p. 18).

No matter how "disgusting" the UN is for the Watch Tower Society in New York, the Society was nonetheless associated with the United Nations from 1991 to 2001 as a non-governmental organization (NGO) member—that is *quite deliberately* a member and not an error as some claim. In fact, this membership may have given the Society some *advantages*.

The Society's branch office in Denmark subsequently explained that "the intention of becoming registered as a NGO by the Department of Public Information in 1991 was to gain access to research on health, ecology and social issues that exist in the United Nations library." This reply continues: "We have used this library many years before 1991, but this year it was necessary to be registered as a NGO to continue to have access" (Email to an Ex-Witness from information officer, Erik Joergensen, at the Watchtower Headquarters in Denmark).

The Society's motive to enter into a formal agreement with the UN for a number of years is not easy for me to understand, especially when the Society's branch in Denmark was reluctant to provide an extensive answer. I had asked the Danish public relations officer whether the Watch Tower Society in New York had put its signature on a document confirming a commitment to the UN Charter. But, after making the same inquiry in three letters only to receive evasive answers, I gave up. I must conclude the Jehovah's Witnesses, on a certain committed level, have been involved in UN work while still claiming the world organization is the guise of the beast now emerged from the abyss. Therefore, they formally cooperated with "Satan's organization" and thus with the Devil himself for years!

When this "close" relationship between the Society, the United Nations and Satan became known through the world press—including *The Guardian*—in 2001, the Watchtower Society immediately withdrew its membership. This is also evident from a March 2004 document from the Department of Public Information (DPI) and addressed to "Whom It May Concern":

"By accepting association with DPI, the organization agreed to meet criteria for association, including support and respect of the principles of the Charter of the United Nations and commitment and means to conduct effective information programmes [sic] with its constituents and to a broader audience about UN activities" (August 4, 2004).[349]

The document was published on the UN website after numerous requests. Many members of Jehovah's Witnesses were pretty shocked when the Society's UN connection became known worldwide, for NGO membership requires, as far as I could discern, a *signature* indicating the member's agreement with the UN's mission statement.

VERSE 16
Revised Standard Version:
"... then let those who are in Judea flee to the mountains; ...."

NWT 1984:
"... then let those in Judea begin fleeing to the mountains."

Comment: The Society teaches that the escape to the "mountains" happened *after* Christ's second *presence* began in 1914; these mountains, it must be understood, are not *literal* but *figurative*. In 1954 an article in *The Watchtower* discusses this:

"Flee where? To the mountains. Literal ones? No, that would bring no safety at Armageddon. (Amos 9:2, 3) The mountains must be outside the realm of Christendom, just as the literal ones to which Christians fled AD 66 were outside Jerusalem and Judah. The mountains to which lovers of righteousness now flee in obedience to Christ's command are the New World theocratic system of things Jehovah has created.... Many thousands are now fleeing there and finding that safety. Thousands more will yet come. Those lovers of righteousness who have not yet fled should remember the typical events of 607 BC and AD 70. As in those cases, Christendom has been warned of her sins, her political alliances, her fate from those political cronies, and she has rejected the warning. She has chosen Caesar governments instead of Christ—a disgusting thing that seals her desolation.... She refuses to flee herself; she hinders those who would flee.... Those fleeing to the symbolical mountains will remember what befell the Jews that delayed flight or tried to salvage worldly wealth, contrary to Jesus' instructions. Without delay and without worldliness they will flee, appreciating that we now live in the urgent period parallel to 609–607 BC and AD 66–70. As Jehovah did then, so now he allows opportunity for flight. Seize it, now or never!" (*WT*, July 15, 1954)

Twenty-nine years later, in 1983, *The Watchtower* expressed in an article titled "Flee While There Is Yet Time!" largely the same views about the mountains the Christians were to flee to in the first century but which would have "a far greater fulfillment in our day." *The Watchtower* realized that the Christians in Jerusalem fled the city between 66 and 70: "The prophecy was first given regarding Jerusalem and its magnificent temple.... Note, first of all, the urgent warning to flee to the mountains..." (*WT*, Nov. 15, 1982, p. 3).

The same article went deeper saying when Jesus "foretold the end of [the] Jewish religious system in the first century, he also had in mind something far greater. He knew that it would be a pattern of what to expect on a much larger scale during the 'last days' of this present system of things..." (*WT*, Nov. 15, 1982, p. 5).

Never at a loss to provide explanation, the article continued:

"What are these symbolic mountains today? They are the divinely provided place of refuge, Jehovah's provision for protecting his people.... Fleeing to God's organization and its exalted pure worship also means fleeing from the false religious systems of this world, severing all connections with them.... No one should delay fleeing, thinking that there will be an exact parallel to the Roman armies' withdrawing in 66 CE, allowing time for flight.... Fleeing now is extremely urgent. Why? Because the evidence shows that soon the 'disgusting thing' will desolate also the 'holy place,' the claimed realm of Christendom's churches.... Since those who will survive the 'great tribulation' are to be searched out before it starts, Jehovah does not need to allow for a long, drawn-out 'siege.' ... Have you already fled to the symbolic "mountains"? If not, then do not delay. It means your very life..." (Ibid., p. 6–7).

The Watchtower of May 1, 1999, using to the same cliché-embossed prescription and rhetoric, stated:

"We must be certain that our refuge continues to be Jehovah and his mountainlike organization.... That is where we will find protection!" (*WT*, May 1, 1999, p. 19)

The three synoptic gospels, Matthew, Mark and Luke, all discuss "the abomination of desolation" (KJ), or "the desolating sacrilege" (RSV), and the fleeing to the mountains, although "the abomination" as concept is not directly mentioned in Luke. But Luke, a gospel certainly written *after* the year 70, was addressed to a Roman, the "most excellent Theophilus." Luke wrote the symbolic Jewish words and concepts so that a non-Jew could understand what Jesus—in the *edited* account and according to the interpretations of Luke—had said and meant. Because of Luke's subsequent identification of the concepts in Matthew 24:15 and 16, we are better able to understand the context:

"But when you see Jerusalem surrounded by armies, then know that its desolation has come near. Then let those who are in Judea flee to the mountains, and let those who are inside the city depart, and let not those who are out in the country enter it, for these are days of vengeance..." (Luke 21:20, 21; RSV).

In Luke the mysterious "abomination of desolation" of Daniel (9:27) and Matthew (24.15) is replaced by "armies" and the parenthetic remark in Matthew 24:15—*let the reader understand* (RSV)—Luke replaces with the explanatory paraphrase: "But when you see Jerusalem surrounded by armies, then know that its desolation has come near" (RSV).

All Luke's text dealing with the Roman armies' siege of Jerusalem, the destruction of the city and the events after AD 70, was perceived by gospel readers as if the words had been spoken by Jesus many years before AD 70. Without doubt Luke's Gospel was penned after AD 70, perhaps around 80 or maybe later. Some people even believe the gospel was written in the early second century, around AD 120–130.[350] British scholar Donald Guthrie writes that a number of scholars assume Luke's gospel was written the decade before the turn of the century, as the Gospel was known before the end of the first century and already accepted by the beginning of the second century. Guthrie treats all the arguments for both an early and a later version (pp. 110–115).[351]

The verses from Luke are as follows:

"But when you see Jerusalem surrounded by armies, then know that its desolation has come near. Then let those who are in Judea flee to the mountains, and let those who are inside the city depart, and let not those who are out in the country enter it; for these are days of vengeance, to fulfill all that is written. Alas for those who are with child and for those who give suck in those days! For great distress shall be upon the earth and wrath upon this people; they will fall by the edge of the sword, and be led captive among all nations; and Jerusalem will be trodden down by the Gentiles, until the times of the Gentiles are fulfilled" (Luke 21:20-24; RSV).

Of course, the writer we call Luke knew, at the time he wrote his gospel, that the Roman conquerors killed thousands of Jews "by the sword" and subsequently deported others to "all heathen people as prisoners" ("be led captive among all nations;" Luke 21:24; RSV). The Jewish historian Flavius Josephus claims that between 600,000 and 1,100,000 people were killed during the siege.

Luke's more reality-based words demonstrate that these early Christian Jews fled Jerusalem literally and likewise literally fled to mountains near Jerusalem.

VERSE 22
Revised Standard Version:
"And if those days had not been shortened, no human being would be saved; but for the sake of the elect those days will be shortened."

NWT 1984:
"In fact, unless those days were cut short, no flesh would be saved; but on account of the chosen ones those days will be cut short."

Comment: The association here indicates that *those days* were the days of the *great tribulation,* as in the siege of Jerusalem and its destruction. This great *time of distress* has not had its equal since the beginning of the world (Matthew 24:21), and because it would overshadow all previous *times of distress,* Christians believed God would "shorten" *the days.*

In time, the Watchtower leaders gained a convenient *clearer understanding,* so now they no longer believe the great tribulation began in 1914. This is astonishing to me! Initially they thought the *shortening* of those days meant a *break* in the great tribulation, which began in 1914. Yet for the sake of the Bible Students, this tribulation was interrupted in such a way that the message about the Kingdom of God, established in October 1914, *in time* could be proclaimed anywhere on earth. (See *You May Survive,* 1955, chapter 7, p. 107.)

In 1996, *The Watchtower* published:
"The tribulation caused by the Romans was cut short, allowing God's anointed chosen ones ample opportunity to escape and remain alive. Thus, we can rest assured that the destructive attack on religion will not be allowed to kill off the global congregation of true worshipers. It will proceed quickly, as if 'in one day.' Somehow, though, it will be cut short, will not be allowed to complete its objective, so that God's people can be 'saved'..." (*WT,* Aug. 15, 1996, p. 19).

The Gospel of Matthew is an ancient writing and its ideas tell us something about its author and what his contemporaries thought. "Those days" would *not be extended* means quite simply that they are shortened, as the remaining time was quite short. By around AD 80, this was still the message for the Christian congregations in Syria, and later in Rome.

VERSE 29
Revised Standard Version:
"Immediately after the tribulation of those days the sun will be darkened, and the moon will not give its light, and the stars will fall from heaven, and the powers of the heavens will be shaken."

NWT 1984:

"Immediately after the tribulation of those days the sun will be darkened, and the moon will not give its light, and the stars will fall from heaven, and the powers of the heavens will be shaken."

Comment: This verse also refers to the events connected with the Jewish-Roman war from 66 to 70. The words "immediately after" perhaps tell the contemporary reader that after the destruction of Jerusalem it won't be long until the world's end. This strengthens the perception that the script was originally written in its enlarged edition during the latter part of the first century of the Christian era.

"Immediately after the tribulation" the firmament will be shaken in its foundations, and the "stars will fall from heaven"—*down* to earth, since at that time mankind imagined earth was the center of the universe. The physical world, the *cosmos*, would be left to *chaos*, disorder and collapse. The world would experience a solar eclipse. The stars, otherwise firmly affixed in the firmament, would rain down all over mankind's world. But Christ, the son of Man, would appear in the clouds of heaven to save his elect. (Matthew 24:29-31)

Russell deduced that verse twenty-nine's literal fulfillment occurred when stars "fell" over North America in 1833. A large meteor shower that year was seen over large parts of North America, Mexico and the Caribbean islands. Russell borrowed this view from the Adventists. He thought the days when the sun was darkened focused on the dark day in Northern America, May 19, 1780 (a natural phenomenon; see *Studies* 4, 1914 edition, p. 585–590).[352]

Since then, the Society has pressed the interpretation of this verse to the extreme:

"When stars fall from heaven where do they drop? Down on this earth? This earth could not endure that; it could not accommodate them all. So that is not to be expected.... The news reports from all over the world since 1914 bear witness to the undeniable fulfillment of Jesus' prophecy, to prove that Michael, the Son of man, stood up. Not to be dismissed from consideration as 'fearful sights' and 'great signs' from heaven are new things that modern science is discovering and bringing to the people's attention, to their own and the people's mental agitation and rising fears. The so-called cosmic rays are more and more commanding scientific study.... Certainly the Creator of cosmic rays, Jehovah God, could use these to affect the minds of his enemies.... In this prophecy [Ezekiel 38:21] God warns that he will also use other natural forces that are at his disposal, possibly a rain of anti-matter that has the property of annihilating any material thing that it meets" (*Your Will Be Done*, 1958, p. 319–322).

In 1970, *The Watchtower* added the new twist I discussed earlier when the magazine stated that in view of what happened in the first century, the modern tribulation could not have an opening part in 1914–1918, followed by an interval, and later a resumption after several decades, and then continue. *The Watchtower* concluded: "The 'great tribulation' such as will not occur again *is yet ahead...*" (*WT*, Jan. 15, 1970; italics are mine).

Meaning: In 1975 or *beyond*.

The problem for the Watchtower's interpreters and editors was that since "immediately after" referred to *immediately after* the destruction of Jerusalem, how could the *larger fulfillment* after 1914 explain immediately after? Through a complicated argument in the context of Joel 2:28–31 (in the *Old* Testament) they concluded that Matthew 24:29 refers to the day of the final clash, Armageddon: "The fulfillment of Joel's prophecy (in harmony with other prophecies using similar language) helps us to understand the words at Matthew 24:29. Clearly, what Jesus said about 'the sun being darkened, the moon not giving light, and the stars falling' does not refer to things occurring over the many decades of the conclusion of the present system, such as space rocketry, moon landings, and the like. No, he pointed to things tied in with 'the great and fear-inspiring day of Jehovah,' the destruction *yet to come*" (*WT*, Feb. 15, 1994, p. 16; italics are mine).

Put another way: What the members previously believed about the sun, the moon and the stars represented in the gospels is now about the Great Tribulation, and its actual start postponed until *sometime in the future*. The article highlights the delay as an illustration of "how the light shines 'more and more unto the perfect day' [Proverbs 4:18, ASV]" (Ibid.). *The Watchtower* writers wander among the available editorial versions, using whichever fits the recent change in teachings. In one article they emphasize a *figurative* version and in another a *literal*.

VERSE 31, 32, 33 and 34
Revised Standard Version:
"[31] ...and he will send out his angels with a loud trumpet call, and they will gather his elect from the four winds, from one end of heaven to the other. [32] From the fig tree learn its lesson: as soon as its branch becomes tender and puts forth its leaves, you know that summer is near. [33] So also, when you see all these things, you know that he is near, at the very gates. [34] Truly, I say to you, this generation will not pass away till all these things take place."

American Standard Version:
"[34] Verily I say unto you, This generation shall not pass away, till all these things be accomplished."
King James Version:
"[34] ...This generation shall not pass, till all these things be fulfilled."

NWT 1984:
"31 And he will send forth his angels with a great trumpet sound, and they will gather his chosen ones together from the four winds, from one extremity of

the heavens to their other extremity. 32 Now learn from the fig tree as an illustration this point: Just as soon as its young branch grows tender and it puts forth leaves, YOU know that summer is near. 33 Likewise also YOU, when YOU see all these things, know that he is near at the doors. 34 Truly I say to YOU that this generation will by no means pass away until all these things occur.

Comment: The Watchtower Society's interpretation of the *trumpet verse* is based on the interpretations of Russell, who said that the separation work was done in the "harvest time." The *angels* were the Bible Students who gathered the selected ones from the Christian churches. The *trumpet* "has been symbolically sounding since October 1874, and will continue to the end of the Millennium" (*Studies* 4, 1914, p. 601). Today's Watchtower leadership builds further on Russell's interpretation, as the "great sound of a trumpet" (KJ) is their witness about the Kingdom.

The coherence of verse thirty-one says the angels, at Christ's return, bring together those who have been selected through the preaching work. The disciples were selected from the moment Jesus announced the "kingdom of heaven is at hand" (Matthew 4:17), and later in large scale, as the disciples obeyed the command to preach (Matthew 28:18-20).

There is no evidence whatsoever that the first Christians saw the angel's trumpet sound as a picture of the disciples preaching. The early Christian congregation lived in the last times and the signs were fulfilled right before their eyes. Even Paul expected the Second Coming would begin in his own lifetime (1 Thessalonians 4:15), and he mentions the trumpet sound as something that is heard in connection with the Second Coming: "We shall not all sleep, but we shall all be changed, in a moment, in the twinkling of an eye, at the last trumpet..." (1 Corinthians 15:51-52; RSV). I will, however, refrain from trying to decipher the ancient apocalyptic imagery further. The religious language's roots are largely lost today.

The following verses—Matthew 24: 32, 33 and 34—all emphasize strongly that the signs must come *before* the Second Coming and not *after*, as the Society falsely teaches. The *leaves* and *branches* must come *before* summer. Some things are true and some things parables, and perhaps, some things are in between. The language was different, flowery at the time of Jesus, and these verses are, unlike the other material in Matthew 24, parables.

In the 1950s, the Watchtower Society interpreted the parable as follows: Christ arrived in 1914 and was from then on *present*. The *branch* and *leaves* are the thirty-nine signs of the *composite sign*, which by its fulfillment proves the Second Coming has taken place. The *summer* pointed toward the battle of Armageddon. That he is near at the door is seen as the Millennium that comes at the conclusion of the time of the end, which began in 1914. Thus, it is the Millennium that is "near at the doors" (NWT). The true meaning of the text is thus again obscured, because one conclusion inevitably follows the other. The portrayed signs must necessarily *precede* the Second Coming, but neither Russell nor the top officials who inherited the founder's *borrowed* ideas realized this as they continued to translate the word *parousia* (coming) as *presence*.

The Watchtower of August 15, 1996 stated:

"In his reply Jesus spoke of the appearance of leaves showing that summer 'is near.' (Matthew 24:32, 33) Hence, many churches teach that the apostles were asking for a sign of Jesus' 'coming,' the sign proving that his return was imminent. They believe that the 'coming' will be the point when he takes Christians to heaven and then brings the end of the world…" (*WT*, Aug. 15, 1996, p. 9–14; see also *The Kingdom Is at Hand,* 1944, chapter 18; *Paradise Regained,* 1958, p. 205).

The above citation clearly shows the Society's writers are well aware of what they do, just as the wearer alone knows where the *shoe pinches*!

Matthew 24:32-34 presumably is an expression of the early church's belief in Christ's imminent return. By saying "this generation," the gospel's writer must, of course, have thought of the eyewitnesses' own time and generation. Elsewhere Jesus also said, according to the Matthew version, "Truly, I say to you, there are some standing here who will not taste death before they see the Son of man coming in his kingdom" (Matthew 16:28).

This seems to confirm that the Gospel According to Matthew was written in the last quarter of the first century.

About Time and Hours

Under this topic Matthew 24:36, 43 and 44 are treated.

VERSE 36

Revised Standard Version:

"[36] But of that day and hour no one knows, not even the angels of heaven, nor the Son, but the Father only.

[43] But know this, that if the householder had known in what part of the night the thief was coming, he would have watched and would not have let his house be broken into.

[44] Therefore you also must be ready; for the Son of man is coming at an hour you do not expect."

NWT 1984:

"36 Concerning that day and hour nobody knows, neither the angels of the heavens nor the Son, but only the Father.

43 But know one thing, that if the householder had known in what watch the thief was coming, he would have kept awake and not allowed his house to be broken into.

44 On this account YOU too prove yourselves ready, because at an hour that YOU do not think to be it, the Son of man is coming."

Comment: These words may have been used by the Early Church to reject the "false prophets" attracting attention to unauthorized predictions about the Second Coming and the Judgment Day. None, absolutely none, not even the Son, could come to know the date in advance. The words and meaning do not stand alone, but are stressed repeatedly. See the following: Matthew 24:42 and Matthew 25:13.

Today the Society also asserts that no one knows the day and hour, and yet they write in nearly every issue of *The Watchtower* that we stand on the threshold of Armageddon. It was precisely these people that the writer of the Gospel of Matthew aimed his words about "that day and hour." As my review of the historical and educational material should have shown, the Society's agitation in this area has only served one purpose: to provide a basis for the "global expansion" and huge literature sales through unethical Judgment-Day hysteria.

VERSE 45
Revised Standard Version:
"Who then is the faithful and wise servant, whom his master has set over his household, to give them their food at the proper time?"

NWT 1984:
"Who really is the faithful and discreet slave whom his master appointed over his domestics, to give them their food at the proper time?"

Comment: Russell's supporters believed that he was the "faithful and wise servant" of Matthew 24:45. The leaders of the Watchtower Society also had this view around the time of Russell's death although they later updated it. Many of the "unprogressive 'elective elders' in the local congregations" insisted on "living in the past, in the time of Pastor Russell, who was claimed by them to be the sole channel of Scriptural enlightenment, whom they called 'the servant' of Matthew 24:45" (*Qualified*, 1955, p. 318).

Since then, Watchtower leaders have often stressed it is not the Society which is the "faithful and wise servant," but the remnant of the 144,000 who fill that role. This remnant, the last survivors of the *anointed generation,* is represented by the Governing Body. Today the members of this board *officially* act as the *spiritual* leadership of the organization. There are indications, however, that in reality this council has become purely ornamental.

The Society has had various positions on this matter, and even though the leaders of today claim *the remnant* is the servant or slave, in the history of the movement it has often been implied the leaders of the Society, *collectively,* are *the servant*. This is evidenced indirectly in an article from 1957:

"In apostolic times a governing body of Christians at Jerusalem directed the work and served as a channel to bring forth spiritual food. To gain an understanding of God's Word and purposes back there one had to get in touch with this body or its representatives. And only those who did received God's holy spirit. / Likewise today Jehovah has an organization channel through which he makes known his will and purposes and through which he directs the work of preaching the good news of his kingdom. Even as Jesus foretold, today we see a 'faithful and discreet slave whom his master appointed over his domestics to give them their food at the proper time.' The facts show that this slave that God is using is not a single person but a composite individual, a group, an instrument, an organization, which uses as its legal instrument the Watch Tower Society..." (*WT*, July 15, 1957, p. 436; see also *WT*, Jan. 1, 1956, p. 28).

The facts also show that in practice the Society, in every respect, *was* and *is* the authority within the movement. When I was young it was forever and always: "The Society says, the Society believes." The Society was synonymous with God's visible leadership and assumed the lofty airs attributed to a divine "tool"—like "the sanctuary"—as that mentioned in Daniel 8:14. (*WT*, Jan. 15, 2001, p. 28)

Only members of the *slave class* (the 144,000 selected) could be elected to the board of the Watch Tower Bible and Tract Society of Pennsylvania (legally founded in 1884). Obviously, the leaders had a revelation, because in 1971, it became clear that members of the Governing Body were not necessarily identical to the directors of the Pennsylvania company, and by the "unforgettable annual meeting in 1971," as it says in a *Watchtower* article from 2001, "a distinction was clearly drawn between the spirit-anointed members of the Governing Body and the directors of the Pennsylvania corporation. Still, members of the Governing Body continued to serve as directors and officers of the Society" (*WT*, Jan. 15, 2001, p. 28-31; *Divine Purpose*, 1959, p. 64; 148).

Today the Society formally distinguishes between the Governing Body and the various legal societies, yet all work so closely together the whole enterprise still seems to me to form a compact, tightly woven symbiosis. However, I have noted members no longer say "the Society believes"; today it's "the Governing Body believes" and they seem a bit at sixes and sevens concerning where the real power is located.

But now the ambiguity is lessening. In 2011–2012 the Society provided greater clarity about who in the future—except Jehovah—is the movement's highest authority, and not least important, the "faithful and wise slave" (or "servant") from Matthew 24:45: The Governing Body that is temporarily manned by the same individuals who currently sit on the Board of Directors in the Watch Tower Society in Brooklyn. "The servant" is not one, two or three of these eight (more or less) individuals, but the entire collective team (of these eight men) who, as far as I have been informed, do not all belong to the anointed. Thus it is also clear the select group of Witnesses known as the anointed, which counts about 10,000 individuals in its membership, has apparently moved out of its role as the Governing Body's *official* steering group.

This was hinted at in *The Watchtower* of August 15, 2011, and is based partly on a members' meeting in the Watch Tower Society's Jersey Assembly Hall (The Stanley Theater in Jersey City, New Jersey) held on October 6, 2012. The participants were told that "the servant" (or "slave") is no longer *all the anointed* who have lived on earth since the year AD 33 (which The Watchtower leaders previously learned), instead "the servant" now only consists of a narrow group of anointed who, particularly since 1919, has served as the Watch Tower Society's board and management—today known as the Governing Body.[353]

At the meeting, the Council's six representatives concluded, among other things:

"From 1919 on, there has always been a small group of anointed Christians at the world headquarters of Jehovah's Witnesses.... In recent years, that group has been closely identified with the Governing Body of Jehovah's Witnesses."

It seems then, everything has returned to the old view. The Society has effectively scrapped the idea of the anointed as a "class" and is thus returned to J. F. Rutherford's vulgar idea of the Society as God's only communication channel on earth. (*WT*, Aug. 15, 2011, p. 22; www.jwsurvey.org; see also endnote 308)

Finally, I am tempted to quote and document once more that the former understanding inside the Jehovah's Witnesses throughout the world was that "the Society" in particular was Jehovah's Witnesses' supreme authority. So it was said in the 1938 statement that congregations throughout the world were instructed to send to the Society's branch offices (previously quoted in Chapter 18):

"We, the company of God's people taken out for his name, and now at -----, recognize that God's government is a pure theocracy and that Christ Jesus is at the temple and in full charge and control of the visible organization of Jehovah, as well as the invisible, and that 'THE SOCIETY' is the visible representative of the Lord on earth, and we therefore request 'The Society' to organize this company for service and to appoint the various servants thereof, so that all of us may work together in peace, righteousness, harmony and complete unity" (*Divine Purpose*, 1959, p. 148, see also *WT*, June 15, 1938, p. 182, 183).

It's interesting that before 1960, they wrote "governing body" with only lower-case letters, while "The Society" was highlighted with initial capitals, as in the 1938 statement. Until 2011–2012, power was apparently shared, and *the authority*, THE SOCIETY, has faded into the background, although I am quite sure that not a whit has changed—the astonishing development in 2011–2012, mentioned above, shows that ("governing body": *Divine Purpose*, 1959, p. 64; p. 148; "Governing Body," *WT*, Sept. 1, 2009, p. 29; the change to initial capitals on Governing Body occurred around 1973).

The words about the good and bad servants are obviously not aimed at Jehovah's Witnesses' leadership in New York in our time, or a group of anonymous board members, but they are, as the context of Matthew's gospel shows, aimed at the congregations in existence immediately after the year AD 70 (70 to 90). Even then the early Christians had a sense of the eschatological drama that could strengthen faith. All members were to be ready and at watch, because the *parousia* could be expected at any moment. The parable had an admonishing and topical aim. Indirectly, the author of the Gospel of Matthew expressed that the return seemed to be dragging on, as the evil servant is supposed to think: "My master is delayed" (Matthew 24:48). But he is warned. If he does not live a life his master finds worthy, then will his master "come in a day when he does not expect him and at an hour he does not know" (Matthew 24:50).

Try to imagine you have been displaced from Israel and must live in neighboring Syria in the decade after the destruction of Jerusalem—far from the Jews' former capital, now largely a heap of ruins, where Jews are forbidden to live.

Flavius Josephus wrote in his historic report on the war that 1,100,000 Jews were killed and 100,000 prisoners were removed along with precious trophies from the Jewish temple. The Roman soldiers set fire to the temple so they could get the melted gold. It burned completely down and was almost totally destroyed. Could the Jewish Christians imagine anything worse? Even though Paul had confronted the Jews' sacrifice cult, we know that he and James, the brother of Jesus, entered the temple of Herod around AD 48–50. According to the Acts of the Apostles, they had sacrificed in the temple, probably for the sake of the Jewish Christian members who were still dominant within the sect. For the Jewish Christians in Syria about AD 80, it was important to wait for final closure, when the Second Coming would convey the reward, a heavenly life reigning as associate kings of Christ with all wants fulfilled and all the sufferings in this life healed.

Something suggests that the words about the "faithful and wise servant" probably are aimed at church leaders *after* AD 70. The growing church organization had, as we have seen, the need of written accounts of Jesus' deeds to be used for regular worship services in the congregations. The message of Matthew 24:45 was likely meant to authorize church leaders and prevent irresponsible and unauthorized "spiritual food" frauds from influencing the church. And the words could now also be regarded as an allegorical parable, which, read in its entirety, could be used by the second and third generation of Christian church leaders.

The Church was moving toward its establishment as a proper cosmopolitan church. Under the leadership of Roman Emperor Constantine in AD 325, the church could enjoy the fruits of its patient waiting: Official recognition by the Roman State, and accompanying power in the secular community.

One can then discuss whether this development was particularly sympathetic, but it was certainly exciting and amazing, and as history shows, it supports what the historical facts emphasize: It's about power and the expansion of this power so that the organization that you belong to can get even more power, coincidentally the kind of power that leads to corruption and the most appalling atrocities.

That is the movement this book is about, certainly not excepted from, even though it neither stones nor burns its heretics. They are only stigmatized, sentenced to perpetual mockery and made a laughing stock for the self-righteous' sacred gathering. Their former brothers and sisters will nevermore see them or greet them. They are made invisible. Separated from who and what they knew. Exterminated! What horror!

Or, maybe, they are being given a chance to start once more on a new, but also narrow and lonely, road that leads neither to heaven nor to Armageddon's battlefield, but to the self-understanding that comes from daring to be yourself, and perhaps even approach God on their own terms.

Epilogue

With this review of Matthew 24, I hope the reader can better understand why I consider the *historical-critical method*[354] is the key to freeing a human being from the mental dominance the fundamentalist Watchtower Society inflicts on its members. This, at least, was my experience more than fifty years ago, between 1959 and 1960.

I hope in this discussion I have succeeded in showing how the Bible interpretations of the Jehovah's Witnesses generally rest on an extremely flawed foundation—to put it mildly—and that the movement's leaders, in my opinion, mislead and exploit their followers. How can the members know this truth when they are regularly warned against the development of personal, individual perceptions and against seeking a higher education as management subjects them to systematic and constant threat of being reduced to bleached bones in the impending Judgment Day War? Education could give them the tools to become autonomous and independent people, free thinkers who might realize how the Society schemes to keep its working sheep in ignorance.

Contact with others who have broken away from the movement clearly shows me that disconnection is much harder than one would assume. At the start, the disconnection process requires that one suspects something is wrong with the situation, and as we know, this very line of thought is thwarted by the organization's deep and continuous mind-control tactics. As a result of lengthy exposure to such brainwashing, the members' condition renders them unable to realistically evaluate the situation. The Jehovah's Witnesses' rhetoric becomes a habitual drug of the mind, something incontrovertible and unquestionable.

Yet despite the great personal difficulties associated with recognizing that one's past beliefs are built on absurd notions and deceptive theology, I hope this book helps people free themselves from what I personally perceive as the pure madness. I also hope readers will accept this book as a kind of model description for other fundamentalist phenomena we are confronted with daily. These controlling and intrusive ideologies can be observed everywhere and some are much more influential, even considerably more serious and frightening than that movement whose history and theology I have tried to elucidate.

This book is not meant as an attack on religion's innermost essence—on the contrary. Humans have found support in religion's ancient universe, which is an unquenchable and rich resource of knowledge able to offer comfort even today when modern life becomes too rational and materialistic. Rather, I would advance this book is an attack on religious leaders and companies who grossly abuse the human need for a deeper explanation of the meaning of life. Hopefully this book documents how wrong things can go if one indiscriminately throws oneself into the arms of such ventures.

Naturally, I have considered whether I should have written this book about a small—viewed on a world scale—extremist religious movement, which nevertheless has managed to capture the entire world's attention. While seeming meek against other more vocal—and, yes, even violent—religious organizations, this movement dominates people who are born into it or who voluntarily choose to engage in it. It controlled my parents, and it controlled me for a short period in my youth, until I fought my way out. Therefore, I want to clarify that I do not criticize the average-member Witnesses; primarily and in principle I censure the legal and legitimate company that, since 1884, has led the movement, setting policy, doctrine and restrictions to further its own aims.

Admittedly, when everything has been said and truths exposed, many people, whom I perceive as *prisoners* in a controlling fundamentalist system, may yet be very happy in their faith and have no desire to reject it. I would not dream of intervening in their contented existence. Always, it is a believer's *personal* decision to assess whether they want to view their faith from a more critical angle.

In any case, I think, the possibility exists for anyone wishing to do so, and perhaps this book can shine lights on dogmatic darkness.

130 Years Later

It is hard to imagine Pittsburgh as it was more than 130 years ago, even though only a moment has passed since, if we look at it in the long context of man's religious and social history. The formerly dusty and smoky city, known as the City of Bridges and the Steel City, would be completely unrecognizable to Russell and his Bible Students. Steel manufacturing and blast furnaces have been replaced by high-tech industry, and gray-belching smokestacks that characterized the city's skyline at the end of the 19th and much of the 20th century are gone. Today, Pittsburgh is said to be one of the greenest and cleanest cities in America. As far as I can tell from contemporary photographs of the city's skyline, it looks more like New York City in the early 20th century.

When I do web searches on Pittsburgh, I find a lot of the usual information one would expect for a thriving city: advertising for fashion, contemporary art, fine hotels and good restaurants. Pittsburgh has a fine airport and public transportation services, promotes arts and culture, supports athletic teams in several sports and maintains its rich historic architectural heritage. The cost of a one-way plane ticket from New York in business class is affordable and the flight is quick, so unlike making the same journey in 1884. Much of this is familiar description, resembling most large American cities to one degree or another. Yet, Pittsburgh is certainly unique in its own ways and undoubtedly much beloved by those who live and visit there.

Whether modern Pittsburgh's residents are also proud that the religious corporation, Watch Tower Bible and Tract Society of Pennsylvania, was founded there back in 1884, I cannot say. The founding occurred only thirty years before 1914—the year when the world would perish, according to association founder Charles Taze Russell. We know now he was so wrong, and luckily enough for us today the end did not come, although some supporters were terribly disappointed that they didn't go to heaven when the designated day came. Before long, however, we will reach 2014, one hundred years after the Day of Judgment should have destroyed Babylon (the false religions), Pittsburgh, America and the rest of the world's countries and kingdoms. At the same time we can recognize this as a fascinating and horrible adventure to illustrate how foolish people can be when they too strongly and uncritically engage in a utopian idea that occupies them, mind and soul, and destroys their judgment.

Once again, according to the Witnesses, we are at the end of the road. Yet, the world is still firm beneath our feet and revolving around the sun. And although there is much that could be improved, we nonetheless live on a wonderful planet we should cherish and preserve, rather than preaching about and cheering for its destruction—something I do not think any *loving god* will allow. Still, with humans, one never knows. They are, at times, the most dangerous, I think, or at least some are. I also know there are a lot of good and bright people in the world.

Thankfully!

Appendixes

Maria F. Russell's "Circular Letter"

Maria F. (Ackley) Russell's controversial pamphlet against her husband, Charles Taze Russell, was released in Pittsburgh, Pennsylvania, around 1902–1903. Maria Russell's pamphlet is said to be very difficult to obtain today, yet I managed to acquire it through my overseas contacts. Below, it is reproduced exactly as I received it, apart from my page references enclosed in brackets. Layout, spelling and possible errors are as found in the original pamphlet of fifteen pages. After its release, Maria Russell had to hear many nasty things about her pamphlet and her reasons for publishing it (see *Proclaimers,* 1993, p. 645), but here, some 100 years later, it remains, despite its subjective nature, a *remarkable* document that sheds light on the breach between the spouses.

I first saw the pamphlet (a copy) after my book was published in Danish in 2006; therefore, I had to rewrite the original chapter where I discussed it because of the new material. It was later expanded into three new chapters, 6, 7 and 8.

I have chosen to let Maria Russell's pamphlet stand in its original form, i.e., in the English language as it was written circa 1900.

December 2012

Has the truth been suppressed?

It has surprised me that Maria Russell's pamphlet is not available today. Yes, it is almost impossible to find! But I know at least two authors, who have written extensively about Jehovah's Witnesses, that possess copies of the pamphlet. Why it has not been published, or even quoted before now, anyone can guess. I think it is because the now over-110-year-old campaign the Watchtower Society has consistently led against Maria Russell keeps such a firm grip on everyone who approaches the topic that it even affects the North American writers who have told the story of Jehovah's Witnesses critically and with detail. However, they forget one of the key witnesses: Maria Frances (Ackley) Russell. Maybe they were victims of the same misinformation that all readers of *The Watch-*

tower have been exposed to over time. I hope by including the pamphlet's contents here, it can help lift or thin the veil.

Note that three stars (***) have been inserted below on page one. On the copy of the pamphlet I received the front cover was not reproduced. Bleed-through of the cover appeared on the photocopy but the line between "Readers" and "Attention" was illegible.

READERS

***
ATTENTION
[End of page 1]
"And judgment is turned away backward and justice standeth afar off; for truth is fallen in the streets and equity cannot enter. Yea, truth faileth and he that departeth from evil maketh himself a prey. And the Lord saw it, and it displeased him that there was no judgment." Isaiah 59:14, 15.
[End of page 2]
Without note or comment from some of like precious faith with you who are preparing and sending out this circular letter, we invite you to a careful comparison of the following extract from the editorial columns of "Zion's Watch Tower" with some other extracts from letters of the editor to his wife against whose Christian character the attack of this item is manifestly aimed. The item evidently is intended as an answer to many inquiries of her friends abroad as to the reason why she is no longer heard from through that journal.

Read for yourselves and draw your own conclusions.

"Zion's Watch Tower," Nov. 1, 1902, fourth column of first article:

"As an illustration of a misguided conscience and its baneful effects in social affairs we mention the case of an editor's wife. She at one time took pleasure in assisting him in his work. By and by a deluded and misguided conscience told her that God wished her to be editor-in-chief and publish what she pleased. When the editor demurred that he dare not abandon his stewardship the deluded conscience told its owner that she should no longer co-operate; but more, that she should break her marriage covenant in deserting her husband and home, and that she should say all manner of evil against him, falsely, until such time as he would yield to her the liberties of the journal—which her conscience told her was God's will."

Compare this with the following clear statement of the editor of "Zion's Watch Tower," Mr. Chas. T. Russell, in a letter to his wife dated Sept. 26, 1896, he oddly preferring to write rather than speak to her—providentially, we believe, so that this testimony can be verified in his own handwriting, which Mrs. Russell has carefully preserved, together with her replies.

Quotation:—"I understand you to request that, instead of being associate editor of the 'Tower,' you be treated as a contributor to its columns, whose name shall appear with each article, and that any article offered not acceptable as a whole shall be treated as the article of any other contributor, viz., either published and publicly criticized, or rejected."
[End of page 3]
Mrs. Russell states that this was exactly what she requested—nothing more and nothing less. He understood her perfectly. But observe that, instead of demanding, either directly or indirectly, that she should be editor-in-chief, she had, as his own words show, refused longer to be called even the associate editor, preferring to be merely a contributor to the columns of the "Tower," whenever her articles were acceptable as a whole to the editor.

The point she sought to guard against by this measure was the mutilation of her articles often to make them express sentiments which she could not endorse, and the claim of the editor that he had a right to do this because she was an irresponsible associate and had no signature to her articles.

So much for the testimony of his own hand and pen against himself in the matter of the editorship.

Now here is more of the same kind of testimony bearing on the other matters—a mere sample of the voluminous testimony on hand in his own penmanship.

July 8, 1896. "I decline a discussion. * * * I am convinced that our difficulty is a growing one generally—that it is a great mistake for strong-minded men and women to marry. If they will marry, the strong-minded would far better marry such as are not too intellectual and high-spirited; for there never can, in the nature of things, be peace under present time conditions where the two are on an equality."

July 9, 1896. Mrs. Russell's reply to the above:

"My dear husband:—After my request of Sunday evening for an interview concerning the difficulties between us and my urging the same in view of the Lord's words,—'If thou bring thy gift to the altar and there rememberest that thy brother hath aught against thee, leave there thy gift before the altar and go thy way, first be reconciled to thy brother, and then come and offer thy gift; and again, 'Agree with thine adversary quickly' (and if with thine adversary, then certainly with thy friend, thy brother or sister or wife); and 'Let not the sun go down upon your wrath,' etc.—I received your letter of Monday evening, and what a revelation it is of the real cause of your opposition to me—that it is envy, jealousy.

"This you freely confess, saying, 'I am convinced that it is a great mistake for strong-minded men [End of page 4] and women to marry. If they will marry, the strong-minded would far better marry such as are not too intellectual and high-spirited; for there never can, in the nature of things, be peace, under present time conditions, where the two are on an equality.'

"Is it possible that you are so full of envy and vainglory, so desirous of out-rivaling every one else, so full of that spirit of 'which shall be greatest?' which the Lord reproved in his early disciples, that you cannot brook being among your peers? Is it indeed possible that 'the nature of things' in your heart forbids your living at peace with one on an 'equality' with you, even though, as you confess, you never met as near your ideal?

"Then if this later statement be true, and you recognize me as a sister in Christ, you must have discerned in me the spirit of Christ, which of course, should be the Christian's ideal. Very true, while you have discerned the spirit of Christ, you must also have observed the imperfections to which the flesh is heir, and which you must also realize in yourself, and against which we must all war a good warfare.

"You have known my manner of life now for seventeen years. You have observed my faithfulness to God,—to his truth, his cause and his righteousness; you have seen how faithfully and studiously I have endeavored to know and do his will and to teach it by precept and example; you have known my loyalty and devotion to you and my efforts to assist and uphold you and to second all your efforts in the good work of the Lord by every means in my power.

"You must also have noted how I have shunned the world and things pertaining to its spirit that I might devote myself entirely to the Lord as, in my imperfect way, I have done in all these years. And now what? You have observed that the humble talents thus employed have somewhat increased, and you are displeased, envious, because the comparison between us does not show a difference sufficiently wide to satisfy your ambition to be much the greater. 'There never can, in the nature of things, be peace where the two are on an equality.'

"O my husband, beware of this spirit of pride, of strife and vain glory. I beg of you to fight against it or it will ruin you. You seem to be getting into a position [End of page 5] now where I can do but little for you except to pray, and this I do without ceasing. When the disciples came to Jesus, saying, who is the greatest in the kingdom of heaven? Jesus called a little child unto him and set him in the midst of them and said, 'Verily I say unto you (you who have believed on me and have left all and followed me, you who are longing for the kingdom of God and who hope to inherit it, verily, I say unto you), except ye be converted (from this envious vain-glorying spirit of rivalry) and become as little children, ye shall not enter into the kingdom of heaven.'

"Let me urge you therefore my dear, to resist this spirit and to 'humble yourself under the mighty hand of God that he may exalt you *in due time*.' I want to see you win in this battle and Satan vanquished under your feet; for the hosts of sin are pressing hard to draw you from the prize. You are a mark for the adversary and you are being besieged by the powers of darkness at an unguarded place. Satan hath desired to have thee that he might sift thee as wheat; but I have prayed for thee and will continue to do so.

"I must add that I cannot admit the claim of your second note that the barrier between us is of my raising, and that therefore it devolves upon me to make all 'the advances in the way of social amenities, such as, good morning, good evening, etc., for, though I sincerely wish you good mornings and good evenings and every other blessing, you have placed me in a position where I cannot now tell you so because it would be misconstrued as an admission on my part that the barrier is of my raising, which, in my estimation, is not true.

"With many prayers and great anxiety for you

Your loving Wife—

though 'only in a legal sense' you say. Yes, so it seems: in heart you have deserted me because of envy and vain glory; but nevertheless, I am still legally—according to the laws of God and man— your wife, deserted thus for the simple reason that there is too much of an equality. This reminds me of that which was prophetically said of our Lord, 'They hated me *without a cause*; and also of the words of Solomon, 'Wrath is cruel, and anger is outrageous; but who is able to stand before envy?' "

July 9, 1896. Mr. Russell's reply to the above:—"Confidence is the only ground of co-operation, love and [End of page 6] harmony. You wish me to discuss the matter and to prove myself worthy of your confidence. I refuse to discuss and will always refuse to discuss and refute the ground- less imaginings and misunderstandings which you and some in whom you have confidence delude yourselves with."

Replying to this Mrs. Russell wrote to her husband as follows:

July 10, 1896. "Perhaps you do not realize it, but you are actually asking a moral impossibility when you demand perfect confidence in all you do and say. That would be almost clothing you with infallibility. The fact is that, while I most earnestly desire to have perfect confidence in you, there are some things in your course of conduct which I cannot reconcile with the principles of righteous- ness expressed in the Word of God, and therefore, in all honesty and candor and love, I must say that, the ground of my confidence having been impaired, my confidence in you has been somewhat weakened, much to my regret and sorrow. But to repair the foundation and make it good and strong again, is *your part*, not mine.

"Most gladly will I step out on the planks when you have shown them to be secure, if they are so; or if they are not, then when you have recognized the fact and made them so. This is my reason for requesting an interview and a very plain, candid consideration of those difficulties in my mind which at present constitute a barrier which I cannot remove."

Replying to this Mr. Russell wrote:

July 10, 1896. "You have declared yourself a doubter, and that without a cause,—merely some evil surmise or suspicion. I take God and Christ for my pattern in deciding that I will never be pleased with doubters, nor choose them for my confidants, nor consider them my true friends. To the queries of the *faith*ful I am ever attentive, as is the Lord, but he that doubts without cause is the waverer who is unstable and unreasonable and who is undeserving of confidence or friendship."

Mrs. Russell understands that *the lordship* of Christ is not to be patterned after and thus as- sumed by any of his people. "One is your master and all ye are brethren." But being anxious to bridge over the chasm and thinking perhaps he had dwelt upon this matter of her lack of [End of page 7] confidence until it had assumed undue proportions in his mind, she wrote him as follows:

July 12, 1896. "Dear Husband, I have been thinking over this matter of confidence in the light in which you have put it, and I can say that I have confidence in the integrity of your heart and purpose.

"I am glad to be able to tell you this and to learn that on this basis you are willing to consider our difficulties, that, as nearly as possible, we may see eye to eye. I greatly desire to fully realize the oneness of spirit in the body of Christ so that there may be no schism between even two of its members, all of whom should be knit together in Christian love and mutual confidence. I am ready at any time that suits you."

To her note to this effect Mr. Russell appended the following reply:

July 13, 1896. "Under all the circumstances this treatment of the subject is not calculated to establish my confidence in you. I must wait for some evidence of a true repentance in a full and hearty recantation, or else I must hold you at a distance and doubt your object and meaning and look for some solution of the meaning and object of your attack as I would with any other attacker and traducer.

"I hope you will express yourself very freely and say just what you mean. I leave no one in doubt as to whom I esteem my friends, and wish to know all my enemies;—not to hurt them, but to withdraw all my confidence from them. If your pencil has told of the full measure of your feelings I reject it with shame, contempt and pain."

NON SUPPORT.

These letters were followed by withdrawal of support, except upon humiliating conditions to which he knew his wife would never descend, and when he refused her even her clothing, claiming that it belonged to him, and she took the wife's privilege of supplying herself from the stores at his expense, he published the following notice in the Pittsburg daily papers:

"Notice.—The public is hereby cautioned to give credit to no one in my name except upon my specific written order, as I will not be responsible for such debts nor pay them.

"CHARLES TAZE RUSSELL,
"No. 58 Arch St., Bible House, Allegheny."

[End of page 8]

Then, to conceal from the general public the fact that this was aimed at his wife, the following statement appeared in the evening papers of the same day. See "Pittsburg Times," February 7, 1898, first page. A copy is on hand here.

"IMPOSED ON CHARITY."

"THE CREDIT OF AN ALLEGHENY PASTOR USED TO GET GOODS WITHOUT HIS KNOWLEDGE."

"Charles T. Russell, pastor of the congregation known as Christians, holding services at No. 58 Arch St., Allegheny, has been taken advantage of by some of the benefactors of his charitable work. During the recent cold weather, Mr. Russell, for the congregation and in a spirit of charity, relieved considerable suffering among the poor of both cities. Toward the later part of last week Mr. Russell began to receive bills from grocers, butchers and others. Several persons who had been helped, and others who had heard of his distribution of food and clothing, took it upon themselves to order goods and have them charged to the account of Mr. Russell. None of the amounts were large and Mr. Russell paid them. Hereafter, however, neither the Christian's congregation, nor its pastor, will stand good for anything bought in their names unless a written order is presented by the purchaser."

We know of no such chartable work ever undertaken by either Mr. Russell or the congregation, and they are taught that the greatest and all-comprehensive charity is the distribution of his literature. It is quite unlikely that, that winter was any exception to all the winters before and since. None of Mrs. Russell's bills were from butchers or grocers, but from dry goods merchants only, and in all amounted to less than two hundred dollars.

HIS IDEA OF MARRIAGE.

Subsequently he wrote to her:—"I may explain why I never address you as 'wife' and why I think it strange that you should address me as 'husband.' My reason for not calling you 'wife' is that you have broken the marriage [End of page 9] tie. What does the word 'wife' mean? Does it not signify a helpmate? What does the word 'husband' mean? Does it not signify a caretaker? Since you have left me, I certainly have not taken care of you; you have no husband so far as I am aware. Nor have I had a wife for some time. You were certainly not a helpmate to me for quite a while before you left.

"To call you a wife under such circumstances, would be to discredit our English language, and for you to call me a husband under the circumstances is equally inappropriate."

INSULTING LETTERS TO HER FRIENDS.

After a deep plot and wide endeavor, by intrigue, insinuation and falsehood, to alienate all the friends which the years of her work had gathered, Mr. Russell, not willing to stop there, addressed letters to her intimate friends and relatives and even to his own father, warning them, under threat of legal proceedings for alienating his wife's affections, not to harbor her in their homes or to have any communication with her by letter or otherwise, and copies of the same were given to Mrs. Russell. But neither she nor any of her friends either replied or heeded them.

These letters were so insulting in their character as to be unfit for publication. They were not sent by mail but were delivered in person by his employees in the office of "Zion's Watch Tower," they, in each case, having read the contents before delivering.

So much, briefly, for the testimony of his own hand and pen as to who broke the marriage covenant, as he will have it. More might be said here, but Mr. Russell himself is the only witness summoned at this hearing. When Mrs. Russell left the house in the fall of 1897 to seek legal counsel of her brother it was with full intent to return in a few days. And this was a very necessary prudential measure in view of a report he was causing to be circulated to the effect that she was of unsound mind, and of measures that were manifestly being taken to deal with her on this pretext.

To this danger she felt she was exposed unprotected. This measure, which she wisely took for self-protection, has resulted, unwittingly on her part, in permanent separation [End of page 10], with little hope, as the reader may judge, of any peaceable settlement.

This, however, could never be construed as "breaking the marriage covenant." According to the

Word of God that covenant can be broken only by one thing, viz., unchastity. Mrs. Russell is too well known in the vicinity of Pittsburg and Allegheny, where she was born and reared and has spent all her life, for any such claim to be openly made; and if this remark is intended as a covered attack, an insinuation to this effect, there is testimony from his own pen on this line also.

This was given in reply to a letter from a lady then in his congregation to whom Mr. Russell had spoken thus slightingly of his wife. We append extracts from both these letters:

PITTSBURG, Nov. 14, 1897.

"Dear Brother Russell:

"My heart condemned me for not replying to you when you said you were sorry to say your wife had not been faithful to you.

"What may seem unfaithfulness to you may prove to be faithfulness to her God. A wife can come to that point where, though her husband may be a Christian, she may have to choose between him and Christ. For though they are one flesh the individuality is not lost, nor can personal responsibility be set aside."

To this Mr. Russell replied as follows:

Nov. 17, 1897.

"Dear Sister C.:

"Your favor of the 14th inst. is at hand and contains one statement which I wish to correct as quickly as possible. You say that I said I was sorry to say that my wife had not been faithful to me.

"I beg to say that you must be mistaken, and I trust that you will not circulate such a slander upon my wife's fair name. This may have been the shape my words took before your mind, but I am confident that I use language too carefully to permit any such slip. To speak of unfaithfulness on the part of married people has a special and peculiarly evil significance. I am positive that I did not use that language.

"Moreover, if I said *anything* evil respecting her I request that you consider it retracted and withdrawn."

[End of page 11]

AN OPEN DOOR.

After a year and a half of quiet residence with her sister and without support from her husband, Providence pointed Mrs. Russell to an open door which she might enter and establish a home of her own. A house of theirs vacated by a tenant was lawfully taken possession of by Mrs. Russell, and the dilemma was before her husband, either of quiet acquiescence or else prompt legal proceedings, for Mrs. Russell had determined to stand on her legal rights. The former measure was preferred, although various efforts were made to intimidate and dispossess her. And since the eyes of the public and of his congregation were upon him, some furnishment of the house was seen to be a necessity of the situation and was also provided.

The following is her note to him informing him of this step.

"April 1, 1899. Husband:—Acting on legal advice from one of the most eminent Pittsburg attorneys I have taken up my abode at No. 79 [new No. 1004] Cedar Ave. Some furniture has been provided me and I am keeping house here by myself with occasional company of Mabel. I have no fears as I have good neighbors on both sides.

"I have taken down the 'To let' notice and purpose by renting the rooms to secure a little income, aside from which, as you know, I have none. If you take this matter kindly and feel like co-operating in it I feel sure it will be for your good no less than mine.

"Your wife, MARIA F. RUSSELL."

To this she received reply as follows:

April 3, 1899. "Dear Mrs. Russell:—Your note of the first inst., informing me that you had burglarized house No. 79 Cedar Ave. and had taken possession of the same, and intend to hold possession of it, and impliedly requesting that I give my assent, came duly. This is my earliest opportunity for reply.

"I regret that you have taken this step, and I now give you formal and legal notice to immediately remove from the said premises any of your belongings, for I can neither rent you the property nor permit you to occupy it. By giving prompt attention to this matter you will save both yourself and me trouble.

"Very Respectfully, C. T. Russell."

[End of page 12]

Mrs. Russell still resides at No. 79—new No. 1004—Cedar Ave., Allegheny, supporting herself by her own exertions, not receiving a dollar from her husband, nor from the literary work so largely hers.

She also still holds in the main the doctrines therein set forth, though some points have been greatly modified by the eye-opening experiences through which she has passed. The fact that some hold the truth in unrighteousness does not invalidate the truth now any more than of old. Though the scribes and pharisees whom Jesus described as whited sepulchres, full of all manner of uncleanness, held and taught the divine law, that law remains as pure today as if they had never touched it. And so it is of all truth that is God's truth.

No attempt is here made to enter into details of explanation. Space will not permit that, but candid minds will see that "truth is fallen in the streets and equity cannot enter."

If a biased or untruthful reply is made to this through the columns of "Zion's Watch Tower," bear in mind that no such medium is open for further explanation and defence. But let us here say in advance that testimony in abundance is on hand to meet any form of defence by any person or persons as against the words of the editor of "Zion's Watch Tower" herin presented.

If "Tower" readers are sincere and honest, and if they would guard against being "partakers of other men's sins" (1 Tim. 5:22) let them take measures to learn the truth and to act accordingly. True, you have no organization and no arrangements for calling any one to account. Consequently you are dominated by one, and that one may be blind to the operations of the principles of righteousness, and following such leading together you may fall into the ditch.

If you would "watch and be sober" here is something to watch against.

"Let him that thinketh he standeth take heed lest he fall."

"Cease ye from man whose breath is in his nostrils, for wherin is he to be accounted of?"

"Put not your trust in princes, nor in the son of man, in whom there is no help."

"Blessed is the man that trusteth in the Lord and whose hope the Lord is."

[End of page 13]

We affirm that we have read the original correspondence from Charles T. Russell, 610 Arch St. (old No. 58 Arch St.), Allegheny City, and copies of replies thereto written by Maria F. Russell, 1004 Cedar Ave. (old No. 79), Allegheny City, and that the quotations herein are accurate.

CHARLES L. CORBETT,
7909 Maderia St.,
Pittsburg, Pa.

F. C. SMITH,
610 Wood St.,
Wilkinsburg, Pa.

COMMONWEALTH PENNSYLVANIA }
COUNTY OF ALLEGHENY.   } *ss.*

On this 10th day of December, A. D., 1902, before me a Notary Public in and for the said County and State came the above named Chas. L. Corbett and F. C. Smith, and acknowledge the foregoing Indenture to be their act and deed and desire the same to be recognized as such.

Witness my hand and notary seal the day, year aforesaid.

Jas. S. Weldon,
SEAL }

CHICAGO, Dec. 2, 1902.

TO WHOM IT MAY CONCERN:

I have seen and read the original letters referred to in the foregoing and hereby affirm the correctness of quotations from same, as also those from her replies.

JNO. H. BROWN,
96 and 98 Lake St.

The foregoing was signed before me, a Notary Public in and for the County of Cook and State of Illinois, on this second day of December, A. D., 1902.

L. S. DICKSON.
SEAL }

[End of page 14]
At the mouth of two witnesses, or
at the mouth of three witnesses,
shall the matter be established.
Deuteronomy
[End of page 15]

Olin R. Moyle's Letter to J. F. Rutherford, 1929:

OLIN R. MOYLE Counselor
117 Adams Street. Brooklyn. New York
Telephone Triangle 5-1474
July 21, 1939

Judge J. F. Rutherford, Brooklyn, N. Y.

Dear Brother Rutherford:
This letter is to give you notice of our intention to leave Bethel on September 1st next. These reasons for leaving are stated herein and we ask that you give them careful and thoughtful consideration.

Conditions at Bethel are a matter of concern to all of the Lord's people. Nowhere among imperfect men can there be perfect freedom from oppression, discrimination and unfair treatment, but at the Lord's headquarters on earth conditions should be such that injustice would be reduced to the minimum. That is not the case here at Bethel and a protest should be made against it. I am in a good position to make such protest because your treatment of me has been generally kind, considerate and fair. I can make this protest in the interests of the Bethel family and of the Kingdom work without any personal interest entering into the matter.

Treatment of Bethel Family
Shortly after coming to Bethel we were shocked to witness the spectacle of our brethren receiving what is designated as a "trimming" from you. The first, if memory serves me correct, was a tongue lashing given to C. J. Woodworth. Woodworth in a personal letter to you stated something to the effect that it would be serving the devil to continue using our present day calendar. For that he was humiliated, called a jackass, and given a public lambasting. Others have been similarly treated. McCaughey, McCormick, Knorr, Prosser, Price, Van Sipma, Ness and others have been similarly scolded. They have been publicly called to account, condemned, and reprimanded without any previous notice. This summer some of the most unfair public reproaches have been given. J. Y. McCauley asked a question which carried with it a criticism of the present method of Watch Tower study. For that he was severely reprimanded. Your action constituted a violation of the principle for which we are fighting, to wit, freedom of speech. It was the action of a boss and not that of a fellow servant. Securing an efficient mode of study with imperfect study leaders is no easy task, and no method yet produced has proved to be one hundred per cent perfect. You stated that no complaints had come to you concerning this method of study. If that be the case you have not had all the facts presented to you. There is complaint in various places that the Watch Tower studies have degenerated into mere reading lessons. It may be that the present method is the best that can be used, but in view of known limitations honest criticism should not be censored nor honest critics punished.

Brother Worsley received a public denunciation from you because he prepared and handed to brethren a list of helpful Scripture citations on fundamental topics. How can we consistently condemn religionists for being intolerant when you exercise intolerance against those who work with you? Doesn't this prove that the only freedom permitted at Bethel is freedom to do and say that which you wish to be said and done? The Lord certainly never authorized you to exercise such high handed authority over your fellow servants.

Since the Madison Square Garden meeting there has been a distressing condition of restraint and suspicion at Bethel. The ushers were placed in a tough spot but did an excellent piece of work. They exercised care and diligence in watching arrivals at the Garden, and prevented a number of suspicious characters from entering. They were on the job immediately when the disturbance started and quelled a disturbance which would have otherwise reached serious proportions. But for two weeks following the convention there has been constant criticism and condemnation of them from you. They have been charged with dereliction of duty and labeled as "sissies". To see some of these boys break down and cry because of your unkind remarks is, to say the least, saddening.

The brethren at Bethel have thoroughly demonstrated their loyalty and devotion to the Lord, and do not need to be berated for wrong doing. A suggestion or a kindly admonition from you would be more than sufficient to check any wrongful action, and would eliminate resentment and induce greater happiness and comfort for the whole family. You have stated many times that there are no bosses in the Lord's organization but the undeniable fact cannot be evaded that your actions in scolding and upbraiding these boys are the actions of a boss. It makes one sick at heart and disgusted to listen to them. If you will cease smiting your fellow servants Bethel will be a happier place and the Kingdom work will prosper accordingly.

Discrimination

We publish to the world that all in the Lord's organization are treated alike, and receive the same as far as this world's goods are concerned. You know that is not the case. The facts cannot be denied. Take for instance the difference between the accommodations furnished to you, and your personal attendants, compared with those furnished to some of your brethren. You have many many homes, to wit, Bethel, Staten Island, California, etc. I am informed that even at the Kingdom Farm one house is kept for your sole use during the short periods you spend there. And what do the brethren at the farm receive? Small rooms, unheated thru the bitter cold winter weather. They live in their trunks like campers. That may be all right if necessary, but there are many houses on the farm standing idle or used for other purposes, which could be used to give some comfort to those who work so long and so hard. You work in a nice air conditioned room. You and your attendants spend a portion of the week in the quiet of country surroundings. The boys at the factory diligently work thru the hot summer months without such helps, or any effort made to give them. That is discrimination which should receive your thoughtful consideration.

Marriage

Here again is shown unequal and discriminatory treatment. One brother left Bethel some time ago for the purpose of getting married, and, so I am informed, was refused the privilege of pioneering in New York, apparently as an official disapproval of his action in leaving Bethel. On the other hand when Bonnie Boyd got married she didn't have to leave Bethel. She was permitted to bring her husband into Bethel in spite of the printed rule providing that both marrying parties should have lived there for five years. Harsh treatment of one and favored treatment of another is discrimination, and should not have a place in the Lord's organization.

Filthy and Vulgar Language

The Biblical injunctions against unclean, filthy speaking and jesting have never been abrogated. It is shocking and nauseating to hear vulgar speaking and smut at Bethel. It was stated by a sister that was one of the things you had to get used to at Bethel. The loudest laughter at the table comes when a filth or near filthy joke goes through, and your skirts are not clear.

Liquor

Under your tutelage there has grown up a glorification of alcohol and condemnation of total abstinence which is unseemly. Whether a servant of Jehovah drinks alcoholic liquor is none of my business, except in giving a helping hand to a brother who is stumbled thereby. Whether I am a total abstainer is nobody's business but my own. But not so at Bethel. There appears to be a definite policy of breaking in newcomers into the use of liquor, and resentment is shown against those who do not join them. The claim is made, "One can't be a real Bethelite without drinking beer." Shortly after we arrived it was arrogantly stated, "we can't do much with Moyle, but we'll make a man out of Peter." A New York brother intimated that I was out of harmony with the truth and with the Society because I didn't drink liquor. A New York sister stated that she had never used liquor or served it until some of the Bethel boys insisted upon it. A brother who used to drink liquor to excess became a total abstainer after getting the truth. He knew that a single drink of liquor would start him off to his former drinking habits, but in spite of that brethren from Bethel insisted upon his imbibing liquor and inferred that he was out of harmony with the organization through refusing.

Total abstainers are looked upon with scorn as weaklings. You have publicly labeled total abstainers as prudes and therefore must assume your share of the responsibility for the Bacchus like attitude exhibited by members of the family.

These are a few of the things which should have no place in the Lord's organization. There are other more grievous injustices but I have had no personal contact with them and therefore do not discuss them.

It hasn't been an easy or pleasant task to write these things to you, and it's still harder to make this protest effective by leaving Bethel.

We sold our home and business when we came to Bethel and fully intended to spend the rest of our lives at this place in the Lord's service. We leave in order to register most emphatically our disagreement with the unjust conditions related in this letter. We are not leaving the Lord's service but will continue to serve Him and His organization as fully as strength and means will allow.

Neither am I running away from battling the Devil's crowd in the courts. I expect to return to the private practice of law, probably in Milwaukee, Wisconsin, and hope to be in the fight in every way possible. With this letter I am enclosing a statement of the major cases now pending in which I am actively participating. It would be unreasonable and unfair to drop these matters into your lap without further assistance or consideration. I am ready and willing to press these issues in the courts just as vigorously and carefully as though I remained at Bethel, and will do so if that is your desire.

We have considered this action for some time, but this letter is delivered to you just as we are leaving on a vacation trip for very specific reasons. First: It is desirable that you take time for thought and consideration of the matters herein set forth before taking any action. Hasty and ill considered action might be regrettable. Second: Frankly I have no desire for a verbal argument with you over these matters. I have had plenty of occasion to observe that a controversial matter does not receive a calm and reasoned discussion of the facts. Too often it turns into a denunciation of some person by you.

I am not interested in that kind of a wordy battle. These statements are the reasons presented by Sister Moyle and myself for leaving Bethel. If we speak erroneously or wrongfully we are responsible before the Lord for so speaking. If we speak truthfully, and we stoutly content that everything here related is the truth, then there is an immediate responsibility on your part to remedy the conditions necessitating this protest. May the Lord direct and guide you into fair and kindly treatment of your fellow servants is my wish and prayer.

Your Brother in the King's service,
Olin R. Moyle

P.S. Should you desire to write to me concerning these matters during vacation a letter will reach me at Ticonderoga, New York, General Delivery after July 29th.

"Rumors" on the Author, Marley Cole

Marley Cole was a Witness when he wrote his book in the 1950s. Here is the documentation, which was printed in my first book on Jehovah's Witnesses, released only in Denmark in 1966:

First letter:
SC 24 August 1960.
Mr Poul Bregninge
Aldershvilevej 103 B
Bagsvaerd.

We have received your letter of August 21, in which you ask if the journalist who has written the book "Jehovah's Witnesses - The New World Society," has been a Jehovah's Witness in about eight [years] before he wrote the book, and that he also had been a pioneer.

We have also heard this rumor but we have nothing in hands by which we can confirm or refute the allegation. We believe, however, that this plays no special role, but if anyone mean it do you can possibly be given this information by applying to the publisher of the book in America.

With regards,
Watchtower Bible & Tract Society

Second letter:
"AB/SE On December 2, 1960
Mr Poul Bregninge
Aldershvilevej 103 B
Bagsvaerd

We have received a response from our headquarters in Brooklyn about Marley Cole, and a request to answer your question.

It is stated that as far as it is known, Marley Cole is a witness and was it at the time he wrote his book. Furthermore, it is announced that the Society has never declared that he was not a witness or made attempt to conceal this fact. The fact is that the Society has not affected the issue in one or another sense, since Cole's books is not published by our company. All advertise material in connection with the book, including Marley Cole's biography that is printed on the wrapper and only mentions his secular background and his qualifications as author of the book, was prepared by the publishers. Since Marley Cole has not seen any reason to mention his connection with Jehovah's Witnesses in the context of the book, the Society has seen no reason, nor has it had any occasion in particular, to make this side of the matter known.

As mentioned book was published, the Society invited the witnesses to read it and recommend it to others, because it was the most detailed history of Jehovah's witnesses which were published in book form at the time, and because the picture was truthful, unbiased and unprejudiced. And since it also was written from a journalistic standpoint, it would seem appealing to many people who would like to learn the truth about Jehovah's witnesses without the preaching for them. We are always interested to see truthful and bias-free books, magazines and newspaper articles about Jehovah's witnesses which indirectly contribute to the spread of the good news of God's kingdom, just as we do everything we can to spread the message about the Kingdom through direct service worldwide.

Yours in the efforts to promote the good news of God's kingdom, Watchtower Bible & Tract SocietyA charitable company
(Translated from Danish)

Jette Svane: Note regarding "genuine" or "false anointed" (Chapter 34)

The management of the Watchtower Society in the coming years is faced with a considerable dilemma. Because, if reports continually arrive saying members of the "great crowd" are beginning to "partake" of the "emblematic bread and wine" and thereby indicate that they have received a *heavenly calling*, it means that an equal number of the "old anointed" have become "renegade anointed." Or are the "new anointed" in fact "false anointed?"

On this topic, *The Watchtower* wrote in 1975:

"As discussed in the book *Life Everlasting—in Freedom of the Sons of God,* pages 147 to 151, evidence indicates that by 1934 God's attention turned to developing the 'great crowd' of persons who will survive the coming 'great tribulation' to enter into an earthly New Order and that by that time the number of those called to the heavenly kingdom had reached its full number of 144,000. (Rev. 7:9-14; 14:1-3) Hence, it would be expected that thenceforth only as a result of an anointed one's proving unfaithful would there be occasion for another person to be called as a replacement" (*WT*, Feb. 15, 1975; see also *WT*, March 15, 1991).

In 2009, it had been seventy-five years since Rutherford (in 1934) proclaimed that the heavenly gate was closed to new members, and that newcomers from

Anointed in 1969	Apostasy from 1969	Faithful from 1969	Unfaithful from 1969	97% dead faithful in 2003	In heaven in 2003	Available places in heaven in 2003	False in 2003	Anointed in 2003
10.368	0%	10.368	0	10.057	143.689	311.0	8.254	8.565
10.368	10%	9.331	1.037	9.051	142.683	1.317	7.248	8.565
10.368	20%	8.294	2.074	8.046	141.678	2.322	6.243	8.565
10.368	30%	7.258	3.110	7.040	140.672	3.328	5.237	8.565
10.368	40%	6.221	4.147	6.034	139.666	4.334	4.231	8.565
10.368	50%	5.184	5.184	5.028	138.660	5.340	3.225	8.565
10.368	60%	4.147	6.221	4.023	137.655	6.345	2.220	8.565
10.368	70%	3.110	7.258	3.017	136.649	7.351	1.214	8.565
10.368	80%	2.074	8.294	2.011	135.643	8.357	208.0	8.565
10.368	90%	1.037	9.331	1.006	134.638	9.362	0	8.565
10.368	100%	0	10.368	0	133.632	10.368	0	8.565

Note that the sum of the numbers on the "In Heaven in 2003" and "Available places in the Heaven in 2003" is constant at 144,000. The figure of "apostates and unfaithful anointed" from 1969 must be inversely proportional to the number of "false anointed" in 2003. If all those of 1969 remained "faithful," there cannot be more than about 311 "truly anointed" (3%) around today, if one assumes that 97% of them have died. This is a low estimate when their age is taken into consideration. So then, 8,254 of the "anointed" of 2003 must therefore be "false." Conversely, assuming that there are only 208 "false anointed" in 2003, then 80% (8,294) of the "anointed" from 1969 have been "unfaithful" using the same precondition.

that time forward belonged to the great crowd. Since all Bible Students until 1934 thought they belonged to the "small crowd," and since we must assume that they were all adults in 1934 (twenty years of age or more), we must conclude that these people are almost extinct.

The figure of those who partook of the bread and the wine has fallen from 39,225 in 1938 to 10,368 in 1969, statistics found in *The Watchtower*, February 15, 1970. If you accept the idea of the organization, some of the "1969s" could theoretically be "substitutes" for the former "apostate anointed." But they should—about forty years later (in 2009)—also now have died, or they should at least be very advanced in age, if you take the opinion of *The Watchtower* at face value:

"Who Really Have a Heavenly Calling? ... But what if an anointed Christian proved unfaithful and a replacement was needed? Then it would be reasonable to conclude that God would give the heavenly calling to someone who had been exemplary in rendering faithful service to our heavenly Father for very many years" (*WT*, March 15, 1991, p. 22).

Against this background it would be interesting to go into this organization's way of thinking and set up its own numbers in a table—*however ridiculous it may look.*

Remember that the organization has no more than 10,368 "anointed" to work with from 1969 to the present, and in 2003 there were still 8,565 that professed to be part of "the anointed flock" (calculation made in 2004).

Note also that the vast majority of the "anointed" in 1969 were older people who must be dead today. Only "substitutes," or "substitutes of substitutes," remain.

The table on the previous page covers the period from 1969 to 2003. But it will not be easy to reach a firm conclusion, since the figure for the remaining anointed changes each year. As previously mentioned (Chapter 27), the number rose in 2008 to just under 10,000. I have, therefore, kept the diagram from the initial Danish edition of this book, which covers the period from 1969 to 2003. But it is hard to follow what is going on, because in 2009 the number of the anointed rose to 10,857. The indirect impact of this increase is, of course, that Armageddon is postponed—at least until 2034.

Conclusion on this note

If the Society claims that most of "the anointed" today are *genuine*, they must simultaneously admit that the majority of 1969 were "unfaithful" and that the "faithful and wise servant" at that time was not so clever indeed. If they choose to say the opposite—that most of the "anointed" from 1969 remained faithful—they must simultaneously recognize that most of today's "anointed" are false, and that the organization is largely no longer headed by a "faithful and wise servant-crowd"—and certainly not in a few years.

As previously written (see Chapter 27), this calculation may seem exaggerated—indeed, almost tasteless compared to the object of faith, which ought to exist *in spite of* knowledge and science—and, as here, mathematics; but the author has simply taken the consequence of the way of thinking, as the Witnesses advocate. Everything is required to be *proved*, which of course is impossible when it comes to religious ideas.

Jette Svane, 2010

Are changes underway in the blood transfusion issue?

The Watchtower in the section "Questions From Readers" from June 2000 hints that changes may be underway in Society's blood policy and sheds new light on the whole issue. The question reads:

"Do Jehovah's Witnesses accept any medical products derived from blood?"

The answer to the reader's question should be quoted here in full, but it is too extensive, so allow me to condense, as follows:

The editors throw themselves into an argument that, among other things, highlights many different blood components, including proteins, hormones, inorganic salts, enzymes, nutrients, proteins as albumin, coagulation factors and antibodies, and gradually arrive at the main issue that Jehovah's Witnesses must get transfusions with *derivatives* of the four main components of blood even the red hemoglobin-based that is oxygen-transporting. The four main components are blood plasma, white and red blood cells, and platelets.

"Such therapies are not transfusions of those primary components; they usually involve parts or fractions thereof. Should Christians accept these fractions in medical treatment? *We cannot say.* The Bible does not give details, *so a Christian must make his own conscientious decision* before God" (*WT*, June 15, 2000, p. 30; italics are mine).

The response is typical and similar to that given—in connection with the Society's position on conscientious objector service—in *The Watchtower* for August 15, 1998. This issue left members, amazingly enough, to their own consciences in the future, even though for years the Society had pushed the young male conscripts of the movement into jail.

Here *The Watchtower* wrote (and take note of the obscure rhetoric):

"In modern times, there have been *some Witnesses* who were very strict in their view of what they would or would not do. For that reason they suffered more than others. Later, increased knowledge helped them to expand their view of matters. But they have no reason to regret having earlier acted in harmony with their conscience, even when this possibly brought extra suffering" (*WT*, Aug. 15, 1998, p. 17; italics are mine).

The somewhat *cryptic* "some Witnesses," probably hiding the Watchtower Society's *own* positions, has driven thousands of young Witnesses to refuse *all* civilian, non-military, national services since the end of World War II, and probably resulted in lengthy prison sentences. I was myself one of the prisoners, but what happened in Denmark was nothing compared to what young Witnesses experienced in other countries, such as South Africa. But with a stroke of the pen, the leadership laid the responsibility for the decisions of the young people, encouraged by a "very strict" view, onto the young men themselves and they didn't dare to go against the Society.

Again, take note of the code words:

"Later, increased knowledge helped them to *expand their view of matters.*" (Ibid.; italics are mine)

In these words we may find a hidden *hint* about the developments around the possible liberalization of blood transfusion, for identical terms are used in the article from *The Watchtower* of June 15, 2000, that sets new, changed guidelines for what the Witnesses must and must not do on the issue of blood fractions.

The article states:

"Does the fact that opinions and conscientious decisions may differ mean that the issue is inconsequential? No. It is serious. Yet, there is a basic simplicity. The above material shows that Jehovah's Witnesses refuse transfusions of both whole blood and its primary blood components.... Beyond that, when it comes to fractions of any of the primary components, each Christian, after careful and prayerful meditation, must conscientiously decide for himself..." (*WT*, June 15, 2000, p. 31; italics are mine).

After having mentioned "some," which refuse "anything derived from blood (even fractions intended to provide temporary passive immunity)," specifically in relation to the Watchtower leaders' own past harsh blood policy, then they write ambiguously, which is striking for this argument:

"*Other Christians decide differently* [that is, the new angles of the Society]. They too refuse transfusions of whole blood, red cells, white cells, platelets, or plasma. Yet, they might allow a physician to treat them with a fraction extracted from the primary components. Even here there may be differences. One Christian may accept a gamma globulin injection, but he may or may not agree to an injection containing something extracted from red or white cells..." (*WT*, June 15, 2000, p. 31; italics are mine; see also *WT*, June 15, 2004).

And this brings me back to my association with the problem of the conscientious objector service, which in 1998 was also left to the young Witnesses' own consciences and decisions.

The article on the *new vision* of derivatives ends as follows:

"The sincere Christian endeavors to have a broader, *more balanced view* that involves more than just the physical aspects.... However, when it comes to products derived from blood, they carefully weigh what God says and their personal relationship with our Life-Giver..." (Ibid.; italics are mine).

One is left with a sneaking feeling that the members of this *growing individualization* of the blood issue—plus a "more balanced view"—have now been left *alone* with their consciences, which of course can *secretly* lead to all sorts of solutions, and perhaps to the decision that one receive both *this* and *that* at the same time—incidentally, without telling the hospital committees of it.

If we can just get rid of them!

As far as I can see, this article has effectively allowed the members, to a greater degree, to receive the substances from the blood that can carry oxygen around in the body, and although "whole-blood" (a term which is rarely used by doctors today) is regarded as "unacceptable" by the Society today, we can read *between the lines* that there is at least something new on its way. It is now entirely left to each member's "personal relationship" with God, which naturally transfers responsibility for the *last 60 years of inhuman blood policy* from the organization's top people to the anonymous lower-level members (*WT*, June 15, 2000).

This response to the readers of the magazine may have a particularly important feature, since it was reprinted four years later, in 2004 (*WT*, June 15).

I think here it has been possible to identify a *Watchtower-jargon* that contains a kind of "cryptogram," a hidden message to suggest some changes are underway. And it could actually be that blood transfusions will gradually be allowed over the next ten to twenty years, but, granted, right now such a change seems unlikely, because the course seems to have tightened in 2004 in a new *Watchtower* article.

May Jehovah's Witnesses now get hemoglobin?

In the above mentioned article, the position on blood is now a Christian core issue: "By his declaration [Genesis 9:5, 6], God was directing humans not to misuse blood. Have you ever wondered why? Yes, what was behind God's view on blood? Actually, the answer involves one of the most important teachings in the Bible. It is at the very core of the Christian message, though many churches choose to ignore it" (*WT*, June 15, 2004, p. 15).

The blood issue seems to be the most central of all now. This article seems to have removed the Society from any future liberalization, which (also) could be seen as an *indirect signal* that there are some changes coming. It seems to zig-zag and confuse, undoubtedly, the members. Leaders appear to run on multiple horses—even in the same article—because the reader is nonetheless given the impression that he or she remains free, and that receipt of blood in the form of derivatives is a matter of *personal conscience* and, therefore, not the Society's responsibility anymore. The leaders' intention here may be that through their ambiguity they shield themselves from *future lawsuits*!

It would seem from the aforementioned issue of the magazine that it is un-acceptable to receive red blood cells, which in turn is one of *full blood's* four components, but that the members themselves decide whether to accept a *derivative* of the red blood cells.

"Some have concluded that such minute fractions are, in effect, no longer blood and hence are not covered by the command 'to abstain from blood.' (Acts 15:29; 21:25; page 31, paragraph 1) That is *their responsibility*. The conscience of others moves them to reject everything obtained from blood (animal or human), *even a tiny fraction of just one primary component*.... Moreover, some products derived from one of the four primary components may be so similar to the function of the whole component and carry on such a *life-sustaining role* in the body that most Christians would find them objectionable" (*WT*, June 15, 2004, p. 23-24; italics are mine).

Clearly, we see from the citation above, the Jehovah's Witnesses may now receive derivatives from all the major components in the blood, just not "life-maintaining," and they circumvent the issue of red blood cells. Whether they may receive *hemoglobin*, the red, iron-containing protein that can absorb and transport oxygen and carbon dioxide throughout the bloodstream, is a little unclear to me.

Glossary

ACA: Advent Christian Association, from 1860 to 1864; from 1864 to today known as Advent Christian Church (ACC).

ACC: The Advent Christian Church, the name of the church from 1864 to the present. Currently, it is the second-largest Adventist church. From 1860 to 1864 its name was The Advent Christian Association (ACA).

actualize: Old writings used in a new way, e.g., in our time.

Advent Christian Association: From 1860 to 1864 this was the name for the Advent Christian Church; it is now the second-largest Adventist church in the world. This church is the direct heir of the original Miller-Adventists. See Chapter 2.

Adventists and Second Adventists: Adherents of the movement founded by William Miller, who waited for Christ's literal return in the clouds of heaven in 1843–1844.

allegorical: Figurative, metaphorical representation.

allusion: Allusion to; covert or indirect reference.

Annihilationism: Belief that sinners are destroyed rather than tormented forever in Hell. Today this doctrine is taught within the Adventists and the Jehovah's Witnesses. It is related to the doctrine of *conditional immortality* (see also).

antagonism: Fight; hostility as active resistance.

antagonist: Opponent, competitor, rival.

Apocalypse: From the Greek *Apokálypsis*; "lifting of the veil" or "revelation." The Apocalypse of John, also known as the Book of Revelation, the last book in the Bible.

apocalyptic: Regarding the world's end.

Apocalypticism: End-time doctrines; obscure, mysterious; about the time of the end.

archaic: Having the characteristics of language of the past

ascension: Ascending, rising; ascension to heaven.

Bethel: The name of Jehovah's Witnesses' headquarters all over the world; it means "the house of God." Here used mainly regarding the central headquarters in Brooklyn, NY.

Bible Students: The original name for Russell's movement and supporters.

Biblicism, Biblicists: Biblical literalism or fundamentalism. First known use of *Biblicism* was in 1850. Biblicists are adherents to this method.

brainwashing: Technique that works on the human brain, using isolation, control, repetition and manipulation. Suggested reading, *Brainwashed in Peking* by Dries van Coillie, 1969.

Brooklyn: Used in this book for the JW-headquarters in Brooklyn, New York. This headquarters is actually a subsidiary of the original Pennsylvania society, The Watch Tower Bible & Tract Society of Pennsylvania. The New York society is now called: Watchtower Bible and Tract Society of New York, Inc. (Previously: People's Pulpit Association).

charismatic: Personal charm, appealing personality or allure; a person who has a captivating quality and is personally and/or intellectually attractive.

circuit overseer: Supervisor of a circuit (or circuits) or a leader of many JW-congregations.

cognitive: About knowledge, reasoning and perception.

cognition: Knowledge, perception.

colporteur: A peddler of religious literature.

conditional immortality: This doctrine means that man does not have an innate immortal soul but acquires this on "condition" when receives eternal life as a gift from God through Jesus Christ.

conglomerate: Mixture of heterogeneous parts; e.g., gravel consisting of large and small stones.

coup d'état: To forcibly overthrow a government or leadership structure. For example, a general may assume power in a country by a *coup d'état*.

cryptogram: Messages or text written in cypher or code.

deism: Belief in a god who is not present in the world and does not intervene in human affairs.

disfellowshipped/disfellowshipping: Excommunication or exclusion from the holy community, particularly used today inside the Jehovah's Witnesses.

DK: The Kingdom of Denmark. Usually used in this book to denote literature published only in the Danish language. It is also used when it has been impossible for the author to find the original quotation in the Society's English-version literature.

eclectic: Selecting or borrowing freely from various sources.

Engram: Neuropsychology term for memory traces in the central nervous system; aftereffects of learning and/or indoctrination (hypothetical). The concept is especially used by Scientology.

Eschatology: The teachings or doctrines about the last days.

full-time service: A regular pioneer using all his or her time to preach door-to-door.

Governing Body: JW's God-guided, central governing council; has only minor importance today.

Great Disappointment: Occurred when Christ failed to appear on earth at the predicted time in the mid-19th century. Afterward, Adventists were divided into many small church communities. The Adventists believed that Christ would return in 1844.

hermeneutic(al): Traditional hermeneutics is the study of the interpretation of written texts, especially texts concerning literature, religion and law (*Wikipedia*).

historical-critical method, The: Evaluating a scripture in context of the era in which it was written.

IBSA: International Bible Students Association; used in articles of the Bible Students and JW.

interregnum: The period when a state or organization has no normal ruler, especially between the end of a king's reign and installment of a successor; interval; pause.

JW: The Jehovah's Witnesses. Frequently used as an abbreviation.

libido: Sexual energy; it can also be triggered by work or dedication to a cause.

Millennium: The thousand year realm coming after the Judgment Day; Christ's thousand-year kingdom. There are different perceptions of the sequence of the concept.

Millerism: Outsiders name for the movement founded by the Baptist William Miller.

Millerites: Followers of William Miller; adherents to Millerism.

omnipotence: Condition of being all powerful. Usually used to denote that God is almighty or has *unlimited* power.

Parousia: Greek word meaning coming; presence; normally, the Second Coming of Christ.

pioneer, regular: Full-time minister/preacher within the Jehovah's Witnesses.

Predestination: In Calvinistic theology this is the doctrine that all events, because God is all-powerful and all-knowing, have been *willed* by God (*Wikipedia; Theopedia*).

Presence: JW's understanding of Christ's second coming (*parousia*), an invisible coming or presence, the central doctrine for the JW.

Preterism: A belief that some or all New Testament prophecies concerning the last days refer to eschatological events fulfilled in the first century, especially around the destruction of Jerusalem, AD 70. Belief that Christ returned in the first century at the destruction of Jerusalem in 70. Adherents of Preterism are known as Preterists. (From the Latin *praeter*, past.)

preterist: Person who believes that Christ has already come (AD 70); Judgment Day and resurrection may be understood as events in the life of individuals. There are "full" and "partial" preterists.

publisher: Ordinary member-preacher inside the JW; the publisher-concept comes, perhaps, from circa 1922, where the members were charged to act as "publicity [agents] for the King and the Kingdom" (*Proclaimers*, 1993, p. 77, 78).

publisher, Kingdom: A Kingdom publisher is an ordinary Witness preacher, canvassing from door-to-door and house-to-house, selling books and magazines produced by the Watchtower Society.

Rapture, The: The rapture is described in 1 Thessalonians 4:17 as the time when Christians will be gathered together to meet Christ in heaven. However, this event occurring in connection with Christ's Second Coming is a matter of hot dispute.

rationalism: The idea that reason is the basis for knowledge rather than experience or divine revelation.

rhetoric: The art of speaking and writing; language artificially ornamented; exaggerated phrasing.

rhetorical: Art of rhetoric; high-sounding, flowery language intended to produce an emotional effect rather than presenting bare facts.

Russelism: Expression used by historians to identify Russell's theology, doctrines and movement; JW do not use this concept; it is seen as disparaging.

Russellites: Adherents of C. T. Russell's teaching both before and after 1916, when Russell died. Also denotes groups that separated themselves from the Watch Tower Society as a result of the power struggle with J. F. Rutherford, 1917 to 1918. Today the Russellites number only about 70,000. It is argued that to separate Rutherford's Bible Students from the opposing Bible Students, he invented the name Jehovah's Witnesses.

SDA: Seventh-day Adventists, both in Denmark and the USA.

self-object: The experience that one person, a group of persons (a gang, a clique) or an organization is made a dominant part of one's self or self-perception (from a psychoanalytic viewpoint). *Self-object* refers to the narcissistic experience where *the other* (a person or group outside the self) serves one's own self, and therefore is a "part" of *the self*, resulting in increased self-esteem.

Society, The: Watch Tower Bible and Tract Society of Pennsylvania, synonymous with the Watch Tower Bible and Tract Society in New York, Inc. This company is formally a subsidiary of the parent company in Pennsylvania, but in reality (in my view), the company in New York is the principal.

theocracy: God's rule and government; state or religion governed by God directly or through a sacerdotal class; for example the Governing Body, the leaders of JW. This concept was also used by Jean (John) Calvin in Geneva, 1541. It was a terror regime.

theocratic: Life according to God's rules and the Watchtower Society's perceptions; God-driven.

Tower, The: The magazine *Zion's Watch Tower* was called "the Tower" by Charles T. Russell's followers. Charles Russell and his wife Maria founded the Watch Tower Society of Pennsylvania in 1884.

Bibliography, Contributors, Source Notes

Sources in General

Regarding Danish theological and church history sources, part of these sources are excluded from the literary list. Instead, they will appear in the text itself, or in the Endnotes in the back of the book.

Using *Wikipedia*

As I wrote in the "Practical Remarks" in the Introduction, I have used *Wikipedia* as an extra source while I worked on my manuscript; this was an excellent experience, as I did not otherwise have access to a large store of books, magazines and encyclopedias in English. I have indicated each time I used *Wikipedia* as a source. I am aware of its less-than-ideal nature as a scholarly resource, but found it to be a useful tool for research purposes.

Publications, Authors and Contributors

Above the Firmament, 1874, by Isaac Newton Vail (on the Water Vapor Canopy theory). See Chapter 4.

Abrahams, Edward H.: *The Pain of the Millennium Charles Taze Russell and the Jehovah's Witnesses, 1879–1916*. Smaller book or article published after 1970.

Acts: The Acts of the Apostles, *Authorized King James Version*.

A Great Battle in the Ecclesiastical Heavens: J. F. Rutherford, author. Copyrighted by the author; New York, 1915. This little book was written to defend against J. J. Ross, author of a strongly critical book on Russell: *Some Facts and More Facts about the Self-Styled "Pastor" Charles T. Russell*, 1913.

Aid to Bible Understanding, 1 and 2: WTS, 1968-1971. Published as a 1,700-page encyclopedia; authored by Raymond Franz (and others) before his break with the Watchtower Society.

Anderson, Barbara: *Secrets of Pedophilia in an American Religion - Jehovah's Witnesses in Crisis* (CD). "Approximately 5,000 pages of court documents have been amassed from twelve court record depositories in four states. These court documents are the result of twelve lawsuits that Defendants Jehovah's Witnesses, et al. were involved with since 1999, although there have been many more lawsuits settled out of court by Defendants in the past decades. The records for the twelve cases along with commentary are being offered on a CD..." (From Lulu.com, 2011).

Anderson, Barbara: *Writings of Maria Russell, The* (eBook). "The Writings of Maria Russell e-document contains Mrs. Russell's last work, a handwritten 600-page unpublished manuscript and hand-drawn end-times chart, meant for a book titled, *The Eternal Purpose*, which outlines her later theological beliefs. To help understand the development of a schism between Maria and her husband, Pastor Charles Taze Russell, and her separation from the religious organization they founded, an enlightening introduction is included as well as a scan of her 1890 ninety-six-page poem, *The Wonderful Story*; two books, *This Gospel of the Kingdom* and *The Twain One*, both published in 1906; eleven of her *Zion's Watch Tower* articles—all meant for excellent comparative study. This e-document contains nearly 1,150 pages for serious C. T. and Maria Russell researchers to review." (From http://Lulu.com, 2011)

Approached, 1973: *God's Kingdom of a Thousand Years Has Approached*. WTS, 1973. Possible author: F. W. Franz.

Arthur, David Tallmadge: *Come out of Babylon; A Study of Millerite Separatism and Denominationalism*. Rochester, New York: The University of Rochester, 1970. (David Arthur is a leading Advent Christian historian.)

ASV: *Holy Bible, American Standard Version*, 1901.

Author's Testimony, The: See Reed, David A.

Awake!: Sister magazine of *The Watchtower*, released by the WTS from 1946 forward. Before 1946, it was called *The Golden Age* (1919–1937) and *Consolation* (1937–1946).

Bartholdy, Christian: 1889–1976, Danish clergyman. Bartholdy had a deep and prolonged influence on the church association for the Home Mission in Denmark (Indre Mission), which he chaired from 1934 to 1959. From 1943 to 1954 he was vicar in Haslev, South Zealand. In sermons and radio lectures he often gave his comments on current events in a challenging form that captured the public's attention. His presentations were seasoned with expressions such as "a robbers' den," and directed at the theological faculty at Aarhus University because of the historical-critical bible research-method, advocated by Professor P. G. Lindhardt. Bartholdy wrote, among his many books, a commentary, *The Revelation of John*. O. Lohses Forlag, Eftf., 1952 (Danish only).

Bergman, Jerry: *The Mental Health of Jehovah's Witnesses*. Clayton, CA: Witness Inc., copyright 1986, 1987 by Jerry Bergman.

Berlingske Tidende: Danish (conservative) morning paper, published since 1749.

Be True: Let God Be True (1952): Published by WTS. First edition, 1946; revised second edition, 1952. Printed in 10,524,830 copies.

Bible Examiner, The (1843–1863; 1871–1879): published by Adventist George Storrs.

Bilde, Per: *En religion bliver til* (Beginning of a religion). Forlaget Anis, publisher, 2001. Introduction to the early Christian history through AD 110 (Danish only).

Bliss, Sylvester: *Memoirs of William Miller*. 1853. Bliss was an early Adventist author and historian close to "the Great Disappointment" in 1844. The 1853 Miller book was reprinted by Leaves of Autumn Books in 1988. Quoting from the back of the book:

"It is a biography of the 'grandfather' of Seventh-day Adventism.... These memoirs give a full and impartial history of Miller's life and the principal incidents of those exciting days..."

Blood, Medicine and the Law of God: WTS, 1961 (leaflet).

Braden, C. S.: *These Also Believe, A Study of Modern American Cults*. New York: The Macmillan Company, 1960. Contains a chapter on Jehovah's Witnesses (p. 358–384).

Bregninge, Poul: *Jehovas Vidner under anklage* (Jehovah's Witnesses on Trial; Danish only). Hans Reitzels Forlag, 1966. The author's first book about JW. First (and only) edition, 5,000 copies produced.

Brown, John Aquila: See *Even-Tide*.

B.T.: Danish tabloid (conservative) founded in 1915.

Briem, Efraim: *Jehovas Vittnen*. Stockholm: Bokförlaget Natur och Kultur, 1944 (Swedish).

"Brooklyn": The author's nickname for the Watchtower Bible and Tract Society located in Brooklyn, New York.

Burridge, J. H.: *"Pastor" Russell's Position and Credentials and His Methods of Interpretation*, 1911.

Carson, D. A., Douglas J. Moo, Leon Morris: *An Introduction to the New Testament*. Zondervan Publishing House, 1992.

Children: J. F. Rutherford, author. WTS, 1941. This was Rutherford's last book. First edition, 3,000,000 copies.

Cole, Marley: *Jehovah's Witnesses—the New World Society*, Vantage Press, 1955. Marley Cole was a Witness when he wrote his book, and it was written with the cooperation and support of WTS. See documentation in Appendix.

Comfort for the Jews: J. F. Rutherford, author. WTS, 1925. In 1925, Rutherford published this little book (128 p.), wherein he argued for the return of the Jews to Palestine as a fulfillment of God's promises: "JUDGE RUTHERFORD, known throughout the world as a friend of the Hebrew people, is vigorously supporting the *daim* of the Jews to the Holy Land" (from the Foreword). "The rebuilding of Palestine is now beginning and is well under way. This is being done clearly in fulfillment of prophecy uttered as promises from Jehovah. The mere fact that the Lord said he would overturn it until a set time, is conclusive proof that it is God's purpose to restore Israel to his favor upon certain conditions" (Foreword and Chapter II, p. 12. See also: Internet *Archive*, free download, Watch Tower publications).

Commandant of Auschwitz: See Hoess, Rudolf.

Conscience: See *Crisis of Conscience*.

Creation: J. F. Rutherford, author; WTS, 1927; 1,100,000 copies. (Based on I. N. Vail's ideas about the Water Vapor Canopy theory.)

Crisis of Conscience: Raymond Franz, author. Atlanta: Commentary Press, 1983. Franz was a former member of the so-called Governing Body of Jehovah's Witnesses. This book upended the Jehovah's Witnesses' history after the catastrophic year 1975 and was followed by *In Search of Christian Freedom*, Commentary Press, Atlanta, 1991. See: Franz, Raymond.

Cunningly Devised Fables of Russellism: W. H. Wilson (Benjamin Wilson's nephew), author. Chicago: A. S. Wilson, 1890 (David Krogh, Registrar at the Atlanta Bible College, Morrow, Georgia, USA, kindly provided a copy of this paper). This document indicates that Benjamin Wilson, the original publisher of *The Emphatic Diaglott* (1864), strongly disagreed with Russell on his core teachings of Christ's *invisible* coming. First mention in this book.

Davies, W. D. and Dale Allison: *The Gospel According to Saint Matthew*, vol. 1–3, International Critical Commentary. Edinburgh: T. & T. Clark, 1988–1997. Here especially, reference vol. 3.

Day Dawn, The: J. H. Paton, author. Watch Tower Society, 1880. This was the first bound book published by WTS. Paton left Russell's movement early, after which he tried to start his own magazine but the project failed.

Dean, David A.: *Reprint of Advent Christian General Conference of America*. Lenox, Massachusetts, 1981 and 2004.

Diaglott, The Emphatic: See *Emphatic Diaglott, The*.

Diary of an Armageddon Survivor, The: Michael Pendley, author. Several versions of Pendley's story can be found on the Internet, often with the characters and locations renamed. See Chapter 32.

Divine Purpose, Jehovah's Witnesses in the: WTS, 1959. First edition: 500,000. The first major historical work from WTS; it was followed by *Jehovah's Witnesses—Proclaimers of God's Kingdom* (known as *Proclaimers*) in 1993. A short history of the JW can be found in *Qualified*, 1955, p. 297–360.Duffield, George: *Millennium, or Second Coming of Christ*, 1843 (book).

Brooklyn Daily Eagle: Tabloid published in New York. It often featured sensational and critical articles about C. T. Russell.

Earth's Annular System, The: Isaac Newton Vail, author. 1902. This book is about the Water Vapor Canopy theory; it and Vail's book from 1874, *Above the Firmament*, were important sources for Rutherford's book, *Creation*, 1927.

Eaton, E. L.: *The Millennial Dawn Heresy: An Examination*. New York: Jennings and Graham, 1911. Very critical towards C. T. Russell. E. L. Eaton is relatively well known from his six debates with Russell in Pittsburgh in 1903; Eaton was a conservative pastor and theologian who defended the Christian doctrines in relation to C. T. Russell's books and teachings.

E.B. (*Ekstra Bladet*): Danish tabloid (politically liberal), published since 1904.

Ecclesiastical Heavens, A Great Battle in the: J. F. Rutherford, author. See *A Great Battle in the Ecclesiastical Heavens*.

Ehrman, Bart D.: *Jesus, Apocalyptic Prophet of the New Millennium*. Oxford University Press, Inc., 1999. An eye-opener of a book about the early Christian's belief in the world's near end. In this highly accessible book, Ehrman reviews the latest textual and archeological research into Jesus's life and the history of the early Church in the first century AD. Ehrman is an American New Testament scholar and textual critic of early Christianity. He is the James A. Gray Distinguished Professor and Chair of the Department of Religious Studies at the University of North Carolina at Chapel Hill. He has written about how the original New Testament texts were frequently altered by scribes for a variety of reasons, and he argues that these alterations affect the interpretation of the texts (from *Wikipedia*).

Ekstra Bladet: See E.B.

Elder Manual: See *Pay Attention to Yourselves and to All the Flock*.

Elliott, Edward Bishop, (E. B.): *Horae Apocalypticae: or, a Commentary on the Apoca-*

lypse, Critical and Historical. Fifth edition, 4 volumes. London: 1862. Elliott was a British clergyman who suggested 1914 as the possible date of the end of the "seven times." (Luke 21:24) See *Gentile*, 2004, p. 68; *Proclaimers*, 1993, p. 134.

Elpis Israel: John Thomas, author. 1849 Thomas established the Christadelphians, a movement related to the Adventists and Age-to-Come, which still exist today.

Emphatic Diaglott, The: Benjamin Wilson, author and translator. The *Diaglott*'s Greek-to-English interlinear rendering was released in 1864. Wilson died in 1900. In 1902 the Watchtower Society came into possession of the printing plates to *The Emphatic Diaglott,* presumably purchased from Wilson's widow, and in 1903 the WTS made its first edition. Reprinted in 1942, WTS. From 1924 till 1993 427,924 copies were printed. This Bible translation has a very high historic and theological status among the Jehovah's Witnesses. Wilson was a printer by trade and editor of *The Gospel Banner and Bible Advocate*, Geneva, Illinois 1854–1869. Wilson was presumably against Russell's doctrines, particularly that of the invisible coming in 1874. See the story of *The Emphatic Diaglott* in Chapter 4.

Ency.: Seventh-day Adventist Encyclopedia (printed). Washington, DC: Review and Herald Publishing Association, 1966.

Even-Tide: John Aquila Brown, author. London: 1823. This book is an interpretation of the so-called "seven times" of the book of Daniel. By means of the "day-year principle," Brown came to the conclusion that there would be 2,520 years from 604 BC to 1917, in other words the same prescription as Barbour and Russell, since these two men embraced this concept, the Watchtower Society used it and still uses it today.

Evidences for the Coming of the Lord in 1873, or The Midnight Cry: N. H. Barbour, author. 1871 (pamphlet).

Ex-Witnesses: Ex-Witnesses is a widespread, global protest movement against the Watchtower Society. The highly committed members of this movement are loosely linked across national borders and language barriers for the sole purpose of unveiling the methods of the Watchtower Society. The movement consists of independent groups that cooperate and coordinate their efforts to disseminate information about the Witnesses.

Facsimiles of the two earliest S.D.A. periodicals: *The Present Truth and the Advent Review*. Washington, DC: Review and Herald Publishing Association, July 1946.

Facts and More Facts, Some: See *Some Facts and More Facts about the Self-Styled "Pastor" Charles T. Russell.*

Family Care and Medical Management for Jehovah's Witnesses: WTS, 1992, revised 1995. Instructional book for members of the hospital committees (discusses blood transfusion and other issues).

Frikirker og sekter (Free Churches and Sects): Michael Neiiendam, author. GEC Gads Forlag, 1948 (DK only). Jehovah's Witnesses are treated on pages 209 to 227.

Franz, Raymond: *In Search of Christian Freedom*. Atlanta: Commentary Press, 1991. Raymond Franz is the nephew of JW president F. W. Franz, and a former member of the Governing Body. The author is world famous for his book, *Crisis of Conscience* (see also). His two books are recommended reading for anyone interested in the JW's story.

From Paradise Lost to Paradise Regained: WTS, 1958. First English printing, 500,000 copies.

Gads Bibelleksikon (*Gads Bible Dictionary*) 1 and 2: Geert Hallbäck, Jorgen Jensen Lundager and Bertil Wiberg, eds. GEC Gads Forlag, second edition, 1998 (DK only).

Gentile: *The Gentile Times Reconsidered* (4th edition). Carl Olof Jonsson, author. Atlanta, Commentary Press, 2004. Jonsson is a Swedish Ex-Witness. He revealed that the doctrine of the "Gentile Times," which must have ended in 1914, was pure nonsense. Regarding Carl Olof Jonsson, see Chapter 28: Brooklyn Shaken to its Foundations.

God's Kingdom of a Thousand Years Has Approached: 1973. See *Approached*.

Gordon, Paul A. (1930-2009): Gordon was a Seventh-day Adventist historian and wrote *Herald of the Midnight Cry*. Boise, Idaho: Pacific Press Publishing Association (an SDA publishing house), 1990. Gordon was director of the Ellen G. White Estate from 1990 to 1995. Ellen G. White Estate is the official organization created by Ellen G. White (see Chapter 2) to act as the custodian of her writings, which are of importance to the Seventh-day Adventist Church. The estate is based at the SDA General Conference in Silver Spring, Maryland, with which it works closely; the White Estate has branch offices and research centers at Adventist universities and colleges around the world (from *Wikipedia*, Nov. 2010).

Gospel Banner and Millennial Advocate, The: magazine published by Benjamin Wilson, 1853–1865.

Goulder, Michael D.: author of *Midrash and Lection in Matthew*. London: SPCK, 1974 (concerning the *lectionary-hypothesis*).

Great Pyramid, a Miracle in Stone, The: J. A. Seiss, author. 1877.

(The) Great Pyramid: Why Was It Built? And Who Built It?: John Taylor, author. 1859.

Guds tider og stunder: C. O. Jonsson, author. 1985 (Swedish only).

Guthrie, Donald: *New Testament Introduction*. England: InterVarsity Press, 1970. Reprinted up to 1981. Printed and bound in Great Britain by Hazell Watson and Viney, Ltd., Aylesbury, Bucks.

Harp of God, The: J. F. Rutherford, his first bound book. WTS, 1921. Between 1921 and 1928, total impressions of 3,710,000.

Herald of the Future Age, The: Christadelphian magazine published by Dr. John Thomas, 1855.

Herald of the Kingdom and Age-to-Come: Christadelphian magazine published by Dr. John Thomas from 1851–1855 and from 1856–1861.

Herald of the Morning: Barbour's magazine (and Barbour and Russell's journal around 1878); 1878–1879, published with C. T. Russell as co-editor and owner to sometime in the spring of 1879. Russell broke off cooperation with N. H. Barbour early in 1879. After the breach with Russell, Barbour continued to publish the magazine, though with breaks, until around 1903, occasionally issuing statements critical of C. T. Russell. He wrote favorably though cautiously that he was persuaded 1896 was the date for Christ's visible return. The last date set by Barbour for Christ's return was 1907. After Barbour's death in 1905 some of his articles from *The Herald of the Morning* were collected and published in a book: *Washed in His Blood*, 1908. Main source, *Wikipedia*; B. W. Schulz and Rachael De Vienne: *Nelson Barbour: The Millennium's Forgotten Prophet*, 2009; and B. W. Schulz and Rachael De Vienne: "Nelson Barbour: The Time-ists Last Breath," *Journal from the Radical Reformation*, Spring 2008, p. 54. See Chapter 4.

Hewitt, Clyde: *Midnight and Morning*. Ventura Books, 1983. A historian associated with Advent Christian Church.

Himes, Joshua Vaughan (1805-1895): Joshua Himes initiated publication of the first Adventist magazine, *The Signs of the Times*, first published in March 1840. In 1842 Himes started a Second Adventist newspaper, *The Midnight Cry*, in New York City. In 1858 he became a leader of the Evangelical Adventists and their American Millennial Association, opposing Sabbatarian Adventism (forerunners of Seventh-day Adventism) and their understanding of the sanctuary, as well as those who believed in conditional immortality and the re-establishment of Israel before Christ's Second Coming. In 1863, Himes accepted the doctrine of "conditional immortality," joined the Advent Christian Church, and moved his family west to Buchanan, Michigan, assuming a prominent leadership role in the church and starting the newspaper, *The Voice of the West*, later *Advent Christian Times*. (Source: Joshua Vaughan Himes at *AllExperts.com*, 2011; *Wikipedia, 2008*)

Hints on the Interpretation of Prophecy: Moses Stuart, author. New York: Allen, Morrill & Wardwell, 1842. Moses Stuart was professor at Andover Theological Seminary, the oldest graduate school of theology in the United States (*Wikipedia*). Concerning Moses Stuart, see Chapter 2.

Hoess, Rudolf: *Commandant of Auschwitz*, originally published by Weidenfeld & Nicolson, 1959. The quotation used in this book is from the reprinted edition of Hoess's book published by Phoenix Press, London, 2000. Jehovah's Witnesses are treated on pages 88–91.

Holmquist, Hjalmar: *Den nyere tids kirkehistorie* (The Recent Church History). J. H. Schultz Forlag, 1927 (DK only). Hjalmar Holmquist, 1873–1945, Swedish church historian, professor at Lund University 1909–1938. Of the extensive writings on Nordic and European issues, his *Kyrkohistoria* (Swedish, vol. 3, 1922–1926) and *Kirkehistorie I and II* (1925–1927, *Church History I and II*, DK only, J. H. Schultz Forlag, 1946) had a particular importance in Denmark.

Holmquist, Hjalmar and Jens Nørregaard: *Kirkehistorie I and II* (Church History I and II). J. H. Schultz Forlag, 1946 (DK only). Professor Jens Nørregaard's (University of Copenhagen) enhanced and enlarged edition was the standard of professional church history at the universities of Copenhagen and Aarhus through most of 1900s; DK only. [Gyldendal's (Internet) *Encyklopædi*, 2009] See also Holmquist entry above.

Horae Apocalypticae: Edward Bishop Elliott, author. 1851. See Elliott.

How Can Blood Save Your Life?: Published in 1990 by the WTS.

Jonsson, Carl Olof and Wolfgang Herbst: *The "Sign" of the Last Days—When?*, Atlanta: Commentary Press. See Chapter 23 and Chapter 34 under the treatment of Matt. 24, verse 7.

Informationer: A Swedish magazine for Ex-JWs.

Insight, 1 and 2: *Insight on the Scriptures*, volumes 1 and 2. WTS, 1988. Each volume has 1,280 pages.

In Search of Christian Freedom: See Franz, Raymond.

Isaiah's Prophecy, 1 and 2: *Isaiah's Prophecy—Light for All Mankind*. WTS, 2000.

Introduction to Maria Russell's Writings: Barbara Anderson, author and editor. 2008. Home page: http://www.watchtowerdocuments.com

Jehovah's Witnesses and the Question of Blood: 1977 (leaflet).JW-CD: Watchtower Library on digital media, 2005. This CD contains all Watchtower magazines from 1950 forward and other important publications, including *Our Kingdom Ministry*,

The Watchtower, from 1950 forward, *Awake!*, etc. This is a vital information source about the Jehovah's Witnesses and the Watchtower Society, which I was allowed to purchase. Further, with the cooperation of an elder, I was able to reference information from a JW-CD of 2008.

Jyllands Posten: Danish morning paper (conservative), published since 1871.

KD: *Kristeligt Dagblad*, Christian Danish newspaper.

Kingdom Come: Let your Kingdom Come. WTS, 1981. First English edition, 2,000,000 copies.

Kingdom Interlinear Translation of the Scriptures, The: WTS, 1985. Total printed through 1985, 800,000.

Kingdom is at Hand, The: WTS, 1944. First edition, 3,000,000 copies.

KJ: authorized King James Version of the Bible, Old and New Testaments.

KM: *Kingdom Ministry*, as of today *Our Kingdom Ministry*. Internal newsletter for members only. Normally on four pages. It can be found on the JW-CD.

Knight, George R.: *Anticipating the Advent: a brief history of Seventh-Day Adventists*. Boise, Idaho: Pacific Press Pub. Association, 1992 (Danish edition: *Forventningen om Jesu genkomst*. Denmark: Dansk Bogforlag,). Knight is a Seventh-day Adventist historian, educator and professor emeritus in church history at Andrews University (a SDA university) in Berrien Springs, Michigan. He has written many books, in fact about thirty-one, all released under the auspices of the Seventh-day Adventist church. Knight gradually developed an interest in Adventist history that led to his transition to the Church History department in the Seventh-day Adventist Theological Seminary. During the 1990s Knight became particularly well-known for his fresh insight and popularization of SDA history. By the year 2000 he was the bestselling SDA author in the denomination with a steady stream of doctoral students and graduate assistants who helped him research his books. (*Wikipedia*, Nov. 2010, and other sources on the Internet)

Knowledge That Leads to Everlasting Life: WTS, 1995 (revised 1997 and 2000). First English edition, 6,000,000 copies.

Kolarz, Walter: *Religion in the Soviet Union*. London: Macmillan & Co. Ltd., 1961; Jehovah's Witnesses in the Soviet Union is treated on the pages 338–344.

Koch, Hal: *Konstantin den Store* (Constantine the Great). Denmark: Gyldendal, 1961 (DK only). *Kristendommens oprindelse* (The Origin of Christianity). Denmark: Gyldendal, 1963 (DK only).

Krogh, David: See *Cunningly Devised Fables of Russellism*.

Kutscher, Brian: For some time, Brian Kutscher has been amassing an archive of Bible Students' literature dating from the 1870s to 1917, covering the ministry of C. T. Russell. Brian kindly agreed to read the proofs of Chapters 22 and 23 of this book. He is an electrical engineer who worked for Ford Motor Company for nearly twenty-five years in fuel injection systems. He has also worked in high speed data acquisition, as an administrator and instructor of graduate-level technical education courses, and as a software design engineer. He has been a member of a Bible Student association for many years.

LaHaye, Tim and Jerry B. Jenkins: *The Beginning of the End*. Wheaton, IL: Tyndall House Publishers, 1972. Expresses similar views on the UN as Jehovah's Witnesses' views. The time-schedule of this book recalls Russell's schedule in his series, *Mil-*

lennial Dawn and *Studies in the Scriptures*, vol. 1. The "left behind series" by Tim LaHaye and Jerry B. Jenkins is a kind of apocalyptic thriller, consisting of twelve volumes. *Time* magazine named LaHaye as one of the twenty-five most influential evangelicals in the United States (from *Wikipedia*).

Learn From the Great Teacher: WTS, 2003. Particularly for children of Jehovah's Witnesses. First English edition, 5,000,000 copies.

Leslie, Jerry: Jerry Leslie is a retired computer systems professional with more than thirty years in the field. He has been an elder of a Bible Student congregation in Portland, Oregon, for about forty-five years. Today he functions as a kind of traveling representative for this congregation. For many years he has visited various Bible Student communities throughout the world. Jerry emphasize that these travels have been conducted as personal ventures, and in recent years, mostly to encourage similar congregations around the world. Jerry kindly read early proofs of Chapters 11 through 17 and provided commentary and notes important to completing this book.

Let God Be True: WTS, 1946, revised 1952. First edition, 10,524,830 copies; second edition, 6,787,000 copies; printed in 50 languages.

Let Your Kingdom Come: WTS, 1981.

Let Your Name be Sanctified: WTS, 1961.

Life Everlasting: *Life Everlasting in Freedom of the Sons of God*. WTS, 1966. First edition, 2,000,000 copies.

Light 1 & 2: J. F. Rutherford, author. WTS, 1930.

Lindén, Dr. Ingemar: Dr. Ingemar Linden (1924–2005), born in Härnösand, North Sweden; he received his primary education in England (1953–1955) and Sweden. He received his master's degree and bachelor's degree in theology from Uppsala University (fil. mag. and teol. Cand. 1962), and four years later "teol. Lic." In 1971 he received his doctorate in theology from Uppsala University. Linden also researched the early history of the Jehovah's Witnesses. Senior associate professor Ingemar Lindén is a well-known researcher in the Nordic countries on the subjects of Millerism and Adventism. He was critical, but friendly toward the Seventh-day's Adventist church. On July16, 2009, Carl Olof Jonsson provided the following information about Lindén via email: "A remarkable development occurred sometime in the late 1990s. In Sweden, Ellen G. White's authority has not been stressed especially among the church's supporters, and the management in Sweden has been quite open to the criticisms of her central position as the prophet of the movement. It was on the background of this that Ingemar, in the 1990s, was suddenly called on by representatives of the SDA-church leadership in Sweden, who appealed to him to return to the movement. Ingemar said that he was surprised because he had not changed his attitude and his criticism. They replied that they did not care about this and that they believed people with Lindén's knowledge and understanding were needed in the movement. He decided then to return to the SDA church to push for reform from within. He died in 2005. I got to know him as a very likeable and open man with a broad knowledge of many issues." Publications by Lindén:

• *Adventismen vid skiljevägen* (Adventism at the Cross-road; Swedish only). Critical to Seventh-day Adventism. Malmö, Sweden: Team Offset, 1983. 166 pages.

• *1844 and the Shut Door Problem*; published in the book series *Studia historico-ecclesiastica Upsaliensia, as volume 35. Stockholm:* Distributor, Almquist & Wiksell

International, 1982 (130 pages). Excellent book by one of the best researchers of Seventh-day Adventism in the United States and Sweden, particularly dealing with one of the movement's central doctrines, the Shut Door ideology; 500 copies printed in English only.

- *Biblicism Apokalyptik Utopi* (*Biblicism Apocalypticism Utopia*), Uppsala University, 1971; 494 pages. The historical development of Adventism in the United States and in Sweden to about 1939, *with a 19-page Summary in English* (outstanding scholarly treatise). When Lindén was translating this treatise into English, he chose instead to write a totally new book, *The Last Trump, see below.*
- *The Last Trump: Historico-genetical Study of Some Important Chapters in the Making and Development of the Seventh-Day Adventist Church,* volume 17 in the series *Studies in the Intercultural History of Christianity* (Peter Lang, Frankfurt am Main, Bern, Las Vegas, 1978), 372 pages. *The Last Trump* was initially to have been an English translation of *Biblicism Apocalypticism Utopia* (1971), but was instead a new work about the history of Adventism, and especially the history of the Seventh-day Adventists.

Lindhardt, Jan: born in 1938, Lindhardt is a Danish theologian and son of Poul Georg Lindhardt, doctor of theology. From 1963 to 1997 Jan was employed at Aarhus University, Jutland, Denmark. He received a doctorate in theology in 1983 and served as bishop of Roskilde 1997–2008. As a theologian and historian of ideas, Jan Lindhardt has, in particular, worked professionally with rhetoric, the Renaissance and Martin Luther's intellectual processes. In Lindhardt's writings he has also dealt with current ethical and pedagogical issues. Few, if any, have discussed the ecclesiastical debate in Denmark as powerfully as Jan Lindhardt. His many books include *Martin Luther, Knowledge and Meditation in the Renaissance.* New York: Edwin Mellen Press, 1986. (Among other sources: *Gyldendal's Free Encyclopedia*)

Lindhardt, Poul Georg (1910–1988): Known as P. G. Lindhardt; beginning in 1942 he served as a professor of church history at the Faculty of Theology at the University of Aarhus, Denmark. P. G. Lindhardt is the father of Roskilde Diocese's now former Bishop Jan Lindhardt and Pastoral Seminary Rector Mogens Lindhardt, and grandfather of the actor Thure Lindhardt. P. G. wrote several books and major works, including *The Scandinavian Church History* (1945, DK only), *Hell Strategy* (1958, DK only) and *The Danish Church History*, vol. 7 (1966). In the religious-political regard, he stood guard on the spaciousness of the Danish national church. P. G. Lindhardt's dissertations and books caused protests, particularly from Christian Bartholdy, the Home Missions chairman, who in 1948 called the Aarhus faculty "a robbers' den."

Lutherans & Adventists in Conversation: Silver Spring, MD: General Conference of Seventh-day Adventist, 2000.

Macmillan, A. H: *Faith on the March*, Prentice-Hall, 1957. Published in agreement with the Watchtower Tract Society. Macmillan, who had been a close associate of C. T. Russell and J. F. Rutherford, until his death was a staff member at JW headquarters in New York. The foreword of his book is written by Nathan H. Knorr, at that time president of the Watchtower Society. *Faith on the March* is a necessary read for those who want to delve into the substance of the JWs.

Make Sure of All Things: WTS, 1953.

Man's Salvation Out of World Distress at Hand!: 1975.

Maria Russell's Writings (2008 release): Author and editor Barbara Anderson wrote the introduction for this release of Mrs. Russell's writings. Can be found at http://www.watchtowerdocuments.com. Barbara Anderson's homepage contains rare Society writings that I've referred to and quoted in this book. See Chapter 32 for Barbara Anderson's story.

Martin and Klann 1959: See below.

Martin, W. R. and N. H. Klann: *Jehovah of the Watch Tower*. Grand Rapids, MI: Zondervan Publishing House, 1959 (5. impression). Both authors were Baptist ministers around 1953 and highly critical of the Witnesses.

"Manner of Christ's Coming, The": J. A. Seiss, 1875. This article appeared in Seiss' magazine, the *Prophetic Times*.

Matt. or Matthew: The Gospel According to St. Matthew, *Authorized King James Version*.

Mattison: Mark M.: "The Provenance of Russellism," as printed in the *History Newsletter of the Church of God General Conference*. J. Stilson, ed. Fall 1991/Winter 1992, No. 2–3. Supplement to *The Restitution Herald*, periodical of the Church of God General Conference. See Chapter 4.

Midnight Cry and Herald of the Morning, The: Periodical produced from March 1874 to 1876.

Millennial Dawn, Books 1, 2, 3, 4, 5 and 6: C. T. Russell, author. In 1904 the name was changed to *Studies in the Scriptures*. Much suggests that Maria Russell co-authored the first four volumes, and especially the fourth volume.

Millions Now Living Will Never Die: J. F. Rutherford, author. WTS, 1920. Incredibly distasteful pamphlet written in regard to the millions who died in the First World War. It's interesting to note the author and most of his supporters are long dead.

Mosbech, Holger (1886–1953): Mosbech was a Danish theologian and lecturer in the New Testament at the University of Copenhagen from 1916–1936, and then a professor until his death. Mosbech, who was under the influence of the religious and historical school of liberal theology, was a lic. theol. since converted to dr. theol. In 1916 he wrote a thesis on The Essenes. Since he released a number of NT-commentaries, for example, *Johannes Aabenbaring* (The Revelation of John), 1943, as well as a comprehensive introduction to the NT (1946–1949), he was a leading force behind the authorized translation of the New Testament from 1948. Highly respected during his lifetime and posthumously, Mosbech was a strong defender of the technical term *tidshistorisk forskning* (DK), which can be translated to time-historical research (or method). The "historical-critical method" (not to be confused with Preterism) covers the same concept. Mosbech's publications include:

- *Apostlenes gerninger, indledet og forklaret* (The Acts, Introduced and Explained). Denmark: Gyldendal, 1938 (DK only).
- *Evangelielitteraturens tilblivelse* (The Arise of Evangelic Literature). Denmark: Gyldendal, 1937 (DK only).
- *Fortolkningen af Johannes' Aabenbaring i fortid og nutid* (Interpretation of the Revelation in the Past and Present). Denmark: Gyldendal, 1934 (DK only).
- *Johannes Aabenbaring, indledet og forklaret* (The Revelation of John, Introduced and Explained). Copenhagen: Gyldendalske Boghandel/Nordisk Forlag, 1943 (DK only).

- *Nytestamentlig Isagogik* (New Testament Isagogic). Copenhagen: Gyldendalske Boghandel/Nordisk Forlag, 1946–1949 (DK only).

MSNBC: Cable news channel based in the United States and available in the US, UK and Canada (*Wikipedia*). Mentioned in Chapter 26 regarding a news program broadcast by MSNBC.

Müller, Mogens: Writer and professor at Copenhagen University, he has produced two books in English on New Testament topics. *The Expression "Son of Man" and the Development of Christology, A History of Interpretation.* London: Equinox Publishing, 2008. *First Bible of the Church: A Plea for the Septuagint.* London: The Continuum International Publishing Group Ltd., 2009. Müller has also published several Danish books on other theological topics on diverse subjects including the Dead Sea Scrolls; a Bible dictionary *Politikens Bibelleksikon* (Politiken's Bible Dictionary, co-authored with his wife, Lizbet Müller), published by Politikens Forlag, 1992 (DK only); and the Essenes, the Dead Sea sect. Mogens Müller has also written an extensive commentary on Matthew, the first gospel in the New Testament, *Kommentar til Matthæusevangeliet* (Commentary to the Gospel of Matthew), Aarhus University, 2000. It is an impressive work of 617 pages (DK only).

Nations Shall Know: *The Nations Shall Know That I Am Jehovah*. WTS, 1971. First English edition, 2,000,000 copies.

Neiiendam, Michael: *Frikirker og sekter* (Free Churches and Sects), GEC Gads Forlag, 1948 (Jehovah's Witnesses are treated on pages 209 to 227; DK only).

(The) New English Bible, New Testament: Great Britain: Oxford University Press, Cambridge University Press, 1961.

New Heavens: *New Heavens and a New Earth*. WTS, 1953. First edition, 3,600,000 copies.

New World Translation of the Christian Greek Scriptures: WTS, 1950. Contains only the New Testament, translated by the WTS and strongly influenced by Benjamin Wilson's translation, *The Emphatic Diaglott*, 1864 (reprinted in 1942).

New World Translation of the Holy Scriptures: WTS, 1960 (published successively from 1953–1960). Released in a single edition in 1963.

NT: *The New Testament.*

NWT and NWT (1963, 1984): *New World Translation of the Holy Scriptures*, 1960 (published successively from 1953–1960). First translation was of the New Testament, *New World Translation of the Christian Greek Scriptures,* WTS, 1950. The following years (1953–1960), all the books in the Old Testament were released until 1963 when the whole Bible was released in one volume. *New World Translation of the Holy Scriptures*, WTS, bound together in one volume and published in 1963. A new, *revised* version of this NWT-translation of the whole Bible was released in 1984. *New World Translation of the Holy Scriptures*, WTS, bound together in one volume and published in 1984. This is a revised version of NWT 1963. Small but telling changes are seen in the 1984 edition when compared to the 1963 edition (for instance in Matt. 24:6).

Object and Manner of Our Lord's Return, The: C. T. Russell, author. Pittsburgh, PA. *Herald of the Morning*, Rochester, New York, 1877 (printed and published by N. H. Barbour, Rochester, NY).

Our Inheritance in the Great Pyramid: Charles Piazzi Smyth, author. London, 1874.

Qualified to Be Ministers: Also known as *Qualified*. WTS, 1955. Revised in 1967. Contains the first full story of Jehovah's Witnesses, pages 197 through 360.

Quest: Articles by Carl Olof Jonsson found in the journal *Quest*, 1988.

Paradise on Earth (1982, 1989): *You Can Live Forever in Paradise on Earth*. WTS, 1982 and 1989 (revised edition, 1989). First English printing, 5,000,000 copies.

Paradise Regained: *From Paradise Lost to Paradise Regained*. WTS, 1958. First English printing, 500,000 copies.

Parkinson, James: James Parkinson is a retired engineer with degrees in mechanical engineering, engineering math, and nuclear engineering from the University of Michigan. He is familiar with the Greek New Testament papyri and other manuscripts and a member of a Bible Student association. James Parkinson proofread Chapters 11 through 17 in cooperation with Jerry Leslie and provided valuable notes and commentary.

Parousia Messenger, The: Paul S. L. Johnson, author. 1938. Circa 1900–1916 Johnson was a close associate and employee of C. T. Russell.

Paton, J. H.: John H. Paton, who was one of Russell's earliest employees, was the author of the first book released by the Bible Students, *The Day Dawn*, published in 1880. See Chapter 6.

Pay Attention: *Pay Attention to Yourselves and to All the Flock*. WTS, 1991. Also called the Elder Manual; this book is only to be owned by elders.

Pay Attention to Daniel's Prophecy: WTS, 1999, revised 2006. This book contains unusual speculative interpretations of the book of Daniel, interpretations which should come with warning lights that flash at any reader. First English printing, 5,000,000 copies.

Penton, M. James: *Apocalypse Delayed, the Story of Jehovah's Witnesses,* University of Toronto Press, 1986 (second printing). When Penton wrote his book, he was professor of History and Religious Studies, University of Lethbridge, Canada. He was a fourth-generation Witness when he was excluded from the movement in 1981. His book is an outstanding analysis of the history and doctrines of JW. He also wrote *Jehovah's Witnesses and the Third Reich: Sectarian Politics under Persecution*, University of Toronto Press, Toronto, 2004.

Pedersen, E. Thestrup: *Apostelen Paulus* (The Apostle Paul), Gjellerup, 1971 (DK only).

Pike, Royston: *Jehovah's Witnesses*. London: C. A. Watts and Co. Ltd., 1954. Very polite book on Jehovah's Witnesses in the 1950s.

Politiken: Danish social-liberal and moderate leftwing morning paper; published since 1884.

Politikens Bible Encyclopedia: Lizbet and Mogens Müller. Politikens Forlag A/S, 1992 (DK only).

Present Truth or Meat in Due Season: Jonas Wendell, 1870 (booklet).

Proclaimers: *Jehovah's Witnesses—Proclaimers of God's Kingdom*. WTS, 1993. First English edition, 500,000 copies.

Prophetic Times (1863-1881): Joseph Augustus Seiss (1823-1904), ed.

Prophetic Times and Watch Tower, The: Joseph Augustus Seiss, ed. 1870 (previously: *Prophetic Times*, see above).

Readers Attention: A pamphlet by Maria F. Russell against C. T. Russell during their separation, published in 1902–1903. This small pamphlet has been heavily criticized by the WTS since its release.

Reed, David A.: Reed is a former JW elder who wrote a 13-page article posted on the Internet, *The Author's Testimony*. It is a critical and pertinent observation of the JW and very readable, as it touches characteristic aspects of the social life of Jehovah's Witnesses, seen from a strong religious perspective. He also authored *Dictionary of J.W.ese,* the unique language of Jehovah's Witnesses. Available in paperback and eBook from online retailers.

Religion: J. F. Rutherford. WTS, 1940. First English printing, 1,500,000 copies.

Report of New World Society Assembly of Jehovah's Witnesses, New York, 1953: WTS, 1953. Report of Jehovah's Witnesses huge assembly held in New York City in 1953. It contains many interviews with top Watchtower officials and delegates.

Report of the Divine Will International Assembly of Jehovah's Witnesses, New York, 1958: WTS, 1959. This is an A-4 publication reporting on the huge assembly held at Yankee Stadium and Polo Grounds in New York in 1958.

Reprints: In this case, reprints of *Zion's Watch Tower* and *Watchtower*, published by WTS. See "Practical remarks" in the Introduction. Used in this book with quotations, for example this reference "Reprints 3411" (number varies), according to its location in the seven volumes of reprints of *Zion's Watch Tower* and *The Watchtower* (new name in 1909). After Charles Taze Russell's death, these reprints were produced by the Watch Tower Society. The last page of this collection is 6622. On each page in the reprints are two page numbers, on the top of the page is the old page from the original magazine at the bottom is the page number of the reprint volume. These volumes can be found in multiple locations on the Internet, including http://www.archive.org/details/WatchTowerBibleandTractSocietyofPennsylvaniaWatchTowerpubs_0

Rev./Revelation: The Revelation of John, New Testament, the last book in the Bible. The author is possibly John, the apostle of Jesus, but probably it was written by a now unknown presbyter of the same name.

Rigets Tjeneste: Danish edition of *Our Kingdom Ministry*, found on the Danish JW-CD.

Rommetveit, Ragnar: Emeritus Professor of Psychology at the University of Oslo, Norway, and author of *Ego i moderne psykologi*, Oslo 1958, s. 43–44; Danish edition by Munksgaard, 1970 (Norwegian and Danish).

Ross, J. J.: See *Some Facts and More Facts about the Self-styled "Pastor" Charles T. Russell*.

RSV: *Revised Standard Version*, containing the Old and New Testaments, The British & Foreign Bible Society, 1946–1952, and Second Edition of The New Testament AD, 1971 (as applied in Chapter 32).

RT: *Russia Today*, English-language news channel.

Russell, Charles Taze (1852–1916): Founder of the Bible Students and second president of WTS from approximately 1881/1884 until 1914. See Chapters 1 to 8. Russell was also author of the book series *Millennial Dawn*, later titled *Studies in the Scriptures*. See *Studies*.

Russell, Maria Frances (nee Ackley): Wife of Charles T. Russell. She produced a pamphlet, *Readers Attention*, 1902–1903, in which she published portions of private correspondence between her and Charles. The publication caused great anger among Bible Students and today's Watchtower Society, which still refers to the pamphlet in very irreconcilable and irascible terms.

Salvation: J. F. Rutherford. WTS, 1939.

Sanctified: Let Your Name Be Sanctified. WTS, 1961. First English printing, 1,000,000 copies.

Scenario of the Photo-Drama of Creation: Book form of the photo drama, 1914.

Schnell, William J.: *Thirty Years a Watch Tower Slave.* London/Edinburgh: Marshall, Morgan & Scott, 1963 (fifth edition, 1963; originally published in 1957). This book attracted much attention since its first publication. At that time it was one of the most devastating exposés on the Jehovah's Witnesses ever released. It was written by a "Watchtower boy" from the inner circles of the movement in Germany and USA. On the dust jacket flap of the 1963 edition, the publisher writes: "Be sure to read this book. You owe it to yourselves to be well posted on this aggressive movement. Sooner or later you will be confronted with its message of perversion." Schnell also wrote:

• *Christians Awake!* Edinburgh: Marshall, Morgan & Scott, 1961. In the book is a reproduction of a "Certificate" issued by the WTS to W. J. Schnell on October 31, 1937 (p. 5). In his Foreword Schnell writes: "In the Watch Tower movement I was for years a Zoneservant. As such I trained thousands of Jehovah's Witnesses in the arts of witnessing, evangelizing and soulwinning..." Schnell later considered himself saved by the Lord (p.8).

• *Into the Light of Christianity.* Baker Book House, 1959.

Schulz, Bruce W., and Rachael De Vienne: "Nelson Barbour: The Time-ists' Last Breath," mentioned in *The Radical Reformation*, vol. 15, No. 1, spring 2008.

Secrets of Pedophilia in an American Religion, Jehovah's Witnesses in Crisis, CD: Circa 2007–2008, edited by Barbara Anderson. See Chapter 30.

Seiss, Joseph Augustus (1823-1904): Theologian, born in Graceham, Frederick County, Maryland, March 18, 1823. Important model and contact person for C. T. Russell around 1877. As far as I can judge, Seiss never accepted the notably younger Charles Russell.

Seventh-day Adventist CD-ROM: Produced by Review and Herald Publishing Association, released by SDA, 1995.

(The) Sign of the Last Days, When?: Carl Olof Jonsson and Wolfgang Herbst, authors. Atlanta: Commentary Press, 1987. Wolfgang Herbst is a pseudonym for Rud Person, a former elder in Sweden, who cooperated with Jonsson on this book.

Signs of the Times: William Miller's fortnightly paper. The *Signs of the Times*, called *the Advent Herald* from 1843–1844. Miller's magazine, *Signs of the Times*, was published in February 1840 with editor Pastor Joshua V. Himes, Chardon Street Chapel in Boston, a key figure in the Millerite movement. *Signs of the Times* is published today by the Seventh-day Adventist Church as a monthly evangelistic magazine. See Chapter 2.

Some Facts and More Facts about the Self-styled "Pastor" Charles T. Russell: By Rev. J. J. Ross, pastor at the James Street Baptist Church, Hamilton, Ontario. He released this very critical pamphlet against "Pastor" Charles T. Russell in 1912. See Chapters 8 and 9.

Steinhaug: This reference is to a manuscript about the Jehovah's Witnesses by Norwegian author Kent Steinhaug, an Ex-Witness. Steinhaug's manuscript is a book about Jehovah's Witnesses; it was posted online in 1993. Kent Steinhaug has frequently posted documents embarrassing to the Watchtower Society on his Watchtower Observer website. In 1996 he published the copyrighted *Pay Attention to Yourselves and to All the Flock*, however, it quickly prompted an angry response from the headquarters of Jehovah's Witnesses in New York (Source: or search for Kent Steinhaug).

Stilson, Jan Turner: Jan Stilson is a life-long member of the Church of God, holds several master's degrees, and is the author of two books and many articles. She penned "An Overview of the Leadership and Development of the Age to Come in the United States: 1832–1971" found in *Journal from the Radical Reformation (JRAD)*, Anthony Buzzard and Kent Ross. Morrow, Georgia: Church of God General Conference, autumn 2001. Also:

- "The Church of God which was and is," article in *History Newsletter*, autumn 1991, winter 1992, Nos. 2–3, supplement to *The Restitution Herald*.
- "The Development of the Church of God Abrahamic Faith 1845-1921" article for the Theological Conference, Atlanta Bible College, Atlanta, Georgia; April 2003 and subsequently published in the *Journal of the Radical Reformation*, vol. 11, 2003.
- "The Publishing Heritage of the Age-to-Come Movement 1808-1985," article in *The Restitution Herald*, October 1985.
- *Biographical Encyclopedia: Chronicling the History of the Church of God Abrahamic Faith, 19th & 20th Centuries*. Stillman Valley, IL: Word Edge, 2011 (Paperback ISBN 9780615465616; also published as eBook available at http://www.bio-cog.com).

Survival: *Survival Into a New Earth*. WTS, 1984.

Stroup, Herbert Hewitt: *The Jehovah's Witnesses*. New York: Columbia University Press, 1945. Stroup's book was an early pioneer work on the Jehovah's Witnesses.

Studies 1, 2, 3, 4, 5, 6 and 7 (seven book series): C. T. Russell. Studies 1 *The Plan of the Ages*, later *The Divine Plan of the Ages*; Studies 2 *The Time Is at Hand*, 1889; Studies 3 *Thy Kingdom Come*, 1891; Studies 4 *The Day of Vengeance*, later *The Battle of Armageddon*, 1897; Studies 5 *At-one-ment Between God and Man*, 1899; Studies 6, *The New Creation*, 1904. The books were first published as *The Millennial Dawn* series, but from 1904 onward called *Studies in the Scriptures*. Studies 7, *The Finished Mystery*, was written after Russell's death and released in 1917. Volume 7 is clearly not written by Russell; it was written by two of his staff members after his death.

Survive Armageddon: *You May Survive Armageddon Into God's New World*. WTS, 1955. First English printing, 1,000,000 copies.

Taylor, Cordon Rattray: *Sex In History*. 1954. Taylor was born in Eastbourne, England, 1911; he was educated at Radley College public school, before studying natural sciences at Trinity College, Cambridge. In 1933 he entered journalism. During the war he worked in the Psychological Warfare division of SHAEF. In 1958 he joined the BBC where he wrote and devised science television programs such as *Eye on Research*. In 1966 he became a full-time author. He served as a member of the Society for Psychical Research, London, 1976–1981 (partially sourced from *Wikipedia*). I received a copy of this book as a gift from my first publisher, Hans Reitzel, in 1966.

Thirty Years a Watch Tower Slave: William J. Schnell. Baker Book House, 1956 (Marshall, Morgan and Scott, Ltd., London). See also Schnell, William J.

Three Worlds: *Three Worlds and the Harvest of this World*. N. H. Barbour and C. T. Russell. Rochester, New York, 1877. This was a joint project by the two men. It contains many of the doctrines JW still maintains.

True Peace and Security—from What Source?: WTS, 1973. Revised in 1986.

True Peace: *True Peace and Security—How Can You Find It?* WTS, 1986 (revised version of *True Peace and Security—from What Source?*). It is said to have been produced in sixty-six languages and for a total printing of 33,000,000 copies.

Truth Book: *The Truth That Leads to Eternal Life*. WTS, 1969/1981. First English printing, 5,000,000 copies. Appeared in 1969 as a deep-blue, pocket-sized book. This new
book was used with a recruiting campaign with a six-month curriculum base that
would lead the "students" to attend the meetings of the movement. Apparently, it was
a mere scare campaign (*Proclaimers*, 1993, p. 105). The *Guinness Book of Records*
1990-series, under the category "Highest Printing," reported that the "Truth Book"
was printed in huge editions. In 1997 it sold 107,000,000 copies in 117 languages. In
the revised edition of 1981 an indirect allusion or reference to the apocalyptic year
1975 has been removed (Ref. "Shaun's Research on the Jehovah's Witnesses, Watchtower Publication Abbreviations"; and *Wikipedia*, 2009; see also the "Truth book"
1968 and 1981, p. 88, 89. See also under the section "Truth or deception?" in Chapter
18, where the subject is treated).

Truth Make Free: *The Truth Shall Make You Free*. WTS, 1943 (a new version was published in 1953). First English printing, 3,000,000 copies.

Truth That Leads to Eternal Life, The: WTS, 1968. Also known as The Truth Book, see
below.

Twain One, The: Maria Frances Russell. 1906 (100 pages). Can be found at Barbara Anderson's http://www.watchtowerdocuments.com.

Vindication, 1, 2 and 3: J. F. Rutherford. WTS, 1931–1932.

VT: Abbreviation for *Vagttårnet*, Danish edition of *The Watchtower*.

Watchman, The: Jonas Wendell, co-editor. 1850. Only one issue of this magazine was
published. See Chapter 3.

Watchtower, The: Sans italics means the Watchtower Society in Brooklyn, New York,
rather than the publication.

Watchtower, The: In italics means the magazine.

Western Mercury, The: Published by Benjamin Wilson around 1850.

What Pastor Russell Said: A publication of Dawn Bible Students Association by Leslie
W. Jones, but in several editions which have different pages. Year of release is not
specified, but it was probably published for the first time around 1919–1923.

What Pastor Russell Taught: Leslie W. Jones. 1919. Published by Dawn Bible Students
Association, probably for the first time 1919-1923.

Wikipedia: This reference work was used as an encyclopedia and dictionary, especially
when I could not readily find information (in English) on topics elsewhere. My experience was very positive, despite the criticisms often leveled against the website. The
information on *Wikipedia* was often very informative, relatively comprehensive and
accurate at least where Jehovah's Witnesses are concerned.

Whitney, Jim: Jim previewed the first 200 pages of *Judgment Day Must Wait*. The
plan was that he proofread my whole manuscript, but Jim was seriously ill in
2011–2012. He has also contributed with historic additions and notes. His article
series on the 1918 trial against J. F. Rutherford and his associates can be found
at http://Jehovah-Witness.net under "Trial-of-JFR" (Part 1 to Part 5a, a total of
fifteen articles).

Wilson, Benjamin: See *Emphatic Diaglott, The*.

Wonderful Story, The: A 96-page poem by Maria F. Russell, 1890. See Maria Russell's
Writings (2008 release). *The Wonderful Story* is available at Barbara Anderson's
http://www.watchtowerdocuments.com

World's Crisis, The: An Adventist magazine published by the Advent Christian Church, from 1854 to approximately 1880.

Writings 2008: See Maria Russell's Writings (2008 release).

WT: *The Watchtower*; published from 1909. Known as *Zion's Watch Tower* (ZWT) from 1879 to 1908.

WT-CD: English edition of the Watchtower Library CD, containing literature from around 1950 to the present (depending on version). Many "older" books, for instance from 1966, are evidently excluded.

WT, Study Edition: In recent years, the WT was produced in an edition dedicated to the public and in a "Student Edition," which is reserved for members only.

WTS: Watch Tower Bible and Tract Society or "the Society," which still, as far as I know, is the *real* and highest authority inside JW.

XJW or X-JW: So called "renegades" or "apostates," now active in many countries providing information about and particularly *against* Jehovah's Witnesses.

XJV: The magazine for the Danish support group for former Jehovah's Witnesses.

YB or Yearbook: *Yearbook of the Jehovah's Witnesses*. WTS annual publication since 1940.

You Can Live Forever in Paradise on Earth: First published in 1982 (revised 1989). See *Paradise on Earth*.

You May Survive: *You May Survive Armageddon Into God's New World, 1955*. First edition, 1,000,000 copies.

Your Will Be Done: *Your Will Be Done on Earth*, 1958. First edition, 1,000,000 copies.

Zion Day Star: Magazine published in 1881 by A. D. Jones, one of Russell's earliest associates.

ZWT: *Zion's Watch Tower* published since 1879; after 1909 known as *The Watchtower*.

Reader Reference

Additional Literature on Jehovah's Witnesses

Bejer, Erik. *Falska Profeter*. Svenska Kyrkans Diakonistyrelses Bogforlag, 1955.

Borregaard, Svend. *Jehovas Vidner*. O. Lohses Forlag, 1954 (DK only).

Doyon, Josy: *Jeg var Jehovas Vidners tjenerinde*. O. Lohses Forlag, 1983 (DK only).

Finnerty, Robert U. *Jehovah's Witnesses on Trial, The Testimony of the Early Church Fathers*. P&R Publishing, 1993.

Geertz-Hansen, Kjeld. *Et katolsk svar til Jehovas Vidner*. Sankt Ansgars Forlag, København 1956 (DK only).

Gustafsson, Axel. *Jehovas Vittnen afslöjas*. Gummessons Bokförlag, 1960 (Swedish only).

Hjeresen, Axel. *Blodhævneren kommer*. Forlaget Aros, 1957 (pamphlet; DK only).

Hvalvik, Reidar. *Drømmen om det tabte paradis*. O. Lohses Forlag (og Credo), 1991 (Norwegian, Danish only).

Jonsson, Carl Olof. *Blodfrågan*. CKI-Förlaget, Göteborg (Swedish only).

Lauridsen, Irma. *Med lyset i øjnene*. Novel written by an ex-Witness. Forlaget Cicero, 1992.

Penton, M. James. *Jehovah's Witnesses and the Third Reich: Sectarian Politics under Persecution*. University of Toronto Press, 2004.

Penton, M. James. *Jehovah's Witnesses in Canada: Champions of Freedom of Speech and Worship.* Toronto: Macmillan of Canada, 1976. (Written by Penton before he broke with the Jehovah's Witnesses.)

Sejergaard, Jørgen. *Tempelgud - om Treenigheden Jesus og Helligånden.* Credo Forlag, 1997. Remarkable book by a Danish vicar intended to prove that the trinity dogma can be documented from the New Testament. Addressed, among others, to members of Jehovah's Witnesses.

Schnell, William J. *Christians Awake!* Edinburgh: Marshall, Morgan & Scott, 1961.

Schnell, William J. *Into the Light of Christianity.* Baker Book House, 1959.

Stevenson, W. C. *The Inside Story of Jehovah's Witnesses.* Originally released in Britain under the title *Year of Doom, 1975.* New York: Hart Publishing Company, Inc., 1967.

Thorell, Folke. *Lögnprofeter.* ÖM's Förlag, Örebro, 1955.

Werge, Asger Dan. *Kirke kontra kætter.* Eget Forlag 1952 (Danish only). A remarkable book written by a young Danish theologian seeking to defend the theological objections to and criticisms of Jehovah's Witnesses at his time. While it appears groundbreaking, the book was never taken seriously by anyone other than Jehovah's Witnesses in Denmark. Many years ago, I met Dan Werge, and his *courteous* treatment has partially inspired me to write about my topic with more restraint and not indulge in scolding—although at times it was quite difficult.

Encyclopedias

Anchor Bible Dictionary, The, (6 volumes). New York: Doubleday, 1992.

Encyclopedia Britannica Online.

Den Store Danske (*The Great Danish*; DK only). Gyldendal's free Internet encyclopedia.

Gads lille leksikon. 1995 (DK only).

Salmonsen. 1915–1925 (DK only).

Store Nordiske Konversationsleksikon. 1916–1924 (DK only).

Svensk Uppslagsbok. Förlagshuset Norden AB, Malmö, 1947–1955 (Swedish only).

Wikipedia. The Free Encyclopedia, http://www.wikipedia.org. Referenced 2006–2011.

Dictionaries

Fowler's Concise English Dictionary, compiled and edited by H. W. Fowler, Great Britain, 1989.

Gyldendals Røde Ordbøger, Engelsk-Dansk, 1976; *Gyldendals Røde Ordbøger, Dansk-Engelsk*, 1976.

Oxford Advanced Learner's Dictionary of Current English, Oxford University Press, 1980.

Webster's New World Dictionary of the American Language, USA, 1959 and 1990.

Wikipedia, Referenced as an auxiliary source; information from this website was always checked and cross-checked. The information on *Wikipedia* was often found to be very informative, relatively comprehensive and accurate.

Apocalyptic Literature from the Christian Right

LaHaye, Tim. *The Beginning of the End.* Wheaton, IL: Tyndale House Publishers, 1972. Expresses similar views on the UN as Jehovah's Witnesses. The tables in this book recall Russell's timetables in his series, *Millennial Dawn* or *Studies in the Scriptures.*

Left Behind. Book series, beginning with the novel *Left Behind* by Tim LaHaye and Jerry B. Jenkins, is an apocalyptic, pop-novel series in twelve volumes, published from 1995. The titles include: *Glorious Appearing, Armageddon, The Remnant, Desecration* and *Soul Harvest.*

Scholarly Literature

Commentary on the Bible (Old and New Testaments):
Peake's Commentary on the Bible. Matthew Black, gen. ed. London: Nelson, 1962.

Commentary on the Book of Revelation:
Aune, David E. *Revelation 1–5.* Word Biblical Commentary (Dallas, Texas: World Books, 1997). *Revelation 6–16.* Word Biblical Commentary (1998). *Revelation 17–22.* Word Biblical Commentary (1998).

Commentary on the Gospel of Matthew:
Luz, Ulrich. *Matthew 1–7. A Commentary.* James E. Crouch, trans. *Hermeneia—A Critical and Historical Commentary on the Bible* (Minneapolis: Fortress Press, 1992; second edition, 2007); *Matthew 8–20. A Commentary* (2001); *Matthew 21–28. A Commentary* (2005).

Commentary on the New Testament:
Carson, D. A., Douglas J. Moo, and Leon Morris: *An Introduction to the New Testament.* Apollos (an imprint of InterVarsity Press), 1992.

Commentary on the New Testament:
Guthrie, Donald. *New Testament Introduction.* InterVarsity Press. Third revised volume, reprinted in 1981. Through four revisions it has proved resilient and today maintains its status as the premier of this type. Guthrie provides an extensive treatment of the history and methodology of New Testament Theology. Guthrie also introduces the reader to critical elements in New Testament scholarship, including authorship, historical questions and other major critical concerns (Christianbook.com).

Dictionary:
The Anchor Bible Dictionary, Vol. 1–6. David Noel Freedman, ed. New York: Doubleday, 1992.

Internet Sources

Internet sites can generally be somewhat unclear and confusing, at least for this author; yet many of the following pages are useful, since they are gateways to even more information that should be measured by the user. In particular, pages that contain older literature can be extremely useful for those who want to investigate issues related to the Jehovah's Witnesses, possibly including former members who have been ostracized, or for researchers and authorities seeking information and insights into the JW literature.

The following addresses are a small sample, of variable quality, and the Internet user may discover an even larger range of JW-related topics through varied searches.

C. T. Russell's Book Series
A2Z.org or
http://www.a2z.org/wtarchive/docs/1916-1918_Studies_in_the_Scriptures.pdf
To view *Studies in the Scriptures 1–7*, 1916–1918. An outstanding resource, where one can search all seven volumes simultaneously.

History
www.amazingforums.com/HGREW or http://amazingforums.com/forum/HGREW/forum.html
Information on Jehovah's Witnesses' earliest history. Proceed to: ZION'S WATCH TOWER SOCIETY: The Early Years.

http://www.jehovahswitnesstruth.com/menu.html
American (anonymous) site that contains many historical details about the origin of the Jehovah's Witnesses' central doctrines.

http://Truthistory.blogspot.com
B. W. Schultz, web master. Historical details including Russell's time.

Zion's Watch Tower Tract Society: The Early Years

http://www.watchtowernews.org/
Historical debate website concerning Jehovah's Witnesses.

William Henry Conley biographical information as found on *Wikipedia* or
http://en.wikipedia.org/wiki/William_Henry_Conley
He was the first president of WTS.

http://wtarchiv.kilu.de/index_e.htm
Watch Tower History and old photos of Russell and Rutherford.

COJ-Correspondence, 1977–1980
http://user.tninet.se/~oof408u/fkf/english/corr.htm
Correspondence from 1977 to 1980 between Carl Olof Jonsson, Göteborg, Sweden, and the headquarters of the Watchtower Society in Brooklyn, NY.

Jehovah's Witnesses' Official Site, www.watchtower.org

Literature, old and new
http://www.a2z.org/wtarchive/archive.htm
Much old literature related to the early years of the Russellites; among other things the *Biography of George Storrs*, 1883, and old Watchtower literature.

The Watchtower from 1879 to 1949, free download available at
http://www.4shared.com/account/dir/4409793/434fff7a/WATCHTOWER_1879_-_1949.htm

Strictly Genteel–Theocratic Resources
http://www.strictlygenteel.co.uk/
Site with older WTS-literature, Russell's books etc.; created and maintained by
members of Jehovah's Witnesses.

http://www.mostholyfaith.com/bible/Reprints/index.asp
Reprint Index (free) of Watch Tower, 1879–1916.

http://www.watchtowerdocuments.com
Barbara Anderson's outstanding site with a lot of old and especially rare literature
established and maintained by X-Witnesses.

http://www.archive.org/details/
WatchTowerBibleandTractSocietyofPennsylvaniaWatchTowerpubs_0
Access to a vast and outstanding library of older and newer Watchtower literature.
Copies of books through 1960 and *Watch Tower* from 1879 to 1949.

http://www.watchtowerwiki.org/index.php5?title=Downloads
Outstanding site for research. Old literature from *The Three Worlds* (Barbour and
Russell), from *Awake!* Oct. 8, 1968 to *2009 Annual Report*, a total of fifty-nine
books and magazines available at the time this was written. All major WTS-
publications are available on this website.

Masoitic symbols in the early Zion's Watch Tower
http://www.theforbiddenknowledge.com/.../dirtywatchtowersecrets.htm
This website is an example of the speculations about Russell's alleged membership
in the Freemasons. I have not found evidence for these assumptions, but they are
exciting. The fact that the "Crown and the Cross" (which can be found near Russell's
gravestone) was found in the earliest copies of *Zion's Watch Tower* has fertilized
the perception that Russell had secret links to Masonic organizations. This has,
however, never been proven.

Newton and Christ's "invisible" return
http://www.isaacnewton.ca or http://www.isaac-newton.org. or http://www.
newtonproject.ic.ac.uk
Professor S. D. Snobelen's personal website on Newton. (S.D. Snobelen is professor
at University of King's College, Halifax, Nova Scotia, Canada) According to
the Watchtower Society, Isaac Newton (1642–1727), in addition to his scientific
research, worked with many theological issues and dealt with the *invisible return* of
Christ ("Christ would return and reign 'invisible to mortals' "; *Proclaimers,* 1993, p.
46). Professor Snobelen kindly informed me about the Watchtower Society's point
of view on Newton, specifically, Frank E. Manuel's *The Religion of Isaac Newton,*
Clarendon Press, Oxford, 1974. (See Chapter 4, "Time of the Gentiles.")

Internal documents
B.O.E. Letters
Various B.O.E. Letters. A collection of letters to the Bodies of Elders organized into folders according to subject.

Statistics
http://www.jwfacts.com//watchtower/statistics.php

Victims of Abuse
http://www.silentlambs.org
Silentlambs helps children within the Jehovah's Witnesses who have been victimized by pedophiles.

http://www.msnbc.msn.com/id/21917798
New evidence in Jehovah's Witness allegations. The Jehovah's Witnesses have settled nine lawsuits alleging church policies protected men who sexually abused children for many years.

http://www.youtube.com/watch?v=QLAC9kS_EqM
NBC report on Jehovah's Witnesses child sexual abuse.

Miscellaneous Websites of various types and quality
Search for Jehovah's Witnesses by Maurice Barnett, dealing with Watchtower history; critical to JW.

http://www.theforbiddenknowledge.com/.../dirtywatchtowersecrets.htm

http://www.watchtowernews.org/
Worldwide news about the Watchtower Bible and Tract Society. Debate home site about Jehovah's Witnesses.

X-JW
http://www.freeminds.org
Maintained by Ex-Witnesses to help previous members.

Locate Books about Jehovah's Witnesses
Danish:
http://www.dci.dk/

English:
http://www.commentarypress.com/ Owned by Raymond Franz, author of *Crisis of Conscience*, Atlanta, 1983. Books are available in many languages.

French:
http://www.aggelia.be/index.html

German:

http://www.ausstieg-info.de/

Spanish:

http://www.extj.org/

Swedish:

http://www.xjw.com/cki-2006.html

CKI-FÖRLAGET by Carl Olof Jonsson. Publisher and dealer of critical books about the Jehovah's Witnesses in several languages: Box 14037, S-40020 Göteborg, Sverige/Sweden.

Notes

1 Maxim Gorky: *My Universities*, 1923, p. 132; published in Penguin Classics 1979; reprinted in Penguin Books, 1991. Gorky wrote his memoirs before he was persuaded by Joseph Stalin to return from his voluntary exile in southern Europe to the Soviet Union, where he later died, possibly a victim of Stalin's bloody purges.

2 Jan Lindhardt was bishop of Roskilde Cathedral from 1997 to 2008. The Danish kings are buried at Roskilde Cathedral. For more, see the publications list (with biographical notes) in this book.

3 SISO: The name in Danish is *Videncenter for Sociale Indsatser ved Seksuelle Overgreb mod Børn.*

4 *Jehovas Vidner under anklage*, published 1966.

5 An expression Sigmund Freud addressed to Carl G. Jung in an attempt to gain Jung's support for his theory of sexuality and occultism. C. G. Jung: *Memories, Dreams, Reflections* (1963).

6 See: *The Pain of the Millennium. Charles Russell and the Jehovah's Witnesses 1879-1916* by Edward H. Abraham, c. 1975; an article, or little book, found on the Internet in 2010, dealing mainly with the movement Jehovah's Witnesses as a "home" for those dissatisfied with our society. This small but interesting treatise deals mainly with the psychosocial aspects.

7 Russell: "We believe that the word of God furnishes us with dubitable proof that we are *now* living in this 'Day of the Lord', that it began in 1874, and is a day of forty years' duration,…" (*ZWT*, October/November 1882, p. 6, 7).

8 "Be not surprised, then, when in subsequent chapters we present proofs that the setting up of the Kingdom of God is already begun, that it is pointed out in prophecy as due to begin the exercise of power in AD 1878, and that the 'battle of the great day of God Almighty' (Rev. 16:14), which will end in AD 1914 with the complete overthrow of earth's present rulership, *is already commenced*. The gathering of the armies is plainly visible from the standpoint of God's Word" (*Studies* 2, 1917 (1891), p. 101; italics are mine).

9 This year, 606 BC, was based on an amateurish chronological calculation of the time of Jerusalem's first destruction, which originally came from the Adventists. It was, in reality, not until the year 587 BC that the first destruction took place. This is further treated in chapter 39.

10 "Although Maryland was established as a refuge for Roman Catholics from England (under the Act of Toleration, 1649 to 1654), most early settlers were Protestants. Members of the Society of Friends (Quakers) were in the Chesapeake Bay area as early as 1657. The Anglican Church was established as the official church in 1692 and continued as such until 1776." (This information is from "Maryland Church Records," found on the Internet, Feb. 7, 2011.)

11 Search for "The Salem Witchcraft Trials" and "Salem Witchcraft Trials 1692" on the Internet. Arthur Miller (1915–2005) wrote the play, *The Crucible*, first performed in 1953, which was a dramatization of the Salem witch persecutions in the years 1692–1693. Miller wrote the play as an allegory of McCarthyism in the late 1940s and early 1950s (*Wikipedia*, 2010, and other sources). Aldous Huxley reported similar incidents in his novel from 1952, *The Devils of Loudun.*

12 Concerning the year 1869, see Chapter 3.

13 In 1870 Wendell published a booklet *The Present Truth, or Meat in Due Season*, in which he concluded that Christ's Second Advent would take place in 1873.

14 *Supplement to Zion's Watch Tower and Herald of Christ's Presence*, June 1879.

15 *Late*, meaning some years after the *early* Second Adventism of 1844; like *late* Judaism.

16 The Puritans were a major religious group and movement within English Protestantism in the 16th and 17th centuries. The Protestant population of England during the 16th century (1550–1600) was divided into three groups: Conformists, Puritans and Separatists. The Puritans objected to many ceremonies in the established Anglican Church. They believed in reform within the church, and opposed separation from the Church of England. The settlers in Massachusetts Bay were Puritans who initially had no intention of breaking with the English mother church. (Several sources, including "Conformists—Puritans—Separatists" found on the Internet, Feb. 2011.)

17 Biblical literalism (literal Biblical interpretation) is associated with the fundamentalist and evangelical hermeneutical approach to Scripture, and is used by many conservative Christians today (*Wikipedia*).

18 Ruth Alden Doan: *The Miller Heresy, Millennialism, and American Culture*; Philadelphia, PA; Temple University Press, 1987. Ruth Doan examined the geographical distribution of correspondents to the Millerite periodical *Signs of the Times* from 1840 to 1847, and found a total of 615 New York, Vermont and New England. Outside of these areas, representation was sparse. However Miller's message was not limited to America. He preached in Canada's eastern townships on at least three occasions in 1835, 1838 and 1840. At least five Millerite papers were published in Canada, among them the *Faithful Watchman* from January 1843, and the influential *Voice of Elijah*, published in Montreal from June 1843 (*Wikipedia*, Millerism; Dec. 2010).

19 In the Danish edition of this book, I used the Danish expression *tidshistorisk forskning*, which literally could be translated to: time-historical research. In a Danish context it is a scholarly expression, tied to church history, free from any religious meaning. But the "historical-critical method," which is used in English speaking countries, covers this concept very well. Otis A. Skinner's book *The Theory of William Miller, Concerning the End of the World in 1843*, can be found on the Internet.

20 Moses Stuart's work *Hints on the Interpretation of Prophecy*, circa 1842, can be found on Internet; it is a lengthy argument with the prophetical literalists (among them George Duffield) or fundamentalists, particularly the Millerites. Moses Stuart's intellectual and scientific point are surprising, and it struck me that such a work could have been read by both W. Miller and C. T. Russell, who both undoubtedly knew him. Stuart's argument rested on a "preteristic" history view (which is an *approximate* variant of the historical-critical method of interpretation at this time, however, basically founded on an apocalyptic Christian faith), namely that biblical prophecies must be assessed from the time they were written. Stuart's argument particularly targets the books of Daniel and Revelation because these books were crucial for the Adventists—and later the Russellites—and today the Jehovah's Witnesses. Moses Stuart died at age seventy-two in 1852, the same year Charles Russell was born. (Concerning "preterism/preterists," see the Glossary.)

21 For an overview of the railways in the United States in the 1840s, see oldrailhistory.com.

22 Miller himself believed not in an *invisible* coming, but preached the second advent as a *visible* event. "Jesus would come in the clouds of heaven, and every eye would see Him. He did not believe in a *secret* coming" (Gordon, 1990, p. 42; italics are mine).

23 George R. Knight, a Seventh-day Adventist historian and professor emeritus in church history at Andrews University (a SDA-university) in Berrien Springs, Michigan, has written many books, in fact about thirty-one, all released under auspices of the Seventh-day Adventist church in USA [*Ministry Magazine* (2011), Wikipedia (2010), and other Internet sources].

24 In 1842 Himes started a Second Adventist newspaper, *The Midnight Cry*, in New York City. In 1858 he became a leader of the Evangelical Adventists and their American Millennial Association, opposing Sabbatarian Adventism (forerunners of the Seventh-day Adventists) and their understanding of the sanctuary, as well as those who believed in conditional immortality and the re-establishment of Israel before Christ's Second Coming. In 1863, Himes accepted the doctrine of "conditional immortality," joined the Advent Christian Church, and moved his family west to Buchanan, Michigan, assuming a prominent leadership role in the church and started the newspaper, *The Voice of the West*, later *Advent Christian Times*. [Source: Joshua Vaughan Himes at AllExperts.com (2011); *Wikipedia* (2008)].

25 According to the oldest traditions (Irenaeus, *Against Heresies*, ca. AD 180), the book of Revelation (Rev.)

was primarily written towards the end of Emperor Domitian's reign (81–96), which means AD 90–95 Most denominations agree on this. New Testament researcher, R. H. Charles (*The Revelation of St. John*, 1920), listed nine different interpretations of Revelation. The following lines of interpretation are the most common: 1) the *ecclesiastical historicism*: the adherents believe that the Rev. describes the Christian church from its beginning to the end of the world in obscure imagery; 2) The *eschatological* or *futuristic* argues that the writing is chiefly about what will happen in the last times; 3) The *historical-critical method* explains the portrayal as a reflection of the period when the Rev. was written, and that its obscure images and predictions concern the near future. *Preterism* recalls that view, but claims that most of the predictions in the New Testament were fulfilled within the generation in which they were spoken; 4) The *religious history* method assumes that in late Judaism and early Christianity there was apocalyptic material already existed, and that the writer of Rev. made use of this material. A fifth method of interpretation is close to the *historical-critical method*, or so-called *preterism*, which holds that the events in Revelation solely concern the first century AD. (I refer here primarily to the late Danish professor Holger Mosbech—who has written epoch-making books on the Revelation—and also to countless websites, among them, *Wikipedia*.)

26 Ingemar Lindén has written three critical books on Seventh-day Adventism: *Biblicism, Apokalyptik, Utopi*, Uppsala, 1971 (Swedish with 19-page summary in English); *The Last Trump*, Peter Lang, Frankfurt, 1978. (*The Last Trump* was initially to have been an English translation of *Biblicism Apocalypticism Utopia*, but became a whole new book on the same topic (English only); and *1844 and the Shut Door Problem*, Uppsala, 1982 (English only), distributed by Almquist & Wiksell International, Stockholm, Sweden.

27 *The Advent Review*, Auburn (NY), August 1850, found in *Facsimile Reproductions of The Present Truth*, and *The Advent Review*, Review and Herald Publishing Association, Washington, D. C., July 1946.

28 The Seventh-day Adventists today experience a yearly increase of some 4%, surpassing the approximately 1.5–3.0% yearly increase of the Jehovah's Witnesses (newset increase: 1.9% in 2012 per 2013 *YB*, p. 178). However, it is difficult to compare the two movements, since the basis for determining the respective numbers of the members are a little different. In the Seventh-day Adventist church the criterion is baptism, but within the Witnesses, it is both baptism and the members' reporting of service hours that count. In the service year 2011, 7,699,019 Witnesses were considered active "peak publishers," which is the latest official list of members reporting their amount of hours spent in the preaching ("average publishers" in 2011: 7,224,930). New members baptized, 263,131 (2011 service year report of Jehovah's Witnesses worldwide). However, if one counts the number of Jehovah's Witnesses all over the world in basically the same way as the Seventh-day Adventists count their supporters, the Witnesses may number near 16–20 million. Only about 7.5 million of those count as *active publishers*, that is the official number of members that report the number of hours given in service from house-to-house (*YB*, 2012).

29 Critics fronted by W. T. Rea (*The White Lie*, 1982) claim that the content of as much as 40% of Ellen White's writings was plagiarised from contemporary writers. The American leadership of the Seventh-day Adventists have declined to provide access to the documents in the archives at the White Estate; the archives contain, among other things, the letters and original manuscripts of Ellen White. (Lindèn, 1983, p. 35-60)

30 See also Ingemar Lindén: *1844 and the Shut Door Problem*, 1982 (written in light of Dr. Desmond Ford's provocative lecture on 1844 and the so-called "sanctuary doctrine," which, according to Ingemar Lindén, resulted in a global discussion inside the Seventh-day Adventists).

31 The Investigative Judgment is a unique Seventh-day Adventist doctrine which asserts that a divine judgment of professed Christians has been in progress since 1844. Ellen G. White, SDA's first leader, believed in the Second Coming in 1844, but in order to explain away the failure, the "investigative judgment" was invented. This doctrine originated from a vision experienced by Adventist Hiram Edson on October 23, 1844 (*Wikipedia*; search also for Hiram Edson on other websites; A general introduction to Adventism is found in Ingemar Lindén's *The Last Trump*, Peter Lang, Frankfurt am Main, 1978; see also the bibliographical listing in this book).

32 Around 1979 Lyman Swingle, coordinator of the Writing Committee of the Watchtower organization in New York, said: "But at least you know that as far as 1914 is concerned, Jehovah's Witnesses got the whole thing—lock, stock and barrel—from the Second Adventists" (*Conscience*, 1983, p. 216).

33 "[O]utsiders" generally called the members "Millennial Dawn people" or "Russellites" (*Divine Purpose*, 1959, p. 125). Also the name "the truth people" was used in *The Watch Tower* around 1910.

34 The Jehovah's Witnesses of today try to give the impression that between 1870 and 1876 Russell and the members of his small group came to the conclusion that Christ's return would *not* be visible, as the Adventists believed, but *invisible*. This view is said to have been a result of the group's Bible study, and it was not until 1876 that Russell—according to his own account from 1879—allegedly was aware that other Adventists had come to similar conclusions. This appears in the book *Jehovah's Witnesses—Proclaimers of God's Kingdom*, in which it is *indirectly* stated that Russell, already *before* 1876, had similar ideas. Russell "learned," as it says, "that there was another group who then believed that Christ's return would be invisible." Russell "came to recognize that although Jesus first came to the earth as a man in the flesh, at his return he would be invisibly present as a spirit person" (*Proclaimers*, 1993, 134; p. 45). In other words, Russell is said to have realized the idea of Jesus' invisible return *simultaneously* or *before* the Adventists (see Chapter 4) he met in 1876. For that reason we must conclude that Russell and his friends, at an early stage *independently of other Adventists,* developed similar ideas about the manner of Jesus' return. This is probably *not* true. The first time he wrote an article was to the *Bible Examiner* in 1876, where he didn't write about Christ's coming, rather "Gentile Times: When do they end?" It was not before 1877 that he, in the booklet *The Object and Manner of Our Lord's Return,* wrote about Christ's return. (Source: "Strictly Genteel—Theocratic Resources" located on the Internet).

35 Another well-known Advent Christian, George W. Stetson, who also played an important role in Russell's early life, replaced Jonas Wendell as pastor in Edinboro, Pennsylvania, in 1871. According to my source, Wendell was arrested for one reason or another. He was not convicted, but his reputation reportedly suffered. This may explain the replacement. The church in Edinboro had something more than 100 members. [Internet: "19th Century Pioneers of Jehovah's Witnesses" discussion board topic, Jonas Wendell and George Stetson (September 2008; January 2011)].

36 The Second Adventists (the main body) "1854 expectation" resulted after the failure to form a new group, later known as Advent Christians. This group was organized in 1860 under the name The Advent Christian Association. In 1864 it was changed to the Advent Christian Church. This church was largely composed of those who held to "conditional immortality" as the principal doctrine. (*Ency.*, volume 10, page 10; subject: Adventist Bodies).

37 Wendell added thirty years to William Miller's 1843-calculation, and got 1873: "The evidence is then clear and conclusive, that the 1,260 years commenced in AD 538 and ended in 1798; and as the 1,290 and 1,335 commence at the same point of time, the 1,290 days would terminate 30 years after the 1,260, viz: 1828, and the 1335 would end 45 years after the 1,290, viz: 1873" (*Present Truth*, 1870, p. 13).

38 "...I confess indebtedness to Adventists as well as to other denominations" (*The Watch Tower*, July 15, 1906).

39 In 1844 Swedish professor Efraim Briem wrote a pamphlet (*Jehovas Vittnen*) in which he claimed that Russell was guilty of plagiarism (p. 21): "Russell was in no way a creating spirit, but a mere copyist, and his success lay primarily in his organizational skills" (Briem, 1844, p. 21).

40 When Russell and Wendell actually met is not completely clear. In *The Finished Mystery* (1917), the year 1868 is mentioned (*Studies* 7, 1917, p. 53), but most sources say 1869 (Penton, 1986, p. 14; *Proclaimers*, 1993, p. 43). Russell wrote in a supplement to the first issue of *Zion's Watch Tower*, July 1879, "to readers of the Herald of the Morning," that this meeting took place "about 1869." Maybe it first happened in 1871 at Wendell's (registered) first visit in Allegheny. Wendell was not, according to one of my sources, in Allegheny in 1869. Operating from this assumption, the 1868 or 1969 dates must not refer to *when* Russell met Wendell, but to the *beginning* of his search among different churches and oriental philosophies. Still referring to my source (B. W. Schulz), it had to be possible to trace Wendell's movements month by month in *The World's Crisis*, published by the Advent Christian Church. But because of Russell's own words in "Supplement to *Zion's Watch Tower*, To the readers of the Herald of the Morning," July 1, 1879, where he also wrote about the "seven years" from 1869 to 1876, I maintain the year 1869 (email from B. W. Schulz, who maintains truthistory.blogspot.com, August 2008).

41 The private correspondence between John Roller and the historians David T. Arthur and Scott Palmer, the Advent Christian Church, from which I have been allowed to cite, reveals that historians within the Advent Christian Church have had a hard time coming to terms with the historical connection between the Advent Christian Church, Russell and the Jehovah's Witnesses of our present day.

42 An article from 1876 was titled "Gentile Times: When do they end?"

43 Henry Grew: *Future Punishment Not Eternal Life In Misery But Destruction* (see Henry Grew, *Wikipedia*; also see http://www.harvestherald.com/grewindex.htm "Writings by Henry Grew," where the above-noted title by Grew can be found).

44 Letter from the Secretary of Lodge 45, Pittsburgh, PA: "Please be advised that the Masonic Fraternity has no connection with the Jehovah Witness group, the Watch Tower Society or the cemetery mentioned which includes the mini-pyramid therein. / The Greater Pittsburgh Masonic Center purchased the ground where is [sic] located and erected the building in 1987 after the sale of the Masonic Temple in Pittsburgh (Oakland) to the University of Pittsburgh" (Aug. 23, 2010).

45 Formerly, the magazine was called *Zion's Watch Tower and Herald of Christ's Presence* (1879); *The Watch Tower and Herald of Christ's Presence* (1909); *The Watchtower and Herald of Christ's Kingdom* (1939); and in the same year, 1939, changed again to *The Watchtower Announcing Jehovah's Kingdom* (from 1939 until today). The magazine is published monthly in approximately 185 languages by the Watch Tower Bible and Tract Society of Pennsylvania and printed in Wallkill, New York, and branch offices around the world (*Wikipedia*, 2010). WTS PRODUCTION, 1998–2008. Books 458,230,708; Magazines 11,292,413,199; Tracts 7,996,906,376; Brochures 862,050,233; CDs/MP3s 34,621,130; DVDs 13,500,125; Other 129,083,031. Total 20,786,804,802. It has published entirely or in part more than 150 million copies of the *New World Translation of the Holy Scriptures* in seventy-two languages. According to the WT-CD, the Watch Tower Society publishes in about 473 languages (JW-CD, 2009).

46 Paton was author of the first book, *The Day Dawn*, released in 1880 by the Watch Tower Society (333 pages). He is not mentioned in the first history book from 1959, *Jehovah's Witnesses in the Divine Purpose*, but in the *Proclaimers*, from 1993, where we read that in 1881 Paton was "serving as a traveling representative of the *Watch Tower*," but "began to turn away…" Thereafter he published a revised version of his first book from 1880, released independently of WTS. Today, he is regarded as one of the earliest apostates. As far as I can see, Paton was a better writer than C. T. Russell, but when Paton published his book in 1880, under WTS auspices, he positioned himself as Russell's competitor, which would later prove to be a problem. Russell tolerated *no competition*. (*Proclaimers*, 1993, p. 620)

47 One source says it happened in December 1871. Wendell died in 1873 (B. W. Schulz, 2008).

48 The subtitle indicated clearly what the booklet (16 pages) addressed: "Giving some of the Evidences for the Coming of our Lord and Savior, this year, 1873."

49 It was entirely my own assumption when I wrote this in the Danish edition of my book. But I now find on the Internet that this subject is under discussion.

50 B. W. Schulz and R. De Vienne: "Nelson Barbour, the Time-ists' Last Breath"—*The Radical Reformation*, p. 54–57, spring 2008 (an Age-to-Come magazine).

51 According to B. W. Schulz at his website truthhistory.blogspot.com, June 2008, Barbour's middle name was Horatio, not Homer. See: Bennet Woodcroft: Alphabetical Index and Applicants of Patents for Invention for the Year 1870, London, 1871, page 12 (Source: B. W. Schulz).

52 *Horæ Apocalypticæ; A Commentary on the Apocalypse, Critical and Historical; Including also an examination of the chief prophecies of Daniel* (4 Volumes), Seeley, Jackson, and Halliday, Fleet Street, London; MDCCCLXII (1862).

53 See more under the subject: "Creation–Days of, How Long?"

54 In the book *The Photo-Drama of Creation*, published in 1914, Russell writes: "We follow the theory that each of the Seven Days of the Creation Week was a period of seven thousand years. This, seven times seven thousand equals forty-nine thousand (7x7,000=49,000) years, ushering in a grand Jubilee Epoch" (*The Photo-Drama of Creation*, 1914, p. 2; see also Penton, 1986, p. 196-197).

55 *Creation, 1927*, p. 29: "It seems to have been the plan of Jehovah God to begin the increase of light upon his great work for the benefit of man about the year 1874 AD. It was in that year that Isaac N. Vail first published a pamphlet titled "The Earth's Annular System." Rutherford is unfortunately wrong concerning the year of publication of *The Earth's Annular System*. It was published in 1902. Vail published a pamphlet in 1874, *Above the Firmament*, which, for the first time, addressed the same subject, the annular system.

56 See Glenn R. Morton's article from the year 2000: *The Demise and Fall of the Water Vapor Canopy: A Fallen Creationist Idea* (Located on the Internet, search for Isaac Newton Vail).

57 In November 2005, Professor Mogens Müller, the University of Copenhagen, wrote to me: "Johann Jakob Griesbach (1745–1812) is a known figure in the research of the New Testament. Besides hermeneutics, he was occupied with text criticism, which resulted in a two-volume edition of the Greek text of the New Testament (1796). He was also the first to publish the initial three synoptic gospels in columns (1774), so we could compare them (a synopsis). His research is described in William Baird's *History of New Testament Research: Vol. 1. From Deism to Tübingen* (Fortress Press, Minneapolis, MN, 1992), p. 138-148."

58 The first council of Nicaea consisted of 1,800 Christian bishops assembled in Nicaea in Bithynia (present-day İznik in Turkey) led by Roman Emperor Constantine. It was the first effort to attain consensus respecting Christian teachings in the form of a Creed. The first words in this creed are: "We believe in one God, the Father Almighty, Maker of all things visible and invisible; and in one Lord Jesus Christ, the only begotten of the Father, that is, of the substance of the Father, God of God, light of light, true God of true God, begotten not made, of the same substance with the Father, through whom all things were made both in heaven and on earth..." (Several sources, including *Catholic Encyclopedia* "First Council of Nicaea"; *Wikipedia*, March 9, 2011).

59 "The diary entry for the 1895 Iowa Conference mentioned 'C.T. Russell' who was paid $1.50 for preaching at the conference on four occasions. Russell was the founder and leader of the Zion's Watch Tower which eventually became known as the Jehovah's Witnesses. There was friendly exchange between Russell and some leaders in the Church of God up to around 1900, but Russell was never part of the development of the Church of God." (Stilson, J. Turner: *Biographical Encyclopedia Chronicling the Development of the Church of God Abrahamic Faith 19th and 20th Centuries*, June 2011).

60 According to the Watchtower Society, Isaac Newton (1642–1727), who in addition to his scientific research worked with many theological issues, dealt with the *invisible return* of Christ ["Christ would return and reign 'invisible to mortals' " (*Proclaimers*, 1993, p. 46)]. But there is no evidence whatsoever that Newton ever stated such thoughts, and the objective of the Society is probably just to put Russell in good company, plus strengthen the invisibility theory, however impossible this theory may be. *Proclaimers* does not note the quote's origin. However, Professor S. D. Snobelen, a specialist regarding Isaac Newton, of the University of King's College, Halifax, Nova Scotia, Canada, who I contacted based on a recommendation, informed me that the editors of *Proclaimers* obtained this quote from Frank E. Manuel's *The Religion of Isaac Newton*, Clarendon Press, Oxford, 1974, Appendix B, p. 135.

61 *Even-Tide*, John Aquila Brown (England), 1823. J. A. Brown's book, *Even-Tide,* is an interpretation of the so-called "seven times" of the book of Daniel. By means of the so-called "day-year principle," Brown came to the conclusion that there had to be 2,520 years from 604 BC to AD 1917 which, so to speak, is the same prescription as Russell, and after him, the Watchtower Society has used. *See,* among others: *Gentile* 2004, p. 32–36; Penton 1986, p. 21.

62 "The Secret Rapture," as well as the idea of a gradual (in stages) return of Christ, initially *invisibly* and later a *visible* manifestation, was promoted early in the 19th century, around 1826–30 by Henry Drummond (1786–1860). Drummond influenced Edward Irving (founder of the Apostolic Catholic Church), and through him, the American Adventists. In 1835 Henry Drummond was chosen as one of the "twelve apostles" of the Apostolic Catholic Church. The apostles were expected to survive until the Second Coming of Jesus, but since the last of them, Francis Woodhouse, died in 1901 at age 96, the church and its members existed in seclusion without any outreach mission. The membership today numbers about six million worldwide (*Gentile*, 2004, p. 36–39; a detailed account by C. O. Jonsson can be found in *Quest*, spring issue, 1988, and *Quest*, summer issue, 1989).

63 The new Catholic Apostolic Church (sectarian) was headed by twelve "apostles," and the first one, John Cardale, was appointed by Drummond. In 1883, Irving was prescribed as a so-called "angel" and bishop of the church in London. He died in 1834 at age 42.

64 Francisco Ribera (1537–1591), a Spanish Jesuit doctor of theology, circa 1590 published a commentary on the book of Revelation titled: *In Sacrum Beati Ioannis Apostoli, & Evangelistiae Apocalypsin Commentarij*. In order to remove the Catholic Church from consideration as Antichrist, Ribera assumed that the first chapters of the Apocalypse refer to ancient imperial Rome, and the rest he limited to a *future period of 3-1/2 literal years*, immediately prior to the return of Christ. This assumption was later called *Futurism*. This 3-1/2 years became important for Barbour, Russell, and today's Jehovah's Witnesses (Internet source: "The Catholic Origins of Futurism and Preterism," which primarily builds on *The Prophetic Faith of Our Fathers*, by Le Roy Edwin Froom, Volume

II, published by the Review and Herald Publishing Association, Washington, D.C., 1948; Chapters 21–23 in particular).

65 John Nelson Darby (1800–1882) was an Anglo-Irish evangelist and an influential figure among the original Plymouth Brethren. He is the father of modern Dispensationalism, and is said to have invented the "secret rapture" idea (Sources: *Wikipedia*, Nov. 2008; *Theopedia*, March 2011; and Internet, search for *John Nelson Darby* bio).

66 *The Midnight Cry and Herald of the Morning*, Volume 1, Number 4, March 1874.

67 Transference: Originally I had used the word "translation," but I admit that the use of the word in this place is not generally found in English, however, in *Fowler's Concise English Dictionary*, 1989, p. 1303, one finds: "translate ... translation ... (bibl.) convey to heaven without death."

68 N. Barbour, September 1875: "When the 'harvest' is ended, I believe the most terrible judgments of war, famine, pestilence, and desolation, this world has ever witnessed; will prevail, until one universal reign of terror obtains, from pole to pole: until life shall be a burden to the most favored; and death earnestly desired" (*Herald*, September 1875).

69 Under the heading, "The year 1881," Russell wrote in *Zion's Watch Tower* of May 1881: "The Watch Tower never claimed that the *body of Christ* [the saints] will be changed to spiritual beings during this year. There is such a *change* due sometime. We have not attempted to say when, but have repeatedly said that it could not take place *before* the fall of 1881.... To our understanding it will be due at any time after October 2nd, 1881, but we know of no *scriptural* evidence as to what time we will be changed from natural to spiritual, from mortal to immortal.... We should be glad to go sooner if it were the Bridegroom's will, but we will be equally glad to remain here in earthly conditions if it is *his will...*" (*ZWT*, May 1881, p. 224). Russell appears here—in good time before October 1881—to prepare his readers that nothing supernatural would happen in the autumn of 1881.

70 Smyth, C. Piazzi: *Our Inheritance in the Great Pyramid*, London, W. Isbister & Co., 1874.

71 You can see images of Russell's gravestone and read an article about his gravesite at http://www.freeminds.org/organization/russell/charles-t.-russell-gravesite-rosemont-united-cemetery.html.

72 Some of Russell's "inches" in *Thy Kingdom Come*, the third volume of the *Millennial Dawn*-series, chapter 10, were altered along the way, presumably because Russell could see that he was rather short of time before the world's predicted end in 1914. Thus, the 3,416 inches, which, translated into years, ranged from 1542 BC to 1874, were changed to 3,457 inches, representing a difference of 41 inches—equal to 41 years, which aptly would bring Russell up to 1915 [the 3,426 inches: *Millennial Dawn* 3, 1891–1904, p. 342; the 3,457 inches: *Studies* 3, 1919 edition (Strictly Genteel); downloaded from the Internet, October 27, 2008, under the theme: "C. Piazzi Smyth, Charles Taze Russell and the Great Pyramid of Gizeh"]. In the same article, the author makes note that the 1891 edition calculates the "Chronological beginning of the time of trouble" to 1874, while the edition published after 1904, calculates that the "close of 1914 will be the beginning of the time of trouble." The "time of trouble" period was *before* 1914 by a length of forty years, and went from 1874 to 1914.

73 In *Herald of the Morning*, September 1875, Barbour wrote: "I believe the earth (or cosmos) abideth forever; but that the ages, (aionies) are continually passing. That we are now in the end of the gospel age, and the commencing of the age of, or 'times of restitution of all things.' That this transition period is called 'the time of harvest.' And that it began in the autumn of 1874, and will end in the spring of 1878; measuring three and a half years. And that the events of this time of harvest, are first the resurrection of the dead in Christ; second, the binding of the tares in bundles; third and last, the translation of the living saints and gathering of them together with the risen ones to the Lord in the air. / I believe that though the gospel dispensation will end in 1878, the Jews will not be restored to Palestine, until 1881; and that the 'times of the Gentiles,' viz. their seven prophetic times, of 2520, or twice 1260 years, which began where God gave all, into the hands of Nebuchadnezzar, 606 BC; do not end until AD 1914; or 40 years from this" (*Herald of the Morning*, September 1875; Here, I assume Barbour did not change his doctrines until 1877).

74 In conjunction with her research on Russell's (possible) connection with the Advent Christians, Age-to-Come and the Seventh-day Adventists, Janet Stilson wrote to me in October 2005: "I am certain C. T. Russell participated in meetings with the Church of God/Age-to-Come, particularly in the congregations comprised of members from both the Church of God/Age-to-Come (Restitutionists), the Advent Christians, as well as the Seventh-day Adventists" (email, 2005). In an article in the *History Newsletter*,

1992/1993 (addition to the *Restitution Herald*), Mark M. Mattison writes that Russell gave speeches to Adventists everywhere, and that on several occasions he gave lectures for Church of God congregations. At a Church of God Conference in Marshalltown, Iowa, in 1885, he even opened his speech with a sermon. It is confirmed that contacts were established as early as 1881. In a lengthy article in the *Zion's Watch Tower* of July 1881 Russell cites a passage by H. V. Reed from the *Restitution*, the official Age-to-Come-magazine. The most interesting evidence of contact, however, is found in the *Zion's Watch Tower* of June 1881, shortly after the magazine had commenced publishing, in which Russell under the headline "The Credibility of the Scriptures" presented a lengthy article authored by Dr. John Thomas, leader of the Christadelphians, who also had ties to the Age-to-Come-magazine *Restitution*. My conclusion is that Russell must have both read this Age-to-Come-magazine, as well as having been interested in the views of John Thomas. (Source: J. Stilson and Mark M. Mattison, Newsletter 1991/1992, addition to *The Restitution Herald*)

75 There is a significant disparity between the total magazines published and those that actually reach the public. Many, if not most, members of the Jehovah's Witnesses order far more magazines than they use themselves. Some members will leave magazines in public places. In recent years the Watchtower Society has scaled back its production of *The Watchtower* magazine, and *Awake!* has been reduced to a monthly publication from semi-monthly (note by Jim Whitney).

76 George Storrs: *The Watch Tower: Or, Man in Death; and the Hope for a Future Life*. See the footnote in *Proclaimers*, 1993, p. 48. Here it states: "The name was also incorporated in the title of various religious periodicals. It stems from the idea of keeping on the watch for the outworking of God's purposes…"

77 For example, a man by the name of H. B. Rice preached and lectured in the Santa Clara Valley around 1885. This can be read in *The Restitution*, an Age-to-Come journal, Jan. 21, 1885. He was probably a member of the Church of God.

78 Full-time publisher: Generally, the preachers of Jehovah's Witnesses are called "publishers," which must be understood as "preachers." Therefore, you can also be a "full-time publisher" or a "pioneer." In 1960 this meant at least 110 hours, and today (in 2011) fifty hours in "field service" per month.

79 During further investigations in 2011, I chanced on William I. Mann's name. He was briefly mentioned in a larger article on the numerous small sects that arose after Russell's death in 1916. Here it is stated under "Various Individuals" that Wm. I. Mann joined a small congregation in Rochester, NY, a few months before his death in 1930 (Source: Bible Students Fragments 1917-1967; or http://www. heraldmag.org / OLB / contents / history / jp% 20history.htm).

80 That W. H. Conley acted as the first president of the Society prior to 1884 is not evident from the first (larger) historic presentation, *Jehovah's Witnesses in the Divine Purpose*, published by the WTS in 1959. Conley is not mentioned. In a footnote (p. 27), it says: "The original leaders were C. T. Russell, president; William I. Mann, vice president; Maria S. Russell, wife of Pastor Russell, secretary and cashier."

81 This is evidenced by the amazing development that the Watchtower Society in New York has, since that time, experienced in the property market of the city. Today, Jehovah's Witnesses in New York are one of the city's largest property and landowners; however, the image began to crack in 2004 when a relocation plan aimed at a reorganization of the movement's activities in New York began. Circa 2004, the printing and shipping department was moved to Walkill, NY, and a number of the movement's well-known buildings, which mainly had served as accommodation for staff members were put up for sale because some of the staff moved to Walkill and other destinations. As I understand from articles, contributions and reports on the Internet, the buildings put up for sale include: 169 Columbia Heights, the former Standish Arms Hotel; 183 Columbia Heights, built in 1920; and 161 Columbia Heights from 1844. The last two buildings have, since 1986 and 1988, been owned by the Watchtower Society. Beyond the aforementioned structures at 360 Furman, 89 Hicks Street and 67 Livingston Street were sold to Brooklyn Law School and a private investor. The sale of these properties is justified in that they no longer had the same need for accommodation of employees at headquarters in Brooklyn. It is also reported that the Watchtower Society will build a four-tower complex at 85 Jay Street in DUMBO (Down Under the Manhattan Bridge Overpass), which will include apartments and may mean they will sell more of the Society's apartment properties in Brooklyn. A spokesman for the Watchtower headquarters, David Semonian, told the *Brooklyn Daily Eagle* (Feb. 2010): "A primary objective of the Watchtower in acquiring additional properties is to find a complex that would be closer to facilities in the Shawangunk and Patterson" (*Brooklyn Daily Eagle*, 2006 and 2010). Patterson is the Watchtower Educational Center, a religious school and office complex operated by Watch-

tower Society. Each year the Patterson facility draws thousands of American and international visitors to its educational programs. In February 2010 the Society announced its intention to establish the World Headquarters of Jehovah's Witnesses at a proposed complex in Warwick, New York (*Wikipedia*, 2010).

82 Under the heading, "A Theological Discussion," *Zion's Watch Tower* of October 15, 1903, we find the following: "On March 10, 1903, Rev. E. L. Eaton, D.D., pastor North Avenue M. E. church, addressed a letter to Pastor C. T. Russell. of the Arch Street (Bible House) Chapel, in which he said: / 'Believing that nothing helps so much to get at the exact truth of a fact or doctrine as a full and free discussion of it; and that any legitimate thing that will attract the attention and arouse the interest of those who are indifferent to Scriptural truth is commendable; I have thought that a public debate of some of those questions about which you and I differ, and which we both believe to be vital to the Christian system, would be of immense interest to the public, and perhaps of great spiritual profit to those who heard, provided that the discussions be carried on—as I feel sure they would be—in a Christian spirit and with moral and spiritual earnestness. Therefore I have decided to call your attention to the matter, and to inquire whether you would be willing to engage with me in a joint discussion, at some suitable time and place in this city. The questions which I have in mind, but which I have not exactly formulated, are concerning the following: / 1—The Second Coming of Christ. / 2--The Millennium. / 3—Post-Mortem Probation. / 4—State of the Dead Between Death and the Resurrection. / 5—Eternal States of the Saved and the Lost. / 6—The Doctrine of Salvation.' "

83 Quote continued from the main text due to length: " 'I therefore accept your proposition, and join you in mutual assurances that the "Golden Rule" shall be observed, which will insure Christian courtesy of the very highest standard.' ... on June 27 the gentlemen concerned appended their signatures to a joint letter embodying the general conditions which should regulate the discussion, viz.: that in debate the first speaker should have fifty minutes, the second speaker fifty minutes; and that each should have ten minutes for reply; that the meetings should be absolutely free to the public, and should be held in Carnegie Hall, Allegheny, on October 18, 20, 22, 27, 29, and November 1" (*ZWT*, Oct. 15, 1903; reprint 3257).

84 *Recycling* was common among those who left the original movement. Thus, Jones copied "Zion" from Russell's *Zion's Watch Tower*, and Russell later re-used "Dawn" from Paton in his own book series, *Millennial Da*wn.

85 John H. Paton, who was one of Russell earliest employees, and author of the first book the Bible Students released. It was called *The Day Dawn* and published in 1880. And as it says on *Strictly Genteel*, where I downloaded the book, it was written "before his [Paton's] apostasy." The citation continues: "Paton later broke with the Bible Students, and altered the text of his book to reflect the apostate views he had espoused (*Strictly Genteel–Theocratic Resources*). This website is published by members of Jehovah's Witnesses. But the site is very useful and applicable, because in addition to Russell's *Studies in the Scripture* it contains many other English publications.

86 "No, the truths I present, as God's mouthpiece, were not revealed in visions or dreams, nor by God's audible voice, nor all at once, but gradually, especially since 1870, and particularly since 1880. Neither is this clear unfolding of truth due to any human ingenuity or acuteness of perception, but to the simple fact that God's due time has come; and if I did not speak, and no other agent could be found, the very stones would cry out" (*Proclaimers*, 1993, p. 143).

87 *The New World Translation*, the Jehovah's Witnesses' Bible translation, says: "Who really is the faithful and discreet slave whom his master appointed over his domestics to give them their food at the proper time?" (*NWT*, 1950) Note, that "servant" in this translation is replaced with "slave." Also *The Emphatic Diaglott*, B. Wilson's translation, has "slave."

88 On the website *Watch Tower History*, Tuesday, April 22, 2008 (site maintained by B. W. Schulz), it is argued that Maria Russell later modified her statements at the trial in 1907 and her claims of a partial authorship was an exaggeration, only due to the desire to reinforce the claim for alimony and a settlement on common property. That at the trial she also called the book series *Millennial Dawn* "Mr. Russell's books" can, however, in my view not be taken as proof that the series was *only* Russell's work. Obviously, they were *Russell's books*, regardless that some of his coreligionists had contributed with their labor. The question is really about the extent to which Maria Russell participated in the authorship.

89 From the testimony of the appeal case of Maria Russell about her writings for the Bible Student movement: "Question: What was the name of this paper that you issued? /Answer: *Zion's Watch Tower*. / Q:

Now, were there any books and writings published by you and your husband? / A: Yes, sir. / Q: Name them. / A: The *Millennial Dawn* series, and the *Hymn Book*, that is all. / Q: Now, you speak of the *Millennial Dawn* series, how many of these books had been published at the time you and your husband separated in 1897? / A: Four volumes. / Q: And that *Millennial Dawn*, of which you speak, I believe is the book which Mr. Russell testified has a circulation at the present time only exceeded by that of the Bible? / A: Yes, sir. / Q: Who wrote the *Millennial Dawn*? / Objected to as immaterial. / A: Well, the books were written by myself and Mr. Russell, all that Mr. Russell wrote was submitted to me for examination; I laid the plans for each of these volumes, and I can testify that at least one-half the work, and I think more, is mine, and of the fourth volume I wrote the entire volume except one chapter, but when seven chapters of that had gone to the printer, Mr. Russell took offense and never wrote the balance of it; he finished it himself, so that is the way the fourth volume ended; the *Hymn Book* was entirely my own work. / Q: Is that *Hymn Book* still in circulation? / A: I believe so. / Q: Did your name appear upon the title page of either of these publications? / A: Of all of them, unless they have been taken off in recent years; I have not seen their recent editions, but it was mentioned in the preface of each volume" (*Maria F. Russell v. Charles T. Russell*, on appeal, April 2, 1907, p. 120, 121).

90 *Libido* (Latin = lust). Psychoanalytic concept; Sigmund Freud explained this as sexual energy or *libido*, which when sublimated could be expressed in forms other than sexuality. Is one of two basic instincts, namely *libido* and *aggression*—or Eros & Thanatos. In man's mental system, libido is channeled to a wider area than sexuality. According to Swiss psychiatrist Carl G. Jung, however, *libido* is identified with psychic energy in general, which according to him was a "constant" in the individual and as Jung asserts expresses itself through symbols. The different definitions fit generally very well with the ordinary experience that *unilateral* energy takes energy from other aspects of life, including sexual life. The concept of *libido* was introduced in the first version of Freud's *Drei Abhandlungen zur Sexualtheorie* from 1905 (*Three Contributions to the Theory of Sex*).

91 "The object in taking out a charter is succinctly stated in the WATCHTOWER for January 1891, page 16, as follows: / 'This is a business association merely. It was chartered as a corporation by the state of Pennsylvania, and authorized to hold or dispose of property in its own name as though it were an individual. It has no creed or confession. It is merely a business convenience in disseminating the truth. Any one subscribing to one copy or more of the Society's quarterly, styled *Old Theology Tracts* (6 cents a year), is considered an active member of this Society—but not a *voting* member. Any one subscribing for $10 worth or more of the *O. T. Tracts*, or any one *donating* $10 or more to the funds of the Society for the spread of the Truth, is a voting member and is entitled to one vote for each $10 he or she may have donated. The affairs of the Society are so arranged that its entire control rests in the care of Brother and Sister Russell as long as they shall live. In fact the only objects in having the corporation are:— / 'First, To provide a channel or fund through which those who wish can employ their money talent, whether small or great, to better advantage for the spread of the Truth than if each interested one acted and published independently of the others. Secondly, The corporation was called for by reason of the uncertainty of the lives of those at present managing the fund. Some wrote that they were doing all that their present necessities permitted, but at their death they desired to do more; and urged the necessity of a legal corporation, as Brother and Sister Russell also might die, and they wanted their donations to go to the spread of the Truth. / 'The Society owns nothing, has nothing, pays no salaries, no rent or other expenses. Its policy is to use in the work every dollar received, to the best advantage, and as speedily as possible. Its success in publishing and circulating among the right kind of readers tons of *Old Theology Tracts,* is phenomenal alike to its friends and its enemies. The latter imagine there must be great wealth connected with the concern, whereas there is really very little. Few of the friends of this cause are able to do *much* financially; but what money there is, under economy and the divine blessing, is like the widow's cruise of oil; it accomplishes about a hundred times as much as other Tract Societies, which spend most of their receipts upon salaries.' / It will be seen from this and other mentions of the subject in the WATCH TOWER that I have never intimated otherwise than that the management of the Tract Society would probably rest entirely in the hands of myself and Sister Russell so long as we live, as provided by the regulations of the charter,—that the majority of voting-shares elect the executive officers. Our reasons for expecting to control the Society while we live, we did not state, because of modesty and a desire not to seem to boast of our good works. But now it is necessary to state matters plainly in order that our good deeds be not evil spoken of and misunderstood, and thus become a stumbling-block to others.—Rom. 14:16. / The fact is that, by the grace of God, Sister R. and myself are been enabled not only to give our own time without charge to the service

of the truth, in writing and overseeing, but also to contribute more money to the Tract Society's fund for the scattering of the good tidings, than all others combined. If I were *selling* my services for money, the Tract Fund receipts could not secure them, as my business ability would command a large remuneration" (*Extra Edition ZWT*, April 25, 1894, p. 57-59).

92 Quotation: "Preface / The Birth of This Question Book / After waiting nearly all summer, for the friends to let me know whether or not they desired copies of the 1916 Souvenir Convention Report, I placed an order with the printer for what I thought would be an ample supply, based upon the orders on hand. / The presses started and about one half of the book was printed and the type disposed of when Pastor Russell died. / Immediately the friends began to send in their orders for Reports, stating they MUST have Brother Russell's words, especially the reports of the various Question Meetings. / The result was, that all the available supply was quickly exhausted, and no prospect of another edition. / What to do for the friends was the question, until we believe, the Lord impressed upon our mind to compile all the questions and answers as they have appeared in the various Souvenir Convention Reports for the past twelve years, with other questions answered by Pastor Russell, making a classified list of all, according to the year answered, and binding them in a substantial book form / The result is the birth of this present volume of about seven hundred pages, which we pray, and trust will be to the glory of God, to whom it is dedicated, and for the blessing of His consecrated children, for whose use it has been prepared.... Yours in HIS service, L. W. Jones, M.D." (*What Pastor Russell Said*, circa 1916, 1917, p. 3; be aware that the page number can vary depending on the edition).

93 "But the servant is merely a steward, and liable to be removed at any moment, should he fail to fully and duly acknowledge in every particular, the Master,—the great Servant of God, and his people,—'the Messenger of the Covenant,'—Christ. / Faithfulness on the part of said steward (both to the 'Master' and to 'his fellow-servants' and 'the household') will be rewarded by his continuance as steward;—so long as he serves faithfully, he may continue, and may serve the household of faith with things new and old,—meat in due season—to the end; bringing forth all the precious things of divine provision. But if unfaithful he will be deposed entirely and put into outer darkness, while presumably another would take the place, subject to the same conditions. / To our understanding this would not imply that 'that servant' or steward, used as a channel for the circulation of the 'meat in due season,' would be the *originator* of that meat, nor *inspired*, nor *infallible*. Quite to the contrary, we may be sure that whoever the Lord will so use, as a truth-distributing agent, will be very humble and unassuming, as well as very zealous for the Master's glory; so that he would not think of claiming authorship or ownership of the truth, but would merely dispense it zealously, as his Master's gift, to his Master's 'servants' and 'household' " (*Studies* 4, 1915 (1897), p. 613, 614; see also strictlygenteel.co.uk).

94 "Go tell the blessed tidings / That legally we're free / From sin and pain and dying / To live eternally" (*The Wonderful Story*, p. 57; published of the Watch Tower Society, Allegheny Pa., 1890; *Writings,* 2008).

95 A rather subjective account, which demonizes Maria F. Russell and simultaneously justifies C. T. Russell's treatment of his wife, is found under the heading "Questions from Readers" in *The Watchtower* November 1, 1972. The article expresses the stigmatizing perception of Maria Russell, which first C. T. Russell and then the Watchtower Society has since constantly expressed. The *WT* editors quote one of Russell's private letters to a friend in England, dated Dec. 27, 1899, in which he explained why his wife had left him: "Our dear Sister Russell became afflicted with the same malady which has smitten others— notably those mentioned in the pamphlet, 'A Conspiracy Exposed.' Their difficulty was the same as that of the great Adversary in the beginning—ambition, and a desire to subvert matters in order to gratify that ambition…" Russell continued to use terms and statements such as that Maria Russell tried to "organize a women's crusade against me in the Allegheny congregation," and that this "female conspiracy" failed and resulted in only a "little sifting." And Russell summed up: "Sister Russell became afflicted with the spirit of ambition, as others have been, and in the Lord's providence it seemed best three years ago now that she should not be further identified with the publications [of the Watch Tower Bible and Tract Society], until such time as she might show a thorough change of heart in this matter" (*WT*, June 15, p. 384). A similar statement can be found in the *Proclaimers,* 1993, p. 642-672, published ninety-six years after the couple's separation in 1897. Other articles can be found in the *Yearbook* for 1975, *The Watchtower*, Jan. 15, 1955 and Aug. 1, 1994. This story is apparently still repeated without much self-criticism.

96 Ernest Charles Henninges died on February 3, 1939. His sect, the New Covenant Fellowship, is still active and offers Henninges books and copies of the *New Covenant Advocate and Kingdom Herald*. Henninges

defection caused the second largest split in the history of the Watch Tower Society, second only to the 1917–1931 schism. Henninges was also married to Rose Ball, Maria and Charles Russell's foster daughter. (For more information search for Ernest C. Henninges and the New Covenant Fellowship on the Internet)

97 In 1909 the name of the magazine *Zion's Watch Tower* was changed to *The Watch Tower*.

98 *The Brooklyn Daily Eagle* wrote eight or more articles about the case, some of them were: 1) October 29, 1911: Girl kissed pastor and sat on his knee. 2) January 1, 1913, pages 1, 2: Miracle Wheat Scandal. 3) January 22, 1913, page 2: Testimony of Russellite beliefs. 4) January 23, 24, 1913, page 3: Testimony on wheat. 5) January 25, 1913, page 16: Financial statements proving Russell's absolute control, made by Secretary-Treasurer VanAmburgh. 6) VanAmburgh's statement: "... We are not responsible to anyone for our expenditures. We are responsible only to God." 7) January 27, 1913, page 3. Government experts testify on "Miracle Wheat" and ascertain beyond doubt that it is not miraculous or overly excellent. 8) January 28, 1913, page 2: Prosecution and Defense sum-up. Russell assailed, but not present to hear it. 9) January 29, 1913, page 16: Russell loses libel suit (among others, Martin and Klann 1959, p. 15; see also J. J. Ross: *Some Facts* 1913).

99 (Continued from the main text due to length): "THE CASE BRIEFLY REVIEWED ... I am interested in everything progressive and tending to prove that we are entering the great thousand years of earth's blessings under Messiah.... Some of our readers purchased seed from Mr. Stoner at $1.25 per pound and approved it. In 1910 one of the friends of our Society, who had raised some of this wheat, sold it for seed at $1.00 per pound, and donated tile proceeds to our Society. In 1911 the same friend, having raised more seed, asked that THE WATCH TOWER give the benefit of this to its readers at $1.00 a pound post-paid, and appropriate the net results to the furtherance of its work.... We made no claim for the wheat on our own knowledge. We merely gave the report of the Government expert, of the originator, and of our friends who had tried the wheat. We merely acted as intermediary. / Nevertheless, everything that was said respecting the wheat was fully proven at this trial by expert witnesses, interested and disinterested, and their testimony was not shaken. It was also shown that farmer Stoner and his business partner, Mr. Knight, made no sales of this wheat under $1.25 per pound until September, 1911; and that they had a written contract between them that none of the wheat was to be sold at any price until the following year—1912. Suddenly in September, 1911, they changed their plans, considering that they had wheat enough accumulated, put the price down to $5.00 per bushel, about the time that THE WATCH TOWER wheat was all sold at a dollar a pound. This *The Eagle's* attorney claimed was proof of fraud on the part of THE WATCH TOWER—sufficient excuse for the slanderous assaults of *The Eagle* upon me. / It was in vain that my attorney sought to show the jury *The Eagle's* malice—that it really was attacking me along religious grounds; that it had set itself as the champion of certain clerical enemies [presumably including Ross] of mine, and, was seeking to destroy my influence and, if possible, to drive me from Brooklyn. In the court-room sat about twenty-five of my friends, who had come long distances at their own expense to have an opportunity to speak a word in my behalf. Through some intricacies of the law respecting evidence, these were unable to be heard in my behalf. Instead, the law gave *The Eagle's* attorney the privilege of saying all manner of evil against me falsely—for the sake of the doctrines of Christ, which I hold and teach. He was allowed to picture me, as *The Eagle* had done in its cartoon—as a thief and robber, masquerading in the garb of a minister of Christ. He was allowed to ridicule the 'Miracle Wheat,' although I had nothing whatever to do with it, nor with the naming of it; and notwithstanding the fact that its superiority was proven.... Presumably because there were seven Catholics on the jury, *The Eagle's* attorney was prompted to refer to the Sisters of Charity and their noble work as nurses in the hospitals, without referring to the fact that those nurses are well paid, and that the hospitals in large measure are supported by State taxation.... *The Eagle* was pictured by its attorney as a dove, a bird of Paradise: For defending it the Protestants on the jury were led to hope for escape from eternal torment through 'the pearly gates' of heaven, welcomed with the words, 'Well done!' for giving *The Eagle* the verdict. Neither I nor my attorneys could offer such inducements conscientiously" (*WT*, February 15, 1913; Reprint 5189).

100 Ross's pamphlet can be found on Barbara Anderson's website: www.watchtowerdocuments.com. This website contains a wealth of old and especially rare releases from The Watchtower Society.

101 Fakir: a Hindu ascetic; self-torment; impostor or malingerer.

102 A term that the foreman of the Grand Jury writes across the face of a bill of indictment (a document drawn up by a prosecutor that states formal criminal charges against a designated individual) to indicate that the criminal charges alleged therein against a suspect have not been sufficiently supported by the

evidence presented before it to warrant his or her criminal prosecution (TheFreeDictionary.com, Oct. 2011).

103   A grand jury's determination that there is inadequate evidence to indict someone. (*Webster's New World Law Dictionary*, 2006 by Wiley Publishing, Inc., Hoboken, New Jersey, USA.)

104   Police Court of the City of Hamilton, Ontario, March 17, 1913. See also *JW Apologetics Encyclopedia: Charges Against Charles Taze Russell*; see also Pastor Charles Taze Russell and the WTB&TS, Bible Students to Jehovah's Witnesses.

105   Rutherford also writes in his book: "He stated to me prior thereto that he would be glad to pay Mrs. Russell, *but he had no money*, which fact I knew to be true" (*Ecclesiastical Heavens*, p. 35; italics are mine).

106   "MR. E. J. COWARD, / Port-of-Spain, Trinidad, B.W.I. / Dear Brother in *Christ:*—Yours of October 3rd is before me. Thanks for its clippings from the *Gazette* and the *Evangelical Christian*. / I am quite familiar with the slanderous screed issued by Rev. J. J. Ross. In Canada they have just two laws governing libel. Under the one the falsifier may be punished by the assessment of damages and money. Under the other, criminal libel, he is subject to imprisonment. I entered suit against Rev. Ross under the criminal act, at the advice of my attorneys, *because, as he has no property, a suit for damages would not intimidate him nor stop him*. The lower Court found him guilty of libel. But when the case went to the second Judge he called up an English precedent, in which it was held that criminal libel would only operate in a case where the jury felt sure that there was danger of rioting or violence. As there was no danger that myself or friends would resort to rioting, the case was thrown out. I could still bring my action for financial damages, but it would be costly to me and impotent as respects Rev. Ross. He, however, is having troubles of his own. Since he began to attack me, he has split two Baptist Congregations—one in Toronto, the other in Hamilton. The last heard of him, he was in London, Ont., and again in trouble with his congregation. A lying spirit is sure to be a boomerang. / As respects my education in Greek and Hebrew: Not only do I not claim very special knowledge of either language, but I claim that not one minister in a thousand is either a Hebrew or a Greek scholar. To be able to spell out a few Greek words is of no earthly value. Nor is it necessary longer to study these languages, in order to have knowledge of the Bible. Our Presbyterian friends have gotten out at great cost *Young's Analytical Hebrew, Chaldaie, Greek and English Lexicon Concordance*, which anyone may procure. And our Methodist friends have issued a similar work—*Strong's Analytical Concordance and Lexicon*. And there is a still older one titled *Englishman's Hebrew, Chaldaic, Greek and English Lexicon and Concordance*. / Additionally, Liddell and Scott's *Greek Lexicon* is a standard authority. The prices of these are not beyond the reach of the average man. By these works scholarly information respecting the original text of the Bible is obtainable. I have all four of these works and have used them faithfully. Very few college professors, even, would risk to give a critical translation of any text of Scripture without consulting these very works of reference, which are standard. To merely learn to read the Greek and Hebrew without a six years' course in their grammars is more likely to hinder than to help in Bible study; far better take the acknowledged scholarship to which I have referred. / Additionally I remind you of the many translations of the Bible now extant—all of them very good. I have all of these and find them useful in comparison in the study of any text—one sometimes giving a thought which another may not. The other day, for curiosity's sake, I counted Bibles in different translations, etc., in my study and found that I have thirty-two" (*WT*, September 15, 1914, p. 286; italics are mine).

107   Actually, the judge wanted to consider the issues related to Rose Ball, but the statute of limitations for Maria's claims had run out, rendering the claim null and void. This is per the trial transcript (note by Jim Whitney).

108   According to a source on the Internet, Rose Ball was later married to one of the Watchtower Society's leaders, Ernest C. Henninges, who was one of C. T. Russell's two closest associates, and who owned a portion of the Society's shares. However, they sat at a tiny fraction of the share capital ($5.00 each). Source: "The Mary Russell Scandal" at http://www.jehovahs-witnesses.info/sscc5.html. Search also for: Pastor Charles Taze Russell and the WTB&TS. The Bible Students and Jehovah's Witnesses. Ernest C. Henninges and the New Covenant Fellowship, May 2011).

109   *Proclaimers* wrote in 1993: "In 1879, Charles Taze Russell married Maria Frances Ackley. They had a good relationship for 13 years. Then flattery of Maria and appeals to pride on her part by others began to undermine that relationship; but when their objective became clear, she seemed to regain her balance. After a former associate had spread falsehoods about Brother Russell, she even asked her husband's

permission to visit a number of congregations to answer the charges, since it had been alleged that he mistreated her. However, the fine reception she was given on that trip in 1894 evidently contributed to a gradual change in her opinion of herself. She sought to secure for herself a stronger voice in directing what would appear in the *Watch Tower*. When she realized that nothing that she wrote would be published unless her husband, the editor of the magazine, agreed with its contents (on the basis of its consistency with the Scriptures), she became greatly disturbed. He put forth earnest effort to help her, but in November 1897 she left him. Nevertheless, he provided her with a place to live and means of maintenance. Years later, after court proceedings that had been initiated by her in 1903, she was awarded, in 1908, a judgment, not of absolute divorce, but of divorce from bed and board, with alimony. / Having failed to force her husband to acquiesce to her demands, she put forth great effort after she left him to bring his name into disrepute. In 1903 she published a tract filled, not with Scriptural truths, but with gross misrepresentations of Brother Russell.... Earlier, Maria Russell had condemned, verbally and in writing, those who charged Brother Russell with the sort of misconduct that she herself now alleged. Using certain unsubstantiated statements made during court proceedings in 1906 (and which statements were struck from the record by order of the court), some religious opposers of Brother Russell have published charges designed to make it appear that he was an immoral man and hence unfit to be a minister of God. However, the court record is clear that such charges are false.... Nine years after Mrs. Russell first brought the case to court, Judge James Macfarlane wrote a letter of reply to a man who was seeking a copy of the court record so that one of his associates could expose Russell. The judge frankly told him that what he wanted would be a waste of time and money. His letter stated: 'The ground for her application and of the decree entered upon the verdict of the jury was 'indignities' and not adultery...'" (*Proclaimers*, 1993, p. 645-647; see also *Divine Purpose* 1959, p. 45).

110 B. W. Schulz uses this name for Barbour's small movement.

111 "Instead of expecting to convert the world, the Bible Students understood from the Scriptures that what was to be done then was to give a *witness* and that this would serve toward the gathering of 'an elect few from *all* nations, peoples, kindreds and tongues for membership in [Christ's] Bride class—to sit with Him in His throne during the thousand years, cooperating in the work of uplifting the race as a whole' " (*Proclaimers*, 1993, p. 419, 420; *WT*, April 15, 1912).

112 Stroup, 1945, p. 11, 12; J. H. Burridge, *Pastor Russell's Position and Credentials and His Methods of Interpretation*, p. 220 (see Stroup and *Wikipedia*).

113 See the section, "He died a Hero," in Chapter 10.

114 "The first volume of the *Millennial Dawn Series* was released in 1886. Its name was: *The Plan of the Ages*, later *The Divine Plan of the Ages*. Five more were published in the course of the years: Volume 2, *The Time Is at Hand*, 1889; Volume 3, *Thy Kingdom Come*, 1891; Volume 4, *The Battle of Armageddon*, originally called *The Day of Vengeance*, 1897; Volume 5, *At-one-ment Between God and Man*, 1899, and the last, volume 6, *The New Creation*, was released in 1904. Sometime after the sixth book was released in 1904 the series was renamed *Studies in the Scriptures* (*Divine Purpose*, 1959, p. 31).

115 The full text of *Millennial Dawn* 2 (1889): "In this chapter we present the Bible evidence proving that the full end of the times of the Gentiles, i.e., the full end of their lease of dominion, will be reached in AD 1914; and that *that date will be the farthest limit of the rule of imperfect man*. And be it observed, that if this is shown to be a fact firmly established by the Scriptures, it will prove:- / Firstly, That at that date the Kingdom of God, for which our Lord taught us to pray, saying, 'Thy Kingdom come,' will have obtained full, universal control, and that it will then be 'set up,' or firmly established, in the earth ..." (*Millennial Dawn* 2, 1889, p. 76, 77; Internet Archive, Free Download, *The Time Is At Hand*; italics in the quote are mine). The revised sentence in *Studies in the Scriptures*, page 76, 77, which *after* 1916 was decisively changed, reads:

"In this chapter we present the Bible evidence proving that the full end of the times of the Gentiles, i.e., the full end of their lease of dominion, will be reached in AD 1914; *and that that date will see the disintegration of the rule of imperfect men*. And be it observed, that if this is shown to be a fact firmly established by the Scriptures, it will prove: Firstly, That at that date the Kingdom of God, for which our Lord taught us to pray, saying, 'Thy Kingdom come,' will begin to assume control, and that it will then shortly be 'set up,' or firmly established, in the earth, on the ruins of present institutions. (p. 76; italics are mine)

116 "How true it is, therefore, in our day, when we are made to see clearly that the year 1914 will be the full end of the Times of the Gentiles, and that the next twenty-four years, therefore, must bring about the full consummation" (*ZWT*, Feb. 1890).

117 See for example *The Advent Review*, No. 4, September 1850, p. 56, 57: "The reason why none but 144,000 can learn or sing this song, will be because the history and deliverance of no other class will be like those who pass through the time of trouble, and are changed 'at the twinkling of an eye' at the coming of the Lord" (*The Advent Review* was edited by Hiram Edson and James White, later of the SDA, among others).

118 Jim Whitney adds: "The Bible Students also taught, however, that the great crowd of unnumbered sheep would attend the bride class of 144,000 into heaven, but hold a lesser position. All this changed in 1931 and again in 1935 when the great crowd of the Revelation of John was told they would live on earth forever. However, many also felt that something was not quite 'right' with going to heaven with the 144,000 as bridesmaids. But they were relieved to learn in 1931 that their hope was to be to live on a paradise earth" (e-mail, 2011).

119 Reference: www.mostholyfaith.com/bible/Reprints/index.asp or http://www.archive.org/details/Watch-TowerBibleandTractSocietyofPennsylvaniaWatchTowerpubs_0

120 See also *Jehovah's Witnesses in the Divine Purpose*, WTS, 1959, p. 47–67.

121 Other Bible students accepted things more calmly. For this, see Chapter 11.

122 *Self-Object*: Is due to Heinz Kohut, 1913-1981, an Austrian-born American psychoanalyst. It means that the experience one or more persons from a psychoanalytic viewpoint is a part of one's own self. Self-object refers to the narcissistic experience where *the other* (a person outside the self) serves one's own self, and therefore a "part" of oneself, resulting in consistency and increased self-esteem; a source of narcissistic feeling. Summary of definitions found on the Internet (March 2011).

123 "Before October closes our dearly Beloved Brother Russell will be with the Lord in glory. We are alone in Car Roseisle on Santa Fe train No. 10, due in Kansas City 7.35 Wednesday morning, and he is dying like a Hero" (Reprints 6005, *WT*, Dec. 1, 1916, p. 365-366).

124 In *The Watch Tower* for April 15, 1916, Russell wrote: "We believe that the dates have proven to be quite right. We believe that Gentile Times have ended, and that God is now allowing the Gentile Governments to destroy themselves, in order to prepare the way for Messiah's kingdom. The Lord did not say that the church would all be glorified by 1914. We merely inferred it and, evidently, erred. We see, however, that the different times and seasons which the Lord's providence sent to his people in hope of resurrection 'change' correspond closely with the different places to which Elijah, the Prophet, was sent before his translation. The last place to which he was sent was Jordan, which, we believe, corresponds to October, 1914. After that, Elijah and Elisha went on without having any definite point in view" (*WT*, Dec. 15, 1916, p. 121–127; Reprints 5888; see also *Proclaimers*, 1993, p. 635).

125 To learn more about W. Reade: http://www.socialaffairsunit.org.uk/blog/archives/000574.php

126 James Parkinson and Jerry Leslie, current Bible Students in the US, have kindly made a first critical and linguistic proofreading of chapters 11 through 17 in an earlier draft; for this reason I have used some of their insightful notes, subsequently placed here as endnotes. This does not necessarily imply that they share my views and conclusions.

127 An example of Rutherford's pompous and hateful rhetoric can be found in the book *Religion*, which appeared in 1940, one year before his death. "Armageddon" is mentioned seventy-five times throughout this book, and the Christian churches, especially Catholic, are attacked the worst. Under the heading, "WIPED OUT," it states: "The battle of that great day of God Almighty will forever put AN END TO RELIGION AND RELIGIOUS PERSECUTORS. That battle of Armageddon is God's appointed time and place to settle all accounts with his enemies.... The blood of those slain at Armageddon will not rest upon the heads of Jehovah's faithful servants. His witnesses and their companions have obediently and zealously sounded the trumpet of warning … and soon the workers of iniquity shall perish" (*Religion*, 1940, p. 348-350).

128 Internet resource, W. Hagen (originally written March 2009): "The Mystery Years of 'The Judge' Joseph Franklin Rutherford in Missouri," Freeminds.org, May 2011.

129 Note by Jim Whitney: "This 'empowerment' is fairly easy to obtain as long as a lawyer is able to practice before his state highest court. And that right is not difficult as long as the lawyer has practiced law in good standing for a certain period, in some states it is at least three years. So, while practicing before the US Supreme Court is an honor, it is not a difficult honor to achieve."

130 Note from James Parkinson: "Rutherford could not have represented anyone in a Canadian court. Dittlieb Felderer has uncovered information about John Jacob Ross. Among them, Ross was defended by the slickest Jesuit lawyer in Ontario, Canada (for a Baptist to be defended by a Catholic was badly looked upon). Forewarned of a coming subpoena, Ross suddenly fled from Hamilton, Ontario. Magistrate Jelfs sent the case up to the court twice for trial, but the court refused to hear it both times [the second time on the basis that there was no danger of public rioting (a criterion for criminal cases under Canadian law)]. Ross was included in 'Who's Who' for a few years, until it was learned that he didn't have the degrees he claimed" (July 25, 2011).

131 The "workers" (not employees) were essentially volunteers, who received minimal living expenses plus room and board.

132 C. T. Russell's editorial wishes published in *The Watch Tower*, December 1916: "In addition to the five named for the committee I have named five others from whom I prefer that selection should be made for any vacancies in the Editorial Committee, before going outside for a general selection—unless in the interim, between the making of this Will and the time of my death, something should occur which would seem to indicate these as less desirable or others more desirable for filling the vacancies mentioned. The names of the Editorial Committee are as follows:

WILLIAM E. PAGE,

WILLIAM E. VAN AMBURGH,

HENRY CLAY ROCKWELL,

E. W. BRENNEISEN,

F. H. ROBISON.

The names of the five whom I suggest as possibly amongst the most suitable from which to fill vacancies in the Editorial Committee are as follows: A. E. Burgess, Robert Hirsh, Isaac Hoskins, Geo. H. Fisher (Scranton), J. F. Rutherford, Dr. John Edgar."

133 The conclusion of Russell's testament: "We shall be satisfied when we awake in his likeness—'Changed from glory unto glory'. [signed by] CHARLES TAZE RUSSELL. PUBLISHED AND DECLARED IN THE PRESENCE OF THE WITNESSES WHOSE NAMES ARE ATTACHED: MAE F. LAND, M. ALMETA NATION, LAURA M. WHITE~IOUSE. DONE AT ALLEGHENY, PA., JUNE TWENTY-NINE, NINETEEN HUNDRED AND SEVEN" (*WT*, December 1, 1916).

134 Note from James Parkinson and Jerry Leslie: "Doubtful if A. I. Ritchie was considered for removal. But seventy Bethel workers were let go in the spring of 1915 due to shortfalls in contributions. See *Watch Tower*, 1915, May 1, p. 140."

135 Note from James Parkinson: "The Troy-Rutherford debates were in Glendale, California, in April 1915; so Rutherford was already in Los Angeles then. Charlotte White's letter in *WT* 1915, Feb. 1, p. 47 adds confirmation."

136 Note from Jerry Leslie: "See: http://governingbodyletters.blogspot.com/2008/07/some-historic-information-about-russell.html notes: Russell did not recommend Rutherford as his successor. He knew that Rutherford could not be trusted and that he was an opportunist. So in 1915 Russell dismissed Rutherford and gave him $1,500 to set up a practice in California. When Russell died, Rutherford was an elder in the Los Angeles Ecclesia of Bible Students. He had a regular job as an attorney for a department store."

137 Brian Kutscher wrote to me about the message J. F. Rutherford received from Macmillan: "Here, if something is 'coded,' it indicates that the message is unreadable to anyone except the recipient, who will have the proper key to decipher it. Macmillan's wire to Rutherford was completely readable. The expression 'old man,' in American usage, generally implies a great lack of respect for the person referred to. As (and if) the message was worded that way, it shows that Rutherford and Macmillan both were only waiting for C. T. Russell to die to hatch their plans for a takeover" (email of Sept. 13, 2011).

138 Quote from the testament of possible changes: "The names of the Editorial Committee (with such changes as may from time to time occur) shall all be published in each number of the journal—but it shall not in any manner be indicated by whom the various articles appearing in the journal are written. It will be sufficient that the fact be recognized that the articles are approved by the majority of the committee" (*WT*, December 1, 1916).

139 Suggested Internet search for more information: The curious case of the mysterious 6th name.

140 www.agsconsulting.com/htdbv5/r5999.html, found on the Internet, May 2011.

141 *Light After Darkness* had, as a matter of fact, five signators who all had (or had had) important positions in the Society: A. N. Pierson (vice president), J. D. Wright, A. I. Ritchie (previous vice president), I. F. Hoskins, R. H. Hirsh. Robert H. Hirsh was a trained journalist, and therefore, I presume he played an important role as author in the creation of this pamphlet.

142 Internet source: *Bible Students Fragments 1917–1967*: "At the 1917 January 6 elders meeting and ensuing Watch Tower annual meeting, several by-laws had been adopted (at Rutherford's urgent insistence, but without being read), among them: votes should be counted only for those nominated, and whoever is elected president of the Peoples' Pulpit Association (subsidiary corporation in New York state) is elected for life."

143 See *Bible Students Fragments 1917–1967* and/or: http://www.heraldmag.org/olb/contents/history/jp%20 history.htm.

144 According to an email from James Parkinson in November 2011: "J. F. Rutherford, and almost certainly A. H. Macmillan, wanted it to appear unanimous when published. They were unwilling to risk Menta Sturgeon, P. S. L. Johnson, or anyone else, being nominated. Moreover, by suspending the rules of balloting it would be possible, with the help of the by-laws surreptitiously passed a few minutes earlier, for JFR to vote CTR's shares as he pleased. By that, Rutherford was apparently able to get A. I. Ritchie out of the way and replace him with a supporter (A. N. Pierson). A year later he dumped A. N. Pierson by another change of by-laws, allowing someone to be elected without having been nominated. In the 1920s Rutherford did away with any pretense of open elections."

145 Robert Hirsh writes: "We rehearse these facts to show how the Brother managed to take the power from the Board of Directors, and to have it in his own hand. One of the by-laws, which was suggested at the shareholders' meeting, reads: 'The President of the Society shall always be the Executive Officer and General Manager of the Corporation, having in charge the management of its affairs and work' "(*Light After Darkness*, 1917).

146 See Note 144 for content of James Parkinson's email.

147 Brian Kutscher, an American who helped with historical details, writes about this: "It is amazing that Rutherford already knew the results of the election before it happened on January 6th, as it was normal to have an issue of *The Watch Tower* fully ready for printing and distribution at least two weeks prior to the issue's date. Hence it is 'amazing' how the results of an election, taking place on the 6th could be reported, typeset and printed for the January 15th issue—only 9 days after the actual events took place! My point is that, although not impossible, it was standard operating procedure to have the next issue ready (in terms of articles that would be used) before the prior one went out. Further, the magazines were probably posted one or more days before the date of issue" (email, Nov. 2011).

Jerry Leslie adds to Brian Kutscher's note: "Now I just wish to add a little support to Brian's comment in regard to the short window of time from the election on January 6 to include any additional articles or material in the scarcely 9 days for typesetting, proofing, printing, and mailing for the January 15 issue of The Watch Tower. Notice the article 'Who will be our Pastor?' on page 29. Here is an insert from Rutherford that compresses the timeline even less than 9 days, unless it was all prepared before the election. 6 January 1917 was a Saturday and the election. From the report we read: 'As it would take a little time for the Committee to complete its work, four o'clock in the afternoon was set to hear its report. It was nearly five when the Chairman called the meeting to order...' After the election Rutherford delivered his acceptance speech, a portion of which was transcribed for this issue of the *Watch Tower*. So it is evening when all return to their residences. There is no mail on Sunday and nothing until the mail delivery on Monday 8 January. Now notice the first letter copied on page 29. 'The following is a sample of inquiries received by J. F. Rutherford since his election as President of the Society, and his reply there to: DEAR BROTHER RUTHERFORD:—Greetings in the name of the Lord! Last night we as a Church elected you as our Pastor. Let me inquire, dear brother, is this the correct procedure or not? [Jerry Leslie: We acknowledge there is no date stating when this letter was written or received.] / Reply / DEAR BRETHREN IN CHRIST—Since my election as President of the Watch Tower Bible and Tract Society, I am advised that your Ecclesia has elected me as its Pastor...' If this is accurate as stated, such a letter could not arrive until Monday 8 January. Then J. F. Rutherford would have read and responded to this singular letter among any other correspondence. Then he would have submitted this reply to the typesetters to be composed in this issue to be printed and delivered to the post office by Friday the 12th or Saturday the 13th, but no later than Monday 15 January, for the 50,000 subscribers. So now we are down to 5-6 days for all the composition, typesetting, proofing, printing and mailing. All this is more than circumstantial evidence. Some of these features were certainly composed prior to the election and not all composed and written in the days afterward. They are only evidences that would raise the attention of any historian. Jerry" (Received Nov. 30, 2011).

148 Continuation from *Harvest Siftings Reviewed*, 1917: "In this account Bro. Rutherford failed to state that by his prearrangement the nominations were so closed, that there could be no other Presidential candidates for whom thousands of voting shares were instructed, and that he prepared the resolution recommending that he be made Executive and Manager. No political convention was ever more completely or more smoothly 'bossed' than the voting shareholders' meeting Jan. 6. Certainly the remark that Bro. Rutherford made to me in July, when he explained how he arranged for the election of Bro. Hirsh to the Board, applies to the proceedings of the Jan. 6 meeting. 'Of course, Bro. Johnson, you know all things of that character are arranged beforehand, just like matters connected with a political convention!' " (Quote can be located on the Internet at several locations using a portion for the search material.)

149 See also Alan Rogerson's book, *Millions Now Living will Never Die*, London: Constable (1969), quoting from P. S. L. Johnson's *Merariism*, p. 83–84, and, of course, P. S. L. Johnson's own book, *Harvest Siftings Reviewed* from Nov. 1917.

150 James Dennis Wright was on the board in 1906 and 1908, before the move to New York, and Isaac Hoskins from 1908.

151 "Brother Russell asked me to see if the WATCH TOWER BIBLE AND TRACT SOCIETY could be registered as a corporation in the State of New York. After a thorough examination of the matter I told him it could not be done, because it is a non-stock corporation organized under the laws of Pennsylvania and there is no provision in the law of the State of New York for registering such a foreign corporation" (*Harvest Siftings*; see THE PEOPLE'S PULPIT ASSOCIATION, approx. p. 42 in the edition, which can be found on the Internet).

152 "Two days after his [Russell's] death the Board met and elected Brother A. N. Pierson as a member of the Board to fill the vacancy caused by Brother Russell's change (*Light After Darkness*, 1917).

153 James Parkinson writes in May 2011 in an email: "F. H. McGee was a Bible Student. He sided with Bros. Ritchie, Wright, Hoskins, Hirsh and the others when JFR [Rutherford] seized power. (See *Light After Darkness*)... It was F. H. McGee who pointed out that officers cannot be elected unless they are first members of the board; so at the 1917 WT Annual Meeting there were either 7 members of the board, or zero. He also got a legal opinion to support that position. And he pointed out that a legal opinion is something you pay lawyers for (like a negotiating position), and it should not be confused with an honest opinion. Objectivity is essential."

154 The quotation from Penton apparently builds on a book (which I have not read) by Barbara G. Harrison: *Visions of Glory: A History and a Memory of Jehovah's Witnesses*, Simon and Schuster, New York, 1978.

155 "NO LAW SUIT We are charged in 'Harvest Siftings' [Rutherford's pamphlet] with great wrong because we consulted an attorney with regard to some legal matters; but it was not until the President himself had repeatedly told us that certain portions of the Charter were illegal that we considered it our duty to consult an attorney, who is a brother, well established in the Truth. And his advice, which proved to be sound, revealed to us that Brother Rutherford's legal opinion was very unsound. Then the President made a trip to Philadelphia to consult a lawyer there with the purpose of securing a legal opinion which would justify his declaring the Board illegal. Was it wrong for us to get legal advice when we saw one after another of the wise safeguards devised by our Pastor being swept away? It was not our desire to go into court proceedings. Far from it. And yet, all corporations are creatures of the law and necessarily subject to it. The law requires that Directors shall direct. They must know what their corporation is doing, and if they allow a President or other official to exceed his powers to the detriment of the corporation, they do so at their own peril, especially if they are driven in the direction of the law and do not take steps to protect their trust" (*Light After Darkness*).

156 James Parkinson writes in *Troubled Years (1916–1918)*: "Rutherford's efforts to establish control met increasing resistance from the majority of the board. On July 17, 1917, Rutherford claimed the Watch

Tower Bible and Tract Society charter provided for the election of directors annually, so only the three officers of the board (elected January 6) were truly members of the board; and so he appointed A. H. MacMillan, G. H. Fisher, J. A. Bohnet, and W. E. Spill to replace Ritchie, Wright, Hoskins, and Hirsh. The board majority, joined by F. H. McGee, countered that officers of the board cannot be elected unless they are first members of the board; therefore there are either seven members or no members. Both sides purchased legal opinions to support their claims. The ousted members decided not to institute legal proceedings, per 1 Corinthians 6:6–7."

157 Note from James Parkinson: "In London, Jesse Hemery was apparently grasping for total control, and he succeeded in getting P. S. L. Johnson to oust Henry J. Shearn, Secretary, and Wm. Crawford, Treasurer. This, of course, exposed the two to the British military draft. A. O. Hudson: *Bible Students in Britain*; Bible Fellowship Union, 1989."

158 Rutherford writes in *Harvest Siftings*, August 1917: "Learning thus that Brother Johnson was on his way to America, it was arranged that brethren should meet him at the dock and bring him to Bethel. I had been personally requested by his wife to keep him here until he recovered. When he appeared in the Bethel Home, to all intents and purposes he was sane upon every point except himself. He asked me if he might have a hearing before the Board. I called the members of the Board to the Study, and several other Brethren, and we listened to Brother Johnson for two hours. I presented to him a copy of the cablegram which he had sent me wherein he claimed to be the 'Steward' of Matt. 20:8, and asked him if he sent it. After much effort he finally acknowledged that he did.... It was the unanimous consent of all present that Brother Johnson was of unsound mind. I then stated to him, in the presence of the other, in substance: Brother Johnson, for the purpose of this matter we will concede that you thought you had authority to do what you did in Great Britain, and that you were acting honestly. Let us drop the matter now and not think of it any more. We all shook hands kindly, and he went to his room. He continued in the Bethel home uninterrupted for two months, except on one occasion he announced at the table that he is the 'Steward' mentioned in Mt [Matt.] 20:8, but in a few days thereafter withdrew the statement. Our hope was that he was recovering, and we rejoiced" (*Harvest Siftings*, August 1917; search term: "unsound mind").

159 Search for "Harvest Siftings Reviewed, P. S. L. Johnson"; a number of Bible Student publications can be downloaded from this website: http://www.biblestudents.net/history/.

160 Concerning the "steward," see Matthew 20:8 and Luke 12:45. As far as I can see, "steward" in Matt. 20:8 and Luke 12: 42 has the same function in the JW's doctrines as the "faithful and wise servant" of Matt. 24:45 (RSV). All the verses here are used partly on Russell, the Watchtower Society and today on members of the "faithful and discreet slave"-class (NW), or the "the faithful steward"-class (*WT*, October 1, 1981) and today on members of the "faithful and discreet slave"-class (*NW*), or the "the faithful steward"-class (*WT*, October 1, 1981).

161 As late as 1993 the Society presented the Johnson case as follows: "Out of respect for Brother Russell's wish, the Society dispatched Johnson to Britain in November 1916. However, once he was in Britain, he dismissed two of the Society's managers. Seeing himself as an important personage, he argued in speeches and correspondence that what he was doing was foreshadowed in the Scriptures by Ezra, Nehemiah, and Mordecai. He claimed to be the steward (or, man in charge) referred to by Jesus in his parable at Matthew 20:8. He tried to take control of the Society's money, and he instituted a suit in the High Court of London to achieve his aims" (*Proclaimers*, 1993, p. 627–628).

162 "'This is Rutherfordism.' Quickly seeing the similarity, but in another sense than he meant, I replied to the following effect: 'Yes, Brother Hoskins, it is Rutherfordism, just as two Board members, Brothers Rutherford and VanAmburgh, and one not on the Board, Brother MacMillan, sought to set aside the voted decision of the Board's majority, so you and Brother Margeson, two members of the Committee, with the assistance of one not on the Committee, Brother Rockwell, are now doing. It is Rutherfordism, indeed.' In fact, it was Rutherfordism repeating itself; but, strange to say, this time it is among ourselves" (*Another Harvest Siftings Reviewed*, August 22, 1918).

163 Later (around 1926) G. H. Fisher encouraged the German branch and ecclesias (congregations) of the Bible Students to expel (disfellowship) J. F. Rutherford of the Watch Tower Bible and Tract Society (*Wikipedia*, May 2011).

164 Ken Raines has written extensively about C. J. Woodworth: http://www.premier1.net/~raines/woodworth.html.

165 C. J. Woodworth - New historical information, article by Lee Elder, dated Oct. 3, 2001, located on Jehovahs-Witness.net; viewed by this author on Sept. 8, 2011.

166 Article by Ken Raines: "C. J. Woodworth: The Demon Possessed Editor of The Golden Age." See also: http://www.premier1.net/~raines/woodworth.html.

167 Jan S. Haugland: *The Successor Problem – A Focused biography of Joseph Rutherford, 2nd leader of the Jehovah's Witnesses*, 1916-1942 (Sept. 2000), available on the Internet.

168 Marley Cole died in 2009, at age 93. Cole's funeral took place at the Jehovah's Witnesses Kingdom Hall, 9140 East River Road, Coon Rapids, MN. Source: StarTribune.com; *Star Tribune* on May 3, 2009. See documentation in the Appendix.

169 Cole's book was released at a self-publishing press, Vantage Press, NY, in 1955, and must, according to information from Vantage Press, have been the publisher's biggest success, even today. It must have sold more than 100,000 copies. A recommendation from the Society's headquarters in New York, 1955, said: "Jehovah's Witnesses—the New World Society. A new book by this name has been published by Vantage Press of New York city. Written in newsy reporter style by Marley Cole, it presents for the first time in book form authentic information on the history, activities and doctrinal views of Jehovah's witnesses. Much of the material was gathered by personal interviews with witnesses, some of them being officials of the Society. Frequently in the news is something about the religion of President Eisenhower's parents. This book gives the facts often overlooked or concealed, with documentary proof that they were Jehovah's witnesses for many years. You will be interested in reading this 229-page book and seeing its many fine photographs. It is $2.95 a copy, and may be had at your local bookstore or from the Watchtower Society, 117 Adams Street, Brooklyn 1, N. Y." (*WT*, August 15, 1955, p. 511). Marley Cole's book could be ordered through the Watchtower Society, which is extremely rare for books that are not published by this organization (Jehovah-Witness.net, June 24, 2010).

170 "Associated Bible Students" is a Millennialist, Restorationist Christian movement that emerged from the teachings and ministry of Charles Taze Russell. Members of the movement have variously referred to themselves as Bible Students, International Bible Students, Associated Bible Students, or Independent Bible Students (*Wikipedia*, July 2011).

171 Note by James Parkinson and Jerry Leslie: "Adolph Ernst Knoch, Universalism; not a branch from the Bible Students, though several Bible Students in America, and the majority who left the Watch Tower in Sweden and Finland, went to them. Among them were first, Fred Robison, then Menta Sturgeon, who accompanied Russell on the last train trip and died in 1935, and Fred Robison and O. L. Sullivan." (Adolph Ernst Knoch [December 19, 1874 to March 28, 1965] was the author of numerous theological writings and a Bible publisher. Knoch founded the Concordant Publishing Concern and the Concordant Version of the Bible (*Wikipedia*, July 2011.)

172 Martin and Klann, 1959, p. 12; Braden, 1960, p. 362; Stroup, 1945, p. 1-21; *Divine Purpose* 1959, p. 72; Penton, 1986, p. 118; "Recent Bible Student History," available on the Internet.

173 Some other of the Bible Student groups (some already mentioned), which were formed in opposition to Rutherford in 1918: Angel of Jehovah Bible and Tract Society; Associated Bible Students; Berean Bible Institute (Australia); Bible Fellowship Union (Britain); Bible Students Publications / Publishing Company; Christian Millennial Fellowship, Inc.; Christian Truth Institute; Dawn Bible Students Association; Elijah Voice Society; Forest Gate Church (London, east side): Goshen Fellowship; Institute of Pyramidology (Britain); Laymen's Home Missionary Movement; Laodicean Home Missionary Movement; Epiphany Bible Students Association (these three all followers of P. S. L. Johnson); New Covenant Believers; New Covenant Fellowship; New Jerusalem Fellowship; Old Paths Publications (Britain); Pastoral Bible Institute, Inc.; Servants of Yah; Stand Fast Bible Students Association; Watchers of the Morning (Isaac Hoskins, April 1937 into early 1950s; sources include http://www.biblestudents.net/history/daughters_tower.htm, James Parkinson and Jerry Leslie).

174 "Walter A. Conkey was called as a witness for the Government. He was the book printer located at the time in Hammond, Indiana, who printed material for the Society. He testified that he printed 'The Finished Mystery' under contract with the Watch Tower Society in 1918. All of the contracts were identified as being written and signed by Joseph F. Rutherford" (Jim Whitney's article series, Part 5a).

175 Quotation: "That period of witnessing, as it were, in the 'sackcloth' of mourning had begun during the first half of the month of November, 1914, and now three and a half years later it was being killed by Sa-

tan's symbolic 'wild beast.' As Revelation 11:7 foretold. Warrants were served the following day by US Marshall Power, and the eight men were arraigned in Federal Court, Judge Garvin presiding..." (*Divine Purpose*, 1959, p. 79).

176 Members of Jehovah's Witnesses today are not familiar with the Bible Students' expectations for the year 1918. On FreeMinds.org, in 2011 I found the following: "Very few Jehovah's Witnesses are familiar with expectations for the year 1918. Russell mentioned 1918 before he died and the first editions of *The Finished Mystery* made some very strong predictions for the heavenly glorification of the Church in 1918. With this understanding, the end of the harvest was moved from 1914 to 1918."

177 In 1910 Russell introduced the name *International Bible Students Association* as a means of identifying his worldwide community of Bible study groups. He wrote regarding IBSA: "It fairly represents our sentiments and endeavors. We are Bible students. We welcome all of God's people to join with us in the study. We believe that the result of such studies is blessed and unifying. We recommend therefore that the little classes everywhere and the larger ones adopt this unobjectionable style and that they use it in the advertising columns of their newspapers" (*Wikipedia*, August 2011).

178 "Woodrow Wilson: Like Roosevelt before him, Woodrow Wilson regarded himself as the personal representative of the people. 'No one but the President,' he said, 'seems to be expected ... to look out for the general interests of the country.' He developed a program of progressive reform and asserted international leadership in building a new world order. In 1917 he proclaimed American entrance into World War I a crusade to make the world 'safe for democracy.'" (Source: Woodrow *Wilson* on Whitehouse.gov, June 2011).

179 Jim Whitney's article series on the 1918 trial against J. F. Rutherford and his associates can be found at: Jehovah-Witness.net; then: Trial-of-JFR (Part 1 to Part 5a, a total of fifteen articles). This refers to Part 5.

180 I've had trouble finding the exact wording of the indictment, since this and the court records use varied wording. I hope, however, that by means of Jim Whitney's articles (see previous endnote) and the Internet search suggested below I have been able to *reconstruct a fair wording* of this part of the indictment. An example of a variation is listed in the square bracket. On page 473, the indictment had another variation: "...disloyalty and refusal of duty, or to obstruct the recruiting and enlistment service"; "mutiny" is mentioned many times in the Indictment, and in transcripts found by searching for "1918 Rutherford vs the United States Trial" and locating the pdf file (See also pp. 79, 473, 502, 506, 1124, 1147).

181 Quote from the start of the banned pages 247–253 in *The Finished Mystery* which Rutherford, at the US government's request, had to remove. The censored portion is an interpretation of Revelation 16:13, an interpretation which expresses the Bible Students' strong anti-militarism and hatred of the churches. That these pages could be perceived as offensive in 1918 is incredible. I quote: "Come out of the mouth of the dragon.—The three fundamental truths of history are man's Fall, Redemption and Restoration. Stated in other language these three truths are the mortal nature of man, the Christ of God and His Millennial Kingdom. Standing opposite to these Satan has placed three great untruths, human immortality, the Antichrist and a certain delusion which is best described by the word Patriotism, but which is in reality murder, the spirit of the very Devil. [p. 247] ... Nowhere in the New Testament is Patriotism (a narrow-minded hatred of other peoples) encouraged. Everywhere and always murder in its every form is forbidden; and yet, under the guise of Patriotism the civil governments of earth demand of peace-loving men the sacrifice of themselves and their loved ones and the butchery of their fellows, and hail it as a duty demanded by the laws of heaven." The text on these pages is supplemented with very long quotations from, among others, C. E. Jefferson and a New York minister named John Hayes Holmes, Church of the Messiah, New York City, and others.

182 Edwin Louis Garvin (1877–1960) was an American lawyer and politician from New York. He was a judge in US District Court for the Eastern District of New York during the lawsuit against Rutherford and his colleagues.

183 Quotation from *The Watchtower*, 1989: "Oh, how the clergy of Christendom—the most prominent part of Babylon the Great—tried to use the world crisis to destroy those outspoken Bible Students! At last, in 1918, they had eight officials of the Watch Tower Society *railroaded into prison* on trumped-up charges of sedition" (*WT*, April 15, 1989; italics are mine).

184 Court to jurors: "What do you say, would you try him fairly and impartially, give him the rights the law

requires, *give him that cheerfully,* justly and with full measure?" (Jim Whitney's investigation of the trial.)

185 The italics in the chapter heading are taken from Daniel 7:18 in the Watchtower Society's own translation of the Bible, *New World Translation*. The verse reads: "But the holy ones of the Supreme One will receive the kingdom, and they will take possession of the kingdom for time indefinite, even for time indefinite upon times indefinite." *Revised Standard Version* says here: "But the saints of the Most High shall receive the kingdom, and possess the kingdom for ever, for ever and ever."

186 Quote from the book of Daniel 7:22, but taken from the Society's *New World Translation*, this verse reads: "... until the Ancient of Days came and judgment itself was given in favor of the holy ones of the Supreme One, and the definite time arrived that the holy ones took possession of the kingdom itself."

187 Quote from the trial: "Mr. Sparks [Rutherford's counsel]: We object on the ground that the defendant Hirsh is alleged as a coconspirator in this indictment, and the motion to dismiss the indictment as to him would result in making him a witness, not governed by the usual rule covering coconspirators. It makes him available as a witness without the disqualification of corroborating his testimony.... The Court: Yes, the Government is quite often wrong. You may enter the motion to dismiss the indictment as to this defendant Robert H. Hirsh, one of the defendants, is granted" (1918_Rutherford_vs_the_United_States_Trial.pdf available from several online sources, p. 108).

188 Note by Jerry Leslie: The Hirshes [Robert H. Hirsh and Rose Leffler] were both put out of the Bethel by Rutherford in July 1917. Afterwards they sided with P. S. L Johnson, until within just a few years they had a falling out with him. Robert H. Hirsh died 81 years old in 1949, and his wife died in 1984 at age 106.

189 "Although Manton was later made a 'knight of the order of St. Gregory the Great' by Pope Pius XI, his disregard for justice was finally revealed when, June 3, 1939, he was sentenced to the maximum penalty of two years' imprisonment plus a fine of $10,000 for shamefully misusing his high federal judgeship by accepting bribes of $186,000 for six decisions" (*Divine Purpose*, 1959, p. 87; search also on the Internet for Martin T. Manton Trial: 1939 – "without regard to the merits," "conspiracy constitutes the offense").

190 "Mr. J. F. Rutherford, 124 Columbia Heights, Brooklyn, N. Y. / Dear Brother: / Having in mind the letter I wrote you several months ago—and which letter was published in the Watch Tower—I feel it is obligatory that I write you again; I shall be brief. / At the time I wrote that letter I had a hope that I might still be able to engage in the work of the Society, in spite of the fact that I could not agree with all the Watch Tower articles; nor was I in full accord with the methods of conducting the work of the Society. However, I had determined to crush my own feelings and preferences with a view to being 'Loyal.' / The more recent articles in the Watch Tower, and the whole of the 'Light' book are to my mind so distinctly misleading that I now have no hesitation in positively separating myself from the 'Society' as it now exists. This letter is absolutely without personal feeling, and is informative only. Respectfully, / E. D. Sexton." (http://www.heraldmag.org/archives/1931_2.htm#_Toc23239531).

191 In the book *Prophecy*, Rutherford still held that 1874 was the date of Christ's second presence: "The Scriptural proof is that the second presence of the Lord Jesus Christ began in 1874 AD..." (*Prophecy*, 1929, p. 65, 66).

192 "The time for the fulfillment of the prophecy of Revelation seems to be from *about 1879* forward until the kingdom is in full sway. It was about that date that the second presence of the Lord began to be observed, and that and other truths began to appear in The Watch Tower" (*Light* 1, 1930, p. 12; italics are mine). See also the book *Prophecy*, bottom of page 65, Rutherford still held that 1874 was the date of Christ's second presence, and demonstrated by scriptural "proofs" – and this was published in 1929 (note from Jim Whitney). This probably means that Rutherford, as late as 1929–1930, still seems to teach that Christ's invisible return began in 1874 ("around 1879"). However, this must have been a part of his transition strategy, as the time not yet had come for the final showdown with Russell's ideas. James Parkinson adds here that as late as 1929, *Studies in the Scriptures* was sold by Rutherford's Bible Students, a campaign that was followed up with another book that contradicted the *Studies*. The Watchtower had a large stockpile of Russell's works, last printed in 1927, and Rutherford's motto must have been that they should look to get rid of "old meat" in time ("Get rid of the stale meat"), books in the past had been "meat in due season."

193 "It is possible that AD 1980 marks the regathering of all of Fleshly Israel from their captivity in death.

It is just 70 years beyond 1910, the date when Pastor Russell gave his great witness to the Jewish people in the New York Hippodrome" (*Studies* 7, 1926 (1917), p. 62).

194 "Sword of Jehovah" is a well-known expression in the terminology of the Witnesses. See *WT*, June, 15, 1950; *WT*, Sept. 15, 1988; *Divine Purpose*, 1959, p. 119).

195 Modern Jehovah's Witnesses' use of the "sword" is in reference to their employment of the Bible, the word of God, as their "oral" sword to win debates, and convince new converts to their faith (note from Jim Whitney).

196 James Parkinson wrote to me concerning the building and ownership of Beth Sarim: "Beth Sarim was built for $75,000 in materials and 0 for labor ('volunteer' workers) on a hundred acres of land (0.42 square kilometer). When complete in 1930, Robert J. Martin deeded the property over to JFR [Rutherford] for $10 (four of us have been completely through the house and over most of the remaining 2.7 acres of unsold land)." "Persistent rumors," continues James Parkinson, "say that Beth Sarim was built to remove Rutherford from headquarters in Brooklyn" (email, Sept. 2011).

197 In 1939, Rutherford wrote about Beth Sarim: "At San Diego, California, there is a small piece of land, on which, in the year 1929, there was built a house, which is called and known as Beth-Sarim. The Hebrew words *Beth Sarim* mean 'House of the Princes'; and the purpose of acquiring that property and building the house was that there might be some tangible proof that there are those on earth today who fully believe God and Christ Jesus and in His kingdom, and who believe that the faithful men of old will soon be resurrected by the Lord, be back on earth, and take charge of the visible affairs of earth. The title to Beth-Sarim is vested in the WATCH TOWER BIBLE & TRACT SOCIETY in trust, to be used by the president of the Society and his assistants for the present, and thereafter to be for ever at the disposal of the aforementioned princes on the earth. To be sure, everything then on the earth will belong to the Lord, and neither the Lord nor the princes need others to build houses for them; but it was thought well and pleasing to God that the aforementioned house be built as a testimony to the name of Jehovah and showing faith in his announced purposes. The house has served as a testimony to many persons throughout the earth, and while the unbelievers have mocked concerning it and spoken contemptuously of it, yet it stands there as a testimony to Jehovah's name; and if and when the princes do return and some of them occupy the property, such will be a confirmation of the faith and hope that induced the building of Beth-Sarim" (*Salvation*, 1939, p. 312).

198 http://www.aggelia.be/Rutherford_Exposed.pdf

199 See the letter from the anonymous debater here: www.aggelia.be/Rutherford_Exposed.pdf or Jehovah's Witnesses - 1 Farkel *Rutherford Exposed*: The ... - *Aggelia* ... a pdf via Internet download.

200 James Penton notes in his book, *Apocalypse Delayed*, that the Witnesses under Rutherford's presidency had a more relaxed attitude to sexual relationships in the movement (Penton, 1986, p. 266).

201 Or "the faithful and discreet slave," as it says in the *New World Translation*, the Jehovah's Witnesses' Bible from 1950.

202 The "Governing Body" (*like*, it is said, the old apostle-council in the first century from the first century) is chosen from among The Board of Directors of the Watch Tower Society: "By amendment to the Charter as voted upon in 1944, the membership of the Society was restricted to five hundred at the most, and these were to be men fully devoted to Jehovah God as dedicated, baptized disciples of Jesus Christ. These are selected by the Board of Directors of the Watch Tower Society. But their spiritual status must also come under scrutiny. Why so? Because not all these present-day members of the Society are spirit-anointed members of the 'faithful and discreet slave' class. At this writing there are just 450 members of the Society, but less than half (or 200) of them are of the anointed remnant of the 'slave' class. So the major number are disciples of Christ who have no heavenly hope. They are of Christ's 'other sheep' whose hope is to gain everlasting life in a Paradise earth under his heavenly kingdom" (*WT*, Dec. 15, 1971).

203 The department had been established by J. F. Rutherford to help the Witnesses throughout the United States defend themselves amid increasing opposition to their preaching, and their stance on flag salute, which the Society vehemently opposed (Stroup, 1945, p. 25, 26; search for Olin R. Moyle on the Internet, *Wikipedia* among other sources).

204 Olin R. Moyle's letter and a transcript from the subsequent trial are available at Barbara Anderson's website: www.watchtowerdocuments.com.

205 Other records of the Moyle trial show he won two $15,000 settlements at trial for a total of $30,000; another source indicates Moyle won his suit, and the court awarded him $30,000 in damages, which was reduced to $15,000 on appeal in 1944 (*Wikipedia*). However, the most important is that *he won his suit*.

206 "In more recent decades, at least since the 1960s, the modern Jehovah's Witness must go through a series of studies and then lengthy questions, which can today number about 120, by the congregation elders, and then is approved for baptism" (note from Jim Whitney).

207 The *King James Version* reads: "When ye therefore shall see the abomination of desolation, spoken of by Daniel the prophet, stand in the holy place, (whoso readeth, let him understand:)" (Matt. 24:15).

208 Quote from *Qualified to Be Ministers*, 1955: "In the advanced conceptions of the new witness work and the more centralized organization necessary to weld the witnesses together into one solid working force, considerable resistance was encountered from unprogressive 'elective elders' in the local congregations. Many of these insisted on living in the past, in the time of Pastor Russell, who was claimed by them to be the sole channel of Scriptural enlightenment, whom they called 'the servant' of Matthew 24:45. The Watch Tower of April 1, 1920, and subsequent studies showed clearly that even Brother Russell conceded in his time that the Watch Tower Society was the instrument or channel being used by Jehovah to teach his people on earth. Now that there was much new spiritual food being flashed from Jehovah's heavenly temple these elective 'elders' should not retard or prevent the local congregations from keeping abreast with the accelerating New World society" (*Qualified*, 1955, p. 318).

209 See Revelation 7:9 (RSV): "After this I looked, and behold, a great multitude which no man could number, from every nation, from all tribes and peoples and tongues, standing before the throne and before the Lamb, clothed in white robes ..."

210 Watchtower.observer.org

211 It should be noted here that from about 1880, C. T. Russell (and later Rutherford) showed favor toward the Jews' return to Palestine, and this is why he was perceived by some as a supporter of the Zionists. About 1910 Russell had, according to Penton, participated in a meeting in New York, where he had to have guided a Jewish gathering during the singing of the Zionist hymn, "Hatikva." And as recently as 1925, J. F. Rutherford published a little book, in which the Jews return to Palestine was considered as part of the fulfillment of the prophecy. The book's title was: *Comfort for the Jews* (125 pages), WTS, 1925. It states, in part: "JUDGE RUTHERFORD, known throughout the world as a friend of the Hebrew people, is vigorously supporting the claim of the Jews to the Holy Land..." (Foreword) "The rebuilding of Palestine is now beginning and is well under way. This is being done clearly in fulfillment of prophecy uttered as promises from Jehovah. The mere fact that the Lord said he would overturn it until a set time, is conclusive proof that it is God's purpose to restore Israel to his favor upon certain conditions" (J. Penton: *Jehovah's Witnesses and the Third Reich: Sectarian Politics under Persecution*, University of Toronto Press, Toronto, 2004; *Comfort for the Jews*, Foreword and Chapter II, p. 12. See also: Amazon. com. Jehovah's Witnesses and the Third Reich; Internet *Archive*: Free Download: Watch Tower pubs).

212 *Commandant of Auschwitz* was originally published by Weidenfeld & Nicolson, 1959. The quotation is from the reprinted edition, published by Phoenix Press, London, 2000.

213 A Swedish minister at Svenska Missionskyrkan (the Swedish Mission Church) and associate professor of theology at the University of Göteborg, Gunnar Samuelsson, has a doctorate in theological dissertation: "Crucifixion in Antiquity: An Inquiry into the Background of the New Testament Terminology of Crucifixion." Therein Samuelsson argues that the "crucifixion" is not mentioned in the New Testament Greek original text and that the word *stauroun* (or substantive *stauros*), which translates to "crucified" in fact refers only to the execution tool on which the Romans hanged criminals up. It translates to "tree," "stick," "pole" or "stake." According to the media, Samuelson has not drawn any absolute conclusion of his investigation, and he assumed himself that Jesus was crucified. His point is that today we cannot say anything definite about it. But it seems to be wrong. The Roman's methods of execution included among other things "Crucifixion," which took place in the way that the soldiers placed a crossbeam, on which the offender was previously attached with iron rivets, up on a vertical pole. Samuelson apparently believes that he is the first who has pointed this out, but the fact is that Jehovah's Witnesses since 1950 have claimed that Jesus did not die on a cross, but on a "stake," and therefore he was "impaled." For Jehovah's Witnesses the "discovery" that *stauroun* could be translated to "stake" was epoch-making, because they could trumpet the news as another indirect attack on "Christianity." This, the Swedish Protestant

clergyman and Bible-researcher ought to have known. Any well-informed theologian and pastor in the United States and Scandinavia knows that it was the Jehovah's Witnesses who first made the claim that Jesus was not crucified, but "impaled on a stake." The "discovery" was made by Jehovah's Witnesses' "New World Bible Translation Committee," which in 1950 began publishing Jehovah's Witnesses' special Bible translation, *New World Translation*. See for example: *The Watch Tower*, Nov. 1, 1950.

214 As mentioned in my introduction, I have chosen some places to call the Watchtower world headquarters simply "Brooklyn," which I think has been used as a synonym for the headquarters in previous years. Now, however, it looks like that the headquarters is currently being slowly moved to Warrick in the State of New York. But I will, until further on, keep using *Brooklyn*, because I am not familiar enough with the pending relocation plans. See the Internet: Watch Tower Will Move World Headquarters to Warwick. *Brooklyn* is far more familiar to most Jehovah's Witnesses.

215 On the title page we read the following: "A copy of this textbook is issued to each appointed elder, and he may retain it as long as he continues to serve as an elder in any congregation. At such time as he should cease to serve in that capacity, his copy of the book must be handed over to the Congregation Service Committee, since this publication is congregation property. No copies are to be made of any part of this publication" (Watch Tower Bible and Tract Society of Pennsylvania (all rights reserved), 1991; located this information on the Internet).

216 Note from Jim Whitney: "In the 1990s Circuit Overseers gave talks to congregations suggesting strongly that excessive and unrepentant masturbation is a form of 'loose conduct' and can be a basis for being disfellowshipped."

217 It is common in the United States for the dead to be buried only at licensed and zoned cemeteries in municipalities (Jim Whitney).

218 http://www.aggelia.be/Rutherford_Exposed.pdf

219 http://www.archive.org/stream/NewsclippingsAboutJudgeRutherford/News_Clippings_ Judge_ Rutherford#page/n25/mode/2up/search/rutherford.

220 *WT*, Dec. 15, 1954. The quotation is partially abbreviated, and the italics are by the author.

221 Former American Witness Jim Whitney wrote to me in 2011 on this topic: "I recall a conversation with a good friend who investigated the education of Fred Franz. It turns out that Fred only had two semesters of Greek. He was the only member of the New World Bible Translation committee who knew any of the "dead" languages. But, when reading the Walsh trial, held in Scotland, it became clear that Fred was not very good at Greek and really did not know Hebrew well."

222 This footnote is taken directly from the *Proclaimers*, which is done deliberately. It tells a little about all the changes within the organization which members must constantly endure: "From 1894 to 1927, traveling speakers sent out by the Society were known first as Tower Tract Society representatives, then as pilgrims. From 1928 to 1936, with increased emphasis on field service, they were called regional *service directors*. Starting with July 1936, to emphasize their proper relationship to the local brothers, they became known as regional *servants*. From 1938 to 1941, zone servants were assigned to work with a limited number of congregations on a rotation basis, thus getting back to the same groups at regular intervals. After an interruption of about a year, this service was revived in 1942 with servants to the brethren. In 1948 the term circuit servant was adopted; now, circuit *overseer*. / From 1938 through 1941, regional servants, in a new role, regularly served local assemblies, where Witnesses from a limited area (a zone) met for a special program. When this work was revived in 1946, these traveling overseers were known as district servants; now, district *overseers*" (*Proclaimers*, 1993, p. 223; italics by the Watchtower Society).

223 Link: http://www.telegraph.co.uk/health/healthnews/7734480/Teenage-Jehovahs-Witness-refuses-blood-transfusion-and-dies.html

224 See: http://www.watchman.org/jw/bloodbulgaria.htm

225 http://www.watchman.org/jw/bloodbulgaria.htm

226 Robert M. Bowman, E. C. Beisner and T. Ehrenborg: *Jehovah's Witnesses*, Zondervan, 1995.

227 Bruce M. Metzger: "Jehovah's Witnesses and Jesus Christ," *Theology Today*, April 1953, p. 74.

228 Mantey concludes his letter with this salute, partially quoted in the main text: "The above are only a

few examples of Watchtower mistranslations and perversions of God's Word. In view of the preceding facts, especially because you have been quoting me out of context I herewith request you not to quote the Manual Grammar of the Greek New Testament again, which you have been doing for 24 years. Also, that you not quote it or me in any of your publications from this time on. Also, that you publicly and immediately apologize in the Watchtower magazine, since my words had no relevance to the absence of the article before theos in John 1:1. And please write to Caris and state that you misused and misquoted my 'rule'. On the page before the Preface in the grammar are these words: 'All rights reserved no part of this book may be reproduced in any form without permission in writing from the publisher'. If you have such permission, please send me a photocopy of it. If you do not heed these requests, you will suffer the consequences." (http://www.towerwatch.com/Witnesses/New_World_Translation/mantey_letter.htm)

229 H. H. Rowley: "How Not to Translate the Bible," *The Expository Times*, Nov. 1953, p. 41, 42 (located on the Internet: Reachout Trust—Jehovah's Witnesses—The New World Translation). The webmaster of the site assures me that all its information is secure and is verified (Doug Harris, Reachout Trust). See also: The New World *Translation*: The Watchtower Society's Corrupt *Bible*.

230 The New World *Translation*: The Watchtower Society's Corrupt *Bible*.

231 See: A critical look at the Jehovah's Witnesses' Bible: The New World Translation by M. Kurt Goedelman (www.focusonthefaulty.com/Pages/jehovahs.html); this website is from a Christian association, critical to many cults which appear in the US, among them: Scientology, Mormonism, the Jehovah's Witnesses and others. I cannot, however, guarantee the credibility of this website.

232 Editor of the newsletter *Comments from the Friends* and co-author of *The Author's Testimony* and *Dictionary of J.W.ese: The Unique Language of Jehovah's Witnesses*, 1997/2010, publisher: lulu.com (Jan. 3, 2010); available at Amazon.com (USA).

233 "Just as that method was so important for them from the first and, later, in Paul's day, so it is our most important work during *this fortieth year* of Jehovah's kingdom. You should get out there in the field, going from house to house, from home to home, meeting the people in their homes, talking to them about the glory of Jehovah's kingdom. Are you doing that, especially now that the Kingdom, Jehovah's permanent government, is here? It is urgent to do so, because the years left before his final battle at Armageddon cannot be too many" (*WT*, Jan. 1, 1954, p. 15; italics are mine).

234 Schnell, 1956, p. 33: "This expectation [concerning 1925] was fanned by every publication of the Organization of that time and it left a deep imprint upon our minds. In fact, it virtually made irrational crack-pots out of many of us."

235 "We must do this for the endurance test that yet lies ahead and for the work that remains to be done" (*WT*, August 15, 1953).

236 The International Geophysical Year (IGY) was an international scientific project which lasted from July 1, 1957, to December 31, 1958 (*Wikipedia*).

237 Regarding *The Habbakkuk Commentary*, see for example: Millar Burrows, *The Dead Sea Scrolls*, 1956, p. 365–370; see also: Geza Vermes, *The Dead Sea Scrolls in English*, Penguin Books, 1992, p. 384–386). See also: James C. VanderKam, *The Dead Sea Scrolls Today*, Wm. E. Eerdmans Publishing Co., 1994. Also the controversial Robert Eisenman, who once published the *Dead Sea Texts*, where among other things he deals with the "Chittims" or the "Kittim": *James the Brother of Jesus—Recovering the True History of Early Christianity*, by Faber and Faber Limited, 1997, p. 19.

238 Antiochus IV Epiphanes (ca. 215–164 BC). He ruled the Seleucid Empire from 175 BC until his death in 164 BC. He was called *Epiphanes*, "God Revealed," but nicknamed *Epimanes*, "the mad." He was a son of King Antiochus III the Great. His original name was Mithridates; he assumed the name Antiochus after he ascended the throne (*Wikipedia*, 2011; and: www.bibarch.com/Biographs/Ancient/Antiochus%20 IV.htm).

239 Jim Whitney made me aware of the psychiatric term, "cognitive dissonance." On the Internet there are many articles on the topic. Leon Festinger developed the "cognitive dissonance" theory in 1957. The Danish author and religion researcher Per Bilde used the concept in his book *En religion bliver til* (*A Religion Arises*). He uses the concept in connection with the early Christians' disappointment over Christ's defaulting return.

240 Quote: "For each of the five years from March, 1952, to April, 1957, there was an average of 500 mem-

bers that were disfellowshipped for flagrant misdeeds that cannot be tolerated inside of Jehovah's congregation" (*WT*, March 15, 1958, p. 165–172).

241 Jim Whitney wrote to me about this issue: "In the mid-1970s, I recall the number of disfellowshipped each year was about 40,000. When I left the Jehovah's Witnesses in the early 1990s, the number of those disfellowshipped reached about 60,000 per year worldwide. The number has consistently stayed around 1% of all JWs are disfellowshipped each year. The number of those who are privately or publicly reproved each year is not reported that I am aware, but I suspect, based on many years' experience, that it represents another yearly 1% of all JWs" (March 2011).

242 Note from Jim Whitney: "I was able to build statistics over a 40-year period, from the late 1950s to the late 1990s, based on the January *Watchtower* magazine. From this, using baptism numbers, the number of deaths and the number of those still active, I estimated that by the mid-1990s, about 2 million people are former JWs that are still alive. Many of these left during the late 1970s and into the mid-1980s over the failure of 1975 ... and with the advent of the Internet in the late 1990s, many more have left the ranks of Jehovah's Witnesses" (March, 2011).

243 Walter Kolarz (1912–1962) was a British-based scholar of the communist world who wrote widely on ethnic and religious issues (*Wikipedia*). As an Englishman, Kolarz has perhaps used words, phrases and spellings that are not common in the US.

244 See: http://www.watchtower.org/e/statistics/wholereport.htm.

245 The Governing Body was in these years not at all a lofty size, as that term has since evolved into. For example they spelled it "governing Body" with only lowercase letters at first. For example, see the *1970 Yearbook*, which states: "So really the governing body of Jehovah's witnesses is the board of directors of the Watch Tower Bible and Tract Society of Pennsylvania, all of whom are dedicated to Jehovah God and anointed by his holy spirit" (p. 65).

246 I have tried to find the original article from the *Watch Tower Library* (JW-CD), in which this quote appeared, but it has been impossible. I searched on the word "opportunity." But as I sought the mentioned article, I found another one—almost as striking. I quote: "May we not waste time; may we not prove lazy in this grandest opportunity.... May we not waste our strength in a calamitous occupation. The time to use our strength in Kingdom service now before Armageddon is too limited. To the fullest may we give our strength to the Kingdom service. Young people have a special opportunity in this regard. If they misspend their youth in vain, calamitous works, God will in due time judge them for it" (*WT*, Nov. 15, 1957).

247 "All animals are equal, but some animals are more equal than others." A proclamation made by the pigs in the novel, *Animal Farm*, by English writer, George Orwell. Orwell's real name was Eric Arthur Blair (b. June 25, 1903; d. January 21, 1950).

248 In *King James Version* the quote from Matthew 24:45 reads: "Who then is a faithful and wise servant, whom his lord hath made ruler over his household, to give them meat in due season?" In the *New World Translation*, the Jehovah's Witnesses' Bible, the same verse reads: "Who really is the faithful and discreet slave whom his master appointed over his domestics to give them their food at the proper time?" (*NWT*, 1953–1960; bound together in one volume and published in 1963)

249 Abrahamson himself tells this part of the story in *The Watchtower*, December 1, 2003: "One of the problems to be dealt with was that a few in responsible positions failed to accept direction from the headquarters in Brooklyn. Also, three of the four who were translating our publications into Danish left Bethel and eventually ceased association with Jehovah's Witnesses" (*WT*, Nov. 1, 2003).

250 In 1925 William Dey from Scotland was assigned to supervise the preaching work of the Bible Students in Denmark. He was reportedly well-liked and he soon became known as the "Big Scotsman" (*WT*, Oct. 1, 1997).

251 W. & P. Paddock: *Famine 1975!: America's decision: Who will survive?*, 286 pages. Publisher: Little, Brown; 1st edition, Boston 1967. A critical mention and review by Wilbur L. Bullock, Zoology Department, University of New Hampshire, Durham, N.H., which can be found on the Internet, evaluates the book as somewhat superficial and sensational, but also serious and thought-provoking. The starting point is Christian, possibly in part Catholic, and it confuses many concepts—such as Matthew 24, verse 7, which includes among others future famines, "but it also sounds ominously like parts of the Revela-

tion," writes W. L. Bullock. William Paddock, one of the authors, must be an experienced agronomist and recognized authority on tropical agriculture. The Paddock brothers' apocalyptic visions fell understandably in good soil of the Witnesses' headquarters in Brooklyn. It was water in their mill! (JASA Book Reviews for December 1968)

252   *Awake!* from October 8, 1973, states: "What is now developing *on a global scale* was predicted several years ago. For example, among others, William and Paul Paddock in their book *Famine 1975* had warned that world population growth was running ahead of food production and that a crisis could be expected in the mid-1970's. In May 1973, a New York *Times* editorial commented: 'It appears that the Paddock brothers' prophecy for 1975 could begin to become a reality as early as 1974.' But the symptoms have already appeared before 1974" (italics by *Awake!).*

253   Quotation from *Awake!* Dec. 22, 1974: "The Paddock brothers' well-known 1967 book *Famine 1975!* based its predictions on population growth and similar factors. Interestingly, a letter in *Science* magazine now reports that the former director of the Smithsonian Institution's Astrophysical Observatory published a prediction in 1938 pointing to 1975 for different reasons. Based on sunspot cycles and water levels of the North American Great Lakes, he said that "there is much reason to expect a ... drought beginning about 1975." In 1963 he added: "I predicted about 1938 [drought] recurrence in the decade of 1950–1960. It proved very severe in [the] Southwest United States." He then repeated his 1938 prediction of a 'great drought' that he said would "probably begin about 1975."

254   Unabridged quote from *the Watchtower*: "In the last five years 323,986 new Kingdom publishers symbolized their dedication to Jehovah God by water baptism. Yet, during that period, there was an increase, on an average, of only 174,088 ministers. What happened to the other 149,898? When one subtracts the approximately 1 percent who normally die each year, it still leaves about 100,000 persons who have ceased to preach in just the past five years. Are you one of these who used to be a Kingdom publisher? If so, what is the reason for it?" (*WT*, March 1, 1967)

255   A similar study is available at http://www.jwfacts.com/watchtower/statistics.php—under the title: "Facts about Jehovah's Witnesses" (located site and article July 2009).

256   Today: "Circuit overseer."

257   Reference to Revelation 17:5–6. The *woman* is "...Babylon the great, the mother of harlots and abominations of the earth. And I saw the woman drunken with the blood of the saints..." Babylon is according to the doctrines of the Watchtower Society the Christian churches, and "the saints" are the Witnesses. See also: *WT*, Oct. 1, 1953, p. 582-607.

258   See *Yearbook* 1975, Part 3: "United States of America," here it states: "During the 1967 service year 74,981 persons were baptized. This was an upswing and it gave renewed reason for optimism. Then came 1968, along with the *Truth* book and the six-months Bible study program. 'In the minds of many,' remarks Edgar C. Kennedy, 'it was closely linked with the announcement two years before of the 6,000 years [of man's existence on earth] ending in 1975.' C. W. Barber similarly cites 'the shortness and urgency of the times,' terming 1968 as a 'turning point,' and states: 'Everywhere the brothers aroused themselves and went at this 'easier' method of spreading the good news, with vigor. The number of publishers started to climb again all over the earth." The mood within the Witnesses was extremely heated at this time (WT-CD, 2005).

259   "Circumstantial evidence" is evidence in a case which can be used to draw inferences about events, therefore, a legal term. The term is also used within the Jehovah's Witnesses in matters of guilt in cases of immoral sexual behavior. Here they would use *strong* "circumstantial evidences" to illustrate such a case. On the English JW-CD, which dates back to 1950, I found this quotation, where "circumstantial evidence" is used in much the same way: "Jesus did not tell them that he would be visibly present with them. Rather, his presence with them would be noted solely by circumstantial evidence..." (*WT*, November 1, 1953, p. 644). See also *Insight*, Volume 1 (WTS), where "circumstantial evidence" is used in connection with archaeology.

260   The Witness doctrine about the 144,000, the "little flock," who from heaven shall govern with Christ in the thousand-year, is founded in a combination of three verses from Revelation 7:4 and 9, and Luke 12:32. The "little flock" will lead the "great multitude" (KJ) into paradise, the New World, where they shall live forever.

261   After 1975 the Society's annual report shows that the "anointed" is now dying out much more slowly

than before 1975, which seems to suggest that the Society is using this as a way to postpone Armageddon. This surprising development is looked at in more depth in Chapter 34.

262 According to a new timetable, which added one hundred year more to Russell's old timetable, the eleventh chapter of the book, *The Truth Shall Make You Free* from 1943, says that the year 1943 was the 5,971st year since the creation of man: "We are therefore near the end of six thousand years of human history, with conditions upon us and tremendous events at hand foreshadowed by those of Noah's day.—Luke 17:26-30." With reference to this book, the new one, *God's Kingdom of a Thousand Years has Approached*, says: "This moved forward the end of six thousand years of man's existence into the decade of the 1970s" (*Approached*, 1973, chapter 1, § 17; p. 209, 210; see also p. 14).

263 Compare with *King James Version*: "For the vision is yet for an appointed time, but at the end it shall speak, and not lie: though it tarries, wait for it; because it will surely come, it will not tarry" (KJ).

264 Interaction is what happens when two or more objects (such as a speaker and his audience) have a reciprocal effect upon one another. The effect could be that the speaker will have an experience of his own "great" importance, especially if the audience is applauding, and that the audience uses the speaker's grandiose self-understanding to expand the importance of their own personality perception (*Wikipedia* among other sources).

265 Quote from 1957: "Being so closely associated with the mother organization, Christ's 'bride' would certainly resemble her mother in all respects, as would even those Christians still on earth in the flesh who are engaged to be married to Christ. These would serve as her representatives and would therefore be easily recognizable by their conformity to God's requirements for his visible channel of communication." Quote from 1991: "That faithful and discreet slave is represented today by the Governing Body of Jehovah's Witnesses, which has as its publicity agent the Watch Tower Bible and Tract Society. Most appropriately, that faithful and discreet slave has also been called God's channel of communication" (*WT*, Sept. 1, 1991).

266 In 1891 Russell already used a similar speculative argument in connection with the period between the creation of Adam and creation of Eve (See: *Studies in the Scripture* 3, 1919 (1891), p. 127, 128).

267 Under the heading, "A Governing Body as Different from a Legal Corporation," *The Watchtower* writes: "ON Friday morning, October 1, 1971, the legal corporation known as Watch Tower Bible and Tract Society of Pennsylvania held its annual corporation meeting, this time in the Assembly Hall of Jehovah's witnesses at Buckingham, Pennsylvania. All seven members of the Board of Directors of said Society attended and had a part in the program presented. The membership of this Society is limited to five hundred at the most, there being at present four hundred and fifty such members throughout the earth. Many of these members attended this annual corporation meeting in person, still more by means of proxy. All together, 2,076 attended this corporation meeting, doubtless all of them being interested Christian witnesses of Jehovah. / At this meeting a question came up and was discussed from the platform. It was as to what the relationship is between the Board of Directors of the Society as a legal corporation and the Governing Body of Jehovah's Christian witnesses. Are they the same, identical, or are they different? Such questions were due to the fact that it has been published in print that the Governing Body of Jehovah's witnesses at headquarters is associated with the Board of Directors of the said Society. How did this come about, and does this make the Board of Directors the same as the Governing Body of Jehovah's witnesses all the earth around?" (*WT*, Dec. 15, 1971)

268 When I needed to find the English word "murmur" or the gerund "murmuring," as part of the "theocratic" terminology, I used the WT-CD to search for the word, and I discovered there were many references in articles from *The Watchtower* and other places in the Watchtower literature where the word occurred. For example in a short article: "Why Murmur?" with thirty-six appearances: "In particular should all those dedicated Christians in the New World society examine themselves when tempted to murmur. Jehovah was leading his organization before we ever became a part of it; so let us humbly put our faith and trust in him and in the instruments he has chosen to act as overseers in various capacities. If conditions really do need correcting, have patience and faith that God will correct them in his due time. In the meantime, do not make yourself and others unhappy by murmuring. Yes, why murmur?" (*WT*, May 1, 1960, p. 259–260). An article from *The Watchtower*, July 15, 2006, has forty-four instances of the word in three forms, "murmur," "murmured," "murmuring/murmurings" (questions to the article included). It resembles brainwashing.

269 In 1951, the perception of the Watchtower Society of the time of trouble: "Christ Jesus groups many such prophecies and enlarges on them when explaining to his disciples some of the things which must come to pass in the last days. (See Matthew 24.) He shows the beginning of this time and how the troubles increase, and mentions some of the sorrows to fall on the world, during the time of trouble. The length of time is indicated by him when he said, 'Truly I say to you that this generation will by no means pass away until all these things occur.' (Matt. 24:34, *NW*) The actual meaning of these words is, beyond question, that which takes a "generation" in the ordinary sense, as at Mark 8:12 and Acts 13:36, or for those who are living at the given period. So it was on 'this generation' that the accumulated judgments were to fall. (Matt. 23:36) This therefore means that from 1914 a generation shall not pass till all is fulfilled, and amidst a great time of trouble" (*WT*, July, 1, 1951).

270 "In December 1973, Nathan Knorr, then president of the Watch Tower Society, wrote both the Bethel Office and the Towers management, saying that the Society planned to 'move out of the Towers Hotel by October 1, 1974.' / Brother Couch said that he was shocked because there was nowhere to house the Bethelites living in the Towers. The Towers management was also shocked, since they were relying on the Society's rent money to keep them going. The upshot was that the Towers management urged Jehovah's Witnesses to buy the hotel. 'You've been growing ever since we've been in the neighborhood,' they said, 'and you need the building.'/ 'It's full of tenants,' was the reply of the Society's representatives. 'If we bought it, we'd want to put our own people in there.'/ 'We'll empty the building for you,' the Towers management promised. Well, shortly afterward Jehovah's Witnesses purchased the Towers building at an appropriate price. 'Why did Brother Knorr write that letter?' Couch asked his fascinated audience. 'He probably didn't know himself, but that is the thing that sold the Towers Hotel to the Watch Tower Society' " (*WT*, April 15, 1996; heading: "Expansion With Jehovah's Blessing").

271 The whole correspondence is now available on the Internet: http://user.tninet.se/~oof408u/fkf/english/corr.htm

272 That the "gentile times" from Luke 21:24 would be a longer time period, which had and still has a special significance in the context of Christ's coming is really difficult to find justification for in the New Testament. When the Gospel of Luke was written, which happened around the years AD 70–90, maybe even later, the city of Jerusalem, conquered and destroyed in AD 70, was still under Roman administration, and the term "gentile times" is without a doubt an allusion to this fact. Maybe in fact a clause, since the term only appears once in the New Testament. It should also to be noted that in the first century, the term "Jerusalem" was not yet removed from the Christian conceptual world, but was still linked to the hope of Christ's immediate coming and Jewish restoration as God's people, including Jerusalem's liberation from oppressors. All the verses in Luke 21:20–28 deal with the Roman occupation of Jerusalem, as seen from a time perspective after the year AD 70. And it's clear to me that the Christians are looking forward to the imminent coming of their Lord, Jesus Christ. But the author pretend that Jesus' words are spoken before the year 70 (verse 20).

273 During the German occupation of Denmark, 1939–1945, *alsang* served as an expression of resistance against the German occupiers.

274 See "Biography of Tom Cabeen," available on the Internet; see also on the Internet: "Tom Cabeen - Former Overseer Of The Watchtower Printing & Pressroom"; both March 2011.

275 The Swedish Elder was Carl Olof Jonsson, who published his great study in 1983: *The Gentile Times Reconsidered,* now in four editions, the latest in 2004, revised and expanded, published by Commentary Press, Atlanta, Georgia.

276 See for example *The Watchtower*, August 1, 1993; and *Awake!*, June 22, 1992, where this terminology, "bad company," is used. This term comes originally from 1 Corinthians 15:33 "Be not deceived: evil communications corrupt good manners."

277 Mors is an island, located in Limfjorden, in the Northwest of Jutland, Denmark.

278 The Limfjord (Danish: *Limfjorden*) is a shallow sound in Denmark that separates the island of Mors from those parts of the country on the Jutland Peninsula known as Thy and Vendsyssel (partly *Wikipedia*, 2011).

279 The "faithful and discreet slave" is taken from Matt. 24:45 in *The New World Translation*, 1963. *The Watchtower* writes about that "slave": "Our Christian brotherhood is another valuable resource in seek-

ing Jehovah's guidance. Central to that brotherhood is "the faithful and discreet slave" with its representative Governing Body, which issues a constant supply of spiritual food in the form of printed material and programs for meetings and assemblies. (Matt. 24:45-47; compare Acts 15:6, 22-31.) In addition, within the Christian brotherhood are mature individuals, especially the elders, who are qualified to give personal help and Scriptural counsel..." (*WT*, April 15, 2008, p. 11).

280 The secret elder manual: *"Pay Attention to Yourselves and to All the Flock;"* Watch Tower Society, 1991.

281 Poul Dal and Jette Svane met each other later at an apostates' meeting, and since they shared similar dramatic events in their lives they created a new life together. They now live in a nice house south of Viborg, not many miles from the place where my wife and I lived with our two sons when we left the movement in 1959.

282 According to the daily Danish paper *Politiken*, the crucial test is 120 questions that the baptismal candidate has to answer in relation to the congregation's committee. To this Erik Jorgensen, public relations director for Jehovah's Witnesses in Denmark, said: "Sometimes the council assess that the person is not mature enough. It is a very meticulous process where we ensure that we really understand what one is getting into." Erik himself was only twelve when he was baptized (*Politiken*, Feb. 12, 2011). In 1993 *The Watchtower* said: "A younger generation is growing up in Jehovah's service, and happily the majority of these are making application of Solomon's words at Ecclesiastes 12:1: 'Remember, now, your Grand Creator in the days of your young manhood.' They are applying themselves in their schoolwork, as well as being trained in spiritual matters by devoted parents. It has been a joy to see a goodly number of teenage youngsters stand up at recent conventions, offering themselves for baptism" (*WT*, Jan., 1, 1993).

283 Auxiliary pioneer: Previously known as "vacation pioneer." It is common that youngsters enroll themselves as "auxiliary pioneers" during vacation, where they spend 100 hours a month preaching from house-to-house (*WT*, Nov. 1, 2006, p. 9).

284 Kingdom Ministry (some other rules concerning the report of hours): "If a student [Bible student] gets baptized before completing both books, then the study should continue until the *"God's Love"* book is finished. Even though the student is baptized, you may report the time, the return visit, and the study. A publisher who accompanies you and participates in the study may also count the time" (*KM*, March 2009).

285 Trade school training.

286 Upper secondary; higher education.

287 In an article, "Helping Minors to Worship God," one finds instructions on how to treat a minor if he or she does something that church leaders judge is wrong: "We see in the congregations the delightful result—hundreds of thousands of exemplary young ones 'who love Jehovah and want to worship him forever. ... / Christian parents also have the primary responsibility to discipline and reprove their children, imposing whatever restrictions or loving punishments they deem necessary. (Ephesians 6:4; Hebrews 12:8, 9; Proverbs 3:11, 12; 22:15) If, though, a minor child who has been associating as an unbaptized publisher becomes involved in serious wrongdoing, it is of concern to the elders who are 'watching over the souls' of the flock.—Hebrews 13:17. / Basically, such wrongdoing should be cared for as outlined earlier in this article. Two elders can be assigned to look into the matter. They might, for example, first discuss with the parents (or parent) what has occurred, what the child's attitude is, and what corrective steps have been taken. (Compare Deuteronomy 21:18-21.) If the Christian parents have the situation in hand, the elders can simply check with them from time to time to offer helpful counsel, suggestions, and loving encouragement. / Sometimes, though, the discussion with the parents shows that it would be best for the elders to meet with the wayward minor and the parents. Bearing in mind the limitations and inclinations of youths, the overseers will endeavor to instruct the young, unbaptized publisher with mildness. (2 Timothy 2:22-26) In some cases, it may be clear that he no longer qualifies to be a publisher and that an appropriate announcement should be made. / Thereafter, what would parents do in behalf of their erring minor child? They are still responsible for their child, though he is disqualified as an unbaptized publisher or even if he is disfellowshipped because of wrongdoing after baptism. Just as they will continue to provide him with food, clothing, and shelter, they need to instruct and discipline him in line with God's Word" (*WT*, Nov. 15, 1988). The same subject is treated in a paragraph with the heading, "Baptized minors," in the elders textbook, "Pay Attention to Yourselves and to All the Flock" (1991, p. 98).

288 This quotation from Matthew 24 is taken from the *New World Translation*, Jehovah's Witnesses Bible,

but in *King James Version* it reads: "Who then is the faithful and wise servant, whom his Lord hath made ruler over his household, to give them meat in due season" (Matthew: 24:45). The "slave" concept is derived from the NWT-version of Matthew 24:45: "faithful and discreet slave." The Roman servants were mostly slaves, however, so this translation seems to be adequate. *The Emphatic Diaglott* also has "slave" in Matthew 24:45.

289 See: Knorr's Policies – Freeminds.org. I quote from Barbara Anderson's article found at the Freeminds site (read by this author in Sept. 2011). "In and around 1953 or '54 ... a number of young Bethelites who were assigned to the Brooklyn Heights Congregation were engaged in wife-swapping with couples who were not Bethelites, but who lived in the area. When the fat hit the fan, so to speak, Knorr was furious. That's when he used DISFELLOWSHIPPING and cleaned house. When I was in the Writing Department, I read the article in the Watchtower which introduced the disfellowshipping tenet to the members. It's quite an article to read, but what's not in the article are the details of the scandal that caused the article to be written in the first place. I remember there is an unspecific statement about immorality occurring amongst JWs and that's why, the Watchtower said, there was a need for disfellowshipping." (See also *WT*, March 1, 1952, two articles, 'Keeping the Organization Clean,' and 'Propriety of Disfellowshiping,' deal with disfellowshipping for the first time."

290 The article in *The Watchtower*, which at the same time appeared in the Danish *Vagttårnet*, stated among other things: "For a man who was a child molester before he was baptized, there may be another consequence. When he learns the truth, he repents and turns around, not bringing that cruel sin into the congregation. He may thereafter make fine progress, completely overcome his wrong impulses, and even be inclined to 'reach out' for a responsible position in the congregation. What, though, if he still has to live down notoriety in the community as a former child molester? Would he 'be irreprehensible ... have a fine testimony from people on the outside ... [be] free from accusation'? (1 Timothy 3:1-7, 10; Titus 1:7) No, he would not. Hence, he would not qualify for congregation privileges ... But a dedicated adult Christian who falls into the sin of child sexual abuse reveals an unnatural fleshly weakness. Experience has shown that such an adult may well molest other children.... For the protection of our children, a man known to have been a child molester does not qualify for a responsible position in the congregation. Moreover, he cannot be a pioneer or serve in any other special, full-time service ... It would be a shocking perversion if one of these authority figures were to misuse that child's innocent trust so as to seduce or force him or her to submit to sexual acts. Those who have been sexually molested in this way often struggle for years to overcome the resulting emotional trauma. Hence, a child molester is subject to severe congregational discipline and restrictions. It is not his status as an authority figure that should be of concern but, rather, the unblemished purity of the congregation ..." (*WT*, Jan 1, 1997, p. 26).

291 Regarding the number of eyewitnesses the Elder Manual states: "There must be two or three eyewitnesses, not just persons repeating what they have heard; no action can be taken if there is only one witness. (Deut. 19:15; John 8:17) ... If there are two or three witnesses to the same kind of wrongdoing but each one is witness to a separate incident, their testimony can be considered. / Such evidence may be used to establish guilt, but it is preferable to have two witnesses to the same occurrence of wrongdoing" (*Pay Attention to Yourselves and to All the Flock* 1991, p. 111). This quote was provided by a former, now-excluded elder, who writes: "It was the way many such cases were previously rejected by Jehovah's Witnesses" (Jan. 15, 2006).

292 Excerpts from the letter in *Awake!* to Barbara and Joe: "Have you ever wondered why I have been able to stay on the straight and narrow? Because, besides my love for Jehovah God, I have always had great respect for you both. This respect has been so strong that coupled with your discipline, it has caused me always to think twice when doing things and making decisions. The success of my life in doing God's will is indeed due in large part to your consistent love and discipline of me and your undying devotion to Jehovah and his organization" (*Awake!*, August 8, 1993).

293 Jean (John) Calvin (b. July 10, 1509; d. May 27, 1564), born as Jean Cauvin in Noyon in Picardy in the north-east France. As a child he was particularly precocious. Originally trained as a humanist lawyer, he broke from the Roman Catholic Church around 1530. Jean Calvin was second only to Martin Luther, the most important reformer. Calvin was expelled from Geneva in 1538, but returned in 1541. He was a tireless polemic and apologetic writer who generated much controversy. However, despite violent protests from opponents in Geneva, Calvin introduced the strictest church discipline, and in 1555 he

established a "theocracy" in the city. On Calvin's order the prominent Spanish doctor Miguel Servet, a mathematical genius and known for his criticism of the Trinity teachings, was denounced by Calvin and executed by the city council (burned at the stake). Servet was the first European to describe the function of pulmonary circulation. Foremost among his many writings are *Religionis Institutio Christiana*, 1536 (Institutes of the Christian Religion; *Wikipedia*, Feb. 2, 2011, and other Internet sources).

294 As I was researching "disfellowshipping," I found this interesting article on the Internet: "Disfellowshipping and Shunning." The article states: "For every 100 Jehovah's Witnesses more than 1 is disfellowshipped each year; over 60,000. Two out of every three are never reinstated. Being disfellowshipped can result in serious emotional side effects because those that continue to believe Watchtower doctrine are told that whilst disfellowshipped they are condemned to everlasting destruction; whereas those who become unbelievers, with no intention of returning to the Watchtower Society, realize they are unlikely to freely associate with Witness family and friends for the remainder of their lives" (Source: http://www.jwfacts.com/watchtower/disfellowship-shunning.php#2).

295 Arianism: The doctrine advocated by the presbyter Arius of Alexandria (Alexandros Arios), who had been priest at the main church in Alexandria in Egypt in AD 312. Since Arius instigated violent unrest on the conflict topic, Christ's divine nature, the Emperor Constantine in AD 325 called the First Council of Nicaea in Bithynia, and from here the emperor settled the future of the doctrines of Arianism and the trinity. For *political reasons*, the choice fell on the trinity doctrine, which was judged as being best suited to bring together *the now Christian Roman Empire*. The Nicaea council banned Arius and his supporters. See the article: "Arius, Arianism," *The Anchor Bible Dictionary* by Dennis E. Groh, NY, Doubleday, 1992, vol. 1, p. 384-386. See also "Arianism" on *Wikipedia* which gives an excellent introduction to the topic.

296 Gangrene appears in the *New World Translation*, but is also found in KJ as "canker."

297 The expression "only true Christians," used about JW, can be found in these sources: *WT*, Sept. 15, 1953; *WT*, Sept. 1, 1957, and *YB*, 1977, p. 199. The last reference is about the few Bible Students in Norway in 1904, a country where many Christian churches exist side by side: "This group, the first in north Norway, now consisted of five persons. For many years these were the *only true Christians* in that part of the country" (italics are mine).

298 *NWT*: "...the disgusting thing that causes desolation, as spoken of through Daniel..." (Matt. 24:15; see also: *WT*, Sept. 1, 1985, p. 24, par. 14).

299 *Slutade hedningernes tider i 1914?* (literally in English: Ended the Gentile Times in 1914?) is an abbreviated Scandinavian edition of Jonsson's *The Gentile Times Reconsidered* from 1983/2004.

300 Then in 2008, a new twist in the changing interpretations about *the generation* came, since the Society *again* proclaimed that when Armageddon breaks out, there will still be some of the anointed alive— which *rewritten* means that again time is relatively short (in 2008). The Watchtower article states: "Those without spiritual understanding today have felt that there has been no 'striking observableness' with regard to the sign of Jesus' presence. They reason that everything is continuing on as it did in the past. (2 Pet. 3:4) On the other hand, Christ's faithful anointed brothers, the modern-day John class, have recognized this sign as if it were a flash of lightning and have understood its true meaning. As a class, these anointed ones make up the modern-day 'generation' of contemporaries that will not pass away 'until all these things occur.' *This suggests that some who are Christ's anointed brothers will still be alive on earth when the foretold great tribulation begins*" (*WT*, Feb. 15, 2008, p. 24; italics are mine; see also *WT*, April 15, 2008, p. 29).

301 I found the last numbers for 2008 on the web. The *2011 Yearbook* is now published on the web, which seems to be an innovation. But when locating the correct figures in the Witnesses' literature, if you are not among the most experienced, you risk the possibility of getting completely lost in a jungle of figures, which is what happened to me. But now that it's easily available it is worth checking out.

302 Quote from *The Watchtower*, 2001: "Brother Barr told the audience that recently certain members of the Governing Body of Jehovah's Witnesses who had been serving as directors and officers voluntarily stepped aside from the boards of directors of all the corporations used by 'the faithful and discreet slave' in the United States. Responsible brothers of the other sheep class were elected as replacements. / This decision is beneficial indeed. It allows members of the Governing Body to spend more time in preparing spiritual food and in otherwise caring for the spiritual needs of the worldwide brotherhood. / In conclu-

sion, the chairman told his delighted audience: 'While various legal and administrative duties have been assigned to experienced overseers, … all of them serve under the spiritual direction of the Governing Body…. All of us prayerfully look to Jehovah for his blessing upon our united efforts in doing his will, to the honor and glory of his great name.'" (*WT*, Jan. 15, 2001)

303 All companies are currently as follows: Watch Tower Bible and Tract Society of Pennsylvania (incorporated 1884), President Don A. Adams; Watchtower Bible and Tract Society of New York, Inc. (incorporated 1909), President Max H. Larson; Christian Congregation of Jehovah's Witnesses (incorporated 2000), President William L. Van De Wall; Religious Order of Jehovah's Witnesses (incorporated 2000), President Patrick J. LaFranca; Kingdom Support Services, Inc. (incorporated 2000), President Harold L. Corkern; Watchtower Bible and Tract Society of New Jersey, Inc. (incorporated 1955), President Charles V. Molohan; Watchtower Bible and Tract Society of Florida, Inc. (incorporated 1986), President Leonard R. Pearson; Valley Farms Corporation (incorporated 1987), President Charles J. Rice; The division into many companies is said to be based on fear of new extensive litigation that may be brought against the companies in the future (Maurice Barnett: *Jehovah's Witnesses*, chapter 18, 2010, available for free on the Internet).

304 *Apparatchik* is a Russian term for a full-time, professional functionary of the Communist Party or the government, i.e., an agent of the state "apparatus" (*Wikipedia*, Nov. 2010).

305 The now 88-year-old Don Alden Adams (born around 1925 in Oak Park, Illinois) is "a long time insider" and a "50-year veteran" at the world headquarters in Brooklyn Heights. Respectively *New York Daily News* and *The Washington Post* described Adams as president of the Watch Tower Bible and Tract Society of Pennsylvania, that is, the principal or original parent corporation, the oldest of the Watchtower corporations. Adams is said to be the "religious leader" of Jehovah's Witnesses. But I think it is Max H. Larson, who as president of the "Society" in New York (which has traditionally served as the power base of the organization) has his finger on the trigger. The two presidents seem to limit each other's sphere of influence within the organization, perhaps the real purpose of the division of the presidency. Some believe, however, that the sharing had legal reasons that may address possible future lawsuits. Adams became president of the original Watchtower Society succeeding Milton G. Henschel in the year 2000, in connection with the demotion of the Governing Body's functions. They simply split up Henschel's presidency between the two companies, so each got its own president. Thus today, a real "strong man" as president of the Jehovah's Witnesses seems to be lacking inside the movement (Don Alden Adams, *Wikipedia*, Jan. 22, 2010; *New York Daily News*, Oct. 14, 2000, *Washington Post,* October 9, 2000). After serving as a full-time preacher, Don Adams was, like Max Larson in 1944, invited to work at world headquarters in Brooklyn. Here Adams served as secretary for N. H. Knorr. Beginning in 1960, Adams served directly as a traveling overseer under the Governing Body, visiting the branch offices in various countries outside the US. Later he worked in the "Bethel Home Committee" (*Wikipedia*, Jan. 2010).

306 "The Theocracy" with capital letters was in common use around 1950. See *WT*, May 15, 1950; *WT*, July 1, 1950; *WT*, Aug. 1, 1950.

307 In 1909 Russell, with assistance from his legal advisor, J. F. Rutherford, formed the subsidiary in Brooklyn, New York, which was named the People's Pulpit Association. Headquarters were at the same time moved to Brooklyn. In 1939 the subsidiary was renamed Watch Tower Bible and Tract Society, Inc. And in 1956 the name was changed again to the Watch Tower Bible and Tract Society of New York, Inc. In 2001 the Watch Tower Bible and Tract Society of New York also registered as a of the forty highest revenue generating companies in New York City (*Wikipedia*, 2012; Jehovahs-witness.net).

308 Newly joined members of the board, or the Governing Body: *Notes on the Governing Body of Jehovah's Witnesses*, available on the Internet.

309 As of December 2010, the following seven people are members of the Governing Body of Jehovah's Witnesses and the Watch Tower and Tract Society in Pittsburgh, Pennsylvania. (year of appointment in parentheses): Samuel Herd (1999); Geoffrey Jackson (2005); M. Stephen Lett (1999); Gerrit Lösch (1994); Anthony Morris (2005); Guy H. Pierce (1999) and David H. Splane (1999). (*Wikipedia*)

310 The internal *Kingdom Ministry* announced in the July issue, 2007, that *The Watchtower* magazine from January 2008 would have to appear in two different versions: The first of the month the edition that is sold from door to door would appear, and the fifteenth of each month, the new and

special *Study Edition*, which is used internally at the Witnesses' weekly meetings, would appear (*KM*, July, 2007, p. 1).

311 In 2006 the following appeared in *The Watchtower*: "With each passing day, it becomes more urgent that we keep Jehovah at our right hand. Soon, starting with the destruction of false religion, Satan's world will experience a tribulation such as it has never experienced before. (Matthew 24:21) Fear will envelop faithless mankind. Yet, during that chaotic time, Jehovah's courageous servants will rejoice in their hope! 'As these things start to occur,' said Jesus, 'raise yourselves erect and lift your heads up, because your deliverance is getting near.'—Luke 21:28." See also *The Watchtower*, May 15, 2008, s. 20: "Since time is running out for Satan's wicked world, entering these avenues of Kingdom service becomes *more urgent every day*. Will you go through the 'large door' while there is still time?" (Italics are mine). *The Watchtower* of March 15, 2009, warns: "The end of this wicked system will come in what is called 'the great tribulation.' (Rev. 7:14) The Bible does not tell us how long that will last, but Jesus said: 'Then there will be great tribulation such as has not occurred since the world's beginning until now, no, nor will occur again.' (Matt. 24:21) When we consider the tribulation that this world has already experienced, such as in World War II when an estimated 50 to 60 million lives were lost, the coming great tribulation will be very severe indeed. It will reach its climax in the battle of Armageddon. That is when Jehovah will unleash his executional forces to destroy every vestige of Satan's earthly system.—Rev. 16:14, 16."

312 The Society has never *directly* mentioned the year *2034*, and not even in the cited article.

313 In 2005, while writing the Danish edition of this book, I didn't know of David A. Reed's report, "The Authors Testimony." I discovered it on the Internet in 2010. David Reed also draws comparisons to Orwell's novel *Nineteen Eighty-Four*, especially "Newspeak." Reed had put his personal story on the Internet under the title: "The Author's Testimony." I recommend reading it. It is pretty interesting, and it is easily translated into many languages through Google Translate.

314 For 2005 the average number of *average* publishers was 6,390,016 (growth 1.3%). In 2006, the number was 6,491,775 (growth 1.6%). From 2005 to 2006, the Witnesses only grew by 101,759 members, which most probably came from the children within the movement, who now count as baptized. So it is an illusion to think Jehovah's Witnesses today is the world's fastest growing religious movement (*YB*, 2006 and 2007). In 2007 the increase was 3.1 over 2006, and in 2008 it was 2.1 over 2007. Therefore, I must assume that the Seventh-day Adventists today both grow faster and form a higher number than the Jehovah's Witnesses (my conclusions are based on Knight, 1992 and other available material from the Seventh-day Adventists, among them the *2009 Yearbook of Seventh-day Adventist Church*, plus the Jehovah's Witnesses yearbooks up to 2008).

315 I quote: "A Freudian slip, also called parapraxis, is an error in speech, memory, or physical action that is interpreted as occurring due to the interference of some unconscious ("dynamically repressed") wish, conflict, or train of thought. The concept is thus part of classical psychoanalysis" (Source: *Wikipedia*, 2011).

316 There is an ongoing discussion among scientists whether the Apostle John is the true author of The Revelation. It is only conservative scholars and fundamentalists—it is said—who maintain that it was the Apostle John who wrote "The Revelation of John." According to these considerations, the author of Revelation can have been an otherwise unknown presbyter (elder), but of the same name. See the article by Adela Yarbro Collins: "Revelation, Book of," in *The Anchor Bible Dictionary*, Vol. 5, p. 694-708.

317 Holger Mosbech: *Johannes' Åbenbaring* (Revelation of John), 1943, p. 257, 297; DK only. See also the list of publications in this book.

318 In other translations, for example the Danish, it is said: "...shortly after 1914."

319 All references to this quotation are to the foreword of the Danish edition (approx. 1916–1927) of the Forth Volume. It was impossible for me to find the quotation in an English edition, because it was changed sometime after 1920. But this quotation covers very well Russell's views before and after 1914.

320 The psychologist, Tue Toft, in a Danish tabloid, *B.T.*, Dec. 11, 1997.

321 In particle physics, "antimatter" is the extension of the concept of the antiparticle to matter, where antimatter is composed of antiparticles in the same way that normal matter is composed of particles (*Wikipedia*). *The Watchtower* editor's use of the term "antimatter" seems to be saying that the wicked should not only be killed, but they also must be destroyed so completely that all traces of them are removed from the universe.

322 1 Corinthians 5:13 in *NWT*, 1984, states: "Remove the wicked man from among yourselves."

323 *Ekstra Bladet*, May 16, 2004.

324 Matthew 24:13.

325 In 2004, the growth was around 2.0% (over 2003). In 2005 it ended at 1.3% (over 2004), in 2006 at 1.6% (over 2005), in 2007 on 3.1% (over 2006) and in 2008 on 2.1% (over 2007).

326 This I wrote long before the movie *Worlds Apart* (Two Worlds) premiered.

327 The movie *Worlds Apart* (Two Worlds/*To Verdener*), by the Danish director, Niels Arden Oplev: Sara and her family belong to Jehovah's Witnesses. But when Sara falls in love with Teis, who is not a Witness, their love grows through stolen, secret meetings. Sara is torn between her conscience, faith and passion, forced to make a choice between her love and her family that are worlds apart (*To Verdener/ Worlds Apart*, on the Internet, Jan. 2011).

328 *New World Translation* says here: "For YOU yourselves know quite well that Jehovah's day is coming exactly as a thief in the night. Whenever it is that they are saying: 'Peace and security!' then sudden destruction is to be instantly upon them just as the pang of distress upon a pregnant woman; and they will by no means escape" (1 Thess. 5:2, 3; *NWT*, 1984). Despite my poor English skills, I feel that here there is a *slight* difference in the meaning of "peace conferences!"

329 "Engram:" A term used in Scientology and *Dianetics* for a "recording" of a past painful event not normally accessible to the conscious mind (*Wikipedia*).

330 See also the article of Duane F. Watson, "Six Hundred and Sixty-six," *The Anchor Bible Dictionary*, vol. 6, p. 54, 55.

331 See the article by Adela Yarbro Collins: "Revelation, Book of," *The Anchor Bible Dictionary*, vol. 5, p. 694–708.

332 A discussion of the origin of the second epistle of Peter is found in an article by John H. Elliott: "Peter, Second Epistle of," in *The Anchor Bible Dictionary*, vol. 5, p. 282–287, Doubleday, 1992.

333 Marcus Aurelius Valerius Maxentius (AD 278–312) was Western Roman Emperor from 306 to 312. He was the son of Emperor Maximian, and the son-in-law of Galerius, also an emperor. Emperor Maxentius died in the battle at the Milvian Bridge in the year 312 (among other sources, *Wikipedia*, March 2011).

334 Donald Guthrie: *New Testament Introduction*, InterVarsity Press, 1970, p. 45–46; see also D. A. Carson, Douglas J. Moo, and Leon Morris: An Introduction to the New Testament, Apollos; Zondervan Publishing House, 1994 (British edition).

335 Concerning the "Lectionary-hypothesis;" see Michael D. Goulder, *Lection and Midrash in Matthew*, London, SPCK, 1974.

336 *The New English Bible*, New Testament, Oxford University Press and Cambridge University Press, 1961.

337 All Bible quotations from the 1984 edition of *New World Translation of the Holy Scriptures* are taken from a JW-CD (2005), which the Watchtower Society in Denmark kindly sold to me.

338 I am especially indebted to Professor Mogens Müller (the Theological Faculty at the University of Copenhagen): *Kommentar til Matthæusevangeliet*, 2000 (Commentary to the Gospel of Matthew; DK only); deceased Professor Holger: *Johannes' Aabenbaring*, 1943 (The Revelation of John; DK only), and *Nytestamentlig Isagogik*, 1949 (New Testament Isagogik; DK only); plus Professor Per Bilde: *En religion bliver til, 2001* (A religion arises; DK only). But naturally, I have studied many other books on Early Christianity, mostly by Danish, German and English scholars, which I will not list here.

339 The *NWT* 1963 edition has here: "consummation."

340 In a recycling business near my home, I found one day (in 2009) among the vintage and antique books an English Bible, namely: *The Youth Bible*. Curious, I opened the Bible to Matthew 24:3 to see how the term "parousia" was translated in this version and found: "Later, as Jesus was sitting on the Mount of Olives, his followers came to be alone with him. They said, 'Tell us, when will these things happen? And what will be the sign that it is time for you to come again and for this age to end?' " (*The Youth Bible*, New Century Version, by Word Publishing, Dallas 1991, p. 950) And the continuation: "Jesus answered, 'Be careful that no one fools you…!' "

341 The twenty-four places are as follows: Matt. 24:3 and 27, 37 and 39; 1 Cor. 15:23, 16:17; 2 Cor. 7:6, 7:7

and 10:10; Philemon 1:26 and2:12; 1 Thess. 2:19, 3:13, 4:15 and 5:23; 2 Thess. 2:1, 2:8 and 2:9; James 5:7 and 5:8; 2 Peter 1:16, 3:4 and 3:12; and 1 John 2:28.

342 *Wikipedia* gives an excellent definition of the original meaning of the Greek "*parousia*." Parousia simply meant "the appearance and the subsequent presence" of a ruler or a king in the ancient world. *Wikipedia* says about *parousia*: "The original Greek of the New Testament uses the term *parousia* (παρουσία from the Greek literal meaning of *parousia*: presence or arrival, derived from 'para-' beside, beyond; and 'ousia' substance)."

343 Barbara Thiering: *Jesus the Man: New Interpretations from the Dead Sea Scrolls*, Simon and Schuster, New York, 1993. Her book is a highly speculative Jesus-interpretation. Barbara Thiering (born 1930) is an Australian nonfiction writer, historian and Biblical exegete specializing in the origins of the early Christian Church and the Dead Sea Scrolls. In books and journal articles, she challenges Christian orthodoxy, drawing on what she claims is new evidence that gives alternative answers to its supernatural beliefs. Her analysis has been rejected by many scholars in the field. (From *Wikipedia* and other sources)

344 The *NWT* 1963 version has this verse as follows: "YOU are going to hear of wars and reports of wars; see that YOU are not terrified. For these things must take place, but *the accomplished end* is not yet" (italics are mine).

345 Released on Commentary Press, P.O. Box 43532, Atlanta, Georgia, 1987.

346 In the version of *NWT* 1963, this verse reads: "And this good news of the kingdom will be preached in all the inhabited earth for the purpose of a witness to all nations, and then the accomplished end will come." Note that the NWT edition from 1963 here has, as in Matt. 24:6, "the accomplished end." In the revised NWT-edition from 1984 this changed to the more plain and less demanding: "the end."

347 Taken from Daniel 12:4 (KJ): "But thou, O Daniel, shut up the words, and seal the book, even to the time of the end: many shall run to and fro, and knowledge shall be increased" (important text-verse for the Adventists and the Witnesses).

348 The quotation from *New Heavens and A New Earth*, 1953, in full: "When Jesus gave this prophecy on the final preaching of 'this good news of the kingdom,' he was there present and the good news that was then being preached was, 'The kingdom of the heavens has drawn near.' (Matt. 4:17; 10:7, NW) 'The appointed time has been fulfilled and the kingdom of God has drawn near.' (Mark 1:15, NW) He had been anointed to the Kingdom and was present in the midst of the people, friends and enemies; and he could correctly say therefore: 'Look! the kingdom of God is in your midst.' 'The kingdom of God has come near to you.' (Luke 17:21; 10:9, NW) That was 'this good news of the kingdom' at that time, at the consummation of the Jewish system of things in Judea. Hence Jesus' prophetic expression 'this good news of the kingdom' for the present 'consummation of the system of things,' the 'time of the end' of this world, must be the good news, *not of a kingdom yet to come in the far-off, indefinite future, but of God's kingdom born, set up, and with the anointed Jesus in the heavenly throne, invisibly present* there and with his attention and the 'rod of [his] strength' directed toward this earth. Such good news the facts prove it to be" (p. 254; italics are mine).

349 Documentation: The following are taken from the Internet: Jehovah's Witnesses and the United Nations at *Wikipedia*: "The Watchtower Society became an Associate member of the United Nations Department of Public Information (UN/DPI) in February 1992 and maintained this membership until October 2001. The association status was ceased the day after it was made known in the *Guardian* newspaper. In a letter dated August 4, 2004, the UN website explains the association it had with the Watchtower Society: 'By accepting association with DPI, the organization agreed to meet criteria for association, including support and respect of the principles of the Charter of the United Nations and commitment and means to conduct effective information programmes with its constituents and to a broader audience about UN activities.' The official UN/DPI Web page explains about associated organizations: 'Please note that association of NGOs with DPI does not constitute their incorporation into the United Nations system, nor does it entitle associated organizations or their staff to any kind of privileges, immunities or special status.' Yet, the associate member must disseminate information about the principles and activities of the United Nations and adhere to the United Nations' principles" (*Wikipedia*, June 5, 2009).

350 Modern researcher's date both "the Gospel According to St. Luke" and "The Acts of the Apostles" to sometime around AD 120, 130.

351 Donald Guthrie: *New Testament Introduction*, InterVarsity Press, 1981.

352 Quote from *The Battle of Armageddon* (series 4), 1914: " 'The dark day in Northern America was one of those wonderful phenomena of nature which will always be read of with interest, but which philosophy is at a loss to explain.' Webster's Dictionary, 1869 edition, under the head of Vocabulary of Noted Names, says: - 'The dark day, May 19, 1780-so called on *account* of a remarkable darkness on that day extending over all New England. In some places, persons could not see to read common print in the open air for several hours together. Birds sang their evening songs, disappeared, and became silent; fowls went to roost; cattle sought the barn-yard; and candles were lighted in the houses. The obscuration began about ten o'clock in the morning, and continued till the middle of the next night, but with differences of degree of duration in different places' " (*Studies* 4, 1914, p. 594–590).

353 The study edition of *The Watchtower* dated August 15, 2011, said this about the anointed that enjoyed the symbols at the Memorial ceremony: "Memorial partakers. This is the number of baptized individuals who partake of the emblems at the Memorial worldwide. Does this total represent the number of anointed ones on earth? Not necessarily. A number of factors—including past religious beliefs or even mental or emotional imbalance—might cause some to assume mistakenly that they have the heavenly calling. We thus have no way of knowing the exact number of anointed ones on earth; nor do we need to know. The Governing Body does not keep a list of all partakers, for it does not maintain a global network of anointed ones. / What we do know is that there will be some of the anointed "slaves of our God" on earth when the destructive winds of the great tribulation are released. (Rev. 7:1-3) Until then, the anointed will take the lead in something that is well-documented by our annual service report—the greatest preaching and teaching work in human history" (*WT*, Aug. 15, 2011, p. 22).

354 This method should not be confused with *Preterism*, the understanding method used by its supporters (*the Preterists*) who still (as far as I can perceive) believe in a future fulfillment of the apocalyptic prophecies of Matthew 24: the Second Coming, the Judgment Day and the resurrection. A supporter of the historical-critical method is neutral to Christian doctrines but only seeks to clarify the historical, linguistic and religious contexts.

Index

The number following "n" indicates a note number.

Food for Thinking Christians, 58

forbidden books, 342

Fort Duquesne, 3

Franz, Frederick William, 191, 220–221, 223–225, 227, 231, 233, 236–237, 290–291, 300, 312–313, 315, 518; 565n221

Franz, Raymond, 217, 222, 266, 273, 291, 311, 315–316, 329

Free Bible Students, 156

Freemasons, 34, 108, 538

Freytag, Alexander, 156, 242

Friends of Jehovah's Witnesses, A Fear–Free Zone, 450

G

Geneva, ix, 8, 40, 369–370, 372–373, 516, 521; 572n293

gentile times, 5, 49, 102, 109–110, 117, 119, 151, 184, 243, 316–317, 323, 326, 328, 332, 336–337, 379, 381, 415, 522; 544n34, 544n42, 555n124, 570n272, 570n275, 573n299

Gentiles, 42, 49, 103, 105–106, 121, 184; 547n73, 554n115–116

Germany, 101, 163, 168, 189, 197, 209–210, 212, 215, 246, 292

Gilead, 227, 241, 245, 255–256, 291, 318

Gileadites, 227

God's mouthpiece, 68

God's stone witness, 47

God's theocratic organization, 333

Gog of Magog, 235–236, 272, 425, 430–431

Golden Age, The, 149, 180–181, 190, 194, 203

Gorgas, C. R. 19

Governing Body, 195, 254, 265–266, 290, 299, 303, 305, 311–316, 318, 323–325, 329–332, 335, 338–340, 360, 362–363, 365, 367, 380–381, 384, 398–401, 403–408, 412, 490–492, 514, 516, 519, 521; 563n202, 567n245, 569n265, 569n267, 570n279, 571n279, 573n302, 574n302, 574n305, 574n308–309, 575n308, 578n353

gramophone record, 205, 226

Grandir avec Jéhovah, 373–374

grasshopper troops, 209

gray eminence, 223, 231, 313, 379

Great Battle in the Ecclesiastical Heavens, A, 84, 88, 97, 517, 520; 553n105

great crowd, 90, 108, 205, 237, 285, 300, 381, 384, 393, 396, 398, 399, 407–408, 420, 507, 508; 555n118

Great Disappointment, 9, 18, 22, 30, 37, 188, 297–298, 322, 514, 518

great multitude, 108–109, 205–206, 239; 564n209, 569n260

Great Pyramid, 46–48, 522, 528; 547n70, 547n72

great tribulation, 104–105, 107, 113, 187, 205, 288–289, 295, 300, 396, 419, 433, 480–481, 483, 485, 487, 507; 573n300, 575n311

Grew, Henry, 34–35, 61

Griffith, Bill, 401

H

Hamilton, E. Louise, 155

Hamilton, Ontario, 89–93, 97–98, 100, 155, 531; 553n104, 553n106, 556n130

Harvest Siftings, 134–136, 142

Harvest Siftings Reviewed, 139–140

Haslett, Donald, 191

Hawaiian Star, 101

headstone (Russell's), 120–121

heavenly crowd, 205, 394, 400

Henninges, E. C., 83, 89; 551n96, 553n108

Henschel, Milton George, 233, 299, 303, 400–402, 405; 574n305

Herald of Christ's Kingdom, 180

Herald of Christ's Presence, Zion's Watch Tower and, 52, 129, 326; 542n14, 545n43, 545n45

Herald of Life and the Coming Kingdom, 47

Herald of the Future Age, 41

Herald of the Kingdom and Age–to–Come, 30

Herald of the Midnight Cry, 522

Herald of the Morning, The Midnight Cry and, 47; 544n39, 547n66

Highland Park Kingdom Hall, 190

Hirsh, Robert H., 130, 134–136, 139–145, 147–148, 151, 154–157, 166, 169, 175–176; 556n132, 557n141, 557n145, 558n148, 558n153, 559n156, 562n187–188

historical–critical method, 13, 456–457, 494, 515, 527; 542n19–20, 543n25, 578n354

Hitler, Adolf, 209–210, 212–213, 215, 242

Hoess, Rudolf, 212–213, 519, 523

Hoskins, Isaac F., 130, 139, 142, 144, 148, 151, 154–155, 444; 556n132, 557n141, 558n150, 558n153, 559n156, 559n162, 560n173

Howe, Judge Harlan B., 168, 179

Howlett, Matthew, 191–192

I

In Search of Christian Freedom, 521

International Bible Students Association, *also* IBSA, xix, 9, 28, 58–59, 90, 109, 136, 138, 156, 160, 163, 171, 515; 560n170, 561n177

CPSIA information can be obtained at www.ICGtesting.com
Printed in the USA
BVOW09s2353070915

416777BV00004B/67/P